D0086710

UNIX™ TIME-SHARING SYSTEM:

UNIX PROGRAMMER'S MANUAL

939521

UNIX™ TIME-SHARING SYSTEM:

UNIX PROGRAMMER'S MANUAL

Seventh Edition, Volume 2

Bell Telephone Laboratories, Incorporated
Murray Hill, New Jersey

HOLT, RINEHART AND WINSTON

New York   Chicago   San Francisco   Philadelphia
Montreal   Toronto   London   Sydney   Tokyo
Mexico City   Rio de Janeiro   Madrid

Copyright © 1983, 1979, Bell Telephone Laboratories, Incorporated.

All rights reserved.
Address correspondence to:
383 Madison Avenue, New York, NY 10017

Library of Congress Cataloging in Publication Data

(Revised for volume 2)

Bell Telephone Laboratories, Inc.
    UNIX time-sharing system.

    Vol. 2 had also special title: Supplementary
documents.
    Includes indexes.
    1. UNIX (Computer system)   I. Title.
QA76.8.U65B44   1982   001.64'2   82-15498

ISBN 0-03-061742-1 (v. 1)
ISBN 0-03-061743-X (v. 2)

Printed in the United States of America

Published simultaneously in Canada

456 073 98765

CBS COLLEGE PUBLISHING
Holt, Rinehart and Winston
The Dryden Press
Saunders College Publishing

QA
76.8
.U65
O44
1983
v.2

CONTENTS

Preface   vii

General Works   1

1. 7th Edition UNIX—Summary.   3
    A concise summary of the facilities available on UNIX.
2. The UNIX Time-Sharing System   20
    D. M. Ritchie and K. Thompson.   The original UNIX paper, reprinted from CACM.

Getting Started   37

3. UNIX for Beginners—Second Edition.   39
    B. W. Kernighan.   An introduction to the most basic use of the system.
4. A Tutorial Introduction to the UNIX Text Editor.   54
    B. W. Kernighan.   An easy way to get started with the editor.
5. Advanced Editing on UNIX.   65
    B. W. Kernighan.   The next step.
6. An Introduction to the UNIX Shell.   82
    S. R. Bourne.   An introduction to the capabilities of the command interpreter, the shell.
7. Learn—Computer Aided Instruction on UNIX.   109
    M. E. Lesk and B. W. Kernighan.   Describes a computer-aided instruction program that walks new users through the basics of files, the editor, and document preparation software.

Document Preparation   123

8. Typing Documents on the UNIX System.   125
    M. E. Lesk.   Describes the basic use of the formatting tools. Also describes "—ms", a standardized package of formatting requests that can be used to lay out most documents (including those in this volume).
9. A System for Typesetting Mathematics.   146
    B. W. Kernighan and L. L. Cherry.   Describes EQN. an easy-to-learn language for doing high-quality mathematical typesetting.
10. TBL—A Program to Format Tables.   157
    M. E. Lesk.   A program to permit easy specification of tabular material for typesetting. Again, easy to learn and use.
11. Some Applications of Inverted Indexes on the UNIX System.   175
    M. E. Lesk.   Describes, among other things, the program REFER which fills in bibliographic citations from a data base automatically.
12. NROFF/TROFF User's Manual.   196
    J. F. Ossanna.   The basic formatting program.
13. A TROFF Tutorial.   230
    B. W. Kernighan.   An introduction to TROFF for those who really want to know such things.

Programming 245

14. The C Programming Language—Reference Manual. 247

   D. M. Ritchie. Official statement of the syntax and semantics of C. Should be supplemented by *The C Programming Language*, B. W. Kernighan and D. M. Ritchie, Prentice-Hall, 1978, which contains a tutorial introduction and many examples.

15. Lint, A C Program Checker. 278

   S. C. Johnson. Checks C programs for syntax errors, type violations, portability problems, and a variety of probable errors.

16. Make—A Program for Maintaining Computer Programs. 291

   S. I. Feldman. Indispensable tool for making sure that large programs are properly compiled with minimal effort.

17. UNIX Programming. 301

   B. W. Kernighan and D. M. Ritchie. Describes the programming interface to the operating system and the standard I/O library.

18. A Tutorial Introduction to ADB. 323

   J. F. Maranzano and S. R. Bourne. How to use the ADB debugger.

Supporting Tools and Languages 351

19. YACC: Yet Another Compiler-Compiler. 353

   S. C. Johnson. Converts a BNF specification of a language and semantic actions written in C into a compiler for the language.

20. LEX—A Lexical Analyzer Generator. 388

   M. E. Lesk and E. Schmidt. Creates a recognizer for a set of regular expressions; each regular expression can be followed by arbitrary C code which will be executed when the regular expression is found.

21. A Portable Fortran 77 Compiler. 401

   S. I. Feldman and P. J. Weinberger. The first Fortran 77 compiler, and still one of the best.

22. Ratfor—A Preprocessor for a Rational Fortran. 421

   B. W. Kernighan. Converts a Fortran with C-like control structures and cosmetics into real, ugly Fortran.

23. The M4 Macro Process. 433

   B. W. Kernighan and D. M. Ritchie. M4 is a macro processor useful as a front end for C, Ratfor, Cobol, and in its own right.

24. SED—A Non-interactive Text Editor. 440

   L. E. McMahon. A variant of the editor for processing large inputs.

25. AWK—A Pattern Scanning and Processing Language. 451

   A. V. Aho, B. W. Kernighan and P. J. Weinberger. Makes it easy to specify many data transformation and selection operations.

26. DC—An Interactive Desk Calculator. 460

   R. H. Morris and L. L. Cherry. A super HP calculator, if you don't need floating point.

27. BC—An Arbitrary Precision Desk-Calculator Language. 469

   L. L. Cherry and R. H. Morris. A front end for DC that provides infix notation, control flow, and built-in functions.

28. UNIX Assembler Reference Manual. 483

   D. M. Ritchie. The ultimate dead language.

Implementation, Maintenance, and Miscellaneous 495

29. Setting Up UNIX—Seventh Edition. 497

   C. B. Haley and D. M. Ritchie. How to configure and get your system running.

30. Regenerating System Software. 506

   C. B. Haley and D. M. Ritchie. What to do when you have to change things.

CONTENTS

31. UNIX Implementation. 512
    K. Thompson. How the system actually works inside.
32. The UNIX I/O System. 522
    D. M. Ritchie. How the I/O system really works.
33. A Tour Through the UNIX C Compiler. 529
    D. M. Ritchie. How the PDP-11 compiler works inside.
34. A Tour Through the Portable C Compiler. 544
    S. C. Johnson. How the portable C compiler works inside.
35. A Dial-Up Network of UNIX Systems. 569
    D. A. Nowitz and M. E. Lesk. Describes UUCP, a program for communicating files between UNIX systems.
36. UUCP Implementation Description. 577
    D. A. Nowitz. How UUCP works, and how to administer it.
37. On the Security of UNIX. 592
    D. M. Ritchie. Hints on how to break UNIX, and how to avoid doing so.
38. Password Security: A Case History. 595
    R. H. Morris and K. Thompson. How the bad guys used to be able to break the password algorithm, and why they can't now, at least not so easily.

Glossary 602

Index 609

PREFACE

In this new form from Holt Rinehart, the *UNIX† Programmer's Manual* becomes a trade book, readily available to the tens of thousands of users of the UNIX system. Its usefulness as a reference work had been enhanced by the addition of a glossary and an index.

This volume contains documents which supplement the information contained in Volume 1. The documents here are grouped roughly into the areas of basics, editing, language tools, document preparation, and system maintenance. Further general information may be found in the Bell System Technical Journal special issue on UNIX, July-August, 1978.

Many of the documents cited within this volume as Bell Laboratories internal memoranda or Computing Science Technical Reports (CSTR) are also contained here.

These documents contain occasional localism, typically references to other operating systems like GCOS and IBM. In all cases, such references may be safely ignored.

---

† UNIX is a Trademark of Bell Laboratories.

GENERAL WORKS

7th Edition UNIX — Summary

September 6, 1978

Bell Laboratories
Murray Hill, New Jersey 07974

A. What's new: highlights of the 7th edition UNIX† System

Aimed at larger systems. Devices are addressable to 2^{31} bytes, files to 2^{30} bytes. 128K memory (separate instruction and data space) is needed for some utilities.

Portability. Code of the operating system and most utilities has been extensively revised to minimize its dependence on particular hardware.

Fortran 77. F77 compiler for the new standard language is compatible with C at the object level. A Fortran structurer, STRUCT, converts old, ugly Fortran into RATFOR, a structured dialect usable with F77.

Shell. Completely new SH program supports string variables, trap handling, structured programming, user profiles, settable search path, multilevel file name generation, etc.

Document preparation. TROFF phototypesetter utility is standard. NROFF (for terminals) is now highly compatible with TROFF. MS macro package provides canned commands for many common formatting and layout situations. TBL provides an easy to learn language for preparing complicated tabular material. REFER fills in bibliographic citations from a data base.

UNIX-to-UNIX file copy. UUCP performs spooled file transfers between any two machines.

Data processing. SED stream editor does multiple editing functions in parallel on a data stream of indefinite length. AWK report generator does free-field pattern selection and arithmetic operations.

Program development. MAKE controls re-creation of complicated software, arranging for minimal recompilation.

Debugging. ADB does postmortem and breakpoint debugging, handles separate instruction and data spaces, floating point, etc.

C language. The language now supports definable data types, generalized initialization, block structure, long integers, unions, explicit type conversions. The LINT verifier does strong type checking and detection of probable errors and portability problems even across separately compiled functions.

Lexical analyzer generator. LEX converts specification of regular expressions and semantic actions into a recognizing subroutine. Analogous to YACC.

Graphics. Simple graph-drawing utility, graphic subroutines, and generalized plotting filters adapted to various devices are now standard.

Standard input-output package. Highly efficient buffered stream I/O is integrated with formatted input and output.

Other. The operating system and utilities have been enhanced and freed of restrictions in many other ways too numerous to relate.

---

† UNIX is a Trademark of Bell Laboratories.

B. Hardware

The 7th edition UNIX operating system runs on a DEC PDP-11/45 or 11/70* with at least the following equipment:

128K to 2M words of managed memory; parity not used.

disk: RP03, RP04, RP06, RK05 (more than 1 RK05) or equivalent.

console typewriter.

clock: KW11-L or KW11-P.

The following equipment is strongly recommended:

communications controller such as DL11 or DH11.

full duplex 96-character ASCII terminals.

9-track tape or extra disk for system backup.

The system is normally distributed on 9-track tape. The minimum memory and disk space specified is enough to run and maintain UNIX. More will be needed to keep all source on line, or to handle a large number of users, big data bases, diversified complements of devices, or large programs. The resident code occupies 12-20K words depending on configuration; system data occupies 10-28K words.

There is no commitment to provide 7th edition UNIX on PDP-11/34, 11/40 and 11/60 hardware.

C. Software

Most of the programs available as UNIX commands are listed. Source code and printed manuals are distributed for all of the listed software except games. Almost all of the code is written in C. Commands are self-contained and do not require extra setup information, unless specifically noted as "interactive." Interactive programs can be made to run from a prepared script simply by redirecting input. Most programs intended for interactive use (e.g., the editor) allow for an escape to command level (the Shell). Most file processing commands can also go from standard input to standard output ("filters"). The piping facility of the Shell may be used to connect such filters directly to the input or output of other programs.

1. Basic Software

This includes the time-sharing operating system with utilities, a machine language assembler and a compiler for the programming language C—enough software to write and run new applications and to maintain or modify UNIX itself.

1.1. Operating System

□ UNIX   The basic resident code on which everything else depends. Supports the system calls, and maintains the file system. A general description of UNIX design philosophy and system facilities appeared in the Communications of the ACM, July, 1974. A more extensive survey is in the Bell System Technical Journal for July-August 1978. Capabilities include:
  ○ Reentrant code for user processes.
  ○ Separate instruction and data spaces.
  ○ "Group" access permissions for cooperative projects, with overlapping memberships.
  ○ Alarm-clock timeouts.

---

*PDP is a Trademark of Digital Equipment Corporation.

     ○ Timer-interrupt sampling and interprocess monitoring for debugging and measurement.

     ○ Multiplexed I/O for machine-to-machine communication.

□ DEVICES   All I/O is logically synchronous. I/O devices are simply files in the file system. Normally, invisible buffering makes all physical record structure and device characteristics transparent and exploits the hardware's ability to do overlapped I/O. Unbuffered physical record I/O is available for unusual applications. Drivers for these devices are available; others can be easily written:

     ○ Asynchronous interfaces: DH11, DL11. Support for most common ASCII terminals.

     ○ Synchronous interface: DP11.

     ○ Automatic calling unit interface: DN11.

     ○ Line printer: LP11.

     ○ Magnetic tape: TU10 and TU16.

     ○ DECtape: TC11.

     ○ Fixed head disk: RS11, RS03 and RS04.

     ○ Pack type disk: RP03, RP04, RP06; minimum-latency seek scheduling.

     ○ Cartridge-type disk: RK05, one or more physical devices per logical device.

     ○ Null device.

     ○ Physical memory of PDP-11, or mapped memory in resident system.

     ○ Phototypesetter: Graphic Systems System/1 through DR11C.

□ BOOT   Procedures to get UNIX started.

□ MKCONF   Tailor device-dependent system code to hardware configuration. As distributed, UNIX can be brought up directly on any acceptable CPU with any acceptable disk, any sufficient amount of core, and either clock. Other changes, such as optimal assignment of directories to devices, inclusion of floating point simulator, or installation of device names in file system, can then be made at leisure.

1.2. User Access Control

□ LOGIN   Sign on as a new user.

     ○ Verify password and establish user's individual and group (project) identity.

     ○ Adapt to characteristics of terminal.

     ○ Establish working directory.

     ○ Announce presence of mail (from MAIL).

     ○ Publish message of the day.

     ○ Execute user-specified profile.

     ○ Start command interpreter or other initial program.

□ PASSWD   Change a password.

     ○ User can change his own password.

     ○ Passwords are kept encrypted for security.

□ NEWGRP   Change working group (project). Protects against unauthorized changes to projects.

1.3. Terminal Handling

□ TABS   Set tab stops appropriately for specified terminal type.

□ STTY   Set up options for optimal control of a terminal. In so far as they are deducible from the input, these options are set automatically by LOGIN.

○ Half vs. full duplex.
○ Carriage return+line feed vs. newline.
○ Interpretation of tabs.
○ Parity.
○ Mapping of upper case to lower.
○ Raw vs. edited input.
○ Delays for tabs, newlines and carriage returns.

1.4. File Manipulation

☐ CAT   Concatenate one or more files onto standard output. Particularly used for una-dorned printing, for inserting data into a pipeline, and for buffering output that comes in dribs and drabs. Works on any file regardless of contents.

☐ CP   Copy one file to another, or a set of files to a directory. Works on any file regardless of contents.

☐ PR   Print files with title, date, and page number on every page.
○ Multicolumn output.
○ Parallel column merge of several files.

☐ LPR   Off-line print. Spools arbitrary files to the line printer.

☐ CMP   Compare two files and report if different.

☐ TAIL   Print last n lines of input
○ May print last n characters, or from n lines or characters to end.

☐ SPLIT   Split a large file into more manageable pieces. Occasionally necessary for editing (ED).

☐ DD   Physical file format translator, for exchanging data with foreign systems, especially IBM 370's.

☐ SUM   Sum the words of a file.

1.5. Manipulation of Directories and File Names

☐ RM   Remove a file. Only the name goes away if any other names are linked to the file.
○ Step through a directory deleting files interactively.
○ Delete entire directory hierarchies.

☐ LN   "Link" another name (alias) to an existing file.

☐ MV   Move a file or files. Used for renaming files.

☐ CHMOD   Change permissions on one or more files. Executable by files' owner.

☐ CHOWN   Change owner of one or more files.

☐ CHGRP   Change group (project) to which a file belongs.

☐ MKDIR   Make a new directory.

☐ RMDIR   Remove a directory.

☐ CD   Change working directory.

☐ FIND   Prowl the directory hierarchy finding every file that meets specified criteria.

○ Criteria include:
  name matches a given pattern,
  creation date in given range,
  date of last use in given range,
  given permissions,
  given owner,
  given special file characteristics,
  boolean combinations of above.
○ Any directory may be considered to be the root.
○ Perform specified command on each file found.

1.6. Running of Programs

□ SH   The Shell, or command language interpreter.
                ○ Supply arguments to and run any executable program.
                ○ Redirect standard input, standard output, and standard error files.
                ○ Pipes: simultaneous execution with output of one process connected to the
                  input of another.
                ○ Compose compound commands using:
                      if ... then ... else,
                      case switches,
                      while loops,
                      for loops over lists,
                      break, continue and exit,
                      parentheses for grouping.
                ○ Initiate background processes.
                ○ Perform Shell programs, i.e., command scripts with substitutable arguments.
                ○ Construct argument lists from all file names satisfying specified patterns.
                ○ Take special action on traps and interrupts.
                ○ User-settable search path for finding commands.
                ○ Executes user-settable profile upon login.
                ○ Optionally announces presence of mail as it arrives.
                ○ Provides variables and parameters with default setting.

□ TEST   Tests for use in Shell conditionals.
                ○ String comparison.
                ○ File nature and accessibility.
                ○ Boolean combinations of the above.

□ EXPR   String computations for calculating command arguments.
                ○ Integer arithmetic
                ○ Pattern matching

□ WAIT   Wait for termination of asynchronously running processes.

□ READ   Read a line from terminal, for interactive Shell procedure.

□ ECHO   Print remainder of command line. Useful for diagnostics or prompts in Shell
                programs, or for inserting data into a pipeline.

□ SLEEP   Suspend execution for a specified time.

□ NOHUP   Run a command immune to hanging up the terminal.

□ NICE   Run a command in low (or high) priority.

☐ KILL   Terminate named processes.

☐ CRON   Schedule regular actions at specified times.
              ○ Actions are arbitrary programs.
              ○ Times are conjunctions of month, day of month, day of week, hour and minute. Ranges are specifiable for each.

☐ AT   Schedule a one-shot action for an arbitrary time.

☐ TEE   Pass data between processes and divert a copy into one or more files.

1.7. Status Inquiries

☐ LS   List the names of one, several, or all files in one or more directories.
              ○ Alphabetic or temporal sorting, up or down.
              ○ Optional information: size, owner, group, date last modified, date last accessed, permissions, i-node number.

☐ FILE   Try to determine what kind of information is in a file by consulting the file system index and by reading the file itself.

☐ DATE   Print today's date and time. Has considerable knowledge of calendric and horological peculiarities.
              ○ May set UNIX's idea of date and time.

☐ DF   Report amount of free space on file system devices.

☐ DU   Print a summary of total space occupied by all files in a hierarchy.

☐ QUOT   Print summary of file space usage by user id.

☐ WHO   Tell who's on the system.
              ○ List of presently logged in users, ports and times on.
              ○ Optional history of all logins and logouts.

☐ PS   Report on active processes.
              ○ List your own or everybody's processes.
              ○ Tell what commands are being executed.
              ○ Optional status information: state and scheduling info, priority, attached terminal, what it's waiting for, size.

☐ IOSTAT   Print statistics about system I/O activity.

☐ TTY   Print name of your terminal.

☐ PWD   Print name of your working directory.

1.8. Backup and Maintenance

☐ MOUNT   Attach a device containing a file system to the tree of directories. Protects against nonsense arrangements.

☐ UMOUNT   Remove the file system contained on a device from the tree of directories. Protects against removing a busy device.

☐ MKFS   Make a new file system on a device.

☐ MKNOD   Make an i-node (file system entry) for a special file. Special files are physical devices, virtual devices, physical memory, etc.

☐ TP

☐ TAR   Manage file archives on magnetic tape or DECtape. TAR is newer.
        ○ Collect files into an archive.
        ○ Update DECtape archive by date.
        ○ Replace or delete DECtape files.
        ○ Print table of contents.
        ○ Retrieve from archive.

☐ DUMP   Dump the file system stored on a specified device, selectively by date, or indiscriminately.

☐ RESTOR   Restore a dumped file system, or selectively retrieve parts thereof.

☐ SU   Temporarily become the super user with all the rights and privileges thereof. Requires a password.

☐ DCHECK

☐ ICHECK

☐ NCHECK   Check consistency of file system.
        ○ Print gross statistics: number of files, number of directories, number of special files, space used, space free.
        ○ Report duplicate use of space.
        ○ Retrieve lost space.
        ○ Report inaccessible files.
        ○ Check consistency of directories.
        ○ List names of all files.

☐ CLRI   Peremptorily expunge a file and its space from a file system. Used to repair damaged file systems.

☐ SYNC   Force all outstanding I/O on the system to completion. Used to shut down gracefully.

1.9. Accounting

The timing information on which the reports are based can be manually cleared or shut off completely.

☐ AC   Publish cumulative connect time report.
        ○ Connect time by user or by day.
        ○ For all users or for selected users.

☐ SA   Publish Shell accounting report. Gives usage information on each command executed.
        ○ Number of times used.
        ○ Total system time, user time and elapsed time.
        ○ Optional averages and percentages.
        ○ Sorting on various fields.

1.10. Communication

☐ MAIL   Mail a message to one or more users. Also used to read and dispose of incoming mail. The presence of mail is announced by LOGIN and optionally by SH.
        ○ Each message can be disposed of individually.
        ○ Messages can be saved in files or forwarded.

☐ CALENDAR Automatic reminder service for events of today and tomorrow.

☐ WRITE   Establish direct terminal communication with another user.

☐ WALL   Write to all users.

☐ MESG   Inhibit receipt of messages from WRITE and WALL.

☐ CU   Call up another time-sharing system.
- ◯ Transparent interface to remote machine.
- ◯ File transmission.
- ◯ Take remote input from local file or put remote output into local file.
- ◯ Remote system need not be UNIX.

☐ UUCP   UNIX to UNIX copy.
- ◯ Automatic queuing until line becomes available and remote machine is up.
- ◯ Copy between two remote machines.
- ◯ Differences, mail, etc., between two machines.

1.11. Basic Program Development Tools

Some of these utilities are used as integral parts of the higher level languages described in section 2.

☐ AR   Maintain archives and libraries. Combines several files into one for housekeeping efficiency.
- ◯ Create new archive.
- ◯ Update archive by date.
- ◯ Replace or delete files.
- ◯ Print table of contents.
- ◯ Retrieve from archive.

☐ AS   Assembler. Similar to PAL-11, but different in detail.
- ◯ Creates object program consisting of
   code, possibly read-only,
   initialized data or read-write code,
   uninitialized data.
- ◯ Relocatable object code is directly executable without further transformation.
- ◯ Object code normally includes a symbol table.
- ◯ Multiple source files.
- ◯ Local labels.
- ◯ Conditional assembly.
- ◯ "Conditional jump" instructions become branches or branches plus jumps depending on distance.

☐ Library   The basic run-time library. These routines are used freely by all software.
- ◯ Buffered character-by-character I/O.
- ◯ Formatted input and output conversion (SCANF and PRINTF) for standard input and output, files, in-memory conversion.
- ◯ Storage allocator.
- ◯ Time conversions.
- ◯ Number conversions.
- ◯ Password encryption.
- ◯ Quicksort.
- ◯ Random number generator.
- ◯ Mathematical function library, including trigonometric functions and inverses, exponential, logarithm, square root, bessel functions.

☐ ADB   Interactive debugger.
          ○ Postmortem dumping.
          ○ Examination of arbitrary files, with no limit on size.
          ○ Interactive breakpoint debugging with the debugger as a separate process.
          ○ Symbolic reference to local and global variables.
          ○ Stack trace for C programs.
          ○ Output formats:
                1-, 2-, or 4-byte integers in octal, decimal, or hex
                single and double floating point
                character and string
                disassembled machine instructions
          ○ Patching.
          ○ Searching for integer, character, or floating patterns.
          ○ Handles separated instruction and data space.

☐ OD   Dump any file. Output options include any combination of octal or decimal by words, octal by bytes, ASCII, opcodes, hexadecimal.
          ○ Range of dumping is controllable.

☐ LD   Link edit. Combine relocatable object files. Insert required routines from specified libraries.
          ○ Resulting code may be sharable.
          ○ Resulting code may have separate instruction and data spaces.

☐ LORDER Places object file names in proper order for loading, so that files depending on others come after them.

☐ NM   Print the namelist (symbol table) of an object program. Provides control over the style and order of names that are printed.

☐ SIZE   Report the core requirements of one or more object files.

☐ STRIP   Remove the relocation and symbol table information from an object file to save space.

☐ TIME   Run a command and report timing information on it.

☐ PROF   Construct a profile of time spent per routine from statistics gathered by time-sampling the execution of a program. Uses floating point.
          ○ Subroutine call frequency and average times for C programs.

☐ MAKE   Controls creation of large programs. Uses a control file specifying source file dependencies to make new version; uses time last changed to deduce minimum amount of work necessary.
          ○ Knows about CC, YACC, LEX, etc.

1.12. UNIX Programmer's Manual

☐ Manual Machine-readable version of the UNIX Programmer's Manual.
          ○ System overview.
          ○ All commands.
          ○ All system calls.
          ○ All subroutines in C and assembler libraries.
          ○ All devices and other special files.
          ○ Formats of file system and kinds of files known to system software.
          ○ Boot and maintenance procedures.

☐ MAN   Print specified manual section on your terminal.

1.13. Computer-Aided Instruction

☐ LEARN   A program for interpreting CAI scripts, plus scripts for learning about UNIX by using it.
○ Scripts for basic files and commands, editor, advanced files and commands, EQN, MS macros, C programming language.

2. Languages

2.1. The C Language

☐ CC   Compile and/or link edit programs in the C language. The UNIX operating system, most of the subsystems and C itself are written in C. For a full description of C, read *The C Programming Language,* Brian W. Kernighan and Dennis M. Ritchie, Prentice-Hall, 1978.
○ General purpose language designed for structured programming.
○ Data types include character, integer, float, double, pointers to all types, functions returning above types, arrays of all types, structures and unions of all types.
○ Operations intended to give machine-independent control of full machine facility, including to-memory operations and pointer arithmetic.
○ Macro preprocessor for parameterized code and inclusion of standard files.
○ All procedures recursive, with parameters by value.
○ Machine-independent pointer manipulation.
○ Object code uses full addressing capability of the PDP-11.
○ Runtime library gives access to all system facilities.
○ Definable data types.
○ Block structure

☐ LINT   Verifier for C programs. Reports questionable or nonportable usage such as:
Mismatched data declarations and procedure interfaces.
Nonportable type conversions.
Unused variables, unreachable code, no-effect operations.
Mistyped pointers.
Obsolete syntax.
○ Full cross-module checking of separately compiled programs.

☐ CB   A beautifier for C programs. Does proper indentation and placement of braces.

2.2. Fortran

☐ F77   A full compiler for ANSI Standard Fortran 77.
○ Compatible with C and supporting tools at object level.
○ Optional source compatibility with Fortran 66.
○ Free format source.
○ Optional subscript-range checking, detection of uninitialized variables.
○ All widths of arithmetic: 2- and 4-byte integer; 4- and 8-byte real; 8- and 16-byte complex.

☐ RATFOR   Ratfor adds rational control structure à la C to Fortran.
○ Compound statements.

○ If-else, do, for, while, repeat-until, break, next statements.
○ Symbolic constants.
○ File insertion.
○ Free format source
○ Translation of relationals like $>$, $>=$.
○ Produces genuine Fortran to carry away.
○ May be used with F77.

□ STRUCT   Converts ordinary ugly Fortran into structured Fortran (i.e., Ratfor), using statement grouping, if-else, while, for, repeat-until.

2.3. Other Algorithmic Languages

□ BAS   An interactive interpreter, similar in style to BASIC. Interpret unnumbered statements immediately, numbered statements upon 'run'.
○ Statements include:
      comment,
      dump,
      for...next,
      goto,
      if...else...fi,
      list,
      print,
      prompt,
      return,
      run,
      save.
○ All calculations double precision.
○ Recursive function defining and calling.
○ Builtin functions include log, exp, sin, cos, atn, int, sqr, abs, rnd.
○ Escape to ED for complex program editing.

□ DC   Interactive programmable desk calculator. Has named storage locations as well as conventional stack for holding integers or programs.
○ Unlimited precision decimal arithmetic.
○ Appropriate treatment of decimal fractions.
○ Arbitrary input and output radices, in particular binary, octal, decimal and hexadecimal.
○ Reverse Polish operators:
      $+ - * /$
    remainder, power, square root,
    load, store, duplicate, clear,
    print, enter program text, execute.

□ BC   A C-like interactive interface to the desk calculator DC.
○ All the capabilities of DC with a high-level syntax.
○ Arrays and recursive functions.
○ Immediate evaluation of expressions and evaluation of functions upon call.
○ Arbitrary precision elementary functions: exp, sin, cos, atan.
○ Go-to-less programming.

2.4. Macroprocessing

☐ M4   A general purpose macroprocessor.
- ○ Stream-oriented, recognizes macros anywhere in text.
- ○ Syntax fits with functional syntax of most higher-level languages.
- ○ Can evaluate integer arithmetic expressions.

2.5. Compiler-compilers

☐ YACC   An LR(1)-based compiler writing system. During execution of resulting parsers, arbitrary C functions may be called to do code generation or semantic actions.
- ○ BNF syntax specifications.
- ○ Precedence relations.
- ○ Accepts formally ambiguous grammars with non-BNF resolution rules.

☐ LEX   Generator of lexical analyzers. Arbitrary C functions may be called upon isolation of each lexical token.
- ○ Full regular expression, plus left and right context dependence.
- ○ Resulting lexical analysers interface cleanly with YACC parsers.

3. Text Processing

3.1. Document Preparation

☐ ED   Interactive context editor. Random access to all lines of a file.
- ○ Find lines by number or pattern. Patterns may include: specified characters, don't care characters, choices among characters, repetitions of these constructs, beginning of line, end of line.
- ○ Add, delete, change, copy, move or join lines.
- ○ Permute or split contents of a line.
- ○ Replace one or all instances of a pattern within a line.
- ○ Combine or split files.
- ○ Escape to Shell (command language) during editing.
- ○ Do any of above operations on every pattern-selected line in a given range.
- ○ Optional encryption for extra security.

☐ PTX   Make a permuted (key word in context) index.

☐ SPELL   Look for spelling errors by comparing each word in a document against a word list.
- ○ 25,000-word list includes proper names.
- ○ Handles common prefixes and suffixes.
- ○ Collects words to help tailor local spelling lists.

☐ LOOK   Search for words in dictionary that begin with specified prefix

☐ TYPO   Look for spelling errors by a statistical technique; not limited to English.

☐ CRYPT   Encrypt and decrypt files for security.

3.2. Document Formatting

☐ ROFF   A typesetting program for terminals. Easy for nontechnical people to learn, and good for simple documents. Input consists of data lines intermixed with control lines, such as

        .sp 2   insert two lines of space
        .ce   center the next line

ROFF is deemed to be obsolete; it is intended only for casual use.

○ Justification of either or both margins.

○ Automatic hyphenation.

○ Generalized running heads and feet, with even-odd page capability, numbering, etc.

○ Definable macros for frequently used control sequences (no substitutable arguments).

○ All 4 margins and page size dynamically adjustable.

○ Hanging indents and one-line indents.

○ Absolute and relative parameter settings.

○ Optional legal-style numbering of output lines.

○ Multiple file capability.

○ Not usable as a filter.

□ TROFF

□ NROFF   Advanced typesetting. TROFF drives a Graphic Systems phototypesetter; NROFF drives ascii terminals of all types. This summary was typeset using TROFF. TROFF and NROFF style is similar to ROFF, but they are capable of much more elaborate feats of formatting, when appropriately programmed. TROFF and NROFF accept the same input language.

○ All ROFF capabilities available or definable.

○ Completely definable page format keyed to dynamically planted ''interrupts'' at specified lines.

○ Maintains several separately definable typesetting environments (e.g., one for body text, one for footnotes, and one for unusually elaborate headings).

○ Arbitrary number of output pools can be combined at will.

○ Macros with substitutable arguments, and macros invocable in mid-line.

○ Computation and printing of numerical quantities.

○ Conditional execution of macros.

○ Tabular layout facility.

○ Positions expressible in inches, centimeters, ems, points, machine units or arithmetic combinations thereof.

○ Access to character-width computation for unusually difficult layout problems.

○ Overstrikes, built-up brackets, horizontal and vertical line drawing.

○ Dynamic relative or absolute positioning and size selection, globally or at the character level.

○ Can exploit the characteristics of the terminal being used, for approximating special characters, reverse motions, proportional spacing, etc.

The Graphic Systems typesetter has a vocabulary of several 102-character fonts (4 simultaneously) in 15 sizes. TROFF provides terminal output for rough sampling of the product.

NROFF will produce multicolumn output on terminals capable of reverse line feed, or through the postprocessor COL.

High programming skill is required to exploit the formatting capabilities of TROFF and NROFF, although unskilled personnel can easily be trained to enter documents according to canned formats such as those provided by MS, below. TROFF and EQN are essentially identical to NROFF and NEQN so it is usually possible to define interchangeable formats to produce approximate proof copy on terminals before actual typesetting. The preprocessors MS, TBL, and REFER are fully compatible with TROFF and NROFF.

□ MS   A standardized manuscript layout package for use with NROFF/TROFF. This document was formatted with MS.

○ Page numbers and draft dates.
○ Automatically numbered subheads.
○ Footnotes.
○ Single or double column.
○ Paragraphing, display and indentation.
○ Numbered equations.

☐ EQN A mathematical typesetting preprocessor for TROFF. Translates easily readable formulas, either in-line or displayed, into detailed typesetting instructions. Formulas are written in a style like this:

sigma sup 2 ˜=˜ 1 over N sum from i=1 to N (x sub i − x bar) sup 2

which produces:

$$\sigma^2 = \frac{1}{N} \sum_{i=1}^{N} (x_i - \bar{x})^2$$

○ Automatic calculation of size changes for subscripts, sub-subscripts, etc.
○ Full vocabulary of Greek letters and special symbols, such as 'gamma', 'GAMMA', 'integral'.
○ Automatic calculation of large bracket sizes.
○ Vertical "piling" of formulae for matrices, conditional alternatives, etc.
○ Integrals, sums, etc., with arbitrarily complex limits.
○ Diacriticals: dots, double dots, hats, bars, etc.
○ Easily learned by nonprogrammers and mathematical typists.

☐ NEQN A version of EQN for NROFF; accepts the same input language. Prepares formulas for display on any terminal that NROFF knows about, for example, those based on Diablo printing mechanism.
○ Same facilities as EQN within graphical capability of terminal.

☐ TBL A preprocessor for NROFF/TROFF that translates simple descriptions of table layouts and contents into detailed typesetting instructions.
○ Computes column widths.
○ Handles left- and right-justified columns, centered columns and decimal-point alignment.
○ Places column titles.
○ Table entries can be text, which is adjusted to fit.
○ Can box all or parts of table.

☐ REFER Fills in bibliographic citations in a document from a data base (not supplied).
○ References may be printed in any style, as they occur or collected at the end.
○ May be numbered sequentially, by name of author, etc.

☐ TC Simulate Graphic Systems typesetter on Tektronix 4014 scope. Useful for checking TROFF page layout before typesetting.

☐ GREEK Fancy printing on Diablo-mechanism terminals like DASI-300 and DASI-450, and on Tektronix 4014.
○ Gives half-line forward and reverse motions.
○ Approximates Greek letters and other special characters by overstriking.

☐ COL Canonicalize files with reverse line feeds for one-pass printing.

☐ DEROFF Remove all TROFF commands from input.

☐ CHECKEQ Check document for possible errors in EQN usage.

4. Information Handling

☐ SORT   Sort or merge ASCII files line-by-line. No limit on input size.
○ Sort up or down.
○ Sort lexicographically or on numeric key.
○ Multiple keys located by delimiters or by character position.
○ May sort upper case together with lower into dictionary order.
○ Optionally suppress duplicate data.

☐ TSORT   Topological sort — converts a partial order into a total order.

☐ UNIQ   Collapse successive duplicate lines in a file into one line.
○ Publish lines that were originally unique, duplicated, or both.
○ May give redundancy count for each line.

☐ TR   Do one-to-one character translation according to an arbitrary code.
○ May coalesce selected repeated characters.
○ May delete selected characters.

☐ DIFF   Report line changes, additions and deletions necessary to bring two files into agreement.
○ May produce an editor script to convert one file into another.
○ A variant compares two new versions against one old one.

☐ COMM   Identify common lines in two sorted files. Output in up to 3 columns shows lines present in first file only, present in both, and/or present in second only.

☐ JOIN   Combine two files by joining records that have identical keys.

☐ GREP   Print all lines in a file that satisfy a pattern as used in the editor ED.
○ May print all lines that fail to match.
○ May print count of hits.
○ May print first hit in each file.

☐ LOOK   Binary search in sorted file for lines with specified prefix.

☐ WC   Count the lines, "words" (blank-separated strings) and characters in a file.

☐ SED   Stream-oriented version of ED. Can perform a sequence of editing operations on each line of an input stream of unbounded length.
○ Lines may be selected by address or range of addresses.
○ Control flow and conditional testing.
○ Multiple output streams.
○ Multi-line capability.

☐ AWK   Pattern scanning and processing language. Searches input for patterns, and performs actions on each line of input that satisfies the pattern.
○ Patterns include regular expressions, arithmetic and lexicographic conditions, boolean combinations and ranges of these.
○ Data treated as string or numeric as appropriate.
○ Can break input into fields; fields are variables.
○ Variables and arrays (with non-numeric subscripts).
○ Full set of arithmetic operators and control flow.
○ Multiple output streams to files and pipes.
○ Output can be formatted as desired.
○ Multi-line capabilities.

5. Graphics

The programs in this section are predominantly intended for use with Tektronix 4014 storage scopes.

☐ GRAPH   Prepares a graph of a set of input numbers.
          ○ Input scaled to fit standard plotting area.
          ○ Abscissae may be supplied automatically.
          ○ Graph may be labeled.
          ○ Control over grid style, line style, graph orientation, etc.

☐ SPLINE   Provides a smooth curve through a set of points intended for GRAPH.

☐ PLOT   A set of filters for printing graphs produced by GRAPH and other programs on various terminals. Filters provided for 4014, DASI terminals, Versatec printer/plotter.

6. Novelties, Games, and Things That Didn't Fit Anywhere Else

☐ BACKGAMMON
          A player of modest accomplishment.

☐ CHESS   Plays good class D chess.

☐ CHECKERS Ditto, for checkers.

☐ BCD   Converts ascii to card-image form.

☐ PPT   Converts ascii to paper tape form.

☐ BJ   A blackjack dealer.

☐ CUBIC   An accomplished player of 4×4×4 tic-tac-toe.

☐ MAZE   Constructs random mazes for you to solve.

☐ MOO   A fascinating number-guessing game.

☐ CAL   Print a calendar of specified month and year.

☐ BANNER   Print output in huge letters.

☐ CHING   The *I Ching*. Place your own interpretation on the output.

☐ FORTUNE   Presents a random fortune cookie on each invocation. Limited jar of cookies included.

☐ UNITS   Convert amounts between different scales of measurement. Knows hundreds of units. For example, how many km/sec is a parsec/megayear?

☐ TTT   A tic-tac-toe program that learns. It never makes the same mistake twice.

☐ ARITHMETIC
          Speed and accuracy test for number facts.

☐ FACTOR   Factor large integers.

☐ QUIZ   Test your knowledge of Shakespeare, Presidents, capitals, etc.

☐ WUMP   Hunt the wumpus, thrilling search in a dangerous cave.

☐ REVERSI   A two person board game, isomorphic to Othello®

☐ HANGMAN Word-guessing game. Uses the dictionary supplied with SPELL.

☐ FISH   Children's card-guessing game.

The UNIX Time-Sharing System*

D. M. Ritchie and K. Thompson

ABSTRACT

UNIX† is a general-purpose, multi-user, interactive operating system for the larger Digital Equipment Corporation PDP-11 and the Interdata 8/32 computers. It offers a number of features seldom found even in larger operating systems, including

i   A hierarchical file system incorporating demountable volumes,

ii   Compatible file, device, and inter-process I/O,

iii The ability to initiate asynchronous processes,

iv   System command language selectable on a per-user basis,

v   Over 100 subsystems including a dozen languages,

vi   High degree of portability.

This paper discusses the nature and implementation of the file system and of the user command interface.

1. INTRODUCTION

There have been four versions of the UNIX time-sharing system. The earliest (circa 1969-70) ran on the Digital Equipment Corporation PDP-7 and -9 computers. The second version ran on the unprotected PDP-11/20 computer. The third incorporated multiprogramming and ran on the PDP-11/34, /40, /45, /60, and /70 computers; it is the one described in the previously published version of this paper, and is also the most widely used today. This paper describes only the fourth, current system that runs on the PDP-11/70 and the Interdata 8/32 computers. In fact, the differences among the various systems is rather small; most of the revisions made to the originally published version of this paper, aside from those concerned with style, had to do with details of the implementation of the file system.

Since PDP-11 UNIX became operational in February, 1971, over 600 installations have been put into service. Most of them are engaged in applications such as computer science education, the preparation and formatting of documents and other textual material, the collection and processing of trouble data from various switching machines within the Bell System, and recording and checking telephone service orders. Our own installation is used mainly for research in operating systems, languages, computer networks, and other topics in computer science, and also for document preparation.

Perhaps the most important achievement of UNIX is to demonstrate that a powerful operating system for interactive use need not be expensive either in equipment or in human effort: it can run on hardware costing as little as $40,000, and less than two man-years were spent on the main system software. We hope, however, that users find that the most important

* Copyright 1974, Association for Computing Machinery, Inc., reprinted by permission. This is a revised version of an article that appeared in Communications of the ACM, *17*, No. 7 (July 1974), pp. 365-375. That article was a revised version of a paper presented at the Fourth ACM Symposium on Operating Systems Principles, IBM Thomas J. Watson Research Center, Yorktown Heights, New York, October 15-17, 1973.
†UNIX is a Trademark of Bell Laboratories.

characteristics of the system are its simplicity, elegance, and ease of use.

Besides the operating system proper, some major programs available under UNIX are

C compiler
Text editor based on QED[1]
Assembler, linking loader, symbolic debugger
Phototypesetting and equation setting programs[2,3]
Dozens of languages including Fortran 77, Basic, Snobol, APL, Algol 68, M6,
TMG, Pascal

There is a host of maintenance, utility, recreation and novelty programs, all written locally. The UNIX user community, which numbers in the thousands, has contributed many more programs and languages. It is worth noting that the system is totally self-supporting. All UNIX software is maintained on the system; likewise, this paper and all other documents in this issue were generated and formatted by the UNIX editor and text formatting programs.

II. HARDWARE AND SOFTWARE ENVIRONMENT

The PDP-11/70 on which the Research UNIX system is installed is a 16-bit word (8-bit byte) computer with 768K bytes of core memory; the system kernel occupies 90K bytes about equally divided between code and data tables. This system, however, includes a very large number of device drivers and enjoys a generous allotment of space for I/O buffers and system tables; a minimal system capable of running the software mentioned above can require as little as 96K bytes of core altogether. There are even larger installations; see the description of the PWB/UNIX systems,[4,5] for example. There are also much smaller, though somewhat restricted, versions of the system.[6]

Our own PDP-11 has two 200-Mb moving-head disks for file system storage and swapping. There are 20 variable-speed communications interfaces attached to 300- and 1200-baud data sets, and an additional 12 communication lines hard-wired to 9600-baud terminals and satellite computers. There are also several 2400- and 4800-baud synchronous communication interfaces used for machine-to-machine file transfer. Finally, there is a variety of miscellaneous devices including nine-track magnetic tape, a line printer, a voice synthesizer, a phototypesetter, a digital switching network, and a chess machine.

The preponderance of UNIX software is written in the abovementioned C language.[7] Early versions of the operating system were written in assembly language, but during the summer of 1973, it was rewritten in C. The size of the new system was about one-third greater than that of the old. Since the new system not only became much easier to understand and to modify but also included many functional improvements, including multiprogramming and the ability to share reentrant code among several user programs, we consider this increase in size quite acceptable.

III. THE FILE SYSTEM

The most important role of the system is to provide a file system. From the point of view of the user, there are three kinds of files: ordinary disk files, directories, and special files.

3.1 Ordinary files

A file contains whatever information the user places on it, for example, symbolic or binary (object) programs. No particular structuring is expected by the system. A file of text consists simply of a string of characters, with lines demarcated by the newline character. Binary programs are sequences of words as they will appear in core memory when the program starts executing. A few user programs manipulate files with more structure; for example, the assembler generates, and the loader expects, an object file in a particular format. However, the structure of files is controlled by the programs that use them, not by the system.

3.2 Directories

Directories provide the mapping between the names of files and the files themselves, and thus induce a structure on the file system as a whole. Each user has a directory of his own files; he may also create subdirectories to contain groups of files conveniently treated together. A directory behaves exactly like an ordinary file except that it cannot be written on by unprivileged programs, so that the system controls the contents of directories. However, anyone with appropriate permission may read a directory just like any other file.

The system maintains several directories for its own use. One of these is the **root** directory. All files in the system can be found by tracing a path through a chain of directories until the desired file is reached. The starting point for such searches is often the **root**. Other system directories contain all the programs provided for general use; that is, all the *commands*. As will be seen, however, it is by no means necessary that a program reside in one of these directories for it to be executed.

Files are named by sequences of 14 or fewer characters. When the name of a file is specified to the system, it may be in the form of a *path name*, which is a sequence of directory names separated by slashes, "/", and ending in a file name. If the sequence begins with a slash, the search begins in the root directory. The name **/alpha/beta/gamma** causes the system to search the root for directory **alpha**, then to search **alpha** for **beta**, finally to find **gamma** in **beta**. **gamma** may be an ordinary file, a directory, or a special file. As a limiting case, the name "/" refers to the root itself.

A path name not starting with "/" causes the system to begin the search in the user's current directory. Thus, the name **alpha/beta** specifies the file named **beta** in subdirectory **alpha** of the current directory. The simplest kind of name, for example, **alpha**, refers to a file that itself is found in the current directory. As another limiting case, the null file name refers to the current directory.

The same non-directory file may appear in several directories under possibly different names. This feature is called *linking*; a directory entry for a file is sometimes called a link. The UNIX system differs from other systems in which linking is permitted in that all links to a file have equal status. That is, a file does not exist within a particular directory; the directory entry for a file consists merely of its name and a pointer to the information actually describing the file. Thus a file exists independently of any directory entry, although in practice a file is made to disappear along with the last link to it.

Each directory always has at least two entries. The name "." in each directory refers to the directory itself. Thus a program may read the current directory under the name "." without knowing its complete path name. The name ".." by convention refers to the parent of the directory in which it appears, that is, to the directory in which it was created.

The directory structure is constrained to have the form of a rooted tree. Except for the special entries "." and "..", each directory must appear as an entry in exactly one other directory, which is its parent. The reason for this is to simplify the writing of programs that visit subtrees of the directory structure, and more important, to avoid the separation of portions of the hierarchy. If arbitrary links to directories were permitted, it would be quite difficult to detect when the last connection from the root to a directory was severed.

3.3 Special files

Special files constitute the most unusual feature of the UNIX file system. Each supported I/O device is associated with at least one such file. Special files are read and written just like ordinary disk files, but requests to read or write result in activation of the associated device. An entry for each special file resides in directory **/dev**, although a link may be made to one of these files just as it may to an ordinary file. Thus, for example, to write on a magnetic tape one may write on the file **/dev/mt**. Special files exist for each communication line, each disk, each tape drive, and for physical main memory. Of course, the active disks and the memory special file are protected from indiscriminate access.

There is a threefold advantage in treating I/O devices this way: file and device I/O are as similar as possible; file and device names have the same syntax and meaning, so that a program expecting a file name as a parameter can be passed a device name; finally, special files are subject to the same protection mechanism as regular files.

3.4 Removable file systems

Although the root of the file system is always stored on the same device, it is not necessary that the entire file system hierarchy reside on this device. There is a **mount** system request with two arguments: the name of an existing ordinary file, and the name of a special file whose associated storage volume (e.g., a disk pack) should have the structure of an independent file system containing its own directory hierarchy. The effect of **mount** is to cause references to the heretofore ordinary file to refer instead to the root directory of the file system on the removable volume. In effect, **mount** replaces a leaf of the hierarchy tree (the ordinary file) by a whole new subtree (the hierarchy stored on the removable volume). After the **mount**, there is virtually no distinction between files on the removable volume and those in the permanent file system. In our installation, for example, the root directory resides on a small partition of one of our disk drives, while the other drive, which contains the user's files, is mounted by the system initialization sequence. A mountable file system is generated by writing on its corresponding special file. A utility program is available to create an empty file system, or one may simply copy an existing file system.

There is only one exception to the rule of identical treatment of files on different devices: no link may exist between one file system hierarchy and another. This restriction is enforced so as to avoid the elaborate bookkeeping that would otherwise be required to assure removal of the links whenever the removable volume is dismounted.

3.5 Protection

Although the access control scheme is quite simple, it has some unusual features. Each user of the system is assigned a unique user identification number. When a file is created, it is marked with the user ID of its owner. Also given for new files is a set of ten protection bits. Nine of these specify independently read, write, and execute permission for the owner of the file, for other members of his group, and for all remaining users.

If the tenth bit is on, the system will temporarily change the user identification (hereafter, user ID) of the current user to that of the creator of the file whenever the file is executed as a program. This change in user ID is effective only during the execution of the program that calls for it. The set-user-ID feature provides for privileged programs that may use files inaccessible to other users. For example, a program may keep an accounting file that should neither be read nor changed except by the program itself. If the set-user-ID bit is on for the program, it may access the file although this access might be forbidden to other programs invoked by the given program's user. Since the actual user ID of the invoker of any program is always available, set-user-ID programs may take any measures desired to satisfy themselves as to their invoker's credentials. This mechanism is used to allow users to execute the carefully written commands that call privileged system entries. For example, there is a system entry invokable only by the "super-user" (below) that creates an empty directory. As indicated above, directories are expected to have entries for ''.'' and ''..''. The command which creates a directory is owned by the super-user and has the set-user-ID bit set. After it checks its invoker's authorization to create the specified directory, it creates it and makes the entries for ''.'' and ''..''.

Because anyone may set the set-user-ID bit on one of his own files, this mechanism is generally available without administrative intervention. For example, this protection scheme easily solves the MOO accounting problem posed by "Aleph-null."[8]

The system recognizes one particular user ID (that of the "super-user") as exempt from the usual constraints on file access; thus (for example), programs may be written to dump and reload the file system without unwanted interference from the protection system.

3.6 I/O calls

The system calls to do I/O are designed to eliminate the differences between the various devices and styles of access. There is no distinction between "random" and "sequential" I/O, nor is any logical record size imposed by the system. The size of an ordinary file is determined by the number of bytes written on it; no predetermination of the size of a file is necessary or possible.

To illustrate the essentials of I/O, some of the basic calls are summarized below in an anonymous language that will indicate the required parameters without getting into the underlying complexities. Each call to the system may potentially result in an error return, which for simplicity is not represented in the calling sequence.

To read or write a file assumed to exist already, it must be opened by the following call:

filep = open (name, flag)

where **name** indicates the name of the file. An arbitrary path name may be given. The **flag** argument indicates whether the file is to be read, written, or "updated," that is, read and written simultaneously.

The returned value **filep** is called a *file descriptor*. It is a small integer used to identify the file in subsequent calls to read, write, or otherwise manipulate the file.

To create a new file or completely rewrite an old one, there is a **create** system call that creates the given file if it does not exist, or truncates it to zero length if it does exist; **create** also opens the new file for writing and, like **open**, returns a file descriptor.

The file system maintains no locks visible to the user, nor is there any restriction on the number of users who may have a file open for reading or writing. Although it is possible for the contents of a file to become scrambled when two users write on it simultaneously, in practice difficulties do not arise. We take the view that locks are neither necessary nor sufficient, in our environment, to prevent interference between users of the same file. They are unnecessary because we are not faced with large, single-file data bases maintained by independent processes. They are insufficient because locks in the ordinary sense, whereby one user is prevented from writing on a file that another user is reading, cannot prevent confusion when, for example, both users are editing a file with an editor that makes a copy of the file being edited.

There are, however, sufficient internal interlocks to maintain the logical consistency of the file system when two users engage simultaneously in activities such as writing on the same file, creating files in the same directory, or deleting each other's open files.

Except as indicated below, reading and writing are sequential. This means that if a particular byte in the file was the last byte written (or read), the next I/O call implicitly refers to the immediately following byte. For each open file there is a pointer, maintained inside the system, that indicates the next byte to be read or written. If n bytes are read or written, the pointer advances by n bytes.

Once a file is open, the following calls may be used:

n = read (filep, buffer, count)
n = write (filep, buffer, count)

Up to **count** bytes are transmitted between the file specified by **filep** and the byte array specified by **buffer**. The returned value **n** is the number of bytes actually transmitted. In the **write** case, **n** is the same as **count** except under exceptional conditions, such as I/O errors or end of physical medium on special files; in a **read**, however, **n** may without error be less than **count**. If the read pointer is so near the end of the file that reading **count** characters would cause reading beyond the end, only sufficient bytes are transmitted to reach the end of the file; also, typewriter-like terminals never return more than one line of input. When a **read** call returns with **n** equal to zero, the end of the file has been reached. For disk files this occurs when the read pointer becomes equal to the current size of the file. It is possible to generate an end-of-file from a terminal by use of an escape sequence that depends on the device used.

Bytes written affect only those parts of a file implied by the position of the write pointer and the count; no other part of the file is changed. If the last byte lies beyond the end of the file, the file is made to grow as needed.

To do random (direct-access) I/O it is only necessary to move the read or write pointer to the appropriate location in the file.

$$location = lseek(filep, offset, base)$$

The pointer associated with **filep** is moved to a position **offset** bytes from the beginning of the file, from the current position of the pointer, or from the end of the file, depending on **base.** **offset** may be negative. For some devices (e.g., paper tape and terminals) seek calls are ignored. The actual offset from the beginning of the file to which the pointer was moved is returned in **location**.

There are several additional system entries having to do with I/O and with the file system that will not be discussed. For example: close a file, get the status of a file, change the protection mode or the owner of a file, create a directory, make a link to an existing file, delete a file.

IV. IMPLEMENTATION OF THE FILE SYSTEM

As mentioned in Section 3.2 above, a directory entry contains only a name for the associated file and a pointer to the file itself. This pointer is an integer called the *i-number* (for index number) of the file. When the file is accessed, its i-number is used as an index into a system table (the *i-list*) stored in a known part of the device on which the directory resides. The entry found thereby (the file's *i-node*) contains the description of the file:

i   the user and group-ID of its owner

ii   its protection bits

iii   the physical disk or tape addresses for the file contents

iv   its size

v   time of creation, last use, and last modification

vi   the number of links to the file, that is, the number of times it appears in a directory

vii   a code indicating whether the file is a directory, an ordinary file, or a special file.

The purpose of an **open** or **create** system call is to turn the path name given by the user into an i-number by searching the explicitly or implicitly named directories. Once a file is open, its device, i-number, and read/write pointer are stored in a system table indexed by the file descriptor returned by the **open** or **create**. Thus, during a subsequent call to read or write the file, the descriptor may be easily related to the information necessary to access the file.

When a new file is created, an i-node is allocated for it and a directory entry is made that contains the name of the file and the i-node number. Making a link to an existing file involves creating a directory entry with the new name, copying the i-number from the original file entry, and incrementing the link-count field of the i-node. Removing (deleting) a file is done by decrementing the link-count of the i-node specified by its directory entry and erasing the directory entry. If the link-count drops to 0, any disk blocks in the file are freed and the i-node is de-allocated.

The space on all disks that contain a file system is divided into a number of 512-byte blocks logically addressed from 0 up to a limit that depends on the device. There is space in the i-node of each file for 13 device addresses. For nonspecial files, the first 10 device addresses point at the first 10 blocks of the file. If the file is larger than 10 blocks, the 11 device address points to an indirect block containing up to 128 addresses of additional blocks in the file. Still larger files use the twelfth device address of the i-node to point to a double-indirect block naming 128 indirect blocks, each pointing to 128 blocks of the file. If required, the thirteenth device address is a triple-indirect block. Thus files may conceptually grow to $[(10+128+128^2+128^3)\cdot 512]$ bytes. Once opened, bytes numbered below 5120 can be read with a single disk access; bytes in the range 5120 to 70,656 require two accesses; bytes in the range 70,656 to 8,459,264 require three accesses; bytes from there to the largest file (1,082,201,088) require four accesses. In practice, a device cache mechanism (see below) proves effective in eliminating most of the indirect fetches.

The foregoing discussion applies to ordinary files. When an I/O request is made to a file whose i-node indicates that it is special, the last 12 device address words are immaterial, and the first specifies an internal *device name*, which is interpreted as a pair of numbers representing, respectively, a device type and subdevice number. The device type indicates which system routine will deal with I/O on that device; the subdevice number selects, for example, a disk drive attached to a particular controller or one of several similar terminal interfaces.

In this environment, the implementation of the **mount** system call (Section 3.4) is quite straightforward. **mount** maintains a system table whose argument is the i-number and device name of the ordinary file specified during the **mount**, and whose corresponding value is the device name of the indicated special file. This table is searched for each i-number/device pair that turns up while a path name is being scanned during an **open** or **create**; if a match is found, the i-number is replaced by the i-number of the root directory and the device name is replaced by the table value.

To the user, both reading and writing of files appear to be synchronous and unbuffered. That is, immediately after return from a **read** call the data are available; conversely, after a **write** the user's workspace may be reused. In fact, the system maintains a rather complicated buffering mechanism that reduces greatly the number of I/O operations required to access a file. Suppose a **write** call is made specifying transmission of a single byte. The system will search its buffers to see whether the affected disk block currently resides in main memory; if not, it will be read in from the device. Then the affected byte is replaced in the buffer and an entry is made in a list of blocks to be written. The return from the **write** call may then take place, although the actual I/O may not be completed until a later time. Conversely, if a single byte is read, the system determines whether the secondary storage block in which the byte is located is already in one of the system's buffers; if so, the byte can be returned immediately. If not, the block is read into a buffer and the byte picked out.

The system recognizes when a program has made accesses to sequential blocks of a file, and asynchronously pre-reads the next block. This significantly reduces the running time of most programs while adding little to system overhead.

A program that reads or writes files in units of 512 bytes has an advantage over a program that reads or writes a single byte at a time, but the gain is not immense; it comes mainly from the avoidance of system overhead. If a program is used rarely or does no great volume of I/O, it may quite reasonably read and write in units as small as it wishes.

The notion of the i-list is an unusual feature of UNIX. In practice, this method of organizing the file system has proved quite reliable and easy to deal with. To the system itself, one of its strengths is the fact that each file has a short, unambiguous name related in a simple way to the protection, addressing, and other information needed to access the file. It also permits a quite simple and rapid algorithm for checking the consistency of a file system, for example, verification that the portions of each device containing useful information and those free to be allocated are disjoint and together exhaust the space on the device. This algorithm is independent of the directory hierarchy, because it need only scan the linearly organized i-list. At the same time the notion of the i-list induces certain peculiarities not found in other file system organizations. For example, there is the question of who is to be charged for the space a file occupies, because all directory entries for a file have equal status. Charging the owner of a file is unfair in general, for one user may create a file, another may link to it, and the first user may delete the file. The first user is still the owner of the file, but it should be charged to the second user. The simplest reasonably fair algorithm seems to be to spread the charges equally among users who have links to a file. Many installations avoid the issue by not charging any fees at all.

V. PROCESSES AND IMAGES

An *image* is a computer execution environment. It includes a memory image, general register values, status of open files, current directory and the like. An image is the current state of a pseudo-computer.

A *process* is the execution of an image. While the processor is executing on behalf of a process, the image must reside in main memory; during the execution of other processes it remains in main memory unless the appearance of an active, higher-priority process forces it to be swapped out to the disk.

The user-memory part of an image is divided into three logical segments. The program text segment begins at location 0 in the virtual address space. During execution, this segment is write-protected and a single copy of it is shared among all processes executing the same program. At the first hardware protection byte boundary above the program text segment in the virtual address space begins a non-shared, writable data segment, the size of which may be extended by a system call. Starting at the highest address in the virtual address space is a stack segment, which automatically grows downward as the stack pointer fluctuates.

5.1 Processes

Except while the system is bootstrapping itself into operation, a new process can come into existence only by use of the **fork** system call:

processid = fork ( )

When **fork** is executed, the process splits into two independently executing processes. The two processes have independent copies of the original memory image, and share all open files. The new processes differ only in that one is considered the parent process: in the parent, the returned **processid** actually identifies the child process and is never 0, while in the child, the returned value is always 0.

Because the values returned by **fork** in the parent and child process are distinguishable, each process may determine whether it is the parent or child.

5.2 Pipes

Processes may communicate with related processes using the same system **read** and **write** calls that are used for file-system I/O. The call:

filep = pipe ( )

returns a file descriptor **filep** and creates an inter-process channel called a *pipe*. This channel, like other open files, is passed from parent to child process in the image by the **fork** call. A **read** using a pipe file descriptor waits until another process writes using the file descriptor for the same pipe. At this point, data are passed between the images of the two processes. Neither process need know that a pipe, rather than an ordinary file, is involved.

Although inter-process communication via pipes is a quite valuable tool (see Section 6.2), it is not a completely general mechanism, because the pipe must be set up by a common ancestor of the processes involved.

5.3 Execution of programs

Another major system primitive is invoked by

execute (file, arg_1, arg_2, ... , arg_n)

which requests the system to read in and execute the program named by **file**, passing it string arguments arg_1, arg_2, ... , arg_n. All the code and data in the process invoking **execute** is replaced from the **file**, but open files, current directory, and inter-process relationships are unaltered. Only if the call fails, for example because **file** could not be found or because its execute-permission bit was not set, does a return take place from the **execute** primitive; it resembles a "jump" machine instruction rather than a subroutine call.

5.4 Process synchronization

Another process control system call:

processid = wait (status)

causes its caller to suspend execution until one of its children has completed execution. Then **wait** returns the **processid** of the terminated process. An error return is taken if the calling process has no descendants. Certain status from the child process is also available.

5.5 Termination

Lastly:

exit (status)

terminates a process, destroys its image, closes its open files, and generally obliterates it. The parent is notified through the **wait** primitive, and **status** is made available to it. Processes may also terminate as a result of various illegal actions or user-generated signals (Section VII below).

VI. THE SHELL

For most users, communication with the system is carried on with the aid of a program called the shell. The shell is a command-line interpreter: it reads lines typed by the user and interprets them as requests to execute other programs. (The shell is described fully elsewhere,[9] so this section will discuss only the theory of its operation.) In simplest form, a command line consists of the command name followed by arguments to the command, all separated by spaces:

command arg$_1$ arg$_2$ ... arg$_n$

The shell splits up the command name and the arguments into separate strings. Then a file with name **command** is sought; **command** may be a path name including the "/" character to specify any file in the system. If **command** is found, it is brought into memory and executed. The arguments collected by the shell are accessible to the command. When the command is finished, the shell resumes its own execution, and indicates its readiness to accept another command by typing a prompt character.

If file **command** cannot be found, the shell generally prefixes a string such as **/bin/** to **command** and attempts again to find the file. Directory **/bin** contains commands intended to be generally used. (The sequence of directories to be searched may be changed by user request.)

6.1 Standard I/O

The discussion of I/O in Section III above seems to imply that every file used by a program must be opened or created by the program in order to get a file descriptor for the file. Programs executed by the shell, however, start off with three open files with file descriptors 0, 1, and 2. As such a program begins execution, file 1 is open for writing, and is best understood as the standard output file. Except under circumstances indicated below, this file is the user's terminal. Thus programs that wish to write informative information ordinarily use file descriptor 1. Conversely, file 0 starts off open for reading, and programs that wish to read messages typed by the user read this file.

The shell is able to change the standard assignments of these file descriptors from the user's terminal printer and keyboard. If one of the arguments to a command is prefixed by ">", file descriptor 1 will, for the duration of the command, refer to the file named after the ">". For example:

ls

ordinarily lists, on the typewriter, the names of the files in the current directory. The command:

ls > there

creates a file called **there** and places the listing there. Thus the argument >**there** means "place output on **there**." On the other hand:

ed

ordinarily enters the editor, which takes requests from the user via his keyboard. The command

ed < script

interprets **script** as a file of editor commands; thus < **script** means "take input from **script**."

Although the file name following "<" or ">" appears to be an argument to the command, in fact it is interpreted completely by the shell and is not passed to the command at all. Thus no special coding to handle I/O redirection is needed within each command; the command need merely use the standard file descriptors 0 and 1 where appropriate.

File descriptor 2 is, like file 1, ordinarily associated with the terminal output stream. When an output-diversion request with ">" is specified, file 2 remains attached to the terminal, so that commands may produce diagnostic messages that do not silently end up in the output file.

6.2 Filters

An extension of the standard I/O notion is used to direct output from one command to the input of another. A sequence of commands separated by vertical bars causes the shell to execute all the commands simultaneously and to arrange that the standard output of each command be delivered to the standard input of the next command in the sequence. Thus in the command line:

ls | pr −2 | opr

ls lists the names of the files in the current directory; its output is passed to **pr**, which paginates its input with dated headings. (The argument "−2" requests double-column output.) Likewise, the output from **pr** is input to **opr**; this command spools its input onto a file for off-line printing.

This procedure could have been carried out more clumsily by:

ls > temp1
pr −2 < temp1 > temp2
opr < temp2

followed by removal of the temporary files. In the absence of the ability to redirect output and input, a still clumsier method would have been to require the **ls** command to accept user requests to paginate its output, to print in multi-column format, and to arrange that its output be delivered off-line. Actually it would be surprising, and in fact unwise for efficiency reasons, to expect authors of commands such as **ls** to provide such a wide variety of output options.

A program such as **pr** which copies its standard input to its standard output (with processing) is called a *filter*. Some filters that we have found useful perform character transliteration, selection of lines according to a pattern, sorting of the input, and encryption and decryption.

6.3 Command separators; multitasking

Another feature provided by the shell is relatively straightforward. Commands need not be on different lines; instead they may be separated by semicolons:

    ls; ed

will first list the contents of the current directory, then enter the editor.

A related feature is more interesting. If a command is followed by "**&**," the shell will not wait for the command to finish before prompting again; instead, it is ready immediately to accept a new command. For example:

    as source >output &

causes **source** to be assembled, with diagnostic output going to **output**; no matter how long the assembly takes, the shell returns immediately. When the shell does not wait for the completion of a command, the identification number of the process running that command is printed. This identification may be used to wait for the completion of the command or to terminate it. The "**&**" may be used several times in a line:

    as source >output & ls >files &

does both the assembly and the listing in the background. In these examples, an output file other than the terminal was provided; if this had not been done, the outputs of the various commands would have been intermingled.

The shell also allows parentheses in the above operations. For example:

    (date; ls) >x &

writes the current date and time followed by a list of the current directory onto the file **x**. The shell also returns immediately for another request.

6.4 The shell as a command; command files

The shell is itself a command, and may be called recursively. Suppose file **tryout** contains the lines:

    as source
    mv a.out testprog
    testprog

The **mv** command causes the file **a.out** to be renamed **testprog. a.out** is the (binary) output of the assembler, ready to be executed. Thus if the three lines above were typed on the keyboard, **source** would be assembled, the resulting program renamed **testprog**, and **testprog** executed. When the lines are in **tryout**, the command:

    sh <tryout

would cause the shell **sh** to execute the commands sequentially.

The shell has further capabilities, including the ability to substitute parameters and to construct argument lists from a specified subset of the file names in a directory. It also provides general conditional and looping constructions.

6.5 Implementation of the shell

The outline of the operation of the shell can now be understood. Most of the time, the shell is waiting for the user to type a command. When the newline character ending the line is typed, the shell's **read** call returns. The shell analyzes the command line, putting the arguments in a form appropriate for **execute**. Then **fork** is called. The child process, whose code of course is still that of the shell, attempts to perform an **execute** with the appropriate arguments. If successful, this will bring in and start execution of the program whose name was given. Meanwhile, the other process resulting from the **fork**, which is the parent process, **waits** for the child process to die. When this happens, the shell knows the command is finished, so it types its prompt and reads the keyboard to obtain another command.

Given this framework, the implementation of background processes is trivial; whenever a command line contains "**&**," the shell merely refrains from waiting for the process that it created to execute the command.

Happily, all of this mechanism meshes very nicely with the notion of standard input and output files. When a process is created by the **fork** primitive, it inherits not only the memory image of its parent but also all the files currently open in its parent, including those with file descriptors 0, 1, and 2. The shell, of course, uses these files to read command lines and to write its prompts and diagnostics, and in the ordinary case its children—the command programs—inherit them automatically. When an argument with "<" or ">" is given, however, the offspring process, just before it performs **execute,** makes the standard I/O file descriptor (0 or 1, respectively) refer to the named file. This is easy because, by agreement, the smallest unused file descriptor is assigned when a new file is **open**ed (or **create**d); it is only necessary to close file 0 (or 1) and open the named file. Because the process in which the command program runs simply terminates when it is through, the association between a file specified after "<" or ">" and file descriptor 0 or 1 is ended automatically when the process dies. Therefore the shell need not know the actual names of the files that are its own standard input and output, because it need never reopen them.

Filters are straightforward extensions of standard I/O redirection with pipes used instead of files.

In ordinary circumstances, the main loop of the shell never terminates. (The main loop includes the branch of the return from **fork** belonging to the parent process; that is, the branch that does a **wait**, then reads another command line.) The one thing that causes the shell to terminate is discovering an end-of-file condition on its input file. Thus, when the shell is executed as a command with a given input file, as in:

    sh <comfile

the commands in **comfile** will be executed until the end of **comfile** is reached; then the instance of the shell invoked by **sh** will terminate. Because this shell process is the child of another instance of the shell, the **wait** executed in the latter will return, and another command may then be processed.

6.6 Initialization

The instances of the shell to which users type commands are themselves children of another process. The last step in the initialization of the system is the creation of a single process and the invocation (via **execute**) of a program called **init**. The role of **init** is to create one process for each terminal channel. The various subinstances of **init** open the appropriate terminals for input and output on files 0, 1, and 2, waiting, if necessary, for carrier to be established on dial-up lines. Then a message is typed out requesting that the user log in. When the user types a name or other identification, the appropriate instance of **init** wakes up, receives the log-in line, and reads a password file. If the user's name is found, and if he is able to supply the correct password, **init** changes to the user's default current directory, sets the process's user ID to that of the person logging in, and performs an **execute** of the shell. At this point, the shell is ready to receive commands and the logging-in protocol is complete.

Meanwhile, the mainstream path of **init** (the parent of all the subinstances of itself that will later become shells) does a **wait**. If one of the child processes terminates, either because a shell found an end of file or because a user typed an incorrect name or password, this path of **init** simply recreates the defunct process, which in turn reopens the appropriate input and output files and types another log-in message. Thus a user may log out simply by typing the end-of-file sequence to the shell.

6.7 Other programs as shell

The shell as described above is designed to allow users full access to the facilities of the system, because it will invoke the execution of any program with appropriate protection mode. Sometimes, however, a different interface to the system is desirable, and this feature is easily arranged for.

Recall that after a user has successfully logged in by supplying a name and password, **init** ordinarily invokes the shell to interpret command lines. The user's entry in the password file may contain the name of a program to be invoked after log-in instead of the shell. This program is free to interpret the user's messages in any way it wishes.

For example, the password file entries for users of a secretarial editing system might specify that the editor **ed** is to be used instead of the shell. Thus when users of the editing system log in, they are inside the editor and can begin work immediately; also, they can be prevented from invoking programs not intended for their use. In practice, it has proved desirable to allow a temporary escape from the editor to execute the formatting program and other utilities.

Several of the games (e.g., chess, blackjack, 3D tic-tac-toe) available on the system illustrate a much more severely restricted environment. For each of these, an entry exists in the password file specifying that the appropriate game-playing program is to be invoked instead of the shell. People who log in as a player of one of these games find themselves limited to the game and unable to investigate the (presumably more interesting) offerings of the UNIX system as a whole.

VII. TRAPS

The PDP-11 hardware detects a number of program faults, such as references to non-existent memory, unimplemented instructions, and odd addresses used where an even address is required. Such faults cause the processor to trap to a system routine. Unless other arrangements have been made, an illegal action causes the system to terminate the process and to write its image on file **core** in the current directory. A debugger can be used to determine the state of the program at the time of the fault.

Programs that are looping, that produce unwanted output, or about which the user has second thoughts may be halted by the use of the **interrupt** signal, which is generated by typing the "delete" character. Unless special action has been taken, this signal simply causes the program to cease execution without producing a **core** file. There is also a **quit** signal used to force an image file to be produced. Thus programs that loop unexpectedly may be halted and the remains inspected without prearrangement.

The hardware-generated faults and the interrupt and quit signals can, by request, be either ignored or caught by a process. For example, the shell ignores quits to prevent a quit from logging the user out. The editor catches interrupts and returns to its command level. This is useful for stopping long printouts without losing work in progress (the editor manipulates a copy of the file it is editing). In systems without floating-point hardware, unimplemented instructions are caught and floating-point instructions are interpreted.

VIII. PERSPECTIVE

Perhaps paradoxically, the success of the UNIX system is largely due to the fact that it was not designed to meet any predefined objectives. The first version was written when one of us (Thompson), dissatisfied with the available computer facilities, discovered a little-used PDP-7 and set out to create a more hospitable environment. This (essentially personal) effort was sufficiently successful to gain the interest of the other author and several colleagues, and later to justify the acquisition of the PDP-11/20, specifically to support a text editing and formatting system. When in turn the 11/20 was outgrown, the system had proved useful enough to persuade management to invest in the PDP-11/45, and later in the PDP-11/70 and Interdata 8/32 machines, upon which it developed to its present form. Our goals throughout the effort, when articulated at all, have always been to build a comfortable relationship with the machine and to explore ideas and inventions in operating systems and other software. We have not been faced with the need to satisfy someone else's requirements, and for this freedom we are grateful.

Three considerations that influenced the design of UNIX are visible in retrospect.

First: because we are programmers, we naturally designed the system to make it easy to write, test, and run programs. The most important expression of our desire for programming convenience was that the system was arranged for interactive use, even though the original version only supported one user. We believe that a properly designed interactive system is much more productive and satisfying to use than a "batch" system. Moreover, such a system is rather easily adaptable to noninteractive use, while the converse is not true.

Second: there have always been fairly severe size constraints on the system and its software. Given the partially antagonistic desires for reasonable efficiency and expressive power, the size constraint has encouraged not only economy, but also a certain elegance of design. This may be a thinly disguised version of the "salvation through suffering" philosophy, but in our case it worked.

Third: nearly from the start, the system was able to, and did, maintain itself. This fact is more important than it might seem. If designers of a system are forced to use that system, they quickly become aware of its functional and superficial deficiencies and are strongly motivated to correct them before it is too late. Because all source programs were always available and easily modified on-line, we were willing to revise and rewrite the system and its software when new ideas were invented, discovered, or suggested by others.

The aspects of UNIX discussed in this paper exhibit clearly at least the first two of these design considerations. The interface to the file system, for example, is extremely convenient from a programming standpoint. The lowest possible interface level is designed to eliminate distinctions between the various devices and files and between direct and sequential access. No large "access method" routines are required to insulate the programmer from the system calls; in fact, all user programs either call the system directly or use a small library program, less than a page long, that buffers a number of characters and reads or writes them all at once.

Another important aspect of programming convenience is that there are no "control blocks" with a complicated structure partially maintained by and depended on by the file system or other system calls. Generally speaking, the contents of a program's address space are the property of the program, and we have tried to avoid placing restrictions on the data structures within that address space.

Given the requirement that all programs should be usable with any file or device as input or output, it is also desirable to push device-dependent considerations into the operating system itself. The only alternatives seem to be to load, with all programs, routines for dealing with each device, which is expensive in space, or to depend on some means of dynamically linking to the routine appropriate to each device when it is actually needed, which is expensive either in overhead or in hardware.

Likewise, the process-control scheme and the command interface have proved both convenient and efficient. Because the shell operates as an ordinary, swappable user program, it consumes no "wired-down" space in the system proper, and it may be made as powerful as desired at little cost. In particular, given the framework in which the shell executes as a process that spawns other processes to perform commands, the notions of I/O redirection, background processes, command files, and user-selectable system interfaces all become essentially trivial to implement.

Influences

The success of UNIX lies not so much in new inventions but rather in the full exploitation of a carefully selected set of fertile ideas, and especially in showing that they can be keys to the implementation of a small yet powerful operating system.

The **fork** operation, essentially as we implemented it, was present in the GENIE time-sharing system.[10] On a number of points we were influenced by Multics, which suggested the particular form of the I/O system calls[11] and both the name of the shell and its general functions. The notion that the shell should create a process for each command was also suggested to us by the early design of Multics, although in that system it was later dropped for efficiency reasons. A similar scheme is used by TENEX.[12]

IX. STATISTICS

The following numbers are presented to suggest the scale of the Research UNIX operation. Those of our users not involved in document preparation tend to use the system for program development, especially language work. There are few important "applications" programs.

Overall, we have today:

125	user population
33	maximum simultaneous users
1,630	directories
28,300	files
301,700	512-byte secondary storage blocks used

There is a "background" process that runs at the lowest possible priority; it is used to soak up any idle CPU time. It has been used to produce a million-digit approximation to the constant e, and other semi-infinite problems. Not counting this background work, we average daily:

13,500	commands
9.6	CPU hours
230	connect hours
62	different users
240	log-ins

X. ACKNOWLEDGMENTS

The contributors to UNIX are, in the traditional but here especially apposite phrase, too numerous to mention. Certainly, collective salutes are due to our colleagues in the Computing Science Research Center. R. H. Canaday contributed much to the basic design of the file system. We are particularly appreciative of the inventiveness, thoughtful criticism, and constant support of R. Morris, M. D. McIlroy, and J. F. Ossanna.

References

1. L. P. Deutsch and B. W. Lampson, "An online editor," *Comm. Assoc. Comp. Mach.* **10**(12) pp. 793-799, 803 (December 1967).

2. B. W. Kernighan and L. L. Cherry, "A System for Typesetting Mathematics," *Comm. Assoc. Comp. Mach.* **18** pp. 151-157 (March 1975).

3. B. W. Kernighan, M. E. Lesk, and J. F. Ossanna, "UNIX Time-Sharing System: Document Preparation," *Bell Sys. Tech. J.* **57**(6) pp. 2115-2135 (1978).

4. T. A. Dolotta and J. R. Mashey, "An Introduction to the Programmer's Workbench," *Proc. 2nd Int. Conf. on Software Engineering*, pp. 164-168 (October 13-15, 1976).

5. T. A. Dolotta, R. C. Haight, and J. R. Mashey, "UNIX Time-Sharing System: The Programmer's Workbench," *Bell Sys. Tech. J.* **57**(6) pp. 2177-2200 (1978).

6. H. Lycklama, "UNIX Time-Sharing System: UNIX on a Microprocessor," *Bell Sys. Tech. J.* **57**(6) pp. 2087-2101 (1978).

7. B. W. Kernighan and D. M. Ritchie, *The C Programming Language,* Prentice-Hall, Englewood Cliffs, New Jersey (1978).

8. Aleph-null, "Computer Recreations," *Software Practice and Experience* **1**(2) pp. 201-204 (April-June 1971).

9. S. R. Bourne, "UNIX Time-Sharing System: The UNIX Shell," *Bell Sys. Tech. J.* **57**(6) pp. 1971-1990 (1978).

10. L. P. Deutsch and B. W. Lampson, "SDS 930 time-sharing system preliminary reference manual," Doc. 30.10.10, Project GENIE, Univ. Cal. at Berkeley (April 1965).

11. R. J. Feiertag and E. I. Organick, "The Multics input-output system," *Proc. Third Symposium on Operating Systems Principles,* pp. 35-41 (October 18-20, 1971).

12. D. G. Bobrow, J. D. Burchfiel, D. L. Murphy, and R. S. Tomlinson, "TENEX, a Paged Time Sharing System for the PDP-10," *Comm. Assoc. Comp. Mach.* **15**(3) pp. 135-143 (March 1972).

GETTING STARTED

UNIX For Beginners — Second Edition

Brian W. Kernighan

Bell Laboratories
Murray Hill, New Jersey 07974

ABSTRACT

This paper is meant to help new users get started on the UNIX† operating system. It includes:

- basics needed for day-to-day use of the system — typing commands, correcting typing mistakes, logging in and out, mail, inter-terminal communication, the file system, printing files, redirecting I/O, pipes, and the shell.
- document preparation — a brief discussion of the major formatting programs and macro packages, hints on preparing documents, and capsule descriptions of some supporting software.
- UNIX programming — using the editor, programming the shell, programming in C, other languages and tools.
- An annotated UNIX bibliography.

September 30, 1978

---

†UNIX is a Trademark of Bell Laboratories.

INTRODUCTION

From the user's point of view, the UNIX operating system is easy to learn and use, and presents few of the usual impediments to getting the job done. It is hard, however, for the beginner to know where to start, and how to make the best use of the facilities available. The purpose of this introduction is to help new users get used to the main ideas of the UNIX system and start making effective use of it quickly.

You should have a couple of other documents with you for easy reference as you read this one. The most important is *The UNIX Programmer's Manual*; it's often easier to tell you to read about something in the manual than to repeat its contents here. The other useful document is *A Tutorial Introduction to the UNIX Text Editor*, which will tell you how to use the editor to get text — programs, data, documents — into the computer.

A word of warning: the UNIX system has become quite popular, and there are several major variants in widespread use. Of course details also change with time. So although the basic structure of UNIX and how to use it is common to all versions, there will certainly be a few things which are different on your system from what is described here. We have tried to minimize the problem, but be aware of it. In cases of doubt, this paper describes Version 7 UNIX.

This paper has five sections:

1. Getting Started: How to log in, how to type, what to do about mistakes in typing, how to log out. Some of this is dependent on which system you log into (phone numbers, for example) and what terminal you use, so this section must necessarily be supplemented by local information.

2. Day-to-day Use: Things you need every day to use the system effectively: generally useful commands; the file system.

3. Document Preparation: Preparing manuscripts is one of the most common uses for UNIX systems. This section contains advice, but not extensive instructions on any of the formatting tools.

4. Writing Programs: UNIX is an excellent system for developing programs. This section talks about some of the tools, but again is not a tutorial in any of the programming languages provided by the system.

5. A UNIX Reading List. An annotated bibliography of documents that new users should be aware of.

I. GETTING STARTED

Logging In

You must have a UNIX login name, which you can get from whoever administers your system. You also need to know the phone number, unless your system uses permanently connected terminals. The UNIX system is capable of dealing with a wide variety of terminals: Terminet 300's; Execuport, TI and similar portables; video (CRT) terminals like the HP2640, etc.; high-priced graphics terminals like the Tektronix 4014; plotting terminals like those from GSI and DASI; and even the venerable Teletype in its various forms. But note: UNIX is strongly oriented towards devices with *lower case*. If your terminal produces only upper case (e.g., model 33 Teletype, some video and portable terminals), life will be so difficult that you should look for another terminal.

Be sure to set the switches appropriately on your device. Switches that might need to be adjusted include the speed, upper/lower case mode, full duplex, even parity, and any others that local wisdom advises. Establish a connection using whatever magic is needed for your terminal; this may involve dialing a telephone call or merely flipping a switch. In either case, UNIX should type "**login:**" at you. If it types garbage, you may be at the wrong speed; check the switches. If that fails, push the "break" or "interrupt" key a few times, slowly. If that fails to produce a login message, consult a guru.

When you get a **login:** message, type your login name *in lower case.* Follow it by a RETURN; the system will not do anything until you type a RETURN. If a password is required, you will be asked for it, and (if possible) printing will be turned off while you type it. Don't forget RETURN.

The culmination of your login efforts is a "prompt character," a single character that indicates that the system is ready to accept commands from you. The prompt character is usually a dollar sign **$** or a percent sign **%**. (You may also get a message of the day just before the prompt character, or a notification that you have mail.)

Typing Commands

Once you've seen the prompt character, you can type commands, which are requests that the system do something. Try typing

date

followed by RETURN. You should get back something like

Mon Jan 16 14:17:10 EST 1978

Don't forget the RETURN after the command, or nothing will happen. If you think you're being ignored, type a RETURN; something should happen. RETURN won't be mentioned again, but don't forget it — it has to be there at the end of each line.

Another command you might try is **who**, which tells you everyone who is currently logged in:

who

gives something like

mb	tty01	Jan 16	09:11
ski	tty05	Jan 16	09:33
gam	tty11	Jan 16	13:07

The time is when the user logged in; "ttyxx" is the system's idea of what terminal the user is on.

If you make a mistake typing the command name, and refer to a non-existent command, you will be told. For example, if you type

whom

you will be told

whom: not found

Of course, if you inadvertently type the name of some other command, it will run, with more or less mysterious results.

Strange Terminal Behavior

Sometimes you can get into a state where your terminal acts strangely. For example, each letter may be typed twice, or the RETURN may not cause a line feed or a return to the left margin. You can often fix this by logging out and logging back in. Or you can read the description of the command **stty** in section I of the manual. To get intelligent treatment of tab characters (which are much used in UNIX) if your terminal doesn't have tabs, type the command

stty —tabs

and the system will convert each tab into the right number of blanks for you. If your terminal does have computer-settable tabs, the command **tabs** will set the stops correctly for you.

Mistakes in Typing

If you make a typing mistake, and see it before RETURN has been typed, there are two ways to recover. The sharp-character # erases the last character typed; in fact successive uses of # erase characters back to the beginning of the line (but not beyond). So if you type badly, you can correct as you go:

dd#atte##e

is the same as **date**.

The at-sign @ erases all of the characters typed so far on the current input line, so if the line is irretrievably fouled up, type an @ and start the line over.

What if you must enter a sharp or at-sign as part of the text? If you precede either # or @ by a backslash \, it loses its erase meaning. So to enter a sharp or at-sign in something, type \# or \@. The system will always echo a newline at you after your at-sign, even if preceded by a backslash. Don't worry — the at-sign has been recorded.

To erase a backslash, you have to type two sharps or two at-signs, as in \##. The backslash is used extensively in UNIX to indicate that the following character is in some way special.

Read-ahead

UNIX has full read-ahead, which means that you can type as fast as you want, whenever you want, even when some command is typing at you. If you type during output, your input characters will appear intermixed with the output characters, but they will be stored away and interpreted in the correct order. So you can type several commands one after another without waiting for the first to finish or even begin.

Stopping a Program

You can stop most programs by typing the character "DEL" (perhaps called "delete" or "rubout" on your terminal). The "interrupt" or "break" key found on most terminals can also be used. In a few programs, like the text editor, DEL stops whatever the program is doing but leaves you in that program. Hanging up the phone will stop most programs.

Logging Out

The easiest way to log out is to hang up the phone. You can also type

> **login**

and let someone else use the terminal you were on. It is usually not sufficient just to turn off the terminal. Most UNIX systems do not use a time-out mechanism, so you'll be there forever unless you hang up.

Mail

When you log in, you may sometimes get the message

> **You have mail.**

UNIX provides a postal system so you can communicate with other users of the system. To read your mail, type the command

> **mail**

Your mail will be printed, one message at a time, most recent message first. After each message, **mail** waits for you to say what to do with it. The two basic responses are **d**, which deletes the message, and RETURN, which does not (so it will still be there the next time you read your mailbox). Other responses are described in the manual. (Earlier versions of **mail** do not process one message at a time, but are otherwise similar.)

How do you send mail to someone else? Suppose it is to go to "joe" (assuming "joe" is someone's login name). The easiest way is this:

> **mail joe**
> *now type in the text of the letter*
> *on as many lines as you like ...*
> *After the last line of the letter*
> *type the character "control—d",*
> *that is, hold down "control" and type*
> *a letter "d".*

And that's it. The "control-d" sequence, often called "EOF" for end-of-file, is used throughout the system to mark the end of input from a terminal, so you might as well get used to it.

For practice, send mail to yourself. (This isn't as strange as it might sound — mail to one-

self is a handy reminder mechanism.)

There are other ways to send mail — you can send a previously prepared letter, and you can mail to a number of people all at once. For more details see **mail**(1). (The notation **mail**(1) means the command **mail** in section 1 of the *UNIX Programmer's Manual.*)

Writing to other users

At some point, out of the blue will come a message like

> **Message from joe tty07...**

accompanied by a startling beep. It means that Joe wants to talk to you, but unless you take explicit action you won't be able to talk back. To respond, type the command

> **write joe**

This establishes a two-way communication path. Now whatever Joe types on his terminal will appear on yours and vice versa. The path is slow, rather like talking to the moon. (If you are in the middle of something, you have to get to a state where you can type a command. Normally, whatever program you are running has to terminate or be terminated. If you're editing, you can escape temporarily from the editor — read the editor tutorial.)

A protocol is needed to keep what you type from getting garbled up with what Joe types. Typically it's like this:

> Joe types **write smith** and waits.
> Smith types **write joe** and waits.
> Joe now types his message (as many lines as he likes). When he's ready for a reply, he signals it by typing (**o**), which stands for "over".
> Now Smith types a reply, also terminated by (**o**).
> This cycle repeats until someone gets tired; he then signals his intent to quit with (**oo**), for "over and out".
> To terminate the conversation, each side must type a "control-d" character alone on a line. ("Delete" also works.) When the other person types his "control-d", you will get the message **EOF** on your terminal.

If you write to someone who isn't logged in, or who doesn't want to be disturbed, you'll be told. If the target is logged in but doesn't answer after a decent interval, simply type "control-d".

On-line Manual

The *UNIX Programmer's Manual* is typically kept on-line. If you get stuck on something, and can't find an expert to assist you, you can print on your terminal some manual section that might help. This is also useful for getting the most up-to-date information on a command. To print a manual section, type "man command-name". Thus to read up on the **who** command, type

man who

and, of course,

man man

tells all about the **man** command.

Computer Aided Instruction

Your UNIX system may have available a program called **learn**, which provides computer aided instruction on the file system and basic commands, the editor, docum nt preparation, and even C programming. Try typing the command

learn

If **learn** exists on your system, it will tell you what to do from there.

II. DAY-TO-DAY USE

Creating Files — The Editor

If you have to type a paper or a letter or a program, how do you get the information stored in the machine? Most of these tasks are done with the UNIX "text editor" **ed**. Since **ed** is thoroughly documented in **ed**(1) and explained in *A Tutorial Introduction to the UNIX Text Editor,* we won't spend any time here describing how to use it. All we want it for right now is to make some *files.* (A file is just a collection of information stored in the machine, a simplistic but adequate definition.)

To create a file called **junk** with some text in it, do the following:

> **ed junk**   (invokes the text editor)
> **a**   (command to "ed", to add text)
> *now type in*
> *whatever text you want ...*
> .   (signals the end of adding text)

The "." that signals the end of adding text must be at the beginning of a line by itself. Don't forget it, for until it is typed, no other **ed** commands will be recognized — everything you type will be treated as text to be added.

At this point you can do various editing operations on the text you typed in, such as correcting spelling mistakes, rearranging paragraphs and the like. Finally, you must write the information you have typed into a file with the editor command **w**:

> **w**

ed will respond with the number of characters it wrote into the file **junk**.

Until the **w** command, nothing is stored permanently, so if you hang up and go home the information is lost.† But after **w** the information is there permanently; you can re-access it any time by typing

> **ed junk**

Type a **q** command to quit the editor. (If you try to quit without writing, **ed** will print a **?** to remind you. A second **q** gets you out regardless.)

Now create a second file called **temp** in the same manner. You should now have two files, **junk** and **temp**.

What files are out there?

The **ls** (for "list") command lists the names (not contents) of any of the files that UNIX knows about. If you type

> **ls**

the response will be

> **junk**
> **temp**

which are indeed the two files just created. The names are sorted into alphabetical order automatically, but other variations are possible. For example, the command

> **ls —t**

causes the files to be listed in the order in which they were last changed, most recent first. The **—l** option gives a "long" listing:

> **ls —l**

will produce something like

> —rw—rw—rw— 1 bwk   41 Jul 22 2:56 junk
> —rw—rw—rw— 1 bwk   78 Jul 22 2:57 temp

The date and time are of the last change to the file. The 41 and 78 are the number of characters (which should agree with the numbers you got from **ed**). **bwk** is the owner of the file, that is, the person who created it. The —rw—rw—rw— tells who has permission to read and write the file, in this case everyone.

---

† This is not strictly true — if you hang up while editing, the data you were working on is saved in a file called **ed.hup**, which you can continue with at your next session.

Options can be combined: **ls −lt** gives the same thing as **ls −l**, but sorted into time order. You can also name the files you're interested in, and **ls** will list the information about them only. More details can be found in **ls**(1).

The use of optional arguments that begin with a minus sign, like **−t** and **−lt**, is a common convention for UNIX programs. In general, if a program accepts such optional arguments, they precede any filename arguments. It is also vital that you separate the various arguments with spaces: **ls−l** is not the same as **ls   −l**.

Printing Files

Now that you've got a file of text, how do you print it so people can look at it? There are a host of programs that do that, probably more than are needed.

One simple thing is to use the editor, since printing is often done just before making changes anyway. You can say

ed junk
1,$p

ed will reply with the count of the characters in **junk** and then print all the lines in the file. After you learn how to use the editor, you can be selective about the parts you print.

There are times when it's not feasible to use the editor for printing. For example, there is a limit on how big a file **ed** can handle (several thousand lines). Secondly, it will only print one file at a time, and sometimes you want to print several, one after another. So here are a couple of alternatives.

First is **cat**, the simplest of all the printing programs. **cat** simply prints on the terminal the contents of all the files named in a list. Thus

cat junk

prints one file, and

cat junk temp

prints two. The files are simply concatenated (hence the name "**cat**") onto the terminal.

pr produces formatted printouts of files. As with **cat**, **pr** prints all the files named in a list. The difference is that it produces headings with date, time, page number and file name at the top of each page, and extra lines to skip over the fold in the paper. Thus,

pr junk temp

will print **junk** neatly, then skip to the top of a new page and print **temp** neatly.

pr can also produce multi-column output:

pr −3 junk

prints **junk** in 3-column format. You can use any reasonable number in place of "3" and **pr** will do its best. **pr** has other capabilities as well; see **pr**(1).

It should be noted that **pr** is *not* a formatting program in the sense of shuffling lines around and justifying margins. The true formatters are **nroff** and **troff**, which we will get to in the section on document preparation.

There are also programs that print files on a high-speed printer. Look in your manual under **opr** and **lpr**. Which to use depends on what equipment is attached to your machine.

Shuffling Files About

Now that you have some files in the file system and some experience in printing them, you can try bigger things. For example, you can move a file from one place to another (which amounts to giving it a new name), like this:

mv junk precious

This means that what used to be "junk" is now "precious". If you do an **ls** command now, you will get

precious
temp

Beware that if you move a file to another one that already exists, the already existing contents are lost forever.

If you want to make a *copy* of a file (that is, to have two versions of something), you can use the **cp** command:

cp precious temp1

makes a duplicate copy of **precious** in **temp1**.

Finally, when you get tired of creating and moving files, there is a command to remove files from the file system, called **rm**.

rm temp temp1

will remove both of the files named.

You will get a warning message if one of the named files wasn't there, but otherwise **rm**, like most UNIX commands, does its work silently. There is no prompting or chatter, and error messages are occasionally curt. This terseness is sometimes disconcerting to newcomers, but experienced users find it desirable.

What's in a Filename

So far we have used filenames without ever saying what's a legal name, so it's time for a couple of rules. First, filenames are limited to 14 characters, which is enough to be descriptive.

Second, although you can use almost any character in a filename, common sense says you should stick to ones that are visible, and that you should probably avoid characters that might be used with other meanings. We have already seen, for example, that in the **ls** command, **ls −t** means to list in time order. So if you had a file whose name was **−t**, you would have a tough time listing it by name. Besides the minus sign, there are other characters which have special meaning. To avoid pitfalls, you would do well to use only letters, numbers and the period until you're familiar with the situation.

On to some more positive suggestions. Suppose you're typing a large document like a book. Logically this divides into many small pieces, like chapters and perhaps sections. Physically it must be divided too, for **ed** will not handle really big files. Thus you should type the document as a number of files. You might have a separate file for each chapter, called

> **chap1**
> **chap2**
> etc...

Or, if each chapter were broken into several files, you might have

> **chap1.1**
> **chap1.2**
> **chap1.3**
> ...
> **chap2.1**
> **chap2.2**
> ...

You can now tell at a glance where a particular file fits into the whole.

There are advantages to a systematic naming convention which are not obvious to the novice UNIX user. What if you wanted to print the whole book? You could say

> **pr chap1.1 chap1.2 chap1.3 ......**

but you would get tired pretty fast, and would probably even make mistakes. Fortunately, there is a shortcut. You can say

> **pr chap***

The * means "anything at all," so this translates into "print all files whose names begin with **chap**", listed in alphabetical order.

This shorthand notation is not a property of the **pr** command, by the way. It is system-wide, a service of the program that interprets commands (the "shell," **sh**(1)). Using that fact, you can see how to list the names of the files in the book:

> **ls chap***

produces

> **chap1.1**
> **chap1.2**
> **chap1.3**
> ...

The * is not limited to the last position in a filename — it can be anywhere and can occur several times. Thus

> **rm *junk* *temp***

removes all files that contain **junk** or **temp** as any part of their name. As a special case, * by itself matches every filename, so

> **pr ***

prints all your files (alphabetical order), and

> **rm ***

removes *all files*. (You had better be *very* sure that's what you wanted to say!)

The * is not the only pattern-matching feature available. Suppose you want to print only chapters 1 through 4 and 9. Then you can say

> **pr chap[12349]***

The [...] means to match any of the characters inside the brackets. A range of consecutive letters or digits can be abbreviated, so you can also do this with

> **pr chap[1−49]***

Letters can also be used within brackets: [a−z] matches any character in the range **a** through **z**.

The **?** pattern matches any single character, so

> **ls ?**

lists all files which have single-character names, and

> **ls −l chap?.1**

lists information about the first file of each chapter (**chap1.1**, **chap2.1**, etc.).

Of these niceties, * is certainly the most useful, and you should get used to it. The others are frills, but worth knowing.

If you should ever have to turn off the special meaning of *, **?**, etc., enclose the entire argument in single quotes, as in

> **ls '?'**

We'll see some more examples of this shortly.

What's in a Filename, Continued

When you first made that file called **junk**, how did the system know that there wasn't another **junk** somewhere else, especially since the person in the next office is also reading this tutorial? The answer is that generally each user has a private *directory*, which contains only the files that belong to him. When you log in, you are "in" your directory. Unless you take special action, when you create a new file, it is made in the directory that you are currently in; this is most often your own directory, and thus the file is unrelated to any other file of the same name that might exist in someone else's directory.

The set of all files is organized into a (usually big) tree, with your files located several branches into the tree. It is possible for you to "walk" around this tree, and to find any file in the system, by starting at the root of the tree and walking along the proper set of branches. Conversely, you can start where you are and walk toward the root.

Let's try the latter first. The basic tools is the command **pwd** ("print working directory"), which prints the name of the directory you are currently in.

Although the details will vary according to the system you are on, if you give the command **pwd**, it will print something like

/usr/your-name

This says that you are currently in the directory **your-name**, which is in turn in the directory **/usr**, which is in turn in the root directory called by convention just **/**. (Even if it's not called **/usr** on your system, you will get something analogous. Make the corresponding changes and read on.)

If you now type

ls /usr/your-name

you should get exactly the same list of file names as you get from a plain **ls**: with no arguments, **ls** lists the contents of the current directory; given the name of a directory, it lists the contents of that directory.

Next, try

ls /usr

This should print a long series of names, among which is your own login name **your-name**. On many systems, **usr** is a directory that contains the directories of all the normal users of the system, like you.

The next step is to try

ls /

You should get a response something like this (although again the details may be different):

> **bin**
> **dev**
> **etc**
> **lib**
> **tmp**
> **usr**

This is a collection of the basic directories of files that the system knows about; we are at the root of the tree.

Now try

cat /usr/your-name/junk

(if **junk** is still around in your directory). The name

/usr/your-name/junk

is called the **pathname** of the file that you normally think of as "junk". "Pathname" has an obvious meaning: it represents the full name of the path you have to follow from the root through the tree of directories to get to a particular file. It is a universal rule in the UNIX system that anywhere you can use an ordinary filename, you can use a pathname.

Here is a picture which may make this clearer:

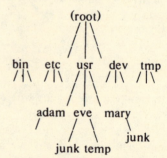

Notice that Mary's **junk** is unrelated to Eve's.

This isn't too exciting if all the files of interest are in your own directory, but if you work with someone else or on several projects concurrently, it becomes handy indeed. For example, your friends can print your book by saying

pr /usr/your-name/chap*

Similarly, you can find out what files your neighbor has by saying

ls /usr/neighbor-name

or make your own copy of one of his files by

cp /usr/your-neighbor/his-file yourfile

If your neighbor doesn't want you poking around in his files, or vice versa, privacy can be arranged. Each file and directory has read-write-execute permissions for the owner, a group, and everyone else, which can be set to control access. See **ls**(1) and **chmod**(1) for details. As a matter of observed fact, most users most of the time find openness of more benefit than privacy.

As a final experiment with pathnames, try

> **ls /bin /usr/bin**

Do some of the names look familiar? When you run a program, by typing its name after the prompt character, the system simply looks for a file of that name. It normally looks first in your directory (where it typically doesn't find it), then in **/bin** and finally in **/usr/bin**. There is nothing magic about commands like **cat** or **ls**, except that they have been collected into a couple of places to be easy to find and administer.

What if you work regularly with someone else on common information in his directory? You could just log in as your friend each time you want to, but you can also say "I want to work on his files instead of my own". This is done by changing the directory that you are currently in:

> **cd /usr/your-friend**

(On some systems, **cd** is spelled **chdir**.) Now when you use a filename in something like **cat** or **pr**, it refers to the file in your friend's directory. Changing directories doesn't affect any permissions associated with a file — if you couldn't access a file from your own directory, changing to another directory won't alter that fact. Of course, if you forget what directory you're in, type

> **pwd**

to find out.

It is usually convenient to arrange your own files so that all the files related to one thing are in a directory separate from other projects. For example, when you write your book, you might want to keep all the text in a directory called **book**. So make one with

> **mkdir book**

then go to it with

> **cd book**

then start typing chapters. The book is now found in (presumably)

> **/usr/your-name/book**

To remove the directory **book**, type

> **rm book/***
> **rmdir book**

The first command removes all files from the directory; the second removes the empty directory.

You can go up one level in the tree of files by saying

> **cd ..**

".." is the name of the parent of whatever directory you are currently in. For completeness, "." is an alternate name for the directory you are in.

Using Files instead of the Terminal

Most of the commands we have seen so far produce output on the terminal; some, like the editor, also take their input from the terminal. It is universal in UNIX systems that the terminal can be replaced by a file for either or both of input and output. As one example,

> **ls**

makes a list of files on your terminal. But if you say

> **ls >filelist**

a list of your files will be placed in the file **filelist** (which will be created if it doesn't already exist, or overwritten if it does). The symbol > means "put the output on the following file, rather than on the terminal." Nothing is produced on the terminal. As another example, you could combine several files into one by capturing the output of **cat** in a file:

> **cat f1 f2 f3 >temp**

The symbol >> operates very much like > does, except that it means "add to the end of." That is,

> **cat f1 f2 f3 >>temp**

means to concatenate **f1**, **f2** and **f3** to the end of whatever is already in **temp**, instead of overwriting the existing contents. As with >, if **temp** doesn't exist, it will be created for you.

In a similar way, the symbol < means to take the input for a program from the following file, instead of from the terminal. Thus, you could make up a script of commonly used editing commands and put them into a file called **script**. Then you can run the script on a file by saying

> **ed file <script**

As another example, you can use **ed** to prepare a letter in file **let**, then send it to several people with

> **mail adam eve mary joe <let**

Pipes

One of the novel contributions of the UNIX system is the idea of a *pipe*. A pipe is simply a way to connect the output of one program to the input of another program, so the two run as a sequence of processes — a pipeline.

For example,

pr f g h

will print the files **f**, **g**, and **h**, beginning each on a new page. Suppose you want them run together instead. You could say

cat f g h >temp
pr <temp
rm temp

but this is more work than necessary. Clearly what we want is to take the output of **cat** and connect it to the input of **pr**. So let us use a pipe:

cat f g h | pr

The vertical bar | means to take the output from **cat**, which would normally have gone to the terminal, and put it into **pr** to be neatly formatted.

There are many other examples of pipes. For example,

ls | pr −3

prints a list of your files in three columns. The program **wc** counts the number of lines, words and characters in its input, and as we saw earlier, **who** prints a list of currently-logged on people, one per line. Thus

who | wc

tells how many people are logged on. And of course

ls | wc

counts your files.

Any program that reads from the terminal can read from a pipe instead; any program that writes on the terminal can drive a pipe. You can have as many elements in a pipeline as you wish.

Many UNIX programs are written so that they will take their input from one or more files if file arguments are given; if no arguments are given they will read from the terminal, and thus can be used in pipelines. **pr** is one example:

pr −3 a b c

prints files **a**, **b** and **c** in order in three columns. But in

cat a b c | pr −3

pr prints the information coming down the pipeline, still in three columns.

The Shell

We have already mentioned once or twice the mysterious "shell," which is in fact **sh**(1). The shell is the program that interprets what you type as commands and arguments. It also looks after translating *, etc., into lists of filenames, and <, >, and | into changes of input and output streams.

The shell has other capabilities too. For example, you can run two programs with one command line by separating the commands with a semicolon; the shell recognizes the semicolon and breaks the line into two commands. Thus

date; who

does both commands before returning with a prompt character.

You can also have more than one program running *simultaneously* if you wish. For example, if you are doing something time-consuming, like the editor script of an earlier section, and you don't want to wait around for the results before starting something else, you can say

ed file <script &

The ampersand at the end of a command line says "start this command running, then take further commands from the terminal immediately," that is, don't wait for it to complete. Thus the script will begin, but you can do something else at the same time. Of course, to keep the output from interfering with what you're doing on the terminal, it would be better to say

ed file <script >script.out &

which saves the output lines in a file called **script.out**.

When you initiate a command with **&**, the system replies with a number called the process number, which identifies the command in case you later want to stop it. If you do, you can say

kill process-number

If you forget the process number, the command **ps** will tell you about everything you have running. (If you are desperate, **kill 0** will kill all your processes.) And if you're curious about other people, **ps a** will tell you about *all* programs that are currently running.

You can say

(command-1; command-2; command-3) &

to start three commands in the background, or you can start a background pipeline with

command-1 | command-2 &

Just as you can tell the editor or some similar program to take its input from a file instead of from the terminal, you can tell the shell to read a file to get commands. (Why not? The shell, after all, is just a program, albeit a clever one.) For instance, suppose you want to set tabs on your terminal, and find out the date and who's on the system every time you log in. Then you can put the three necessary commands (**tabs**, **date**, **who**) into a file, let's call it **startup**, and then run it with

> **sh startup**

This says to run the shell with the file **startup** as input. The effect is as if you had typed the contents of **startup** on the terminal.

If this is to be a regular thing, you can eliminate the need to type **sh**: simply type, once only, the command

> **chmod +x startup**

and thereafter you need only say

> **startup**

to run the sequence of commands. The **chmod**(1) command marks the file executable; the shell recognizes this and runs it as a sequence of commands.

If you want **startup** to run automatically every time you log in, create a file in your login directory called **.profile**, and place in it the line **startup**. When the shell first gains control when you log in, it looks for the **.profile** file and does whatever commands it finds in it. We'll get back to the shell in the section on programming.

III. DOCUMENT PREPARATION

UNIX systems are used extensively for document preparation. There are two major formatting programs, that is, programs that produce a text with justified right margins, automatic page numbering and titling, automatic hyphenation, and the like. **nroff** is designed to produce output on terminals and line-printers. **troff** (pronounced "tee-roff") instead drives a photo-typesetter, which produces very high quality output on photographic paper. This paper was formatted with **troff**.

Formatting Packages

The basic idea of **nroff** and **troff** is that the text to be formatted contains within it "formatting commands" that indicate in detail how the formatted text is to look. For example, there might be commands that specify how long lines are, whether to use single or double spacing, and what running titles to use on each page.

Because **nroff** and **troff** are relatively hard to learn to use effectively, several "packages" of canned formatting requests are available to let you specify paragraphs, running titles, footnotes, multi-column output, and so on, with little effort and without having to learn **nroff** and **troff**. These packages take a modest effort to learn, but the rewards for using them are so great that it is time well spent.

In this section, we will provide a hasty look at the "manuscript" package known as −**ms**. Formatting requests typically consist of a period and two upper-case letters, such as **.TL**, which is used to introduce a title, or **.PP** to begin a new paragraph.

A document is typed so it looks something like this:

```
.TL
title of document
.AU
author name
.SH
section heading
.PP
paragraph ...
.PP
another paragraph ...
.SH
another section heading
.PP
etc.
```

The lines that begin with a period are the formatting requests. For example, **.PP** calls for starting a new paragraph. The precise meaning of **.PP** depends on what output device is being used (typesetter or terminal, for instance), and on what publication the document will appear in. For example, −**ms** normally assumes that a paragraph is preceded by a space (one line in **nroff**, ½ line in **troff**), and the first word is indented. These rules can be changed if you like, but they are changed by changing the interpretation of **.PP**, not by re-typing the document.

To actually produce a document in standard format using −**ms**, use the command

> **troff −ms files ...**

for the typesetter, and

> **nroff −ms files ...**

for a terminal. The −**ms** argument tells **troff** and **nroff** to use the manuscript package of formatting requests.

There are several similar packages; check with a local expert to determine which ones are in common use on your machine.

Supporting Tools

In addition to the basic formatters, there is a host of supporting programs that help with document preparation. The list in the next few paragraphs is far from complete, so browse through the manual and check with people around you for other possibilities.

eqn and **neqn** let you integrate mathematics into the text of a document, in an easy-to-learn language that closely resembles the way you would speak it aloud. For example, the **eqn** input

sum from i=0 to n x sub i ˜=˜ pi over 2

produces the output

$$\sum_{i=0}^{n} x_i = \frac{\pi}{2}$$

The program **tbl** provides an analogous service for preparing tabular material; it does all the computations necessary to align complicated columns with elements of varying widths.

refer prepares bibliographic citations from a data base, in whatever style is defined by the formatting package. It looks after all the details of numbering references in sequence, filling in page and volume numbers, getting the author's initials and the journal name right, and so on.

spell and **typo** detect possible spelling mistakes in a document. **spell** works by comparing the words in your document to a dictionary, printing those that are not in the dictionary. It knows enough about English spelling to detect plurals and the like, so it does a very good job. **typo** looks for words which are "unusual", and prints those. Spelling mistakes tend to be more unusual, and thus show up early when the most unusual words are printed first.

grep looks through a set of files for lines that contain a particular text pattern (rather like the editor's context search does, but on a bunch of files). For example,

grep 'ing$' chap*

will find all lines that end with the letters **ing** in the files **chap***. (It is almost always a good practice to put single quotes around the pattern you're searching for, in case it contains characters like * or $ that have a special meaning to the shell.) **grep** is often useful for finding out in which of a set of files the misspelled words detected by **spell** are actually located.

diff prints a list of the differences between two files, so you can compare two versions of something automatically (which certainly beats proofreading by hand).

wc counts the words, lines and characters in a set of files. **tr** translates characters into other characters; for example it will convert upper to lower case and vice versa. This translates upper into lower:

tr A−Z a−z <input >output

sort sorts files in a variety of ways; **cref** makes cross-references; **ptx** makes a permuted index (keyword-in-context listing). **sed** provides many of the editing facilities of **ed**, but can apply them to arbitrarily long inputs. **awk** provides the ability to do both pattern matching and numeric computations, and to conveniently process fields within lines. These programs are for more advanced users, and they are not limited to document preparation. Put them on your list of things to learn about.

Most of these programs are either independently documented (like **eqn** and **tbl**), or are sufficiently simple that the description in the *UNIX Programmer's Manual* is adequate explanation.

Hints for Preparing Documents

Most documents go through several versions (always more than you expected) before they are finally finished. Accordingly, you should do whatever possible to make the job of changing them easy.

First, when you do the purely mechanical operations of typing, type so that subsequent editing will be easy. Start each sentence on a new line. Make lines short, and break lines at natural places, such as after commas and semicolons, rather than randomly. Since most people change documents by rewriting phrases and adding, deleting and rearranging sentences, these precautions simplify any editing you have to do later.

Keep the individual files of a document down to modest size, perhaps ten to fifteen thousand characters. Larger files edit more slowly, and of course if you make a dumb mistake it's better to have clobbered a small file than a big one. Split into files at natural boundaries in the document, for the same reasons that you start each sentence on a new line.

The second aspect of making change easy is to not commit yourself to formatting details too early. One of the advantages of formatting packages like −ms is that they permit you to delay decisions to the last possible moment. Indeed, until a document is printed, it is not even decided whether it will be typeset or put on a line printer.

As a rule of thumb, for all but the most trivial jobs, you should type a document in terms of a set of requests like **.PP**, and then define them appropriately, either by using one of the canned packages (the better way) or by defining your own **nroff** and **troff** commands. As long as you have entered the text in some systematic way, it can always be cleaned up and reformatted by a judicious combination of editing commands and request definitions.

IV. PROGRAMMING

There will be no attempt made to teach any of the programming languages available but a few words of advice are in order. One of the reasons why the UNIX system is a productive programming environment is that there is already a rich set of tools available, and facilities like pipes, I/O redirection, and the capabilities of the shell often make it possible to do a job by pasting together programs that already exist instead of writing from scratch.

The Shell

The pipe mechanism lets you fabricate quite complicated operations out of spare parts that already exist. For example, the first draft of the **spell** program was (roughly)

```
cat ...      collect the files
| tr ...     put each word on a new line
| tr ...     delete punctuation, etc.
| sort       into dictionary order
| uniq       discard duplicates
| comm       print words in text
             but not in dictionary
```

More pieces have been added subsequently, but this goes a long way for such a small effort.

The editor can be made to do things that would normally require special programs on other systems. For example, to list the first and last lines of each of a set of files, such as a book, you could laboriously type

```
ed
e chap1.1
1p
$p
e chap1.2
1p
$p
etc.
```

But you can do the job much more easily. One way is to type

```
ls chap* >temp
```

to get the list of filenames into a file. Then edit this file to make the necessary series of editing commands (using the global commands of **ed**), and write it into **script**. Now the command

```
ed <script
```

will produce the same output as the laborious hand typing. Alternately (and more easily), you can use the fact that the shell will perform loops, repeating a set of commands over and over again for a set of arguments:

```
for i in chap*
do
        ed $i <script
done
```

This sets the shell variable **i** to each file name in turn, then does the command. You can type this command at the terminal, or put it in a file for later execution.

Programming the Shell

An option often overlooked by newcomers is that the shell is itself a programming language, with variables, control flow (**if-else, while, for, case**), subroutines, and interrupt handling. Since there are many building-block programs, you can sometimes avoid writing a new program merely by piecing together some of the building blocks with shell command files.

We will not go into any details here; examples and rules can be found in *An Introduction to the UNIX Shell*, by S. R. Bourne.

Programming in C

If you are undertaking anything substantial, C is the only reasonable choice of programming language: everything in the UNIX system is tuned to it. The system itself is written in C, as are most of the programs that run on it. It is also an easy language to use once you get started. C is introduced and fully described in *The C Programming Language* by B. W. Kernighan and D. M. Ritchie (Prentice-Hall, 1978). Several sections of the manual describe the system interfaces, that is, how you do I/O and similar functions. Read *UNIX Programming* for more complicated things.

Most input and output in C is best handled with the standard I/O library, which provides a set of I/O functions that exist in compatible form on most machines that have C compilers. In general, it's wisest to confine the system interactions in a program to the facilities provided by this library.

C programs that don't depend too much on special features of UNIX (such as pipes) can be moved to other computers that have C compilers. The list of such machines grows daily; in addition to the original PDP-11, it currently includes at least Honeywell 6000, IBM 370, Interdata 8/32, Data General Nova and Eclipse, HP 2100, Harris /7, VAX 11/780, SEL 86, and Zilog Z80. Calls to the standard I/O library will work on all of these machines.

There are a number of supporting programs that go with C. **lint** checks C programs for potential portability problems, and detects errors such as mismatched argument types and uninitialized variables.

For larger programs (anything whose source is on more than one file) **make** allows you to specify the dependencies among the source files and the processing steps needed to make a new version; it then checks the times that the pieces were last changed and does the minimal amount of recompiling to create a consistent updated version.

The debugger **adb** is useful for digging through the dead bodies of C programs, but is rather hard to learn to use effectively. The most effective debugging tool is still careful thought, coupled with judiciously placed print statements.

The C compiler provides a limited instrumentation service, so you can find out where programs spend their time and what parts are worth optimizing. Compile the routines with the −p option; after the test run, use **prof** to print an execution profile. The command **time** will give you the gross run-time statistics of a program, but they are not super accurate or reproducible.

Other Languages

If you *have* to use Fortran, there are two possibilities. You might consider Ratfor, which gives you the decent control structures and free-form input that characterize C, yet lets you write code that is still portable to other environments. Bear in mind that UNIX Fortran tends to produce large and relatively slow-running programs. Furthermore, supporting software like **adb**, **prof**, etc., are all virtually useless with Fortran programs. There may also be a Fortran 77 compiler on your system. If so, this is a viable alternative to Ratfor, and has the non-trivial advantage that it is compatible with C and related programs. (The Ratfor processor and C tools can be used with Fortran 77 too.)

If your application requires you to translate a language into a set of actions or another language, you are in effect building a compiler, though probably a small one. In that case, you should be using the **yacc** compiler-compiler, which helps you develop a compiler quickly. The **lex** lexical analyzer generator does the same job for the simpler languages that can be expressed as regular expressions. It can be used by itself, or as a front end to recognize inputs for a **yacc**-based program. Both **yacc** and **lex** require some sophistication to use, but the initial effort of learning them can be repaid many times over in programs that are easy to change later on.

Most UNIX systems also make available other languages, such as Algol 68, APL, Basic, Lisp, Pascal, and Snobol. Whether these are useful depends largely on the local environment: if someone cares about the language and has worked on it, it may be in good shape. If not, the odds are strong that it will be more trouble than it's worth.

V. UNIX READING LIST

General:

K. L. Thompson and D. M. Ritchie, *The UNIX Programmer's Manual,* Bell Laboratories, 1978. Lists commands, system routines and interfaces, file formats, and some of the maintenance procedures. You can't live without this, although you will probably only need to read section 1.

Documents for Use with the UNIX Time-sharing System. Volume 2 of the Programmer's Manual. This contains more extensive descriptions of major commands, and tutorials and reference manuals. All of the papers listed below are in it, as are descriptions of most of the programs mentioned above.

D. M. Ritchie and K. L. Thompson, "The UNIX Time-sharing System," CACM, July 1974. An overview of the system, for people interested in operating systems. Worth reading by anyone who programs. Contains a remarkable number of one-sentence observations on how to do things right.

The Bell System Technical Journal (BSTJ) Special Issue on UNIX, July/August, 1978, contains many papers describing recent developments, and some retrospective material.

The 2nd International Conference on Software Engineering (October, 1976) contains several papers describing the use of the Programmer's Workbench (PWB) version of UNIX.

Document Preparation:

B. W. Kernighan, "A Tutorial Introduction to the UNIX Text Editor" and "Advanced Editing on UNIX," Bell Laboratories, 1978. Beginners need the introduction; the advanced material will help you get the most out of the editor.

M. E. Lesk, "Typing Documents on UNIX," Bell Laboratories, 1978. Describes the −ms macro package, which isolates the novice from the vagaries of **nroff** and **troff**, and takes care of most formatting situations. If this specific package isn't available on your system, something similar probably is. The most likely alternative is the PWB/UNIX macro package −**mm**; see your local guru if you use PWB/UNIX.

B. W. Kernighan and L. L. Cherry, "A System for Typesetting Mathematics," Bell Laboratories Computing Science Tech. Rep. 17.

M. E. Lesk, "Tbl — A Program to Format Tables," Bell Laboratories CSTR 49, 1976.

J. F. Ossanna, Jr., "NROFF/TROFF User's Manual," Bell Laboratories CSTR 54, 1976. **troff** is the basic formatter used by −**ms**, **eqn** and **tbl**. The reference manual is indispensable if you are going to write or maintain these or similar programs. But start with:

B. W. Kernighan, "A TROFF Tutorial," Bell Laboratories, 1976. An attempt to unravel the intricacies of **troff**.

Programming:

B. W. Kernighan and D. M. Ritchie, *The C Programming Language*, Prentice-Hall, 1978. Contains a tutorial introduction, complete discussions of all language features, and the reference manual.

B. W. Kernighan and D. M. Ritchie, "UNIX Programming," Bell Laboratories, 1978. Describes how to interface with the system from C programs: I/O calls, signals, processes.

S. R. Bourne, "An Introduction to the UNIX Shell," Bell Laboratories, 1978. An introduction and reference manual for the Version 7 shell. Mandatory reading if you intend to make effective use of the programming power of this shell.

S. C. Johnson, "Yacc — Yet Another Compiler-Compiler," Bell Laboratories CSTR 32, 1978.

M. E. Lesk, "Lex — A Lexical Analyzer Generator," Bell Laboratories CSTR 39, 1975.

S. C. Johnson, "Lint, a C Program Checker," Bell Laboratories CSTR 65, 1977.

S. I. Feldman, "MAKE — A Program for Maintaining Computer Programs," Bell Laboratories CSTR 57, 1977.

J. F. Maranzano and S. R. Bourne, "A Tutorial Introduction to ADB," Bell Laboratories CSTR 62, 1977. An introduction to a powerful but complex debugging tool.

S. I. Feldman and P. J. Weinberger, "A Portable Fortran 77 Compiler," Bell Laboratories, 1978. A full Fortran 77 for UNIX systems.

A Tutorial Introduction to the UNIX Text Editor

Brian W. Kernighan

Bell Laboratories
Murray Hill, New Jersey 07974

ABSTRACT

Almost all text input on the UNIX† operating system is done with the text-editor *ed.* This memorandum is a tutorial guide to help beginners get started with text editing.

Although it does not cover everything, it does discuss enough for most users' day-to-day needs. This includes printing, appending, changing, deleting, moving and inserting entire lines of text; reading and writing files; context searching and line addressing; the substitute command; the global commands; and the use of special characters for advanced editing.

September 21, 1978

---

†UNIX is a Trademark of Bell Laboratories.

Introduction

Ed is a "text editor", that is, an interactive program for creating and modifying "text", using directions provided by a user at a terminal. The text is often a document like this one, or a program or perhaps data for a program.

This introduction is meant to simplify learning *ed*. The recommended way to learn *ed* is to read this document, simultaneously using *ed* to follow the examples, then to read the description in section I of the *UNIX Programmer's Manual*, all the while experimenting with *ed*. (Solicitation of advice from experienced users is also useful.)

Do the exercises! They cover material not completely discussed in the actual text. An appendix summarizes the commands.

Disclaimer

This is an introduction and a tutorial. For this reason, no attempt is made to cover more than a part of the facilities that *ed* offers (although this fraction includes the most useful and frequently used parts). When you have mastered the Tutorial, try *Advanced Editing on UNIX*. Also, there is not enough space to explain basic UNIX procedures. We will assume that you know how to log on to UNIX, and that you have at least a vague understanding of what a file is. For more on that, read *UNIX for Beginners*.

You must also know what character to type as the end-of-line on your particular terminal. This character is the RETURN key on most terminals. Throughout, we will refer to this character, whatever it is, as RETURN.

Getting Started

We'll assume that you have logged in to your system and it has just printed the prompt character, usually either a $ or a %. The easiest way to get *ed* is to type

    ed   (followed by a return)

You are now ready to go — *ed* is waiting for you to tell it what to do.

Creating Text — the Append command "a"

As your first problem, suppose you want to create some text starting from scratch. Perhaps you are typing the very first draft of a paper; clearly it will have to start somewhere, and undergo modifications later. This section will show how to get some text in, just to get started. Later we'll talk about how to change it.

When *ed* is first started, it is rather like working with a blank piece of paper — there is no text or information present. This must be supplied by the person using *ed;* it is usually done by typing in the text, or by reading it into *ed* from a file. We will start by typing in some text, and return shortly to how to read files.

First a bit of terminology. In *ed* jargon, the text being worked on is said to be "kept in a buffer." Think of the buffer as a work space, if you like, or simply as the information that you are going to be editing. In effect the buffer is like the piece of paper, on which we will write things, then change some of them, and finally file the whole thing away for another day.

The user tells *ed* what to do to his text by typing instructions called "commands." Most commands consist of a single letter, which must be typed in lower case. Each command is typed on a separate line. (Sometimes the command is preceded by information about what line or lines of text are to be affected — we will discuss these shortly.) *Ed* makes no response to most commands — there is no prompting or typing of messages like "ready". (This silence is preferred by experienced users, but sometimes a hangup for beginners.)

The first command is *append*, written as the letter

    a

all by itself. It means "append (or add) text lines to the buffer, as I type them in." Appending is rather like writing fresh material on a piece of paper.

So to enter lines of text into the buffer, just type an **a** followed by a RETURN, followed by the lines of text you want, like this:

    a
    Now is the time
    for all good men
    to come to the aid of their party.

The only way to stop appending is to type a line that contains only a period. The "." is used to tell *ed* that you have finished appending. (Even experienced users forget that terminating "." sometimes. If *ed* seems to be ignoring you, type an extra line with just "." on it. You may then find you've added some garbage lines to your text, which you'll have to take out later.)

After the append command has been done, the buffer will contain the three lines

    Now is the time
    for all good men
    to come to the aid of their party.

The "a" and "." aren't there, because they are not text.

To add more text to what you already have, just issue another **a** command, and continue typing.

Error Messages — "?"

If at any time you make an error in the commands you type to *ed,* it will tell you by typing

    ?

This is about as cryptic as it can be, but with practice, you can usually figure out how you goofed.

Writing text out as a file — the Write command "w"

It's likely that you'll want to save your text for later use. To write out the contents of the buffer onto a file, use the *write* command

    w

followed by the filename you want to write on. This will copy the buffer's contents onto the specified file (destroying any previous information on the file). To save the text on a file named **junk**, for example, type

    w junk

Leave a space between **w** and the file name. *Ed* will respond by printing the number of characters it wrote out. In this case, *ed* would respond with

    68

(Remember that blanks and the return character at the end of each line are included in the character count.) Writing a file just makes a copy of the text — the buffer's contents are not disturbed, so you can go on adding lines to it. This is an important point. *Ed* at all times works on a copy of a file, not the file itself. No change in the contents of a file takes place until you give a **w** command. (Writing out the text onto a file from time to time as it is being created is a good idea, since if the system crashes or if you make some horrible mistake, you will lose all the text in the buffer but any text that was written onto a file is relatively safe.)

Leaving ed — the Quit command "q"

To terminate a session with *ed*, save the text you're working on by writing it onto a file using the **w** command, and then type the command

    q

which stands for *quit.* The system will respond with the prompt character ($ or %). At this point your buffer vanishes, with all its text, which is why you want to write it out before quitting.†

Exercise 1:

Enter *ed* and create some text using

    a
    . . . text . . .

Write it out using **w**. Then leave *ed* with the **q** command, and print the file, to see that everything worked. (To print a file, say

    pr filename

or

    cat filename

in response to the prompt character. Try both.)

Reading text from a file — the Edit command "e"

A common way to get text into the buffer is to read it from a file in the file system. This is what you do to edit text that you saved with the **w** command in a previous session. The *edit* command **e** fetches the entire contents of a file into the buffer. So if you had saved the three lines "Now is the time", etc., with a **w** command in an earlier session, the *ed* command

    e junk

would fetch the entire contents of the file **junk** into the buffer, and respond

---

† Actually, *ed* will print **?** if you try to quit without writing. At that point, write if you want; if not, another **q** will get you out regardless.

68

which is the number of characters in **junk**. *If anything was already in the buffer, it is deleted first.*

If you use the **e** command to read a file into the buffer, then you need not use a file name after a subsequent **w** command; *ed* remembers the last file name used in an **e** command, and **w** will write on this file. Thus a good way to operate is

    ed
    e file
    [editing session]
    w
    q

This way, you can simply say **w** from time to time, and be secure in the knowledge that if you got the file name right at the beginning, you are writing into the proper file each time.

You can find out at any time what file name *ed* is remembering by typing the *file* command **f**. In this example, if you typed

    f

ed would reply

    junk

Reading text from a file — the Read command "r"

Sometimes you want to read a file into the buffer without destroying anything that is already there. This is done by the *read* command **r**. The command

    r junk

will read the file **junk** into the buffer; it adds it to the end of whatever is already in the buffer. So if you do a read after an edit:

    e junk
    r junk

the buffer will contain *two* copies of the text (six lines).

    Now is the time
    for all good men
    to come to the aid of their party.
    Now is the time
    for all good men
    to come to the aid of their party.

Like the **w** and **e** commands, **r** prints the number of characters read in, after the reading operation is complete.

Generally speaking, **r** is much less used than **e**.

Exercise 2:

Experiment with the **e** command — try reading and printing various files. You may get an error **?name**, where **name** is the name of a file; this means that the file doesn't exist, typically because you spelled the file name wrong, or perhaps that you are not allowed to read or write it. Try alternately reading and appending to see that they work similarly. Verify that

    ed filename

is exactly equivalent to

    ed
    e filename

What does

    f filename

do?

Printing the contents of the buffer — the Print command "p"

To *print* or list the contents of the buffer (or parts of it) on the terminal, use the print command

    p

The way this is done is as follows. Specify the lines where you want printing to begin and where you want it to end, separated by a comma, and followed by the letter **p**. Thus to print the first two lines of the buffer, for example, (that is, lines 1 through 2) say

    1,2p   (starting line=1, ending line=2 p)

Ed will respond with

    Now is the time
    for all good men

Suppose you want to print *all* the lines in the buffer. You could use **1,3p** as above if you knew there were exactly 3 lines in the buffer. But in general, you don't know how many there are, so what do you use for the ending line number? *Ed* provides a shorthand symbol for "line number of last line in buffer" — the dollar sign **$**. Use it this way:

    1,$p

This will print *all* the lines in the buffer (line 1 to last line.) If you want to stop the printing before it is finished, push the DEL or Delete key; *ed* will type

    ?

and wait for the next command.

To print the *last* line of the buffer, you could use

$,$p

but *ed* lets you abbreviate this to

$p

You can print any single line by typing the line number followed by a **p**. Thus

1p

produces the response

Now is the time

which is the first line of the buffer.

In fact, *ed* lets you abbreviate even further: you can print any single line by typing *just* the line number — no need to type the letter **p**. So if you say

$

ed will print the last line of the buffer.

You can also use $ in combinations like

$-1,$p

which prints the last two lines of the buffer. This helps when you want to see how far you got in typing.

Exercise 3:

As before, create some text using the **a** command and experiment with the **p** command. You will find, for example, that you can't print line 0 or a line beyond the end of the buffer, and that attempts to print a buffer in reverse order by saying

3,1p

don't work.

The current line — "Dot" or "."

Suppose your buffer still contains the six lines as above, that you have just typed

1,3p

and *ed* has printed the three lines for you. Try typing just

p   (no line numbers)

This will print

to come to the aid of their party.

which is the third line of the buffer. In fact it is the last (most recent) line that you have done anything with. (You just printed it!) You can repeat this **p** command without line numbers, and it will continue to print line 3.

The reason is that *ed* maintains a record of the last line that you did anything to (in this case, line 3, which you just printed) so that it

can be used instead of an explicit line number. This most recent line is referred to by the shorthand symbol

(pronounced "dot").

Dot is a line number in the same way that $ is; it means exactly "the current line", or loosely, "the line you most recently did something to." You can use it in several ways — one possibility is to say

.,$p

This will print all the lines from (including) the current line to the end of the buffer. In our example these are lines 3 through 6.

Some commands change the value of dot, while others do not. The **p** command sets dot to the number of the last line printed; the last command will set both . and $ to 6.

Dot is most useful when used in combinations like this one:

.+1   (or equivalently, .+1p)

This means "print the next line" and is a handy way to step slowly through a buffer. You can also say

.−1   (or .−1p)

which means "print the line *before* the current line." This enables you to go backwards if you wish. Another useful one is something like

.−3,.−1p

which prints the previous three lines.

Don't forget that all of these change the value of dot. You can find out what dot is at any time by typing

.=

Ed will respond by printing the value of dot.

Let's summarize some things about the **p** command and dot. Essentially **p** can be preceded by 0, 1, or 2 line numbers. If there is no line number given, it prints the "current line", the line that dot refers to. If there is one line number given (with or without the letter **p**), it prints that line (and dot is set there); and if there are two line numbers, it prints all the lines in that range (and sets dot to the last line printed.) If two line numbers are specified the first can't be bigger than the second (see Exercise 2.)

Typing a single return will cause printing of the next line — it's equivalent to .+1p. Try it. Try typing a −; you will find that it's equivalent to .−1p.

Deleting lines: the "d" command

Suppose you want to get rid of the three extra lines in the buffer. This is done by the *delete* command

d

Except that **d** deletes lines instead of printing them, its action is similar to that of **p**. The lines to be deleted are specified for **d** exactly as they are for **p**:

starting line, ending line **d**

Thus the command

4,$d

deletes lines 4 through the end. There are now three lines left, as you can check by using

1,$p

And notice that **$** now is line 3! Dot is set to the next line after the last line deleted, unless the last line deleted is the last line in the buffer. In that case, dot is set to **$**.

Exercise 4:

Experiment with **a**, **e**, **r**, **w**, **p** and **d** until you are sure that you know what they do, and until you understand how dot, **$**, and line numbers are used.

If you are adventurous, try using line numbers with **a**, **r** and **w** as well. You will find that **a** will append lines *after* the line number that you specify (rather than after dot); that **r** reads a file in *after* the line number you specify (not necessarily at the end of the buffer); and that **w** will write out exactly the lines you specify, not necessarily the whole buffer. These variations are sometimes handy. For instance you can insert a file at the beginning of a buffer by saying

0r filename

and you can enter lines at the beginning of the buffer by saying

0a
. . . *text* . . .
.

Notice that **.w** is *very* different from

.
w

Modifying text: the Substitute command "s"

We are now ready to try one of the most important of all commands — the substitute command

s

This is the command that is used to change individual words or letters within a line or group of lines. It is what you use, for example, for correcting spelling mistakes and typing errors.

Suppose that by a typing error, line 1 says

Now is th time

— the *e* has been left off *the*. You can use **s** to fix this up as follows:

1s/th/the/

This says: "in line 1, substitute for the characters *th* the characters *the*." To verify that it works (*ed* will not print the result automatically) say

p

and get

Now is the time

which is what you wanted. Notice that dot must have been set to the line where the substitution took place, since the **p** command printed that line. Dot is always set this way with the **s** command.

The general way to use the substitute command is

starting-line, ending-line **s/** *change this/ to this/*

Whatever string of characters is between the first pair of slashes is replaced by whatever is between the second pair, in *all* the lines between *starting-line* and *ending-line*. Only the first occurrence on each line is changed, however. If you want to change *every* occurrence, see Exercise 5. The rules for line numbers are the same as those for **p**, except that dot is set to the last line changed. (But there is a trap for the unwary: if no substitution took place, dot is *not* changed. This causes an error **?** as a warning.)

Thus you can say

1,$s/speling/spelling/

and correct the first spelling mistake on each line in the text. (This is useful for people who are consistent misspellers!)

If no line numbers are given, the **s** command assumes we mean "make the substitution on line dot", so it changes things only on the current line. This leads to the very common sequence

s/something/something else/p

which makes some correction on the current line, and then prints it, to make sure it worked out right. If it didn't, you can try again. (Notice that there is a **p** on the same line as the **s** command. With few exceptions, **p** can follow any command; no other multi-command lines are legal.)

It's also legal to say

    s/ . . .//

which means "change the first string of characters to "*nothing*", i.e., remove them. This is useful for deleting extra words in a line or removing extra letters from words. For instance, if you had

    Nowxx is the time

you can say

    s/xx//p

to get

    Now is the time

Notice that **//** (two adjacent slashes) means "no characters", not a blank. There *is* a difference! (See below for another meaning of **//**.)

Exercise 5:

Experiment with the substitute command. See what happens if you substitute for some word on a line with several occurrences of that word. For example, do this:

    a
    the other side of the coin
    .

    s/the/on the/p

You will get

    on the other side of the coin

A substitute command changes only the first occurrence of the first string. You can change all occurrences by adding a **g** (for "global") to the **s** command, like this:

    s/ . . ./ . . ./gp

Try other characters instead of slashes to delimit the two sets of characters in the **s** command — anything should work except blanks or tabs.

(If you get funny results using any of the characters

    ^   . $ [*   \   &

read the section on "Special Characters".)

Context searching — "/ . . . /"

With the substitute command mastered, you can move on to another highly important idea of *ed* — context searching.

Suppose you have the original three line text in the buffer:

    Now is the time
    for all good men
    to come to the aid of their party.

Suppose you want to find the line that contains *their* so you can change it to *the*. Now with only three lines in the buffer, it's pretty easy to keep track of what line the word *their* is on. But if the buffer contained several hundred lines, and you'd been making changes, deleting and rearranging lines, and so on, you would no longer really know what this line number would be. Context searching is simply a method of specifying the desired line, regardless of what its number is, by specifying some context on it.

The way to say "search for a line that contains this particular string of characters" is to type

    / *string of characters we want to find***/**

For example, the *ed* command

    /their/

is a context search which is sufficient to find the desired line — it will locate the next occurrence of the characters between slashes ("their"). It also sets dot to that line and prints the line for verification:

    to come to the aid of their party.

"Next occurrence" means that *ed* starts looking for the string at line **.+1**, searches to the end of the buffer, then continues at line 1 and searches to line dot. (That is, the search "wraps around" from **$** to 1.) It scans all the lines in the buffer until it either finds the desired line or gets back to dot again. If the given string of characters can't be found in any line, *ed* types the error message

    ?

Otherwise it prints the line it found.

You can do both the search for the desired line *and* a substitution all at once, like this:

    /their/s/their/the/p

which will yield

    to come to the aid of the party.

There were three parts to that last command: context search for the desired line, make the substitution, print the line.

The expression **/their/** is a context search expression. In their simplest form, all context search expressions are like this — a string of characters surrounded by slashes. Context searches are interchangeable with line numbers, so they can be used by themselves to find and print a desired line, or as line numbers for some other command, like **s**. They were used both ways in the examples above.

Suppose the buffer contains the three familiar lines

> **Now** is the time
> for all good men
> to come to the aid of their party.

Then the *ed* line numbers

> /Now/+1
> /good/
> /party/−1

are all context search expressions, and they all refer to the same line (line 2). To make a change in line 2, you could say

> /Now/+1s/good/bad/

or

> /good/s/good/bad/

or

> /party/−1s/good/bad/

The choice is dictated only by convenience. You could print all three lines by, for instance

> /Now/,/party/p

or

> /Now/,/Now/+2p

or by any number of similar combinations. The first one of these might be better if you don't know how many lines are involved. (Of course, if there were only three lines in the buffer, you'd use

> 1,$p

but not if there were several hundred.)

The basic rule is: a context search expression is *the same as* a line number, so it can be used wherever a line number is needed.

Exercise 6:

Experiment with context searching. Try a body of text with several occurrences of the same string of characters, and scan through it using the same context search.

Try using context searches as line numbers for the substitute, print and delete commands. (They can also be used with **r**, **w**, and **a**.)

Try context searching using **?text?** instead of **/text/**. This scans lines in the buffer in reverse order rather than normal. This is sometimes useful if you go too far while looking for some string of characters — it's an easy way to back up.

(If you get funny results with any of the characters

> ^   . $ [*   \   &

read the section on "Special Characters".)

Ed provides a shorthand for repeating a context search for the same string. For example, the *ed* line number

> /string/

will find the next occurrence of **string**. It often happens that this is not the desired line, so the search must be repeated. This can be done by typing merely

> //

This shorthand stands for "the most recently used context search expression." It can also be used as the first string of the substitute command, as in

> /string1/s//string2/

which will find the next occurrence of **string1** and replace it by **string2**. This can save a lot of typing. Similarly

> ??

means "scan backwards for the same expression."

Change and Insert — "c" and "i"

This section discusses the *change* command

> c

which is used to change or replace a group of one or more lines, and the *insert* command

> i

which is used for inserting a group of one or more lines.

"Change", written as

> c

is used to replace a number of lines with different lines, which are typed in at the terminal. For example, to change lines **.+1** through **$** to something else, type

> .+1,$c
> *. . . type the lines of text you want here . . .*
> .

The lines you type between the **c** command and the **.** will take the place of the original lines between start line and end line. This is most useful in replacing a line or several lines which have errors in them.

If only one line is specified in the **c** command, then just that line is replaced. (You can type in as many replacement lines as you like.) Notice the use of **.** to end the input — this works just like the **.** in the append command

and must appear by itself on a new line. If no line number is given, line dot is replaced. The value of dot is set to the last line you typed in.

"Insert" is similar to append — for instance

>   /string/i
>   . . . type the lines to be inserted here . . .
>   .

will insert the given text *before* the next line that contains "string". The text between i and . is *inserted before* the specified line. If no line number is specified dot is used. Dot is set to the last line inserted.

Exercise 7:

"Change" is rather like a combination of delete followed by insert. Experiment to verify that

>   *start, end* **d**
>   **i**
>   . . . *text* . . .
>   .

is almost the same as

>   *start, end* **c**
>   . . . *text* . . .
>   .

These are not *precisely* the same if line **$** gets deleted. Check this out. What is dot?

Experiment with **a** and **i**, to see that they are similar, but not the same. You will observe that

>   *line-number* **a**
>   . . . *text* . . .
>   .

appends *after* the given line, while

>   *line-number* **i**
>   . . . *text* . . .
>   .

inserts *before* it. Observe that if no line number is given, **i** inserts before line dot, while **a** appends after line dot.

Moving text around: the "m" command

The move command **m** is used for cutting and pasting — it lets you move a group of lines from one place to another in the buffer. Suppose you want to put the first three lines of the buffer at the end instead. You could do it by saying:

>   1,3w temp
> $r temp
>   1,3d

(Do you see why?) but you can do it a lot easier with the **m** command:

>   1,3m$

The general case is

>   *start line, end line* **m** *after this line*

Notice that there is a third line to be specified — the place where the moved stuff gets put. Of course the lines to be moved can be specified by context searches; if you had

>   **First paragraph**
>   . . .
>   **end of first paragraph.**
>   **Second paragraph**
>   . . .
>   **end of second paragraph.**

you could reverse the two paragraphs like this:

>   /Second/,/end of second/m/First/−1

Notice the −1: the moved text goes *after* the line mentioned. Dot gets set to the last line moved.

The global commands "g" and "v"

The *global* command g is used to execute one or more *ed* commands on all those lines in the buffer that match some specified string. For example

>   g/peling/p

prints all lines that contain **peling**. More usefully,

>   g/peling/s//pelling/gp

makes the substitution everywhere on the line, then prints each corrected line. Compare this to

>   1,$s/peling/pelling/gp

which only prints the last line substituted. Another subtle difference is that the g command does not give a **?** if **peling** is not found where the s command will.

There may be several commands (including **a, c, i, r, w**, but not **g**); in that case, every line except the last must end with a backslash \:

>   g/xxx/.−1s/abc/def/B
>   .+2s/ghi/jkl/B
>   .−2,.p

makes changes in the lines before and after each line that contains **xxx**, then prints all three lines.

The **v** command is the same as g, except that the commands are executed on every line that does *not* match the string following v:

>   v/ /d

deletes every line that does not contain a blank.

Special Characters

You may have noticed that things just don't work right when you used some characters like ., *, $, and others in context searches and the substitute command. The reason is rather complex, although the cure is simple. Basically, *ed* treats these characters as special, with special meanings. For instance, *in a context search or the first string of the substitute command only,* . means "any character," not a period, so

/x.y/

means "a line with an **x**, *any character,* and a **y**," *not* just "a line with an **x**, a period, and a **y**." A complete list of the special characters that can cause trouble is the following:

^   . $ [*   \

Warning: The backslash character \ is special to *ed*. For safety's sake, avoid it where possible. If you have to use one of the special characters in a substitute command, you can turn off its magic meaning temporarily by preceding it with the backslash. Thus

s/\\\.*/backslash dot star/

will change \.* into "backslash dot star".

Here is a hurried synopsis of the other special characters. First, the circumflex ^ signifies the beginning of a line. Thus

/^string/

finds **string** only if it is at the beginning of a line: it will find .

string

but not

the string...

The dollar-sign $ is just the opposite of the circumflex; it means the end of a line:

/string$/

will only find an occurrence of **string** that is at the end of some line. This implies, of course, that

/^string$/

will find only a line that contains just **string**, and

/^.$/

finds a line containing exactly one character.

The character ., as we mentioned above, matches anything;

/x.y/

matches any of

x+y
x−y
x y
x.y

This is useful in conjunction with *, which is a repetition character; a* is a shorthand for "any number of a's," so .* matches any number of anythings. This is used like this:

s/.*/stuff/

which changes an entire line, or

s/.*,//

which deletes all characters in the line up to and including the last comma. (Since .* finds the longest possible match, this goes up to the last comma.)

[is used with] to form "character classes"; for example,

/[0123456789]/

matches any single digit − any one of the characters inside the braces will cause a match. This can be abbreviated to [0−9].

Finally, the & is another shorthand character − it is used only on the right-hand part of a substitute command where it means "whatever was matched on the left-hand side". It is used to save typing. Suppose the current line contained

Now is the time

and you wanted to put parentheses around it. You could just retype the line, but this is tedious. Or you could say

s/^/(/
s/$/)/

using your knowledge of ^ and $. But the easiest way uses the &:

s/.*/(&)/

This says "match the whole line, and replace it by itself surrounded by parentheses." The & can be used several times in a line; consider using

s/.*/&? &!!/

to produce

Now is the time? Now is the time!!

You don't have to match the whole line, of course: if the buffer contains

the end of the world

you could type

/world/s//& is at hand/

to produce

the end of the world is at hand

Observe this expression carefully, for it illustrates how to take advantage of *ed* to save typing. The string **/world/** found the desired line; the shorthand **//** found the same word in the line; and the **&** saves you from typing it again.

The **&** is a special character only within the replacement text of a substitute command, and has no special meaning elsewhere. You can turn off the special meaning of **&** by preceding it with a ****:

s/ampersand/\&/

will convert the word "ampersand" into the literal symbol **&** in the current line.

Summary of Commands and Line Numbers

The general form of *ed* commands is the command name, perhaps preceded by one or two line numbers, and, in the case of **e**, **r**, and **w**, followed by a file name. Only one command is allowed per line, but a **p** command may follow any other command (except for **e**, **r**, **w** and **q**).

a: Append, that is, add lines to the buffer (at line dot, unless a different line is specified). Appending continues until . is typed on a new line. Dot is set to the last line appended.

c: Change the specified lines to the new text which follows. The new lines are terminated by a **.**, as with **a**. If no lines are specified, replace line dot. Dot is set to last line changed.

d: Delete the lines specified. If none are specified, delete line dot. Dot is set to the first undeleted line, unless **$** is deleted, in which case dot is set to **$**.

e: Edit new file. Any previous contents of the buffer are thrown away, so issue a **w** beforehand.

f: Print remembered filename. If a name follows **f** the remembered name will be set to it.

g: The command

g/---/commands

will execute the commands on those lines that contain ---, which can be any context search expression.

i: Insert lines before specified line (or dot) until a . is typed on a new line. Dot is set to last line inserted.

m: Move lines specified to after the line named after **m**. Dot is set to the last line moved.

p: Print specified lines. If none specified, print line dot. A single line number is equivalent to *line-number* **p**. A single return prints .**+1**, the next line.

q: Quit *ed*. Wipes out all text in buffer if you give it twice in a row without first giving a **w** command.

r: Read a file into buffer (at end unless specified elsewhere.) Dot set to last line read.

s: The command

s/string1/string2/

substitutes the characters **string1** into **string2** in the specified lines. If no lines are specified, make the substitution in line dot. Dot is set to last line in which a substitution took place, which means that if no substitution took place, dot is not changed. **s** changes only the first occurrence of **string1** on a line; to change all of them, type a **g** after the final slash.

v: The command

v/---/commands

executes **commands** on those lines that *do not* contain ---.

w: Write out buffer onto a file. Dot is not changed.

.=: Print value of dot. (**=** by itself prints the value of **$**.)

!: The line

!command-line

causes **command-line** to be executed as a UNIX command.

/-----/: Context search. Search for next line which contains this string of characters. Print it. Dot is set to the line where string was found. Search starts at .**+1**, wraps around from **$** to 1, and continues to dot, if necessary.

?-----?: Context search in reverse direction. Start search at .**−1**, scan to 1, wrap around to **$**.

Advanced Editing on UNIX

Brian W. Kernighan

Bell Laboratories
Murray Hill, New Jersey 07974

ABSTRACT

This paper is meant to help secretaries, typists and programmers to make effective use of the UNIX† facilities for preparing and editing text. It provides explanations and examples of

- special characters, line addressing and global commands in the editor **ed**;
- commands for "cut and paste" operations on files and parts of files, including the **mv**, **cp**, **cat** and **rm** commands, and the **r**, **w**, **m** and t commands of the editor;
- editing scripts and editor-based programs like **grep** and **sed**.

Although the treatment is aimed at non-programmers, new users with any background should find helpful hints on how to get their jobs done more easily.

August 4, 1978

---

†UNIX is a Trademark of Bell Laboratories.

1. INTRODUCTION

Although UNIX† provides remarkably effective tools for text editing, that by itself is no guarantee that everyone will automatically make the most effective use of them. In particular, people who are not computer specialists — typists, secretaries, casual users — often use the system less effectively than they might.

This document is intended as a sequel to *A Tutorial Introduction to the UNIX Text Editor* [1], providing explanations and examples of how to edit with less effort. (You should also be familiar with the material in *UNIX For Beginners* [2].) Further information on all commands discussed here can be found in *The UNIX Programmer's Manual* [3].

Examples are based on observations of users and the difficulties they encounter. Topics covered include special characters in searches and substitute commands, line addressing, the global commands, and line moving and copying. There are also brief discussions of effective use of related tools, like those for file manipulation, and those based on **ed**, like **grep** and **sed**.

A word of caution. There is only one way to learn to use something, and that is to *use* it. Reading a description is no substitute for trying something. A paper like this one should give you ideas about what to try, but until you actually try something, you will not learn it.

2. SPECIAL CHARACTERS

The editor **ed** is the primary interface to the system for many people, so it is worthwhile to know how to get the most out of **ed** for the least effort.

The next few sections will discuss shortcuts and labor-saving devices. Not all of these will be instantly useful to any one person, of course, but a few will be, and the others should give you ideas to store away for future use. And as always, until you try these things,

---

†UNIX is a Trademark of Bell Laboratories.

they will remain theoretical knowledge, not something you have confidence in.

The List command 'l'

ed provides two commands for printing the contents of the lines you're editing. Most people are familiar with **p**, in combinations like

    1,$p

to print all the lines you're editing, or

    s/abc/def/p

to change 'abc' to 'def' on the current line. Less familiar is the *list* command **l** (the letter 'l'), which gives slightly more information than **p**. In particular, **l** makes visible characters that are normally invisible, such as tabs and backspaces. If you list a line that contains some of these, **l** will print each tab as ≫ and each backspace as ≪. This makes it much easier to correct the sort of typing mistake that inserts extra spaces adjacent to tabs, or inserts a backspace followed by a space.

The **l** command also 'folds' long lines for printing — any line that exceeds 72 characters is printed on multiple lines; each printed line except the last is terminated by a backslash \, so you can tell it was folded. This is useful for printing long lines on short terminals.

Occasionally the **l** command will print in a line a string of numbers preceded by a backslash, such as \07 or \16. These combinations are used to make visible characters that normally don't print, like form feed or vertical tab or bell. Each such combination is a single character. When you see such characters, be wary — they may have surprising meanings when printed on some terminals. Often their presence means that your finger slipped while you were typing; you almost never want them.

The Substitute Command 's'

Most of the next few sections will be taken up with a discussion of the substitute command **s**. Since this is the command for changing the contents of individual lines, it probably has the most complexity of any **ed** command, and the most potential for effective use.

As the simplest place to begin, recall the meaning of a trailing **g** after a substitute command. With

    s/this/that/

and

    s/this/that/g

the first one replaces the *first* 'this' on the line with 'that'. If there is more than one 'this' on the line, the second form with the trailing **g** changes *all* of them.

Either form of the **s** command can be followed by **p** or **l** to 'print' or 'list' (as described in the previous section) the contents of the line:

    s/this/that/p
    s/this/that/l
    s/this/that/gp
    s/this/that/gl

are all legal, and mean slightly different things. Make sure you know what the differences are.

Of course, any **s** command can be preceded by one or two 'line numbers' to specify that the substitution is to take place on a group of lines. Thus

    1,$s/mispell/misspell/

changes the *first* occurrence of 'mispell' to 'misspell' on every line of the file. But

    1,$s/mispell/misspell/g

changes *every* occurrence in every line (and this is more likely to be what you wanted in this particular case).

You should also notice that if you add a **p** or **l** to the end of any of these substitute commands, only the last line that got changed will be printed, not all the lines. We will talk later about how to print all the lines that were modified.

The Undo Command 'u'

Occasionally you will make a substitution in a line, only to realize too late that it was a ghastly mistake. The 'undo' command **u** lets you 'undo' the last substitution: the last line that was substituted can be restored to its previous state by typing the command

    u

The Metacharacter '.'

As you have undoubtedly noticed when you use **ed**, certain characters have unexpected meanings when they occur in the left side of a substitute command, or in a search for a particular line. In the next several sections, we will talk about these special characters, which are often called 'metacharacters'.

The first one is the period '.'. On the left side of a substitute command, or in a search with '/.../', '.' stands for *any* single character. Thus the search

    /x.y/

finds any line where 'x' and 'y' occur separated by a single character, as in

    x+y
    x−y
    x□y
    x.y

and so on. (We will use □ to stand for a space whenever we need to make it visible.)

Since '.' matches a single character, that gives you a way to deal with funny characters printed by **l**. Suppose you have a line that, when printed with the **l** command, appears as

    .... th\07is ....

and you want to get rid of the \07 (which represents the bell character, by the way).

The most obvious solution is to try

    s/\07//

but this will fail. (Try it.) The brute force solution, which most people would now take, is to re-type the entire line. This is guaranteed, and is actually quite a reasonable tactic if the line in question isn't too big, but for a very long line, re-typing is a bore. This is where the metacharacter '.' comes in handy. Since '\07' really represents a single character, if we say

    s/th.is/this/

the job is done. The '.' matches the mysterious character between the 'h' and the 'i', *whatever it is*.

Bear in mind that since '.' matches any single character, the command

    s/./,/

converts the first character on a line into a ',', which very often is not what you intended.

As is true of many characters in **ed**, the '.' has several meanings, depending on its context. This line shows all three:

.s/./.

The first '.' is a line number, the number of the line we are editing, which is called 'line dot'. (We will discuss line dot more in Section 3.) The second '.' is a metacharacter that matches any single character on that line. The third '.' is the only one that really is an honest literal period. On the *right* side of a substitution, '.' is not special. If you apply this command to the line

    Now is the time.

the result will be

    .ow is the time.

which is probably not what you intended.

The Backslash '\'

Since a period means 'any character', the question naturally arises of what to do when you really want a period. For example, how do you convert the line

    Now is the time.

into

    Now is the time?

The backslash '\' does the job. A backslash turns off any special meaning that the next character might have; in particular, '\.' converts the '.' from a 'match anything' into a period, so you can use it to replace the period in

    Now is the time.

like this:

    s/\./?/

The pair of characters '\.' is considered by **ed** to be a single real period.

The backslash can also be used when searching for lines that contain a special character. Suppose you are looking for a line that contains

    .PP

The search

    /.PP/

isn't adequate, for it will find a line like

    THE APPLICATION OF ...

because the '.' matches the letter 'A'. But if you say

    /\.PP/

you will find only lines that contain '.PP'.

The backslash can also be used to turn off special meanings for characters other than '.'. For example, consider finding a line that contains a backslash. The search

    /\/

won't work, because the '\' isn't a literal '\', but instead means that the second '/' no longer delimits the search. But by preceding a backslash with another one, you can search for a literal backslash. Thus

    /\\/

does work. Similarly, you can search for a forward slash '/' with

    /\//

The backslash turns off the meaning of the immediately following '/' so that it doesn't terminate the /.../ construction prematurely.

As an exercise, before reading further, find two substitute commands each of which will convert the line

    \x\.\y

into the line

    \x\y

Here are several solutions; verify that each works as advertised.

    s/\\\.//
    s/x../x/
    s/..y/y/

A couple of miscellaneous notes about backslashes and special characters. First, you can use any character to delimit the pieces of an **s** command: there is nothing sacred about slashes. (But you must use slashes for context searching.) For instance, in a line that contains a lot of slashes already, like

    //exec //sys.fort.go // etc...

you could use a colon as the delimiter — to delete all the slashes, type

    s:/::g

Second, if # and @ are your character erase and line kill characters, you have to type \# and \@; this is true whether you're talking to **ed** or any other program.

When you are adding text with **a** or **i** or **c**, backslash is not special, and you should only put in one backslash for each one you really want.

The Dollar Sign '$'

The next metacharacter, the '$', stands for 'the end of the line'. As its most obvious use, suppose you have the line

Now is the

and you wish to add the word 'time' to the end. Use the $ like this:

s/$/□time/

to get

Now is the time

Notice that a space is needed before 'time' in the substitute command, or you will get

Now is thetime

As another example, replace the second comma in the following line with a period without altering the first:

Now is the time, for all good men,

The command needed is

s/,$/./

The $ sign here provides context to make specific which comma we mean. Without it, of course, the s command would operate on the first comma to produce

Now is the time. for all good men,

As another example, to convert

Now is the time.

into

Now is the time?

as we did earlier, we can use

s/.$/?/

Like '.', the '$' has multiple meanings depending on context. In the line

$s/$/$/

the first '$' refers to the last line of the file, the second refers to the end of that line, and the third is a literal dollar sign, to be added to that line.

The Circumflex '^'

The circumflex (or hat or caret) '^' stands for the beginning of the line. For example, suppose you are looking for a line that begins with 'the'. If you simply say

/the/

you will in all likelihood find several lines that contain 'the' in the middle before arriving at the one you want. But with

/^the/

you narrow the context, and thus arrive at the desired one more easily.

The other use of '^' is of course to enable you to insert something at the beginning of a line:

s/^/□/

places a space at the beginning of the current line.

Metacharacters can be combined. To search for a line that contains *only* the characters

.PP

you can use the command

/^\.PP$/

The Star '*'

Suppose you have a line that looks like this:

text x   y *text*

where *text* stands for lots of text, and there are some indeterminate number of spaces between the x and the y. Suppose the job is to replace all the spaces between x and y by a single space. The line is too long to retype, and there are too many spaces to count. What now?

This is where the metacharacter '*' comes in handy. A character followed by a star stands for as many consecutive occurrences of that character as possible. To refer to all the spaces at once, say

s/x□*y/x□y/

The construction '□*' means 'as many spaces as possible'. Thus 'x□*y' means 'an x, as many spaces as possible, then a y'.

The star can be used with any character, not just space. If the original example was instead

text x————————y *text*

then all '—' signs can be replaced by a single space with the command

s/x—*y/x□y/

Finally, suppose that the line was

text x..................y *text*

Can you see what trap lies in wait for the unwary? If you blindly type

s/x.*y/x□y/

what will happen? The answer, naturally, is that it depends. If there are no other x's or y's on the line, then everything works, but it's blind luck, not good management. Remember that '.' matches *any* single character? Then '.*' matches as many single characters as possible, and unless you're careful, it can eat up a lot more of the line than you expected. If the line was, for example, like this:

    text x text x...............y text y text

then saying

    s/x.*y/x□y/

will take everything from the *first* 'x' to the *last* 'y', which, in this example, is undoubtedly more than you wanted.

The solution, of course, is to turn off the special meaning of '.' with '\.':

    s/x\.*y/x□y/

Now everything works, for '\.*' means 'as many *periods* as possible'.

There are times when the pattern '.*' is exactly what you want. For example, to change

    Now is the time for all good men ....

into

    Now is the time.

use '.*' to eat up everything after the 'for':

    s/□for.*/./

There are a couple of additional pitfalls associated with '*' that you should be aware of. Most notable is the fact that 'as many as possible' means *zero* or more. The fact that zero is a legitimate possibility is sometimes rather surprising. For example, if our line contained

    text xy text x   y text

and we said

    s/x□*y/x□y/

the *first* 'xy' matches this pattern, for it consists of an 'x', zero spaces, and a 'y'. The result is that the substitute acts on the first 'xy', and does not touch the later one that actually contains some intervening spaces.

The way around this, if it matters, is to specify a pattern like

    /x□□*y/

which says 'an x, a space, then as many more spaces as possible, then a y', in other words, one or more spaces.

The other startling behavior of '*' is again related to the fact that zero is a legitimate number of occurrences of something followed by a star. The command

    s/x*/y/g

when applied to the line

    abcdef

produces

    yaybycydyeyfy

which is almost certainly not what was intended. The reason for this behavior is that zero is a legal number of matches, and there are no x's at the beginning of the line (so that gets converted into a 'y'), nor between the 'a' and the 'b' (so that gets converted into a 'y'), nor ... and so on. Make sure you really want zero matches; if not, in this case write

    s/xx*/y/g

'xx*' is one or more x's.

The Brackets '[ ]'

Suppose that you want to delete any numbers that appear at the beginning of all lines of a file. You might first think of trying a series of commands like

    1,$s/^1*//
    1,$s/^2*//
    1,$s/^3*//

and so on, but this is clearly going to take forever if the numbers are at all long. Unless you want to repeat the commands over and over until finally all numbers are gone, you must get all the digits on one pass. This is the purpose of the brackets [and].

The construction

    [0123456789]

matches any single digit — the whole thing is called a 'character class'. With a character class, the job is easy. The pattern '[0123456789]*' matches zero or more digits (an entire number), so

    1,$s/^[0123456789]*//

deletes all digits from the beginning of all lines.

Any characters can appear within a character class, and just to confuse the issue there are essentially no special characters inside the brackets; even the backslash doesn't have a special meaning. To search for special characters, for example, you can say

    /[.\$^[]/

Within [...], the '[' is not special. To get a ']' into a character class, make it the first character.

It's a nuisance to have to spell out the digits, so you can abbreviate them as [0−9]; similarly, [a−z] stands for the lower case letters, and [A−Z] for upper case.

As a final frill on character classes, you can

specify a class that means 'none of the following characters'. This is done by beginning the class with a '^':

[^0−9]

stands for 'any character *except* a digit'. Thus you might find the first line that doesn't begin with a tab or space by a search like

/^[^(space)(tab)]/

Within a character class, the circumflex has a special meaning only if it occurs at the beginning. Just to convince yourself, verify that

/^[^^]/

finds a line that doesn't begin with a circumflex.

The Ampersand '&'

The ampersand '&' is used primarily to save typing. Suppose you have the line

Now is the time

and you want to make it

Now is the best time

Of course you can always say

s/the/the best/

but it seems silly to have to repeat the 'the'. The '&' is used to eliminate the repetition. On the *right* side of a substitute, the ampersand means 'whatever was just matched', so you can say

s/the/& best/

and the '&' will stand for 'the'. Of course this isn't much of a saving if the thing matched is just 'the', but if it is something truly long or awful, or if it is something like '.*' which matches a lot of text, you can save some tedious typing. There is also much less chance of making a typing error in the replacement text. For example, to parenthesize a line, regardless of its length,

s/.*/(&)/

The ampersand can occur more than once on the right side:

s/the/& best and & worst/

makes

Now is the best and the worst time

and

s/.*/&? &!!/

converts the original line into

Now is the time? Now is the time!!

To get a literal ampersand, naturally the backslash is used to turn off the special meaning:

s/ampersand/\&/

converts the word into the symbol. Notice that '&' is not special on the left side of a substitute, only on the *right* side.

Substituting Newlines

ed provides a facility for splitting a single line into two or more shorter lines by 'substituting in a newline'. As the simplest example, suppose a line has gotten unmanageably long because of editing (or merely because it was unwisely typed). If it looks like

text xy *text*

you can break it between the 'x' and the 'y' like this:

s/xy/x\
y/

This is actually a single command, although it is typed on two lines. Bearing in mind that '\' turns off special meanings, it seems relatively intuitive that a '\' at the end of a line would make the newline there no longer special.

You can in fact make a single line into several lines with this same mechanism. As a large example, consider underlining the word 'very' in a long line by splitting 'very' onto a separate line, and preceding it by the **roff** or **nroff** formatting command '.ul'.

text a very big *text*

The command

s/□very□/\
.ul\
very\
/

converts the line into four shorter lines, preceding the word 'very' by the line '.ul', and eliminating the spaces around the 'very', all at the same time.

When a newline is substituted in, dot is left pointing at the last line created.

Joining Lines

Lines may also be joined together, but this is done with the **j** command instead of **s**. Given the lines

Now is
□the time

and supposing that dot is set to the first of them,

then the command

    j

joins them together. No blanks are added, which is why we carefully showed a blank at the beginning of the second line.

All by itself, a **j** command joins line dot to line dot+1, but any contiguous set of lines can be joined. Just specify the starting and ending line numbers. For example,

    1,$jp

joins all the lines into one big one and prints it. (More on line numbers in Section 3.)

Rearranging a Line with \(... \)

(This section should be skipped on first reading.) Recall that '&' is a shorthand that stands for whatever was matched by the left side of an s command. In much the same way you can capture separate pieces of what was matched; the only difference is that you have to specify on the left side just what pieces you're interested in.

Suppose, for instance, that you have a file of lines that consist of names in the form

    Smith, A. B.
    Jones, C.

and so on, and you want the initials to precede the name, as in

    A. B. Smith
    C. Jones

It is possible to do this with a series of editing commands, but it is tedious and error-prone. (It is instructive to figure out how it is done, though.)

The alternative is to 'tag' the pieces of the pattern (in this case, the last name, and the initials), and then rearrange the pieces. On the left side of a substitution, if part of the pattern is enclosed between \(and \), whatever matched that part is remembered, and available for use on the right side. On the right side, the symbol '\1' refers to whatever matched the first \(...\) pair, '\2' to the second \(...\), and so on.

The command

    1,$s/^\([^,]*\),□*\(.*\)/\2□\1/

although hard to read, does the job. The first \(...\) matches the last name, which is any string up to the comma; this is referred to on the right side with '\1'. The second \(...\) is whatever follows the comma and any spaces, and is referred to as '\2'.

Of course, with any editing sequence this complicated, it's foolhardy to simply run it and

hope. The global commands **g** and **v** discussed in section 4 provide a way for you to print exactly those lines which were affected by the substitute command, and thus verify that it did what you wanted in all cases.

3. LINE ADDRESSING IN THE EDITOR

The next general area we will discuss is that of line addressing in **ed**, that is, how you specify what lines are to be affected by editing commands. We have already used constructions like

    1,$s/x/y/

to specify a change on all lines. And most users are long since familiar with using a single newline (or return) to print the next line, and with

    /thing/

to find a line that contains 'thing'. Less familiar, surprisingly enough, is the use of

    ?thing?

to scan *backwards* for the previous occurrence of 'thing'. This is especially handy when you realize that the thing you want to operate on is back up the page from where you are currently editing.

The slash and question mark are the only characters you can use to delimit a context search, though you can use essentially any character in a substitute command.

Address Arithmetic

The next step is to combine the line numbers like '.', '$', '/.../' and '?...?' with '+' and '−'. Thus

    $−1

is a command to print the next to last line of the current file (that is, one line before line '$'). For example, to recall how far you got in a previous editing session,

    $−5,$p

prints the last six lines. (Be sure you understand why it's six, not five.) If there aren't six, of course, you'll get an error message.

As another example,

    .−3,.+3p

prints from three lines before where you are now (at line dot) to three lines after, thus giving you a bit of context. By the way, the '+' can be omitted:

    .−3,.3p

is absolutely identical in meaning.

Another area in which you can save typing effort in specifying lines is to use '−' and '+' as line numbers by themselves.

> −

by itself is a command to move back up one line in the file. In fact, you can string several minus signs together to move back up that many lines:

> − − −

moves up three lines, as does '−3'. Thus

> −3,+3p

is also identical to the examples above.

Since '−' is shorter than '.−1', constructions like

> −,.s/bad/good/

are useful. This changes 'bad' to 'good' on the previous line and on the current line.

'+' and '−' can be used in combination with searches using '/.../' and '?...?', and with '$'. The search

> /thing/ − −

finds the line containing 'thing', and positions you two lines before it.

Repeated Searches

Suppose you ask for the search

> /horrible thing/

and when the line is printed you discover that it isn't the horrible thing that you wanted, so it is necessary to repeat the search again. You don't have to re-type the search, for the construction

> //

is a shorthand for 'the previous thing that was searched for', whatever it was. This can be repeated as many times as necessary. You can also go backwards:

> ??

searches for the same thing, but in the reverse direction.

Not only can you repeat the search, but you can use '//' as the left side of a substitute command, to mean 'the most recent pattern'.

> /horrible thing/
> .... *ed prints line with 'horrible thing'* ...
> s//good/p

To go backwards and change a line, say

> ??s//good/

Of course, you can still use the '&' on the right hand side of a substitute to stand for whatever got matched:

> //s//&␣&/p

finds the next occurrence of whatever you searched for last, replaces it by two copies of itself, then prints the line just to verify that it worked.

Default Line Numbers and the Value of Dot

One of the most effective ways to speed up your editing is always to know what lines will be affected by a command if you don't specify the lines it is to act on, and on what line you will be positioned (i.e., the value of dot) when a command finishes. If you can edit without specifying unnecessary line numbers, you can save a lot of typing.

As the most obvious example, if you issue a search command like

> /thing/

you are left pointing at the next line that contains 'thing'. Then no address is required with commands like **s** to make a substitution on that line, or **p** to print it, or **l** to list it, or **d** to delete it, or **a** to append text after it, or **c** to change it, or **i** to insert text before it.

What happens if there was no 'thing'? Then you are left right where you were — dot is unchanged. This is also true if you were sitting on the only 'thing' when you issued the command. The same rules hold for searches that use '?...?'; the only difference is the direction in which you search.

The delete command **d** leaves dot pointing at the line that followed the last deleted line. When line '$' gets deleted, however, dot points at the *new* line '$'.

The line-changing commands **a**, **c** and **i** by default all affect the current line — if you give no line number with them, **a** appends text after the current line, **c** changes the current line, and **i** inserts text before the current line.

a, **c**, and **i** behave identically in one respect — when you stop appending, changing or inserting, dot points at the last line entered. This is exactly what you want for typing and editing on the fly. For example, you can say

> a
> ... text ...
> ... botch ...   (minor error)
> .
> s/botch/correct/   (fix botched line)
> a
> ... more text ...

without specifying any line number for the substitute command or for the second append command. Or you can say

    a
    ... text ...
    ... horrible botch ...   (major error)
    .
    c   (replace entire line)
    ... fixed up line ...

You should experiment to determine what happens if you add *no* lines with **a**, **c** or **i**.

The **r** command will read a file into the text being edited, either at the end if you give no address, or after the specified line if you do. In either case, dot points at the last line read in. Remember that you can even say **0r** to read a file in at the beginning of the text. (You can also say **0a** or **1i** to start adding text at the beginning.)

The **w** command writes out the entire file. If you precede the command by one line number, that line is written, while if you precede it by two line numbers, that range of lines is written. The **w** command does *not* change dot: the current line remains the same, regardless of what lines are written. This is true even if you say something like

    /^\.AB/,/^\.AE/w abstract

which involves a context search.

Since the **w** command is so easy to use, you should save what you are editing regularly as you go along just in case the system crashes, or in case you do something foolish, like clobbering what you're editing.

The least intuitive behavior, in a sense, is that of the **s** command. The rule is simple — you are left sitting on the last line that got changed. If there were no changes, then dot is unchanged.

To illustrate, suppose that there are three lines in the buffer, and you are sitting on the middle one:

    x1
    x2
    x3

Then the command

    −,+s/x/y/p

prints the third line, which is the last one changed. But if the three lines had been

    x1
    y2
    y3

and the same command had been issued while

dot pointed at the second line, then the result would be to change and print only the first line, and that is where dot would be set.

Semicolon ';'

Searches with '/.../' and '?...?' start at the current line and move forward or backward respectively until they either find the pattern or get back to the current line. Sometimes this is not what is wanted. Suppose, for example, that the buffer contains lines like this:

    .
    .
    .
    ab
    .
    .
    bc
    .

Starting at line 1, one would expect that the command

    /a/,/b/p

prints all the lines from the 'ab' to the 'bc' inclusive. Actually this is not what happens. *Both* searches (for 'a' and for 'b') start from the same point, and thus they both find the line that contains 'ab'. The result is to print a single line. Worse, if there had been a line with a 'b' in it before the 'ab' line, then the print command would be in error, since the second line number would be less than the first, and it is illegal to try to print lines in reverse order.

This is because the comma separator for line numbers doesn't set dot as each address is processed; each search starts from the same place. In **ed**, the semicolon ';' can be used just like comma, with the single difference that use of a semicolon forces dot to be set at that point as the line numbers are being evaluated. In effect, the semicolon 'moves' dot. Thus in our example above, the command

    /a/;/b/p

prints the range of lines from 'ab' to 'bc', because after the 'a' is found, dot is set to that line, and then 'b' is searched for, starting beyond that line.

This property is most often useful in a very simple situation. Suppose you want to find the *second* occurrence of 'thing'. You could say

    /thing/
    //

but this prints the first occurrence as well as the

second, and is a nuisance when you know very well that it is only the second one you're interested in. The solution is to say

    /thing/;//

This says to find the first occurrence of 'thing', set dot to that line, then find the second and print only that.

Closely related is searching for the second previous occurrence of something, as in

    ?something?;??

Printing the third or fourth or ... in either direction is left as an exercise.

Finally, bear in mind that if you want to find the first occurrence of something in a file, starting at an arbitrary place within the file, it is not sufficient to say

    1;/thing/

because this fails if 'thing' occurs on line 1. But it is possible to say

    0;/thing/

(one of the few places where 0 is a legal line number), for this starts the search at line 1.

Interrupting the Editor

As a final note on what dot gets set to, you should be aware that if you hit the interrupt or delete or rubout or break key while **ed** is doing a command, things are put back together again and your state is restored as much as possible to what it was before the command began. Naturally, some changes are irrevocable — if you are reading or writing a file or making substitutions or deleting lines, these will be stopped in some clean but unpredictable state in the middle (which is why it is not usually wise to stop them). Dot may or may not be changed.

Printing is more clear cut. Dot is not changed until the printing is done. Thus if you print until you see an interesting line, then hit delete, you are *not* sitting on that line or even near it. Dot is left where it was when the **p** command was started.

4. GLOBAL COMMANDS

The global commands **g** and **v** are used to perform one or more editing commands on all lines that either contain (**g**) or don't contain (**v**) a specified pattern.

As the simplest example, the command

    g/UNIX/p

prints all lines that contain the word 'UNIX'. The pattern that goes between the slashes can be anything that could be used in a line search or in a substitute command; exactly the same rules and limitations apply.

As another example, then,

    g/^\./p

prints all the formatting commands in a file (lines that begin with '.').

The **v** command is identical to **g**, except that it operates on those line that do *not* contain an occurrence of the pattern. (Don't look too hard for mnemonic significance to the letter 'v'.) So

    v/^\./p

prints all the lines that don't begin with '.' — the actual text lines.

The command that follows **g** or **v** can be anything:

    g/^\./d

deletes all lines that begin with '.', and

    g/^$/d

deletes all empty lines.

Probably the most useful command that can follow a global is the substitute command, for this can be used to make a change and print each affected line for verification. For example, we could change the word 'Unix' to 'UNIX' everywhere, and verify that it really worked, with

    g/Unix/s//UNIX/gp

Notice that we used '//' in the substitute command to mean 'the previous pattern', in this case, 'Unix'. The **p** command is done on every line that matches the pattern, not just those on which a substitution took place.

The global command operates by making two passes over the file. On the first pass, all lines that match the pattern are marked. On the second pass, each marked line in turn is examined, dot is set to that line, and the command executed. This means that it is possible for the command that follows a **g** or **v** to use addresses, set dot, and so on, quite freely.

    g/^\.PP/+

prints the line that follows each '.PP' command (the signal for a new paragraph in some formatting packages). Remember that '+' means 'one line past dot'. And

    g/topic/?^\.SH?1

searches for each line that contains 'topic', scans backwards until it finds a line that begins '.SH' (a section heading) and prints the line that follows that, thus showing the section headings under which 'topic' is mentioned. Finally,

  g/^\.EQ/+,/^\.EN/−p

prints all the lines that lie between lines beginning with '.EQ' and '.EN' formatting commands.

The g and v commands can also be preceded by line numbers, in which case the lines searched are only those in the range specified.

Multi-line Global Commands

It is possible to do more than one command under the control of a global command, although the syntax for expressing the operation is not especially natural or pleasant. As an example, suppose the task is to change 'x' to 'y' and 'a' to 'b' on all lines that contain 'thing'. Then

  g/thing/s/x/y/\
  s/a/b/

is sufficient. The '\' signals the g command that the set of commands continues on the next line; it terminates on the first line that does not end with '\'. (As a minor blemish, you can't use a substitute command to insert a newline within a g command.)

You should watch out for this problem: the command

  g/x/s//y/\
  s/a/b/

does *not* work as you expect. The remembered pattern is the last pattern that was actually executed, so sometimes it will be 'x' (as expected), and sometimes it will be 'a' (not expected). You must spell it out, like this:

  g/x/s/x/y/\
  s/a/b/

It is also possible to execute **a**, **c** and **i** commands under a global command; as with other multi-line constructions, all that is needed is to add a '\' at the end of each line except the last. Thus to add a '.nf' and '.sp' command before each '.EQ' line, type

  g/^\.EQ/i\
  .nf\
  .sp

There is no need for a final line containing a '.' to terminate the **i** command, unless there are further commands being done under the global. On the other hand, it does no harm to put it in either.

5. CUT AND PASTE WITH UNIX COMMANDS

One editing area in which non-programmers seem not very confident is in what might be called 'cut and paste' operations — changing the name of a file, making a copy of a file somewhere else, moving a few lines from one place to another in a file, inserting one file in the middle of another, splitting a file into pieces, and splicing two or more files together.

Yet most of these operations are actually quite easy, if you keep your wits about you and go cautiously. The next several sections talk about cut and paste. We will begin with the UNIX commands for moving entire files around, then discuss **ed** commands for operating on pieces of files.

Changing the Name of a File

You have a file named 'memo' and you want it to be called 'paper' instead. How is it done?

The UNIX program that renames files is called **mv** (for 'move'); it 'moves' the file from one name to another, like this:

  mv memo paper

That's all there is to it: **mv** from the old name to the new name.

  mv oldname newname

Warning: if there is already a file around with the new name, its present contents will be silently clobbered by the information from the other file. The one exception is that you can't move a file to itself —

  mv x x

is illegal.

Making a Copy of a File

Sometimes what you want is a copy of a file — an entirely fresh version. This might be because you want to work on a file, and yet save a copy in case something gets fouled up, or just because you're paranoid.

In any case, the way to do it is with the **cp** command. (**cp** stands for 'copy'; the system is big on short command names, which are appreciated by heavy users, but sometimes a strain for novices.) Suppose you have a file called 'good' and you want to save a copy before you make some dramatic editing changes. Choose a name — 'savegood' might be acceptable — then type

  cp good savegood

This copies 'good' onto 'savegood', and you now

have two identical copies of the file 'good'. (If 'savegood' previously contained something, it gets overwritten.)

Now if you decide at some time that you want to get back to the original state of 'good', you can say

    mv savegood good

(if you're not interested in 'savegood' any more), or

    cp savegood good

if you still want to retain a safe copy.

In summary, **mv** just renames a file; **cp** makes a duplicate copy. Both of them clobber the 'target' file if it already exists, so you had better be sure that's what you want to do *before* you do it.

Removing a File

If you decide you are really done with a file forever, you can remove it with the **rm** command:

    rm savegood

throws away (irrevocably) the file called 'savegood'.

Putting Two or More Files Together

The next step is the familiar one of collecting two or more files into one big one. This will be needed, for example, when the author of a paper decides that several sections need to be combined into one. There are several ways to do it, of which the cleanest, once you get used to it, is a program called **cat**. (Not *all* programs have two-letter names.) **cat** is short for 'concatenate', which is exactly what we want to do.

Suppose the job is to combine the files 'file1' and 'file2' into a single file called 'bigfile'. If you say

    cat file

the contents of 'file' will get printed on your terminal. If you say

    cat file1 file2

the contents of 'file1' and then the contents of 'file2' will *both* be printed on your terminal, in that order. So **cat** combines the files, all right, but it's not much help to print them on the terminal — we want them in 'bigfile'.

Fortunately, there is a way. You can tell the system that instead of printing on your terminal, you want the same information put in a file. The way to do it is to add to the command line the character > and the name of the file

where you want the output to go. Then you can say

    cat file1 file2 >bigfile

and the job is done. (As with **cp** and **mv**, you're putting something into 'bigfile', and anything that was already there is destroyed.)

This ability to 'capture' the output of a program is one of the most useful aspects of the system. Fortunately it's not limited to the **cat** program — you can use it with *any* program that prints on your terminal. We'll see some more uses for it in a moment.

Naturally, you can combine several files, not just two:

    cat file1 file2 file3 ... >bigfile

collects a whole bunch.

Question: is there any difference between

    cp good savegood

and

    cat good >savegood

Answer: for most purposes, no. You might reasonably ask why there are two programs in that case, since **cat** is obviously all you need. The answer is that **cp** will do some other things as well, which you can investigate for yourself by reading the manual. For now we'll stick to simple usages.

Adding Something to the End of a File

Sometimes you want to add one file to the end of another. We have enough building blocks now that you can do it; in fact before reading further it would be valuable if you figured out how. To be specific, how would you use **cp**, **mv** and/or **cat** to add the file 'good1' to the end of the file 'good'?

You could try

    cat good good1 >temp
    mv temp good

which is probably most direct. You should also understand why

    cat good good1 >good

doesn't work. (Don't practice with a good 'good'!)

The easy way is to use a variant of >, called >>. In fact, >> is identical to > except that instead of clobbering the old file, it simply tacks stuff on at the end. Thus you could say

    cat good1 >>good

and 'good1' is added to the end of 'good'. (And

if 'good' didn't exist, this makes a copy of 'good1' called 'good'.)

6. CUT AND PASTE WITH THE EDITOR

Now we move on to manipulating pieces of files — individual lines or groups of lines. This is another area where new users seem unsure of themselves.

Filenames

The first step is to ensure that you know the **ed** commands for reading and writing files. Of course you can't go very far without knowing **r** and **w**. Equally useful, but less well known, is the 'edit' command **e**. Within **ed**, the command

        e newfile

says 'I want to edit a new file called *newfile*, without leaving the editor.' The e command discards whatever you're currently working on and starts over on *newfile*. It's exactly the same as if you had quit with the **q** command, then re-entered **ed** with a new file name, except that if you have a pattern remembered, then a command like // will still work.

If you enter **ed** with the command

        ed file

ed remembers the name of the file, and any subsequent **e**, **r** or **w** commands that don't contain a filename will refer to this remembered file. Thus

        ed file1
        ... (editing) ...
        w   (writes back in file1)
        e file2   (edit new file, without leaving editor)
        ... (editing on file2) ...
        w   (writes back on file2)

(and so on) does a series of edits on various files without ever leaving **ed** and without typing the name of any file more than once. (As an aside, if you examine the sequence of commands here, you can see why many UNIX systems use e as a synonym for **ed**.)

You can find out the remembered file name at any time with the **f** command; just type **f** without a file name. You can also change the name of the remembered file name with **f**; a useful sequence is

        ed precious
        f junk
        ... (editing) ...

which gets a copy of a precious file, then uses **f** to guarantee that a careless **w** command won't clobber the original.

Inserting One File into Another

Suppose you have a file called 'memo', and you want the file called 'table' to be inserted just after the reference to Table 1. That is, in 'memo' somewhere is a line that says

        Table 1 shows that ...

and the data contained in 'table' has to go there, probably so it will be formatted properly by **nroff** or **troff**. Now what?

This one is easy. Edit 'memo', find 'Table 1', and add the file 'table' right there:

        ed memo
        /Table 1/
        Table 1 shows that ... [response from ed]
        .r table

The critical line is the last one. As we said earlier, the **r** command reads a file; here you asked for it to be read in right after line dot. An **r** command without any address adds lines at the end, so it is the same as **$r**.

Writing out Part of a File

The other side of the coin is writing out part of the document you're editing. For example, maybe you want to split out into a separate file that table from the previous example, so it can be formatted and tested separately. Suppose that in the file being edited we have

        .TS
        ...[lots of stuff]
        .TE

which is the way a table is set up for the **tbl** program. To isolate the table in a separate file called 'table', first find the start of the table (the '.TS' line), then write out the interesting part:

        /^\.TS/
        .TS [ed prints the line it found]
        .,/^\.TE/w table

and the job is done. If you are confident, you can do it all at once with

        /^\.TS/;/^\.TE/w table

The point is that the **w** command can write out a group of lines, instead of the whole file. In fact, you can write out a single line if you like; just give one line number instead of two. For example, if you have just typed a horribly complicated line and you know that it (or something like it) is going to be needed later, then save it — don't re-type it. In the editor, say

```
a
...lots of stuff...
...horrible line...
.
.w  temp
a
...more stuff...
.
.r  temp
a
...more stuff...
.
```

This last example is worth studying, to be sure you appreciate what's going on.

Moving Lines Around

Suppose you want to move a paragraph from its present position in a paper to the end. How would you do it? As a concrete example, suppose each paragraph in the paper begins with the formatting command '.PP'. Think about it and write down the details before reading on.

The brute force way (not necessarily bad) is to write the paragraph onto a temporary file, delete it from its current position, then read in the temporary file at the end. Assuming that you are sitting on the '.PP' command that begins the paragraph, this is the sequence of commands:

```
.,/^\.PP/−w temp
.,//−d
$r temp
```

That is, from where you are now ('.') until one line before the next '.PP' ('/^\.PP/−') write onto 'temp'. Then delete the same lines. Finally, read 'temp' at the end.

As we said, that's the brute force way. The easier way (often) is to use the *move* command **m** that **ed** provides — it lets you do the whole set of operations at one crack, without any temporary file.

The **m** command is like many other **ed** commands in that it takes up to two line numbers in front that tell what lines are to be affected. It is also *followed* by a line number that tells where the lines are to go. Thus

```
line1, line2 m line3
```

says to move all the lines between 'line1' and 'line2' after 'line3'. Naturally, any of 'line1' etc., can be patterns between slashes, $ signs, or other ways to specify lines.

Suppose again that you're sitting at the first line of the paragraph. Then you can say

```
.,/^\.PP/−m$
```

That's all.

As another example of a frequent operation, you can reverse the order of two adjacent lines by moving the first one to after the second. Suppose that you are positioned at the first. Then

```
m+
```

does it. It says to move line dot to after one line after line dot. If you are positioned on the second line,

```
m− −
```

does the interchange.

As you can see, the **m** command is more succinct and direct than writing, deleting and re-reading. When is brute force better anyway? This is a matter of personal taste — do what you have most confidence in. The main difficulty with the **m** command is that if you use patterns to specify both the lines you are moving and the target, you have to take care that you specify them properly, or you may well not move the lines you thought you did. The result of a botched **m** command can be a ghastly mess. Doing the job a step at a time makes it easier for you to verify at each step that you accomplished what you wanted to. It's also a good idea to issue a **w** command before doing anything complicated; then if you goof, it's easy to back up to where you were.

Marks

ed provides a facility for marking a line with a particular name so you can later reference it by name regardless of its actual line number. This can be handy for moving lines, and for keeping track of them as they move. The *mark* command is **k**; the command

```
kx
```

marks the current line with the name 'x'. If a line number precedes the **k**, that line is marked. (The mark name must be a single lower case letter.) Now you can refer to the marked line with the address

```
'x
```

Marks are most useful for moving things around. Find the first line of the block to be moved, and mark it with *'a*. Then find the last line and mark it with *'b*. Now position yourself at the place where the stuff is to go and say

```
'a,'bm.
```

Bear in mind that only one line can have a particular mark name associated with it at any given time.

Copying Lines

We mentioned earlier the idea of saving a line that was hard to type or used often, so as to cut down on typing time. Of course this could be more than one line; then the saving is presumably even greater.

ed provides another command, called **t** (for 'transfer') for making a copy of a group of one or more lines at any point. This is often easier than writing and reading.

The **t** command is identical to the **m** command, except that instead of moving lines it simply duplicates them at the place you named. Thus

    1,t

duplicates the entire contents that you are editing. A more common use for **t** is for creating a series of lines that differ only slightly. For example, you can say

    a
    .... x .... (long line)
    .
    t.   (make a copy)
    s/x/y/   (change it a bit)
    t.   (make third copy)
    s/y/z/   (change it a bit)

and so on.

The Temporary Escape '!'

Sometimes it is convenient to be able to temporarily escape from the editor to do some other UNIX command, perhaps one of the file copy or move commands discussed in section 5, without leaving the editor. The 'escape' command **!** provides a way to do this.

If you say

    !any UNIX command

your current editing state is suspended, and the UNIX command you asked for is executed. When the command finishes, **ed** will signal you by printing another **!**; at that point you can resume editing.

You can really do *any* UNIX command, including another **ed**. (This is quite common, in fact.) In this case, you can even do another **!**.

7. SUPPORTING TOOLS

There are several tools and techniques that go along with the editor, all of which are relatively easy once you know how **ed** works, because they are all based on the editor. In this section we will give some fairly cursory examples of these tools, more to indicate their existence than to provide a complete tutorial. More information on each can be found in [3].

Grep

Sometimes you want to find all occurrences of some word or pattern in a set of files, to edit them or perhaps just to verify their presence or absence. It may be possible to edit each file separately and look for the pattern of interest, but if there are many files this can get very tedious, and if the files are really big, it may be impossible because of limits in **ed**.

The program **grep** was invented to get around these limitations. The search patterns that we have described in the paper are often called 'regular expressions', and 'grep' stands for

    g/re/p

That describes exactly what **grep** does — it prints every line in a set of files that contains a particular pattern. Thus

    grep 'thing' file1 file2 file3 ...

finds 'thing' wherever it occurs in any of the files 'file1', 'file2', etc. **grep** also indicates the file in which the line was found, so you can later edit it if you like.

The pattern represented by 'thing' can be any pattern you can use in the editor, since **grep** and **ed** use exactly the same mechanism for pattern searching. It is wisest always to enclose the pattern in the single quotes '...' if it contains any non-alphabetic characters, since many such characters also mean something special to the UNIX command interpreter (the 'shell'). If you don't quote them, the command interpreter will try to interpret them before **grep** gets a chance.

There is also a way to find lines that *don't* contain a pattern:

    grep —v 'thing' file1 file2 ...

finds all lines that don't contains 'thing'. The —v must occur in the position shown. Given **grep** and **grep** —v, it is possible to do things like selecting all lines that contain some combination of patterns. For example, to get all lines that contain 'x' but not 'y':

    grep x file... | grep —v y

(The notation | is a 'pipe', which causes the output of the first command to be used as input to the second command; see [2].)

Editing Scripts

If a fairly complicated set of editing operations is to be done on a whole set of files, the easiest thing to do is to make up a 'script', i.e., a file that contains the operations you want to perform, then apply this script to each file in turn.

For example, suppose you want to change every 'Unix' to 'UNIX' and every 'Gcos' to 'GCOS' in a large number of files. Then put into the file 'script' the lines

```
g/Unix/s//UNIX/g
g/Gcos/s//GCOS/g
w
q
```

Now you can say

```
ed file1 <script
ed file2 <script
...
```

This causes **ed** to take its commands from the prepared script. Notice that the whole job has to be planned in advance.

And of course by using the UNIX command interpreter, you can cycle through a set of files automatically, with varying degrees of ease.

Sed

sed ('stream editor') is a version of the editor with restricted capabilities but which is capable of processing unlimited amounts of input. Basically **sed** copies its input to its output, applying one or more editing commands to each line of input.

As an example, suppose that we want to do the 'Unix' to 'UNIX' part of the example given above, but without rewriting the files. Then the command

```
sed 's/Unix/UNIX/g' file1  file2 ...
```

applies the command 's/Unix/UNIX/g' to all lines from 'file1', 'file2', etc., and copies all lines to the output. The advantage of using **sed** in such a case is that it can be used with input too large for **ed** to handle. All the output can be collected in one place, either in a file or perhaps piped into another program.

If the editing transformation is so complicated that more than one editing command is needed, commands can be supplied from a file, or on the command line, with a slightly more complex syntax. To take commands from a file, for example,

```
sed  -f  cmdfile  input-files...
```

sed has further capabilities, including conditional testing and branching, which we cannot go into here.

Acknowledgement

I am grateful to Ted Dolotta for his careful reading and valuable suggestions.

References

[1] Brian W. Kernighan, *A Tutorial Introduction to the UNIX Text Editor*, Bell Laboratories internal memorandum.

[2] Brian W. Kernighan, *UNIX For Beginners*, Bell Laboratories internal memorandum.

[3] Ken L. Thompson and Dennis M. Ritchie, *The UNIX Programmer's Manual*, Bell Laboratories.

An Introduction to the UNIX Shell

S. R. Bourne

Bell Laboratories
Murray Hill, New Jersey 07974

ABSTRACT

The *shell* is a command programming language that provides an interface to the
UNIX† operating system. Its features include control-flow primitives, parameter
passing, variables and string substitution. Constructs such as *while, if then else,
case* and *for* are available. Two-way communication is possible between the
shell and commands. String-valued parameters, typically file names or flags,
may be passed to a command. A return code is set by commands that may be
used to determine control-flow, and the standard output from a command may
be used as shell input.

The *shell* can modify the environment in which commands run. Input and output can be redirected to files, and processes that communicate through 'pipes'
can be invoked. Commands are found by searching directories in the file system in a sequence that can be defined by the user. Commands can be read
either from the terminal or from a file, which allows command procedures to be
stored for later use.

November 12, 1978

---

† UNIX is a Trademark of Bell Laboratories.

1.0 Introduction

The shell is both a command language and a programming language that provides an interface to the UNIX operating system. This memorandum describes, with examples, the UNIX shell. The first section covers most of the everyday requirements of terminal users. Some familiarity with UNIX is an advantage when reading this section; see, for example, "UNIX for beginners".[1] Section 2 describes those features of the shell primarily intended for use within shell procedures. These include the control-flow primitives and string-valued variables provided by the shell. A knowledge of a programming language would be a help when reading this section. The last section describes the more advanced features of the shell. References of the form "see *pipe* (2)" are to a section of the UNIX manual.[2]

1.1 Simple commands

Simple commands consist of one or more words separated by blanks. The first word is the name of the command to be executed; any remaining words are passed as arguments to the command. For example,

        who

is a command that prints the names of users logged in. The command

        ls −l

prints a list of files in the current directory. The argument −*l* tells *ls* to print status information, size and the creation date for each file.

1.2 Background commands

To execute a command the shell normally creates a new *process* and waits for it to finish. A command may be run without waiting for it to finish. For example,

        cc pgm.c &

calls the C compiler to compile the file *pgm.c*. The trailing **&** is an operator that instructs the shell not to wait for the command to finish. To help keep track of such a process the shell reports its process number following its creation. A list of currently active processes may be obtained using the *ps* command.

1.3 Input output redirection

Most commands produce output on the standard output that is initially connected to the terminal. This output may be sent to a file by writing, for example,

        ls −l >file

The notation >*file* is interpreted by the shell and is not passed as an argument to *ls*. If *file* does not exist then the shell creates it; otherwise the original contents of *file* are replaced with the output from *ls*. Output may be appended to a file using the notation ls −l >>file

In this case *file* is also created if it does not already exist.

The standard input of a command may be taken from a file instead of the terminal by writing, for example,

        wc <file

The command *wc* reads its standard input (in this case redirected from *file*) and prints the number of characters, words and lines found. If only the number of lines is required then

        wc −l <file

could be used.

1.4 Pipelines and filters

The standard output of one command may be connected to the standard input of another by writing the 'pipe' operator, indicated by |, as in,

        ls −l | wc

Two commands connected in this way constitute a *pipeline* and the overall effect is the same as

        ls −l >file; wc <file

except that no *file* is used. Instead the two processes are connected by a pipe (see *pipe* (2)) and are run in parallel. Pipes are unidirectional and synchronization is achieved by halting *wc* when there is nothing to read and halting *ls* when the pipe is full.

A *filter* is a command that reads its standard input, transforms it in some way, and prints the result as output. One such filter, *grep*, selects from its input those lines that contain some specified string. For example,

        ls | grep old

prints those lines, if any, of the output from *ls* that contain the string *old*. Another useful filter is *sort*. For example,

        who | sort

will print an alphabetically sorted list of logged in users.

A pipeline may consist of more than two commands, for example,

        ls | grep old | wc −l

prints the number of file names in the current directory containing the string *old*.

1.5 File name generation

Many commands accept arguments which are file names. For example,

        ls −l main.c

prints information relating to the file *main.c*.

The shell provides a mechanism for generating a list of file names that match a pattern. For example,

        ls −l *.c

generates, as arguments to *ls*, all file names in the current directory that end in *.c*. The character * is a pattern that will match any string including the null string. In general *patterns* are specified as follows.

*	Matches any string of characters including the null string.
?	Matches any single character.
[. . .]	Matches any one of the characters enclosed. A pair of characters separated by a minus will match any character lexically between the pair.

For example,

        [a−z]*

matches all names in the current directory beginning with one of the letters *a* through *z*.

        /usr/fred/test/?

matches all names in the directory **/usr/fred/test** that consist of a single character. If no file name is found that matches the pattern then the pattern is passed, unchanged, as an argument.

This mechanism is useful both to save typing and to select names according to some pattern. It may also be used to find files. For example,

        echo /usr/fred/*/core

finds and prints the names of all *core* files in sub-directories of **/usr/fred**. (*echo* is a standard UNIX command that prints its arguments, separated by blanks.) This last feature can be expensive, requiring a scan of all sub-directories of **/usr/fred**.

There is one exception to the general rules given for patterns. The character '.' at the start of a file name must be explicitly matched.

        echo *

will therefore echo all file names in the current directory not beginning with '.'.

        echo .*

will echo all those file names that begin with '.'. This avoids inadvertent matching of the names '.' and '..' which mean 'the current directory' and 'the parent directory' respectively. (Notice that *ls* suppresses information for the files '.' and '..'.)

1.6 Quoting

Characters that have a special meaning to the shell, such as $<\ >\ *\ ?\ |\ \&$, are called metacharacters. A complete list of metacharacters is given in appendix B. Any character preceded by a \ is *quoted* and loses its special meaning, if any. The \ is elided so that

        echo \?

will echo a single **?** , and

        echo \\

will echo a single \. To allow long strings to be continued over more than one line the sequence **newline** is ignored.

\ is convenient for quoting single characters. When more than one character needs quoting the above mechanism is clumsy and error prone. A string of characters may be quoted by enclosing the string between single quotes. For example,

        echo xx´****´xx

will echo

        xx****xx

The quoted string may not contain a single quote but may contain newlines, which are preserved. This quoting mechanism is the most simple and is recommended for casual use.

A third quoting mechanism using double quotes is also available that prevents interpretation of some but not all metacharacters. Discussion of the details is deferred to section 3.4.

1.7 Prompting

When the shell is used from a terminal it will issue a prompt before reading a command. By default this prompt is '**$** '. It may be changed by saying, for example,

> PS1 =yesdear

that sets the prompt to be the string *yesdear*. If a newline is typed and further input is needed then the shell will issue the prompt ' > '. Sometimes this can be caused by mistyping a quote mark. If it is unexpected then an interrupt (DEL) will return the shell to read another command. This prompt may be changed by saying, for example,

> PS2 =more

1.8 The shell and login

Following *login* (1) the shell is called to read and execute commands typed at the terminal. If the user's login directory contains the file **.profile** then it is assumed to contain commands and is read by the shell before reading any commands from the terminal.

1.9 Summary

- **ls**
  Print the names of files in the current directory.

- **ls >file**
  Put the output from *ls* into *file*.

- **ls | wc −l**
  Print the number of files in the current directory.

- **ls | grep old**
  Print those file names containing the string *old*.

- **ls | grep old | wc −l**
  Print the number of files whose name contains the string *old*.

- **cc pgm.c &**
  Run *cc* in the background.

2.0 Shell procedures

The shell may be used to read and execute commands contained in a file. For example,

> sh file [args ...]

calls the shell to read commands from *file*. Such a file is called a *command procedure* or *shell procedure*. Arguments may be supplied with the call and are referred to in *file* using the positional parameters $1, $2, ... For example, if the file *wg* contains

> who | grep $1

then

> sh wg fred

is equivalent to

> who | grep fred

UNIX files have three independent attributes, *read, write* and *execute*. The UNIX command *chmod* (1) may be used to make a file executable. For example,

> chmod +x wg

will ensure that the file *wg* has execute status. Following this, the command

> wg fred

is equivalent to

> sh wg fred

This allows shell procedures and programs to be used interchangeably. In either case a new process is created to run the command.

As well as providing names for the positional parameters, the number of positional parameters in the call is available as $#. The name of the file being executed is available as $0.

A special shell parameter $* is used to substitute for all positional parameters except $0. A typical use of this is to provide some default arguments, as in,

> nroff −T450 −ms $*

which simply prepends some arguments to those already given.

2.1 Control flow - for

A frequent use of shell procedures is to loop through the arguments ($1, $2, ...) executing commands once for each argument. An example of such a procedure is *tel* that searches the file **/usr/lib/telnos** that contains lines of the form

> ...
> fred mh0123
> bert mh0789
> ...

The text of *tel* is

> for i
> do grep $i /usr/lib/telnos; done

The command

> tel fred

prints those lines in **/usr/lib/telnos** that contain the string *fred*.

>   tel fred bert

prints those lines containing *fred* followed by those for *bert*.

The **for** loop notation is recognized by the shell and has the general form

>   **for** *name* **in** *w1 w2* . . .
>   **do** *command-list*
>   **done**

A *command-list* is a sequence of one or more simple commands separated or terminated by a newline or semicolon. Furthermore, reserved words like **do** and **done** are only recognized following a newline or semicolon. *name* is a shell variable that is set to the words *w1 w2* . . . in turn each time the *command-list* following **do** is executed. If **in** *w1 w2* . . . is omitted then the loop is executed once for each positional parameter; that is, **in** $*$ * is assumed.

Another example of the use of the **for** loop is the *create* command whose text is

>   for i do > $i; done

The command

>   create alpha beta

ensures that two empty files *alpha* and *beta* exist and are empty. The notation > *file* may be used on its own to create or clear the contents of a file. Notice also that a semicolon (or newline) is required before **done**.

2.2 Control flow - case

A multiple way branch is provided for by the **case** notation. For example,

>   case $# in
>   1) cat >> $1 ;;
>   2) cat >> $2 < $1 ;;
>   *) echo ´usage: append [from] to´ ;;
>   esac

is an *append* command. When called with one argument as

>   append file

$# is the string *1* and the standard input is copied onto the end of *file* using the *cat* command.

>   append file1 file2

appends the contents of *file1* onto *file2*. If the number of arguments supplied to *append* is other than 1 or 2 then a message is printed indicating proper usage.

The general form of the **case** command is

>   **case** *word* **in**
>   *pattern*) *command-list* ;;
>   . . .
>   **esac**

The shell attempts to match *word* with each *pattern*, in the order in which the patterns appear. If a match is found the associated *command-list* is executed and execution of the **case** is complete. Since * is the pattern that matches any string it can be used for the default case.

A word of caution: no check is made to ensure that only one pattern matches the case argument. The first match found defines the set of commands to be executed. In the example below the commands following the second * will never be executed.

```
            case $# in
                *) ... ;;
                *) ... ;;
            esac
```

Another example of the use of the **case** construction is to distinguish between different forms of an argument. The following example is a fragment of a *cc* command.

```
            for i
            do case $i in
                −[ocs])      ... ;;
                −*) echo 'unknown flag $i' ;;
                *.c) /lib/c0 $i ... ;;
                *)   echo 'unexpected argument $i' ;;
            esac
            done
```

To allow the same commands to be associated with more than one pattern the **case** command provides for alternative patterns separated by a | . For example,

```
            case $i in
                −x | −y)   ...
            esac
```

is equivalent to

```
            case $i in
                −[xy])   ...
            esac
```

The usual quoting conventions apply so that

```
            case $i in
                \?)        ...
            esac
```

will match the character ? .

2.3 Here documents

The shell procedure *tel* in section 2.1 uses the file **/usr/lib/telnos** to supply the data for *grep*. An alternative is to include this data within the shell procedure as a *here* document, as in,

```
            for i
            do grep $i <<!
            ...
            fred mh0123
            bert mh0789
            ...
            !
            done
```

In this example the shell takes the lines between <<! and ! as the standard input for *grep*. The string ! is arbitrary, the document being terminated by a line that consists of the string following << .

Parameters are substituted in the document before it is made available to *grep* as illustrated by the following procedure called *edg* .

```
ed $3 <<%
g/$1/s//$2/g
w
%
```

The call

```
edg string1 string2 file
```

is then equivalent to the command

```
ed file <<%
g/string1/s//string2/g
w
%
```

and changes all occurrences of *string1* in *file* to *string2*. Substitution can be prevented using \ to quote the special character $ as in

```
ed $3 << +
1,\$s/$1/$2/g
w
+
```

(This version of *edg* is equivalent to the first except that *ed* will print a ? if there are no occurrences of the string $1.) Substitution within a *here* document may be prevented entirely by quoting the terminating string, for example,

```
grep $i <<\#
...
#
```

The document is presented without modification to *grep*. If parameter substitution is not required in a *here* document this latter form is more efficient.

2.4 Shell variables

The shell provides string-valued variables. Variable names begin with a letter and consist of letters, digits and underscores. Variables may be given values by writing, for example,

```
user=fred box=m000 acct=mh0000
```

which assigns values to the variables **user, box** and **acct.** A variable may be set to the null string by saying, for example,

```
null=
```

The value of a variable is substituted by preceding its name with $; for example,

```
echo $user
```

will echo *fred*.

Variables may be used interactively to provide abbreviations for frequently used strings. For example,

```
b=/usr/fred/bin
mv pgm $b
```

will move the file *pgm* from the current directory to the directory **/usr/fred/bin** . A more general notation is available for parameter (or variable) substitution, as in,

```
echo ${user}
```

which is equivalent to

        echo $user

and is used when the parameter name is followed by a letter or digit. For example,

        tmp=/tmp/ps
        ps a >${tmp}a

will direct the output of *ps* to the file **/tmp/psa,** whereas,

        ps a >$tmpa

would cause the value of the variable **tmpa** to be substituted.

Except for **$?** the following are set initially by the shell. **$?** is set after executing each command.

$?   The exit status (return code) of the last command executed as a decimal string. Most commands return a zero exit status if they complete successfully, otherwise a non-zero exit status is returned. Testing the value of return codes is dealt with later under **if** and **while** commands.

$#   The number of positional parameters (in decimal). Used, for example, in the *append* command to check the number of parameters.

$$ The process number of this shell (in decimal). Since process numbers are unique among all existing processes, this string is frequently used to generate unique temporary file names. For example,

            ps a >/tmp/ps$$
            ...
            rm /tmp/ps$$

$!   The process number of the last process run in the background (in decimal).

$−   The current shell flags, such as −**x** and −**v**.

Some variables have a special meaning to the shell and should be avoided for general use.

$MAIL   When used interactively the shell looks at the file specified by this variable before it issues a prompt. If the specified file has been modified since it was last looked at the shell prints the message *you have mail* before prompting for the next command. This variable is typically set in the file **.profile,** in the user's login directory. For example,

            MAIL=/usr/mail/fred

$HOME The default argument for the *cd* command. The current directory is used to resolve file name references that do not begin with a **/**, and is changed using the *cd* command. For example,

            cd /usr/fred/bin

makes the current directory **/usr/fred/bin**.

            cat wn

will print on the terminal the file *wn* in this directory. The command *cd* with no argument is equivalent to

            cd $HOME

This variable is also typically set in the the user's login profile.

$PATH A list of directories that contain commands (the *search path*). Each time a command is executed by the shell a list of directories is searched for an executable file. If $PATH is not set then the current directory, **/bin**, and **/usr/bin** are searched by default. Otherwise $PATH consists of directory names separated by **:**. For example,

PATH = :/usr/fred/bin :/bin :/usr/bin

specifies that the current directory (the null string before the first **:**), **/usr/fred/bin, /bin** and **/usr/bin** are to be searched in that order. In this way individual users can have their own 'private' commands that are accessible independently of the current directory. If the command name contains a **/** then this directory search is not used; a single attempt is made to execute the command.

$PS1   The primary shell prompt string, by default, '**$** '.

$PS2   The shell prompt when further input is needed, by default, '**>** '.

$IFS   The set of characters used by *blank interpretation* (see section 3.4).

2.5 The test command

The *test* command, although not part of the shell, is intended for use by shell programs. For example,

test −f file

returns zero exit status if *file* exists and non-zero exit status otherwise. In general *test* evaluates a predicate and returns the result as its exit status. Some of the more frequently used *test* arguments are given here, see *test* (1) for a complete specification.

test s	true if the argument *s* is not the null string
test −f file	true if *file* exists
test −r file	true if *file* is readable
test −w file	true if *file* is writable
test −d file	true if *file* is a directory

2.6 Control flow - while

The actions of the **for** loop and the **case** branch are determined by data available to the shell. A **while** or **until** loop and an **if then else** branch are also provided whose actions are determined by the exit status returned by commands. A **while** loop has the general form

> **while** *command-list$_1$*
> **do** *command-list$_2$*
> **done**

The value tested by the **while** command is the exit status of the last simple command following **while**. Each time round the loop *command-list$_1$* is executed; if a zero exit status is returned then *command-list$_2$* is executed; otherwise, the loop terminates. For example,

> while test $1
> do ...
>   shift
> done

is equivalent to

> for i
> do ...
> done

shift is a shell command that renames the positional parameters $2, $3, ... as $1, $2, ... and loses **$1** .

Another kind of use for the **while/until** loop is to wait until some external event occurs and then run some commands. In an **until** loop the termination condition is reversed. For example,

        until test −f file
        do sleep 300; done
        commands

will loop until *file* exists. Each time round the loop it waits for 5 minutes before trying again. (Presumably another process will eventually create the file.)

2.7 Control flow - if

Also available is a general conditional branch of the form,

        if *command-list*
        then   *command-list*
        else   *command-list*
        fi

that tests the value returned by the last simple command following **if**.

The **if** command may be used in conjunction with the *test* command to test for the existence of a file as in

        if test −f file
        then   *process file*
        else   *do something else*
        fi

An example of the use of **if, case** and **for** constructions is given in section 2.10.

A multiple test **if** command of the form

        if ...
        then   ...
        else   if ...
                then   ...
                else   if ...
                        ...
                        fi
                fi
        fi

may be written using an extension of the **if** notation as,

        if ...
        then   ...
        elif   ...
        then   ...
        elif   ...
        ...
        fi

The following example is the *touch* command which changes the 'last modified' time for a list of files. The command may be used in conjunction with *make* (1) to force recompilation of a list of files.

```
flag=
for i
do case $i in
   -c)  flag=N ;;
   *)   if test -f $i
        then    ln $i junk$$; rm junk$$
        elif test $flag
        then    echo file \'$i\' does not exist
        else    >$i
        fi
   esac
done
```

The −c flag is used in this command to force subsequent files to be created if they do not already exist. Otherwise, if the file does not exist, an error message is printed. The shell variable *flag* is set to some non-null string if the −c argument is encountered. The commands

```
ln ...; rm ...
```

make a link to the file and then remove it thus causing the last modified date to be updated. The sequence

```
if command1
then    command2
fi
```

may be written

```
command1 && command2
```

Conversely,

```
command1 || command2
```

executes *command2* only if *command1* fails. In each case the value returned is that of the last simple command executed.

2.8 Command grouping

Commands may be grouped in two ways,

```
{ command-list ; }
```

and

```
( command-list )
```

In the first *command-list* is simply executed. The second form executes *command-list* as a separate process. For example,

```
(cd x; rm junk )
```

executes *rm junk* in the directory **x** without changing the current directory of the invoking shell. The commands

```
cd x; rm junk
```

have the same effect but leave the invoking shell in the directory **x**.

2.9 Debugging shell procedures

The shell provides two tracing mechanisms to help when debugging shell procedures. The first is invoked within the procedure as

        set −v

(**v** for verbose) and causes lines of the procedure to be printed as they are read. It is useful to help isolate syntax errors. It may be invoked without modifying the procedure by saying

        sh −v proc ...

where *proc* is the name of the shell procedure. This flag may be used in conjunction with the −**n** flag which prevents execution of subsequent commands. (Note that saying *set −n* at a terminal will render the terminal useless until an end-of-file is typed.)

The command

        set −x

will produce an execution trace. Following parameter substitution each command is printed as it is executed. (Try these at the terminal to see what effect they have.) Both flags may be turned off by saying

        set −

and the current setting of the shell flags is available as $− .

2.10 The man command

The following is the *man* command which is used to print sections of the UNIX manual. It is called, for example, as

           man sh
           man −t ed
           man 2 fork

In the first the manual section for *sh* is printed. Since no section is specified, section 1 is used. The second example will typeset (−t option) the manual section for *ed*. The last prints the *fork* manual page from section 2.

```
cd /usr/man

: 'colon is the comment command'
: 'default is nroff ($N), section 1 ($s)'
N=n s=1

for i
do case $i in
    [1−9]*)      s=$i ;;

    −t)  N=t ;;

    −n)  N=n ;;

    −*)  echo unknown flag \'$i\' ;;

    *)   if test −f man$s/$i.$s
         then    ${N}roff man0/${N}aa man$s/$i.$s
         else    : 'look through all manual sections'
                 found=no
                 for j in 1 2 3 4 5 6 7 8 9
                 do if test −f man$j/$i.$j
                    then man $j $i
                         found=yes
                    fi
                 done
                 case $found in
                     no) echo '$i: manual page not found'
                 esac
         fi
    esac
done
```

Figure 1. A version of the man command

3.0 Keyword parameters

Shell variables may be given values by assignment or when a shell procedure is invoked. An argument to a shell procedure of the form *name=value* that precedes the command name causes *value* to be assigned to *name* before execution of the procedure begins. The value of *name* in the invoking shell is not affected. For example,

        user=fred command

will execute *command* with **user** set to *fred.* The −**k** flag causes arguments of the form *name=value* to be interpreted in this way anywhere in the argument list. Such *names* are sometimes called keyword parameters. If any arguments remain they are available as positional parameters **$1, $2, ...**

The *set* command may also be used to set positional parameters from within a procedure. For example,

        set − *

will set **$1** to the first file name in the current directory, **$2** to the next, and so on. Note that the first argument, −, ensures correct treatment when the first file name begins with a −.

3.1 Parameter transmission

When a shell procedure is invoked both positional and keyword parameters may be supplied with the call. Keyword parameters are also made available implicitly to a shell procedure by specifying in advance that such parameters are to be exported. For example,

        export user box

marks the variables **user** and **box** for export. When a shell procedure is invoked copies are made of all exportable variables for use within the invoked procedure. Modification of such variables within the procedure does not affect the values in the invoking shell. It is generally true of a shell procedure that it may not modify the state of its caller without explicit request on the part of the caller. (Shared file descriptors are an exception to this rule.)

Names whose value is intended to remain constant may be declared *readonly*. The form of this command is the same as that of the *export* command,

        readonly name . . .

Subsequent attempts to set readonly variables are illegal.

3.2 Parameter substitution

If a shell parameter is not set then the null string is substituted for it. For example, if the variable **d** is not set

        echo $d

or

        echo ${d}

will echo nothing. A default string may be given as in

        echo ${d−.}

which will echo the value of the variable **d** if it is set and '.' otherwise. The default string is evaluated using the usual quoting conventions so that

        echo ${d−'*'}

will echo * if the variable **d** is not set. Similarly

        echo ${d-$1}

will echo the value of **d** if it is set and the value (if any) of **$1** otherwise. A variable may be assigned a default value using the notation

        echo ${d=.}

which substitutes the same string as

        echo ${d-.}

and if **d** were not previously set then it will be set to the string '.'. (The notation ${...=...} is not available for positional parameters.)

If there is no sensible default then the notation

        echo ${d?message}

will echo the value of the variable **d** if it has one, otherwise *message* is printed by the shell and execution of the shell procedure is abandoned. If *message* is absent then a standard message is printed. A shell procedure that requires some parameters to be set might start as follows.

        : ${user?} ${acct?} ${bin?}
        ...

Colon (:) is a command that is built in to the shell and does nothing once its arguments have been evaluated. If any of the variables **user, acct** or **bin** are not set then the shell will abandon execution of the procedure.

3.3 Command substitution

The standard output from a command can be substituted in a similar way to parameters. The command *pwd* prints on its standard output the name of the current directory. For example, if the current directory is **/usr/fred/bin** then the command

        d=`pwd`

is equivalent to

        d=/usr/fred/bin

The entire string between grave accents (`...`) is taken as the command to be executed and is replaced with the output from the command. The command is written using the usual quoting conventions except that a ` must be escaped using a \ . For example,

        ls `echo "$1"`

is equivalent to

        ls $1

Command substitution occurs in all contexts where parameter substitution occurs (including *here* documents) and the treatment of the resulting text is the same in both cases. This mechanism allows string processing commands to be used within shell procedures. An example of such a command is *basename* which removes a specified suffix from a string. For example,

        basename main.c .c

will print the string *main*. Its use is illustrated by the following fragment from a *cc* command.

        case $A in
        ...
        *.c)   B=`basename $A .c`
        ...
        esac

that sets **B** to the part of **$A** with the suffix **.c** stripped.

Here are some composite examples.

- **for i in `ls −t`; do ...**
  The variable **i** is set to the names of files in time order, most recent first.
- **set `date`; echo $6 $2 $3, $4**
  will print, e.g., *1977 Nov 1, 23:59:59*

3.4 Evaluation and quoting

The shell is a macro processor that provides parameter substitution, command substitution and file name generation for the arguments to commands. This section discusses the order in which these evaluations occur and the effects of the various quoting mechanisms.

Commands are parsed initially according to the grammar given in appendix A. Before a command is executed the following substitutions occur.

- parameter substitution, e.g. **$user**
- command substitution, e.g. **`pwd`**

  Only one evaluation occurs so that if, for example, the value of the variable **X** is the string *$y* then

  echo $X

  will echo *$y*.

- blank interpretation

  Following the above substitutions the resulting characters are broken into non-blank words (*blank interpretation*). For this purpose 'blanks' are the characters of the string **$IFS**. By default, this string consists of blank, tab and newline. The null string is not regarded as a word unless it is quoted. For example,

  echo ″

  will pass on the null string as the first argument to *echo*, whereas

  echo $null

  will call *echo* with no arguments if the variable **null** is not set or set to the null string.

- file name generation

  Each word is then scanned for the file pattern characters *****, **?** and **[...]** and an alphabetical list of file names is generated to replace the word. Each such file name is a separate argument.

The evaluations just described also occur in the list of words associated with a **for** loop. Only substitution occurs in the *word* used for a **case** branch.

As well as the quoting mechanisms described earlier using \ and ´...´ a third quoting mechanism is provided using double quotes. Within double quotes parameter and command substitution occurs but file name generation and the interpretation of blanks does not. The following characters have a special meaning within double quotes and may be quoted using \.

$	parameter substitution
`	command substitution
"	ends the quoted string
\	quotes the special characters $ ` " \

For example,

echo "$x"

will pass the value of the variable **x** as a single argument to *echo*. Similarly,

```
echo "$*"
```

will pass the positional parameters as a single argument and is equivalent to

```
echo "$1 $2 ..."
```

The notation **$@** is the same as **$*** except when it is quoted.

```
echo "$@"
```

will pass the positional parameters, unevaluated, to *echo* and is equivalent to

```
echo "$1" "$2" ...
```

The following table gives, for each quoting mechanism, the shell metacharacters that are evaluated.

	metacharacter					
	\	$	*	`	"	'
'	n	n	n	n	n	t
`	y	n	n	t	n	n
"	y	y	n	y	t	n

t	terminator
y	interpreted
n	not interpreted

Figure 2. Quoting mechanisms

In cases where more than one evaluation of a string is required the built-in command *eval* may be used. For example, if the variable **X** has the value *$y*, and if **y** has the value *pqr* then

```
eval echo $X
```

will echo the string *pqr*.

In general the *eval* command evaluates its arguments (as do all commands) and treats the result as input to the shell. The input is read and the resulting command(s) executed. For example,

```
wg='eval who|grep'
$wg fred
```

is equivalent to

```
who|grep fred
```

In this example, *eval* is required since there is no interpretation of metacharacters, such as | , **following substitution.**

3.5 Error handling

The treatment of errors detected by the shell depends on the type of error and on whether the shell is being used interactively. An interactive shell is one whose input and output are connected to a terminal (as determined by *gtty* (2)). A shell invoked with the **−i** flag is also interactive.

Execution of a command (see also 3.7) may fail for any of the following reasons.

- Input output redirection may fail. For example, if a file does not exist or cannot be created.

- The command itself does not exist or cannot be executed.
- The command terminates abnormally, for example, with a "bus error" or "memory fault". See Figure 2 below for a complete list of UNIX signals.
- The command terminates normally but returns a non-zero exit status.

In all of these cases the shell will go on to execute the next command. Except for the last case an error message will be printed by the shell. All remaining errors cause the shell to exit from a command procedure. An interactive shell will return to read another command from the terminal. Such errors include the following.

- Syntax errors. e.g., if ... then ... done
- A signal such as interrupt. The shell waits for the current command, if any, to finish execution and then either exits or returns to the terminal.
- Failure of any of the built-in commands such as *cd*.

The shell flag −e causes the shell to terminate if any error is detected.

1	hangup
2	interrupt
3*	quit
4*	illegal instruction
5*	trace trap
6*	IOT instruction
7*	EMT instruction
8*	floating point exception
9	kill (cannot be caught or ignored)
10*	bus error
11*	segmentation violation
12*	bad argument to system call
13	write on a pipe with no one to read it
14	alarm clock
15	software termination (from *kill* (1))

Figure 3. UNIX signals

Those signals marked with an asterisk produce a core dump if not caught. However, the shell itself ignores quit which is the only external signal that can cause a dump. The signals in this list of potential interest to shell programs are 1, 2, 3, 14 and 15.

3.6 Fault handling

Shell procedures normally terminate when an interrupt is received from the terminal. The *trap* command is used if some cleaning up is required, such as removing temporary files. For example,

        trap ´rm /tmp/ps$$; exit´ 2

sets a trap for signal 2 (terminal interrupt), and if this signal is received will execute the commands

        rm /tmp/ps$$; exit

exit is another built-in command that terminates execution of a shell procedure. The *exit* is required; otherwise, after the trap has been taken, the shell will resume executing the procedure at the place where it was interrupted.

UNIX signals can be handled in one of three ways. They can be ignored, in which case the signal is never sent to the process. They can be caught, in which case the process must decide what action to take when the signal is received. Lastly, they can be left to cause termination of the process without it having to take any further action. If a signal is being ignored on entry to the shell procedure, for example, by invoking it in the background (see 3.7) then *trap* commands (and the signal) are ignored.

The use of *trap* is illustrated by this modified version of the *touch* command (Figure 4). The cleanup action is to remove the file **junk$$**.

```
flag=
trap ´rm −f junk$$; exit´ 1 2 3 15
for i
do case $i in
   −c) flag=N ;;
   *)  if test −f $i
       then    ln $i junk$$; rm junk$$
       elif test $flag
       then    echo file \´$i\´ does not exist
       else    >$i
       fi
   esac
done
```

Figure 4. The touch command

The *trap* command appears before the creation of the temporary file; otherwise it would be possible for the process to die without removing the file.

Since there is no signal 0 in UNIX it is used by the shell to indicate the commands to be executed on exit from the shell procedure.

A procedure may, itself, elect to ignore signals by specifying the null string as the argument to trap. The following fragment is taken from the *nohup* command.

```
trap ″ 1 2 3 15
```

which causes *hangup, interrupt, quit* and *kill* to be ignored both by the procedure and by invoked commands.

Traps may be reset by saying

```
trap 2 3
```

which resets the traps for signals 2 and 3 to their default values. A list of the current values of traps may be obtained by writing

```
trap
```

The procedure *scan* (Figure 5) is an example of the use of *trap* where there is no exit in the trap command. *scan* takes each directory in the current directory, prompts with its name, and then executes commands typed at the terminal until an end of file or an interrupt is received. Interrupts are ignored while executing the requested commands but cause termination when *scan* is waiting for input.

```
d=`pwd`
for i in *
do if test −d $d/$i
    then cd $d/$i
            while echo "$i:"
                    trap exit 2
                    read x
            do trap : 2; eval $x; done
    fi
done
```

Figure 5. The scan command

read x is a built-in command that reads one line from the standard input and places the result in the variable **x**. It returns a non-zero exit status if either an end-of-file is read or an interrupt is received.

3.7 Command execution

To run a command (other than a built-in) the shell first creates a new process using the system call *fork*. The execution environment for the command includes input, output and the states of signals, and is established in the child process before the command is executed. The built-in command *exec* is used in the rare cases when no fork is required and simply replaces the shell with a new command. For example, a simple version of the *nohup* command looks like

```
trap ″ 1 2 3 15
exec $*
```

The *trap* turns off the signals specified so that they are ignored by subsequently created commands and *exec* replaces the shell by the command specified.

Most forms of input output redirection have already been described. In the following *word* is only subject to parameter and command substitution. No file name generation or blank interpretation takes place so that, for example,

```
echo ... >*.c
```

will write its output into a file whose name is ***.c**. Input output specifications are evaluated left to right as they appear in the command.

> word   The standard output (file descriptor 1) is sent to the file *word* which is created if it does not already exist.

>> word   The standard output is sent to file *word*. If the file exists then output is appended (by seeking to the end); otherwise the file is created.

< word   The standard input (file descriptor 0) is taken from the file *word*.

<< word   The standard input is taken from the lines of shell input that follow up to but not including a line consisting only of *word*. If *word* is quoted then no interpretation of the document occurs. If *word* is not quoted then parameter and command substitution occur and \ is used to quote the characters \ **$** ` and the first character of *word*. In the latter case **newline** is ignored (c.f. quoted strings).

>& digit   The file descriptor *digit* is duplicated using the system call *dup* (2) and the result is used as the standard output.

<& digit   The standard input is duplicated from file descriptor *digit*.

<&−	The standard input is closed.
>&−	The standard output is closed.

Any of the above may be preceded by a digit in which case the file descriptor created is that specified by the digit instead of the default 0 or 1. For example,

... 2>file

runs a command with message output (file descriptor 2) directed to *file*.

... 2>&1

runs a command with its standard output and message output merged. (Strictly speaking file descriptor 2 is created by duplicating file descriptor 1 but the effect is usually to merge the two streams.)

The environment for a command run in the background such as

list *.c | lpr &

is modified in two ways. Firstly, the default standard input for such a command is the empty file **/dev/null**. This prevents two processes (the shell and the command), which are running in parallel, from trying to read the same input. Chaos would ensue if this were not the case. For example,

ed file &

would allow both the editor and the shell to read from the same input at the same time.

The other modification to the environment of a background command is to turn off the QUIT and INTERRUPT signals so that they are ignored by the command. This allows these signals to be used at the terminal without causing background commands to terminate. For this reason the UNIX convention for a signal is that if it is set to 1 (ignored) then it is never changed even for a short time. Note that the shell command *trap* has no effect for an ignored signal.

3.8 Invoking the shell

The following flags are interpreted by the shell when it is invoked. If the first character of argument zero is a minus, then commands are read from the file **.profile**.

−**c** *string*
> If the −**c** flag is present then commands are read from *string*.

−**s** If the −**s** flag is present or if no arguments remain then commands are read from the standard input. Shell output is written to file descriptor 2.

−**i** If the −**i** flag is present or if the shell input and output are attached to a terminal (as told by *gtty*) then this shell is *interactive*. In this case TERMINATE is ignored (so that **kill 0** does not kill an interactive shell) and INTERRUPT is caught and ignored (so that **wait** is interruptable). In all cases QUIT is ignored by the shell.

Acknowledgements

The design of the shell is based in part on the original UNIX shell[3] and the PWB/UNIX shell,[4] some features having been taken from both. Similarities also exist with the command interpreters of the Cambridge Multiple Access System[5] and of CTSS.[6]

I would like to thank Dennis Ritchie and John Mashey for many discussions during the design of the shell. I am also grateful to the members of the Computing Science Research Center and to Joe Maranzano for their comments on drafts of this document.

References

1.   B. W. Kernighan, *UNIX for Beginners*, Bell Laboratories internal memorandum (1978).

2.   K. Thompson and D. M. Ritchie, *UNIX Programmer's Manual*, Bell Laboratories (1978). Seventh Edition.

3.   K. Thompson, "The UNIX Command Language," pp. 375-384 in *Structured Programming—Infotech State of the Art Report*, Infotech International Ltd., Nicholson House, Maidenhead, Berkshire, England (March 1975).

4.   J. R. Mashey, *PWB/UNIX Shell Tutorial*, Bell Laboratories internal memorandum (September 30, 1977).

5.   D. F. Hartley (Ed.), *The Cambridge Multiple Access System — Users Reference Manual*, University Mathematical Laboratory, Cambridge, England (1968).

6.   P. A. Crisman (Ed.), *The Compatible Time-Sharing System*, M.I.T. Press, Cambridge, Mass. (1965).

Appendix A - Grammar

item:	*word*
	input-output
	name = *value*
simple-command:	*item*
	simple-command item
command:	*simple-command*
	(*command-list*)
	{ *command-list* }
	for *name* **do** *command-list* **done**
	for *name* **in** *word* . . . **do** *command-list* **done**
	while *command-list* **do** *command-list* **done**
	until *command-list* **do** *command-list* **done**
	case *word* **in** *case-part* . . . **esac**
	if *command-list* **then** *command-list else-part* **fi**
pipeline:	*command*
	pipeline | *command*
andor:	*pipeline*
	andor **&&** *pipeline*
	andor || *pipeline*
command-list:	*andor*
	command-list ;
	command-list **&**
	command-list ; *andor*
	command-list **&** *andor*
input-output:	> *file*
	< *file*
	>> *word*
	<< *word*
file:	*word*
	& *digit*
	& −
case-part:	*pattern*) *command-list* ;;
pattern:	*word*
	pattern | *word*
else-part:	**elif** *command-list* **then** *command-list else-part*
	else *command-list*
	empty
empty:	
word:	a sequence of non-blank characters
name:	a sequence of letters, digits or underscores starting with a letter
digit:	**0 1 2 3 4 5 6 7 8 9**

Appendix B - Meta-characters and Reserved Words

a) syntactic

|	pipe symbol
&&	'andf' symbol
||	'orf' symbol
;	command separator
;;	case delimiter
&	background commands
( )	command grouping
<	input redirection
<<	input from a here document
>	output creation
>>	output append

b) patterns

*	match any character(s) including none
?	match any single character
[...]	match any of the enclosed characters

c) substitution

${...}	substitute shell variable
`...`	substitute command output

d) quoting

\	quote the next character
'...'	quote the enclosed characters except for '
"..."	quote the enclosed characters except for $ ` \ "

e) reserved words

if then else elif fi
case in esac
for while until do done
{ }

LEARN — Computer-Aided Instruction on UNIX
(Second Edition)

Brian W. Kernighan

Michael E. Lesk

Bell Laboratories
Murray Hill, New Jersey 07974

ABSTRACT

This paper describes the second version of the *learn* program for interpreting CAI scripts on the UNIX† operating system, and a set of scripts that provide a computerized introduction to the system.

Six current scripts cover basic commands and file handling, the editor, additional file handling commands, the *eqn* program for mathematical typing, the "−ms" package of formatting macros, and an introduction to the C programming language. These scripts now include a total of about 530 lessons.

Many users from a wide variety of backgrounds have used *learn* to acquire basic UNIX skills. Most usage involves the first two scripts, an introduction to files and commands, and the text editor.

The second version of *learn* is about four times faster than the previous one in CPU utilization, and much faster in perceived time because of better overlap of computing and printing. It also requires less file space than the first version. Many of the lessons have been revised; new material has been added to reflect changes and enhancements in the UNIX system itself. Script-writing is also easier because of revisions to the script language.

January 30, 1979

---

†UNIX is a Trademark of Bell Laboratories.

1. Introduction.

Learn is a driver for CAI scripts. It is intended to permit the easy composition of lessons and lesson fragments to teach people computer skills. Since it is teaching the same system on which it is implemented, it makes direct use of UNIX† facilities to create a controlled UNIX environment. The system includes two main parts: (1) a driver that interprets the lesson scripts; and (2) the lesson scripts themselves. At present there are six scripts:

- basic file handling commands
- the UNIX text editor *ed*
- advanced file handling
- the *eqn* language for typing mathematics
- the "−ms" macro package for document formatting
- the C programming language

The purported advantages of CAI scripts for training in computer skills include the following:

(a) students are forced to perform the exercises that are in fact the basis of training in any case;

(b) students receive immediate feedback and confirmation of progress;

(c) students may progress at their own rate;

(d) no schedule requirements are imposed; students may study at any time convenient for them;

(e) the lessons may be improved individually and the improvements are immediately available to new users;

(f) since the student has access to a computer for the CAI script there is a place to do exercises;

(g) the use of high technology will improve student motivation and the interest of their management.

Opposed to this, of course, is the absence of anyone to whom the student may direct questions. If CAI is used without a "counselor" or other assistance, it should properly be compared to a textbook, lecture series, or taped course, rather than to a seminar. CAI has been used for many years in a variety of educational areas.[1,2,3] The use of a computer to teach itself, however, offers unique advantages. The skills developed to get through the script are exactly those needed to use the computer; there is no waste effort.

The scripts written so far are based on some familiar assumptions about education; these

---

†UNIX is a Trademark of Bell Laboratories.

assumptions are outlined in the next section. The remaining sections describe the operation of the script driver and the particular scripts now available. The driver puts few restrictions on the script writer, but the current scripts are of a rather rigid and stereotyped form in accordance with the theory in the next section and practical limitations.

2. Educational Assumptions and Design.

First, the way to teach people how to do something is to have them do it. Scripts should not contain long pieces of explanation; they should instead frequently ask the student to do some task. So teaching is always by example: the typical script fragment shows a small example of some technique and then asks the user to either repeat that example or produce a variation on it. All are intended to be easy enough that most students will get most questions right, reinforcing the desired behavior.

Most lessons fall into one of three types. The simplest presents a lesson and asks for a yes or no answer to a question. The student is given a chance to experiment before replying. The script checks for the correct reply. Problems of this form are sparingly used.

The second type asks for a word or number as an answer. For example a lesson on files might say

How many files are there in the current directory? Type "answer N", where N is the number of files.

The student is expected to respond (perhaps after experimenting) with

answer 17

or whatever. Surprisingly often, however, the idea of a substitutable argument (i.e., replacing N by 17) is difficult for non-programmer students, so the first few such lessons need real care.

The third type of lesson is open-ended — a task is set for the student, appropriate parts of the input or output are monitored, and the student types *ready* when the task is done. Figure 1 shows a sample dialog that illustrates the last of these, using two lessons about the *cat* (concatenate, i.e., print) command taken from early in the script that teaches file handling. Most *learn* lessons are of this form.

After each correct response the computer congratulates the student and indicates the lesson number that has just been completed, permitting the student to restart the script after that lesson. If the answer is wrong, the student is offered a chance to repeat the lesson. The "speed" rating of the student (explained in section 5) is given after the lesson number when the lesson is completed successfully; it is printed only for the aid of script authors checking out possible errors in the lessons.

It is assumed that there is no foolproof way to determine if the student truly "understands" what he or she is doing; accordingly, the current *learn* scripts only measure performance, not comprehension. If the student can perform a given task, that is deemed to be "learning."[4]

The main point of using the computer is that what the student does is checked for correctness immediately. Unlike many CAI scripts, however, these scripts provide few facilities for dealing with wrong answers. In practice, if most of the answers are not right the script is a failure; the universal solution to student error is to provide a new, easier script. Anticipating possible wrong answers is an endless job, and it is really easier as well as better to provide a simpler script.

Along with this goes the assumption that anything can be taught to anybody if it can be broken into sufficiently small pieces. Anything not absorbed in a single chunk is just subdivided.

To avoid boring the faster students, however, an effort is made in the files and editor scripts to provide three tracks of different difficulty. The fastest sequence of lessons is aimed at roughly the bulk and speed of a typical tutorial manual and should be adequate for review and for well-prepared students. The next track is intended for most users and is roughly twice as

---

Figure 1: Sample dialog from basic files script

(Student responses in italics; '$' is the prompt)

A file can be printed on your terminal
by using the "cat" command. Just say
"cat file" where "file" is the file name.
For example, there is a file named
"food" in this directory. List it
by saying "cat food"; then type "ready".
$ *cat food*
  this is the file
  named food.
$ *ready*

Good. Lesson 3.3a (1)

Of course, you can print any file with "cat".
In particular, it is common to first use
"ls" to find the name of a file and then "cat"
to print it. Note the difference between
"ls", which tells you the name of the file,
and "cat", which tells you the contents.
One file in the current directory is named for
a President. Print the file, then type "ready".
$ *cat President*
cat: can't open President
$ *ready*

Sorry, that's not right. Do you want to try again? *yes*
Try the problem again.
$ *ls*
.ocopy
X1
roosevelt
$ *cat roosevelt*
  this file is named roosevelt
  and contains three lines of
  text.
$ *ready*

Good. Lesson 3.3b (0)

The "cat" command can also print several files
at once. In fact, it is named "cat" as an abbreviation
for "concatenate"....

---

long. Typically, for example, the fast track might present an idea and ask for a variation on the example shown; the normal track will first ask the student to repeat the example that was shown before attempting a variation. The third and slowest track, which is often three or four times the length of the fast track, is intended to be adequate for anyone. (The lessons of Figure 1 are from the third track.) The multiple tracks also mean that a student repeating a course is unlikely to hit the same series of lessons; this makes it profitable for a shaky user to back up and try again, and many students have done so.

The tracks are not completely distinct, however. Depending on the number of correct answers the student has given for the last few lessons, the program may switch tracks. The driver is actually capable of following an arbitrary directed graph of lesson sequences, as discussed in section 5. Some more structured arrangement, however, is used in all current scripts to aid the script writer in organizing the material into lessons. It is sufficiently difficult to write lessons that the three-track theory is not followed very closely except in the files and editor scripts. Accordingly, in some cases, the fast track is produced merely by skipping lessons from the slower track. In others, there is essentially only one track.

The main reason for using the *learn* program rather than simply writing the same material as a workbook is not the selection of tracks, but actual hands-on experience. Learning by doing is much more effective than pencil and paper exercises.

Learn also provides a mechanical check on performance. The first version in fact would not let the student proceed unless it received correct answers to the questions it set and it would not tell a student the right answer. This somewhat Draconian approach has been moderated in version 2. Lessons are sometimes badly worded or even just plain wrong; in such cases, the student has no recourse. But if a student is simply unable to complete one lesson, that should not prevent access to the rest. Accordingly, the current version of *learn* allows the student to skip a lesson that he cannot pass; a "no" answer to the "Do you want to try again?" question in Figure 1 will pass to the next lesson. It is still true that *learn* will not tell the student the right answer.

Of course, there are valid objections to the assumptions above. In particular, some students may object to not understanding what they are doing; and the procedure of smashing everything into small pieces may provoke the retort "you can't cross a ditch in two jumps." Since writing CAI scripts is considerably more tedious than ordinary manuals, however, it is safe to assume that there will always be alternatives to the scripts as a way of learning. In fact, for a reference manual of 3 or 4 pages it would not be surprising to have a tutorial manual of 20 pages and a (multi-track) script of 100 pages. Thus the reference manual will exist long before the scripts.

3. Scripts.

As mentioned above, the present scripts try at most to follow a three-track theory. Thus little of the potential complexity of the possible directed graph is employed, since care must be taken in lesson construction to see that every necessary fact is presented in every possible path through the units. In addition, it is desirable that every unit have alternate successors to deal with student errors.

In most existing courses, the first few lessons are devoted to checking prerequisites. For example, before the student is allowed to proceed through the editor script the script verifies that the student understands files and is able to type. It is felt that the sooner lack of student preparation is detected, the easier it will be on the student. Anyone proceeding through the scripts should be getting mostly correct answers; otherwise, the system will be unsatisfactory both because the wrong habits are being learned and because the scripts make little effort to deal with wrong answers. Unprepared students should not be encouraged to continue with scripts.

There are some preliminary items which the student must know before any scripts can be tried. In particular, the student must know how to connect to a UNIX system, set the terminal properly, log in, and execute simple commands (e.g., *learn* itself). In addition, the character erase and line kill conventions (# and @) should be known. It is hard to see how this much could be taught by computer-aided instruction, since a student who does not know these basic skills will not be able to run the learning program. A brief description on paper is provided (see Appendix A), although assistance will be needed for the first few minutes. This assistance, however, need not be highly skilled.

The first script in the current set deals with files. It assumes the basic knowledge above and teaches the student about the *ls*, *cat*, *mv*, *rm*, *cp* and *diff* commands. It also deals with the abbreviation characters *, ?, and [ ] in file names. It does not cover pipes or I/O redirection, nor does it present the many options on the *ls* command.

This script contains 31 lessons in the fast track; two are intended as prerequisite checks, seven are review exercises. There are a total of 75 lessons in all three tracks, and the instructional passages typed at the student to begin each lesson total 4,476 words. The average lesson thus begins with a 60-word message. In general, the fast track lessons have somewhat longer introductions, and the slow tracks somewhat shorter ones. The longest message is 144 words and the shortest 14.

The second script trains students in the use of the context editor *ed*, a sophisticated editor using regular expressions for searching.[5] All editor features except encryption, mark names and ';' in addressing are covered. The fast track contains 2 prerequisite checks, 93 lessons, and a review lesson. It is supplemented by 146 additional lessons in other tracks.

A comparison of sizes may be of interest. The *ed* description in the reference manual is 2,572 words long. The *ed* tutorial[6] is 6,138 words long. The fast track through the *ed* script is 7,407 words of explanatory messages, and the total *ed* script, 242 lessons, has 15,615 words. The average *ed* lesson is thus also about 60 words; the largest is 171 words and the smallest 10. The original *ed* script represents about three man-weeks of effort.

The advanced file handling script deals with *ls* options, I/O diversion, pipes, and supporting programs like *pr*, *wc*, *tail*, *spell* and *grep*. (The basic file handling script is a prerequisite.) It is not as refined as the first two scripts; this is reflected at least partly in the fact that it provides much less of a full three-track sequence than they do. On the other hand, since it is perceived as "advanced," it is hoped that the student will have somewhat more sophistication and be better able to cope with it at a reasonably high level of performance.

A fourth script covers the *eqn* language for typing mathematics. This script must be run on a terminal capable of printing mathematics, for instance the DASI 300 and similar Diablo-based terminals, or the nearly extinct Model 37 teletype. Again, this script is relatively short of tracks: of 76 lessons, only 17 are in the second track and 2 in the third track. Most of these provide additional practice for students who are having trouble in the first track.

The −*ms* script for formatting macros is a short one-track only script. The macro package it describes is no longer the standard, so this script will undoubtedly be superseded in the future. Furthermore, the linear style of a single learn script is somewhat inappropriate for the macros, since the macro package is composed of many independent features, and few users need all of them. It would be better to have a selection of short lesson sequences dealing with the features independently.

The script on C is in a state of transition. It was originally designed to follow a tutorial on C, but that document has since become obsolete. The current script has been partially converted to follow the order of presentation in *The C Programming Language,*[7] but this job is not complete. The C script was never intended to teach C; rather it is supposed to be a series of exercises for which the computer provides checking and (upon success) a suggested solution.

This combination of scripts covers much of the material which any user will need to know to make effective use of the UNIX system. With enlargement of the advanced files course to include more on the command interpreter, there will be a relatively complete introduction to UNIX available via *learn*. Although we make no pretense that *learn* will replace other instructional materials, it should provide a useful supplement to existing tutorials and reference manuals.

4. Experience with Students.

Learn has been installed on many different UNIX systems. Most of the usage is on the first two scripts, so these are more thoroughly debugged and polished. As a (random) sample of user experience, the *learn* program has been used at Bell Labs at Indian Hill for 10,500 lessons in a four month period. About 3600 of these are in the files script, 4100 in the editor, and 1400 in advanced files. The passing rate is about 80%, that is, about 4 lessons are passed for every one failed. There have been 86 distinct users of the files script, and 58 of the editor. On our system at Murray Hill, there have been nearly 4000 lessons over four weeks that include Christmas and New Year. Users have ranged in age from six up.

It is difficult to characterize typical sessions with the scripts; many instances exist of someone doing one or two lessons and then logging out, as do instances of someone pausing in a script for twenty minutes or more. In the earlier version of *learn*, the average session in the files course took 32 minutes and covered 23 lessons. The distribution is quite broad and skewed, however; the longest session was 130 minutes and there were five sessions shorter than five minutes. The average lesson took about 80 seconds. These numbers are roughly typical for non-programmers; a UNIX expert can do the scripts at approximately 30 seconds per lesson, most of which is the system printing.

At present working through a section of the middle of the files script took about 1.4 seconds of processor time per lesson, and a system expert typing quickly took 15 seconds of real time per lesson. A novice would probably take at least a minute. Thus, as a rough approximation, a UNIX system could support ten students working simultaneously with some spare capacity.

5. The Script Interpreter.

The *learn* program itself merely interprets scripts. It provides facilities for the script writer to capture student responses and their effects, and simplifies the job of passing control to and recovering control from the student. This section describes the operation and usage of the driver program, and indicates what is required to produce a new script. Readers only interested in the existing scripts may skip this section.

The file structure used by *learn* is shown in Figure 2. There is one parent directory (named *lib*) containing the script data. Within this directory are subdirectories, one for each subject in which a course is available, one for logging (named *log*), and one in which user subdirectories are created (named *play*). The subject directory contains master copies of all lessons, plus any supporting material for that subject. In a given subdirectory, each lesson is a single text file. Lessons are usually named systematically; the file that contains lesson *n* is called *Ln*.

When *learn* is executed, it makes a private directory for the user to work in, within the *learn* portion of the file system. A fresh copy of all the files used in each lesson (mostly data for the student to operate upon) is made each time a student starts a lesson, so the script writer may assume that everything is reinitialized each time a lesson is entered. The student directory is deleted after each session; any permanent records must be kept elsewhere.

The script writer must provide certain basic items in each lesson:

(1)   the text of the lesson;

(2)   the set-up commands to be executed before the user gets control;

(3)   the data, if any, which the user is supposed to edit, transform, or otherwise process;

(4)   the evaluating commands to be executed after the user has finished the lesson, to decide whether the answer is right; and

(5)   a list of possible successor lessons.

Learn tries to minimize the work of bookkeeping and installation, so that most of the effort involved in script production is in planning lessons, writing tutorial paragraphs, and coding tests of student performance.

Figure 2: Directory structure for *learn*

lib

    play

                student1

                        files for student1...

                student2

                        files for student2...

    files

                L0.1a   lessons for files course
                L0.1b
                ...

    editor

                ...

    (other courses)

    log

The basic sequence of events is as follows. First, *learn* creates the working directory. Then, for each lesson, *learn* reads the script for the lesson and processes it a line at a time. The lines in the script are: (1) commands to the script interpreter to print something, to create a files, to test something, etc.; (2) text to be printed or put in a file; (3) other lines, which are sent to the shell to be executed. One line in each lesson turns control over to the user; the user can run any UNIX commands. The user mode terminates when the user types *yes*, *no*, *ready*, or *answer*. At this point, the user's work is tested; if the lesson is passed, a new lesson is selected, and if not the old one is repeated.

Let us illustrate this with the script for the second lesson of Figure 1; this is shown in Figure 3.

Lines which begin with # are commands to the *learn* script interpreter. For example,

    #print

causes printing of any text that follows, up to the next line that begins with a sharp.

    #print file

prints the contents of *file*; it is the same as *cat file* but has less overhead. Both forms of *#print* have the added property that if a lesson is failed, the *#print* will not be executed the second time through; this avoids annoying the student by repeating the preamble to a lesson.

    #create filename

creates a file of the specified name, and copies any subsequent text up to a # to the file. This is used for creating and initializing working files and reference data for the lessons.

    #user

gives control to the student; each line he or she types is passed to the shell for execution. The *#user* mode is terminated when the student types one of *yes*, *no*, *ready* or *answer*. At that time, the driver resumes interpretation of the script.

    #copyin
    #uncopyin

Anything the student types between these commands is copied onto a file called *.copy*. This lets the script writer interrogate the student's responses upon regaining control.

```
┌─────────────────────────────────────────────┐
│ Figure 3:  Sample Lesson                      │
│                                               │
│ #print                                        │
│ Of course, you can print any file with "cat". │
│ In particular, it is common to first use      │
│ "ls" to find the name of a file and then "cat"│
│ to print it.  Note the difference between     │
│ "ls", which tells you the name of the files,  │
│ and "cat", which tells you the contents.      │
│ One file in the current directory is named for│
│ a President.  Print the file, then type "ready".│
│ #create roosevelt                             │
│   this file is named roosevelt                │
│   and contains three lines of                 │
│   text.                                       │
│ #copyout                                      │
│ #user                                         │
│ #uncopyout                                    │
│ tail −3 .ocopy >X1                            │
│ #cmp X1 roosevelt                             │
│ #log                                          │
│ #next                                         │
│ 3.2b 2                                        │
└─────────────────────────────────────────────┘
```

#copyout
#uncopyout

Between these commands, any material typed at the student by any program is copied to the file *ocopy*. This lets the script writer interrogate the effect of what the student typed, which true believers in the performance theory of learning usually prefer to the student's actual input.

#pipe
#unpipe

Normally the student input and the script commands are fed to the UNIX command interpreter (the "shell") one line at a time. This won't do if, for example, a sequence of editor commands is provided, since the input to the editor must be handed to the editor, not to the shell. Accordingly, the material between *#pipe* and *#unpipe* commands is fed continuously through a pipe so that such sequences work. If *copyout* is also desired the *copyout* brackets must include the *pipe* brackets.

There are several commands for setting status after the student has attempted the lesson.

#cmp file1 file2

is an in-line implementation of *cmp*, which compares two files for identity.

#match stuff

The last line of the student's input is compared to *stuff*, and the success or fail status is set according to it. Extraneous things like the word *answer* are stripped before the comparison is made. There may be several *#match* lines; this provides a convenient mechanism for handling multiple "right" answers. Any text up to a # on subsequent lines after a successful *#match* is printed; this is illustrated in Figure 4, another sample lesson.

#bad stuff

This is similar to *#match*, except that it corresponds to specific failure answers; this can be used to produce hints for particular wrong answers that have been anticipated by the script

---

Figure 4: Another Sample Lesson

```
#print
What command will move the current line
to the end of the file?  Type
"answer COMMAND", where COMMAND is the command.
#copyin
#user
#uncopyin
#match m$
#match .m$
"m$" is easier.
#log
#next
63.1d 10
```

---

writer.

> #*succeed*
> #*fail*

print a message upon success or failure (as determined by some previous mechanism).

When the student types one of the "commands" *yes*, *no*, *ready*, or *answer*, the driver terminates the #*user* command, and evaluation of the student's work can begin. This can be done either by the built-in commands above, such as #*match* and #*cmp*, or by status returned by normal UNIX commands, typically *grep* and *test*. The last command should return status true (0) if the task was done successfully and false (non-zero) otherwise; this status return tells the driver whether or not the student has successfully passed the lesson.

Performance can be logged:

> #*log file*

writes the date, lesson, user name and speed rating, and a success/failure indication on *file*. The command

> #*log*

by itself writes the logging information in the logging directory within the *learn* hierarchy, and is the normal form.

> #*next*

is followed by a few lines, each with a successor lesson name and an optional speed rating on it. A typical set might read

> 25.1a   10
> 25.2a   5
> 25.3a   2

indicating that unit 25.1a is a suitable follow-on lesson for students with a speed rating of 10 units, 25.2a for student with speed near 5, and 25.3a for speed near 2. Speed ratings are maintained for each session with a student; the rating is increased by one each time the student gets a lesson right and decreased by four each time the student gets a lesson wrong. Thus the driver tries to maintain a level such that the users get 80% right answers. The maximum rating is limited to 10 and the minimum to 0. The initial rating is zero unless the student specifies a different rating when starting a session.

If the student passes a lesson, a new lesson is selected and the process repeats. If the student fails, a false status is returned and the program reverts to the previous lesson and tries another alternative. If it can not find another alternative, it skips forward a lesson. The student can terminate a session at any time by typing *bye*, which causes a graceful exit from *learn*. Hanging up is the usual novice's way out.

The lessons may form an arbitrary directed graph, although the present program imposes a limitation on cycles in that it will not present a lesson twice in the same session. If the student is unable to answer one of the exercises correctly, the driver searches for a previous lesson with a set of alternatives as successors (following the *#next* line). From the previous lesson with alternatives one route was taken earlier; the program simply tries a different one.

It is perfectly possible to write sophisticated scripts that evaluate the student's speed of response, or try to estimate the elegance of the answer, or provide detailed analysis of wrong answers. Lesson writing is so tedious already, however, that most of these abilities are likely to go unused.

The driver program depends heavily on features of the UNIX system that are not available on many other operating systems. These include the ease of manipulating files and directories, file redirection, the ability to use the command interpreter as just another program (even in a pipeline), command status testing and branching, the ability to catch signals like interrupts, and of course the pipeline mechanism itself. Although some parts of *learn* might be transferable to other systems, some generality will probably be lost.

A bit of history: The first version of *learn* had fewer built-in commands in the driver program, and made more use of the facilities of the UNIX system itself. For example, file comparison was done by creating a *cmp* process, rather than comparing the two files within *learn*. Lessons were not stored as text files, but as archives. There was no concept of the in-line document; even *#print* had to be followed by a file name. Thus the initialization for each lesson was to extract the archive into the working directory (typically 4-8 files), then *#print* the lesson text.

The combination of such things made *learn* rather slow and demanding of system resources. The new version is about 4 or 5 times faster, because fewer files and processes are created. Furthermore, it appears even faster to the user because in a typical lesson, the printing of the message comes first, and file setup with *#create* can be overlapped with printing, so that when the program finishes printing, it is really ready for the user to type at it.

It is also a great advantage to the script maintainer that lessons are now just ordinary text files, rather than archives. They can be edited without any difficulty, and UNIX text manipulation tools can be applied to them. The result has been that there is much less resistance to going in and fixing substandard lessons.

6. Conclusions

The following observations can be made about secretaries, typists, and other non-programmers who have used *learn*:

(a)   A novice must have assistance with the mechanics of communicating with the computer to get through to the first lesson or two; once the first few lessons are passed people can proceed on their own.

(b)   The terminology used in the first few lessons is obscure to those inexperienced with computers. It would help if there were a low level reference card for UNIX to supplement the existing programmer oriented bulky manual and bulky reference card.

(c)   The concept of "substitutable argument" is hard to grasp, and requires help.

(d)   They enjoy the system for the most part. Motivation matters a great deal, however.

It takes an hour or two for a novice to get through the script on file handling. The total time for a reasonably intelligent and motivated novice to proceed from ignorance to a reasonable ability to create new files and manipulate old ones seems to be a few days, with perhaps half of each day spent on the machine.

The normal way of proceeding has been to have students in the same room with someone who knows the UNIX system and the scripts. Thus the student is not brought to a halt by difficult questions. The burden on the counselor, however, is much lower than that on a teacher of a course. Ideally, the students should be encouraged to proceed with instruction immediately prior to their actual use of the computer. They should exercise the scripts on the same computer and the same kind of terminal that they will later use for their real work, and their first few jobs for the computer should be relatively easy ones. Also, both training and initial work should take place on days when the hardware and software are working reliably. Rarely is all of this possible, but the closer one comes the better the result. For example, if it is known that the hardware is shaky one day, it is better to attempt to reschedule training for another one. Students are very frustrated by machine downtime; when nothing is happening, it takes some sophistication and experience to distinguish an infinite loop, a slow but functioning program, a program waiting for the user, and a broken machine.*

One disadvantage of training with *learn* is that students come to depend completely on the CAI system, and do not try to read manuals or use other learning aids. This is unfortunate, not only because of the increased demands for completeness and accuracy of the scripts, but because the scripts do not cover all of the UNIX system. New users should have manuals (appropriate for their level) and read them; the scripts ought to be altered to recommend suitable documents and urge students to read them.

There are several other difficulties which are clearly evident. From the student's viewpoint, the most serious is that lessons still crop up which simply can't be passed. Sometimes this is due to poor explanations, but just as often it is some error in the lesson itself — a botched setup, a missing file, an invalid test for correctness, or some system facility that doesn't work on the local system in the same way it did on the development system. It takes knowledge and a certain healthy arrogance on the part of the user to recognize that the fault is not his or hers, but the script writer's. Permitting the student to get on with the next lesson regardless does alleviate this somewhat, and the logging facilities make it easy to watch for lessons that no one can pass, but it is still a problem.

The biggest problem with the previous *learn* was speed (or lack thereof) — it was often excruciatingly slow and a significant drain on the system. The current version so far does not seem to have that difficulty, although some scripts, notably *eqn*, are intrinsically slow. *eqn*, for example, must do a lot of work even to print its introductions, let alone check the student responses, but delay is perceptible in all scripts from time to time.

Another potential problem is that it is possible to break *learn* inadvertently, by pushing interrupt at the wrong time, or by removing critical files, or any number of similar slips. The defenses against such problems have steadily been improved, to the point where most students should not notice difficulties. Of course, it will always be possible to break *learn* maliciously, but this is not likely to be a problem.

One area is more fundamental — some commands are sufficiently global in their effect that *learn* currently does not allow them to be executed at all. The most obvious is *cd*, which changes to another directory. The prospect of a student who is learning about directories inadvertently moving to some random directory and removing files has deterred us from even writing lessons on *cd*, but ultimately lessons on such topics probably should be added.

7. Acknowledgments

We are grateful to all those who have tried *learn,* for we have benefited greatly from their suggestions and criticisms. In particular, M. E. Bittrich, J. L. Blue, S. I. Feldman, P. A. Fox, and M. J. McAlpin have provided substantial feedback. Conversations with E. Z. Rothkopf also provided many of the ideas in the system. We are also indebted to Don Jackowski for serving

---

* We have even known an expert programmer to decide the computer was broken when he had simply left his terminal in local mode. Novices have great difficulties with such problems.

as a guinea pig for the second version, and to Tom Plum for his efforts to improve the C script.

References

1. D. L. Bitzer and D. Skaperdas, "The Economics of a Large Scale Computer Based Education System: Plato IV," pp. 17-29 in *Computer Assisted Instruction, Testing and Guidance*, ed. Wayne Holtzman, Harper and Row, New York (1970).

2. D. C. Gray, J. P. Hulskamp, J. H. Kumm, S. Lichtenstein, and N. E. Nimmervoll, "COALA - A Minicomputer CAI System," *IEEE Trans. Education* **E-20**(1), pp.73-77 (Feb. 1977).

3. P. Suppes, "On Using Computers to Individualize Instruction," pp. 11-24 in *The Computer in American Education*, ed. D. D. Bushnell and D. W. Allen, John Wiley, New York (1967).

4. B. F. Skinner, "Why We Need Teaching Machines," *Harv. Educ. Review* **31**, pp.377-398, Reprinted in *Educational Technology,* ed. J. P. DeCecco, Holt, Rinehart & Winston (New York, 1964). (1961).

5. K. Thompson and D. M. Ritchie, *UNIX Programmer's Manual,* Bell Laboratories (1978). See section *ed* (I).

6. B. W. Kernighan, *A tutorial introduction to the UNIX text editor*, Bell Laboratories internal memorandum (1974).

7. B. W. Kernighan and D. M. Ritchie, *The C Programming Language,* Prentice-Hall, Englewood Cliffs, New Jersey (1978).

How to Get Started

Absolutely basic information for using the UNIX system
from DASI, Terminet, or HP terminals

First time. BRING A FRIEND. Anyone who has used UNIX before, however briefly, will be of enormous help for the first fifteen minutes to show you where all the switches are and supply information missing from this page.

Terminals. Turn the power on. There are many kinds of terminals. Look at the telephone used with the terminal to distinguish them. Terminals may have
— *old style datasets* (if the phone set is a small gray box with "talk" and "data" buttons at the right above the handset)
— *new style datasets* (if the phone set is a black six button phone with a red "data" button on the left, sitting on a rectangular box with a glass front)
— *acoustic couplers* (if an ordinary telephone is used to call and the terminal has rubber receptacles that the handset fits into) or
— *modems* (if the phone used for calling has a white button for the left button of the pair of buttons the handset usually rests on).
— *none of the above* (in which case there is probably a switch somewhere that should be flipped to signal the computer).

Calling in. For your local UNIX call _____.
— If the terminal doesn't use a phone, ignore this section, and proceed to *Login.*.
— On terminals with datasets you must push the "talk" button to get a dial tone.
— If the terminal has a separate coupler turn the coupler power on.
— If the line is busy UNIX is probably full.
— If there is no answer UNIX is broken.
Usually the phone rings only once; UNIX answers and whistles at you.

Connecting the terminal. Remember what kind of terminal you have. If it uses a
— *dataset,* push down the "data" button, let it spring back up, and then hang up the handset (IN THAT ORDER).
— *coupler,* place the handset in the rubber receptacles. There will be an indication of where the phone cord should be (it matters). You may get better results by placing the handset in the receptacles as you dial.
— *modem,* pull up the white button on the telephone and put the handset down somewhere (but don't hang up the phone!).

Login. UNIX should type "login:". If it does not:
— Your terminal may be in "local" mode — check that the "local/line" switch is on "line". Also, Terminets may have their "interrupt" light on — turn it off by pushing "ready."
— If the message is garbled, the speed is wrong. Somewhere on the terminal is a switch labeled "rate" or "baud" with positions of either "10,15,30" or "110,150,300". Set it to 30 or 300. Push the break or interrupt button slowly a few times. If "login:" doesn't appear, call for help.
— UNIX may be broken (call ext. _____ to check on that).
Type your userid, followed by "return". Your userid is _____.
— If each letter appears twice, find the switch labeled "full/half duplex" and set it to "full".
— If the computer typed back your userid in upper case, find the "all caps" switch or "shift lock" and turn it off. Then dial in again.
Normally UNIX says "Password:" and you should enter your password; printing will be turned off while you do.
    If you misspell it, UNIX will say "Login incorrect. login:" and you can then retype your userid and password correctly.
UNIX will say "$". You have successfully logged in.

Commands. When UNIX has typed "$" you can type commands, one per line. For example, you can type "date" to find out what day and time it is, or "who" to find out who is logged on. Every command must end with a "return". After typing a command, wait for the next "$" to see what happens. For example, your terminal paper might look like this (what the computer typed is in italics):

> *login:* myid
> *Password:* <you can't see it>
> *$* date
> *Thu Jan 15 10:58:21 EST 1979*
> *$*

There are a great many other commands you can type (see the guides below) and in particular the *learn* command can help you learn some features of UNIX.

— If you make a mistake typing: the character # will erase the previous character, so that typing

> dax#te

is the same as typing

> date

and the character @ will erase the entire line; typing

> xxxxx@
> date

is the same as typing "date". UNIX supplies the carriage return after the @.

— You must hit return if you expect the computer to notice what you typed· otherwise it will wait patiently and silently for you to do so. When in doubt, type return and see what happens.

— If you make a typing error and don't correct it with # or @ before hitting return, the computer will typically say

> *datr: not found*

where "datr" is the erroneous input line.

— Other messages that may arise from mistyping include *"cannot execute"* or *"No match"* or just *"?"*. The cure is almost always to retype the offending line correctly.

Terminology. Everything stored on the computer is saved in *files*. A file might contain, for example, a memo or a chapter of a book or a letter. Every file has a name, which is used whenever you want to refer to it. Sample names might be "chap3" or "memo2". The files are grouped into *directories;* each directory contains the names of several files. All users have directories containing their own files.

Logging out. Just hang up. On a terminal with a data set, push the "talk" button. On other terminals hang up the handset. Turn the terminal power off.

Guides. You should have copies of *UNIX For Beginners* and *A Tutorial Introduction to the UNIX Text Editor.*

DOCUMENT
PREPARATION

Typing Documents on the UNIX System:
Using the −ms Macros with Troff and Nroff

M. E. Lesk

Bell Laboratories
Murray Hill, New Jersey 07974

ABSTRACT

This document describes a set of easy-to-use macros for preparing documents on the UNIX system. Documents may be produced on either the photo-typesetter or a on a computer terminal, without changing the input.

The macros provide facilities for paragraphs, sections (optionally with automatic numbering), page titles, footnotes, equations, tables, two-column format, and cover pages for papers.

This memo includes, as an appendix, the text of the "Guide to Preparing Documents with −ms" which contains additional examples of features of −ms.

This manual is a revision of, and replaces, "Typing Documents on UNIX," dated November 22, 1974.

November 13, 1978

Introduction. This memorandum describes a package of commands to produce papers using the *troff* and *nroff* formatting programs on the UNIX system. As with other *roff*-derived programs, text is prepared interspersed with formatting commands. However, this package, which itself is written in *troff* commands, provides higher-level commands than those provided with the basic **troff** program. The commands available in this package are listed in Appendix A.

Text. Type normally, except that instead of indenting for paragraphs, place a line reading ".PP" before each paragraph. This will produce indenting and extra space.

Alternatively, the command .LP that was used here will produce a left-aligned (block) paragraph. The paragraph spacing can be changed: see below under "Registers."

Beginning. For a document with a paper-type cover sheet, the input should start as follows:

        [optional overall format .RP − see below]
        .TL
        Title of document (one or more lines)
        .AU
        Author(s) (may also be several lines)
        .AI
        Author's institution(s)
        .AB
        Abstract; to be placed on the cover sheet of a paper.
        Line length is 5/6 of normal; use .ll here to change.
        .AE (abstract end)
        text ... (begins with .PP, which see)

To omit some of the standard headings (e.g. no abstract, or no author's institution) just omit the corresponding fields and command lines. The word ABSTRACT can be suppressed by writing ".AB no" for ".AB". Several interspersed .AU and .AI lines can be used for multiple authors. The headings are not compulsory: beginning with a .PP command is perfectly OK and will just start printing an ordinary paragraph. *Warning:* You can't just begin a document with a line of text. Some −ms command must precede any text input. When in doubt, use .LP to get proper initialization, although any of the commands .PP, .LP, .TL, .SH, .NH is good enough. Figure 1 shows the legal arrangement of commands at the start of a document.

Cover Sheets and First Pages. The first line of a document signals the general format of the first page. In particular, if it is ".RP" a cover sheet with title and abstract is prepared. The default format is useful for scanning drafts.

In general −ms is arranged so that only one form of a document need be stored, containing all information; the first command gives the format, and unnecessary items for that format are ignored.

Warning: don't put extraneous material between the .TL and .AE commands. Processing of the titling items is special, and other data placed in them may not behave as you expect. Don't forget that some −ms command must precede any input text.

Page headings. The −ms macros, by default, will print a page heading containing a page number (if greater than 1). A default page footer is provided only in *nroff*, where the date is used. The user can make minor adjustments to the page headings/footings by redefining the strings LH, CH, and RH which are the left, center and right portions of the page headings, respectively; and the strings LF, CF, and RF, which are the left, center and right portions of the page footer. For more complex formats, the user can redefine the macros PT and BT, which are invoked respectively at the top and bottom of each page. The margins (taken from registers HM and FM for the top and bottom margin respectively) are normally 1 inch; the page header/footer are in the middle of that space. The user who redefines these macros should be careful not to change parameters such as point size or font without resetting them to default values.

Multi-column formats. If you place the command ".2C" in your document, the document will be printed in double column format beginning at that point. This feature is not too useful in computer terminal output, but is often desirable on the typesetter. The command ".1C" will go back to one-column format and also skip to a new page. The ".2C" command is actually a special case of the command

.MC [column width [gutter width]]

which makes multiple columns with the specified column and gutter width; as many columns as will fit across the page are used. Thus triple, quadruple, ... column pages can be printed. Whenever the number of columns is changed (except going from full width to some larger number of columns) a new page is started.

Headings. To produce a special heading, there are two commands. If you type

.NH
type section heading here
may be several lines

you will get automatically numbered section headings (1, 2, 3, ...), in boldface. For example,

.NH
Care and Feeding of Department Heads

produces

1. Care and Feeding of Department Heads

Alternatively,

.SH
Care and Feeding of Directors

will print the heading with no number added:

Care and Feeding of Directors

Every section heading, of either type, should be followed by a paragraph beginning with .PP or .LP, indicating the end of the heading. Headings may contain more than one line of text.

The .NH command also supports more complex numbering schemes. If a numerical argument is given, it is taken to be a "level" number and an appropriate sub-section number is generated. Larger level numbers indicate deeper sub-sections, as in this example:

.NH
Erie-Lackawanna
.NH 2
Morris and Essex Division
.NH 3
Gladstone Branch
.NH 3
Montclair Branch
.NH 2
Boonton Line

generates:

2. Erie-Lackawanna

2.1. Morris and Essex Division

2.1.1. Gladstone Branch

2.1.2. Montclair Branch

2.2. Boonton Line

An explicit ".NH 0" will reset the numbering of level 1 to one, as here:

.NH 0
Penn Central

1. Penn Central

Indented paragraphs. (Paragraphs with hanging numbers, e.g. references.) The sequence

```
.IP [1]
Text for first paragraph, typed
normally for as long as you would
like on as many lines as needed.
.IP [2]
Text for second paragraph, ...
```

produces

[1] Text for first paragraph, typed normally for as long as you would like on as many lines as needed.

[2] Text for second paragraph, ...

A series of indented paragraphs may be followed by an ordinary paragraph beginning with .PP or .LP, depending on whether you wish indenting or not. The command .LP was used here.

More sophisticated uses of .IP are also possible. If the label is omitted, for example, a plain block indent is produced.

```
.IP
This material will
just be turned into a
block indent suitable for quotations or
such matter.
.LP
```

will produce

This material will just be turned into a block indent suitable for quotations or such matter.

If a non-standard amount of indenting is required, it may be specified after the label (in character positions) and will remain in effect until the next .PP or .LP. Thus, the general form of the .IP command contains two additional fields: the label and the indenting length. For example,

```
.IP first: 9
Notice the longer label, requiring larger
indenting for these paragraphs.
.IP second:
And so forth.
.LP
```

produces this:

first: Notice the longer label, requiring larger indenting for these paragraphs.

second: And so forth.

It is also possible to produce multiple nested indents; the command .RS indicates that the next .IP starts from the current indentation level. Each .RE will eat up one level of indenting so you should balance .RS and .RE commands. The .RS command should be thought of as "move right" and the .RE command as "move left". As an example

```
.IP 1.
Bell Laboratories
.RS
.IP 1.1
Murray Hill
.IP 1.2
Holmdel
.IP 1.3
Whippany
.RS
.IP 1.3.1
Madison
.RE
.IP 1.4
Chester
.RE
.LP
```

will result in

1.   Bell Laboratories

   1.1   Murray Hill

   1.2   Holmdel

   1.3   Whippany

      1.3.1 Madison

   1.4   Chester

All of these variations on .LP leave the right margin untouched. Sometimes, for purposes such as setting off a quotation, a paragraph indented on both right and left is required.

A single paragraph like this is obtained by preceding it with .QP. More complicated material (several paragraphs) should be bracketed with .QS and .QE.

Emphasis. To get italics (on the typesetter) or underlining (on the terminal) say

```
.I
as much text as you want
can be typed here
.R
```

as was done for *these three words*. The .R command restores the normal (usually Roman) font. If only one word is to be italicized, it may be just given on the line with the .I command,

```
.I word
```

and in this case no .R is needed to restore the previous font. **Boldface** can be produced by

```
.B
Text to be set in boldface
goes here
.R
```

and also will be underlined on the terminal or line printer. As with .I, a single word can be placed in boldface by placing it on the same line as the .B command.

A few size changes can be specified similarly with the commands .LG (make larger), .SM (make smaller), and .NL (return to normal size). The size change is two points; the commands may be repeated for increased effect (here one .NL canceled two .SM commands).

If actual <u>underlining</u> as opposed to italicizing is required on the typesetter, the command

```
.UL word
```

will underline a word. There is no way to underline multiple words on the typesetter.

Footnotes. Material placed between lines with the commands .FS (footnote) and .FE (footnote end) will be collected, remembered, and finally placed at the bottom of the current page*. By default, footnotes are 11/12th the length of normal text, but this can be changed using the FL register (see below).

Displays and Tables. To prepare displays of lines, such as tables, in which the lines should not be re-arranged, enclose them in the commands .DS and .DE

---

* Like this.

```
.DS
table lines, like the
examples here, are placed
between .DS and .DE
.DE
```

By default, lines between .DS and .DE are indented and left-adjusted. You can also center lines, or retain the left margin. Lines bracketed by .DS C and .DE commands are centered (and not re-arranged); lines bracketed by .DS L and .DE are left-adjusted, not indented, and not re-arranged. A plain .DS is equivalent to .DS I, which indents and left-adjusts. Thus,

these lines were preceded
by .DS C and followed by
a .DE command;

whereas

```
these lines were preceded
by .DS L and followed by
a .DE command.
```

Note that .DS C centers each line; there is a variant .DS B that makes the display into a left-adjusted block of text, and then centers that entire block. Normally a display is kept together, on one page. If you wish to have a long display which may be split across page boundaries, use .CD, .LD, or .ID in place of the commands .DS C, .DS L, or .DS I respectively. An extra argument to the .DS I or .DS command is taken as an amount to indent. Note: it is tempting to assume that .DS R will right adjust lines, but it doesn't work.

Boxing words or lines. To draw rectangular boxes around words the command

```
.BX word
```

will print word as shown. The boxes will not be neat on a terminal, and this should not be used as a substitute for italics.

> Longer pieces of text may be boxed by enclosing them with .B1 and .B2:
>
> ```
> .B1
> text...
> .B2
> ```
>
> as has been done here.

Keeping blocks together. If you wish to keep a table or other block of lines together on a page, there are "keep -

release'' commands. If a block of lines preceded by .KS and followed by .KE does not fit on the remainder of the current page, it will begin on a new page. Lines bracketed by .DS and .DE commands are automatically kept together this way. There is also a "keep floating" command: if the block to be kept together is preceded by .KF instead of .KS and does not fit on the current page, it will be moved down through the text until the top of the next page. Thus, no large blank space will be introduced in the document.

Nroff/Troff commands. Among the useful commands from the basic formatting programs are the following. They all work with both typesetter and computer terminal output:

.bp - begin new page.
.br - "break", stop running text from line to line.
.sp n - insert n blank lines.
.na - don't adjust right margins.

Date. By default, documents produced on computer terminals have the date at the bottom of each page; documents produced on the typesetter don't. To force the date, say ".DA". To force no date, say ".ND". To lie about the date, say ".DA July 4, 1776" which puts the specified date at the bottom of each page. The command

.ND May 8, 1945

in ".RP" format places the specified date on the cover sheet and nowhere else. Place this line before the title.

Signature line. You can obtain a signature line by placing the command .SG in the document. The authors' names will be output in place of the .SG line. An argument to .SG is used as a typing identification line, and placed after the signatures. The .SG command is ignored in released paper format.

Registers. Certain of the registers used by −ms can be altered to change default settings. They should be changed with .nr commands, as with

.nr PS 9

to make the default point size 9 point. If the effect is needed immediately, the normal

troff command should be used in addition to changing the number register.

Register	Defines	Takes effect	Default
PS	point size	next para.	10
VS	line spacing	next para.	12 pts
LL	line length	next para.	6″
LT	title length	next para.	6″
PD	para. spacing	next para.	0.3 VS
PI	para. indent	next para.	5 ens
FL	footnote length	next FS	11/12 LL
CW	column width	next 2C	7/15 LL
GW	intercolumn gap	next 2C	1/15 LL
PO	page offset	next page	26/27″
HM	top margin	next page	1″
FM	bottom margin	next page	1″

You may also alter the strings LH, CH, and RH which are the left, center, and right headings respectively; and similarly LF, CF, and RF which are strings in the page footer. The page number on *output* is taken from register PN, to permit changing its output style. For more complicated headers and footers the macros PT and BT can be redefined, as explained earlier.

Accents. To simplify typing certain foreign words, strings representing common accent marks are defined. They precede the letter over which the mark is to appear. Here are the strings:

Input	Output	Input	Output
*'e	é	*~a	ã
*`e	è	*Ce	ě
*:u	ü	*,c	ç
*^e	ê		

Use. After your document is prepared and stored on a file, you can print it on a terminal with the command*

nroff −ms file

and you can print it on the typesetter with the command

troff −ms file

(many options are possible). In each case, if your document is stored in several files, just list all the filenames where we have used "file". If equations or tables are used, *eqn* and/or *tbl* must be invoked as preprocessors.

---

* If .2C was used, pipe the *nroff* output through *col;* make the first line of the input ".pi /usr/bin/col."

References and further study. If you have to do Greek or mathematics, see *eqn* [1] for equation setting. To aid *eqn* users, *—ms* provides definitions of .EQ and .EN which normally center the equation and set it off slightly. An argument on .EQ is taken to be an equation number and placed in the right margin near the equation. In addition, there are three special arguments to EQ: the letters C, I, and L indicate centered (default), indented, and left adjusted equations, respectively. If there is both a format argument and an equation number, give the format argument first, as in

.EQ L (1.3a)

for a left-adjusted equation numbered (1.3a).

Similarly, the macros .TS and .TE are defined to separate tables (see [2]) from text with a little space. A very long table with a heading may be broken across pages by beginning it with .TS H instead of .TS, and placing the line .TH in the table data after the heading. If the table has no heading repeated from page to page, just use the ordinary .TS and .TE macros.

To learn more about *troff* see [3] for a general introduction, and [4] for the full details (experts only). Information on related UNIX commands is in [5]. For jobs that do not seem well-adapted to —ms, consider other macro packages. It is often far easier to write a specific macro packages for such tasks as imitating particular journals than to try to adapt —ms.

Acknowledgment. Many thanks are due to Brian Kernighan for his help in the design and implementation of this package, and for his assistance in preparing this manual.

References

[1]   B. W. Kernighan and L. L. Cherry, *Typesetting Mathematics — Users Guide (2nd edition),* Bell Laboratories Computing Science Report no. 17.

[2]   M. E. Lesk, *Tbl — A Program to Format Tables,* Bell Laboratories Computing Science Report no. 45.

[3]   B. W. Kernighan, *A Troff Tutorial,* Bell Laboratories, 1976.

[4]   J. F. Ossanna, *Nroff/Troff Reference Manual,* Bell Laboratories Computing Science Report no. 51.

[5]   K. Thompson and D. M. Ritchie, *UNIX Programmer's Manual,* Bell Laboratories, 1978.

Appendix A
List of Commands

1C	Return to single column format.	LG	Increase type size.
2C	Start double column format.	LP	Left aligned block paragraph.
AB	Begin abstract.		
AE	End abstract.		
AI	Specify author's institution.		
AU	Specify author.	ND	Change or cancel date.
B	Begin boldface.	NH	Specify numbered heading.
DA	Provide the date on each page.	NL	Return to normal type size.
DE	End display.	PP	Begin paragraph.
DS	Start display (also CD, LD, ID).		
EN	End equation.	R	Return to regular font (usually Roman).
EQ	Begin equation.	RE	End one level of relative indenting.
FE	End footnote.	RP	Use released paper format.
FS	Begin footnote.	RS	Relative indent increased one level.
		SG	Insert signature line.
I	Begin italics.	SH	Specify section heading.
		SM	Change to smaller type size.
IP	Begin indented paragraph.	TL	Specify title.
KE	Release keep.		
KF	Begin floating keep.	UL	Underline one word.
KS	Start keep.		

Register Names

The following register names are used by −ms internally. Independent use of these names in one's own macros may produce incorrect output. Note that no lower case letters are used in any −ms internal name.

Number registers used in −ms

:	DW	GW	HM	IQ	LL	NA	OJ	PO	T.	TV
#T	EF	H1	HT	IR	LT	NC	PD	PQ	TB	VS
1T	FL	H3	IK	KI	MM	NF	PF	PX	TD	YE
AV	FM	H4	IM	L1	MN	NS	PI	RO	TN	YY
CW	FP	H5	IP	LE	MO	OI	PN	ST	TQ	ZN

String registers used in −ms

'	A5	CB	DW	EZ	I	KF	MR	R1	RT	TL
`	AB	CC	DY	FA	I1	KQ	ND	R2	S0	TM
^	AE	CD	E1	FE	I2	KS	NH	R3	S1	TQ
~	AI	CF	E2	FJ	I3	LB	NL	R4	S2	TS
:	AU	CH	E3	FK	I4	LD	NP	R5	SG	TT
,	B	CM	E4	FN	I5	LG	OD	RC	SH	UL
1C	BG	CS	E5	FO	ID	LP	OK	RE	SM	WB
2C	BT	CT	EE	FQ	IE	ME	PP	RF	SN	WH
A1	C	D	EL	FS	IM	MF	PT	RH	SY	WT
A2	C1	DA	EM	FV	IP	MH	PY	RP	TA	XD
A3	C2	DE	EN	FY	IZ	MN	QF	RQ	TE	XF
A4	CA	DS	EQ	HO	KE	MO	R	RS	TH	XK

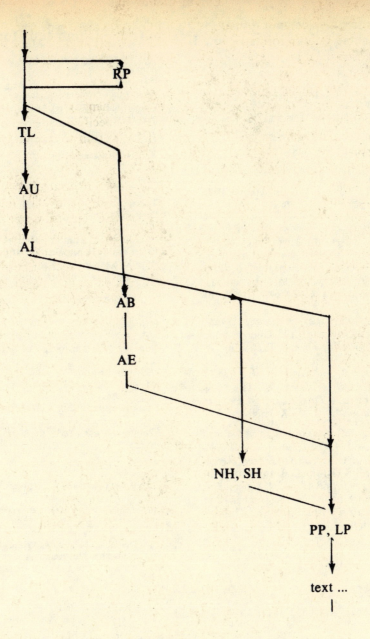

Figure 1

A Guide to Preparing Documents with −ms

M. E. Lesk

Bell Laboratories   August 1978

This guide gives some simple examples of document preparation on Bell Labs computers, emphasizing the use of the −ms macro package. It enormously abbreviates information in

1. *Typing Documents on UNIX and GCOS,* by M. E. Lesk;
2. *Typesetting Mathematics − User's Guide,* by B. W. Kernighan and L. L. Cherry; and
3. *Tbl − A Program to Format Tables,* by M. E. Lesk.

These memos are all included in the *UNIX Programmer's Manual, Volume 2.* The new user should also have *A Tutorial Introduction to the UNIX Text Editor,* by B. W. Kernighan.

For more detailed information, read *Advanced Editing on UNIX* and *A Troff Tutorial,* by B. W. Kernighan, and (for experts) *Nroff/Troff Reference Manual* by J. F. Ossanna. Information on related commands is found (for UNIX users) in *UNIX for Beginners* by B. W. Kernighan and the *UNIX Programmer's Manual* by K. Thompson and D. M. Ritchie.

Contents

A TM 2
A released paper 3
An internal memo, and headings . . . 4
Lists, displays, and footnotes 5
Indents, keeps, and double column . 6
Equations and registers 7
Tables and usage 8

Throughout the examples, input is shown in
  this Helvetica sans serif font
while the resulting output is shown in
  this Times Roman font.

UNIX Document no. 1111

Commands for a TM

```
.TM 1978-5b3 99999 99999-11
.ND April 1, 1976
.TL
The Role of the Allen Wrench in Modern
Electronics
.AU "MH 2G-111" 2345
J. Q. Pencilpusher
.AU "MH 1K-222" 5432
X. Y. Hardwired
.AI
.MH
.OK
Tools
Design
.AB
This abstract should be short enough to
fit on a single page cover sheet.
It must attract the reader into sending for
the complete memorandum.
.AE
.CS 10 2 12 5 6 7
.NH
Introduction.
.PP
Now the first paragraph of actual text ...
...
Last line of text.
.SG MH-1234-JQP/XYH-unix
.NH
References ...
```

Commands not needed in a particular format are ignored.

 Bell Laboratories   Cover Sheet for TM

This information is for employees of Bell Laboratories. (GEI 13.9-3)

Title- **The Role of the Allen Wrench**   Date- **April 1, 1976**
  in Modern Electronics
                                             TM- **1978-5b3**

Other Keywords- **Tools**
               Design

Author	Location	Ext.	
J. Q. Pencilpusher	MH 2G-111	2345	Charging Case- **99999**
X. Y. Hardwired	MH 1K-222	5432	Filing Case- **99999a**

ABSTRACT

This abstract should be short enough to fit on a single page cover sheet. It must attract the reader into sending for the complete memorandum.

Pages Text 10	Other 2	Total 12	
No. Figures 5	No. Tables 6	No. Refs. 7	

E-1932-U (6-73)   **SEE REVERSE SIDE FOR DISTRIBUTION LIST**

A Released Paper with Mathematics

```
.EQ
delim $$
.EN
.RP
```

... (as for a TM)

```
.CS 10 2 12 5 6 7
.NH
Introduction
.PP
The solution to the torque handle equation
.EQ (1)
sum from 0 to inf F ( x sub i ) = G ( x )
.EN
is found with the transformation $ x = rho over
theta $ where $ rho = G prime (x) $ and $theta$
is derived ...
```

The Role of the Allen Wrench
in Modern Electronics

J. Q. Pencilpusher

X. Y. Hardwired

Bell Laboratories
Murray Hill, New Jersey 07974

ABSTRACT

This abstract should be short enough to fit on a single page cover sheet. It must attract the reader into sending for the complete memorandum.

April 1, 1976

The Role of the Allen Wrench
in Modern Electronics

J. Q. Pencilpusher

X. Y. Hardwired

Bell Laboratories
Murray Hill, New Jersey 07974

1. Introduction

The solution to the torque handle equation

$$\sum_0^\infty F(x_i) = G(x) \qquad (1)$$

is found with the transformation $x = \dfrac{\rho}{\theta}$ where $\rho = G'(x)$ and θ is derived from well-known principles.

An Internal Memorandum

```
.IM
.ND January 24, 1956
.TL
The 1956 Consent Decree
.AU
Able, Baker &
Charley, Attys.
.PP
```
Plaintiff, United States of America, having filed its complaint herein on January 14, 1949; the defendants having appeared and filed their answer to such complaint denying the substantive allegations thereof; and the parties, by their attorneys, ...

Bell Laboratories

Subject: **The 1956 Consent Decree**   date: **January 24, 1956**

from: **Able, Baker &**
Charley, Attys.

Plaintiff, United States of America, having filed its complaint herein on January 14, 1949; the defendants having appeared and filed their answer to such complaint denying the substantive allegations thereof; and the parties, by their attorneys, having severally consented to the entry of this Final Judgment without trial or adjudication of any issues of fact or law herein and without this Final Judgment constituting any evidence or admission by any party in respect of any such issues;

Now, therefore before any testimony has been taken herein, and without trial or adjudication of any issue of fact or law herein, and upon the consent of all parties hereto, it is hereby

Ordered, adjudged and decreed as follows:

I. [Sherman Act]

This Court has jurisdiction of the subject matter herein and of all the parties hereto. The complaint states a claim upon which relief may be granted against each of the defendants under Sections 1, 2 and 3 of the Act of Congress of July 2, 1890, entitled "An act to protect trade and commerce against unlawful restraints and monopolies," commonly known as the Sherman Act, as amended.

II. [Definitions]

For the purposes of this Final Judgment:

(a) "Western" shall mean the defendant Western Electric Company, Incorporated.

Other formats possible (specify before .TL) are: .MR ("memo for record"), .MF ("memo for file"), .EG ("engineer's notes") and .TR (Computing Science Tech. Report).

Headings

```
.NH
Introduction.
.PP
text text text
```

1. Introduction
   text text text

```
.SH
Appendix I
.PP
text text text
```

Appendix I
   text text text

A Simple List

```
.IP 1.
J. Pencilpusher and X. Hardwired,
.I
A New Kind of Set Screw,
.R
Proc. IEEE
.B 75
(1976), 23-255.
.IP 2.
H. Nails and R. Irons,
.I
Fasteners for Printed Circuit Boards,
.R
Proc. ASME
.B 23
(1974), 23-24.
.LP  (terminates list)
```

1. J. Pencilpusher and X. Hardwired, *A New Kind of Set Screw*, Proc. IEEE **75** (1976), 23-255.
2. H. Nails and R. Irons, *Fasteners for Printed Circuit Boards*, Proc. ASME **23** (1974), 23-24.

Displays

```
text text text text text text
.DS
and now
for something
completely different
.DE
text text text text text text
```

hoboken harrison newark roseville avenue grove street east orange brick church orange highland avenue mountain station south orange maplewood millburn short hills summit new providence

```
            and now
            for something
            completely different
```

murray hill berkeley heights gillette stirling millington lyons basking ridge bernardsville far hills peapack gladstone

Options: .DS L: left-adjust; .DS C: line-by-line center; .DS B: make block, then center.

Footnotes

```
Among the most important occupants
of the workbench are the long-nosed pliers.
Without these basic tools*
.FS
* As first shown by Tiger & Leopard
(1975).
.FE
few assemblies could be completed.  They may
lack the popular appeal of the sledgehammer
```

Among the most important occupants of the workbench are the long-nosed pliers. Without these basic tools* few assemblies could be completed. They may lack the popular appeal of the sledgehammer

---

* As first shown by Tiger & Leopard (1975).

Multiple Indents

```
This is ordinary text to point out
the margins of the page.
.IP 1.
First level item
.RS
.IP a)
Second level.
.IP b)
Continued here with another second
level item, but somewhat longer.
.RE
.IP 2.
Return to previous value of the
indenting at this point.
.IP 3.
Another
line.
```

This is ordinary text to point out the margins of the page.
1. First level item
   a) Second level.
   b) Continued here with another second level item, but somewhat longer.
2. Return to previous value of the indenting at this point.
3. Another line.

Keeps

Lines bracketed by the following commands are kept together, and will appear entirely on one page:

```
.KS    not moved        .KF    may float
.KE    through text      .KE    in text
```

Double Column

```
.TL
The Declaration of Independence
.2C
.PP
```

When in the course of human events, it becomes necessary for one people to dissolve the political bonds which have connected them with another, and to assume among the powers of the earth the separate and equal station to which the laws of Nature and of Nature's God entitle them, a decent respect to the opinions of

The Declaration of Independence

When in the course of human events, it becomes necessary for one people to dissolve the political bonds which have connected them with another, and to assume among the powers of the earth the separate and equal station to which the laws of Nature and of Nature's God entitle them, a decent respect to the opinions of mankind requires that they should declare the causes which impel them to the separation.

We hold these truths to be self-evident, that all men are created equal, that they are endowed by their creator with certain unalienable rights, that among these are life, liberty, and the pursuit of happiness. That to secure these rights, governments are instituted among men,

Equations

A displayed equation is marked
with an equation number at the right margin
by adding an argument to the EQ line:
.EQ (1.3)
x sup 2 over a sup 2 ~=~ sqrt {p z sup 2 +qz+r}
.EN

A displayed equation is marked with an equation
number at the right margin by adding an argument
to the EQ line:

$$\frac{x^2}{a^2} = \sqrt{pz^2+qz+r} \qquad (1.3)$$

.EQ I (2.2a)
bold V bar sub nu ~=~ left [pile {a above b above
c } right] + left [matrix { col { A(11) above .
above . } col { . above . above .} col { . above .
above A(33) }} right] cdot left [pile { alpha
above beta above gamma } right]
.EN

$$\bar{\mathbf{V}}_\nu = \begin{bmatrix} a \\ b \\ c \end{bmatrix} + \begin{bmatrix} A(11) & . & . \\ . & . & . \\ . & . & A(33) \end{bmatrix} \cdot \begin{bmatrix} \alpha \\ \beta \\ \gamma \end{bmatrix} \qquad (2.2a)$$

.EQ L
F hat (chi) ~ mark = ~ | del V | sup 2
.EN
.EQ L
lineup = ~ {left ({partial V} over {partial x} right)
} sup 2 + { left ({partial V} over {partial y} right
) } sup 2 ~~~~~~ lambda -> inf
.EN

$$\hat{F}(\chi) = |\nabla V|^2$$

$$= \left(\frac{\partial V}{\partial x}\right)^2 + \left(\frac{\partial V}{\partial y}\right)^2 \qquad \lambda \to \infty$$

$ a dot $, $ b dotdot$, $ xi tilde times y vec$:

$\dot{a}$, $\ddot{b}$, $\tilde{\xi} \times \bar{v}$.   (with delim $$ on, see panel 3).

See also the equations in the second table, panel 8.

Some Registers You Can Change

Line length
   .nr LL 7i
	Paragraph spacing
	   .nr PD 0

Title length
   .nr LT 7i
	Page offset
	   .nr PO 0.5i

Point size
   .nr PS 9
	Page heading
	   .ds CH Appendix
	     (center)

Vertical spacing
   .nr VS 11
	.ds RH 7-25-76
	     (right)

Column width
   .nr CW 3i
	.ds LH Private
	     (left)

Intercolumn spacing
   .nr GW .5i
	Page footer
	   .ds CF Draft

Margins — head and foot
   .nr HM .75i
   .nr FM .75i
	.ds LF
	   .ds RF similar

Paragraph indent
   .nr PI 2n
	Page numbers
	   .nr % 3

Tables

.TS   (⊤ indicates a tab)
allbox;
c s s
c c c
n n n.
AT&T Common Stock
Year ⊤ Price ⊤ Dividend
1971 ⊤ 41-54 ⊤ $2.60
2 ⊤ 41-54 ⊤ 2.70
3 ⊤ 46-55 ⊤ 2.87
4 ⊤ 40-53 ⊤ 3.24
5 ⊤ 45-52 ⊤ 3.40
6 ⊤ 51-59 ⊤ .95*
.TE
* (first quarter only)

AT&T Common Stock		
Year	Price	Dividend
1971	41-54	$2.60
2	41-54	2.70
3	46-55	2.87
4	40-53	3.24
5	45-52	3.40
6	51-59	.95*

* (first quarter only)

The meanings of the key-letters describing the alignment of each entry are:

c	center	n	numerical
r	right-adjust	a	subcolumn
l	left-adjust	s	spanned

The global table options are center, expand, box,
doublebox, allbox, tab (x) and linesize (n).

.TS   (with delim $$ on, see panel 3)
doublebox, center;
c c
l l.
Name ⊤ Definition
.sp
Gamma ⊤ $GAMMA (z) = int sub 0 sup inf \
  t sup {z-1} e sup -t dt$
Sine ⊤ $sin (x) = 1 over 2i (e sup ix - e sup -ix)$
Error ⊤ $ roman erf (z) = 2 over sqrt pi \
  int sub 0 sup z e sup {-t sup 2} dt$
Bessel ⊤ $ J sub 0 (z) = 1 over pi \
  int sub 0 sup pi cos (z sin theta) d theta $
Zeta ⊤ $ zeta (s) = \
  sum from k=1 to inf k sup -s ~~(Re~s > 1)$
.TE

Name	Definition
Gamma	$\Gamma(z) = \int_0^\infty t^{z-1} e^{-t} dt$
Sine	$\sin(x) = \frac{1}{2i}(e^{ix} - e^{-ix})$
Error	$\operatorname{erf}(z) = \frac{2}{\sqrt{\pi}} \int_0^z e^{-t^2} dt$
Bessel	$J_0(z) = \frac{1}{\pi} \int_0^\pi \cos(z \sin\theta) d\theta$
Zeta	$\zeta(s) = \sum_{k=1}^{\infty} k^{-s} \quad (\text{Re } s > 1)$

Usage

    Documents with just text:
troff -ms files
    With equations only:
eqn files | troff -ms
    With tables only:
tbl files | troff -ms
    With both tables and equations:
tbl files|eqn|troff -ms

The above generates STARE output on GCOS: replace
−st with −ph for typesetter output.

A System for Typesetting Mathematics

Brian W. Kernighan and Lorinda L. Cherry

Bell Laboratories
Murray Hill, New Jersey 07974

ABSTRACT

This paper describes the design and implementation of a system for typesetting mathematics. The language has been designed to be easy to learn and to use by people (for example, secretaries and mathematical typists) who know neither mathematics nor typesetting. Experience indicates that the language can be learned in an hour or so, for it has few rules and fewer exceptions. For typical expressions, the size and font changes, positioning, line drawing, and the like necessary to print according to mathematical conventions are all done automatically. For example, the input

sum from i=0 to infinity x sub i = pi over 2

produces

$$\sum_{i=0}^{\infty} x_i = \frac{\pi}{2}$$

The syntax of the language is specified by a small context-free grammar; a compiler-compiler is used to make a compiler that translates this language into typesetting commands. Output may be produced on either a phototypesetter or on a terminal with forward and reverse half-line motions. The system interfaces directly with text formatting programs, so mixtures of text and mathematics may be handled simply.

This paper is a revision of a paper originally published in CACM, March, 1975.

1. Introduction

"Mathematics is known in the trade as *difficult*, or *penalty*, *copy* because it is slower, more difficult, and more expensive to set in type than any other kind of copy normally occurring in books and journals." [1]

One difficulty with mathematical text is the multiplicity of characters, sizes, and fonts. An expression such as

$$\lim_{x \to \pi/2} (\tan x)^{\sin 2x} = 1$$

requires an intimate mixture of roman, italic and greek letters, in three sizes, and a special character or two. ("Requires" is perhaps the wrong word, but mathematics has its own typographical conventions which are quite different from those of ordinary text.) Typesetting such an expression by traditional methods is still an essentially manual operation.

A second difficulty is the two dimensional character of mathematics, which the superscript and limits in the preceding example showed in its simplest form. This is carried further by

$$a_0 + \cfrac{b_1}{a_1 + \cfrac{b_2}{a_2 + \cfrac{b_3}{a_3 + \cdots}}}$$

and still further by

$$\int \frac{dx}{ae^{mx} - be^{-mx}} = \begin{cases} \dfrac{1}{2m\sqrt{ab}} \log \dfrac{\sqrt{a}\,e^{mx} - \sqrt{b}}{\sqrt{a}\,e^{mx} + \sqrt{b}} \\ \dfrac{1}{m\sqrt{ab}} \tanh^{-1}(\dfrac{\sqrt{a}}{\sqrt{b}} e^{mx}) \\ \dfrac{-1}{m\sqrt{ab}} \coth^{-1}(\dfrac{\sqrt{a}}{\sqrt{b}} e^{mx}) \end{cases}$$

These examples also show line-drawing, built-up characters like braces and radicals, and a spectrum of positioning problems. (Section 6 shows what a user has to type to produce these on our system.)

2. Photocomposition

Photocomposition techniques can be used to solve some of the problems of typesetting mathematics. A phototypesetter is a device which exposes a piece of photographic paper or film, placing characters wherever they are wanted. The Graphic Systems phototypesetter[2] on the UNIX operating system[3] works by shining light through a character stencil. The character is made the right size by lenses, and the light beam directed by fiber optics to the desired place on a piece of photographic paper. The exposed paper is developed and typically used in some form of photo-offset reproduction.

On UNIX, the phototypesetter is driven by a formatting program called TROFF [4]. TROFF was designed for setting running text. It also provides all of the facilities that one needs for doing mathematics, such as arbitrary horizontal and vertical motions, line-drawing, size changing, but the syntax for describing these special operations is difficult to learn, and difficult even for experienced users to type correctly.

For this reason we decided to use TROFF as an "assembly language," by designing a language for describing mathematical expressions, and compiling it into TROFF.

3. Language Design

The fundamental principle upon which we based our language design is that the language should be easy to use by people (for example, secretaries) who know neither mathematics nor typesetting.

This principle implies several things. First, "normal" mathematical conventions about operator precedence, parentheses, and the like cannot be used, for to give special meaning to such characters means that the user has to understand what he or she is typing. Thus the language should not assume, for instance, that parentheses are always balanced, for they are not in the half-open interval $(a,b]$. Nor should it assume that that $\sqrt{a+b}$ can be replaced by $(a+b)^{1/2}$, or that $1/(1-x)$ is better written as $\frac{1}{1-x}$ (or vice versa).

Second, there should be relatively few rules, keywords, special symbols and operators, and the like. This keeps the language easy to learn and remember. Furthermore, there should be few exceptions to the rules that do exist: if something works in one situation, it should work everywhere. If a variable can have a subscript, then a subscript can have a subscript, and so on without limit.

Third, "standard" things should happen automatically. Someone who types "$x=y+z+1$" should get "$x=y+z+1$". Subscripts and superscripts should automatically be printed in an appropriately smaller size, with no special intervention. Fraction bars have to be made the right length and positioned at the right height. And so on. Indeed a mechanism for overriding default actions has to exist, but its application is the exception, not the rule.

We assume that the typist has a reasonable picture (a two-dimensional representation) of the desired final form, as might be handwritten by the author of a paper. We also assume that the input is typed on a computer terminal much like an ordinary typewriter. This implies an input alphabet of perhaps 100 characters, none of them special.

A secondary, but still important, goal in our design was that the system should be easy to implement, since neither of the authors had any desire to make a long-term project of it. Since our design was not firm, it was also necessary that the program be easy to change at any time.

To make the program easy to build and to change, and to guarantee regularity ("it should work everywhere"), the language is defined by a context-free grammar, described in Section 5. The compiler for the language was built using a compiler-compiler.

A priori, the grammar/compiler-compiler approach seemed the right thing to do. Our subsequent experience leads us to believe that any other course would have been folly. The original language was designed in a few days. Construction of a working system sufficient to try significant examples required perhaps a person-month. Since then, we have spent a modest amount of additional time over several years tuning, adding facilities, and occasionally changing the language as users make criticisms and suggestions.

We also decided quite early that we would let TROFF do our work for us whenever possible. TROFF is quite a powerful program, with a macro facility, text and arithmetic variables, numerical computation and testing, and conditional branching. Thus we have been able to avoid writing a lot of mundane but tricky software. For example, we store no text strings, but simply pass them on to TROFF. Thus we avoid having to write a storage management package. Furthermore, we have been able to isolate ourselves from most details of the particular device and character set currently in use. For example, we let TROFF compute the widths of all strings of characters; we need know nothing about them.

A third design goal is special to our environment. Since our program is only useful for typesetting mathematics, it is necessary that it interface cleanly with the underlying typesetting language for the benefit of users who want to set intermingled mathematics and text (the usual case). The standard mode of operation is that when a document is typed, mathematical expressions are input as part of the text, but marked by user settable delimiters. The program reads this input and treats as comments those things which are not mathematics, simply passing them through untouched. At the same time it converts the mathematical input into the necessary TROFF commands. The resulting ioutput is passed directly to TROFF where the comments and the mathematical parts both become text and/or TROFF commands.

4. The Language

We will not try to describe the language precisely here; interested readers may refer to the appendix for more details. Throughout this section, we will write expressions exactly as they are handed to the typesetting program (hereinafter called "EQN"), except that we won't show the delimiters that the user types to mark the beginning and end of the expression. The interface between EQN and TROFF is described at the end of this section.

As we said, typing x=y+z+1 should produce $x=y+z+1$, and indeed it does. Variables are made italic, operators and digits become roman, and normal spacings between letters and operators are altered slightly to give a more pleasing appearance.

Input is free-form. Spaces and new lines in the input are used by EQN to separate pieces of the input; they are not used to create space in the output. Thus

```
x   =   y
  + z + 1
```

also gives $x=y+z+1$. Free-form input is easier to type initially; subsequent editing is also easier, for an expression may be typed as many short lines.

Extra white space can be forced into the output by several characters of various sizes. A tilde "˜" gives a space equal to the normal word spacing in text; a circumflex gives half this much, and a tab charcter spaces to the next tab stop.

Spaces (or tildes, etc.) also serve to delimit pieces of the input. For example, to get

$$f(t)=2\pi \int \sin(\omega t)dt$$

we write

```
f(t) = 2 pi int sin ( omega t )dt
```

Here spaces are *necessary* in the input to indicate that *sin, pi, int,* and *omega* are special, and potentially worth special treatment. EQN looks up each such string of characters in a table, and if appropriate gives it a translation. In this case, *pi* and *omega* become their greek equivalents, *int* becomes the integral sign (which must be moved down and enlarged so it looks "right"), and *sin* is made roman, following conventional mathematical practice. Parentheses, digits and operators are automatically made roman wherever found.

Fractions are specified with the keyword *over:*

```
a+b over c+d+e = 1
```

produces

$$\frac{a+b}{c+d+e}=1$$

Similarly, subscripts and superscripts are introduced by the keywords *sub* and *sup:*

$$x^2+y^2=z^2$$

is produced by

```
x sup 2 + y sup 2 = z sup 2
```

The spaces after the 2's are necessary to mark the end of the superscripts; similarly the keyword *sup* has to be marked off by spaces or some equivalent delimiter. The return to the proper baseline is automatic. Multiple levels of subscripts or superscripts are of course allowed: "x sup y sup z" is x^{y^z}. The construct "something *sub* something *sup* something" is recognized as a special case, so "x sub i sup 2" is x_i^2 instead of $x_i{}^2$.

More complicated expressions can now be formed with these primitives:

$$\frac{\partial^2 f}{\partial x^2}=\frac{x^2}{a^2}+\frac{y^2}{b^2}$$

is produced by

```
{partial sup 2 f} over {partial x sup 2} =
x sup 2 over a sup 2 + y sup 2 over b sup 2
```

Braces {} are used to group objects together; in this case they indicate unambiguously what goes over what on the left-hand side of the expression. The language defines the precedence of *sup* to be higher than that of *over*, so no braces are needed to get the correct association on the right side. Braces can always be used when in doubt about precedence.

The braces convention is an example of

the power of using a recursive grammar to define the language. It is part of the language that if a construct can appear in some context, then *any expression* in braces can also occur in that context.

There is a *sqrt* operator for making square roots of the appropriate size: "sqrt a+b" produces $\sqrt{a+b}$, and

x = {−b +− sqrt{b sup 2 −4ac}} over 2a

is

$$x=\frac{-b\pm\sqrt{b^2-4ac}}{2a}$$

Since large radicals look poor on our typesetter, *sqrt* is not useful for tall expressions.

Limits on summations, integrals and similar constructions are specified with the keywords *from* and *to*. To get

$$\sum_{i=0}^{\infty}x_i\rightarrow0$$

we need only type

sum from i=0 to inf x sub i −> 0

Centering and making the Σ big enough and the limits smaller are all automatic. The *from* and *to* parts are both optional, and the central part (e.g., the Σ) can in fact be anything:

lim from {x −> pi /2} (tan˜x) = inf

is

$$\lim_{x\to\pi/2}(\tan x)=\infty$$

Again, the braces indicate just what goes into the *from* part.

There is a facility for making braces, brackets, parentheses, and vertical bars of the right height, using the keywords *left* and *right:*

left [x+y over 2a right]˜=˜1

makes

$$\left[\frac{x+y}{2a}\right]=1$$

A *left* need not have a corresponding *right*, as we shall see in the next example. Any characters may follow *left* and *right*, but generally only various parentheses and bars are meaningful.

Big brackets, etc., are often used with another facility, called *piles*, which make vertical piles of objects. For example, to get

$$sign\,(x)\equiv\begin{cases}1 & if\ \ x>0\\0 & if\ \ x=0\\-1 & if\ \ x<0\end{cases}$$

we can type

sign (x) ˜=˜ left {
    rpile {1 above 0 above −1}
    ˜˜lpile {if above if above if}
    ˜˜lpile {x>0 above x=0 above x<0}

The construction "left {" makes a left brace big enough to enclose the "rpile {...}", which is a right-justified pile of "above ... above ...". "lpile" makes a left-justified pile. There are also centered piles. Because of the recursive language definition, a pile can contain any number of elements; any element of a pile can of course contain piles.

Although EQN makes a valiant attempt to use the right sizes and fonts, there are times when the default assumptions are simply not what is wanted. For instance the italic *sign* in the previous example would conventionally be in roman. Slides and transparencies often require larger characters than normal text. Thus we also provide size and font changing commands: "size 12 bold {A˜x˜=˜y}" will produce $\mathbf{A\ x = y}$. *Size* is followed by a number representing a character size in points. (One point is 1/72 inch; this paper is set in 9 point type.)

If necessary, an input string can be quoted in "...", which turns off grammatical significance, and any font or spacing changes that might otherwise be done on it. Thus we can say

lim˜ roman "sup" ˜x sub n = 0

to ensure that the supremum doesn't become a superscript:

$$\lim\,sup\,x_n=0$$

Diacritical marks, long a problem in traditional typesetting, are straightforward:

$$\dot{x}+\hat{x}+\tilde{y}+\hat{X}+\ddot{Y}=\overline{z+Z}$$

is made by typing

x dot under + x hat + y tilde
+ X hat + Y dotdot = z+Z bar

There are also facilities for globally changing default sizes and fonts, for example for making viewgraphs or for setting chemical equations. The language allows for matrices, and for lining up equations at the same horizontal position.

Finally, there is a definition facility, so a user can say

define name "..."

at any time in the document; henceforth, any occurrence of the token "name" in an expression will be expanded into whatever was inside the double quotes in its definition. This lets users tailor the language to their own specifications, for it is quite possible to redefine keywords like *sup* or *over*. Section 6 shows an example of definitions.

The EQN preprocessor reads intermixed text and equations, and passes its output to TROFF. Since TROFF uses lines beginning with a period as control words (e.g., ".ce" means "center the next output line"), EQN uses the sequence ".EQ" to mark the beginning of an equation and ".EN" to mark the end. The ".EQ" and ".EN" are passed through to TROFF untouched, so they can also be used by a knowledgeable user to center equations, number them automatically, etc. By default, however, ".EQ" and ".EN" are simply ignored by TROFF, so by default equations are printed in-line.

".EQ" and ".EN" can be supplemented by TROFF commands as desired; for example, a centered display equation can be produced with the input:

```
.ce
.EQ
x sub i = y sub i ...
.EN
```

Since it is tedious to type ".EQ" and ".EN" around very short expressions (single letters, for instance), the user can also define two characters to serve as the left and right delimiters of expressions. These characters are recognized anywhere in subsequent text. For example if the left and right delimiters have both been set to "#", the input:

Let #x sub i#, #y# and #alpha# be positive

produces:

Let x_i, y and α be positive

Running a preprocessor is strikingly easy on UNIX. To typeset text stored in file "f", one issues the command:

eqn f | troff

The vertical bar connects the output of one process (EQN) to the input of another (TROFF).

5. Language Theory

The basic structure of the language is not a particularly original one. Equations are pictured as a set of "boxes," pieced together in various ways. For example, something with a subscript is just a box followed by another box moved downward and shrunk by an appropriate amount. A fraction is just a box centered above another box, at the right altitude, with a line of correct length drawn between them.

The grammar for the language is shown below. For purposes of exposition, we have collapsed some productions. In the original grammar, there are about 70 productions, but many of these are simple ones used only to guarantee that some keyword is recognized early enough in the parsing process. Symbols in capital letters are terminal symbols; lower case symbols are non-terminals, i.e., syntactic categories. The vertical bar | indicates an alternative; the brackets [ ] indicate optional material. A TEXT is a string of non-blank characters or any string inside double quotes; the other terminal symbols represent literal occurrences of the corresponding keyword.

```
eqn  : box | eqn box

box  : text
     | { eqn }
     | box OVER box
     | SQRT box
     | box SUB box | box SUP box
     | [ L | C | R ]PILE { list }
     | LEFT text eqn [ RIGHT text ]
     | box [ FROM box ] [ TO box ]
     | SIZE text box
     | [ROMAN | BOLD | ITALIC] box
     | box [HAT | BAR | DOT | DOTDOT | TILDE]
     | DEFINE text text

list : eqn | list ABOVE eqn

text : TEXT
```

The grammar makes it obvious why there are few exceptions. For example, the observation that something can be replaced by a more complicated something in braces is implicit in the productions:

```
eqn  : box | eqn box
box  : text | { eqn }
```

Anywhere a single character could be used, *any* legal construction can be used.

Clearly, our grammar is highly ambiguous. What, for instance, do we do with the input

a over b over c ?

Is it

{a over b} over c

or is it

a over {b over c} ?

To answer questions like this, the grammar is supplemented with a small set of rules that describe the precedence and associativity of operators. In particular, we specify (more or less arbitrarily) that *over* associates to the left, so the first alternative above is the one chosen. On the other hand, *sub* and *sup* bind to the right, because this is closer to standard mathematical practice. That is, we assume x^{a^b} is $x^{(a^b)}$, not $(x^a)^b$.

The precedence rules resolve the ambiguity in a construction like

a sup 2 over b

We define *sup* to have a higher precedence than *over*, so this construction is parsed as $\dfrac{a^2}{b}$ instead of $a^{\frac{2}{b}}$.

Naturally, a user can always force a particular parsing by placing braces around expressions.

The ambiguous grammar approach seems to be quite useful. The grammar we use is small enough to be easily understood, for it contains none of the productions that would be normally used for resolving ambiguity. Instead the supplemental information about precedence and associativity (also small enough to be understood) provides the compiler-compiler with the information it needs to make a fast, deterministic parser for the specific language we want. When the language is supplemented by the disambiguating rules, it is in fact LR(1) and thus easy to parse[5].

The output code is generated as the input is scanned. Any time a production of the grammar is recognized, (potentially) some TROFF commands are output. For example, when the lexical analyzer reports that it has found a TEXT (i.e., a string of contiguous characters), we have recognized the production:

text   : TEXT

The translation of this is simple. We generate a local name for the string, then hand the name and the string to TROFF, and let TROFF perform the storage management. All we save is the name of the string, its height, and its baseline.

As another example, the translation associated with the production

box   : box OVER box

is:

Width of output box =
  slightly more than largest input width
Height of output box =
  slightly more than sum of input heights
Base of output box =
  slightly more than height of bottom input box
String describing output box =
  move down;
  move right enough to center bottom box;
  draw bottom box (i.e., copy string for bottom box);
  move up; move left enough to center top box;
  draw top box (i.e., copy string for top box);
  move down and left; draw line full width;
  return to proper base line.

Most of the other productions have equally simple semantic actions. Picturing the output as a set of properly placed boxes makes the right sequence of positioning commands quite obvious. The main difficulty is in finding the right numbers to use for esthetically pleasing positioning.

With a grammar, it is usually clear how to extend the language. For instance, one of our users suggested a TENSOR operator, to make constructions like

$$\,_m^l \mathbf{T}_{n\,i}^{k\,j}$$

Grammatically, this is easy: it is sufficient to add a production like

box   : TENSOR { list }

Semantically, we need only juggle the boxes to the right places.

6. Experience

There are really three aspects of interest—how well EQN sets mathematics, how well it satisfies its goal of being "easy to use," and how easy it was to build.

The first question is easily addressed. This entire paper has been set by the program. Readers can judge for themselves whether it is good enough for their purposes. One of our users commented that although the output is not as good as the best hand-set material, it is still better than average, and much better than the worst. In any case, who cares? Printed books cannot compete with the birds and flowers of illuminated manuscripts on esthetic grounds, either, but they have some clear economic advantages.

Some of the deficiencies in the output could be cleaned up with more work on our part. For example, we sometimes leave too much space between a roman letter and an italic one. If we were willing to keep track of the fonts involved, we could do this better more of the time.

Some other weaknesses are inherent in our output device. It is hard, for instance, to draw a line of an arbitrary length without getting a perceptible overstrike at one end.

As to ease of use, at the time of writing, the system has been used by two distinct groups. One user population consists of mathematicians, chemists, physicists, and computer scientists. Their typical reaction has been something like:

(1) It's easy to write, although I make the following mistakes...

(2) How do I do...?

(3) It botches the following things.... Why don't you fix them?

(4) You really need the following features...

The learning time is short. A few minutes gives the general flavor, and typing a page or two of a paper generally uncovers most of the misconceptions about how it works.

The second user group is much larger, the secretaries and mathematical typists who were the original target of the system. They tend to be enthusiastic converts. They find the language easy to learn (most are largely self-taught), and have little trouble producing the output they want. They are of course less critical of the esthetics of their output than users trained in mathematics. After a transition period, most find using a computer more interesting than a regular typewriter.

The main difficulty that users have seems to be remembering that a blank is a delimiter; even experienced users use blanks where they shouldn't and omit them when they are needed. A common instance is typing

    f(x sub i)

which produces

$$f(x_i)$$

instead of

$$f(x_i)$$

Since the EQN language knows no mathematics, it cannot deduce that the right parenthesis is not part of the subscript.

The language is somewhat prolix, but this doesn't seem excessive considering how much is being done, and it is certainly more compact than the corresponding TROFF commands. For example, here is the source for the continued fraction expression in Section 1 of this paper:

```
a sub 0 + b sub 1 over
  {a sub 1 + b sub 2 over
    {a sub 2 + b sub 3 over
      {a sub 3 + ... }}}
```

This is the input for the large integral of Section 1; notice the use of definitions:

```
define emx "{e sup mx}"
define mab "{m sqrt ab}"
define sa "{sqrt a}"
define sb "{sqrt b}"
int dx over {a emx − be sup −mx} ~=~
left { lpile {
  1 over {2 mab} ~log~
      {sa emx − sb} over {sa emx + sb}
  above
  1 over mab ~ tanh sup −1 ( sa over sb emx )
  above
  −1 over mab ~ coth sup −1 ( sa over sb emx )
}
```

As to ease of construction, we have already mentioned that there are really only a few person-months invested. Much of this time has gone into two things—fine-tuning (what is the most esthetically pleasing space to use between the numerator and denominator of a fraction?), and changing things found deficient by our users (shouldn't a tilde be a delimiter?).

The program consists of a number of small, essentially unconnected modules for code generation, a simple lexical analyzer, a canned parser which we did not have to write, and some miscellany associated with input files and the macro facility. The program is now about 1600 lines of C [6], a high-level language reminiscent of BCPL. About 20 percent of these lines are ''print'' statements, generating the output code.

The semantic routines that generate the actual TROFF commands can be changed to accommodate other formatting languages and devices. For example, in less than 24 hours, one of us changed the entire semantic package to drive NROFF, a variant of TROFF, for typesetting mathematics on teletypewriter devices capable of reverse line motions. Since many potential users do not have access to a typesetter, but still have to type mathematics, this provides a way to get a typed version of the final output which is close enough for debugging purposes, and sometimes even for ultimate use.

7. Conclusions

We think we have shown that it is possible to do acceptably good typesetting of mathematics on a phototypesetter, with an input language that is easy to learn and use and that satisfies many users' demands. Such a package can be implemented in short order, given a compiler-compiler and a decent typesetting program underneath.

Defining a language, and building a compiler for it with a compiler-compiler seems like the only sensible way to do business. Our experience with the use of a grammar and a compiler-compiler has been uniformly favorable. If we had written everything into code directly, we would have been locked into our original design. Furthermore, we would have never been sure where the exceptions and special cases were. But because we have a grammar, we can change our minds readily and still be reasonably sure that if a construction works in one place it will work everywhere.

Acknowledgements

We are deeply indebted to J. F. Ossanna, the author of TROFF, for his willingness to modify TROFF to make our task easier and for his continuous assistance during the development of our program. We are also grateful to A. V. Aho for help with language theory, to S. C. Johnson for aid with the compiler-compiler, and to our early users A. V. Aho, S. I. Feldman, S. C. Johnson, R. W. Hamming, and M. D. McIlroy for their constructive criticisms.

References

[1] *A Manual of Style,* 12th Edition. University of Chicago Press, 1969. p 295.

[2] *Model C/A/T Phototypesetter.* Graphic Systems, Inc., Hudson, N. H.

[3] Ritchie, D. M., and Thompson, K. L., "The UNIX time-sharing system." *Comm. ACM 17,* 7 (July 1974), 365-375.

[4] Oşsanna, J. F., TROFF User's Manual. Bell Laboratories Computing Science Technical Report 54, 1977.

[5] Aho, A. V., and Johnson, S. C., "LR Parsing." *Comp. Surv. 6,* 2 (June 1974), 99-124.

[6] B. W. Kernighan and D. M. Ritchie, *The C Programming Language.* Prentice-Hall, Inc., 1978.

Typesetting Mathematics — User's Guide   (Second Edition)

Brian W. Kernighan and Lorinda L. Cherry

Bell Laboratories
Murray Hill, New Jersey 07974

ABSTRACT

This is the user's guide for a system for typesetting mathematics, using the photo-typesetters on the UNIX† and GCOS operating systems.

Mathematical expressions are described in a language designed to be easy to use by people who know neither mathematics nor typesetting. Enough of the language to set in-line expressions like $\lim_{x \to \pi/2} (\tan x)^{\sin 2x} = 1$ or display equations like

$$G(z) = e^{\ln G(z)} = \exp\left(\sum_{k \geqslant 1} \frac{S_k z^k}{k}\right) = \prod_{k \geqslant 1} e^{S_k z^k / k}$$

$$= \left(1 + S_1 z + \frac{S_1^2 z^2}{2!} + \cdots\right)\left(1 + \frac{S_2 z^2}{2} + \frac{S_2^2 z^4}{2^2 \cdot 2!} + \cdots\right)\cdots$$

$$= \sum_{m \geqslant 0}\left\{\sum_{\substack{k_1, k_2, \ldots, k_m \geqslant 0 \\ k_1 + 2k_2 + \cdots + mk_m = m}} \frac{S_1^{k_1}}{1^{k_1} k_1!} \frac{S_2^{k_2}}{2^{k_2} k_2!} \cdots \frac{S_m^{k_m}}{m^{k_m} k_m!}\right\} z^m$$

can be learned in an hour or so.

The language interfaces directly with the phototypesetting language TROFF, so mathematical expressions can be embedded in the running text of a manuscript, and the entire document produced in one process. This user's guide is an example of its output.

The same language may be used with the UNIX formatter NROFF to set mathematical expressions on DASI and GSI terminals and Model 37 teletypes.

August 15, 1978

---

†UNIX is a Trademark of Bell Laboratories.

1. Introduction

EQN is a program for typesetting mathematics on the Graphics Systems phototypesetters on UNIX and GCOS. The EQN language was designed to be easy to use by people who know neither mathematics nor typesetting. Thus EQN knows relatively little about mathematics. In particular, mathematical symbols like $+$, $-$, $\times$, parentheses, and so on have no special meanings. EQN is quite happy to set garbage (but it will look good).

EQN works as a preprocessor for the typesetter formatter, TROFF[1], so the normal mode of operation is to prepare a document with both mathematics and ordinary text interspersed, and let EQN set the mathematics while TROFF does the body of the text.

On UNIX, EQN will also produce mathematics on DASI and GSI terminals and on Model 37 teletypes. The input is identical, but you have to use the programs NEQN and NROFF instead of EQN and TROFF. Of course, some things won't look as good because terminals don't provide the variety of characters, sizes and fonts that a typesetter does, but the output is usually adequate for proofreading.

To use EQN on UNIX,

    eqn files | troff

GCOS use is discussed in section 26.

2. Displayed Equations

To tell EQN where a mathematical expression begins and ends, we mark it with lines beginning .EQ and .EN. Thus if you type the lines

```
.EQ
x=y+z
.EN
```

your output will look like

$$x=y+z$$

The .EQ and .EN are copied through untouched; they are not otherwise processed by EQN. This means that you have to take care of things like centering, numbering, and so on yourself. The most common way is to use the TROFF and NROFF macro package package '−ms' developed by M. E. Lesk[3], which allows you to center, indent, left-justify and number equations.

With the '−ms' package, equations are centered by default. To left-justify an equation, use .EQ L instead of .EQ. To indent it, use .EQ I. Any of these can be followed by an arbitrary 'equation number' which will be placed at the right margin. For example, the input

```
.EQ I (3.1a)
x = f(y/2) + y/2
.EN
```

produces the output

$$x=f(y/2)+y/2 \hspace{2cm} (3.1a)$$

There is also a shorthand notation so in-line expressions like π_i^2 can be entered without .EQ and .EN. We will talk about it in section 19.

3. Input spaces

Spaces and newlines within an expression are thrown away by EQN. (Normal text is left absolutely alone.) Thus between .EQ and .EN,

$$x=y+z$$

147

and

$$x = y + z$$

and

$$x = y$$
$$+ z$$

and so on all produce the same output

$$x=y+z$$

You should use spaces and newlines freely to make your input equations readable and easy to edit. In particular, very long lines are a bad idea, since they are often hard to fix if you make a mistake.

4. Output spaces

To force extra spaces into the *output*, use a tilde "~" for each space you want:

$$x~=~y~+~z$$

gives

$$x = y + z$$

You can also use a circumflex "^", which gives a space half the width of a tilde. It is mainly useful for fine-tuning. Tabs may also be used to position pieces of an expression, but the tab stops must be set by TROFF commands.

5. Symbols, Special Names, Greek

EQN knows some mathematical symbols, some mathematical names, and the Greek alphabet. For example,

$$x=2 \text{ pi int sin (omega t)dt}$$

produces

$$x=2\pi \int \sin(\omega t)\, dt$$

Here the spaces in the input are **necessary** to tell EQN that *int, pi, sin* and *omega* are separate entities that should get special treatment. The *sin*, digit 2, and parentheses are set in roman type instead of italic; *pi* and *omega* are made Greek; and *int* becomes the integral sign.

When in doubt, leave spaces around separate parts of the input. A *very* common error is to type *f(pi)* without leaving spaces on both sides of the *pi*. As a result, EQN does not recognize *pi* as a special word, and it appears as $f(pi)$ instead of $f(\pi)$.

A complete list of EQN names appears in section 23. Knowledgeable users can also use TROFF four-character names for anything EQN doesn't know about, like \(bs for the Bell System sign Ⓐ.

6. Spaces, Again

The only way EQN can deduce that some sequence of letters might be special is if that sequence is separated from the letters on either side of it. This can be done by surrounding a special word by ordinary spaces (or tabs or newlines), as we did in the previous section.

You can also make special words stand out by surrounding them with tildes or circumflexes:

$$x~=~2~pi~int~sin~(~omega~t~)~dt$$

is much the same as the last example, except that the tildes not only separate the magic words like *sin, omega,* and so on, but also add extra spaces, one space per tilde:

$$x = 2 \pi \int \sin (\omega t)\, dt$$

Special words can also be separated by braces { } and double quotes "...", which have special meanings that we will see soon.

7. Subscripts and Superscripts

Subscripts and superscripts are obtained with the words *sub* and *sup*.

$$x \text{ sup } 2 + y \text{ sub } k$$

gives

$$x^2+y_k$$

EQN takes care of all the size changes and vertical motions needed to make the output look right. The words *sub* and *sup* must be surrounded by spaces; *x sub2* will give you *xsub2* instead of x_2. Furthermore, don't forget to leave a space (or a tilde, etc.) to mark the end of a subscript or superscript. A common error is to say something like

$$y = (x \text{ sup } 2)+1$$

which causes

$$y=(x^{2)+1}$$

instead of the intended

$$y=(x^2)+1$$

Subscripted subscripts and superscripted superscripts also work:

x sub i sub 1

is

$$x_{i_1}$$

A subscript and superscript on the same thing are printed one above the other if the subscript comes *first:*

x sub i sup 2

is

$$x_i^2$$

Other than this special case, *sub* and *sup* group to the right, so x sup y sub z means x^{y_z}, not $x^y{}_z$.

8. Braces for Grouping

Normally, the end of a subscript or superscript is marked simply by a blank (or tab or tilde, etc.) What if the subscript or superscript is something that has to be typed with blanks in it? In that case, you can use the braces { and } to mark the beginning and end of the subscript or superscript:

e sup {i omega t}

is

$$e^{i\omega t}$$

Rule: Braces can *always* be used to force EQN to treat something as a unit, or just to make your intent perfectly clear. Thus:

x sub {i sub 1} sup 2

is

$$x_{i_1}^2$$

with braces, but

x sub i sub 1 sup 2

is

$$x_{i_1^2}$$

which is rather different.

Braces can occur within braces if necessary:

e sup {i pi sup {rho +1}}

is

The general rule is that anywhere you could use some single thing like *x*, you can use an arbitrarily complicated thing if you enclose it in braces. EQN will look after all the details of positioning it and making it the right size.

In all cases, make sure you have the right number of braces. Leaving one out or adding an extra will cause EQN to complain bitterly.

Occasionally you will have to print braces. To do this, enclose them in double quotes, like "{". Quoting is discussed in more detail in section 14.

9. Fractions

To make a fraction, use the word *over:*

a+b over 2c = 1

gives

$$\frac{a+b}{2c}=1$$

The line is made the right length and positioned automatically. Braces can be used to make clear what goes over what:

{alpha + beta} over {sin (x)}

is

$$\frac{\alpha+\beta}{\sin(x)}$$

What happens when there is both an *over* and a *sup* in the same expression? In such an apparently ambiguous case, EQN does the *sup* before the *over,* so

−b sup 2 over pi

is $\frac{-b^2}{\pi}$ instead of $-b^{\frac{2}{\pi}}$ The rules which decide which operation is done first in cases like this are summarized in section 23. When in doubt, however, *use braces* to make clear what goes with what.

10. Square Roots

To draw a square root, use *sqrt:*

sqrt a+b + 1 over sqrt {ax sup 2 +bx+c}

is

$$\sqrt{a+b}+\frac{1}{\sqrt{ax^2+bx+c}}$$

Warning — square roots of tall quantities look lousy, because a root-sign big enough to cover the quantity is too dark and heavy:

sqrt {a sup 2 over b sub 2}

is

$$\sqrt{\dfrac{a^2}{b_2}}$$

Big square roots are generally better written as something to the power ½:

$$(a^2/b_2)^{1/2}$$

which is

(a sup 2 /b sub 2) sup half

11. Summation, Integral, Etc.

Summations, integrals, and similar constructions are easy:

sum from i=0 to {i= inf} x sup i

produces

$$\sum_{i=0}^{i=\infty} x^i$$

Notice that we used braces to indicate where the upper part $i=\infty$ begins and ends. No braces were necessary for the lower part $i=0$, because it contained no blanks. The braces will never hurt, and if the *from* and *to* parts contain any blanks, you must use braces around them.

The *from* and *to* parts are both optional, but if both are used, they have to occur in that order.

Other useful characters can replace the *sum* in our example:

int   prod   union   inter

become, respectively,

$$\int \quad \Pi \quad \cup \quad \cap$$

Since the thing before the *from* can be anything, even something in braces, *from-to* can often be used in unexpected ways:

lim from {n −> inf} x sub n =0

is

$$\lim_{n \to \infty} x_n = 0$$

12. Size and Font Changes

By default, equations are set in 10-point type (the same size as this guide), with standard mathematical conventions to determine what characters are in roman and what in italic. Although EQN makes a valiant attempt to use esthetically pleasing sizes and fonts, it is not perfect. To change sizes and fonts, use *size n* and *roman, italic, bold* and *fat*. Like *sub* and *sup*, size and font changes affect only the thing that follows them, and revert to the normal situation at the end of it. Thus

bold x y

is

$$\mathbf{x}y$$

and

size 14 bold x = y +
  size 14 {alpha + beta}

gives

$$\mathbf{x}{=}y{+}\alpha{+}\beta$$

As always, you can use braces if you want to affect something more complicated than a single letter. For example, you can change the size of an entire equation by

size 12 { ... }

Legal sizes which may follow *size* are 6, 7, 8, 9, 10, 11, 12, 14, 16, 18, 20, 22, 24, 28, 36. You can also change the size *by* a given amount; for example, you can say *size +2* to make the size two points bigger, or *size −3* to make it three points smaller. This has the advantage that you don't have to know what the current size is.

If you are using fonts other than roman, italic and bold, you can say *font X* where X is a one character TROFF name or number for the font. Since EQN is tuned for roman, italic and bold, other fonts may not give quite as good an appearance.

The *fat* operation takes the current font and widens it by overstriking: *fat grad* is ∇ and *fat {x sub i}* is $\boldsymbol{x}_i$.

If an entire document is to be in a non-standard size or font, it is a severe nuisance to have to write out a size and font change for each equation. Accordingly, you can set a "global" size or font which thereafter affects all equations. At the beginning of any equation, you might say, for instance,

```
.EQ
gsize 16
gfont R
...
EN
```

to set the size to 16 and the font to roman thereafter. In place of R, you can use any of the TROFF font names. The size after *gsize* can be a relative change with $+$ or $-$.

Generally, *gsize* and *gfont* will appear at the beginning of a document but they can also appear thoughout a document: the global font and size can be changed as often as needed. For example, in a footnote‡ you will typically want the size of equations to match the size of the footnote text, which is two points smaller than the main text. Don't forget to reset the global size at the end of the footnote.

13. Diacritical Marks

To get funny marks on top of letters, there are several words:

x dot	$\dot{x}$
x dotdot	$\ddot{x}$
x hat	$\hat{x}$
x tilde	$\tilde{x}$
x vec	$\vec{x}$
x dyad	$\overleftrightarrow{x}$
x bar	$\bar{x}$
x under	$\underline{x}$

The diacritical mark is placed at the right height. The *bar* and *under* are made the right length for the entire construct, as in $\overline{x+y+z}$; other marks are centered.

14. Quoted Text

Any input entirely within quotes ("...") is not subject to any of the font changes and spacing adjustments normally done by the equation setter. This provides a way to do your own spacing and adjusting if needed:

italic "sin(x)" + sin (x)

is

$$sin(x)+\sin(x)$$

Quotes are also used to get braces and other EQN keywords printed:

"{ size alpha }"

is

$$\{\ size\ alpha\ \}$$

and

roman "{ size alpha }"

is

$$\{\ size\ alpha\ \}$$

The construction "" is often used as a place-holder when grammatically EQN needs something, but you don't actually want anything in your output. For example, to make ^{2}He, you can't just type *sup 2 roman He* because a *sup* has to be a superscript *on* something. Thus you must say

"" sup 2 roman He

To get a literal quote use ``\"''. TROFF characters like \(bs can appear unquoted, but more complicated things like horizontal and vertical motions with \h and \v should always be quoted. (If you've never heard of \h and \v, ignore this section.)

15. Lining Up Equations

Sometimes it's necessary to line up a series of equations at some horizontal position, often at an equals sign. This is done with two operations called *mark* and *lineup*.

The word *mark* may appear once at any place in an equation. It remembers the horizontal position where it appeared. Successive equations can contain one occurrence of the word *lineup*. The place where *lineup* appears is made to line up with the place marked by the previous *mark* if at all possible. Thus, for example, you can say

---

‡Like this one, in which we have a few random expressions like x_i and π^2. The sizes for these were set by the command *gsize* -2.

```
.EQ I
x+y mark = z
.EN
.EQ I
x lineup = 1
.EN
```

to produce

$$x+y=z$$

$$x=1$$

For reasons too complicated to talk about, when you use EQN and '−ms', use either .EQ I or .EQ L. mark and *lineup* don't work with centered equations. Also bear in mind that *mark* doesn't look ahead;

```
x mark =1
...
x+y lineup =z
```

isn't going to work, because there isn't room for the $x+y$ part after the *mark* remembers where the x is.

16. Big Brackets, Etc.

To get big brackets [ ], braces { }, parentheses ( ), and bars ‖ around things, use the *left* and *right* commands:

```
left { a over b + 1 right }
~=~ left ( c over d right )
+ left [ e right ]
```

is

$$\left\{\frac{a}{b}+1\right\} = \left(\frac{c}{d}\right)+\left[e\right]$$

The resulting brackets are made big enough to cover whatever they enclose. Other characters can be used besides these, but the are not likely to look very good. One exception is the *floor* and *ceiling* characters:

```
left floor x over y right floor
< = left ceiling a over b right ceiling
```

produces

$$\left\lfloor\frac{x}{y}\right\rfloor \leqslant \left\lceil\frac{a}{b}\right\rceil$$

Several warnings about brackets are in order. First, braces are typically bigger than brackets and parentheses, because they are made up of three, five, seven, etc., pieces, while brackets can be made up of two,

three, etc. Second, big left and right parentheses often look poor, because the character set is poorly designed.

The *right* part may be omitted: a "left something" need not have a corresponding "right something". If the *right* part is omitted, put braces around the thing you want the left bracket to encompass. Otherwise, the resulting brackets may be too large.

If you want to omit the *left* part, things are more complicated, because technically you can't have a *right* without a corresponding *left*. Instead you have to say

```
left "" ..... right )
```

for example. The *left* "" means a "left nothing". This satisfies the rules without hurting your output.

17. Piles

There is a general facility for making vertical piles of things; it comes in several flavors. For example:

```
A ~=~ left [
  pile { a above b above c }
  ~~ pile { x above y above z }
  right ]
```

will make

$$A = \begin{bmatrix} a & x \\ b & y \\ c & z \end{bmatrix}$$

The elements of the pile (there can be as many as you want) are centered one above another, at the right height for most purposes. The keyword *above* is used to separate the pieces; braces are used around the entire list. The elements of a pile can be as complicated as needed, even containing more piles.

Three other forms of pile exist: *lpile* makes a pile with the elements left-justified; *rpile* makes a right-justified pile; and *cpile* makes a centered pile, just like *pile*. The vertical spacing between the pieces is somewhat larger for *l-*, *r-* and *cpiles* than it is for ordinary piles.

```
roman sign (x)~=~
left {
  lpile {1 above 0 above −1}
  ~~ lpile
  {if~x>0 above if~x=0 above if~x<0}
```

makes

$$\text{sign}(x) = \begin{cases} 1 & \text{if } x > 0 \\ 0 & \text{if } x = 0 \\ -1 & \text{if } x < 0 \end{cases}$$

Notice the left brace without a matching right one.

18. Matrices

It is also possible to make matrices. For example, to make a neat array like

$$\begin{matrix} x_i & x^2 \\ y_i & y^2 \end{matrix}$$

you have to type

```
matrix {
  ccol { x sub i above y sub i }
  ccol { x sup 2 above y sup 2 }
}
```

This produces a matrix with two centered columns. The elements of the columns are then listed just as for a pile, each element separated by the word *above*. You can also use *lcol* or *rcol* to left or right adjust columns. Each column can be separately adjusted, and there can be as many columns as you like.

The reason for using a matrix instead of two adjacent piles, by the way, is that if the elements of the piles don't all have the same height, they won't line up properly. A matrix forces them to line up, because it looks at the entire structure before deciding what spacing to use.

A word of warning about matrices — *each column must have the same number of elements in it*. The world will end if you get this wrong.

19. Shorthand for In-line Equations

In a mathematical document, it is necessary to follow mathematical conventions not just in display equations, but also in the body of the text, for example by making variable names like x italic. Although this could be done by surrounding the appropriate parts with .EQ and .EN, the continual repetition of .EQ and .EN is a nuisance. Furthermore, with '−ms', .EQ and .EN imply a displayed equation.

EQN provides a shorthand for short in-line expressions. You can define two characters to mark the left and right ends of an in-line equation, and then type expressions right in the middle of text lines. To set both the left and right characters to dollar signs, for example, add to the beginning of your document the three lines

```
.EQ
delim $$
.EN
```

Having done this, you can then say things like

Let $alpha sub i$ be the primary variable, and let $beta$ be zero. Then we can show that $x sub 1$ is $> =0$.

This works as you might expect — spaces, newlines, and so on are significant in the text, but not in the equation part itself. Multiple equations can occur in a single input line.

Enough room is left before and after a line that contains in-line expressions that something like $\sum_{i=1}^{n} x_i$ does not interfere with the lines surrounding it.

To turn off the delimiters,

```
.EQ
delim off
.EN
```

Warning: don't use braces, tildes, circumflexes, or double quotes as delimiters — chaos will result.

20. Definitions

EQN provides a facility so you can give a frequently-used string of characters a name, and thereafter just type the name instead of the whole string. For example, if the sequence

```
x sub i sub 1 + y sub i sub 1
```

appears repeatedly throughout a paper, you can save re-typing it each time by defining it like this:

```
define xy 'x sub i sub 1 + y sub i sub 1'
```

This makes *xy* a shorthand for whatever characters occur between the single quotes in the definition. You can use any character instead of quote to mark the ends of the definition, so long as it doesn't appear inside the definition.

Now you can use *xy* like this:

```
.EQ
f(x) = xy ...
.EN
```

and so on. Each occurrence of *xy* will expand into what it was defined as. Be careful to leave spaces or their equivalent around the name when you actually use it, so EQN will be able to identify it as special.

There are several things to watch out for. First, although definitions can use previous definitions, as in

```
.EQ
define xi ' x sub i '
define xi1 ' xi sub 1 '
.EN
```

don't define something in terms of itself. A favorite error is to say

```
define  X  ' roman X '
```

This is a guaranteed disaster, since X *is* now defined in terms of itself. If you say

```
define  X  ' roman "X" '
```

however, the quotes protect the second X, and everything works fine.

EQN keywords can be redefined. You can make / mean *over* by saying

```
define  /  ' over '
```

or redefine *over* as / with

```
define  over  ' / '
```

If you need different things to print on a terminal and on the typesetter, it is sometimes worth defining a symbol differently in NEQN and EQN. This can be done with *ndefine* and *tdefine*. A definition made with *ndefine* only takes effect if you are running NEQN; if you use *tdefine,* the definition only applies for EQN. Names defined with plain *define* apply to both EQN and NEQN.

21. Local Motions

Although EQN tries to get most things at the right place on the paper, it isn't perfect, and occasionally you will need to tune the output to make it just right. Small extra

horizontal spaces can be obtained with tilde and circumflex. You can also say *back n* and *fwd n* to move small amounts horizontally. *n* is how far to move in 1/100's of an em (an em is about the width of the letter 'm'.) Thus *back 50* moves back about half the width of an m. Similarly you can move things up or down with *up n* and *down n.* As with *sub* or *sup,* the local motions affect the next thing in the input, and this can be something arbitrarily complicated if it is enclosed in braces.

22. A Large Example

Here is the complete source for the three display equations in the abstract of this guide.

```
.EQ I
G(z)~mark =~ e sup { ln ~ G(z) }
~=~ exp left (
sum from k>=1 {S sub k z sup k} over k right )
~=~ prod from k>=1 e sup {S sub k z sup k /k}
.EN
.EQ I
lineup = left ( 1 + S sub 1 z +
{ S sub 1 sup 2 z sup 2 } over 2! + ... right )
left ( 1+ { S sub 2 z sup 2 } over 2
+ { S sub 2 sup 2 z sup 4 } over { 2 sup 2 cdot 2! }
+ ... right ) ...
.EN
.EQ I
lineup =  sum from m>=0 left (
sum from
pile { k sub 1 ,k sub 2 ,..., k sub m  >=0
above
k sub 1 +2k sub 2 + ... +mk sub m =m}
{ S sub 1 sup {k sub 1} } over {1 sup k sub 1 k sub 1 !} ~
{ S sub 2 sup {k sub 2} } over {2 sup k sub 2 k sub 2 !} ~
...
{ S sub m sup {k sub m} } over {m sup k sub m k sub m !}
right ) z sup m
.EN
```

23. Keywords, Precedences, Etc.

If you don't use braces, EQN will do operations in the order shown in this list.

dyad vec under bar tilde hat dot dotdot
fwd back down up
fat roman italic bold size
sub sup sqrt over
from to

These operations group to the left:

over sqrt left right

All others group to the right.

Digits, parentheses, brackets, punctuation marks, and these mathematical words are converted to Roman font when encountered:

    sin cos tan sinh cosh tanh arc
    max min lim log ln exp
    Re Im and if for det

These character sequences are recognized and translated as shown.

>=	$\geq$
<=	$\leq$
==	$\equiv$
!=	$\neq$
+-	$\pm$
->	$\rightarrow$
<-	$\leftarrow$
<<	$\ll$
>>	$\gg$
inf	∞
partial	∂
half	$\frac{1}{2}$
prime	$'$
approx	$\approx$
nothing	
cdot	$\cdot$
times	$\times$
del	∇
grad	∇
...	$\cdots$
,...,	$, \cdots ,$
sum	$\sum$
int	$\int$
prod	$\prod$
union	$\bigcup$
inter	$\bigcap$

To obtain Greek letters, simply spell them out in whatever case you want:

DELTA	Δ	iota	ι
GAMMA	Γ	kappa	κ
LAMBDA	Λ	lambda	λ
OMEGA	Ω	mu	μ
PHI	Φ	nu	ν
PI	Π	omega	ω
PSI	Ψ	omicron	o
SIGMA	Σ	phi	ϕ
THETA	Θ	pi	π
UPSILON	Υ	psi	ψ
XI	Ξ	rho	ρ
alpha	α	sigma	σ

beta	β	tau	τ
chi	χ	theta	θ
delta	δ	upsilon	υ
epsilon	ϵ	xi	ξ
eta	η	zeta	ζ
gamma	γ		

These are all the words known to EQN (except for characters with names), together with the section where they are discussed.

above	17, 18	lpile	17
back	21	mark	15
bar	13	matrix	18
bold	12	ndefine	20
ccol	18	over	9
col	18	pile	17
cpile	17	rcol	18
define	20	right	16
delim	19	roman	12
dot	13	rpile	17
dotdot	13	size	12
down	21	sqrt	10
dyad	13	sub	7
fat	12	sup	7
font	12	tdefine	20
from	11	tilde	13
fwd	21	to	11
gfont	12	under	13
gsize	12	up	21
hat	13	vec	13
italic	12	˜, ^	4, 6
lcol	18	{ }	8
left	16	"..."	8, 14
lineup	15		

24. Troubleshooting

If you make a mistake in an equation, like leaving out a brace (very common) or having one too many (very common) or having a *sup* with nothing before it (common), EQN will tell you with the message

syntax error between lines x and y, file z

where *x* and *y* are approximately the lines between which the trouble occurred, and *z* is the name of the file in question. The line numbers are approximate — look nearby as well. There are also self-explanatory messages that arise if you leave out a quote or try to run EQN on a non-existent file.

If you want to check a document before actually printing it (on UNIX only),

```
eqn  files >/dev/null
```

will throw away the output but print the messages.

If you use something like dollar signs as delimiters, it is easy to leave one out. This causes very strange troubles. The program *checkeq* (on GCOS, use *./checkeq* instead) checks for misplaced or missing dollar signs and similar troubles.

In-line equations can only be so big because of an internal buffer in TROFF. If you get a message "word overflow", you have exceeded this limit. If you print the equation as a displayed equation this message will usually go away. The message "line overflow" indicates you have exceeded an even bigger buffer. The only cure for this is to break the equation into two separate ones.

On a related topic, EQN does not break equations by itself — you must split long equations up across multiple lines by yourself, marking each by a separate .EQ ... .EN sequence. EQN does warn about equations that are too long to fit on one line.

25. Use on UNIX

To print a document that contains mathematics on the UNIX typesetter,

```
eqn files | troff
```

If there are any TROFF options, they go after the TROFF part of the command. For example,

```
eqn files | troff −ms
```

To run the same document on the GCOS typesetter, use

```
eqn files | troff −g (other options) | gcat
```

A compatible version of EQN can be used on devices like teletypes and DASI and GSI terminals which have half-line forward and reverse capabilities. To print equations on a Model 37 teletype, for example, use

```
neqn files | nroff
```

The language for equations recognized by NEQN is identical to that of EQN, although of course the output is more restricted.

To use a GSI or DASI terminal as the output device,

```
neqn files | nroff −Tx
```

where x is the terminal type you are using, such as *300* or *300S*.

EQN and NEQN can be used with the TBL program [2] for setting tables that contain mathematics. Use TBL before [N]EQN, like this:

```
tbl files | eqn | troff
tbl files | neqn | nroff
```

26. Acknowledgments

We are deeply indebted to J. F. Ossanna, the author of TROFF, for his willingness to extend TROFF to make our task easier, and for his continuous assistance during the development and evolution of EQN. We are also grateful to A. V. Aho for advice on language design, to S. C. Johnson for assistance with the YACC compiler-compiler, and to all the EQN users who have made helpful suggestions and criticisms.

References

[1] J. F. Ossanna, "NROFF/TROFF User's Manual", Bell Laboratories Computing Science Technical Report #54, 1976.

[2] M. E. Lesk, "Typing Documents on UNIX", Bell Laboratories, 1976.

[3] M. E. Lesk, "TBL — A Program for Setting Tables", Bell Laboratories Computing Science Technical Report #49, 1976.

Tbl — A Program to Format Tables

M. E. Lesk

Bell Laboratories
Murray Hill, New Jersey 07974

ABSTRACT

Tbl is a document formatting preprocessor for *troff* or *nroff* which makes even fairly complex tables easy to specify and enter. It is available on the PDP-11 UNIX* system and on Honeywell 6000 GCOS. Tables are made up of columns which may be independently centered, right-adjusted, left-adjusted, or aligned by decimal points. Headings may be placed over single columns or groups of columns. A table entry may contain equations, or may consist of several rows of text. Horizontal or vertical lines may be drawn as desired in the table, and any table or element may be enclosed in a box. For example:

1970 Federal Budget Transfers (in billions of dollars)			
State	Taxes collected	Money spent	Net
New York	22.91	21.35	−1.56
New Jersey	8.33	6.96	−1.37
Connecticut	4.12	3.10	−1.02
Maine	0.74	0.67	−0.07
California	22.29	22.42	+0.13
New Mexico	0.70	1.49	+0.79
Georgia	3.30	4.28	+0.98
Mississippi	1.15	2.32	+1.17
Texas	9.33	11.13	+1.80

January 16, 1979

---

* UNIX is a Trademark/Service Mark of the Bell System

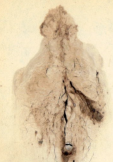

Introduction.

Tbl turns a simple description of a table into a *troff* or *nroff* [1] program (list of commands) that prints the table. *Tbl* may be used on the PDP-11 UNIX [2] system and on the Honeywell 6000 GCOS system. It attempts to isolate a portion of a job that it can successfully handle and leave the remainder for other programs. Thus *tbl* may be used with the equation formatting program *eqn* [3] or various layout macro packages [4,5,6], but does not duplicate their functions.

This memorandum is divided into two parts. First we give the rules for preparing *tbl* input; then some examples are shown. The description of rules is precise but technical, and the beginning user may prefer to read the examples first, as they show some common table arrangements. A section explaining how to invoke *tbl* precedes the examples. To avoid repetition, henceforth read *troff* as *"troff* or *nroff."*

The input to *tbl* is text for a document, with tables preceded by a ".TS".(table start) command and followed by a ".TE" (table end) command. *Tbl* processes the tables, generating *troff* formatting commands, and leaves the remainder of the text unchanged. The ".TS" and ".TE" lines are copied, too, so that *troff* page layout macros (such as the memo formatting macros [4]) can use these lines to delimit and place tables as they see fit. In particular, any arguments on the ".TS" or ".TE" lines are copied but otherwise ignored, and may be used by document layout macro commands.

The format of the input is as follows:

```
    text
    .TS
    table
    .TE
    text
    .TS
    table
    .TE
    text
    . . .
```

where the format of each table is as follows:

```
    .TS
    options ;
    format .
    data
    .TE
```

Each table is independent, and must contain formatting information followed by the data to be entered in the table. The formatting information, which describes the individual columns and rows of the table, may be preceded by a few options that affect the entire table. A detailed description of tables is given in the next section.

158

Input commands.

As indicated above, a table contains, first, global options, then a format section describing the layout of the table entries, and then the data to be printed. The format and data are always required, but not the options. The various parts of the table are entered as follows:

1)   OPTIONS. There may be a single line of options affecting the whole table. If present, this line must follow the .TS line immediately and must contain a list of option names separated by spaces, tabs, or commas, and must be terminated by a semicolon. The allowable options are:

   center   — center the table (default is left-adjust);

   expand   — make the table as wide as the current line length;

   box   — enclose the table in a box;

   allbox   — enclose each item in the table in a box;

   doublebox — enclose the table in two boxes;

   tab (x)   — use x instead of tab to separate data items.

   linesize (n) — set lines or rules (e.g. from **box**) in n point type;

   delim (xy) — recognize x and y as the *eqn* delimiters.

The *tbl* program tries to keep boxed tables on one page by issuing appropriate "need" (*.ne*) commands. These requests are calculated from the number of lines in the tables, and if there are spacing commands embedded in the input, these requests may be inaccurate; use normal *troff* procedures, such as keep-release macros, in that case. The user who must have a multi-page boxed table should use macros designed for this purpose, as explained below under 'Usage.'

2)   FORMAT. The format section of the table specifies the layout of the columns. Each line in this section corresponds to one line of the table (except that the last line corresponds to all following lines up to the next .T&, if any — see below), and each line contains a key-letter for each column of the table. It is good practice to separate the key letters for each column by spaces or tabs. Each key-letter is one of the following:

   L or l   to indicate a left-adjusted column entry;

   R or r   to indicate a right-adjusted column entry;

   C or c   to indicate a centered column entry;

   N or n   to indicate a numerical column entry, to be aligned with other numerical entries so that the units digits of numbers line up;

   A or a   to indicate an alphabetic subcolumn; all corresponding entries are aligned on the left, and positioned so that the widest is centered within the column (see example on page 12);

   S or s   to indicate a spanned heading, i.e. to indicate that the entry from the previous column continues across this column (not allowed for the first column, obviously); or

   ^   to indicate a vertically spanned heading, i.e. to indicate that the entry from the previous row continues down through this row. (Not allowed for the first row of the table, obviously).

When numerical alignment is specified, a location for the decimal point is sought. The rightmost dot (.) adjacent to a digit is used as a decimal point; if there is no dot adjoining a digit, the rightmost digit is used as a units digit; if no alignment is indicated, the item is centered in the column. However, the special non-printing character string \& may be used to override unconditionally dots and digits, or to align alphabetic data; this string lines up where a dot normally would, and then disappears from the final output. In the example below, the items shown at the left will be aligned (in a numerical column) as shown on the right:

13	13
4.2	4.2
26.4.12	26.4.12
abc	abc
abc\&	abc
43\&3.22	433.22
749.12	749.12

Note: If numerical data are used in the same column with wider **L** or **r** type table entries, the widest *number* is centered relative to the wider **L** or **r** items (**L** is used instead of **l** for readability; they have the same meaning as key-letters). Alignment within the numerical items is preserved. This is similar to the behavior of **a** type data, as explained above. However, alphabetic subcolumns (requested by the **a** key-letter) are always slightly indented relative to **L** items; if necessary, the column width is increased to force this. This is not true for **n** type entries.

Warning: the **n** and **a** items should not be used in the same column.

For readability, the key-letters describing each column should be separated by spaces. The end of the format section is indicated by a period. The layout of the key-letters in the format section resembles the layout of the actual data in the table. Thus a simple format might appear as:

```
c s s
l n n .
```

which specifies a table of three columns. The first line of the table contains a heading centered across all three columns; each remaining line contains a left-adjusted item in the first column followed by two columns of numerical data. A sample table in this format might be:

Overall title		
Item-a	34.22	9.1
Item-b	12.65	.02
Items: c,d,e	23	5.8
Total	69.87	14.92

There are some additional features of the key-letter system:

Horizontal lines — A key-letter may be replaced by '_' (underscore) to indicate a horizontal line in place of the corresponding column entry, or by '=' to indicate a double horizontal line. If an adjacent column contains a horizontal line, or if there are vertical lines adjoining this column, this horizontal line is extended to meet the nearby lines. If any data entry is provided for this column, it is ignored and a warning message is printed.

Vertical lines — A vertical bar may be placed between column key-letters. This will cause a vertical line between the corresponding columns of the table. A vertical bar to the left of the first key-letter or to the right of the last one produces a line at the edge of the table. If two vertical bars appear between key-letters, a double vertical line is drawn.

Space between columns — A number may follow the key-letter. This indicates the amount of separation between this column and the next column. The number normally specifies the separation in *ens* (one en is about the width of the letter 'n').* If the "expand" option is used, then these numbers are multiplied by a constant such that the table is as wide as the current line length. The default column separation

---

* More precisely, an en is a number of points (1 point = 1/72 inch) equal to half the current type size.

number is 3. If the separation is changed the worst case (largest space requested) governs.

Vertical spanning — Normally, vertically spanned items extending over several rows of the table are centered in their vertical range. If a key-letter is followed by **t** or **T**, any corresponding vertically spanned item will begin at the top line of its range.

Font changes — A key-letter may be followed by a string containing a font name or number preceded by the letter **f** or **F**. This indicates that the corresponding column should be in a different font from the default font (usually Roman). All font names are one or two letters; a one-letter font name should be separated from whatever follows by a space or tab. The single letters **B**, **b**, **I**, and **i** are shorter synonyms for **fB** and **fI**. Font change commands given with the table entries override these specifications.

Point size changes — A key-letter may be followed by the letter **p** or **P** and a number to indicate the point size of the corresponding table entries. The number may be a signed digit, in which case it is taken as an increment or decrement from the current point size. If both a point size and a column separation value are given, one or more blanks must separate them.

Vertical spacing changes — A key-letter may be followed by the letter **v** or **V** and a number to indicate the vertical line spacing to be used within a multi-line corresponding table entry. The number may be a signed digit, in which case it is taken as an increment or decrement from the current vertical spacing. A column separation value must be separated by blanks or some other specification from a vertical spacing request. This request has no effect unless the corresponding table entry is a text block (see below).

Column width indication — A key-letter may be followed by the letter **w** or **W** and a width value in parentheses. This width is used as a minimum column width. If the largest element in the column is not as wide as the width value given after the **w**, the largest element is assumed to be that wide. If the largest element in the column is wider than the specified value, its width is used. The width is also used as a default line length for included text blocks. Normal *troff* units can be used to scale the width value; if none are used, the default is ens. If the width specification is a unitless integer the parentheses may be omitted. If the width value is changed in a column, the *last* one given controls.

Equal width columns — A key-letter may be followed by the letter **e** or **E** to indicate equal width columns. All columns whose key-letters are followed by **e** or **E** are made the same width. This permits the user to get a group of regularly spaced columns.

Note: The order of the above features is immaterial; they need not be separated by spaces, except as indicated above to avoid ambiguities involving point size and font changes. Thus a numerical column entry in italic font and 12 point type with a minimum width of 2.5 inches and separated by 6 ens from the next column could be specified as

  np12w(2.5i)fI 6

Alternative notation — Instead of listing the format of successive lines of a table on consecutive lines of the format section, successive line formats may be given on the same line, separated by commas, so that the format for the example above might have been written:

  c s s,l n n .

Default — Column descriptors missing from the end of a format line are assumed to be L. The longest line in the format section, however, defines the number of columns in the table; extra columns in the data are ignored silently.

3)   DATA. The data for the table are typed after the format. Normally, each table line is typed as one line of data. Very long input lines can be broken: any line whose last character is \ is combined with the following line (and the \ vanishes). The data for different columns (the table entries) are separated by tabs, or by whatever character has been specified in the option *tabs* option. There are a few special cases:

Troff commands within tables — An input line beginning with a '.' followed by anything but a number is assumed to be a command to *troff* and is passed through unchanged, retaining its position in the table. So, for example, space within a table may be produced by ".sp" commands in the data.

Full width horizontal lines — An input *line* containing only the character _ (underscore) or = (equal sign) is taken to be a single or double line, respectively, extending the full width of the *table*.

Single column horizontal lines — An input table *entry* containing only the character _ or = is taken to be a single or double line extending the full width of the *column*. Such lines are extended to meet horizontal or vertical lines adjoining this column. To obtain these characters explicitly in a column, either precede them by \& or follow them by a space before the usual tab or newline.

Short horizontal lines — An input table *entry* containing only the string _ is taken to be a single line as wide as the contents of the column. It is not extended to meet adjoining lines.

Repeated characters — An input table *entry* containing only a string of the form \R*x* where *x* is any character is replaced by repetitions of the character *x* as wide as the data in the column. The sequence of *x*'s is not extended to meet adjoining columns.

Vertically spanned items — An input table entry containing only the character string \^ indicates that the table entry immediately above spans downward over this row. It is equivalent to a table format key-letter of '^'

Text blocks — In order to include a block of text as a table entry, precede it by **T{** and follow it by **T}**. Thus the sequence

     . . . **T{**
     block of
     text
     T} . . .

is the way to enter, as a single entry in the table, something that cannot conveniently be typed as a simple string between tabs. Note that the **T}** end delimiter must begin a line; additional columns of data may follow after a tab on the same line. See the example on page 10 for an illustration of included text blocks in a table. If more than twenty or thirty text blocks are used in a table, various limits in the *troff* program are likely to be exceeded, producing diagnostics such as 'too many string/macro names' or 'too many number registers.'

Text blocks are pulled out from the table, processed separately by *troff*, and replaced in the table as a solid block. If no line length is specified in the *block of text* itself, or in the table format, the default is to use $L \times C/(N+1)$ where L is the current line length, C is the number of table columns spanned by the text, and N is the total number of columns in the table. The other parameters (point size, font, etc.) used in setting the *block of text* are those in effect at the beginning of the table (including the effect of the ".TS" macro) and any table format specifications of size, spacing and font, using the **p**, **v** and **f** modifiers to the column key-letters. Commands within the text block itself are also recognized, of course. However, *troff* commands within the table data but not within the text block do not affect that block.

Warnings: — Although any number of lines may be present in a table, only the first 200 lines are used in calculating the widths of the various columns. A multi-page table, of course, may be arranged as several single-page tables if this proves to be a problem. Other difficulties with formatting may arise because, in the calculation of column widths all table entries are assumed to be in the font and size being used when the ".TS" command was encountered, except for font and size changes indicated (a) in the table format section and (b) within the table data (as in the entry \s+3\fIdata\fP\s0). Therefore, although arbitrary *troff* requests may be sprinkled in a table, care must be taken to avoid confusing the width calculations; use requests such as '.ps' with care.

4) ADDITIONAL COMMAND LINES. If the format of a table must be changed after many similar lines, as with sub-headings or summarizations, the ".T&" (table continue) command can be used to change column parameters. The outline of such a table input is:

```
.TS
options ;
format .
data
. . .
.T&
format .
data
.T&
format .
data
.TE
```

as in the examples on pages 10 and 12. Using this procedure, each table line can be close to its corresponding format line.

Warning: it is not possible to change the number of columns, the space between columns, the global options such as *box,* or the selection of columns to be made equal width.

Usage.

On UNIX, *tbl* can be run on a simple table with the command

    tbl input-file | troff

but for more complicated use, where there are several input files, and they contain equations and *ms* memorandum layout commands as well as tables, the normal command would be

    tbl file-1 file-2 . . . | eqn | troff −ms

and, of course, the usual options may be used on the *troff* and *eqn* commands. The usage for *nroff* is similar to that for *troff,* but only TELETYPE® Model 37 and Diablo-mechanism (DASI or GSI) terminals can print boxed tables directly.

For the convenience of users employing line printers without adequate driving tables or post-filters, there is a special −TX command line option to *tbl* which produces output that does not have fractional line motions in it. The only other command line options recognized by *tbl* are −ms and −mm which are turned into commands to fetch the corresponding macro files; usually it is more convenient to place these arguments on the *troff* part of the command line, but they are accepted by *tbl* as well.

Note that when *eqn* and *tbl* are used together on the same file *tbl* should be used first. If there are no equations within tables, either order works, but it is usually faster to run *tbl* first, since *eqn* normally produces a larger expansion of the input than *tbl*. However, if there are equations within tables (using the *delim* mechanism in *eqn*), *tbl* must be first or the output will be scrambled. Users must also beware of using equations in **n**-style columns; this is nearly always wrong, since *tbl* attempts to split numerical format items into two parts and this is not possible with equations. The user can defend against this by giving the *delim(xx)* table option; this prevents splitting of numerical columns within the delimiters. For example, if the *eqn* delimiters are *$$*, giving *delim($$)* a numerical column such as "1245 $+- 16$" will be divided after 1245, not after 16.

Tbl limits tables to twenty columns; however, use of more than 16 numerical columns may fail because of limits in *troff*, producing the 'too many number registers' message. *Troff* number registers used by *tbl* must be avoided by the user within tables; these include two-digit names from 31 to 99, and names of the forms #x, x+, x|, ^x, and x−, where x is any lower case letter. The names ##, #−, and #ˆ are also used in certain circumstances. To conserve number register names, the **n** and **a** formats share a register; hence the restriction above that they may not be used in the same column.

For aid in writing layout macros, *tbl* defines a number register TW which is the table width; it is defined by the time that the ".TE" macro is invoked and may be used in the expansion of that macro. More importantly, to assist in laying out multi-page boxed tables the macro T# is defined to produce the bottom lines and side lines of a boxed table, and then invoked at its end. By use of this macro in the page footer a multi-page table can be boxed. In particular, the *ms* macros can be used to print a multi-page boxed table with a repeated heading by giving the argument H to the ".TS" macro. If the table start macro is written

    .TS H

a line of the form

    .TH

must be given in the table after any table heading (or at the start if none). Material up to the ".TH" is placed at the top of each page of table; the remaining lines in the table are placed on several pages as required. Note that this is *not* a feature of *tbl*, but of the *ms* layout macros.

Examples.

Here are some examples illustrating features of *tbl*. The symbol ⊕ in the input represents a tab character.

Input:

    .TS
    box;
    c c c
    l l l.
    Language ⊕ Authors ⊕ Runs on

    Fortran ⊕ Many ⊕ Almost anything
    PL/1 ⊕ IBM ⊕ 360/370
    C ⊕ BTL ⊕ 11/45,H6000,370
    BLISS ⊕ Carnegie-Mellon ⊕ PDP-10,11
    IDS ⊕ Honeywell ⊕ H6000
    Pascal ⊕ Stanford ⊕ 370
    .TE

Output:

Language	Authors	Runs on
Fortran	Many	Almost anything
PL/1	IBM	360/370
C	BTL	11/45,H6000,370
BLISS	Carnegie-Mellon	PDP-10,11
IDS	Honeywell	H6000
Pascal	Stanford	370

Input:

```
.TS
allbox;
c s s
c c c
n n n.
AT&T Common Stock
Year ⊕ Price ⊕ Dividend
1971 ⊕ 41-54 ⊕ $2.60
2 ⊕ 41-54 ⊕ 2.70
3 ⊕ 46-55 ⊕ 2.87
4 ⊕ 40-53 ⊕ 3.24
5 ⊕ 45-52 ⊕ 3.40
6 ⊕ 51-59 ⊕ .95*
.TE
* (first quarter only)
```

Output:

AT&T Common Stock		
Year	Price	Dividend
1971	41-54	$2.60
2	41-54	2.70
3	46-55	2.87
4	40-53	3.24
5	45-52	3.40
6	51-59	.95*

* (first quarter only)

Input:

```
.TS
box;
c s s
c | c | c
l | l | n.
Major New York Bridges
=
Bridge ⊕ Designer ⊕ Length
_
Brooklyn ⊕ J. A. Roebling ⊕ 1595
Manhattan ⊕ G. Lindenthal ⊕ 1470
Williamsburg ⊕ L. L. Buck ⊕ 1600
_
Queensborough ⊕ Palmer & ⊕ 1182
⊕ Hornbostel
_
⊕ ⊕ 1380
Triborough ⊕ O. H. Ammann ⊕ _
⊕ ⊕ 383
_
Bronx Whitestone ⊕ O. H. Ammann ⊕ 2300
Throgs Neck ⊕ O. H. Ammann ⊕ 1800
_
George Washington ⊕ O. H. Ammann ⊕ 3500
.TE
```

Output:

Major New York Bridges		
Bridge	Designer	Length
Brooklyn	J. A. Roebling	1595
Manhattan	G. Lindenthal	1470
Williamsburg	L. L. Buck	1600
Queensborough	Palmer & Hornbostel	1182
Triborough	O. H. Ammann	1380
		383
Bronx Whitestone	O. H. Ammann	2300
Throgs Neck	O. H. Ammann	1800
George Washington	O. H. Ammann	3500

Input:

```
.TS
c c
np-2 |n| .
ⓉStack
Ⓣ _
1Ⓣ46
Ⓣ _
2Ⓣ23
Ⓣ _
3Ⓣ15
Ⓣ _
4Ⓣ6.5
Ⓣ _
5Ⓣ2.1
Ⓣ _
.TE
```

Output:

	Stack
1	46
2	23
3	15
4	6.5
5	2.1

Input:

```
.TS
box;
L L L
L L _
L L |LB
L L _
L L L.
januaryⓉfebruaryⓉmarch
aprilⓉmay
juneⓉjulyⓉMonths
augustⓉseptember
octoberⓉnovemberⓉdecember
.TE
```

Output:

january	february	march
april	may	
june	july	**Months**
august	september	
october	november	december

Input:

```
.TS
box;
cfB s s s.
Composition of Foods

.T&
c |c s s
c |c s s
c |c |c |c.
Food ⊕ Percent by Weight
\^⊕_
\^⊕ Protein ⊕ Fat ⊕ Carbo-
\^⊕\^⊕\^⊕ hydrate

.T&
l |n |n |n.
Apples ⊕.4⊕.5⊕13.0
Halibut ⊕18.4⊕5.2⊕...
Lima beans ⊕7.5⊕.8⊕22.0
Milk ⊕3.3⊕4.0⊕5.0
Mushrooms ⊕3.5⊕.4⊕6.0
Rye bread ⊕9.0⊕.6⊕52.7
.TE
```

Output:

Composition of Foods			
Food	Percent by Weight		
	Protein	Fat	Carbo-hydrate
Apples	.4	.5	13.0
Halibut	18.4	5.2	...
Lima beans	7.5	.8	22.0
Milk	3.3	4.0	5.0
Mushrooms	3.5	.4	6.0
Rye bread	9.0	.6	52.7

Input:

```
.TS
allbox;
cfI s s
c   cw(1i)  cw(1i)
lp9 lp9 lp9.
New York Area Rocks
Era ⊕ Formation ⊕ Age (years)
Precambrian ⊕ Reading Prong ⊕ >1 billion
Paleozoic ⊕ Manhattan Prong ⊕ 400 million
Mesozoic ⊕ T{
.na
Newark Basin, incl.
Stockton, Lockatong, and Brunswick
formations; also Watchungs
and Palisades.
T} ⊕ 200 million
Cenozoic ⊕ Coastal Plain ⊕ T{
On Long Island 30,000 years;
Cretaceous sediments redeposited
by recent glaciation.
.ad
T}
.TE
```

Output:

New York Area Rocks		
Era	Formation	Age (years)
Precambrian	Reading Prong	>1 billion
Paleozoic	Manhattan Prong	400 million
Mesozoic	Newark Basin, incl. Stockton, Lockatong, and Brunswick formations; also Watchungs and Palisades.	200 million
Cenozoic	Coastal Plain	On Long Island 30,000 years; Cretaceous sediments redeposited by recent glaciation.

Input:

```
.EQ
delim $$
.EN


. . .


.TS
doublebox;
c c
l l.
Name Ⓣ Definition
.sp
.vs +2p
Gamma Ⓣ $GAMMA (z) = int sub 0 sup inf  t sup {z-1} e sup -t dt$
Sine Ⓣ $sin (x) = 1 over 2i ( e sup ix - e sup -ix )$
Error Ⓣ $ roman erf (z) = 2 over sqrt pi int sub 0 sup z e sup {-t sup 2} dt$
Bessel Ⓣ $ J sub 0 (z) = 1 over pi int sub 0 sup pi cos ( z sin theta ) d theta $
Zeta Ⓣ $ zeta (s) = sum from k=1 to inf k sup -s ~~( Re~s > 1)$
.vs -2p
.TE
```

Output:

Name	Definition
Gamma	$\Gamma(z) = \int_0^\infty t^{z-1} e^{-t}\,dt$
Sine	$\sin(x) = \dfrac{1}{2i}(e^{ix} - e^{-ix})$
Error	$\mathrm{erf}(z) = \dfrac{2}{\sqrt{\pi}} \int_0^z e^{-t^2}\,dt$
Bessel	$J_0(z) = \dfrac{1}{\pi} \int_0^\pi \cos(z\sin\theta)\,d\theta$
Zeta	$\zeta(s) = \sum\limits_{k=1}^{\infty} k^{-s} \quad (\mathrm{Re}\ s > 1)$

Input:

```
.TS
box, tab(:);
cb s s s s
cp-2 s s s s
c || c | c | c | c
c || c | c | c | c
r2 || n2 | n2 | n2 | n.
Readability of Text
Line Width and Leading for 10-Point Type
=
Line : Set : 1-Point : 2-Point : 4-Point
Width : Solid : Leading : Leading : Leading

9 Pica :\-9.3:\-6.0:\-5.3:\-7.1
14 Pica :\-4.5:\-0.6:\-0.3:\-1.7
19 Pica :\-5.0:\-5.1: 0.0:\-2.0
31 Pica :\-3.7:\-3.8:\-2.4:\-3.6
43 Pica :\-9.1:\-9.0:\-5.9:\-8.8
.TE
```

Output:

Readability of Text				
Line Width and Leading for 10-Point Type				
Line Width	Set Solid	1-Point Leading	2-Point Leading	4-Point Leading
9 Pica	−9.3	−6.0	−5.3	−7.1
14 Pica	−4.5	−0.6	−0.3	−1.7
19 Pica	−5.0	−5.1	0.0	−2.0
31 Pica	−3.7	−3.8	−2.4	−3.6
43 Pica	−9.1	−9.0	−5.9	−8.8

Input:

```
.TS
c s
cip-2 s
l n
a n.
Some London Transport Statistics
(Year 1964)
Railway route miles ⊤ 244
Tube ⊤ 66
Sub-surface ⊤ 22
Surface ⊤ 156
.sp .5
.T&
l r
a r.
Passenger traffic \- railway
Journeys ⊤ 674 million
Average length ⊤ 4.55 miles
Passenger miles ⊤ 3,066 million
.T&
l r
a r.
Passenger traffic \- road
Journeys ⊤ 2,252 million
Average length ⊤ 2.26 miles
Passenger miles ⊤ 5,094 million
.T&
l n
a n.
.sp .5
Vehicles ⊤ 12,521
Railway motor cars ⊤ 2,905
Railway trailer cars ⊤ 1,269
Total railway ⊤ 4,174
Omnibuses ⊤ 8,347
.T&
l n
a n.
.sp .5
Staff ⊤ 73,739
Administrative, etc. ⊤ 5,582
Civil engineering ⊤ 5,134
Electrical eng. ⊤ 1,714
Mech. eng. \- railway ⊤ 4,310
Mech. eng. \- road ⊤ 9,152
Railway operations ⊤ 8,930
Road operations ⊤ 35,946
Other ⊤ 2,971
.TE
```

Output:

Some London Transport Statistics

(Year 1964)

Railway route miles	244
Tube	66
Sub-surface	22
Surface	156
Passenger traffic — railway	
Journeys	674 million
Average length	4.55 miles
Passenger miles	3,066 million
Passenger traffic — road	
Journeys	2,252 million
Average length	2.26 miles
Passenger miles	5,094 million
Vehicles	12,521
Railway motor cars	2,905
Railway trailer cars	1,269
Total railway	4,174
Omnibuses	8,347
Staff	73,739
Administrative, etc.	5,582
Civil engineering	5,134
Electrical eng.	1,714
Mech. eng. — railway	4,310
Mech. eng. — road	9,152
Railway operations	8,930
Road operations	35,946
Other	2,971

Input:

```
.ps 8
.vs 10p
.TS
center box;
c s s
ci s s
c c c
lB l n.
New Jersey Representatives
(Democrats)
.sp .5
Name ⊤ Office address ⊤ Phone
.sp .5
James J. Florio ⊤ 23 S. White Horse Pike, Somerdale 08083 ⊤ 609-627-8222
William J. Hughes ⊤ 2920 Atlantic Ave., Atlantic City 08401 ⊤ 609-345-4844
James J. Howard ⊤ 801 Bangs Ave., Asbury Park 07712 ⊤ 201-774-1600
Frank Thompson, Jr. ⊤ 10 Rutgers Pl., Trenton 08618 ⊤ 609-599-1619
Andrew Maguire ⊤ 115 W. Passaic St., Rochelle Park 07662 ⊤ 201-843-0240
Robert A. Roe ⊤ U.S.P.O., 194 Ward St., Paterson 07510 ⊤ 201-523-5152
Henry Helstoski ⊤ 666 Paterson Ave., East Rutherford 07073 ⊤ 201-939-9090
Peter W. Rodino, Jr. ⊤ Suite 1435A, 970 Broad St., Newark 07102 ⊤ 201-645-3213
Joseph G. Minish ⊤ 308 Main St., Orange 07050 ⊤ 201-645-6363
Helen S. Meyner ⊤ 32 Bridge St., Lambertville 08530 ⊤ 609-397-1830
Dominick V. Daniels ⊤ 895 Bergen Ave., Jersey City 07306 ⊤ 201-659-7700
Edward J. Patten ⊤ Natl. Bank Bldg., Perth Amboy 08861 ⊤ 201-826-4610
.sp .5
.T&
ci s s
lB l n.
(Republicans)
.sp .5v
Millicent Fenwick ⊤ 41 N. Bridge St., Somerville 08876 ⊤ 201-722-8200
Edwin B. Forsythe ⊤ 301 Mill St., Moorestown 08057 ⊤ 609-235-6622
Matthew J. Rinaldo ⊤ 1961 Morris Ave., Union 07083 ⊤ 201-687-4235
.TE
.ps 10
.vs 12p
```

Output:

New Jersey Representatives		
(Democrats)		
Name	Office address	Phone
James J. Florio	23 S. White Horse Pike, Somerdale 08083	609-627-8222
William J. Hughes	2920 Atlantic Ave., Atlantic City 08401	609-345-4844
James J. Howard	801 Bangs Ave., Asbury Park 07712	201-774-1600
Frank Thompson, Jr.	10 Rutgers Pl., Trenton 08618	609-599-1619
Andrew Maguire	115 W. Passaic St., Rochelle Park 07662	201-843-0240
Robert A. Roe	U.S.P.O., 194 Ward St., Paterson 07510	201-523-5152
Henry Helstoski	666 Paterson Ave., East Rutherford 07073	201-939-9090
Peter W. Rodino, Jr.	Suite 1435A, 970 Broad St., Newark 07102	201-645-3213
Joseph G. Minish	308 Main St., Orange 07050	201-645-6363
Helen S. Meyner	32 Bridge St., Lambertville 08530	609-397-1830
Dominick V. Daniels	895 Bergen Ave., Jersey City 07306	201-659-7700
Edward J. Patten	Natl. Bank Bldg., Perth Amboy 08861	201-826-4610
(Republicans)		
Millicent Fenwick	41 N. Bridge St., Somerville 08876	201-722-8200
Edwin B. Forsythe	301 Mill St., Moorestown 08057	609-235-6622
Matthew J. Rinaldo	1961 Morris Ave., Union 07083	201-687-4235

This is a paragraph of normal text placed here only to indicate where the left and right margins are. In this way the reader can judge the appearance of centered tables or expanded tables, and observe how such tables are formatted.

Input:

```
.TS
expand;
c s s s
c c c c
l l n n.
Bell Labs Locations
Name ⊕ Address ⊕ Area Code ⊕ Phone
Holmdel ⊕ Holmdel, N. J. 07733 ⊕ 201 ⊕ 949-3000
Murray Hill ⊕ Murray Hill, N. J. 07974 ⊕ 201 ⊕ 582-6377
Whippany ⊕ Whippany, N. J. 07981 ⊕ 201 ⊕ 386-3000
Indian Hill ⊕ Naperville, Illinois 60540 ⊕ 312 ⊕ 690-2000
.TE
```

Output:

Bell Labs Locations			
Name	Address	Area Code	Phone
Holmdel	Holmdel, N. J. 07733	201	949-3000
Murray Hill	Murray Hill, N. J. 07974	201	582-6377
Whippany	Whippany, N. J. 07981	201	386-3000
Indian Hill	Naperville, Illinois 60540	312	690-2000

Input:

```
.TS
box;
cb  s  s  s
c│c│c  s
ltiw(1i) │ ltw(2i) │ lp8 │ lw(1.6i)p8.
Some Interesting Places

Name Ⓣ Description Ⓣ Practical Information

T{
American Museum of Natural History
T}ⓉT{
The collections fill 11.5 acres (Michelin) or 25 acres (MTA)
of exhibition halls on four floors.  There is a full-sized replica
of a blue whale and the world's largest star sapphire (stolen in 1964).
T}ⓉHoursⓉ10-5, ex. Sun 11-5, Wed. to 9
\^Ⓣ\^ⓉLocationⓉT{
Central Park West & 79th St.
T}
\^Ⓣ\^ⓉAdmissionⓉDonation: $1.00 asked
\^Ⓣ\^ⓉSubwayⓉAA to 81st St.
\^Ⓣ\^ⓉTelephoneⓉ212-873-4225

Bronx ZooⓉT{
About a mile long and .6 mile wide, this is the largest zoo in America.
A lion eats 18 pounds
of meat a day while a sea lion eats 15 pounds of fish.
T}ⓉHoursⓉT{
10-4:30 winter, to 5:00 summer
T}
\^Ⓣ\^ⓉLocationⓉT{
185th St. & Southern Blvd, the Bronx.
T}
\^Ⓣ\^ⓉAdmissionⓉ$1.00, but Tu,We,Th free
\^Ⓣ\^ⓉSubwayⓉ2, 5 to East Tremont Ave.
\^Ⓣ\^ⓉTelephoneⓉ212-933-1759

Brooklyn MuseumⓉT{
Five floors of galleries contain American and ancient art.
There are American period rooms and architectural ornaments saved
from wreckers, such as a classical figure from Pennsylvania Station.
T}ⓉHoursⓉWed-Sat, 10-5, Sun 12-5
\^Ⓣ\^ⓉLocationⓉT{
Eastern Parkway & Washington Ave., Brooklyn.
T}
\^Ⓣ\^ⓉAdmissionⓉFree
\^Ⓣ\^ⓉSubwayⓉ2,3 to Eastern Parkway.
\^Ⓣ\^ⓉTelephoneⓉ212-638-5000

T{
New-York Historical Society
T}ⓉT{
All the original paintings for Audubon's
.I
Birds of America
.R
are here, as are exhibits of American decorative arts, New York history,
Hudson River school paintings, carriages, and glass paperweights.
T}ⓉHoursⓉT{
Tues-Fri & Sun, 1-5; Sat 10-5
T}
\^Ⓣ\^ⓉLocationⓉT{
Central Park West & 77th St.
T}
\^Ⓣ\^ⓉAdmissionⓉFree
\^Ⓣ\^ⓉSubwayⓉAA to 81st St.
\^Ⓣ\^ⓉTelephoneⓉ212-873-3400
.TE
```

Output:

Some Interesting Places		
Name	Description	Practical Information
American Museum of Natural History	The collections fill 11.5 acres (Michelin) or 25 acres (MTA) of exhibition halls on four floors. There is a full-sized replica of a blue whale and the world's largest star sapphire (stolen in 1964).	Hours 10-5, ex. Sun 11-5, Wed. to 9 Location Central Park West & 79th St. Admission Donation: $1.00 asked Subway AA to 81st St. Telephone 212-873-4225
Bronx Zoo	About a mile long and .6 mile wide, this is the largest zoo in America. A lion eats 18 pounds of meat a day while a sea lion eats 15 pounds of fish.	Hours 10-4:30 winter, to 5:00 summer Location 185th St. & Southern Blvd, the Bronx. Admission $1.00, but Tu,We,Th free Subway 2, 5 to East Tremont Ave. Telephone 212-933-1759
Brooklyn Museum	Five floors of galleries contain American and ancient art. There are American period rooms and architectural ornaments saved from wreckers, such as a classical figure from Pennsylvania Station.	Hours Wed-Sat, 10-5, Sun 12-5 Location Eastern Parkway & Washington Ave., Brooklyn. Admission Free Subway 2,3 to Eastern Parkway. Telephone 212-638-5000
New-York Historical Society	All the original paintings for Audubon's *Birds of America* are here, as are exhibits of American decorative arts, New York history, Hudson River school paintings, carriages, and glass paperweights.	Hours Tues-Fri & Sun, 1-5; Sat 10-5 Location Central Park West & 77th St. Admission Free Subway AA to 81st St. Telephone 212-873-3400

Acknowledgments.

Many thanks are due to J. C. Blinn, who has done a large amount of testing and assisted with the design of the program. He has also written many of the more intelligible sentences in this document and helped edit all of it. All phototypesetting programs on UNIX are dependent on the work of the late J. F. Ossanna, whose assistance with this program in particular had been most helpful. This program is patterned on a table formatter originally written by J. F. Gimpel. The assistance of T. A. Dolotta, B. W. Kernighan, and J. N. Sturman is gratefully acknowledged.

References.

[1]   J. F. Ossanna, *NROFF/TROFF User's Manual*, Computing Science Technical Report No. 54, Bell Laboratories, 1976.

[2]   K. Thompson and D. M. Ritchie, "The UNIX Time-Sharing System," *Comm. ACM.* **17**, pp. 365–75 (1974).

[3]   B. W. Kernighan and L. L. Cherry, "A System for Typesetting Mathematics," *Comm. ACM.* **18**, pp. 151–57 (1975).

[4]   M. E. Lesk, *Typing Documents on UNIX*, UNIX Programmer's Manual, Volume 2.

[5]   M. E. Lesk and B. W. Kernighan, *Computer Typesetting of Technical Journals on UNIX, Proc. AFIPS NCC*, vol. 46, pp. 879-888 (1977).

[6]   J. R. Mashey and D. W. Smith, "Documentation Tools and Techniques," *Proc. 2nd Int. Conf. on Software Engineering*, pp. 177-181 (October, 1976).

List of Tbl Command Characters and Words

Command	Meaning	Section
a A	Alphabetic subcolumn	2
allbox	Draw box around all items	1
b B	Boldface item	2
box	Draw box around table	1
c C	Centered column	2
center	Center table in page	1
doublebox	Doubled box around table	1
e E	Equal width columns	2
expand	Make table full line width	1
f F	Font change	2
i I	Italic item	2
l L	Left adjusted column	2
n N	Numerical column	2
nnn	Column separation	2
p P	Point size change	2
r R	Right adjusted column	2
s S	Spanned item	2
t T	Vertical spanning at top	2
tab (x)	Change data separator character	1
T{ T}	Text block	3
v V	Vertical spacing change	2
w W	Minimum width value	2
.xx	Included *troff* command	3
|	Vertical line	2
||	Double vertical line	2
^	Vertical span	2
\^	Vertical span	3
=	Double horizontal line	2,3
_	Horizontal line	2,3
_	Short horizontal line	3
\Rx	Repeat character	3

Some Applications of Inverted Indexes on the UNIX System

M. E. Lesk

Bell Laboratories
Murray Hill, New Jersey 07974

1. Introduction.

The UNIX[†] system has many utilities (e.g. *grep, awk, lex, egrep, fgrep,* ...) to search through files of text, but most of them are based on a linear scan through the entire file, using some deterministic automaton. This memorandum discusses a program which uses inverted indexes[1] and can thus be used on much larger data bases.

As with any indexing system, of course, there are some disadvantages; once an index is made, the files that have been indexed can not be changed without remaking the index. Thus applications are restricted to those making many searches of relatively stable data. Furthermore, these programs depend on hashing, and can only search for exact matches of whole keywords. It is not possible to look for arithmetic or logical expressions (e.g. "date greater than 1970") or for regular expression searching such as that in *lex.*[2]

Currently there are two uses of this software, the *refer* preprocessor to format references, and the *lookall* command to search through all text files on the UNIX system.

The remaining sections of this memorandum discuss the searching programs and their uses. Section 2 explains the operation of the searching algorithm and describes the data collected for use with the *lookall* command. The more important application, *refer* has a user's description in section 3. Section 4 goes into more detail on reference files for the benefit of those who wish to add references to data bases or write new *troff* macros for use with *refer*. The options to make *refer* collect identical citations, or otherwise relocate and adjust references, are described in section 5. The UNIX manual sections for *refer, lookall,* and associated commands are attached as appendices.

2. Searching.

The indexing and searching process is divided into two phases, each made of two parts. These are shown below.

A.   Construct the index.

(1)   Find keys — turn the input files into a sequence of tags and keys, where each tag identifies a distinct item in the input and the keys for each such item are the strings under which it is to be indexed.

(2)   Hash and sort — prepare a set of inverted indexes from which, given a set of keys, the appropriate item tags can be found quickly.

B.   Retrieve an item in response to a query.

---

†UNIX is a Trademark of Bell Laboratories.

1.   D. Knuth, *The Art of Computer Programming: Vol. 3, Sorting and Searching,* Addison-Wesley, Reading, Mass. (1977). See section 6.5.

2.   M. E. Lesk, "Lex — A Lexical Analyzer Generator," Comp. Sci. Tech. Rep. No. 39, Bell Laboratories, Murray Hill, New Jersey (D).

(3) Search — Given some keys, look through the files prepared by the hashing and sorting facility and derive the appropriate tags.

(4) Deliver — Given the tags, find the original items. This completes the searching process.

The first phase, making the index, is presumably done relatively infrequently. It should, of course, be done whenever the data being indexed change. In contrast, the second phase, retrieving items, is presumably done often, and must be rapid.

An effort is made to separate code which depends on the data being handled from code which depends on the searching procedure. The search algorithm is involved only in steps (2) and (3), while knowledge of the actual data files is needed only by steps (1) and (4). Thus it is easy to adapt to different data files or different search algorithms.

To start with, it is necessary to have some way of selecting or generating keys from input files. For dealing with files that are basically English, we have a key-making program which automatically selects words and passes them to the hashing and sorting program (step 2). The format used has one line for each input item, arranged as follows:

> name:start,length (tab) key1 key2 key3 ...

where *name* is the file name, *start* is the starting byte number, and *length* is the number of bytes in the entry.

These lines are the only input used to make the index. The first field (the file name, byte position, and byte count) is the tag of the item and can be used to retrieve it quickly. Normally, an item is either a whole file or a section of a file delimited by blank lines. After the tab, the second field contains the keys. The keys, if selected by the automatic program, are any alphanumeric strings which are not among the 100 most frequent words in English and which are not entirely numeric (except for four-digit numbers beginning 19, which are accepted as dates). Keys are truncated to six characters and converted to lower case. Some selection is needed if the original items are ver lrge. We normally just take the first n keys, with n less than 100 or so; this replaces any attempt at intelligent selection. One file in our system is a complete English dictionary; it would presumably be retrieved for all queries.

To generate an inverted index to the list of record tags and keys, the keys are hashed and sorted to produce an index. What is wanted, ideally, is a series of lists showing the tags associated with each key. To condense this, what is actually produced is a list showing the tags associated with each hash code, and thus with some set of keys. To speed up access and further save space, a set of three or possibly four files is produced. These files are:

File	Contents
entry	Pointers to posting file for each hash code
posting	Lists of tag pointers for each hash code
tag	Tags for each item
key	Keys for each item (optional)

The posting file comprises the real data: it contains a sequence of lists of items posted under each hash code. To speed up searching, the entry file is an array of pointers into the posting file, one per potential hash code. Furthermore, the items in the lists in the posting file are not referred to by their complete tag, but just by an address in the tag file, which gives the complete tags. The key file is optional and contains a copy of the keys used in the indexing.

The searching process starts with a query, containing several keys. The goal is to obtain all items which were indexed under these keys. The query keys are hashed, and the pointers in the entry file used to access the lists in the posting file. These lists are addresses in the tag file of documents posted under the hash codes derived from the query. The common items from all lists are determined; this must include the items indexed by every key, but may also contain some items which are false drops, since items referenced by the correct hash codes need not actually have contained the correct keys. Normally, if there are several keys in the query, there are not likely to be many false drops in the final combined list even though each hash code is somewhat ambiguous. The actual tags are then obtained from the tag file, and to guard against the possibility that an item has false-dropped on some hash code in the query, the original items are normally obtained from the delivery program (4) and the query keys checked against them by string comparison.

Usually, therefore, the check for bad drops is made against the original file. However, if the key derivation procedure is complex, it may be preferable to check against the keys fed to program (2). In this case the optional key file which contains the keys associated with each item is generated, and the item tag is supplemented by a string

    ;start,length

which indicates the starting byte number in the key file and the length of the string of keys for each item. This file is not usually necessary with the present key-selection program, since the keys always appear in the original document.

There is also an option ($-Cn$) for coordination level searching. This retrieves items which match all but n of the query keys. The items are retrieved in the order of the number of keys that they match. Of course, n must be less than the number of query keys (nothing is retrieved unless it matches at least one key).

As an example, consider one set of 4377 references, comprising 660,000 bytes. This included 51,000 keys, of which 5,900 were distinct keys. The hash table is kept full to save space (at the expense of time); 995 of 997 possible hash codes were used. The total set of index files (no key file) included 171,000 bytes, about 26% of the original file size. It took 8 minutes of processor time to hash, sort, and write the index. To search for a single query with the resulting index took 1.9 seconds of processor time, while to find the same paper with a sequential linear search using *grep* (reading all of the tags and keys) took 12.3 seconds of processor time.

We have also used this software to index all of the English stored on our UNIX system. This is the index searched by the *lookall* command. On a typical day there were 29,000 files in our user file system, containing about 152,000,000 bytes. Of these 5,300 files, containing 32,000,000 bytes (about 21%) were English text. The total number of 'words' (determined mechanically) was 5,100,000. Of these 227,000 were selected as keys; 19,000 were distinct, hashing to 4,900 (of 5,000 possible) different hash codes. The resulting inverted file indexes used 845,000 bytes, or about 2.6% of the size of the original files. The particularly small indexes are caused by the fact that keys are taken from only the first 50 non-common words of some very long input files.

Even this large *lookall* index can be searched quickly. For example, to find this document by looking for the keys "lesk inverted indexes" required 1.7 seconds of processor time and system time. By comparison, just to search the 800,000 byte dictionary (smaller than even the inverted indexes, let alone the 32,000,000 bytes of text files) with *grep* takes 29 seconds of processor time. The *lookall* program is thus useful when looking for a document which you believe is stored on-line, but do not know where. For example, many memos from the Computing Science Research Center are in its UNIX file system, but it is often difficult to guess where a particular memo might be (it might have several authors, each with many directories, and have been worked on by a secretary with yet more directories). Instructions for the use of the *lookall* command are given in the manual section, shown in the appendix to this memorandum.

The only indexes maintained routinely are those of publication lists and all English files. To make other indexes, the programs for making keys, sorting them, searching the indexes, and delivering answers must be used. Since they are usually invoked as parts of higher-level commands, they are not in the default command directory, but are available to any user in the directory *lusr/lib/refer*. Three programs are of interest: *mkey*, which isolates keys from input files; *inv*, which makes an index from a set of keys; and *hunt*, which searches the index and delivers the items. Note that the two parts of the retrieval phase are combined into one program, to avoid the excessive system work and delay which would result from running these as separate processes.

These three commands have a large number of options to adapt to different kinds of input. The user not interested in the detailed description that now follows may skip to section 3, which describes the *refer* program, a packaged-up version of these tools specifically oriented towards formatting references.

Make Keys. The program *mkey* is the key-making program corresponding to step (1) in phase A. Normally, it reads its input from the file names given as arguments, and if there are no arguments it reads from the standard input. It assumes that blank lines in the input delimit separate items, for each of which a different line of keys should be generated. The lines of keys are written on the standard output. Keys are any alphanumeric string in the input not among the most frequent words in English and not entirely numeric (except that all-numeric strings are acceptable if they are between 1900 and 1999). In the output, keys are translated to lower case, and truncated to six characters in length; any associated punctuation is removed. The following flag arguments are recognized by *mkey:*

−**c** *name*	Name of file of common words; default is */usr/lib/eign*.
−**f** *name*	Read a list of files from *name* and take each as an input argument.
−**i** *chars*	Ignore all lines which begin with '%' followed by any character in *chars*.
−**k***n*	Use at most *n* keys per input item.
−**l***n*	Ignore items shorter than *n* letters long.
−**n***m*	Ignore as a key any word in the first *m* words of the list of common English words. The default is 100.
−**s**	Remove the labels *(file:start,length)* from the output; just give the keys. Used when searching rather than indexing.
−**w**	Each whole file is a separate item; blank lines in files are irrelevant.

The normal arguments for indexing references are the defaults, which are −*c /usr/lib/eign*, −*n100*, and −*l3*. For searching, the −*s* option is also needed. When the big *lookall* index of all English files is run, the options are −*w*, −*k50*, and −*f (filelist)*. When running on textual input, the *mkey* program processes about 1000 English words per processor second. Unless the −*k* option is used (and the input files are long enough for it to take effect) the output of *mkey* is comparable in size to its input.

Hash and invert. The *inv* program computes the hash codes and writes the inverted files. It reads the output of *mkey* and writes the set of files described earlier in this section. It expects one argument, which is used as the base name for the three (or four) files to be written. Assuming an argument of *Index* (the default) the entry file is named *Index.ia*, the posting file *Index.ib*, the tag file *Index.ic*, and the key file (if present) *Index.id*. The *inv* program recognizes the following options:

−**a**	Append the new keys to a previous set of inverted files, making new files if there is no old set using the same base name.
−**d**	Write the optional key file. This is needed when you can not check for false drops by looking for the keys in the original inputs, i.e. when the key derivation procedure is complicated and the output keys are not words from the input files.
−**h***n*	The hash table size is *n* (default 997); *n* should be prime. Making *n* bigger saves search time and spends disk space.

−i[u] *name*	Take input from file *name*, instead of the standard input; if **u** is present *name* is unlinked when the sort is started. Using this option permits the sort scratch space to overlap the disk space used for input keys.
−n	Make a completely new set of inverted files, ignoring previous files.
−p	Pipe into the sort program, rather than writing a temporary input file. This saves disk space and spends processor time.
−v	Verbose mode; print a summary of the number of keys which finished indexing.

About half the time used in *inv* is in the contained sort. Assuming the sort is roughly linear, however, a guess at the total timing for *inv* is 250 keys per second. The space used is usually of more importance: the entry file uses four bytes per possible hash (note the **−h** option), and the tag file around 15-20 bytes per item indexed. Roughly, the posting file contains one item for each key instance and one item for each possible hash code; the items are two bytes long if the tag file is less than 65336 bytes long, and the items are four bytes wide if the tag file is greater than 65536 bytes long. To minimize storage, the hash tables should be over-full; for most of the files indexed in this way, there is no other real choice, since the *entry* file must fit in memory.

Searching and Retrieving. The *hunt* program retrieves items from an index. It combines, as mentioned above, the two parts of phase (B): search and delivery. The reason why it is efficient to combine delivery and search is partly to avoid starting unnecessary processes, and partly because the delivery operation must be a part of the search operation in any case. Because of the hashing, the search part takes place in two stages: first items are retrieved which have the right hash codes associated with them, and then the actual items are inspected to determine false drops, i.e. to determine if anything with the right hash codes doesn't really have the right keys. Since the original item is retrieved to check on false drops, it is efficient to present it immediately, rather than only giving the tag as output and later retrieving the item again. If there were a separate key file, this argument would not apply, but separate key files are not common.

Input to *hunt* is taken from the standard input, one query per line. Each query should be in *mkey −s* output format; all lower case, no punctuation. The *hunt* program takes one argument which specifies the base name of the index files to be searched. Only one set of index files can be searched at a time, although many text files may be indexed as a group, of course. If one of the text files has been changed since the index, that file is searched with *fgrep;* this may occasionally slow down the searching, and care should be taken to avoid having many out of date files. The following option arguments are recognized by *hunt:*

−a	Give all output; ignore checking for false drops.
−C*n*	Coordination level *n;* retrieve items with not more than *n* terms of the input missing; default *C0*, implying that each search term must be in the output items.
−F[yn*d*]	"−Fy" gives the text of all the items found; "−Fn" suppresses them. "−F*d*" where *d* is an integer gives the text of the first *d* items. The default is *−Fy*.
−g	Do not use *fgrep* to search files changed since the index was made; print an error comment instead.
−i *string*	Take *string* as input, instead of reading the standard input.
−l *n*	The maximum length of internal lists of candidate items is *n;* default 1000.
−o *string*	Put text output ("−Fy") in *string;* of use *only* when invoked from another program.

−p	Print hash code frequencies; mostly for use in optimizing hash table sizes.
−T[yn*d***]**	"−Ty" gives the tags of the items found; "−Tn" suppresses them. "−T*d*" where *d* is an integer gives the first *d* tags. The default is −*Tn*.
−t *string*	Put tag output ("−Ty") in *string;* of use *only* when invoked from another program.

The timing of *hunt* is complex. Normally the hash table is overfull, so that there will be many false drops on any single term; but a multi-term query will have few false drops on all terms. Thus if a query is underspecified (one search term) many potential items will be examined and discarded as false drops, wasting time. If the query is overspecified (a dozen search terms) many keys will be examined only to verify that the single item under consideration has that key posted. The variation of search time with number of keys is shown in the table below. Queries of varying length were constructed to retrieve a particular document from the file of references. In the sequence to the left, search terms were chosen so as to select the desired paper as quickly as possible. In the sequence on the right, terms were chosen inefficiently, so that the query did not uniquely select the desired document until four keys had been used. The same document was the target in each case, and the final set of eight keys are also identical; the differences at five, six and seven keys are produced by measurement error, not by the slightly different key lists.

Efficient Keys				Inefficient Keys			
No. keys	Total drops (incl. false)	Retrieved Documents	Search time (seconds)	No. keys	Total drops (incl. false)	Retrieved Documents	Search time (seconds)
1	15	3	1.27	1	68	55	5.96
2	1	1	0.11	2	29	29	2.72
3	1	1	0.14	3	8	8	0.95
4	1	1	0.17	4	1	1	0.18
5	1	1	0.19	5	1	1	0.21
6	1	1	0.23	6	1	1	0.22
7	1	1	0.27	7	1	1	0.26
8	1	1	0.29	8	1	1	0.29

As would be expected, the optimal search is achieved when the query just specifies the answer; however, overspecification is quite cheap. Roughly, the time required by *hunt* can be approximated as 30 milliseconds per search key plus 75 milliseconds per dropped document (whether it is a false drop or a real answer). In general, overspecification can be recommended; it protects the user against additions to the data base which turn previously uniquely-answered queries into ambiguous queries.

The careful reader will have noted an enormous discrepancy between these times and the earlier quoted time of around 1.9 seconds for a search. The times here are purely for the search and retrieval: they are measured by running many searches through a single invocation of the *hunt* program alone. Usually, the UNIX command processor (the shell) must start both the *mkey* and *hunt* processes for each query, and arrange for the output of *mkey* to be fed to the *hunt* program. This adds a fixed overhead of about 1.7 seconds of processor time to any single search. Furthermore, remember that all these times are processor times: on a typical morning on our PDP 11/70 system, with about one dozen people logged on, to obtain 1 second of processor time for the search program took between 2 and 12 seconds of real time, with a median of 3.9 seconds and a mean of 4.8 seconds. Thus, although the work involved in a single search may be only 200 milliseconds, after you add the 1.7 seconds of startup processor time and then assume a 4:1 elapsed/processor time ratio, it will be 8 seconds before any response is printed.

3. Selecting and Formatting References for TROFF

The major application of the retrieval software is *refer,* which is a *troff* preprocessor like *eqn*.[3] It scans its input looking for items of the form

```
.[
imprecise citation
.]
```

where an imprecise citation is merely a string of words found in the relevant bibliographic citation. This is translated into a properly formatted reference. If the imprecise citation does not correctly identify a single paper (either selecting no papers or too many) a message is given. The data base of citations searched may be tailored to each system, and individual users may specify their own citation files. On our system, the default data base is accumulated from the publication lists of the members of our organization, plus about half a dozen personal bibliographies that were collected. The present total is about 4300 citations, but this increases steadily. Even now, the data base covers a large fraction of local citations.

For example, the reference for the *eqn* paper above was specified as

```
...
preprocessor like
.I eqn.
.[
kernighan cherry acm 1975
.]
It scans its input looking for items
...
```

This paper was itself printed using *refer.* The above input text was processed by *refer* as well as *tbl* and *troff* by the command

refer memo-file | tbl | troff −ms

and the reference was automatically translated into a correct citation to the ACM paper on mathematical typesetting.

The procedure to use to place a reference in a paper using *refer* is as follows. First, use the *lookbib* command to check that the paper is in the data base and to find out what keys are necessary to retrieve it. This is done by typing *lookbib* and then typing some potential queries until a suitable query is found. For example, had one started to find the *eqn* paper shown above by presenting the query

```
$ lookbib
kernighan cherry
(EOT)
```

lookbib would have found several items; experimentation would quickly have shown that the query given above is adequate. Overspecifying the query is of course harmless; it is even desirable, since it decreases the risk that a document added to the publication data base in the future will be retrieved in addition to the intended document. The extra time taken by even a grossly overspecified query is quite small. A particularly careful reader may have noticed that "acm" does not appear in the printed citation; we have supplemented some of the data base items with extra keywords, such as common abbreviations for journals or other sources, to aid in searching.

If the reference is in the data base, the query that retrieved it can be inserted in the text, between .[and .] brackets. If it is not in the data base, it can be typed into a private file of

---

3.   B. W. Kernighan and L. L. Cherry, "A System for Typesetting Mathematics," *Comm. Assoc. Comp. Mach.* **18,** pp.151-157 (March 1975).

references, using the format discussed in the next section, and then the −**p** option used to search this private file. Such a command might read (if the private references are called *myfile*)

   refer −p myfile document| tbl | eqn | troff −ms . . .

where *tbl* and/or *eqn* could be omitted if not needed. The use of the −*ms* macros[4] or some other macro package, however, is essential. *Refer* only generates the data for the references; exact formatting is done by some macro package, and if none is supplied the references will not be printed.

By default, the references are numbered sequentially, and the −*ms* macros format references as footnotes at the bottom of the page. This memorandum is an example of that style. Other possibilities are discussed in section 5 below.

4. Reference Files.

A reference file is a set of bibliographic references usable with *refer*. It can be indexed using the software described in section 2 for fast searching. What *refer* does is to read the input document stream, looking for imprecise citation references. It then searches through reference files to find the full citations, and inserts them into the document. The format of the full citation is arranged to make it convenient for a macro package, such as the −*ms* macros, to format the reference for printing. Since the format of the final reference is determined by the desired style of output, which is determined by the macros used, *refer* avoids forcing any kind of reference appearance. All it does is define a set of string registers which contain the basic information about the reference; and provide a macro call which is expanded by the macro package to format the reference. It is the responsibility of the final macro package to see that the reference is actually printed; if no macros are used, and the output of *refer* fed untranslated to *troff,* nothing at all will be printed.

The strings defined by *refer* are taken directly from the files of references, which are in the following format. The references should be separated by blank lines. Each reference is a sequence of lines beginning with % and followed by a key-letter. The remainder of that line, and successive lines until the next line beginning with %, contain the information specified by the key-letter. In general, *refer* does not interpret the information, but merely presents it to the macro package for final formatting. A user with a separate macro package, for example, can add new key-letters or use the existing ones for other purposes without bothering *refer*. ·

The meaning of the key-letters given below, in particular, is that assigned by the −*ms* macros. Not all information, obviously, is used with each citation. For example, if a document is both an internal memorandum and a journal article, the macros ignore the memorandum version and cite only the journal article. Some kinds of information are not used at all in printing the reference; if a user does not like finding references by specifying title or author keywords, and prefers to add specific keywords to the citation, a field is available which is searched but not printed (**K**).

The key letters currently recognized by *refer* and −*ms,* with the kind of information implied, are:

---

4.   M. E. Lesk, *Typing Documents on UNIX and GCOS: The -ms Macros for Troff,* Bell Laboratories internal memorandum (1977).

Key	Information specified	Key	Information specified
A	Author's name	N	Issue number
B	Title of book containing item	O	Other information
C	City of publication	P	Page(s) of article
D	Date	R	Technical report reference
E	Editor of book containing item	T	Title
G	Government (NTIS) ordering number	V	Volume number
I	Issuer (publisher)		
J	Journal name		
K	Keys (for searching)	X	or
L	Label	Y	or
M	Memorandum label	Z	Information not used by *refer*

For example, a sample reference could be typed as:

```
%T Bounds on the Complexity of the Maximal
Common Subsequence Problem
%Z ctr127
%A A. V. Aho
%A D. S. Hirschberg
%A J. D. Ullman
%J J. ACM
%V 23
%N 1
%P 1-12
%M abcd-78
%D Jan. 1976
```

Order is irrelevant, except that authors are shown in the order given. The output of *refer* is a stream of string definitions, one for each of the fields of each reference, as shown below.

```
.]-
.ds [A authors' names ...
.ds [T title ...
.ds [J journal ...
...
.] [ type-number
```

The *refer* program, in general, does not concern itself with the significance of the strings. The different fields are treated identically by *refer*, except that the X, Y and Z fields are ignored (see the −i option of *mkey*) in indexing and searching. All *refer* does is select the appropriate citation, based on the keys. The macro package must arrange the strings so as to produce an appropriately formatted citation. In this process, it uses the convention that the 'T' field is the title, the 'J' field the journal, and so forth.

The *refer* program does arrange the citation to simplify the macro package's job, however. The special macro .]− precedes the string definitions and the special macro .][follows. These are changed from the input .[and .] so that running the same file through *refer* again is harmless. The .]− macro can be used by the macro package to initialize. The .][macro, which should be used to print the reference, is given an argument *type-number* to indicate the kind of reference, as follows:

Value	Kind of reference
1	Journal article
2	Book
3	Article within book
4	Technical report
5	Bell Labs technical memorandum
0	Other

The type is determined by the presence or absence of particular fields in the citation (a journal article must have a 'J' field, a book must have an 'I' field, and so forth). To a small extent, this violates the above rule that *refer* does not concern itself with the contents of the citation; however, the classification of the citation in *troff* macros would require a relatively expensive and obscure program. Any macro writer may, of course, preserve consistency by ignoring the argument to the .][macro.

The reference is flagged in the text with the sequence

([.number(.]

where *number* is the footnote number. The strings [. and .] should be used by the macro package to format the reference flag in the text. These strings can be replaced for a particular footnote, as described in section 5. The footnote number (or other signal) is available to the reference macro .][as the string register [F. To simplify dealing with a text reference that occurs at the end of a sentence, *refer* treats a reference which follows a period in a special way. The period is removed, and the reference is preceded by a call for the string <. and followed by a call for the string >. For example, if a reference follows "end." it will appear as

end*(<.*([.number*(.]*(>.

where *number* is the footnote number. The macro package should turn either the string >. or <. into a period and delete the other one. This permits the output to have either the form "end[31]." or "end.[31]" as the macro package wishes. Note that in one case the period precedes the number and in the other it follows the number.

In some cases users wish to suspend the searching, and merely use the reference macro formatting. That is, the user doesn't want to provide a search key between .[and .] brackets, but merely the reference lines for the appropriate document. Alternatively, the user can wish to add a few fields to those in the reference as in the standard file, or override some fields. Altering or replacing fields, or supplying whole references, is easily done by inserting lines beginning with %; any such line is taken as direct input to the reference processor rather than keys to be searched. Thus

```
.[
key1 key2 key3 ...
%Q New format item
%R Override report name
.]
```

makes the indicates changes to the result of searching for the keys. All of the search keys must be given before the first % line.

If no search keys are provided, an entire citation can be provided in-line in the text. For example, if the *eqn* paper citation were to be inserted in this way, rather than by searching for it in the data base, the input would read

```
...
preprocessor like
.I eqn.
.[
%A B. W. Kernighan
%A L. L. Cherry
%T A System for Typesetting Mathematics
%J Comm. ACM
%V 18
%N 3
%P 151-157
%D March 1975
.]
It scans its input looking for items
...
```

This would produce a citation of the same appearance as that resulting from the file search.

As shown, fields are normally turned into *troff* strings. Sometimes users would rather have them defined as macros, so that other *troff* commands can be placed into the data. When this is necessary, simply double the control character **%** in the data. Thus the input

```
.[
%V 23
%%M
Bell Laboratories,
Murray Hill, N.J. 07974
.]
```

is processed by *refer* into

```
.ds [V 23
.de [M
Bell Laboratories,
Murray Hill, N.J. 07974
..
```

The information after **%%M** is defined as a macro to be invoked by **.[M** while the information after **%V** is turned into a string to be invoked by ***([V**. At present −*ms* expects all information as strings.

5. Collecting References and other Refer Options

Normally, the combination of *refer* and −*ms* formats output as *troff* footnotes which are consecutively numbered and placed at the bottom of the page. However, options exist to place the references at the end; to arrange references alphabetically by senior author; and to indicate references by strings in the text of the form [Name1975a] rather than by number. Whenever references are not placed at the bottom of a page identical references are coalesced.

For example, the −**e** option to *refer* specifies that references are to be collected; in this case they are output whenever the sequence

```
.[
$LIST$
.]
```

is encountered. Thus, to place references at the end of a paper, the user would run *refer* with the −*e* option and place the above $LIST$ commands after the last line of the text. *Refer* will then move all the references to that point. To aid in formatting the collected references, *refer* writes the references preceded by the line

```
.]<
```

and followed by the line

```
.]>
```

to invoke special macros before and after the references.

Another possible option to *refer* is the −s option to specify sorting of references. The default, of course, is to list references in the order presented. The −s option implies the −e option, and thus requires a

```
.[
$LIST$
.]
```

entry to call out the reference list. The −s option may be followed by a string of letters, numbers, and '+' signs indicating how the references are to be sorted. The sort is done using the fields whose key-letters are in the string as sorting keys; the numbers indicate how many of the fields are to be considered, with '+' taken as a large number. Thus the default is −sAD meaning "Sort on senior author, then date." To sort on all authors and then title, specify −sA+T. And to sort on two authors and then the journal, write −sA2J.

Other options to *refer* change the signal or label inserted in the text for each reference. Normally these are just sequential numbers, and their exact placement (within brackets, as superscripts, etc.) is determined by the macro package. The −l option replaces reference numbers by strings composed of the senior author's last name, the date, and a disambiguating letter. If a number follows the l as in −l3 only that many letters of the last name are used in the label string. To abbreviate the date as well the form -lm,n shortens the last name to the first m letters and the date to the last n digits. For example, the option −l3,2 would refer to the *eqn* paper (reference 3) by the signal *Ker75a*, since it is the first cited reference by Kernighan in 1975.

A user wishing to specify particular labels for a private bibliography may use the −k option. Specifying −kx causes the field x to be used as a label. The default is L. If this field ends in −, that character is replaced by a sequence letter; otherwise the field is used exactly as given.

If none of the *refer*-produced signals are desired, the −b option entirely suppresses automatic text signals.

If the user wishes to override the −*ms* treatment of the reference signal (which is normally to enclose the number in brackets in *nroff* and make it a superscript in *troff*) this can be done easily. If the lines .[or .] contain anything following these characters, the remainders of these lines are used to surround the reference signal, instead of the default. Thus, for example, to say "See reference (2)." and avoid "See reference.[2]" the input might appear

```
See reference
.[ (
imprecise citation ...
.]).
```

Note that blanks are significant in this construction. If a permanent change is desired in the style of reference signals, however, it is probably easier to redefine the strings [. and .] (which are used to bracket each signal) than to change each citation.

Although normally *refer* limits itself to retrieving the data for the reference, and leaves to a macro package the job of arranging that data as required by the local format, there are two special options for rearrangements that can not be done by macro packages. The −c option puts fields into all upper case (CAPS-SMALL CAPS in *troff* output). The key-letters indicated what information is to be translated to upper case follow the c, so that −cAJ means that authors' names and journals are to be in caps. The −a option writes the names of authors last name first, that is *A. D. Hall, Jr.* is written as *Hall, A. D. Jr.* The citation form of the *Journal of the ACM*, for example, would require both −cA and −a options. This produces authors' names in the style KERNIGHAN, B. W. AND CHERRY, L. L. for the previous example. The −a option may be followed by a number to indicate how many author names should be reversed; −a1 (without any −c option) would produce *Kernighan, B. W. and L. L. Cherry,* for example.

Finally, there is also the previously-mentioned −p option to let the user specify a private file of references to be searched before the public files. Note that *refer* does not insist on a previously made index for these files. If a file is named which contains reference data but is not indexed, it will be searched (more slowly) by *refer* using *fgrep*. In this way it is easy for users to keep small files of new references, which can later be added to the public data bases.

Updating Publication Lists

M. E. Lesk

1. Introduction.

This note describes several commands to update the publication lists. The data base consisting of these lists is kept in a set of files in the directory */usr/dict/papers* on the Version 7 UNIX† system. The reason for having special commands to update these files is that they are indexed, and the only reasonable way to find the items to be updated is to use the index. However, altering the files destroys the usefulness of the index, and makes further editing difficult. So the recommended procedure is to

(1) Prepare additions, deletions, and changes in separate files.

(2) Update the data base and reindex.

Whenever you make changes, etc. it is necessary to run the "add & index" step before logging off; otherwise the changes do not take effect. The next section shows the format of the files in the data base. After that, the procedures for preparing additions, preparing changes, preparing deletions, and updating the public data base are given.

2. Publication Format.

The format of a data base entry is given completely in "Some Applications of Inverted Indexes on UNIX" by M. E. Lesk, the first part of this report, and is summarized here via a few examples. In each example, first the output format for an item is shown, and then the corresponding data base entry.

Journal article:

> A. V. Aho, D. J. Hirschberg, and J. D. Ullman, "Bounds on the Complexity of the Maximal Common Subsequence Problem," *J. Assoc. Comp. Mach.*, vol. 23, no. 1, pp. 1-12 (Jan. 1976).

> %T Bounds on the Complexity of the Maximal Common
> Subsequence Problem
> %A A. V. Aho
> %A D. S. Hirschberg
> %A J. D. Ullman
> %J J. Assoc. Comp. Mach.
> %V 23
> %N 1
> %P 1-12
> %D Jan. 1976
> %M Memo abcd...

---

†UNIX is a Trademark of Bell Laboratories.

Conference proceedings:

B. Prabhala and R. Sethi, "Efficient Computation of Expressions with Common Subexpressions," *Proc. 5th ACM Symp. on Principles of Programming Languages,* pp. 222-230, Tucson, Ariz. (January 1978).

```
%A B. Prabhala
%A R. Sethi
%T Efficient Computation of Expressions with
Common Subexpressions
%J Proc. 5th ACM Symp. on Principles
of Programming Languages
%C Tucson, Ariz.
%D January 1978
%P 222-230
```

Book:

B. W. Kernighan and P. J. Plauger, *Software Tools,* Addison-Wesley, Reading, Mass. (1976).

```
%T Software Tools
%A B. W. Kernighan
%A P. J. Plauger
%I Addison-Wesley
%C Reading, Mass.
%D 1976
```

Article within book:

J. W. de Bakker, "Semantics of Programming Languages," pp. 173-227 in *Advances in Information Systems Science, Vol. 2,* ed. J. T. Tou, Plenum Press, New York, N. Y. (1969).

```
%A J. W. de Bakker
%T Semantics of programming languages
%E J. T. Tou
%B Advances in Information Systems Science, Vol. 2
%I Plenum Press
%C New York, N. Y.
%D 1969
%P 173-227
```

Technical Report:

F. E. Allen, "Bibliography on Program Optimization," Report RC-5767, IBM T. J. Watson Research Center, Yorktown Heights, N. Y. (1975).

```
%A F. E. Allen
%D 1975
%T Bibliography on Program Optimization
%R Report RC-5767
%I IBM T. J. Watson Research Center
%C Yorktown Heights, N. Y.
```

Other forms of publication can be entered similarly. Note that conference proceedings are entered as if journals, with the conference name on a %J line. This is also sometimes appropriate for obscure publications such as series of lecture notes. When something is both a report and an article, or both a memorandum and an article, enter all necessary information for both; see the first article above, for example. Extra information (such as "In preparation" or "Japanese translation") should be placed on a line beginning %O. The most common use of %O lines now is for "Also in ..." to give an additional reference to a secondary appearance of the same paper.

Some of the possible fields of a citation are:

Letter	Meaning	Letter	Meaning
A	Author	K	Extra keys
B	Book including item	N	Issue number
C	City of publication	O	Other
D	Date	P	Page numbers
E	Editor of book	R	Report number
I	Publisher (issuer)	T	Title of item
J	Journal name	V	Volume number

Note that %B is used to indicate the title of a book containing the article being entered; when an item is an entire book, the title should be entered with a %T as usual.

Normally, the order of items does not matter. The only exception is that if there are multiple authors (%A lines) the order of authors should be that on the paper. If a line is too long, it may be continued on to the next line; any line not beginning with % or . (dot) is assumed to be a continuation of the previous line. Again, see the first article above for an example of a long title. Except for authors, do not repeat any items; if two %J lines are given, for example, the first is ignored. Multiple items on the same file should be separated by blank lines.

Note that in formatted printouts of the file, the exact appearance of the items is determined by a set of macros and the formatting programs. Do not try to adjust fonts, punctuation, etc. by editing the data base; it is wasted effort. In case someone has a real need for a differently-formatted output, a new set of macros can easily be generated to provide alternative appearances of the citations.

3. Updating and Re-indexing.

This section describes the commands that are used to manipulate and change the data base. It explains the procedures for (a) finding references in the data base, (b) adding new references, (c) changing existing references, and (d) deleting references. Remember that all changes, additions, and deletions are done by preparing separate files and then running an 'update and reindex' step.

Checking what's there now. Often you will want to know what is currently in the data base. There is a special command *lookbib* to look for things and print them out. It searches for articles based on words in the title, or the author's name, or the date. For example, you could find the first paper above with

        lookbib aho ullman maximal subsequence 1976

or

        lookbib aho ullman hirschberg

If you don't give enough words, several items will be found; if you spell some wrong, nothing will be found. There are around 4300 papers in the public file; you should always use this command to check when you are not sure whether a certain paper is there or not.

Additions. To add new papers, just type in, on one or more files, the citations for the new papers. Remember to check first if the papers are already in the data base. For example, if a paper has a previous memo version, this should be treated as a change to an existing entry, rather than a new entry. If several new papers are being typed on the same file, be sure that there is a blank line between each two papers.

Changes. To change an item, it should be extracted onto a file. This is done with the command

     pub.chg key1 key2 key3 ...

where the items key1, key2, key3, etc. are a set of keys that will find the paper, as in the *lookbib* command. That is, if

     lookbib johnson yacc cstr

will find a item (to, in this case, Computing Science Technical Report No. 32, "YACC: Yet Another Compiler-Compiler," by S. C. Johnson) then

     pub.chg johnson yacc cstr

will permit you to edit the item. The *pub.chg* command extracts the item onto a file named "bibxxx" where "xxx" is a 3-digit number, e.g. "bib234". The command will print the file name it has chosen. If the set of keys finds more than one paper (or no papers) an error message is printed and no file is written. Each reference to be changed must be extracted with a separate *pub.chg* command, and each will be placed on a separate file. You should then edit the "bibxxx" file as desired to change the item, using the UNIX editor. Do not delete or change the first line of the file, however, which begins %# and is a special code line to tell the update program which item is being altered. You may delete or change other lines, or add lines, as you wish. The changes are not actually made in the public data base until you run the update command *pub.run* (see below). Thus, if after extracting an item and modifying it, you decide that you'd rather leave things as they were, delete the "bibxxx" file, and your change request will disappear.

Deletions. To delete an entry from the data base, type the command

     pub.del key1 key2 key3 ...

where the items key1, key2, etc. are a set of keys that will find the paper, as with the *lookbib* command. That is, if

     lookbib Aho hirschberg ullman

will find a paper,

     pub.del aho hirschberg ullman

deletes it. Note that upper and lower case are equivalent in keys. The *pub.del* command will print the entry being deleted. It also gives the name of a "bibxxx" file on which the deletion command is stored. The actual deletion is not done until the changes, additions, etc. are processed, as with the *pub.chg* command. If, after seeing the item to be deleted, you change your mind about throwing it away, delete the "bibxxx" file and the delete request disappears. Again, if the list of keys does not uniquely identify one paper, an error message is given.

Remember that the default versions of the commands described here edit a public data base. Do not delete items unless you are sure deletion is proper; usually this means that there are duplicate entries for the same paper. Otherwise, view requests for deletion with skepticism; even if one person has no need for a particular item in the data base, someone else may want it there.

If an item is correct, but should not appear in the "List of Publications" as normally produced, add the line

     %K DNL

to the item. This preserves the item intact, but implies "Do Not List" to the to the commands that print publication lists. The DNL line is normally used for some technical reports, minor memoranda, or other low-grade publications.

Update and reindex. When you have completed a session of changes, you should type the command

    pub.run file1 file2 ...

where the names "file1", ... are the new files of additions you have prepared. You need not list the "bibxxx" files representing changes and deletions; they are processed automatically. All of the new items are edited into the standard public data base, and then a new index is made. This process takes about 15 minutes; during this time, searches of the data base will be slower.

Normally, you should execute *pub.run* just before you logoff after performing some edit requests. However, if you don't, the various change request files remain in your directory until you finally do execute *pub.run*. When the changes are processed, the "bibxxx" files are deleted. It is not desirable to wait too long before processing changes, however, to avoid conflicts with someone else who wishes to change the same file. If executing *pub.run* produces the message "File bibxxx too old" it means that someone else has been editing the same file between the time you prepared your changes, and the time you typed *pub.run*. You must delete such old change files and re-enter them.

Note that although *pub.run* discards the "bibxxx" files after processing them, your files of additions are left around even after *pub.run* is finished. If they were typed in only for purposes of updating the data base, you may delete them after they have been processed by *pub.run*.

Example. Suppose, for example, that you wish to

(1)   Add to the data base the memos "The Dilogarithm Function of a Real Argument" by R. Morris, and "UNIX Software Distribution by Communication Link," by M. E. Lesk and A. S. Cohen;

(2)   Delete from the data base the item "Cheap Typesetters", by M. E. Lesk, SIGLASH Newsletter, 1973; and

(3)   Change "J. Assoc. Comp. Mach." to "Jour. ACM" in the citation for Aho, Hirschberg, and Ullman shown above.

The procedure would be as follows. First, you would make a file containing the additions, here called "new.1", in the normal way using the UNIX editor. In the script shown below, the computer prompts are in italics.

```
$ ed new.1
?
a
%T The Dilogarithm Function of a Real Argument
%A Robert Morris
%M abcd
%D 1978

%T UNIX Software Distribution by Communication Link
%A M. E. Lesk
%A A. S. Cohen
%M abcd
%D 1978
w new.1
199
q
```

Next you would specify the deletion, which would be done with the *pub.del* command:

$ pub.del lesk cheap typesetters siglash
to which the computer responds:

Will delete: (file bib176)

%T Cheap Typesetters
%A M. E. Lesk
%J ACM SIGLASH Newsletter
%V 6
%N 4
%P 14-16
%D October 1973

And then you would extract the Aho, Hirschberg and Ullman paper. The dialogue involved is shown below. First run *pub.chg* to extract the paper; it responds by printing the citation and informing you that it was placed on file *bib123*. That file is then edited.

```
$ pub.chg aho hirschberg ullman
Extracting as file bib123
%T Bounds on the Complexity of the Maximal
Common Subsequence Problem
%A A. V. Aho
%A D. S. Hirschberg
%A J. D. Ullman
%J J. Assoc. Comp. Mach.
%V 23
%N 1
%P 1-12
%M abcd
%D Jan. 1976

$ ed bib123
312
/Assoc/s/ J/ Jour/p
%J Jour. Assoc. Comp. Mach.
s/Assoc.*/ACM/p
%J Jour. ACM
1,$p
%# /usr/dict/papers/p76 233 245 change
%T Bounds on the Complexity of the Maximal
Common Subsequence Problem
%A A. V. Aho
%A D. S. Hirschberg
%A J. D. Ullman
%J Jour. ACM
%V 23
%N 1
%P 1-12
%M abcd
%D Jan. 1976

w
292
q
$
```

Finally, execute *pub.run*, making sure to remember that you have prepared a new file "new.1":

```
$ pub.run new.1
```

and about fifteen minutes later the new index would be complete and all the changes would be included.

4. Printing a Publication List

There are two commands for printing a publication list, depending on whether you want to print one person's list, or the list of many people. To print a list for one person, use the *pub.indiv* command:

```
pub.indiv M Lesk
```

This runs off the list for M. Lesk and puts it in file "output". Note that no '.' is given after the initial. In case of ambiguity two initials can be used. Similarly, to get the list for group of people, say

```
pub.org xxx
```

which prints all the publications of the members of organization *xxx*, taking the names for the list in the file */usr/dict/papers/centlist/xxx*. This command should normally be run in the background; it takes perhaps 15 minutes. Two options are available with these commands:

```
pub.indiv −p M Lesk
```

prints only the papers, leaving out unpublished notes, patents, etc. Also

```
pub.indiv −t M Lesk | gcat
```

prints a typeset copy, instead of a computer printer copy. In this case it has been directed to an alternate typesetter with the 'gcat' command. These options may be used together, and may be used with the *pub.org* command as well. For example, to print only the papers for all of organization zzz and typeset them, you could type

```
pub.center −t −p zzz | gcat &
```

These publication lists are printed double column with a citation style taken from a set of publication list macros; the macros, of course, can be changed easily to adjust the format of the lists.

NROFF/TROFF User's Manual

Joseph F. Ossanna

Bell Laboratories
Murray Hill, New Jersey 07974

Introduction

NROFF and TROFF are text processors under the PDP-11 UNIX Time-Sharing System[1] that format text for typewriter-like terminals and for a Graphic Systems phototypesetter, respectively. They accept lines of text interspersed with lines of format control information and format the text into a printable paginated document having a user-designed style. NROFF and TROFF offer unusual freedom in document styling, including: arbitrary style headers and footers; arbitrary style footnotes; multiple automatic sequence numbering for paragraphs, sections, etc; multiple column output; dynamic font and point-size control; arbitrary horizontal and vertical local motions at any point; and a family of automatic overstriking, bracket construction, and line drawing functions.

NROFF and TROFF are highly compatible with each other and it is almost always possible to prepare input acceptable to both. Conditional input is provided that enables the user to embed input expressly destined for either program. NROFF can prepare output directly for a variety of terminal types and is capable of utilizing the full resolution of each terminal.

Usage

The general form of invoking NROFF (or TROFF) at UNIX command level is

    nroff *options files*   (or **troff** *options files*)

where *options* represents any of a number of option arguments and *files* represents the list of files containing the document to be formatted. An argument consisting of a single minus (−) is taken to be a file name corresponding to the standard input. If no file names are given input is taken from the standard input. The options, which may appear in any order so long as they appear before the files, are:

Option	Effect
−o*list*	Print only pages whose page numbers appear in *list*, which consists of comma-separated numbers and number ranges. A number range has the form $N-M$ and means pages N through M; a initial $-N$ means from the beginning to page N; and a final $N-$ means from N to the end.
−n*N*	Number first generated page *N*.
−s*N*	Stop every *N* pages. NROFF will halt prior to every *N* pages (default *N*=1) to allow paper loading or changing, and will resume upon receipt of a newline. TROFF will stop the phototypesetter every *N* pages, produce a trailer to allow changing cassettes, and will resume after the phototypesetter START button is pressed.
−m*name*	Prepends the macro file **/usr/lib/tmac.***name* to the input *files*.
−r*aN*	Register *a* (one-character) is set to *N*.
−i	Read standard input after the input files are exhausted.
−q	Invoke the simultaneous input-output mode of the **rd** request.

NROFF Only

−T*name*   Specifies the name of the output terminal type. Currently defined names are **37** for the (default) Model 37 Teletype®, **tn300** for the GE TermiNet 300 (or any terminal without half-line capabilities), **300S** for the DASI-300S, **300** for the DASI-300, and **450** for the DASI-450 (Diablo Hyterm).

−e   Produce equally-spaced words in adjusted lines, using full terminal resolution.

TROFF Only

−t   Direct output to the standard output instead of the phototypesetter.

−f   Refrain from feeding out paper and stopping phototypesetter at the end of the run.

−w   Wait until phototypesetter is available, if currently busy.

−b   TROFF will report whether the phototypesetter is busy or available. No text processing is done.

−a   Send a printable (ASCII) approximation of the results to the standard output.

−p*N*   Print all characters in point size *N* while retaining all prescribed spacings and motions, to reduce phototypesetter elasped time.

−g   Prepare output for the Murray Hill Computation Center phototypesetter and direct it to the standard output.

Each option is invoked as a separate argument; for example,

      nroff −o*4,8−10* −T*300S* −m*abc file1 file2*

requests formatting of pages 4, 8, 9, and 10 of a document contained in the files named *file1* and *file2*, specifies the output terminal as a DASI-300S, and invokes the macro package *abc*.

Various pre- and post-processors are available for use with NROFF and TROFF. These include the equation preprocessors NEQN and EQN[2] (for NROFF and TROFF respectively), and the table-construction preprocessor TBL[3]. A reverse-line postprocessor COL[4] is available for multiple-column NROFF output on terminals without reverse-line ability; COL expects the Model 37 Teletype escape sequences that NROFF produces by default. TK[4] is a 37 Teletype simulator postprocessor for printing NROFF output on a Tektronix 4014. TCAT[4] is phototypesetter-simulator postprocessor for TROFF that produces an approximation of phototypesetter output on a Tektronix 4014. For example, in

      tbl *files* | **eqn** | **troff** −t *options* | **tcat**

the first | indicates the piping of TBL's output to EQN's input; the second the piping of EQN's output to TROFF's input; and the third indicates the piping of TROFF's output to TCAT. GCAT[4] can be used to send TROFF (−g) output to the Murray Hill Computation Center.

The remainder of this manual consists of: a Summary and Index; a Reference Manual keyed to the index; and a set of Tutorial Examples. Another tutorial is [5].

                                        Joseph F. Ossanna

References

[1] K. Thompson, D. M. Ritchie, *UNIX Programmer's Manual*, Sixth Edition (May 1975).

[2] B. W. Kernighan, L. L. Cherry, *Typesetting Mathematics — User's Guide (Second Edition)*, Bell Laboratories internal memorandum.

[3] M. E. Lesk, *Tbl — A Program to Format Tables*, Bell Laboratories internal memorandum.

[4] Internal on-line documentation, on UNIX.

[5] B. W. Kernighan, *A TROFF Tutorial*, Bell Laboratories internal memorandum.

SUMMARY AND INDEX

Request Form	Initial Value*	If No Argument	Notes#	Explanation
1. General Explanation				
2. Font and Character Size Control				
.ps $\pm N$	10 point	previous	E	Point size; also $\backslash s \pm N$.†
.ss N	12/36 em	ignored	E	Space-character size set to N/36 em.†
.cs $F N M$	off	-	P	Constant character space (width) mode (font F).†
.bd $F N$	off	-	P	Embolden font F by $N-1$ units.†
.bd S $F N$	off	-	P	Embolden Special Font when current font is F.†
.ft F	Roman	previous	E	Change to font $F = x$, xx, or 1-4. Also $\backslash\mathbf{f}x$, $\backslash\mathbf{f}(xx$, $\backslash\mathbf{f}N$.
.fp $N F$	R,I,B,S	ignored	-	Font named F mounted on physical position $1 \leqslant N \leqslant 4$.
3. Page Control				
.pl $\pm N$	11 in	11 in	v	Page length.
.bp $\pm N$	$N{=}1$	-	B‡,v	Eject current page; next page number N.
.pn $\pm N$	$N{=}1$	ignored	-	Next page number N.
.po $\pm N$	0; 26/27 in	previous	v	Page offset.
.ne N	-	$N{=}1 V$	D,v	Need N vertical space (V = vertical spacing).
.mk R	none	internal	D	Mark current vertical place in register R.
.rt $\pm N$	none	internal	D,v	Return *(upward only)* to marked vertical place.
4. Text Filling, Adjusting, and Centering				
.br	-	-	B	Break.
.fi	fill	-	B,E	Fill output lines.
.nf	fill	-	B,E	No filling or adjusting of output lines.
.ad c	adj,both	adjust	E	Adjust output lines with mode c.
.na	adjust	-	E	No output line adjusting.
.ce N	off	$N{=}1$	B,E	Center following N input text lines.
5. Vertical Spacing				
.vs N	1/6in;12pts	previous	E,p	Vertical base line spacing (V).
.ls N	$N{=}1$	previous	E	Output $N-1$ Vs after each text output line.
.sp N	-	$N{=}1 V$	B,v	Space vertical distance N *in either direction*.
.sv N	-	$N{=}1 V$	v	Save vertical distance N.
.os	-	-	-	Output saved vertical distance.
.ns	space	-	D	Turn no-space mode on.
.rs	-	-	D	Restore spacing; turn no-space mode off.
6. Line Length and Indenting				
.ll $\pm N$	6.5 in	previous	E,m	Line length.
.in $\pm N$	$N{=}0$	previous	B,E,m	Indent.
.ti $\pm N$	-	ignored	B,E,m	Temporary indent.
7. Macros, Strings, Diversion, and Position Traps				
.de $xx\ yy$	-	.$yy{=}..$	-	Define or redefine macro xx; end at call of yy.
.am $xx\ yy$	-	.$yy{=}..$	-	Append to a macro.
.ds xx string	-	ignored	-	Define a string xx containing *string*.
.as xx string	-	ignored	-	Append *string* to string xx.

---

*Values separated by ";" are for NROFF and TROFF respectively.

#Notes are explained at the end of this Summary and Index

†No effect in NROFF.

‡The use of " ´ " as control character (instead of ".") suppresses the break function.

Request Form	Initial Value	If No Argument	Notes	Explanation
.rm *xx*	-	ignored	-	Remove request, macro, or string.
.rn *xx yy*	-	ignored	-	Rename request, macro, or string *xx* to *yy*.
.di *xx*	-	end	D	Divert output to macro *xx*.
.da *xx*	-	end	D	Divert and append to *xx*.
.wh *N xx*	-	-	v	Set location trap; negative is w.r.t. page bottom.
.ch *xx N*	-	-	v	Change trap location.
.dt *N xx*	-	off	D,v	Set a diversion trap.
.it *N xx*	-	off	E	Set an input-line count trap.
.em *xx*	none	none	-	End macro is *xx*.

8. Number Registers

Request Form	Initial Value	If No Argument	Notes	Explanation
.nr *R* $\pm N M$	-		u	Define and set number register *R*; auto-increment by *M*.
.af *R c*	arabic	-	-	Assign format to register *R* (*c*=**1**, **i**, **I**, **a**, **A**).
.rr *R*	-	-	-	Remove register *R*.

9. Tabs, Leaders, and Fields

Request Form	Initial Value	If No Argument	Notes	Explanation
.ta *Nt* ...	0.8; 0.5in	none	E,m	Tab settings; *left* type, unless *t*=**R**(right), **C**(centered).
.tc *c*	none	none	E	Tab repetition character.
.lc *c*	.	none	E	Leader repetition character.
.fc *a b*	off	off	-	Set field delimiter *a* and pad character *b*.

10. Input and Output Conventions and Character Translations

Request Form	Initial Value	If No Argument	Notes	Explanation
.ec *c*	\	\	-	Set escape character.
.eo	on	-	-	Turn off escape character mechanism.
.lg *N*	-; on.	on	-	Ligature mode on if *N*>0.
.ul *N*	off	*N*=1	E	Underline (italicize in TROFF) *N* input lines.
.cu *N*	off	*N*=1	E	Continuous underline in NROFF; like **ul** in TROFF.
.uf *F*	Italic	Italic	-	Underline font set to *F* (to be switched to by **ul**).
.cc *c*	.	.	E	Set control character to *c*.
.c2 *c*	'	'	E	Set nobreak control character to *c*.
.tr *abcd*....	none	-	O	Translate *a* to *b*, etc. on output.

11. Local Horizontal and Vertical Motions, and the Width Function

12. Overstrike, Bracket, Line-drawing, and Zero-width Functions

13. Hyphenation.

Request Form	Initial Value	If No Argument	Notes	Explanation
.nh	hyphenate	-	E	No hyphenation.
.hy *N*	hyphenate	hyphenate	E	Hyphenate; *N* = mode.
.hc *c*	\%	\%	E	Hyphenation indicator character *c*.
.hw *word1* ...		ignored	-	Exception words.

14. Three Part Titles.

Request Form	Initial Value	If No Argument	Notes	Explanation
.tl 'left' center' right'	-	-		Three part title.
.pc *c*	%	off	-	Page number character.
.lt $\pm N$	6.5 in	previous	E,m	Length of title.

15. Output Line Numbering.

Request Form	Initial Value	If No Argument	Notes	Explanation
.nm $\pm N M S I$		off	E	Number mode on or off, set parameters.
.nn *N*	-	*N*=1	E	Do not number next *N* lines.

16. Conditional Acceptance of Input

Request Form	Initial Value	If No Argument	Notes	Explanation
.if *c anything*				If condition *c* true, accept *anything* as input, for multi-line use \\{*anything*\\}.

Request Form	Initial Value	If No Argument	Notes	Explanation
.if !*c* *anything*	-	-		If condition *c* false, accept *anything*.
.if *N* *anything*	-	u		If expression $N > 0$, accept *anything*.
.if !*N* *anything*	-	u		If expression $N \leq 0$, accept *anything*.
.if ´*string1*´*string2*´ *anything*	-	-		If *string1* identical to *string2*, accept *anything*.
.if !´*string1*´*string2*´ *anything*	-	-		If *string1* not identical to *string2*, accept *anything*.
.ie *c* *anything*	-	u		If portion of if-else; all above forms (like **if**).
.el *anything*	-	-		Else portion of if-else.

17. Environment Switching.

.ev *N*	*N*=0	previous	-	Environment switched (*push down*).

18. Insertions from the Standard Input

.rd *prompt*	-	*prompt*=BEL	-	Read insertion.
.ex	-	-	-	Exit from NROFF/TROFF.

19. Input/Output File Switching

.so *filename*	-	-		Switch source file (*push down*).
.nx *filename*		end-of-file	-	Next file.
.pi *program*	-	-		Pipe output to *program* (NROFF only).

20. Miscellaneous

.mc *c N*	-	off	E,m	Set margin character *c* and separation *N*.
.tm *string*	-	newline	-	Print *string* on terminal (UNIX standard message output).
.ig *yy*	-	*yy*=..	-	Ignore till call of *yy*.
.pm *t*	-	all	-	Print macro names and sizes; if *t* present, print only total of sizes.
.fl	-	-	B	Flush output buffer.

21. Output and Error Messages

Notes-

B	Request normally causes a break.
D	Mode or relevant parameters associated with current diversion level.
E	Relevant parameters are a part of the current environment.
O	Must stay in effect until logical output.
P	Mode must be still or again in effect at the time of physical output.
v,p,m,u	Default scale indicator; if not specified, scale indicators are *ignored*.

Alphabetical Request and Section Number Cross Reference

ad 4	cc 10	ds 7	fc 9	ie 16	ll 6	nh 13	pi 19	rn 7	ta 9	vs 5
af 8	ce 4	dt 7	fi 4	if 16	ls 5	nm 15	pl 3	rr 8	tc 9	wh 7
am 7	ch 7	ec 10	fl 20	ig 20	lt 14	nn 15	pm 20	rs 5	ti 6	
as 7	cs 2	el 16	fp 2	in 6	mc 20	nr 8	pn 3	rt 3	tl 14	
bd 2	cu 10	em 7	ft 2	it 7	mk 3	ns 5	po 3	so 19	tm 20	
bp 3	da 7	eo 10	hc 13	lc 9	na 4	nx 19	ps 2	sp 5	tr 10	
br 4	de 7	ev 17	hw 13	lg 10	ne 3	os 5	rd 18	ss 2	uf 10	
c2 10	di 7	ex 18	hy 13	li 10	nf 4	pc 14	rm 7	sv 5	ul 10	

Escape Sequences for Characters, Indicators, and Functions

Section Reference	Escape Sequence	Meaning
10.1	\\	\ (to prevent or delay the interpretation of \)
10.1	\e	Printable version of the *current* escape character.
2.1	\´	´ (acute accent); equivalent to \(**aa**
2.1	\`	` (grave accent); equivalent to \(**ga**
2.1	\−	− Minus sign in the *current* font
7	\.	Period (dot) (see **de**)
11.1	\(space)	Unpaddable space-size space character
11.1	\0	Digit width space
11.1	\\|	1/6 em narrow space character (zero width in NROFF)
11.1	\^	1/12 em half-narrow space character (zero width in NROFF)
4.1	\&	Non-printing, zero width character
10.6	\!	Transparent line indicator
10.7	\"	Beginning of comment
7.3	\$N	Interpolate argument $1 \leqslant N \leqslant 9$
13	\%	Default optional hyphenation character
2.1	\(xx	Character named xx
7.1	*x, *(xx	Interpolate string x or xx
9.1	\a	Non-interpreted leader character
12.3	\b´abc...´	Bracket building function
4.2	\c	Interrupt text processing
11.1	\d	Forward (down) 1/2 em vertical motion (1/2 line in NROFF)
2.2	\fx,\f(xx,\fN	Change to font named x or xx, or position N
11.1	\h´N´	Local horizontal motion; move right N *(negative left)*
11.3	\kx	Mark horizontal *input* place in register x
12.4	\l´Nc´	Horizontal line drawing function (optionally with c)
12.4	\L´Nc´	Vertical line drawing function (optionally with c)
8	\nx,\n(xx	Interpolate number register x or xx
12.1	\o´abc...´	Overstrike characters a, b, c, ...
4.1	\p	Break and spread output line
11.1	\r	Reverse 1 em vertical motion (reverse line in NROFF)
2.3	\sN, \s±N	Point-size change function
9.1	\t	Non-interpreted horizontal tab
11.1	\u	Reverse (up) 1/2 em vertical motion (1/2 line in NROFF)
11.1	\v´N´	Local vertical motion; move down N *(negative up)*
11.2	\w´string´	Interpolate width of *string*
5.2	\x´N´	Extra line-space function *(negative before, positive after)*
12.2	\zc	Print c with zero width (without spacing)
16	\{	Begin conditional input
16	\}	End conditional input
10.7	\(newline)	Concealed (ignored) newline
	\X	X, any character *not* listed above

The escape sequences \\, \., \", \$, *, \a, \n, \t, and \(newline) are interpreted in *copy mode* (§7.2).

Predefined General Number Registers

Section Reference	Register Name	Description
3	%	Current page number.
11.2	ct	Character type (set by *width* function).
7.4	dl	Width (maximum) of last completed diversion.
7.4	dn	Height (vertical size) of last completed diversion.
-	dw	Current day of the week (1-7).
-	dy	Current day of the month (1-31).
11.3	hp	Current horizontal place on *input* line.
15	ln	Output line number.
-	mo	Current month (1-12).
4.1	nl	Vertical position of last printed text base-line.
11.2	sb	Depth of string below base line (generated by *width* function).
11.2	st	Height of string above base line (generated by *width* function).
-	yr	Last two digits of current year.

Predefined Read-Only Number Registers

Section Reference	Register Name	Description
7.3	.$	Number of arguments available at the current macro level.
-	.A	Set to 1 in TROFF, if −a option used; always 1 in NROFF.
11.1	.H	Available horizontal resolution in basic units.
-	.T	Set to 1 in NROFF, if −T option used; always 0 in TROFF.
11.1	.V	Available vertical resolution in basic units.
5.2	.a	Post-line extra line-space most recently utilized using $\backslash\mathbf{x}'N'$.
-	.c	Number of *lines* read from current input file.
7.4	.d	Current vertical place in current diversion; equal to **nl**, if no diversion.
2.2	.f	Current font as physical quadrant (1-4).
4	.h	Text base-line high-water mark on current page or diversion.
6	.i	Current indent.
6	.l	Current line length.
4	.n	Length of text portion on previous output line.
3	.o	Current page offset.
3	.p	Current page length.
2.3	.s	Current point size.
7.5	.t	Distance to the next trap.
4.1	.u	Equal to 1 in fill mode and 0 in nofill mode.
5.1	.v	Current vertical line spacing.
11.2	.w	Width of previous character.
-	.x	Reserved version-dependent register.
-	.y	Reserved version-dependent register.
7.4	.z	Name of current diversion.

REFERENCE MANUAL

1. General Explanation

1.1. Form of input. Input consists of *text lines*, which are destined to be printed, interspersed with *control lines*, which set parameters or otherwise control subsequent processing. Control lines begin with a *control character*—normally . (period) or ´ (acute accent)—followed by a one or two character name that specifies a basic *request* or the substitution of a user-defined *macro* in place of the control line. The control character ´ suppresses the *break* function—the forced output of a partially filled line—caused by certain requests. The control character may be separated from the request/macro name by white space (spaces and/or tabs) for esthetic reasons. Names must be followed by either space or newline. Control lines with unrecognized names are ignored.

Various special functions may be introduced anywhere in the input by means of an *escape* character, normally \. For example, the function \n$R$ causes the interpolation of the contents of the *number register R* in place of the function; here R is either a single character name as in \n$x$, or left-parenthesis-introduced, two-character name as in \n(xx.

1.2. Formatter and device resolution. TROFF internally uses 432 units/inch, corresponding to the Graphic Systems phototypesetter which has a horizontal resolution of 1/432 inch and a vertical resolution of 1/144 inch. NROFF internally uses 240 units/inch, corresponding to the least common multiple of the horizontal and vertical resolutions of various typewriter-like output devices. TROFF rounds horizontal/vertical numerical parameter input to the actual horizontal/vertical resolution of the Graphic Systems typesetter. NROFF similarly rounds numerical input to the actual resolution of the output device indicated by the −**T** option (default Model 37 Teletype).

1.3. Numerical parameter input. Both NROFF and TROFF accept numerical input with the appended scale indicators shown in the following table, where S is the current type size in points, V is the current vertical line spacing in basic units, and C is a *nominal character width* in basic units.

Scale Indicator	Meaning	Number of basic units	
		TROFF	NROFF
i	Inch	432	240
c	Centimeter	432×50/127	240×50/127
P	Pica = 1/6 inch	72	240/6
m	Em = S points	6×S	C
n	En = Em/2	3×S	C, *same as Em*
p	Point = 1/72 inch	6	240/72
u	Basic unit	1	1
v	Vertical line space	V	V
none	Default, see below		

In NROFF, *both* the em and the en are taken to be equal to the C, which is output-device dependent; common values are 1/10 and 1/12 inch. Actual character widths in NROFF need not be all the same and constructed characters such as −> (→) are often extra wide. The default scaling is ems for the horizontally-oriented requests and functions **ll**, **in**, **ti**, **ta**, **lt**, **po**, **mc**, \h, and \l; Vs for the vertically-oriented requests and functions **pl**, **wh**, **ch**, **dt**, **sp**, **sv**, **ne**, **rt**, \v, \x, and \L; **p** for the **vs** request; and **u** for the requests **nr**, **if**, and **ie**. *All* other requests ignore any scale indicators. When a number register containing an already appropriately scaled number is interpolated to provide numerical input, the unit scale indicator **u** may need to be appended to prevent an additional inappropriate default scaling.

The number, N, may be specified in decimal-fraction form but the parameter finally stored is rounded to an integer number of basic units.

The *absolute position* indicator | may be prepended to a number N to generate the distance to the vertical or horizontal place N. For vertically-oriented requests and functions, $|N$ becomes the distance in basic units from the current vertical place on the page or in a *diversion* (§7.4) to the the vertical place N. For *all* other requests and functions, $|N$ becomes the distance from the current horizontal place on the *input* line to the horizontal place N. For example,

    .sp |3.2c

will space *in the required direction* to 3.2 centimeters from the top of the page.

1.4. Numerical expressions. Wherever numerical input is expected an expression involving parentheses, the arithmetic operators $+$, $-$, $/$, $*$, % (mod), and the logical operators $<$, $>$, $<=$, $>=$, $=$ (or $==$), & (and), : (or) may be used. Except where controlled by parentheses, evaluation of expressions is left-to-right; there is no operator precedence. In the case of certain requests, an initial $+$ or $-$ is stripped and interpreted as an increment or decrement indicator respectively. In the presence of default scaling, the desired scale indicator must be attached to *every* number in an expression for which the desired and default scaling differ. For example, if the number register **x** contains 2 and the current point size is 10, then

    .ll   (4.25i+\nxP+3)/2u

will set the line length to 1/2 the sum of 4.25 inches + 2 picas + 30 points.

1.5. Notation. Numerical parameters are indicated in this manual in two ways. $\pm N$ means that the argument may take the forms N, $+N$, or $-N$ and that the corresponding effect is to set the affected parameter to N, to increment it by N, or to decrement it by N respectively. Plain N means that an initial algebraic sign is *not* an increment indicator, but merely the sign of N. Generally, unreasonable numerical input is either ignored or truncated to a reasonable value. For example, most requests expect to set parameters to non-negative values; exceptions are **sp**, **wh**, **ch**, **nr**, and **if**. The requests **ps**, **ft**, **po**, **vs**, **ls**, **ll**, **in**, and **lt** restore the *previous* parameter value in the *absence* of an argument.

Single character arguments are indicated by single lower case letters and one/two character arguments are indicated by a pair of lower case letters. Character string arguments are indicated by multi-character mnemonics.

2. Font and Character Size Control

2.1. Character set. The TROFF character set consists of the Graphics Systems Commercial II character set plus a Special Mathematical Font character set—each having 102 characters. These character sets are shown in the attached Table I. All ASCII characters are included, with some on the Special Font. With three exceptions, the ASCII characters are input as themselves, and non-ASCII characters are input in the form \\(*xx* where *xx* is a two-character name given in the attached Table II. The three ASCII exceptions are mapped as follows:

ASCII Input		Printed by TROFF	
Character	Name	Character	Name
´	acute accent	'	close quote
`	grave accent	'	open quote
−	minus	-	hyphen

The characters ´, `, and − may be input by \\´, \\`, and \\− respectively or by their names (Table II). The ASCII characters @, #, ", ´, `, <, >, \\, {, }, ~, ^, and _ exist only on the Special Font and are printed as a 1-em space if that Font is not mounted.

NROFF understands the entire TROFF character set, but can in general print only ASCII characters, additional characters as may be available on the output device, such characters as may be able to be constructed by overstriking or other combination, and those that can reasonably be mapped into other printable characters. The exact behavior is determined by a driving table prepared for each device. The characters ´, `, and _ print as themselves.

2.2. Fonts. The default mounted fonts are Times Roman (**R**), Times Italic (**I**), Times Bold (**B**), and the Special Mathematical Font (**S**) on physical typesetter positions 1, 2, 3, and 4 respectively. These fonts are used in this document. The *current* font, initially Roman, may be changed (among the mounted fonts) by use of the **ft** request, or by imbedding at any desired point either \f*x*, \f(*xx*, or \f*N* where *x* and *xx* are the name of a mounted font and *N* is a numerical font position. It is *not* necessary to change to the Special font; characters on that font are automatically handled. A request for a named but not-mounted font is *ignored*. TROFF can be informed that any particular font is mounted by use of the **fp** request. The list of known fonts is installation dependent. In the subsequent discussion of font-related requests, *F* represents either a one/two-character font name or the numerical font position, 1-4. The current font is available (as numerical position) in the read-only number register .f.

NROFF understands font control and normally underlines Italic characters (see §10.5).

2.3. Character size. Character point sizes available on the Graphic Systems typesetter are 6, 7, 8, 9, 10, 11, 12, 14, 16, 18, 20, 22, 24, 28, and 36. This is a range of 1/12 inch to 1/2 inch. The **ps** request is used to change or restore the point size. Alternatively the point size may be changed between any two characters by imbedding a \s*N* at the desired point to set the size to *N*, or a \s±*N* ($1 \leq N \leq 9$) to increment/decrement the size by *N*; \s0 restores the *previous* size. Requested point size values that are between two valid sizes yield the larger of the two. The current size is available in the .s register. NROFF ignores type size control.

Request Form	Initial Value	If No Argument	Notes*	Explanation
.ps ±*N*	10 point	previous	E	Point size set to ±*N*. Alternatively imbed \s*N* or \s±*N*. Any positive size value may be requested; if invalid, the next larger valid size will result, with a maximum of 36. A paired sequence +*N*, −*N* will work because the previous requested value is also remembered. Ignored in NROFF.
.ss *N*	12/36 em	ignored	E	Space-character size is set to *N*/36 ems. This size is the minimum word spacing in adjusted text. Ignored in NROFF.
.cs *F N M*	off	-	P	Constant character space (width) mode is set on for font *F* (if mounted); the width of every character will be taken to be *N*/36 ems. If *M* is absent, the em is that of the character's point size; if *M* is given, the em is *M*-points. All affected characters are centered in this space, including those with an actual width larger than this space. Special Font characters occurring while the current font is *F* are also so treated. If *N* is absent, the mode is turned off. The mode must be still or again in effect when the characters are physically printed. Ignored in NROFF.
.bd *F N*	off	-	P	The characters in font *F* will be artificially emboldened by printing each one twice, separated by *N*−1 basic units. A reasonable value for *N* is 3 when the character size is in the vicinity of 10 points. If *N* is missing the embolden mode is turned off. The column heads above were printed with **.bd I 3**. The mode must be still or again in effect when the characters are physically printed. Ignored in NROFF.

*Notes are explained at the end of the Summary and Index above.

.bd S *F N*	off	-	P	The characters in the Special Font will be emboldened whenever the current font is *F*. This manual was printed with **.bd S B** 3. The mode must be still or again in effect when the characters are physically printed.
.ft *F*	Roman	previous	E	Font changed to *F*. Alternatively, imbed \f*F*. The font name **P** is reserved to mean the previous font.
.fp *N F*	R,I,B,S	ignored	-	Font position. This is a statement that a font named *F* is mounted on position *N* (1-4). It is a fatal error if *F* is not known. The phototypesetter has four fonts physically mounted. Each font consists of a film strip which can be mounted on a numbered quadrant of a wheel. The default mounting sequence assumed by TROFF is R, I, B, and S on positions 1, 2, 3 and 4.

3. Page control

Top and bottom margins are *not* automatically provided; it is conventional to define two *macros* and to set *traps* for them at vertical positions 0 (top) and −*N* (*N* from the bottom). See §7 and Tutorial Examples §T2. A pseudo-page transition onto the *first* page occurs either when the first *break* occurs or when the first *non-diverted* text processing occurs. Arrangements for a trap to occur at the top of the first page must be completed before this transition. In the following, references to the *current diversion* (§7.4) mean that the mechanism being described works during both ordinary and diverted output (the former considered as the top diversion level).

The useable page width on the Graphic Systems phototypesetter is about 7.54 inches, beginning about 1/27 inch from the left edge of the 8 inch wide, continuous roll paper. The physical limitations on NROFF output are output-device dependent.

Request Form	*Initial Value*	*If No Argument*	*Notes*	*Explanation*
.pl ±*N*	11 in	11 in	v	Page length set to ±*N*. The internal limitation is about 75 inches in TROFF and about 136 inches in NROFF. The current page length is available in the **.p** register.
.bp ±*N*	*N*=1	-	B*,v	Begin page. The current page is ejected and a new page is begun. If ±*N* is given, the new page number will be ±*N*. Also see request **ns**.
.pn ±*N*	*N*=1	ignored	-	Page number. The next page (when it occurs) will have the page number ±*N*. A **pn** must occur before the initial pseudo-page transition to effect the page number of the first page. The current page number is in the **%** register.
.po ±*N*	0; 26/27 in†	previous	v	Page offset. The current *left margin* is set to ±*N*. The TROFF initial value provides about 1 inch of paper margin including the physical typesetter margin of 1/27 inch. In TROFF the maximum (line-length) + (page-offset) is about 7.54 inches. See §6. The current page offset is available in the **.o** register.
.ne *N*	-	*N*=1 *V*	D,v	Need *N* vertical space. If the distance, *D*, to the next trap position (see §7.5) is less than *N*, a forward vertical space of size *D* occurs, which will spring the trap. If there are no remaining traps on the page, *D* is the

---

*The use of " ' " as control character (instead of ".") suppresses the break function.

†Values separated by ";" are for NROFF and TROFF respectively.

distance to the bottom of the page. If $D < V$, another line could still be output and spring the trap. In a diversion, D is the distance to the *diversion trap*, if any, or is very large.

.mk *R*	none·	internal	D	Mark the *current* vertical place in an internal register (both associated with the current diversion level), or in register *R*, if given. See **rt** request.
.rt $\pm N$	none	internal	D,v	Return *upward only* to a marked vertical place in the current diversion. If $\pm N$ (w.r.t. current place) is given, the place is $\pm N$ from the top of the page or diversion or, if *N* is absent, to a place marked by a previous **mk**. Note that the **sp** request (§5.3) may be used in all cases instead of **rt** by spacing to the absolute place stored in a explicit register; e. g. using the sequence **.mk** *R* ... **.sp** $\backslash$n*R***u**.

4. Text Filling, Adjusting, and Centering

4.1. Filling and adjusting. Normally, words are collected from input text lines and assembled into a output text line until some word doesn't fit. An attempt is then made the hyphenate the word in effort to assemble a part of it into the output line. The spaces between the words on the output line are then increased to spread out the line to the current *line length* minus any current *indent*. A *word* is any string of characters delimited by the *space* character or the beginning/end of the input line. Any adjacent pair of words that must be kept together (neither split across output lines nor spread apart in the adjustment process) can be tied together by separating them with the *unpaddable space* character "\ " (backslash-space). The adjusted word spacings are uniform in TROFF and the minimum interword spacing can be controlled with the **ss** request (§2). In NROFF, they are normally nonuniform because of quantization to character-size spaces; however, the command line option −e causes uniform spacing with full output device resolution. Filling, adjustment, and hyphenation (§13) can all be prevented or controlled. The *text length* on the last line output is available in the **.n** register, and text base-line position on the page for this line is in the **nl** register. The text base-line high-water mark (lowest place) on the current page is in the **.h** register.

An input text line ending with **.**, **?**, or **!** is taken to be the end of a *sentence*, and an additional space character is automatically provided during filling. Multiple inter-word space characters found in the input are retained, except for trailing spaces; initial spaces also cause a *break.*

When filling is in effect, a **\p** may be imbedded or attached to a word to cause a *break* at the *end* of the word and have the resulting output line *spread out* to fill the current line length.

A text input line that happens to begin with a control character can be made to not look like a control line by prefacing it with the non-printing, zero-width filler character **\&**. Still another way is to specify output translation of some convenient character into the control character using **tr** (§10.5).

4.2. Interrupted text. The copying of a input line in *nofill* (non-fill) mode can be *interrupted* by terminating the partial line with a **\c**. The *next* encountered input text line will be considered to be a continuation of the same line of input text. Similarly, a word within *filled* text may be interrupted by terminating the word (and line) with **\c**; the next encountered text will be taken as a continuation of the interrupted word. If the intervening control lines cause a break, any partial line will be forced out along with any partial word.

Request Form	Initial Value	If No Argument	Notes	Explanation
.br	-	-	B	Break. The filling of the line currently being collected is stopped and the line is output without adjustment. Text lines beginning with space characters and empty text lines (blank lines) also cause a break.

.fi	fill on	-	B,E	Fill subsequent output lines. The register **.u** is 1 in fill mode and 0 in nofill mode.
.nf	fill on	-	B,E	Nofill. Subsequent output lines are *neither* filled *nor* adjusted. Input text lines are copied directly to output lines *without regard* for the current line length.
.ad *c*	adj,both	adjust	E	Line adjustment is begun. If fill mode is not on, adjustment will be deferred until fill mode is back on. If the type indicator *c* is present, the adjustment type is changed as shown in the following table.

Indicator	Adjust Type
l	adjust left margin only
r	adjust right margin only
c	center
b or **n**	adjust both margins
absent	unchanged

.na	adjust	-	E	Noadjust. Adjustment is turned off; the right margin will be ragged. The adjustment type for **ad** is not changed. Output line filling still occurs if fill mode is on.
.ce *N*	off	*N*=1	B,E	Center the next *N* input text lines within the current (line-length minus indent). If *N*=0, any residual count is cleared. A break occurs after each of the *N* input lines. If the input line is too long, it will be left adjusted.

5. Vertical Spacing

5.1. Base-line spacing. The vertical spacing (V) between the base-lines of successive output lines can be set using the **vs** request with a resolution of 1/144 inch = 1/2 point in TROFF, and to the output device resolution in NROFF. V must be large enough to accommodate the character sizes on the affected output lines. For the common type sizes (9-12 points), usual typesetting practice is to set V to 2 points greater than the point size; TROFF default is 10-point type on a 12-point spacing (as in this document). The current V is available in the **.v** register. Multiple-V line separation (e.g. double spacing) may be requested with **ls**.

5.2. Extra line-space. If a word contains a vertically tall construct requiring the output line containing it to have extra vertical space before and/or after it, the *extra-line-space* function $\x'N'$ can be imbedded in or attached to that word. In this and other functions having a pair of delimiters around their parameter (here $'$), the delimiter choice is arbitrary, except that it can't look like the continuation of a number expression for N. If N is negative, the output line containing the word will be preceded by N extra vertical space; if N is positive, the output line containing the word will be followed by N extra vertical space. If successive requests for extra space apply to the same line, the maximum values are used. The most recently utilized post-line extra line-space is available in the **.a** register.

5.3. Blocks of vertical space. A block of vertical space is ordinarily requested using **sp**, which honors the *no-space* mode and which does not space *past* a trap. A contiguous block of vertical space may be reserved using **sv**.

Request Form	Initial Value	If No Argument	Notes	Explanation
.vs *N*	1/6in;12pts	previous	E,**p**	Set vertical base-line spacing size V. Transient *extra* vertical space available with $\x'N'$ (see above).
.ls *N*	*N*=1	previous	E	*Line* spacing set to $\pm N$. $N-1$ Vs *(blank lines)* are appended to each output text line. Appended blank lines are omitted, if the text or previous appended blank line

reached a trap position.

.sp N	-	$N=1V$	B,v	Space vertically in *either* direction. If N is negative, the motion is *backward* (upward) and is limited to the distance to the top of the page. Forward (downward) motion is truncated to the distance to the nearest trap. If the no-space mode is on, no spacing occurs (see **ns**, and **rs** below).
.sv N	-	$N=1V$	v	Save a contiguous vertical block of size N. If the distance to the next trap is greater than N, N vertical space is output. No-space mode has *no* effect. If this distance is less than N, no vertical space is immediately output, but N is remembered for later output (see **os**). Subsequent **sv** requests will overwrite any still remembered N.
.os	-	-	-	Output saved vertical space. No-space mode has *no* effect. Used to finally output a block of vertical space requested by an earlier **sv** request.
.ns	space	-	D	No-space mode turned on. When on, the no-space mode inhibits **sp** requests and **bp** requests *without* a next page number. The no-space mode is turned off when a line of output occurs, or with **rs**.
.rs	space	-	D	Restore spacing. The no-space mode is turned off.
Blank text line.		-	B	Causes a break and output of a blank line exactly like **sp 1**.

6. Line Length and Indenting

The maximum line length for fill mode may be set with **ll**. The indent may be set with **in**; an indent applicable to *only* the *next* output line may be set with **ti**. The line length includes indent space but *not* page offset space. The line-length minus the indent is the basis for centering with **ce**. The effect of **ll**, **in**, or **ti** is delayed, if a partially collected line exists, until after that line is output. In fill mode the length of text on an output line is less than or equal to the line length minus the indent. The current line length and indent are available in registers **.l** and **.i** respectively. The length of *three-part titles* produced by **tl** (see §14) is *independently* set by **lt**.

Request Form	Initial Value	If No Argument	Notes	Explanation
.ll $\pm N$	6.5 in	previous	E,m	Line length is set to $\pm N$. In TROFF the maximum (line-length) + (page-offset) is about 7.54 inches.
.in $\pm N$	$N=0$	previous	B,E,m	Indent is set to $\pm N$. The indent is prepended to each output line.
.ti $\pm N$	-	ignored	B,E,m	Temporary indent. The *next* output text line will be indented a distance $\pm N$ with respect to the current indent. The resulting total indent may not be negative. The current indent is not changed.

7. Macros, Strings, Diversion, and Position Traps

7.1. Macros and strings. A *macro* is a named set of arbitrary *lines* that may be invoked by name or with a *trap*. A *string* is a named string of *characters*, *not* including a newline character, that may be interpolated by name at any point. Request, macro, and string names share the *same* name list. Macro and string names may be one or two characters long and may usurp previously defined request, macro, or string names. Any of these entities may be renamed with **rn** or removed with **rm**. Macros are created by **de** and **di**, and appended to by **am** and **da**; **di** and **da** cause normal output to be stored in a macro. Strings are created by **ds** and appended to by **as**. A macro is invoked in the same way as a request; a control line beginning .*xx* will interpolate the contents of macro *xx*. The remainder of the line may contain up to nine *arguments*. The strings *x* and *xx* are interpolated at any desired point with *x and *(*xx* respectively. String references and macro invocations may be nested.

7.2. Copy mode input interpretation. During the definition and extension of strings and macros (not by diversion) the input is read in *copy mode*. The input is copied without interpretation *except* that:

- The contents of number registers indicated by \n are interpolated.
- Strings indicated by * are interpolated.
- Arguments indicated by \$ are interpolated.
- Concealed newlines indicated by \(newline) are eliminated.
- Comments indicated by \" are eliminated.
- \t and \a are interpreted as ASCII horizontal tab and SOH respectively (§9).
- \\ is interpreted as \.
- \. is interpreted as ".".

These interpretations can be suppressed by prepending a \. For example, since \\ maps into a \, \\n will copy as \n which will be interpreted as a number register indicator when the macro or string is reread.

7.3. Arguments. When a macro is invoked by name, the remainder of the line is taken to contain up to nine arguments. The argument separator is the space character, and arguments may be surrounded by double-quotes to permit imbedded space characters. Pairs of double-quotes may be imbedded in double-quoted arguments to represent a single double-quote. If the desired arguments won't fit on a line, a concealed newline may be used to continue on the next line.

When a macro is invoked the *input level* is *pushed down* and any arguments available at the previous level become unavailable until the macro is completely read and the previous level is restored. A macro's own arguments can be interpolated at *any* point within the macro with \$*N*, which interpolates the *N*th argument ($1 \leqslant N \leqslant 9$). If an invoked argument doesn't exist, a null string results. For example, the macro *xx* may be defined by

> .de xx   \"begin definition
> **Today is \\$1 the \\$2.**
> ..   \"end definition

and called by

> .xx Monday 14th

to produce the text

> **Today is Monday the 14th.**

Note that the \$ was concealed in the definition with a prepended \. The number of currently available arguments is in the .$ register.

No arguments are available at the top (non-macro) level in this implementation. Because string referencing is implemented as a input-level push down, no arguments are available from *within* a string. No arguments are available within a trap-invoked macro.

Arguments are copied in *copy mode* onto a stack where they are available for reference. The mechanism does not allow an argument to contain a direct reference to a *long* string (interpolated at copy time) and it is advisable to conceal string references (with an extra \) to delay interpolation until argument reference time.

7.4. Diversions. Processed output may be diverted into a macro for purposes such as footnote processing (see Tutorial §T5) or determining the horizontal and vertical size of some text for conditional changing of pages or columns. A single diversion trap may be set at a specified vertical position. The number registers **dn** and **dl** respectively contain the vertical and horizontal size of the most recently ended diversion. Processed text that is diverted into a macro retains the vertical size of each of its lines when reread in *nofill* mode regardless of the current *V*. Constant-spaced (**cs**) or emboldened (**bd**) text that is diverted can be reread correctly only if these modes are again or still in effect at reread time. One way to do this is to imbed in the diversion the appropriate **cs** or **bd** requests with the *transparent* mechanism described in §10.6.

Diversions may be nested and certain parameters and registers are associated with the current diversion level (the top non-diversion level may be thought of as the 0th diversion level). These are the diversion trap and associated macro, no-space mode, the internally-saved marked place (see **mk** and **rt**), the current vertical place (**.d** register), the current high-water text base-line (**.h** register), and the current diversion name (**.z** register).

7.5. Traps. Three types of trap mechanisms are available—page traps, a diversion trap, and an input-line-count trap. Macro-invocation traps may be planted using **wh** at any page position including the top. This trap position may be changed using **ch**. Trap positions at or below the bottom of the page have no effect unless or until moved to within the page or rendered effective by an increase in page length. Two traps may be planted at the *same* position only by first planting them at different positions and then moving one of the traps; the first planted trap will conceal the second unless and until the first one is moved (see Tutorial Examples §T5). If the first one is moved back, it again conceals the second trap. The macro associated with a page trap is automatically invoked when a line of text is output whose vertical size *reaches* or *sweeps past* the trap position. Reaching the bottom of a page springs the top-of-page trap, if any, provided there is a next page. The distance to the next trap position is available in the **.t** register; if there are no traps between the current position and the bottom of the page, the distance returned is the distance to the page bottom.

A macro-invocation trap effective in the current diversion may be planted using **dt**. The **.t** register works in a diversion; if there is no subsequent trap a *large* distance is returned. For a description of input-line-count traps, see **it** below.

Request Form	Initial Value	If No Argument	Notes	Explanation
.de *xx yy*	-	*.yy*=..	-	Define or redefine the macro *xx*. The contents of the macro begin on the next input line. Input lines are copied in *copy mode* until the definition is terminated by a line beginning with *.yy*, whereupon the macro *yy* is called. In the absence of *yy*, the definition is terminated by a line beginning with "..". A macro may contain **de** requests provided the terminating macros differ or the contained definition terminator is concealed. ".." can be concealed as \\.. which will copy as \.. and be reread as "..".
.am *xx yy*	-	*.yy*=..	-	Append to macro (append version of **de**).
.ds *xx string*	-	ignored	-	Define a string *xx* containing *string*. Any initial double-quote in *string* is stripped off to permit initial blanks.
.as *xx string*	-	ignored	-	Append *string* to string *xx* (append version of **ds**).
.rm *xx*	-	ignored	-	Remove request, macro, or string. The name *xx* is removed from the name list and any related storage space is freed. Subsequent references will have no effect.
.rn *xx yy*	-	ignored	-	Rename request, macro, or string *xx* to *yy*. If *yy* exists, it is first removed.
.di *xx*	-	end	D	Divert output to macro *xx*. Normal text processing occurs during diversion except that page offsetting is not done. The diversion ends when the request **di** or **da** is encountered without an argument; extraneous requests of this type should not appear when nested diversions are being used.

.da *xx*	-	end	D		Divert, appending to *xx* (append version of **di**).
.wh *N xx*	-	-	v		Install a trap to invoke *xx* at page position *N;* a *negative N* will be interpreted with respect to the page *bottom*. Any macro previously planted at *N* is replaced by *xx*. A zero *N* refers to the *top* of a page. In the absence of *xx*, the first found trap at *N*, if any, is removed.
.ch *xx N*	-	-	v		Change the trap position for macro *xx* to be *N*. In the absence of *N*, the trap, if any, is removed.
.dt *N xx*	-	off	D,v		Install a diversion trap at position *N* in the *current* diversion to invoke macro *xx*. Another **dt** will redefine the diversion trap. If no arguments are given, the diversion trap is removed.
.it *N xx*	-	off	E		Set an input-line-count trap to invoke the macro *xx* after *N* lines of *text* input have been read (control or request lines don't count). The text may be in-line text or text interpolated by inline or trap-invoked macros.
.em *xx*	none	none	-		The macro *xx* will be invoked when all input has ended. The effect is the same as if the contents of *xx* had been at the end of the last file processed.

8. Number Registers

A variety of parameters are available to the user as predefined, named *number registers* (see Summary and Index, page 7). In addition, the user may define his own named registers. Register names are one or two characters long and *do not* conflict with request, macro, or string names. Except for certain predefined read-only registers, a number register can be read, written, automatically incremented or decremented, and interpolated into the input in a variety of formats. One common use of user-defined registers is to automatically number sections, paragraphs, lines, etc. A number register may be used any time numerical input is expected or desired and may be used in numerical *expressions* (§1.4).

Number registers are created and modified using **nr**, which specifies the name, numerical value, and the auto-increment size. Registers are also modified, if accessed with an auto-incrementing sequence. If the registers *x* and *xx* both contain *N* and have the auto-increment size *M*, the following access sequences have the effect shown:

Sequence	Effect on Register	Value Interpolated
\n*x*	none	N
\n(*xx*	none	N
\n+*x*	*x* incremented by *M*	$N+M$
\n−*x*	*x* decremented by *M*	$N-M$
\n+(*xx*	*xx* incremented by *M*	$N+M$
\n−(*xx*	*xx* decremented by *M*	$N-M$

When interpolated, a number register is converted to decimal (default), decimal with leading zeros, lower-case Roman, upper-case Roman, lower-case sequential alphabetic, or upper-case sequential alphabetic according to the format specified by **af**.

Request Form	Initial Value	If No Argument	Notes	Explanation
.nr *R* ±*N M*	-		u	The number register *R* is assigned the value ±*N* with respect to the previous value, if any. The increment for auto-incrementing is set to *M*.

| .af *R c* | arabic | - | - | Assign format *c* to register *R*. The available formats are: |

Format	Numbering Sequence
1	0,1,2,3,4,5,...
001	000,001,002,003,004,005,...
i	0,i,ii,iii,iv,v,...
I	0,I,II,III,IV,V,...
a	0,a,b,c,...,z,aa,ab,...,zz,aaa,...
A	0,A,B,C,...,Z,AA,AB,...,ZZ,AAA,...

An arabic format having *N* digits specifies a field width of *N* digits (example 2 above). The read-only registers and the *width* function (§11.2) are always arabic.

| .rr *R* | - | ignored | - | Remove register *R*. If many registers are being created dynamically, it may become necessary to remove no longer used registers to recapture internal storage space for newer registers. |

9. Tabs, Leaders, and Fields

9.1. Tabs and leaders. The ASCII horizontal tab character and the ASCII SOH (hereafter known as the *leader* character) can both be used to generate either horizontal motion or a string of repeated characters. The length of the generated entity is governed by internal *tab stops* specifiable with **ta**. The default difference is that tabs generate motion and leaders generate a string of periods; **tc** and **lc** offer the choice of repeated character or motion. There are three types of internal tab stops—*left* adjusting, *right* adjusting, and *centering*. In the following table: *D* is the distance from the current position on the *input* line (where a tab or leader was found) to the next tab stop; *next-string* consists of the input characters following the tab (or leader) up to the next tab (or leader) or end of line; and *W* is the width of *next-string*.

Tab type	Length of motion or repeated characters	Location of *next-string*
Left	D	Following *D*
Right	$D-W$	Right adjusted within *D*
Centered	$D-W/2$	Centered on right end of *D*

The length of generated motion is allowed to be negative, but that of a repeated character string cannot be. Repeated character strings contain an integer number of characters, and any residual distance is prepended as motion. Tabs or leaders found after the last tab stop are ignored, but may be used as *next-string* terminators.

Tabs and leaders are not interpreted in *copy mode*. \t and \a always generate a non-interpreted tab and leader respectively, and are equivalent to actual tabs and leaders in *copy mode*.

9.2. Fields. A *field* is contained between a *pair* of *field delimiter* characters, and consists of sub-strings separated by *padding* indicator characters. The field length is the distance on the *input* line from the position where the field begins to the next tab stop. The difference between the total length of all the sub-strings and the field length is incorporated as horizontal padding space that is divided among the indicated padding places. The incorporated padding is allowed to be negative. For example, if the field delimiter is # and the padding indicator is ˆ, #ˆ*xxx*ˆ*right*# specifies a right-adjusted string with the string *xxx* centered in the remaining space.

Request Form	Initial Value	If No Argument	Notes	Explanation
.ta Nt ...	0.8; 0.5in	none	E,m	Set tab stops and types. t=**R**, right adjusting; t=**C**, centering; t absent, left adjusting. TROFF tab stops are preset every 0.5in.; NROFF every 0.8in. The stop values are separated by spaces, and a value preceded by **+** is treated as an increment to the previous stop value.
.tc c	none	none	E	The tab repetition character becomes c, or is removed specifying motion.
.lc c	.	none	E	The leader repetition character becomes c, or is removed specifying motion.
.fc a b	off	off	-	The field delimiter is set to a; the padding indicator is set to the *space* character or to b, if given. In the absence of arguments the field mechanism is turned off.

10. Input and Output Conventions and Character Translations

10.1. Input character translations. Ways of inputting the graphic character set were discussed in §2.1. The ASCII control characters horizontal tab (§9.1), SOH (§9.1), and backspace (§10.3) are discussed elsewhere. The newline delimits input lines. In addition, STX, ETX, ENQ, ACK, and BEL are accepted, and may be used as delimiters or translated into a graphic with **tr** (§10.5). *All* others are ignored.

The *escape* character \ introduces *escape sequences*—causes the following character to mean another character, or to indicate some function. A complete list of such sequences is given in the Summary and Index on page 6. \ should not be confused with the ASCII control character ESC of the same name. The escape character \ can be input with the sequence \\. The escape character can be changed with **ec**, and all that has been said about the default \ becomes true for the new escape character. \e can be used to print whatever the current escape character is. If necessary or convenient, the escape mechanism may be turned off with **eo**, and restored with **ec**.

Request Form	Initial Value	If No Argument	Notes	Explanation
.ec c	\	\	-	Set escape character to \, or to c, if given.
.eo	on	-	-	Turn escape mechanism off.

10.2. Ligatures. Five ligatures are available in the current TROFF character set — fi, fl, ff, ffi, and ffl. They may be input (even in NROFF) by \(fi, \(fl, \(ff, \(Fi, and \(Fl respectively. The ligature mode is normally on in TROFF, and *automatically* invokes ligatures during input.

Request Form	Initial Value	If No Argument	Notes	Explanation
.lg N	off; on	on	-	Ligature mode is turned on if N is absent or non-zero, and turned off if N=0. If N=2, only the two-character ligatures are automatically invoked. Ligature mode is inhibited for request, macro, string, register, or file names, and in *copy mode*. No effect in NROFF.

10.3. Backspacing, underlining, overstriking, etc. Unless in *copy mode*, the ASCII backspace character is replaced by a backward horizontal motion having the width of the space character. Underlining as a form of line-drawing is discussed in §12.4. A generalized overstriking function is described in §12.1.

NROFF automatically underlines characters in the *underline* font, specifiable with **uf**, normally that on font position 2 (normally Times Italic, see §2.2). In addition to **ft** and \f$F$, the underline font may be selected by **ul** and **cu**. Underlining is restricted to an output-device-dependent subset of *reasonable* characters.

Request Form	Initial Value	If No Argument	Notes	Explanation
.ul *N*	off	*N*=1	E	Underline in NROFF (italicize in TROFF) the next *N* input text lines. Actually, switch to *underline* font, saving the current font for later restoration; *other* font changes within the span of a **ul** will take effect, but the restoration will undo the last change. Output generated by **tl** (§14) *is* affected by the font change, but does *not* decrement *N*. If *N*>1, there is the risk that a trap interpolated macro may provide text lines within the span; environment switching can prevent this.
.cu *N*	off	*N*=1	E	A variant of **ul** that causes *every* character to be underlined in NROFF. Identical to **ul** in TROFF.
.uf *F*	Italic	Italic	-	Underline font set to *F*. In NROFF, *F* may *not* be on position 1 (initially Times Roman).

10.4. Control characters. Both the control character . and the *no-break* control character may be changed, if desired. Such a change must be compatible with the design of any macros used in the span of the change, and particularly of any trap-invoked macros.

Request Form	Initial Value	If No Argument	Notes	Explanation
.cc *c*	.	.	E	The basic control character is set to *c*, or reset to ".".
.c2 *c*	'	'	E	The *nobreak* control character is set to *c*, or reset to "'".

10.5. Output translation. One cháracter can be made a stand-in for another character using **tr**. All text processing (e. g. character comparisons) takes place with the input (stand-in) character which appears to have the width of the final character. The graphic translation occurs at the moment of output (including diversion).

Request Form	Initial Value	If No Argument	Notes	Explanation
.tr *abcd....*	none	-	O	Translate *a* into *b*, *c* into *d*, etc. If an odd number of characters is given, the last one will be mapped into the space character. To be consistent, a particular translation must stay in effect from *input* to *output* time.

10.6. Transparent throughput. An input line beginning with a \! is read in *copy mode* and *transparently* output (without the initial \!); the text processor is otherwise unaware of the line's presence. This mechanism may be used to pass control information to a post-processor or to imbed control lines in a macro created by a diversion.

10.7. Comments and concealed newlines. An uncomfortably long input line that must stay one line (e. g. a string definition, or nofilled text) can be split into many physical lines by ending all but the last one with the escape \. The sequence \(newline) is *always* ignored—except in a comment. Comments may be imbedded at the *end* of any line by prefacing them with \". The newline at the end of a comment cannot be concealed. A line beginning with \" will appear as a blank line and behave like **.sp 1**; a comment can be on a line by itself by beginning the line with **.\"**.

11. Local Horizontal and Vertical Motions, and the Width Function

11.1. Local Motions. The functions \v'*N*' and \h'*N*' can be used for *local* vertical and horizontal motion respectively. The distance *N* may be negative; the *positive* directions are *rightward* and *downward*. A *local* motion is one contained *within* a line. To avoid unexpected vertical dislocations, it is necessary that the *net* vertical local motion within a word in filled text and otherwise within a line balance to zero. The above and certain other escape sequences providing local motion are summarized in the following table.

Vertical Local Motion	Effect in TROFF	NROFF	Horizontal Local Motion	Effect in TROFF	NROFF
\v´*N*´	Move distance *N*		\h´*N*´ \(space) \0	Move distance *N* Unpaddable space-size space Digit-size space	
\u \d \r	½ em up ½ em down 1 em up	½ line up ½ line down 1 line up	\\| \^	1/6 em space 1/12 em space	ignored ignored

As an example, E^2 could be generated by the sequence **E\s−2\v´−0.4m´2\v´0.4m´\s+2**; it should be noted in this example that the 0.4 em vertical motions are at the smaller size.

11.2. Width Function. The *width* function **\w´*string*´** generates the numerical width of *string* (in basic units). Size and font changes may be safely imbedded in *string*, and will not affect the current environment. For example, **.ti −\w´1. ´u** could be used to temporarily indent leftward a distance equal to the size of the string "**1. **".

The width function also sets three number registers. The registers **st** and **sb** are set respectively to the highest and lowest extent of *string* relative to the baseline; then, for example, the total *height* of the string is **\n(stu−\n(sbu**. In TROFF the number register **ct** is set to a value between 0 and 3: 0 means that all of the characters in *string* were short lower case characters without descenders (like **e**); 1 means that at least one character has a descender (like **y**); 2 means that at least one character is tall (like **H**); and 3 means that both tall characters and characters with descenders are present.

11.3. Mark horizontal place. The escape sequence **\k***x* will cause the *current* horizontal position in the *input line* to be stored in register *x*. As an example, the construction **\k***x*word**\h´|\n***xu***+2u´** *word* will embolden *word* by backing up to almost its beginning and overprinting it, resulting in **word**.

12. Overstrike, Bracket, Line-drawing, and Zero-width Functions

12.1. Overstriking. Automatically centered overstriking of up to nine characters is provided by the *overstrike* function **\o´*string*´**. The characters in *string* overprinted with centers aligned; the total width is that of the widest character. *string* should *not* contain local vertical motion. As examples, **\o´e\'´** produces é, and **\o´\(mo\(sl´** produces ∉.

12.2. Zero-width characters. The function **\z***c* will output *c* without spacing over it, and can be used to produce left-aligned overstruck combinations. As examples, **\z\(ci\(pl** will produce ⊕, and **\(br\z\(rn\(ul\(br** will produce the smallest possible constructed box ⬚.

12.3. Large Brackets. The Special Mathematical Font contains a number of bracket construction pieces (⎛⎝⎞⎠⎧⎨⎩⎫⎬⎭) that can be combined into various bracket styles. The function **\b´*string*´** may be used to pile up vertically the characters in *string* (the first character on top and the last at the bottom); the characters are vertically separated by 1 em and the total pile is centered 1/2 em above the current baseline (½ line in NROFF). For example, **\b´\(lc\(lf´E\\|\b´\(rc\(rf´\x´−0.5m´\x´0.5m´** produces ⎡E⎤.

12.4. Line drawing. The function **\l´*Nc*´** will draw a string of repeated *c*'s towards the right for a distance *N*. (\l is \(lower case L). If *c* looks like a continuation of an expression for *N*, it may insulated from *N* with a **\&**. If *c* is not specified, the _ (baseline rule) is used (underline character in NROFF). If *N* is negative, a backward horizontal motion of size *N* is made *before* drawing the string. Any space resulting from *N*/(size of *c*) having a remainder is put at the beginning (left end) of the string. In the case of characters that are designed to be connected such as baseline-rule _, underrule _, and root-en ¯, the remainder space is covered by over-lapping. If *N* is *less* than the width of *c*, a single *c* is centered on a distance *N*. As an example, a macro to underscore a string can be written

```
.de us
\\$1\l´|0\(ul´
..
```

or one to draw a box around a string

```
.de bx
\(br\|\\$1\|\(br\1´|0\(rn´\1´|0\(ul´
..
```

such that

.ul "underlined words"

and

.bx "words in a box"

yield underlined words and words in a box.

The function \L´ Nc´ will draw a vertical line consisting of the (optional) character c stacked vertically apart 1 em (1 line in NROFF), with the first two characters overlapped, if necessary, to form a continuous line. The default character is the *box rule* | (\(br); the other suitable character is the *bold vertical* | (\(bv). The line is begun without any initial motion relative to the current base line. A positive N specifies a line drawn downward and a negative N specifies a line drawn upward. After the line is drawn *no* compensating motions are made; the instantaneous baseline is at the *end* of the line.

The horizontal and vertical line drawing functions may be used in combination to produce large boxes. The zero-width *box-rule* and the ½-em wide *underrule* were *designed* to form corners when using 1-em vertical spacings. For example the macro

```
.de eb
.sp −1        \"compensate for next automatic base-line spacing
.nf           \"avoid possibly overflowing word buffer
\h´−.5n´\L´|\\nau−1´l´\\n(.lu+1n\(ul´\L´−|\\nau+1´l´|0u−.5n\(ul´    \"draw box
.fi
..
```

will draw a box around some text whose beginning vertical place was saved in number register a (e. g. using **.mk a**) as done for this paragraph.

---

13. Hyphenation.

The automatic hyphenation may be switched off and on. When switched on with **hy**, several variants may be set. A *hyphenation indicator* character may be imbedded in a word to specify desired hyphenation points, or may be prepended to suppress hyphenation. In addition, the user may specify a small exception word list.

Only words that consist of a central alphabetic string surrounded by (usually null) non-alphabetic strings are considered candidates for automatic hyphenation. Words that were input containing hyphens (minus), em-dashes (\(em), or hyphenation indicator characters—such as mother-in-law—are *always* subject to splitting after those characters, whether or not automatic hyphenation is on or off.

Request Form	Initial Value	If No Argument	Notes	Explanation
.nh	hyphenate	-	E	Automatic hyphenation is turned off.
.hy N	on, N=1	on, N=1	E	Automatic hyphenation is turned on for $N \geqslant 1$, or off for $N=0$. If $N=2$, *last* lines (ones that will cause a trap) are not hyphenated. For $N=4$ and 8, the last and first two characters respectively of a word are not split off. These values are additive; i. e. $N=14$ will invoke all three restrictions.
.hc c	\%	\%	E	Hyphenation indicator character is set to c or to the default \%. The indicator does not appear in the output.
.hw word1 ...		ignored	-	Specify hyphenation points in words with imbedded minus signs. Versions of a word with terminal s are

implied; i. e. *dig—it* implies *dig—its*. This list is examined initially *and* after each suffix stripping. The space available is small—about 128 characters.

14. Three Part Titles.

The titling function **tl** provides for automatic placement of three fields at the left, center, and right of a line with a title-length specifiable with **lt**. **tl** may be used anywhere, and is independent of the normal text collecting process. A common use is in header and footer macros.

Request Form	Initial Value	If No Argument	Notes	Explanation
.tl ´left´center´right´	-	-		The strings *left*, *center*, and *right* are respectively left-adjusted, centered, and right-adjusted in the current title-length. Any of the strings may be empty, and overlapping is permitted. If the page-number character (initially %) is found within any of the fields it is replaced by the current page number having the format assigned to register %. Any character may be used as the string delimiter.
.pc *c*	%	off	-	The page number character is set to *c*, or removed. The page-number register remains %.
.lt $\pm N$	6.5 in	previous	E,**m**	Length of title set to $\pm N$. The line-length and the title-length are *independent*. Indents do not apply to titles; page-offsets do.

15. Output Line Numbering.

Automatic sequence numbering of output lines may be requested with **nm**. When in effect, a three-digit, arabic number plus a digit-space is prepended to output text lines. The text lines are

3 thus offset by four digit-spaces, and otherwise retain their line length; a reduction in line length may be desired to keep the right margin aligned with an earlier margin. Blank lines, other vertical spaces, and lines generated by **tl** are *not* numbered. Numbering can be temporarily suspended with

6 **nn**, or with an **.nm** followed by a later **.nm +0**. In addition, a line number indent I, and the number-text separation S may be specified in digit-spaces. Further, it can be specified that only those line numbers that are multiples of some number M are to be printed (the others will appear

9 as blank number fields).

Request Form	Initial Value	If No Argument	Notes	Explanation
.nm $\pm N$ M S I		off	E	Line number mode. If $\pm N$ is given, line numbering is turned on, and the next output line numbered is numbered $\pm N$. Default values are $M=1$, $S=1$, and $I=0$. Parameters corresponding to missing arguments are unaffected; a non-numeric argument is considered missing. In the absence of all arguments, numbering is turned off; the next line number is preserved for possible further use in number register **ln**.
.nn *N*	-	*N*=1	E	The next N text output lines are not numbered.

As an example, the paragraph portions of this section are numbered with $M=3$: **.nm 1 3** was placed at the beginning; **.nm** was placed at the end of the first paragraph; and **.nm +0** was placed

12 in front of this paragraph; and **.nm** finally placed at the end. Line lengths were also changed (by \w´0000´u) to keep the right side aligned. Another example is **.nm +5 5 x 3** which turns on numbering with the line number of the next line to be 5 greater than the last numbered line, with

15 $M=5$, with spacing S untouched, and with the indent I set to 3.

16. Conditional Acceptance of Input

In the following, c is a one-character, built-in *condition* name, ! signifies *not*, N is a numerical expression, *string1* and *string2* are strings delimited by any non-blank, non-numeric character *not* in the strings, and *anything* represents what is conditionally accepted.

Request Form	Initial Value	If No Argument	Notes	Explanation
.if c *anything*	-	-		If condition c true, accept *anything* as input; in multi-line case use \{*anything*\}.
.if !c *anything*	-	-		If condition c false, accept *anything*.
.if N *anything*	-		u	If expression $N > 0$, accept *anything*.
.if !N *anything*	-		u	If expression $N \leqslant 0$, accept *anything*.
.if ´*string1*´*string2*´ *anything*	-		-	If *string1* identical to *string2*, accept *anything*.
.if !´*string1*´*string2*´ *anything*	-		-	If *string1* not identical to *string2*, accept *anything*.
.ie c *anything*	-		u	If portion of if-else; all above forms (like **if**).
.el *anything*	-		-	Else portion of if-else.

The built-in condition names are:

Condition Name	True If
o	Current page number is odd
e	Current page number is even
t	Formatter is TROFF
n	Formatter is NROFF

If the condition c is *true*, or if the number N is greater than zero, or if the strings compare identically (including motions and character size and font), *anything* is accepted as input. If a ! precedes the condition, number, or string comparison, the sense of the acceptance is reversed.

Any spaces between the condition and the beginning of *anything* are skipped over. The *anything* can be either a single input line (text, macro, or whatever) or a number of input lines. In the multi-line case, the first line must begin with a left delimiter \{ and the last line must end with a right delimiter \}.

The request **ie** (if-else) is identical to **if** except that the acceptance state is remembered. A subsequent and matching **el** (else) request then uses the reverse sense of that state. **ie** - **el** pairs may be nested.

Some examples are:

```
.if e .tl ´Even Page %´´´
```

which outputs a title if the page number is even; and

```
.ie \n%>1 \{\
´sp 0.5i
.tl ´Page %´´´
´sp |1.2i \}
.el .sp |2.5i
```

which treats page 1 differently from other pages.

17. Environment Switching.

A number of the parameters that control the text processing are gathered together into an *environment*, which can be switched by the user. The environment parameters are those associated with requests noting E in their *Notes* column; in addition, partially collected lines and words are in the environment. Everything else is global; examples are page-oriented parameters, diversion-oriented parameters, number registers, and macro and string definitions. All environments are initialized with default parameter values.

Request Form	Initial Value	If No Argument	Notes	Explanation
.ev N	N=0	previous	-	Environment switched to environment $0 \leqslant N \leqslant 2$. Switching is done in push-down fashion so that restoring a previous environment *must* be done with **.ev** rather than specific reference.

18. Insertions from the Standard Input

The input can be temporarily switched to the system *standard input* with **rd**, which will switch back when *two* newlines in a row are found (the *extra* blank line is not used). This mechanism is intended for insertions in form-letter-like documentation. On UNIX, the *standard input* can be the user's keyboard, a *pipe*, or a *file*.

Request Form	Initial Value	If No Argument	Notes	Explanation
.rd *prompt*	-	*prompt*=BEL	-	Read insertion from the standard input until two newlines in a row are found. If the standard input is the user's keyboard, *prompt* (or a BEL) is written onto the user's terminal. **rd** behaves like a macro, and arguments may be placed after *prompt*.
.ex	-	-	-	Exit from NROFF/TROFF. Text processing is terminated exactly as if all input had ended.

If insertions are to be taken from the terminal keyboard *while* output is being printed on the terminal, the command line option −q will turn off the echoing of keyboard input and prompt only with BEL. The regular input and insertion input *cannot* simultaneously come from the standard input.

As an example, multiple copies of a form letter may be prepared by entering the insertions for all the copies in one file to be used as the standard input, and causing the file containing the letter to reinvoke itself using **nx** (§19); the process would ultimately be ended by an **ex** in the insertion file.

19. Input/Output File Switching

Request Form	Initial Value	If No Argument	Notes	Explanation
.so *filename*	-	-	-	Switch source file. The top input (file reading) level is switched to *filename*. The effect of an **so** encountered in a macro is not felt until the input level returns to the file level. When the new file ends, input is again taken from the original file. **so**'s may be nested.
.nx *filename*	end-of-file	-	-	Next file is *filename*. The current file is considered ended, and the input is immediately switched to *filename*.
.pi *program*	-	-	-	Pipe output to *program* (NROFF only). This request must occur *before* any printing occurs. No arguments are transmitted to *program*.

20. Miscellaneous

Request Form	Initial Value	If No Argument	Notes	Explanation
.mc *c N*	-	off	E,m	Specifies that a *margin* character *c* appear a distance *N* to the right of the right margin after each non-empty text line (except those produced by **tl**). If the output line is too-long (as can happen in nofill mode) the character will

be appended to the line. If *N* is not given, the previous *N* is used; the initial *N* is 0.2 inches in NROFF and 1 em in TROFF. The margin character used with this paragraph was a 12-point box-rule.

.tm *string*	-	newline	-	After skipping initial blanks, *string* (rest of the line) is read in *copy mode* and written on the user's terminal.
.ig *yy*	-	.*yy*=..	-	Ignore input lines. **ig** behaves exactly like **de** (§7) except that the input is discarded. The input is read in *copy mode*, and any auto-incremented registers will be affected.
.pm *t*	-	all	-	Print macros. The names and sizes of all of the defined macros and strings are printed on the user's terminal; if *t* is given, only the total of the sizes is printed. The sizes is given in *blocks* of 128 characters.
.fl	-	-	B	Flush output buffer. Used in interactive debugging to force output.

21. Output and Error Messages.

The output from **tm**, **pm**, and the prompt from **rd**, as well as various *error* messages are written onto UNIX's *standard message* output. The latter is different from the *standard output*, where NROFF formatted output goes. By default, both are written onto the user's terminal, but they can be independently redirected.

Various *error* conditions may occur during the operation of NROFF and TROFF. Certain less serious errors having only local impact do not cause processing to terminate. Two examples are *word overflow*, caused by a word that is too large to fit into the word buffer (in fill mode), and *line overflow*, caused by an output line that grew too large to fit in the line buffer; in both cases, a message is printed, the offending excess is discarded, and the affected word or line is marked at the point of truncation with a * in NROFF and a ▀◣ in TROFF. The philosophy is to continue processing, if possible, on the grounds that output useful for debugging may be produced. If a serious error occurs, processing terminates, and an appropriate message is printed. Examples are the inability to create, read, or write files, and the exceeding of certain internal limits that make future output unlikely to be useful.

TUTORIAL EXAMPLES

T1. Introduction

Although NROFF and TROFF have by design a syntax reminiscent of earlier text processors* with the intent of easing their use, it is almost always necessary to prepare at least a small set of macro definitions to describe most documents. Such common formatting needs as page margins and footnotes are deliberately not built into NROFF and TROFF. Instead, the macro and string definition, number register, diversion, environment switching, page-position trap, and conditional input mechanisms provide the basis for user-defined implementations.

The examples to be discussed are intended to be useful and somewhat realistic, but won't necessarily cover all relevant contingencies. Explicit numerical parameters are used in the examples to make them easier to read and to illustrate typical values. In many cases, number registers would really be used to reduce the number of places where numerical information is kept, and to concentrate conditional parameter initialization like that which depends on whether TROFF or NROFF is being used.

T2. Page Margins

As discussed in §3, *header* and *footer* macros are usually defined to describe the top and bottom page margin areas respectively. A trap is planted at page position 0 for the header, and at $-N$ (N from the page bottom) for the footer. The simplest such definitions might be

```
.de hd            \"define header
´sp 1i

..                \"end definition
.de fo            \"define footer
´bp
..                \"end definition
.wh 0 hd
.wh −1i fo
```

which provide blank 1 inch top and bottom margins. The header will occur on the *first* page, only if the definition and trap exist prior to the

initial pseudo-page transition (§3). In fill mode, the output line that springs the footer trap was typically forced out because some part or whole word didn't fit on it. If anything in the footer and header that follows causes a *break*, that word or part word will be forced out. In this and other examples, requests like **bp** and **sp** that normally cause breaks are invoked using the *no-break* control character   to avoid this. When the header/footer design contains material requiring independent text processing, the environment may be switched, avoiding most interaction with the running text.

A more realistic example would be

```
.de hd               \"header
.if t .tl ´\(rn´´\(rn´  \"troff cut mark
.if \\n%>1 \{\
´sp |0.5i−1        \"tl base at 0.5i
.tl ´´− % −´´       \"centered page number
.ps                \"restore size
.ft                \"restore font
.vs \}             \"restore vs
´sp |1.0i          \"space to 1.0i
.ns                \"turn on no-space mode
..
.de fo               \"footer
.ps 10             \"set footer/header size
.ft R              \"set font
.vs 12p            \"set base-line spacing
.if \\n%=1 \{\
´sp |\\n(.pu−0.5i−1  \"tl base 0.5i up
.tl ´´− % −´´ \}   \"first page number
´bp
..
.wh 0 hd
.wh −1i fo
```

which sets the size, font, and base-line spacing for the header/footer material, and ultimately restores them. The material in this case is a page number at the bottom of the first page and at the top of the remaining pages. If TROFF is used, a *cut mark* is drawn in the form of *root-en*'s at each margin. The **sp**'s refer to absolute positions to avoid dependence on the base-line spacing. Another reason for this in the footer is that the footer is invoked by printing a line whose vertical spacing swept past the trap position by possibly as

---

*For example: P. A. Crisman, Ed., *The Compatible Time-Sharing System,* MIT Press, 1965, Section AH9.01 (Description of RUNOFF program on MIT's CTSS system).

much as the base-line spacing. The *no-space* mode is turned on at the end of **hd** to render ineffective accidental occurrences of **sp** at the top of the running text.

The above method of restoring size, font, etc. presupposes that such requests (that set *previous* value) are *not* used in the running text. A better scheme is save and restore both the current *and* previous values as shown for size in the following:

```
.de fo
.nr s1 \\n(.s        \"current size
.ps
.nr s2 \\n(.s        \"previous size
. ---                \"rest of footer
..
.de hd
. ---                \"header stuff
.ps \\n(s2           \"restore previous size
.ps \\n(s1           \"restore current size
..
```

Page numbers may be printed in the bottom margin by a separate macro triggered during the footer's page ejection:

```
.de bn               \"bottom number
.tl ''— % —''        \"centered page number
..
.wh −0.5i−1v bn \"tl base 0.5i up
```

T3. Paragraphs and Headings

The housekeeping associated with starting a new paragraph should be collected in a paragraph macro that, for example, does the desired preparagraph spacing, forces the correct font, size, base-line spacing, and indent, checks that enough space remains for *more than one* line, and requests a temporary indent.

```
.de pg               \"paragraph
.br                  \"break
.ft R                \"force font,
.ps 10               \"size,
.vs 12p              \"spacing,
.in 0                \"and indent
.sp 0.4              \"prespace
.ne 1+\\n(.Vu \"want more than 1 line
.ti 0.2i             \"temp indent
..
```

The first break in **pg** will force out any previous partial lines, and must occur before the **vs**. The forcing of font, etc. is partly a defense against prior error and partly to permit things like section heading macros to set parameters only once.

The prespacing parameter is suitable for TROFF; a larger space, at least as big as the output device vertical resolution, would be more suitable in NROFF. The choice of remaining space to test for in the **ne** is the smallest amount greater than one line (the **.V** is the available vertical resolution).

A macro to automatically number section headings might look like:

```
.de sc               \"section
. ---                \"force font, etc.
.sp 0.4              \"prespace
.ne 2.4+\\n(.Vu \"want 2.4+ lines
.fi
\\n+S.
..
.nr S 0 1            \"init S
```

The usage is **.sc**, followed by the section heading text, followed by **.pg**. The **ne** test value includes one line of heading, 0.4 line in the following **pg**, and one line of the paragraph text. A word consisting of the next section number and a period is produced to begin the heading line. The format of the number may be set by **af** (§8).

Another common form is the labeled, indented paragraph, where the label protrudes left into the indent space.

```
.de lp               \"labeled paragraph
.pg
.in 0.5i             \"paragraph indent
.ta 0.2i 0.5i        \"label, paragraph
.ti 0
\t\\$1\t\c           \"flow into paragraph
..
```

The intended usage is ".lp *label*"; *label* will begin at 0.2 inch, and cannot exceed a length of 0.3 inch without intruding into the paragraph. The label could be right adjusted against 0.4 inch by setting the tabs instead with **.ta 0.4iR 0.5i**. The last line of **lp** ends with \c so that it will become a part of the first line of the text that follows.

T4. Multiple Column Output

The production of multiple column pages requires the footer macro to decide whether it was invoked by other than the last column, so that it will begin a new column rather than produce the bottom margin. The header can initialize a column register that the footer will increment and test. The following is arranged for two columns, but is easily modified for more.

```
.de hd           \"header
. ---
.nr cl 0 1       \"init column count
.mk              \"mark top of text
..
.de fo           \"footer
.ie \\n+(cl<2 \{\
.po +3.4i        \"next column; 3.1+0.3
.rt              \"back to mark
.ns \}           \"no-space mode
.el \{\
.po \\nMu        \"restore left margin
. ---
'bp \}
..
.ll 3.1i         \"column width
.nr M \\n(.o     \"save left margin
```

Typically a portion of the top of the first page contains full width text; the request for the narrower line length, as well as another **.mk** would be made where the two column output was to begin.

T5. Footnote Processing

The footnote mechanism to be described is used by imbedding the footnotes in the input text at the point of reference, demarcated by an initial **.fn** and a terminal **.ef**:

```
.fn
Footnote text and control lines...
.ef
```

In the following, footnotes are processed in a separate environment and diverted for later printing in the space immediately prior to the bottom margin. There is provision for the case where the last collected footnote doesn't completely fit in the available space.

```
.de hd           \"header
. ---
.nr x 0 1        \"init footnote count
.nr y 0-\\nb     \"current footer place
.ch fo -\\nbu    \"reset footer trap
.if \\n(dn .fz   \"leftover footnote
..
.de fo           \"footer
.nr dn 0         \"zero last diversion size
.if \\nx \{\
.ev 1            \"expand footnotes in ev1
.nf              \"retain vertical size
.FN              \"footnotes
.rm FN           \"delete it
.if "\\n(.z"fy" .di \"end overflow diversion
.nr x 0          \"disable fx
```

```
.ev \}           \"pop environment
. ---
'bp
..
.de fx           \"process footnote overflow
.if \\nx .di fy  \"divert overflow
..
.de fn           \"start footnote
.da FN           \"divert (append) footnote
.ev 1            \"in environment 1
.if \\n+x=1 .fs  \"if first, include separator
.fi              \"fill mode
..
.de ef           \"end footnote
.br              \"finish output
.nr z \\n(.v     \"save spacing
.ev              \"pop ev
.di              \"end diversion
.nr y -\\n(dn \"new footer position,
.if \\nx=1 .nr y -(\\n(.v-\\nz) \
                 \"uncertainty correction
.ch fo \\nyu     \"y is negative
.if (\\n(nl+1v)>(\\n(.p+\\ny) \
.ch fo \\n(nlu+1v \"it didn't fit
..
.de fs           \"separator
\l'1i'           \"1 inch rule
.br
..
.de fz           \"get leftover footnote
.fn
.nf              \"retain vertical size
.fy              \"where fx put it
.ef
..
.nr b 1.0i       \"bottom margin size
.wh 0 hd         \"header trap
.wh 12i fo       \"footer trap, temp position
.wh -\\nbu fx \"fx at footer position
.ch fo -\\nbu    \"conceal fx with fo
```

The header **hd** initializes a footnote count register **x**, and sets both the current footer trap position register **y** and the footer trap itself to a nominal position specified in register **b**. In addition, if the register **dn** indicates a leftover footnote, **fz** is invoked to reprocess it. The footnote start macro **fn** begins a diversion (append) in environment 1, and increments the count **x**; if the count is one, the footnote separator **fs** is interpolated. The separator is kept in a separate macro to permit user redefinition. The footnote end macro **ef** restores the previous environment and ends the diversion after saving the spacing size in register **z**. **y** is then decremented by the size of the footnote, available in **dn**; then on the first foot-note, **y** is further decremented by the difference in vertical base-line spacings of the two environments, to prevent the late triggering the footer trap from causing the last line of the combined footnotes to overflow. The footer trap is then set to the lower (on the page) of **y** or the current page position (**nl**) plus one line, to allow for printing the reference line. If indicated by **x**, the footer **fo** rereads the footnotes from **FN** in nofill mode in environment 1, and deletes **FN**. If the footnotes were too large to fit, the macro **fx** will be trap-invoked to redivert the overflow into **fy**, and the register **dn** will later indicate to the header whether **fy** is empty. Both **fo** and **fx** are planted in the nominal footer trap position in an order that causes **fx** to be concealed unless the **fo** trap is moved. The footer then terminates the overflow diversion, if necessary, and zeros **x** to disable **fx**, because the uncertainty correction together with a not-too-late triggering of the footer can result in the footnote rereading finishing before reaching the **fx** trap.

A good exercise for the student is to combine the multiple-column and footnote mechanisms.

T6. The Last Page

After the last input file has ended, NROFF and TROFF invoke the *end macro* (§7), if any, and when it finishes, eject the remainder of the page. During the eject, any traps encountered are processed normally. At the *end* of this last page, processing terminates *unless* a partial line, word, or partial word remains. If it is desired that another page be started, the end-macro

```
.de en          \"end-macro
\c
'bp
..
.em en
```

will deposit a null partial word, and effect another last page.

Table I

Font Style Examples

The following fonts are printed in 12-point, with a vertical spacing of 14-point, and with non-alphanumeric characters separated by ¼ em space. The Special Mathematical Font was specially prepared for Bell Laboratories by Graphic Systems, Inc. of Hudson, New Hampshire. The Times Roman, Italic, and Bold are among the many standard fonts available from that company.

Times Roman

abcdefghijklmnopqrstuvwxyz
ABCDEFGHIJKLMNOPQRSTUVWXYZ
1234567890
! $ % & ( ) ' ' * + − . , / : ; = ? [ ] |
● □ — - _ ¼ ½ ¾ fi fl ff ffi ffl ° † ' ¢ ® ©

Times Italic

abcdefghijklmnopqrstuvwxyz
ABCDEFGHIJKLMNOPQRSTUVWXYZ
1234567890
*! $ % & ( ) ' ' * + − . , / : ; = ? [ ] |*
● □ — - _ ¼ ½ ¾ fi fl ff ffi ffl ° † ' ¢ ® ©

Times Bold

abcdefghijklmnopqrstuvwxyz
ABCDEFGHIJKLMNOPQRSTUVWXYZ
1234567890
! $ % & ( ) ' ' * + − . , / : ; = ? [ ] |
● □ — - _ ¼ ½ ¾ fi fl ff ffi ffl ° † ' ¢ ® ©

Special Mathematical Font

" ´ \ ^ _ ` ˜ / < > { } # @ + − = *
$\alpha \beta \gamma \delta \epsilon \zeta \eta \theta \iota \kappa \lambda \mu \nu \xi o \pi \rho \sigma s \tau \upsilon \phi \chi \psi \omega$
$\Gamma \Delta \Theta \Lambda \Xi \Pi \Sigma \Upsilon \Phi \Psi \Omega$
$\sqrt{} \geqslant \leqslant \equiv \sim \simeq \neq \rightarrow \leftarrow \uparrow \downarrow \times \div \pm \cup \cap \subset \supset \subseteq \supseteq \infty \partial$
$\S \nabla \neg \int \propto \emptyset \in \ddagger$ ☛ ☚ Ⓐ | ○ ⎛⎝ ⎞⎠ ⎧⎫ ⎨⎬ ⎩⎭ ⎡ ⎤

Table II

Input Naming Conventions for ´, `, and —
and for Non-ASCII Special Characters

Non-ASCII characters and *minus* on the standard fonts.

Char	Input Name	Character Name	Char	Input Name	Character Name
´	´	close quote	fi	\(fi	fi
`	`	open quote	fl	\(fl	fl
—	\(em	3/4 Em dash	ff	\(ff	ff
-	—	hyphen or	ffi	\(Fi	ffi
-	\(hy	hyphen	ffl	\(Fl	ffl
—	\-	current font minus	°	\(de	degree
●	\(bu	bullet	†	\(dg	dagger
□	\(sq	square	´	\(fm	foot mark
_	\(ru	rule	¢	\(ct	cent sign
¼	\(14	1/4	®	\(rg	registered
½	\(12	1/2	©	\(co	copyright
¾	\(34	3/4			

Non-ASCII characters and ´, `, _, +, −, =, and * on the special font.

The ASCII characters @, #, ", ´, `, <, >, \, {, }, ˜, ˆ, and _ exist *only* on the special font and are printed as a 1-em space if that font is not mounted. The following characters exist only on the special font except for the upper case Greek letter names followed by † which are mapped into upper case English letters in whatever font is mounted on font position one (default Times Roman). The special math plus, minus, and equals are provided to insulate the appearance of equations from the choice of standard fonts.

Char	Input Name	Character Name	Char	Input Name	Character Name
+	\(pl	math plus	κ	\(*k	kappa
−	\(mi	math minus	λ	\(*l	lambda
=	\(eq	math equals	μ	\(*m	mu
*	\(**	math star	ν	\(*n	nu
§	\(sc	section	ξ	\(*c	xi
´	\(aa	acute accent	o	\(*o	omicron
`	\(ga	grave accent	π	\(*p	pi
	\(ul	underrule	ρ	\(*r	rho
⁄	\(sl	slash (matching backslash)	σ	\(*s	sigma
α	\(*a	alpha	ς	\(ts	terminal sigma
β	\(*b	beta	τ	\(*t	tau
γ	\(*g	gamma	υ	\(*u	upsilon
δ	\(*d	delta	φ	\(*f	phi
ε	\(*e	epsilon	χ	\(*x	chi
ζ	\(*z	zeta	ψ	\(*q	psi
η	\(*y	eta	ω	\(*w	omega
θ	\(*h	theta	A	\(*A	Alpha†
ι	\(*i	iota	B	\(*B	Beta†

Input Char	Name	Character Name
Γ	\(*G	Gamma
Δ	\(*D	Delta
E	\(*E	Epsilon†
Z	\(*Z	Zeta†
H	\(*Y	Eta†
Θ	\(*H	Theta
I	\(*I	Iota†
K	\(*K	Kappa†
Λ	\(*L	Lambda
M	\(*M	Mu†
N	\(*N	Nu†
Ξ	\(*C	Xi
O	\(*O	Omicron†
Π	\(*P	Pi
P	\(*R	Rho†
Σ	\(*S	Sigma
T	\(*T	Tau†
Υ	\(*U	Upsilon
Φ	\(*F	Phi
X	\(*X	Chi†
Ψ	\(*Q	Psi
Ω	\(*W	Omega
√	\(sr	square root
	\(rn	root en extender
≥	\(>=	>=
≤	\(<=	<=
≡	\(==	identically equal
≃	\(~=	approx =
~	\(ap	approximates
≠	\(!=	not equal
→	\(->	right arrow
←	\(<-	left arrow
↑	\(ua	up arrow
↓	\(da	down arrow
×	\(mu	multiply
÷	\(di	divide
±	\(+-	plus-minus
∪	\(cu	cup (union)
∩	\(ca	cap (intersection)
⊂	\(sb	subset of
⊃	\(sp	superset of
⊆	\(ib	improper subset
⊇	\(ip	improper superset
∞	\(if	infinity
∂	\(pd	partial derivative
∇	\(gr	gradient
¬	\(no	not
∫	\(is	integral sign
∝	\(pt	proportional to
∅	\(es	empty set
∈	\(mo	member of

Input Char	Name	Character Name
|	\(br	box vertical rule
‡	\(dd	double dagger
☛	\(rh	right hand
☚	\(lh	left hand
⌖	\(bs	Bell System logo
|	\(or	or
O	\(ci	circle
⌈	\(lt	left top of big curly bracket
⌊	\(lb	left bottom
⌉	\(rt	right top
⌋	\(rb	right bot
{	\(lk	left center of big curly bracket
}	\(rk	right center of big curly bracket
|	\(bv	bold vertical
⌊	\(lf	left floor (left bottom of big square bracket)
⌋	\(rf	right floor (right bottom)
⌈	\(lc	left ceiling (left top)
⌉	\(rc	right ceiling (right top)

Summary of Changes to N/TROFF Since October 1976 Manual

Options

-h   (Nroff only) Output tabs used during horizontal spacing to speed output as well as reduce output byte count. Device tab settings assumed to be every 8 nominal character widths. The default settings of input (logical) tabs is also initialized to every 8 nominal character widths.

-z   Efficiently suppresses formatted output. Only message output will occur (from "tm"s and diagnostics).

Old Requests

.ad c   The adjustment type indicator "c" may now also be a number previously obtained from the ".j" register (see below).

.so name The contents of file "name" will be interpolated at the point the "so" is encountered. Previously, the interpolation was done upon return to the file-reading input level.

New Request

.ab text Prints "text" on the message output and terminates without further processing. If "text" is missing, "User Abort." is printed. Does not cause a break. The output buffer is flushed.

.fz F N   forces font "F" to be in size N. N may have the form N, +N, or -N. For example,
          .fz 3 -2
          will cause an implicit \s-2 every time font 3 is entered, and a corresponding \s+2 when it is left. Special font characters occurring during the reign of font F will have the same size modification. If special characters are to be treated differently,
          .fz S F N
          may be used to specify the size treatment of special characters during font F. For example,
          .fz 3 -3
          .fz S 3 -0
          will cause automatic reduction of font 3 by 3 points while the special characters would not be affected. Any ".fp" request specifying a font on some position must precede ".fz" requests relating to that position.

New Predefined Number Registers.

.k   Read-only. Contains the horizontal size of the text portion (without indent) of the current partially collected output line, if any, in the current environment.

.j   Read-only. A number representing the current adjustment mode and type. Can be saved and later given to the "ad" request to restore a previous mode.

.P   Read-only. 1 if the current page is being printed, and zero otherwise.

.L   Read-only. Contains the current line-spacing parameter ("ls").

c.   General register access to the input line-number in the current input file. Contains the same value as the read-only ".c" register.

A TROFF Tutorial

Brian W. Kernighan

Bell Laboratories
Murray Hill, New Jersey 07974

ABSTRACT

troff is a text-formatting program for driving the Graphic Systems photo-typesetter on the UNIX† and GCOS operating systems. This device is capable of producing high quality text; this paper is an example of **troff** output.

The phototypesetter itself normally runs with four fonts, containing roman, italic and bold letters (as on this page), a full greek alphabet, and a substantial number of special characters and mathematical symbols. Characters can be printed in a range of sizes, and placed anywhere on the page.

troff allows the user full control over fonts, sizes, and character positions, as well as the usual features of a formatter — right-margin justification, automatic hyphenation, page titling and numbering, and so on. It also provides macros, arithmetic variables and operations, and conditional testing, for complicated formatting tasks.

This document is an introduction to the most basic use of **troff**. It presents just enough information to enable the user to do simple formatting tasks like making viewgraphs, and to make incremental changes to existing packages of **troff** commands. In most respects, the UNIX formatter **nroff** is identical to **troff**, so this document also serves as a tutorial on **nroff**.

August 4, 1978

---

†UNIX is a Trademark of Bell Laboratories.

1. Introduction

troff [1] is a text-formatting program, written by J. F. Ossanna, for producing high-quality printed output from the phototypesetter on the UNIX and GCOS operating systems. This document is an example of **troff** output.

The single most important rule of using **troff** is not to use it directly, but through some intermediary. In many ways, **troff** resembles an assembly language — a remarkably powerful and flexible one — but nonetheless such that many operations must be specified at a level of detail and in a form that is too hard for most people to use effectively.

For two special applications, there are programs that provide an interface to **troff** for the majority of users. **eqn** [2] provides an easy to learn language for typesetting mathematics; the **eqn** user need know no **troff** whatsoever to typeset mathematics. **tbl** [3] provides the same convenience for producing tables of arbitrary complexity.

For producing straight text (which may well contain mathematics or tables), there are a number of 'macro packages' that define formatting rules and operations for specific styles of documents, and reduce the amount of direct contact with **troff**. In particular, the '−ms' [4] and PWB/MM [5] packages for Bell Labs internal memoranda and external papers provide most of the facilities needed for a wide range of document preparation. (This memo was prepared with '−ms'.) There are also packages for viewgraphs, for simulating the older **roff** formatters on UNIX and GCOS, and for other special applications. Typically you will find these packages easier to use than **troff** once you get beyond the most trivial operations; you should always consider them first.

In the few cases where existing packages don't do the whole job, the solution is *not* to write an entirely new set of **troff** instructions from scratch, but to make small changes to adapt packages that already exist.

In accordance with this philosophy of letting someone else do the work, the part of **troff** described here is only a small part of the whole, although it tries to concentrate on the more useful parts. In any case, there is no attempt to be complete. Rather, the emphasis is on showing how to do simple things, and how to make incremental changes to what already exists. The contents of the remaining sections are:

2. Point sizes and line spacing
3. Fonts and special characters
4. Indents and line length
5. Tabs
6. Local motions: Drawing lines and characters
7. Strings
8. Introduction to macros
9. Titles, pages and numbering
10. Number registers and arithmetic
11. Macros with arguments
12. Conditionals
13. Environments
14. Diversions
    Appendix: Typesetter character set

The **troff** described here is the C-language version running on UNIX at Murray Hill, as documented in [1].

To use **troff** you have to prepare not only the actual text you want printed, but some information that tells *how* you want it printed. (Readers who use **roff** will find the approach familiar.) For **troff** the text and the formatting information are often intertwined quite intimately. Most commands to **troff** are placed on a line separate from the text itself, beginning with a period (one command per line). For example,

    Some text.
    .ps 14
    Some more text.

will change the 'point size', that is, the size of the letters being printed, to '14 point' (one point is 1/72 inch) like this:

Some text. Some more text.

Occasionally, though, something special occurs in the middle of a line — to produce

$$Area = \pi r^2$$

you have to type

Area = \(*p\fIr\fR\|\s8\u2\d\s0

(which we will explain shortly). The backslash character \ is used to introduce **troff** commands and special characters within a line of text.

2. Point Sizes; Line Spacing

As mentioned above, the command **.ps** sets the point size. One point is 1/72 inch, so 6-point characters are at most 1/12 inch high, and 36-point characters are ½ inch. There are 15 point sizes, listed below.

6 point: Pack my box with five dozen liquor jugs.

7 point: Pack my box with five dozen liquor jugs.

8 point: Pack my box with five dozen liquor jugs.

9 point: Pack my box with five dozen liquor jugs.

10 point: Pack my box with five dozen liquor

11 point: Pack my box with five dozen

12 point: Pack my box with five dozen

14 point: Pack my box with five

16 point 18 point 20 point

22 24 28 36

If the number after **.ps** is not one of these legal sizes, it is rounded up to the next valid value, with a maximum of 36. If no number follows **.ps**, **troff** reverts to the previous size, whatever it was. **troff** begins with point size 10, which is usually fine. This document is in 9 point.

The point size can also be changed in the middle of a line or even a word with the in-line command \s. To produce

UNIX runs on a PDP-11/45

type

\s8UNIX\s10 runs on a \s8PDP-\s1011/45

As above, \s should be followed by a legal point size, except that \s0 causes the size to revert to its previous value. Notice that \s1011 can be understood correctly as 'size 10, followed by an 11', if the size is legal, but not otherwise. Be cautious with similar constructions.

Relative size changes are also legal and useful:

\s-2UNIX\s+2

temporarily decreases the size, whatever it is, by two points, then restores it. Relative size changes have the advantage that the size difference is independent of the starting size of the document. The amount of the relative change is restricted to a single digit.

The other parameter that determines what the type looks like is the spacing between lines, which is set independently of the point size. Vertical spacing is measured from the bottom of one line to the bottom of the next. The command to control vertical spacing is **.vs**. For running text, it is usually best to set the vertical spacing about 20% bigger than the character size. For example, so far in this document, we have used "9 on 11", that is,

.ps 9
.vs 11p

If we changed to

.ps 9
.vs 9p

the running text would look like this. After a few lines, you will agree it looks a little cramped. The right vertical spacing is partly a matter of taste, depending on how much text you want to squeeze into a given space, and partly a matter of traditional printing style. By default, **troff** uses 10 on 12.

Point size and vertical spacing make a substantial difference in the amount of text per square inch. This is 12 on 14.

Point size and vertical spacing make a substantial difference in the amount of text per square inch. For example, 10 on 12 uses about twice as much space as 7 on 8. This is 6 on 7, which is even smaller. It packs a lot more words per line, but you can go blind trying to read it.

When used without arguments, **.ps** and **.vs** revert to the previous size and vertical spacing respectively.

The command **.sp** is used to get extra vertical space. Unadorned, it gives you one extra blank line (one **.vs**, whatever that has been set to). Typically, that's more or less than you want, so **.sp** can be followed by information about how much space you want —

.sp 2i

means 'two inches of vertical space'.

.sp 2p

means 'two points of vertical space'; and

.sp 2

means 'two vertical spaces' — two of whatever

.**vs** is set to (this can also be made explicit with .**sp 2v**); **troff** also understands decimal fractions in most places, so

.sp 1.5i

is a space of 1.5 inches. These same scale factors can be used after .**vs** to define line spacing, and in fact after most commands that deal with physical dimensions.

It should be noted that all size numbers are converted internally to 'machine units', which are 1/432 inch (1/6 point). For most purposes, this is enough resolution that you don't have to worry about the accuracy of the representation. The situation is not quite so good vertically, where resolution is 1/144 inch (1/2 point).

3. Fonts and Special Characters

troff and the typesetter allow four different fonts at any one time. Normally three fonts (Times roman, italic and bold) and one collection of special characters are permanently mounted.

abcdefghijklmnopqrstuvwxyz 0123456789
ABCDEFGHIJKLMNOPQRSTUVWXYZ
abcdefghijklmnopqrstuvwxyz 0123456789
ABCDEFGHIJKLMNOPQRSTUVWXYZ
abcdefghijklmnopqrstuvwxyz 0123456789
ABCDEFGHIJKLMNOPQRSTUVWXYZ

The greek, mathematical symbols and miscellany of the special font are listed in Appendix A.

troff prints in roman unless told otherwise. To switch into bold, use the .**ft** command

.ft B

and for italics,

.ft I

To return to roman, use .**ft R**; to return to the previous font, whatever it was, use either .**ft P** or just .ft. The 'underline' command

.ul

causes the next input line to print in italics. .ul can be followed by a count to indicate that more than one line is to be italicized.

Fonts can also be changed within a line or word with the in-line command \f:

bold*face* text

is produced by

\fBbold\fIface\fR text

If you want to do this so the previous font, whatever it was, is left undisturbed, insert extra \fP commands, like this:

\fBbold\fP\fIface\fP\fR text\fP

Because only the immediately previous font is remembered, you have to restore the previous font after each change or you can lose it. The same is true of .**ps** and .**vs** when used without an argument.

There are other fonts available besides the standard set, although you can still use only four at any given time. The command .**fp** tells **troff** what fonts are physically mounted on the typesetter:

.fp 3 H

says that the Helvetica font is mounted on position 3. (For a complete list of fonts and what they look like, see the **troff** manual.) Appropriate .**fp** commands should appear at the beginning of your document if you do not use the standard fonts.

It is possible to make a document relatively independent of the actual fonts used to print it by using font numbers instead of names; for example, \f3 and .ft~3 mean 'whatever font is mounted at position 3', and thus work for any setting. Normal settings are roman font on 1, italic on 2, bold on 3, and special on 4.

There is also a way to get 'synthetic' bold fonts by overstriking letters with a slight offset. Look at the .**bd** command in [1].

Special characters have four-character names beginning with \(, and they may be inserted anywhere. For example,

¼ + ½ = ¾

is produced by

\(14 + \(12 = \(34

In particular, greek letters are all of the form \(*−, where − is an upper or lower case roman letter reminiscent of the greek. Thus to get

$\Sigma(\alpha \times \beta) \rightarrow \infty$

in bare **troff** we have to type

\(*S(\(*a\(mu\(*b) \(−> \(if

That line is unscrambled as follows:

\(*S	Σ
(	(
\(*a	α
\(mu	$\times$
\(*b	β
)	)
\(−>	$\rightarrow$
\(if	∞

A complete list of these special names occurs in Appendix A.

In **eqn** [2] the same effect can be achieved with the input

SIGMA (alpha times beta) − > inf

which is less concise, but clearer to the uninitiated.

Notice that each four-character name is a single character as far as **troff** is concerned — the 'translate' command

.tr \(mi\(em

is perfectly clear, meaning

.tr −−

that is, to translate − into −.

Some characters are automatically translated into others: grave ` and acute ´ accents (apostrophes) become open and close single quotes ' '; the combination of "..." is generally preferable to the double quotes "...". Similarly a typed minus sign becomes a hyphen -. To print an explicit − sign, use \-. To get a backslash printed, use \e.

4. Indents and Line Lengths

troff starts with a line length of 6.5 inches, too wide for 8½×11 paper. To reset the line length, use the .ll command, as in

.ll 6i

As with .sp, the actual length can be specified in several ways; inches are probably the most intuitive.

The maximum line length provided by the typesetter is 7.5 inches, by the way. To use the full width, you will have to reset the default physical left margin ("page offset"), which is normally slightly less than one inch from the left edge of the paper. This is done by the .po command.

.po 0

sets the offset as far to the left as it will go.

The indent command .in causes the left margin to be indented by some specified amount from the page offset. If we use .in to move the left margin in, and .ll to move the right margin to the left, we can make offset blocks of text:

.in 0.3i
.ll −0.3i
text to be set into a block
.ll +0.3i
.in −0.3i

will create a block that looks like this:

Pater noster qui est in caelis sanctificetur nomen tuum; adveniat regnum tuum; fiat voluntas tua, sicut in caelo, et in terra. ... Amen.

Notice the use of '+' and '−' to specify the amount of change. These change the previous setting by the specified amount, rather than just overriding it. The distinction is quite important: .ll +1i makes lines one inch longer; .ll 1i makes them one inch *long*.

With .in, .ll and .po, the previous value is used if no argument is specified.

To indent a single line, use the 'temporary indent' command .ti. For example, all paragraphs in this memo effectively begin with the command

.ti 3

Three of what? The default unit for .ti, as for most horizontally oriented commands (.ll, .in, .po), is ems; an em is roughly the width of the letter 'm' in the current point size. (Precisely, a em in size p is p points.) Although inches are usually clearer than ems to people who don't set type for a living, ems have a place: they are a measure of size that is proportional to the current point size. If you want to make text that keeps its proportions regardless of point size, you should use ems for all dimensions. Ems can be specified as scale factors directly, as in .ti 2.5m.

Lines can also be indented negatively if the indent is already positive:

.ti −0.3i

causes the next line to be moved back three tenths of an inch. Thus to make a decorative initial capital, we indent the whole paragraph, then move the letter 'P' back with a .ti command:

P ater noster qui est in caelis sanctificetur nomen tuum; adveniat regnum tuum; fiat voluntas tua, sicut in caelo, et in terra. ... Amen.

Of course, there is also some trickery to make the 'P' bigger (just a '\s36P\s0'), and to move it down from its normal position (see the section on local motions).

5. Tabs

Tabs (the ASCII 'horizontal tab' character) can be used to produce output in columns, or to set the horizontal position of output. Typically tabs are used only in unfilled text. Tab stops are set by default every half inch from the current indent, but can be changed by the **.ta** command. To set stops every inch, for example,

.ta 1i 2i 3i 4i 5i 6i

Unfortunately the stops are left-justified only (as on a typewriter), so lining up columns of right-justified numbers can be painful. If you have many numbers, or if you need more complicated table layout, *don't* use **troff** directly; use the **tbl** program described in [3].

For a handful of numeric columns, you can do it this way: Precede every number by enough blanks to make it line up when typed.

```
.nf
.ta 1i 2i 3i
   1 tab    2 tab    3
  40 tab   50 tab   60
 700 tab  800 tab 900
.fi
```

Then change each leading blank into the string \0. This is a character that does not print, but that has the same width as a digit. When printed, this will produce

1	2	3
40	50	60
700	800	900

It is also possible to fill up tabbed-over space with some character other than blanks by setting the 'tab replacement character' with the .tc command:

```
.ta 1.5i 2.5i
.tc \(ru        (\(ru is "_")
Name tab Age tab
```

produces

Name _____ Age _____

To reset the tab replacement character to a blank, use .tc with no argument. (Lines can also be drawn with the \l command, described in Section 6.)

troff also provides a very general mechanism called 'fields' for setting up complicated columns. (This is used by **tbl**). We will not go into it in this paper.

6. Local Motions: Drawing lines and characters

Remember 'Area = πr^2' and the big 'P' in the Paternoster. How are they done? **troff** provides a host of commands for placing characters of any size at any place. You can use them to draw special characters or to tune your output for a particular appearance. Most of these commands are straightforward, but messy to read and tough to type correctly.

If you won't use **eqn**, subscripts and superscripts are most easily done with the half-line local motions \u and \d. To go back up the page half a point-size, insert a \u at the desired place; to go down, insert a \d. (\u and \d should always be used in pairs, as explained below.) Thus

Area = \(*pr\u2\d

produces

Area = πr^2

To make the '2' smaller, bracket it with \s−2...\s0. Since \u and \d refer to the current point size, be sure to put them either both inside or both outside the size changes, or you will get an unbalanced vertical motion.

Sometimes the space given by \u and \d isn't the right amount. The \v command can be used to request an arbitrary amount of vertical motion. The in-line command

\v'(amount)'

causes motion up or down the page by the amount specified in '(amount)'. For example, to move the 'P' down, we used

```
.in +0.6i        (move paragraph in)
.ll −0.3i        (shorten lines)
.ti −0.3i        (move P back)
\v'2'\s36P\s0\v'−2'ater noster qui est
in caelis ...
```

A minus sign causes upward motion, while no sign or a plus sign means down the page. Thus \v'−2' causes an upward vertical motion of two line spaces.

There are many other ways to specify the amount of motion —

```
\v'0.1i'
\v'3p'
\v'−0.5m'
```

and so on are all legal. Notice that the scale specifier i or p or m goes inside the quotes. Any character can be used in place of the quotes; this is also true of all other **troff** commands described in this section.

Since **troff** does not take within-the-line vertical motions into account when figuring out where it is on the page, output lines can have unexpected positions if the left and right ends aren't at the same vertical position. Thus \v, like \u and \d, should always balance upward vertical motion in a line with the same amount in the downward direction.

Arbitrary horizontal motions are also available — \h is quite analogous to \v, except that the default scale factor is ems instead of line spaces. As an example,

\h'−0.1i'

causes a backwards motion of a tenth of an inch. As a practical matter, consider printing the mathematical symbol '>>'. The default spacing is too wide, so **eqn** replaces this by

>\h´−0.3m´>

to produce >>.

Frequently \h is used with the 'width function' \w to generate motions equal to the width of some character string. The construction

\w´thing´

is a number equal to the width of 'thing' in machine units (1/432 inch). All **troff** computations are ultimately done in these units. To move horizontally the width of an 'x', we can say

\h´\w´x´u´

As we mentioned above, the default scale factor for all horizontal dimensions is **m**, ems, so here we must have the **u** for machine units, or the motion produced will be far too large. **troff** is quite happy with the nested quotes, by the way, so long as you don't leave any out.

As a live example of this kind of construction, all of the command names in the text, like .sp, were done by overstriking with a slight offset. The commands for .sp are

.sp\h´−\w´.sp´u´\h´1u´.sp

That is, put out '.sp', move left by the width of '.sp', move right 1 unit, and print '.sp' again. (Of course there is a way to avoid typing that much input for each command name, which we will discuss in Section 11.)

There are also several special-purpose **troff** commands for local motion. We have already seen \0, which is an unpaddable white space of the same width as a digit. 'Unpaddable' means that it will never be widened or split across a line by line justification and filling. There is also \(blank), which is an unpaddable character the width of a space, \|, which is half that width, \^, which is one quarter of the width of a space, and \&, which has zero width. (This last one is useful, for example, in entering a text line which would otherwise begin with a '.'.)

The command \o, used like

\o´set of characters´

causes (up to 9) characters to be overstruck, centered on the widest. This is nice for accents, as in

syst\o"e\(ga"me t\o"e\(aa"l\o"e\(aa"phonique

which makes

système téléphonique

The accents are \(ga and \(aa, or \` and \´; remember that each is just one character to **troff**.

You can make your own overstrikes with another special convention, \z, the zero-motion command. \zx suppresses the normal horizontal motion after printing the single character **x**, so another character can be laid on top of it. Although sizes can be changed within \o, it centers the characters on the widest, and there can be no horizontal or vertical motions, so \z may be the only way to get what you want:

is produced by

.sp 2
\s8\z\(sq\s14\z\(sq\s22\z\(sq\s36\(sq

The .sp is needed to leave room for the result.

As another example, an extra-heavy semicolon that looks like

; instead of ; or ;

can be constructed with a big comma and a big period above it:

\s+6\z,\v´−0.25m´.\v´0.25m´\s0

'0.25m' is an empirical constant.

A more ornate overstrike is given by the bracketing function \b, which piles up characters vertically, centered on the current baseline. Thus we can get big brackets, constructing them with piled-up smaller pieces:

$$\left\{\left[x \right]\right\}$$

by typing in only this:

.sp
\b´\(lt\(lk\(lb´ \b´\(lc\(lf´ x \b´\(rc\(rf´ \b´\(rt\(rk\(rb´

troff also provides a convenient facility for drawing horizontal and vertical lines of arbitrary length with arbitrary characters. \l´1i´ draws a line one inch long, like this: _____. The length can be followed by the character to use if the _ isn't appropriate; \l´0.5i.´ draws a half-inch line of dots: .... The construction \L is entirely analogous, except that it draws a vertical line instead of horizontal.

7. Strings

Obviously if a paper contains a large number of occurrences of an acute accent over a letter 'e', typing \o"e\´" for each é would be a great nuisance.

Fortunately, **troff** provides a way in which you can store an arbitrary collection of text in a 'string', and thereafter use the string name as a shorthand for its contents. Strings are one of several **troff** mechanisms whose judicious use lets you type a document with less effort and organize it so that extensive format changes can be made with few editing changes.

A reference to a string is replaced by whatever text the string was defined as. Strings are defined with the command **.ds**. The line

    .ds e \o"e\'"

defines the string e to have the value \o"e\'"

String names may be either one or two characters long, and are referred to by *x for one character names or *(xy for two character names. Thus to get téléphone, given the definition of the string e as above, we can say t*el*ephone.

If a string must begin with blanks, define it as

    .ds xx "   text

The double quote signals the beginning of the definition. There is no trailing quote; the end of the line terminates the string.

A string may actually be several lines long; if **troff** encounters a \ at the end of *any* line, it is thrown away and the next line added to the current one. So you can make a long string simply by ending each line but the last with a backslash:

    .ds xx this \
    is a very \
    long string

Strings may be defined in terms of other strings, or even in terms of themselves; we will discuss some of these possibilities later.

8. Introduction to Macros

Before we can go much further in **troff**, we need to learn a bit about the macro facility. In its simplest form, a macro is just a shorthand notation quite similar to a string. Suppose we want every paragraph to start in exactly the same way — with a space and a temporary indent of two ems:

    .sp
    .ti +2m

Then to save typing, we would like to collapse these into one shorthand line, a **troff** 'command' like

    .PP

that would be treated by **troff** exactly as

    .sp
    .ti +2m

.PP is called a *macro*. The way we tell **troff** what **.PP** means is to *define* it with the **.de** command:

    .de PP
    .sp
    .ti +2m
    ..

The first line names the macro (we used '.PP' for 'paragraph', and upper case so it wouldn't conflict with any name that **troff** might already know about). The last line .. marks the end of the definition. In between is the text, which is simply inserted whenever **troff** sees the 'command' or macro call

    .PP

A macro can contain any mixture of text and formatting commands.

The definition of **.PP** has to precede its first use; undefined macros are simply ignored. Names are restricted to one or two characters.

Using macros for commonly occurring sequences of commands is critically important. Not only does it save typing, but it makes later changes much easier. Suppose we decide that the paragraph indent is too small, the vertical space is much too big, and roman font should be forced. Instead of changing the whole document, we need only change the definition of **.PP** to something like

    .de PP   \" paragraph macro
    .sp 2p
    .ti +3m
    .ft R
    ..

and the change takes effect everywhere we used **.PP**.

\" is a **troff** command that causes the rest of the line to be ignored. We use it here to add comments to the macro definition (a wise idea once definitions get complicated).

As another example of macros, consider these two which start and end a block of offset, unfilled text, like most of the examples in this paper:

```
.de BS        \" start indented block
.sp
.nf
.in +0.3i
..
.de BE        \" end indented block
.sp
.fi
.in −0.3i
..
```

Now we can surround text like

```
Copy to
John Doe
Richard Roberts
Stanley Smith
```

by the commands .BS and .BE, and it will come out as it did above. Notice that we indented by **.in +0.3i** instead of .in 0.3i. This way we can nest our uses of .BS and BE to get blocks within blocks.

If later on we decide that the indent should be 0.5i, then it is only necessary to change the definitions of .BS and .BE, not the whole paper.

9. Titles, Pages and Numbering

This is an area where things get tougher, because nothing is done for you automatically. Of necessity, some of this section is a cookbook, to be copied literally until you get some experience.

Suppose you want a title at the top of each page, saying just

```
~~~~left top          center top          right top~~~~
```

In **roff**, one can say

```
.he 'left top'center top'right top'
.fo 'left bottom'center bottom'right bottom'
```

to get headers and footers automatically on every page. Alas, this doesn't work in **troff**, a serious hardship for the novice. Instead you have to do a lot of specification.

You have to say what the actual title is (easy); when to print it (easy enough); and what to do at and around the title line (harder). Taking these in reverse order, first we define a macro .NP (for 'new page') to process titles and the like at the end of one page and the beginning of the next:

```
.de NP
'bp
'sp 0.5i
.tl 'left top'center top'right top'
'sp 0.3i
..
```

To make sure we're at the top of a page, we issue a 'begin page' command **'bp**, which causes a skip to top-of-page (we'll explain the ' shortly). Then we space down half an inch, print the title (the use of .tl should be self explanatory; later we will discuss parameterizing the titles), space another 0.3 inches, and we're done.

To ask for .NP at the bottom of each page, we have to say something like 'when the text is within an inch of the bottom of the page, start the processing for a new page.' This is done with a 'when' command .**wh**:

```
.wh −1i NP
```

(No '.' is used before NP; this is simply the name of a macro, not a macro call.) The minus sign means 'measure up from the bottom of the page', so '−1i' means 'one inch from the bottom'.

The .**wh** command appears in the input outside the definition of .NP; typically the input would be

```
.de NP
...
..
.wh −1i NP
```

Now what happens? As text is actually being output, **troff** keeps track of its vertical position on the page, and after a line is printed within one inch from the bottom, the .NP macro is activated. (In the jargon, the .wh command sets a *trap* at the specified place, which is 'sprung' when that point is passed.) .NP causes a skip to the top of the next page (that's what the **'bp** was for), then prints the title with the appropriate margins.

Why **'bp** and **'sp** instead of .bp and .sp? The answer is that .sp and .bp, like several other commands, cause a *break* to take place. That is, all the input text collected but not yet printed is flushed out as soon as possible, and the next input line is guaranteed to start a new line of output. If we had used .sp or .bp in the .NP macro, this would cause a break in the middle of the current output line when a new page is started. The effect would be to print the left-over part of that line at the top of the page, followed by the next input line on a new output line. This is *not* what we want. Using ' instead of . for a command tells **troff** that no break is to take place — the output line currently being filled should *not* be forced out before the space or new page.

The list of commands that cause a break is short and natural:

```
.bp  .br  .ce  .fi  .nf  .sp  .in  .ti
```

All others cause *no* break, regardless of whether

you use a . or a '. If you really need a break, add a **.br** command at the appropriate place.

One other thing to beware of — if you're changing fonts or point sizes a lot, you may find that if you cross a page boundary in an unexpected font or size, your titles come out in that size and font instead of what you intended. Furthermore, the length of a title is independent of the current line length, so titles will come out at the default length of 6.5 inches unless you change it, which is done with the **.lt** command.

There are several ways to fix the problems of point sizes and fonts in titles. For the simplest applications, we can change **.NP** to set the proper size and font for the title, then restore the previous values, like this:

```
.de NP
'bp
'sp 0.5i
.ft R          \" set title font to roman
.ps 10         \" and size to 10 point
.lt 6i         \" and length to 6 inches
.tl 'left'center'right'
.ps            \" revert to previous size
.ft P          \" and to previous font
'sp 0.3i
..
```

This version of **.NP** does *not* work if the fields in the **.tl** command contain size or font changes. To cope with that requires **troff**'s 'environment' mechanism, which we will discuss in Section 13.

To get a footer at the bottom of a page, you can modify **.NP** so it does some processing before the '**bp** command, or split the job into a footer macro invoked at the bottom margin and a header macro invoked at the top of the page. These variations are left as exercises.

Output page numbers are computed automatically as each page is produced (starting at 1), but no numbers are printed unless you ask for them explicitly. To get page numbers printed, include the character % in the **.tl** line at the position where you want the number to appear. For example

```
.tl ''- % -''
```

centers the page number inside hyphens, as on this page. You can set the page number at any time with either **.bp** n, which immediately starts a new page numbered n, or with **.pn** n, which sets the page number for the next page but doesn't cause a skip to the new page. Again, **bp** +n sets the page number to n more than its current value; **.bp** means **.bp** +1.

10. Number Registers and Arithmetic

troff has a facility for doing arithmetic, and for defining and using variables with numeric values, called *number registers*. Number registers, like strings and macros, can be useful in setting up a document so it is easy to change later. And of course they serve for any sort of arithmetic computation.

Like strings, number registers have one or two character names. They are set by the **.nr** command, and are referenced anywhere by \nx (one character name) or \n(xy (two character name).

There are quite a few pre-defined number registers maintained by **troff**, among them % for the current page number; nl for the current vertical position on the page; **dy**, **mo** and **yr** for the current day, month and year; and .s and .f for the current size and font. (The font is a number from 1 to 4.) Any of these can be used in computations like any other register, but some, like .s and .f, cannot be changed with .nr.

As an example of the use of number registers, in the —ms macro package [4], most significant parameters are defined in terms of the values of a handful of number registers. These include the point size for text, the vertical spacing, and the line and title lengths. To set the point size and vertical spacing for the following paragraphs, for example, a user may say

```
.nr PS 9
.nr VS 11
```

The paragraph macro **.PP** is defined (roughly) as follows:

```
.de PP
.ps \\n(PS        \" reset size
.vs \\n(VSp       \" spacing
.ft R             \" font
.sp 0.5v          \" half a line
.ti +3m
..
```

This sets the font to Roman and the point size and line spacing to whatever values are stored in the number registers **PS** and **VS**.

Why are there two backslashes? This is the eternal problem of how to quote a quote. When **troff** originally reads the macro definition, it peels off one backslash to see what's coming next. To ensure that another is left in the definition when the macro is *used,* we have to put in two backslashes in the definition. If only one backslash is used, point size and vertical spacing will be frozen at the time the macro is defined, not when it is used.

Protecting by an extra layer of backslashes

is only needed for \n, *, \$ (which we haven't come to yet), and \ itself. Things like \s, \f, \h, \v, and so on do not need an extra backslash, since they are converted by **troff** to an internal code immediately upon being seen.

Arithmetic expressions can appear anywhere that a number is expected. As a trivial example,

.nr PS \\n(PS−2

decrements PS by 2. Expressions can use the arithmetic operators +, −, *, /, % (mod), the relational operators >, >=, <, <=, =, and != (not equal), and parentheses.

Although the arithmetic we have done so far has been straightforward, more complicated things are somewhat tricky. First, number registers hold only integers. **troff** arithmetic uses truncating integer division, just like Fortran. Second, in the absence of parentheses, evaluation is done left-to-right without any operator precedence (including relational operators). Thus

7*−4+3/13

becomes '−1'. Number registers can occur anywhere in an expression, and so can scale indicators like **p**, **i**, **m**, and so on (but no spaces). Although integer division causes truncation, each number and its scale indicator is converted to machine units (1/432 inch) before any arithmetic is done, so 1i/2u evaluates to 0.5i correctly.

The scale indicator **u** often has to appear when you wouldn't expect it − in particular, when arithmetic is being done in a context that implies horizontal or vertical dimensions. For example,

.ll 7/2i

would seem obvious enough − 3½ inches. Sorry. Remember that the default units for horizontal parameters like .ll are ems. That's really '7 ems / 2 inches', and when translated into machine units, it becomes zero. How about

.ll 7i/2

Sorry, still no good − the '2' is '2 ems', so '7i/2' is small, although not zero. You *must* use

.ll 7i/2u

So again, a safe rule is to attach a scale indicator to every number, even constants.

For arithmetic done within a .nr command, there is no implication of horizontal or vertical dimension, so the default units are 'units', and 7i/2 and 7i/2u mean the same thing. Thus

.nr ll 7i/2
.ll \\n(llu

does just what you want, so long as you don't forget the **u** on the .ll command.

11. Macros with arguments

The next step is to define macros that can change from one use to the next according to parameters supplied as arguments. To make this work, we need two things: first, when we define the macro, we have to indicate that some parts of it will be provided as arguments when the macro is called. Then when the macro is called we have to provide actual arguments to be plugged into the definition.

Let us illustrate by defining a macro .SM that will print its argument two points smaller than the surrounding text. That is, the macro call

.SM TROFF

will produce TROFF.

The definition of .SM is

.de SM
\s−2\\$1\s+2
..

Within a macro definition, the symbol \\$n refers to the nth argument that the macro was called with. Thus \\$1 is the string to be placed in a smaller point size when .SM is called.

As a slightly more complicated version, the following definition of .SM permits optional second and third arguments that will be printed in the normal size:

.de SM
\\$3\s−2\\$1\s+2\\$2
..

Arguments not provided when the macro is called are treated as empty, so

.SM TROFF),

produces TROFF), while

.SM TROFF). (

produces (TROFF). It is convenient to reverse the order of arguments because trailing punctuation is much more common than leading.

By the way, the number of arguments that a macro was called with is available in number register .$.

The following macro .**BD** is the one used to make the 'bold roman' we have been using for **troff** command names in text. It combines horizontal motions, width computations, and argument rearrangement.

```
.de BD
\&\\$3\f1\\$1\h'-\w'\\$1'u+1u'\\$1\fP\\$2
..
```

The \h and \w commands need no extra backslash, as we discussed above. The \& is there in case the argument begins with a period.

Two backslashes are needed with the \\$n commands, though, to protect one of them when the macro is being defined. Perhaps a second example will make this clearer. Consider a macro called .SH which produces section headings rather like those in this paper, with the sections numbered automatically, and the title in bold in a smaller size. The use is

```
.SH "Section title ..."
```

(If the argument to a macro is to contain blanks, then it must be *surrounded* by double quotes, unlike a string, where only one leading quote is permitted.)

Here is the definition of the .SH macro:

```
.nr SH 0      \" initialize section number
.de SH
.sp 0.3i
.ft B
.nr SH \\n(SH+1   \" increment number
.ps \\n(PS−1      \" decrease PS
\\n(SH. \\$1      \" number. title
.ps \\n(PS        \" restore PS
.sp 0.3i
.ft R
..
```

The section number is kept in number register SH, which is incremented each time just before it is used. (A number register may have the same name as a macro without conflict but a string may not.)

We used \\n(SH instead of \n(SH and \\n(PS instead of \n(PS. If we had used \n(SH, we would get the value of the register at the time the macro was *defined*, not at the time it was *used*. If that's what you want, fine, but not here. Similarly, by using \\n(PS, we get the point size at the time the macro is called.

As an example that does not involve numbers, recall our .NP macro which had a

```
.tl 'left'center'right'
```

We could make these into parameters by using instead

```
.tl '\\*(LT'\\*(CT'\\*(RT'
```

so the title comes from three strings called LT, CT and RT. If these are empty, then the title will be a blank line. Normally CT would be set with something like

```
.ds CT - % -
```

to give just the page number between hyphens (as on the top of this page), but a user could supply private definitions for any of the strings.

12. Conditionals

Suppose we want the .SH macro to leave two extra inches of space just before section 1, but nowhere else. The cleanest way to do that is to test inside the .SH macro whether the section number is 1, and add some space if it is. The .if command provides the conditional test that we can add just before the heading line is output:

```
.if \\n(SH=1 .sp 2i       \" first section only
```

The condition after the .if can be any arithmetic or logical expression. If the condition is logically true, or arithmetically greater than zero, the rest of the line is treated as if it were text — here a command. If the condition is false, or zero or negative, the rest of the line is skipped.

It is possible to do more than one command if a condition is true. Suppose several operations are to be done before section 1. One possibility is to define a macro .S1 and invoke it if we are about to do section 1 (as determined by an .if).

```
.de S1
--- processing for section 1 ---
..
.de SH
...
.if \\n(SH=1 .S1
...
..
```

An alternate way is to use the extended form of the .if, like this:

```
.if \\n(SH=1 \{--- processing
for section 1 ----\}
```

The braces \{ and \} must occur in the positions shown or you will get unexpected extra lines in your output. **troff** also provides an 'if-else' construction, which we will not go into here.

A condition can be negated by preceding it with !; we get the same effect as above (but less clearly) by using

```
.if !\\n(SH>1 .S1
```

There are a handful of other conditions that can be tested with .if. For example, is the current page even or odd?

```
.if e .tl "even page title"
.if o .tl "odd page title"
```

gives facing pages different titles when used inside an appropriate new page macro.

Two other conditions are t and n, which tell you whether the formatter is **troff** or **nroff**.

```
.if t troff stuff ...
.if n nroff stuff ...
```

Finally, string comparisons may be made in an **.if**:

```
.if 'string1'string2' stuff
```

does 'stuff' if *string1* is the same as *string2*. The character separating the strings can be anything reasonable that is not contained in either string. The strings themselves can reference strings with *, arguments with \$, and so on.

13. Environments

As we mentioned, there is a potential problem when going across a page boundary: parameters like size and font for a page title may well be different from those in effect in the text when the page boundary occurs. **troff** provides a very general way to deal with this and similar situations. There are three 'environments', each of which has independently settable versions of many of the parameters associated with processing, including size, font, line and title lengths, fill/nofill mode, tab stops, and even partially collected lines. Thus the titling problem may be readily solved by processing the main text in one environment and titles in a separate one with its own suitable parameters.

The command **.ev n** shifts to environment n; n must be 0, 1 or 2. The command **.ev** with no argument returns to the previous environment. Environment names are maintained in a stack, so calls for different environments may be nested and unwound consistently.

Suppose we say that the main text is processed in environment 0, which is where **troff** begins by default. Then we can modify the new page macro **.NP** to process titles in environment 1 like this:

```
.de NP
.ev 1         \" shift to new environment
.lt 6i        \" set parameters here
.ft R
.ps 10
... any other processing ...
.ev           \" return to previous environment
..
```

It is also possible to initialize the parameters for an environment outside the **.NP** macro, but the version shown keeps all the processing in one place and is thus easier to understand and change.

14. Diversions

There are numerous occasions in page layout when it is necessary to store some text for a period of time without actually printing it. Footnotes are the most obvious example: the text of the footnote usually appears in the input well before the place on the page where it is to be printed is reached. In fact, the place where it is output normally depends on how big it is, which implies that there must be a way to process the footnote at least enough to decide its size without printing it.

troff provides a mechanism called a diversion for doing this processing. Any part of the output may be diverted into a macro instead of being printed, and then at some convenient time the macro may be put back into the input.

The command **.di xy** begins a diversion — all subsequent output is collected into the macro **xy** until the command **.di** with no arguments is encountered. This terminates the diversion. The processed text is available at any time thereafter, simply by giving the command

```
.xy
```

The vertical size of the last finished diversion is contained in the built-in number register **dn**.

As a simple example, suppose we want to implement a 'keep-release' operation, so that text between the commands **.KS** and **.KE** will not be split across a page boundary (as for a figure or table). Clearly, when a **.KS** is encountered, we have to begin diverting the output so we can find out how big it is. Then when a **.KE** is seen, we decide whether the diverted text will fit on the current page, and print it either there if it fits, or at the top of the next page if it doesn't. So:

```
.de KS        \" start keep
.br           \" start fresh line
.ev 1         \" collect in new environment
.fi           \" make it filled text
.di XX         \" collect in XX
..

.de KE        \" end keep
.br           \" get last partial line
.di           \" end diversion
.if \\n(dn>=\\n(.t .bp   \" bp if doesn't fit
.nf           \" bring it back in no-fill
.XX           \" text
.ev           \" return to normal environment
..
```

Recall that number register **nl** is the current

position on the output page. Since output was being diverted, this remains at its value when the diversion started. **dn** is the amount of text in the diversion; .t (another built-in register) is the distance to the next trap, which we assume is at the bottom margin of the page. If the diversion is large enough to go past the trap, the **.if** is satisfied, and a **.bp** is issued. In either case, the diverted output is then brought back with **.XX**. It is essential to bring it back in no-fill mode so **troff** will do no further processing on it.

This is not the most general keep-release, nor is it robust in the face of all conceivable inputs, but it would require more space than we have here to write it in full generality. This section is not intended to teach everything about diversions, but to sketch out enough that you can read existing macro packages with some comprehension.

Acknowledgements

I am deeply indebted to J. F. Ossanna, the author of **troff**, for his repeated patient explanations of fine points, and for his continuing willingness to adapt **troff** to make other uses easier. I am also grateful to Jim Blinn, Ted Dolotta, Doug McIlroy, Mike Lesk and Joel Sturman for helpful comments on this paper.

References

[1]   J. F. Ossanna, *NROFF/TROFF* User's Manual, Bell Laboratories Computing Science Technical Report 54, 1976.

[2]   B. W. Kernighan, *A System for Typesetting Mathematics — User's Guide (Second Edition)*, Bell Laboratories Computing Science Technical Report 17, 1977.

[3]   M. E. Lesk, *TBL — A Program to Format Tables*, Bell Laboratories Computing Science Technical Report 49, 1976.

[4]   M. E. Lesk, *Typing Documents on UNIX*, Bell Laboratories, 1978.

[5]   J. R. Mashey and D. W. Smith, *PWB/MM — Programmer's Workbench Memorandum Macros*, Bell Laboratories internal memorandum.

Appendix A: Phototypesetter Character Set

These characters exist in roman, italic, and bold. To get the one on the left, type the four-character name on the right.

ff	\\(ff	fi	\\(fi	fl	\\(fl	ffi	\\(Fi	ffl	\\(Fl
_	\\(ru	—	\\(em	¼	\\(14	½	\\(12	¾	\\(34
©	\\(co	°	\\(de	†	\\(dg	'	\\(fm	¢	\\(ct
®	\\(rg	•	\\(bu	□	\\(sq	-	\\(hy		

(In bold, \\(sq is ■.)

The following are special-font characters:

+	\\(pl	−	\\(mi	×	\\(mu	÷	\\(di
=	\\(eq	≡	\\(==	≥	\\(>=	≤	\\(<=
≠	\\(!=	±	\\(+-	¬	\\(no	/	\\(sl
∼	\\(ap	≃	\\(~=	∝	\\(pt	∇	\\(gr
→	\\(->	←	\\(<-	↑	\\(ua	↓	\\(da
∫	\\(is	∂	\\(pd	∞	\\(if	√	\\(sr
⊂	\\(sb	⊃	\\(sp	∪	\\(cu	∩	\\(ca
⊆	\\(ib	⊇	\\(ip	∈	\\(mo	ø	\\(es
´	\\(aa	`	\\(ga	○	\\(ci	ⓐ	\\(bs
§	\\(sc	‡	\\(dd	☜	\\(lh	☞	\\(rh
⌠	\\(lt	⌡	\\(rt	⌈	\\(lc	⌉	\\(rc
⌊	\\(lb	⌋	\\(rb	⎣	\\(lf	⎦	\\(rf
{	\\(lk	}	\\(rk	|	\\(bv	ς	\\(ts
|	\\(br	⎮	\\(or	_	\\(ul	¯	\\(rn
*	\\(**						

These four characters also have two-character names. The ´ is the apostrophe on terminals; the ` is the other quote mark.

´	\\'	`	\\`	−	\\-	_	_

These characters exist only on the special font, but they do not have four-character names:

"   {   }   <   >   ~   ^   \\   #   @

For greek, precede the roman letter by \\(* to get the corresponding greek; for example, \\(*a is α.

a b g d e z y h i k l m n c o p r s t u f x q w
α β γ δ ε ζ η θ ι κ λ μ ν ξ ο π ρ σ τ υ φ χ ψ ω

A B G D E Z Y H I K L M N C O P R S T U F X Q W
Α Β Γ Δ Ε Ζ Η Θ Ι Κ Λ Μ Ν Ξ Ο Π Ρ Σ Τ Υ Φ Χ Ψ Ω

PROGRAMMING

The C Programming Language — Reference Manual

Dennis M. Ritchie

Bell Laboratories, Murray Hill, New Jersey

This manual is reprinted, with minor changes, from *The C Programming Language*, by Brian W. Kernighan and Dennis M. Ritchie, Prentice-Hall, Inc., 1978.

1. Introduction

This manual describes the C language on the DEC PDP-11, the DEC VAX-11, the Honeywell 6000, the IBM System/370, and the Interdata 8/32. Where differences exist, it concentrates on the PDP-11, but tries to point out implementation-dependent details. With few exceptions, these dependencies follow directly from the underlying properties of the hardware; the various compilers are generally quite compatible.

2. Lexical conventions

There are six classes of tokens: identifiers, keywords, constants, strings, operators, and other separators. Blanks, tabs, newlines, and comments (collectively, "white space") as described below are ignored except as they serve to separate tokens. Some white space is required to separate otherwise adjacent identifiers, keywords, and constants.

If the input stream has been parsed into tokens up to a given character, the next token is taken to include the longest string of characters which could possibly constitute a token.

2.1 Comments

The characters /* introduce a comment, which terminates with the characters */. Comments do not nest.

2.2 Identifiers (Names)

An identifier is a sequence of letters and digits; the first character must be a letter. The underscore _ counts as a letter. Upper and lower case letters are different. No more than the first eight characters are significant, although more may be used. External identifiers, which are used by various assemblers and loaders, are more restricted:

DEC PDP-11	7 characters, 2 cases
DEC VAX-11	8 characters, 2 cases
Honeywell 6000	6 characters, 1 case
IBM 360/370	7 characters, 1 case
Interdata 8/32	8 characters, 2 cases

2.3 Keywords

The following identifiers are reserved for use as keywords, and may not be used otherwise:

int	extern	else
char	register	for
float	typedef	do
double	static	while
struct	goto	switch
union	return	case
long	sizeof	default
short	break	entry
unsigned	continue	
auto	if	

The entry keyword is not currently implemented by any compiler but is reserved for future use. Some

---

† UNIX is a Trademark of Bell Laboratories.

implementations also reserve the words `fortran` and `asm.`

2.4 Constants

There are several kinds of constants, as listed below. Hardware characteristics which affect sizes are summarized in §2.6.

2.4.1 Integer constants

An integer constant consisting of a sequence of digits is taken to be octal if it begins with 0 (digit zero), decimal otherwise. The digits 8 and 9 have octal value 10 and 11 respectively. A sequence of digits preceded by 0x or 0X (digit zero) is taken to be a hexadecimal integer. The hexadecimal digits include a or A through f or F with values 10 through 15. A decimal constant whose value exceeds the largest signed machine integer is taken to be `long`; an octal or hex constant which exceeds the largest unsigned machine integer is likewise taken to be `long`.

2.4.2 Explicit long constants

A decimal, octal, or hexadecimal integer constant immediately followed by l (letter ell) or L is a long constant. As discussed below, on some machines integer and long values may be considered identical.

2.4.3 Character constants

A character constant is a character enclosed in single quotes, as in `'x'`. The value of a character constant is the numerical value of the character in the machine's character set.

Certain non-graphic characters, the single quote `'` and the backslash `\`, may be represented according to the following table of escape sequences:

newline	NL (LF)	\n
horizontal tab	HT	\t
backspace	BS	\b
carriage return	CR	\r
form feed	FF	\f
backslash	\	\\
single quote	'	\'
bit pattern	*ddd*	*ddd*

The escape *ddd* consists of the backslash followed by 1, 2, or 3 octal digits which are taken to specify the value of the desired character. A special case of this construction is \0 (not followed by a digit), which indicates the character NUL. If the character following a backslash is not one of those specified, the backslash is ignored.

2.4.4 Floating constants

A floating constant consists of an integer part, a decimal point, a fraction part, an e or E, and an optionally signed integer exponent. The integer and fraction parts both consist of a sequence of digits. Either the integer part or the fraction part (not both) may be missing; either the decimal point or the e and the exponent (not both) may be missing. Every floating constant is taken to be double-precision.

2.5 Strings

A string is a sequence of characters surrounded by double quotes, as in `"..."`. A string has type "array of characters" and storage class `static` (see §4 below) and is initialized with the given characters. All strings, even when written identically, are distinct. The compiler places a null byte \0 at the end of each string so that programs which scan the string can find its end. In a string, the double quote character `"` must be preceded by a `\`; in addition, the same escapes as described for character constants may be used. Finally, a `\` and an immediately following newline are ignored.

2.6 Hardware characteristics

The following table summarizes certain hardware properties which vary from machine to machine. Although these affect program portability, in practice they are less of a problem than might be thought *a priori.*

	DEC PDP-11	Honeywell 6000	IBM 370	Interdata 8/32
	ASCII	ASCII	EBCDIC	ASCII
char	8 bits	9 bits	8 bits	8 bits
int	16	36	32	32
short	16	36	16	16
long	32	36	32	32
float	32	36	32	32
double	64	72	64	64
range	$\pm 10^{\pm 38}$	$\pm 10^{\pm 38}$	$\pm 10^{\pm 76}$	$\pm 10^{\pm 76}$

The VAX-11 is identical to the PDP-11 except that integers have 32 bits.

3. Syntax notation

In the syntax notation used in this manual, syntactic categories are indicated by *italic* type, and literal words and characters in bold type. Alternative categories are listed on separate lines. An optional terminal or non-terminal symbol is indicated by the subscript "opt," so that

$$\{ \ expression_{opt} \ \}$$

indicates an optional expression enclosed in braces. The syntax is summarized in §18.

4. What's in a name?

C bases the interpretation of an identifier upon two attributes of the identifier: its *storage class* and its *type*. The storage class determines the location and lifetime of the storage associated with an identifier; the type determines the meaning of the values found in the identifier's storage.

There are four declarable storage classes: automatic, static, external, and register. Automatic variables are local to each invocation of a block (§9.2), and are discarded upon exit from the block; static variables are local to a block, but retain their values upon reentry to a block even after control has left the block; external variables exist and retain their values throughout the execution of the entire program, and may be used for communication between functions, even separately compiled functions. Register variables are (if possible) stored in the fast registers of the machine; like automatic variables they are local to each block and disappear on exit from the block.

C supports several fundamental types of objects:

Objects declared as characters (char) are large enough to store any member of the implementation's character set, and if a genuine character from that character set is stored in a character variable, its value is equivalent to the integer code for that character. Other quantities may be stored into character variables, but the implementation is machine-dependent.

Up to three sizes of integer, declared short int, int, and long int, are available. Longer integers provide no less storage than shorter ones, but the implementation may make either short integers, or long integers, or both, equivalent to plain integers. "Plain" integers have the natural size suggested by the host machine architecture; the other sizes are provided to meet special needs.

Unsigned integers, declared unsigned, obey the laws of arithmetic modulo 2^n where n is the number of bits in the representation. (On the PDP-11, unsigned long quantities are not supported.)

Single-precision floating point (float) and double-precision floating point (double) may be synonymous in some implementations.

Because objects of the foregoing types can usefully be interpreted as numbers, they will be referred to as *arithmetic* types. Types char and int of all sizes will collectively be called *integral* types. float and double will collectively be called *floating* types.

Besides the fundamental arithmetic types there is a conceptually infinite class of derived types constructed from the fundamental types in the following ways:

arrays of objects of most types;

functions which return objects of a given type;

pointers to objects of a given type;

structures containing a sequence of objects of various types;

unions capable of containing any one of several objects of various types.

In general these methods of constructing objects can be applied recursively.

5. Objects and lvalues

An *object* is a manipulatable region of storage; an *lvalue* is an expression referring to an object. An obvious example of an lvalue expression is an identifier. There are operators which yield lvalues: for example, if E is an expression of pointer type, then *E is an lvalue expression referring to the object to which E points. The name "lvalue" comes from the assignment expression E1 = E2 in which the left operand E1 must be an lvalue expression. The discussion of each operator below indicates whether it expects lvalue operands and whether it yields an lvalue.

6. Conversions

A number of operators may, depending on their operands, cause conversion of the value of an operand from one type to another. This section explains the result to be expected from such conversions. §6.6 summarizes the conversions demanded by most ordinary operators; it will be supplemented as required by the discussion of each operator.

6.1 Characters and integers

A character or a short integer may be used wherever an integer may be used. In all cases the value is converted to an integer. Conversion of a shorter integer to a longer always involves sign extension; integers are signed quantities. Whether or not sign-extension occurs for characters is machine dependent, but it is guaranteed that a member of the standard character set is non-negative. Of the machines treated by this manual, only the PDP-11 sign-extends. On the PDP-11, character variables range in value from −128 to 127; the characters of the ASCII alphabet are all positive. A character constant specified with an octal escape suffers sign extension and may appear negative; for example, '\377' has the value −1.

When a longer integer is converted to a shorter or to a char, it is truncated on the left; excess bits are simply discarded.

6.2 Float and double

All floating arithmetic in C is carried out in double-precision; whenever a float appears in an expression it is lengthened to double by zero-padding its fraction. When a double must be converted to float, for example by an assignment, the double is rounded before truncation to float length.

6.3 Floating and integral

Conversions of floating values to integral type tend to be rather machine-dependent; in particular the direction of truncation of negative numbers varies from machine to machine. The result is undefined if the value will not fit in the space provided.

Conversions of integral values to floating type are well behaved. Some loss of precision occurs if the destination lacks sufficient bits.

6.4 Pointers and integers

An integer or long integer may be added to or subtracted from a pointer; in such a case the first is converted as specified in the discussion of the addition operator.

Two pointers to objects of the same type may be subtracted; in this case the result is converted to an integer as specified in the discussion of the subtraction operator.

6.5 Unsigned

Whenever an unsigned integer and a plain integer are combined, the plain integer is converted to unsigned and the result is unsigned. The value is the least unsigned integer congruent to the signed integer (modulo $2^{wordsize}$). In a 2's complement representation, this conversion is conceptual and there is no actual change in the bit pattern.

When an unsigned integer is converted to long, the value of the result is the same numerically as that of the unsigned integer. Thus the conversion amounts to padding with zeros on the left.

6.6 Arithmetic conversions

A great many operators cause conversions and yield result types in a similar way. This pattern will be called the "usual arithmetic conversions."

First, any operands of type char or short are converted to int, and any of type float are converted to double.

Then, if either operand is `double`, the other is converted to `double` and that is the type of the result.

Otherwise, if either operand is `long`, the other is converted to `long` and that is the type of the result.

Otherwise, if either operand is `unsigned`, the other is converted to `unsigned` and that is the type of the result.

Otherwise, both operands must be `int`, and that is the type of the result.

7. Expressions

The precedence of expression operators is the same as the order of the major subsections of this section, highest precedence first. Thus, for example, the expressions referred to as the operands of + (§7.4) are those expressions defined in §§7.1-7.3   Within each subsection, the operators have the same precedence. Left- or right-associativity is specified in each subsection for the operators discussed therein. The precedence and associativity of all the expression operators is summarized in the grammar of §18.

Otherwise the order of evaluation of expressions is undefined. In particular the compiler considers itself free to compute subexpressions in the order it believes most efficient, even if the subexpressions involve side effects. The order in which side effects take place is unspecified. Expressions involving a commutative and associative operator (`*`, `+`, `&`, `|`, `^`) may be rearranged arbitrarily, even in the presence of parentheses; to force a particular order of evaluation an explicit temporary must be used.

The handling of overflow and divide check in expression evaluation is machine-dependent. All existing implementations of C ignore integer overflows; treatment of division by 0, and all floating-point exceptions, varies between machines, and is usually adjustable by a library function.

7.1 Primary expressions

Primary expressions involving `.`, `->`, subscripting, and function calls group left to right.

> *primary-expression:*
>> *identifier*
>> *constant*
>> *string*
>> (*expression*)
>> *primary-expression* [*expression*]
>> *primary-expression* (*expression-list$_{opt}$*)
>> *primary-lvalue* . *identifier*
>> *primary-expression* -> *identifier*

> *expression-list:*
>> *expression*
>> *expression-list* , *expression*

An identifier is a primary expression, provided it has been suitably declared as discussed below. Its type is specified by its declaration. If the type of the identifier is "array of ...", however, then the value of the identifier-expression is a pointer to the first object in the array, and the type of the expression is "pointer to ...". Moreover, an array identifier is not an lvalue expression. Likewise, an identifier which is declared "function returning ...", when used except in the function-name position of a call, is converted to "pointer to function returning ...".

A constant is a primary expression. Its type may be `int`, `long`, or `double` depending on its form. Character constants have type `int`; floating constants are `double`.

A string is a primary expression. Its type is originally "array of `char`"; but following the same rule given above for identifiers, this is modified to "pointer to `char`" and the result is a pointer to the first character in the string. (There is an exception in certain initializers; see §8.6.)

A parenthesized expression is a primary expression whose type and value are identical to those of the unadorned expression. The presence of parentheses does not affect whether the expression is an lvalue.

A primary expression followed by an expression in square brackets is a primary expression. The intuitive meaning is that of a subscript. Usually, the primary expression has type "pointer to ...", the subscript expression is `int`, and the type of the result is "...". The expression `E1[E2]` is identical (by definition) to `*((E1)+(E2))`. All the clues needed to understand this notation are contained in this section together with the discussions in §§ 7.1, 7.2, and 7.4 on identifiers, `*`, and + respectively; §14.3 below summarizes the implications.

A function call is a primary expression followed by parentheses containing a possibly empty, comma-separated list of expressions which constitute the actual arguments to the function. The primary expression must be of type "function returning ...", and the result of the function call is of type "...". As indicated below, a hitherto unseen identifier followed immediately by a left parenthesis is contextually declared to represent a function returning an integer; thus in the most common case, integer-valued functions need not be declared.

Any actual arguments of type `float` are converted to `double` before the call; any of type `char` or `short` are converted to `int`; and as usual, array names are converted to pointers. No other conversions are performed automatically; in particular, the compiler does not compare the types of actual arguments with those of formal arguments. If conversion is needed, use a cast; see §7.2, 8.7.

In preparing for the call to a function, a copy is made of each actual parameter; thus, all argument-passing in C is strictly by value. A function may change the values of its formal parameters, but these changes cannot affect the values of the actual parameters. On the other hand, it is possible to pass a pointer on the understanding that the function may change the value of the object to which the pointer points. An array name is a pointer expression. The order of evaluation of arguments is undefined by the language; take note that the various compilers differ.

Recursive calls to any function are permitted.

A primary expression followed by a dot followed by an identifier is an expression. The first expression must be an lvalue naming a structure or a union, and the identifier must name a member of the structure or union. The result is an lvalue referring to the named member of the structure or union.

A primary expression followed by an arrow (built from a – and a >) followed by an identifier is an expression. The first expression must be a pointer to a structure or a union and the identifier must name a member of that structure or union. The result is an lvalue referring to the named member of the structure or union to which the pointer expression points.

Thus the expression `E1->MOS` is the same as `(*E1).MOS`. Structures and unions are discussed in §8.5. The rules given here for the use of structures and unions are not enforced strictly, in order to allow an escape from the typing mechanism. See §14.1.

7.2 Unary operators

Expressions with unary operators group right-to-left.

> *unary-expression:*
> > `*` *expression*
> > `&` *lvalue*
> > `–` *expression*
> > `!` *expression*
> > `~` *expression*
> > `++` *lvalue*
> > `--` *lvalue*
> > *lvalue* `++`
> > *lvalue* `--`
> > (*type-name*) *expression*
> > `sizeof` *expression*
> > `sizeof` (*type-name*)

The unary `*` operator means *indirection*: the expression must be a pointer, and the result is an lvalue referring to the object to which the expression points. If the type of the expression is "pointer to ...", the type of the result is "...".

The result of the unary `&` operator is a pointer to the object referred to by the lvalue. If the type of the lvalue is "...", the type of the result is "pointer to ...".

The result of the unary `–` operator is the negative of its operand. The usual arithmetic conversions are performed. The negative of an unsigned quantity is computed by subtracting its value from 2^n, where n is the number of bits in an `int`. There is no unary `+` operator.

The result of the logical negation operator `!` is 1 if the value of its operand is 0, 0 if the value of its operand is non-zero. The type of the result is `int`. It is applicable to any arithmetic type or to pointers.

The `~` operator yields the one's complement of its operand. The usual arithmetic conversions are performed. The type of the operand must be integral.

The object referred to by the lvalue operand of prefix `++` is incremented. The value is the new value of the operand, but is not an lvalue. The expression `++x` is equivalent to `x+=1`. See the discussions of addition (§7.4) and assignment operators (§7.14) for information on conversions.

The lvalue operand of prefix −− is decremented analogously to the prefix ++ operator.

When postfix ++ is applied to an lvalue the result is the value of the object referred to by the lvalue. After the result is noted, the object is incremented in the same manner as for the prefix ++ operator. The type of the result is the same as the type of the lvalue expression.

When postfix −− is applied to an lvalue the result is the value of the object referred to by the lvalue. After the result is noted, the object is decremented in the manner as for the prefix −− operator. The type of the result is the same as the type of the lvalue expression.

An expression preceded by the parenthesized name of a data type causes conversion of the value of the expression to the named type. This construction is called a *cast*. Type names are described in §8.7.

The sizeof operator yields the size, in bytes, of its operand. (A *byte* is undefined by the language except in terms of the value of sizeof. However, in all existing implementations a byte is the space required to hold a char.) When applied to an array, the result is the total number of bytes in the array. The size is determined from the declarations of the objects in the expression. This expression is semantically an integer constant and may be used anywhere a constant is required. Its major use is in communication with routines like storage allocators and I/O systems.

The sizeof operator may also be applied to a parenthesized type name. In that case it yields the size, in bytes, of an object of the indicated type.

The construction sizeof(*type*) is taken to be a unit, so the expression sizeof(*type*)−2 is the same as (sizeof(*type*))−2.

7.3 Multiplicative operators

The multiplicative operators *, /, and % group left-to-right. The usual arithmetic conversions are performed.

> *multiplicative-expression:*
>   *expression * expression*
>   *expression / expression*
>   *expression % expression*

The binary * operator indicates multiplication. The * operator is associative and expressions with several multiplications at the same level may be rearranged by the compiler.

The binary / operator indicates division. When positive integers are divided truncation is toward 0, but the form of truncation is machine-dependent if either operand is negative. On all machines covered by this manual, the remainder has the same sign as the dividend. It is always true that (a/b)*b + a%b is equal to a (if b is not 0).

The binary % operator yields the remainder from the division of the first expression by the second. The usual arithmetic conversions are performed. The operands must not be float.

7.4 Additive operators

The additive operators + and − group left-to-right. The usual arithmetic conversions are performed. There are some additional type possibilities for each operator.

> *additive-expression:*
>   *expression + expression*
>   *expression − expression*

The result of the + operator is the sum of the operands. A pointer to an object in an array and a value of any integral type may be added. The latter is in all cases converted to an address offset by multiplying it by the length of the object to which the pointer points. The result is a pointer of the same type as the original pointer, and which points to another object in the same array, appropriately offset from the original object. Thus if P is a pointer to an object in an array, the expression P+1 is a pointer to the next object in the array.

No further type combinations are allowed for pointers.

The + operator is associative and expressions with several additions at the same level may be rearranged by the compiler.

The result of the − operator is the difference of the operands. The usual arithmetic conversions are performed. Additionally, a value of any integral type may be subtracted from a pointer, and then the same conversions as for addition apply.

If two pointers to objects of the same type are subtracted, the result is converted (by division by the length of the object) to an int representing the number of objects separating the pointed-to objects. This conversion will in general give unexpected results unless the pointers point to objects in the same array, since pointers, even to objects of the same type, do not necessarily differ by a multiple of the object-length.

7.5 Shift operators

The shift operators << and >> group left-to-right. Both perform the usual arithmetic conversions on their operands, each of which must be integral. Then the right operand is converted to int; the type of the result is that of the left operand. The result is undefined if the right operand is negative, or greater than or equal to the length of the object in bits.

> *shift-expression:*
>   *expression* << *expression*
>   *expression* >> *expression*

The value of E1<<E2 is E1 (interpreted as a bit pattern) left-shifted E2 bits; vacated bits are 0-filled. The value of E1>>E2 is E1 right-shifted E2 bit positions. The right shift is guaranteed to be logical (0-fill) if E1 is unsigned; otherwise it may be (and is, on the PDP-11) arithmetic (fill by a copy of the sign bit).

7.6 Relational operators

The relational operators group left-to-right, but this fact is not very useful; a<b<c does not mean what it seems to.

> *relational-expression:*
>   *expression* < *expression*
>   *expression* > *expression*
>   *expression* <= *expression*
>   *expression* >= *expression*

The operators < (less than), > (greater than), <= (less than or equal to) and >= (greater than or equal to) all yield 0 if the specified relation is false and 1 if it is true. The type of the result is int. The usual arithmetic conversions are performed. Two pointers may be compared; the result depends on the relative locations in the address space of the pointed-to objects. Pointer comparison is portable only when the pointers point to objects in the same array.

7.7 Equality operators

> *equality-expression:*
>   *expression* == *expression*
>   *expression* != *expression*

The == (equal to) and the != (not equal to) operators are exactly analogous to the relational operators except for their lower precedence. (Thus a<b == c<d is 1 whenever a<b and c<d have the same truth-value).

A pointer may be compared to an integer, but the result is machine dependent unless the integer is the constant 0. A pointer to which 0 has been assigned is guaranteed not to point to any object, and will appear to be equal to 0; in conventional usage, such a pointer is considered to be null.

7.8 Bitwise AND operator

> *and-expression:*
>   *expression* & *expression*

The & operator is associative and expressions involving & may be rearranged. The usual arithmetic conversions are performed; the result is the bitwise AND function of the operands. The operator applies only to integral operands.

7.9 Bitwise exclusive OR operator

> *exclusive-or-expression:*
>   *expression* ^ *expression*

The ^ operator is associative and expressions involving ^ may be rearranged. The usual arithmetic conversions are performed; the result is the bitwise exclusive OR function of the operands. The operator applies only to integral operands.

7.10 Bitwise inclusive OR operator

> *inclusive-or-expression:*
> *expression* | *expression*

The | operator is associative and expressions involving | may be rearranged. The usual arithmetic conversions are performed; the result is the bitwise inclusive OR function of its operands. The operator applies only to integral operands.

7.11 Logical AND operator

> *logical-and-expression:*
> *expression* && *expression*

The && operator groups left-to-right. It returns 1 if both its operands are non-zero, 0 otherwise. Unlike &, && guarantees left-to-right evaluation; moreover the second operand is not evaluated if the first operand is 0.

   The operands need not have the same type, but each must have one of the fundamental types or be a pointer. The result is always int.

7.12 Logical OR operator

> *logical-or-expression:*
> *expression* || *expression*

The || operator groups left-to-right. It returns 1 if either of its operands is non-zero, and 0 otherwise. Unlike |, || guarantees left-to-right evaluation; moreover, the second operand is not evaluated if the value of the first operand is non-zero.

   The operands need not have the same type, but each must have one of the fundamental types or be a pointer. The result is always int.

7.13 Conditional operator

> *conditional-expression:*
> *expression* ? *expression* : *expression*

Conditional expressions group right-to-left. The first expression is evaluated and if it is non-zero, the result is the value of the second expression, otherwise that of third expression. If possible, the usual arithmetic conversions are performed to bring the second and third expressions to a common type; otherwise, if both are pointers of the same type, the result has the common type; otherwise, one must be a pointer and the other the constant 0, and the result has the type of the pointer. Only one of the second and third expressions is evaluated.

7.14 Assignment operators

   There are a number of assignment operators, all of which group right-to-left. All require an lvalue as their left operand, and the type of an assignment expression is that of its left operand. The value is the value stored in the left operand after the assignment has taken place. The two parts of a compound assignment operator are separate tokens.

> *assignment-expression:*
> *lvalue* = *expression*
> *lvalue* += *expression*
> *lvalue* −= *expression*
> *lvalue* *= *expression*
> *lvalue* /= *expression*
> *lvalue* %= *expression*
> *lvalue* >>= *expression*
> *lvalue* <<= *expression*
> *lvalue* &= *expression*
> *lvalue* ^= *expression*
> *lvalue* |= *expression*

   In the simple assignment with =, the value of the expression replaces that of the object referred to by the lvalue. If both operands have arithmetic type, the right operand is converted to the type of the left preparatory to the assignment.

The behavior of an expression of the form E1 *op*= E2 may be inferred by taking it as equivalent to E1 = E1 *op* (E2); however, E1 is evaluated only once. In += and −=, the left operand may be a pointer, in which case the (integral) right operand is converted as explained in §7.4; all right operands and all non-pointer left operands must have arithmetic type.

The compilers currently allow a pointer to be assigned to an integer, an integer to a pointer, and a pointer to a pointer of another type. The assignment is a pure copy operation, with no conversion. This usage is nonportable, and may produce pointers which cause addressing exceptions when used. However, it is guaranteed that assignment of the constant 0 to a pointer will produce a null pointer distinguishable from a pointer to any object.

7.15 Comma operator

> *comma-expression:*
>> *expression , expression*

A pair of expressions separated by a comma is evaluated left-to-right and the value of the left expression is discarded. The type and value of the result are the type and value of the right operand. This operator groups left-to-right. In contexts where comma is given a special meaning, for example in a list of actual arguments to functions (§7.1) and lists of initializers (§8.6), the comma operator as described in this section can only appear in parentheses; for example,

```
    f(a, (t=3, t+2), c)
```

has three arguments, the second of which has the value 5.

8. Declarations

Declarations are used to specify the interpretation which C gives to each identifier; they do not necessarily reserve storage associated with the identifier. Declarations have the form

> *declaration:*
>> *decl-specifiers declarator-list$_{opt}$;*

The declarators in the declarator-list contain the identifiers being declared. The decl-specifiers consist of a sequence of type and storage class specifiers.

> *decl-specifiers:*
>> *type-specifier decl-specifiers$_{opt}$*
>> *sc-specifier decl-specifiers$_{opt}$*

The list must be self-consistent in a way described below.

8.1 Storage class specifiers
The sc-specifiers are:

> *sc-specifier:*
>> auto
>> static
>> extern
>> register
>> typedef

The typedef specifier does not reserve storage and is called a "storage class specifier" only for syntactic convenience; it is discussed in §8.8. The meanings of the various storage classes were discussed in §4.

The auto, static, and register declarations also serve as definitions in that they cause an appropriate amount of storage to be reserved. In the extern case there must be an external definition (§10) for the given identifiers somewhere outside the function in which they are declared.

A register declaration is best thought of as an auto declaration, together with a hint to the compiler that the variables declared will be heavily used. Only the first few such declarations are effective. Moreover, only variables of certain types will be stored in registers; on the PDP-11, they are int, char, or pointer. One other restriction applies to register variables: the address-of operator & cannot be applied to them. Smaller, faster programs can be expected if register declarations are used appropriately, but future improvements in code generation may render them unnecessary.

At most one sc-specifier may be given in a declaration. If the sc-specifier is missing from a declaration, it is taken to be auto inside a function, extern outside. Exception: functions are never automatic.

8.2 Type specifiers

The type-specifiers are

> *type-specifier:*
> > char
> > short
> > int
> > long
> > unsigned
> > float
> > double
> > *struct-or-union-specifier*
> > *typedef-name*

The words long, short, and unsigned may be thought of as adjectives; the following combinations are acceptable.

> > short int
> > long int
> > unsigned int
> > long float

The meaning of the last is the same as double. Otherwise, at most one type-specifier may be given in a declaration. If the type-specifier is missing from a declaration, it is taken to be int.

Specifiers for structures and unions are discussed in §8.5; declarations with typedef names are discussed in §8.8.

8.3 Declarators

The declarator-list appearing in a declaration is a comma-separated sequence of declarators, each of which may have an initializer.

> *declarator-list:*
> > *init-declarator*
> > *init-declarator , declarator-list*

> *init-declarator:*
> > *declarator initializer$_{opt}$*

Initializers are discussed in §8.6. The specifiers in the declaration indicate the type and storage class of the objects to which the declarators refer. Declarators have the syntax:

> *declarator:*
> > *identifier*
> > (*declarator*)
> > * *declarator*
> > *declarator* ( )
> > *declarator* [*constant-expression$_{opt}$*]

The grouping is the same as in expressions.

8.4 Meaning of declarators

Each declarator is taken to be an assertion that when a construction of the same form as the declarator appears in an expression, it yields an object of the indicated type and storage class. Each declarator contains exactly one identifier; it is this identifier that is declared.

If an unadorned identifier appears as a declarator, then it has the type indicated by the specifier heading the declaration.

A declarator in parentheses is identical to the unadorned declarator, but the binding of complex declarators may be altered by parentheses. See the examples below.

Now imagine a declaration

T   D1

where T is a type-specifier (like int, etc.) and D1 is a declarator. Suppose this declaration makes the identifier have type "... T," where the "..." is empty if D1 is just a plain identifier (so that the type of x in "int x" is just int). Then if D1 has the form

*D

the type of the contained identifier is "... pointer to T."

If D1 has the form

D()

then the contained identifier has the type "... function returning T."

If D1 has the form

D[*constant-expression*]

or

D[]

then the contained identifier has type "... array of T." In the first case the constant expression is an expression whose value is determinable at compile time, and whose type is int. (Constant expressions are defined precisely in §15.) When several "array of" specifications are adjacent, a multi-dimensional array is created; the constant expressions which specify the bounds of the arrays may be missing only for the first member of the sequence. This elision is useful when the array is external and the actual definition, which allocates storage, is given elsewhere. The first constant-expression may also be omitted when the declarator is followed by initialization. In this case the size is calculated from the number of initial elements supplied.

An array may be constructed from one of the basic types, from a pointer, from a structure or union, or from another array (to generate a multi-dimensional array).

Not all the possibilities allowed by the syntax above are actually permitted. The restrictions are as follows: functions may not return arrays, structures, unions or functions, although they may return pointers to such things; there are no arrays of functions, although there may be arrays of pointers to functions. Likewise a structure or union may not contain a function, but it may contain a pointer to a function.

As an example, the declaration

```
int i, *ip, f(), *fip(), (*pfi)();
```

declares an integer i, a pointer ip to an integer, a function f returning an integer, a function fip returning a pointer to an integer, and a pointer pfi to a function which returns an integer. It is especially useful to compare the last two. The binding of *fip() is *(fip()), so that the declaration suggests, and the same construction in an expression requires, the calling of a function fip, and then using indirection through the (pointer) result to yield an integer. In the declarator (*pfi)(), the extra parentheses are necessary, as they are also in an expression, to indicate that indirection through a pointer to a function yields a function, which is then called; it returns an integer.

As another example,

```
float fa[17], *afp[17];
```

declares an array of float numbers and an array of pointers to float numbers. Finally,

```
static int x3d[3][5][7];
```

declares a static three-dimensional array of integers, with rank 3×5×7. In complete detail, x3d is an array of three items; each item is an array of five arrays; each of the latter arrays is an array of seven integers. Any of the expressions x3d, x3d[i], x3d[i][j], x3d[i][j][k] may reasonably appear in an expression. The first three have type "array," the last has type int.

8.5 Structure and union declarations

A structure is an object consisting of a sequence of named members. Each member may have any type. A union is an object which may, at a given time, contain any one of several members. Structure and union specifiers have the same form.

```
        struct-or-union-specifier:
                struct-or-union { struct-decl-list }
                struct-or-union identifier { struct-decl-list }
                struct-or-union identifier
```

```
        struct-or-union:
                struct
                union
```

The struct-decl-list is a sequence of declarations for the members of the structure or union:

```
        struct-decl-list:
                struct-declaration
                struct-declaration struct-decl-list
```

```
        struct-declaration:
                type-specifier struct-declarator-list ;
```

```
        struct-declarator-list:
                struct-declarator
                struct-declarator , struct-declarator-list
```

In the usual case, a struct-declarator is just a declarator for a member of a structure or union. A structure member may also consist of a specified number of bits. Such a member is also called a *field*; its length is set off from the field name by a colon.

```
        struct-declarator:
                declarator
                declarator : constant-expression
                : constant-expression
```

Within a structure, the objects declared have addresses which increase as their declarations are read left-to-right. Each non-field member of a structure begins on an addressing boundary appropriate to its type; therefore, there may be unnamed holes in a structure. Field members are packed into machine integers; they do not straddle words. A field which does not fit into the space remaining in a word is put into the next word. No field may be wider than a word. Fields are assigned right-to-left on the PDP-11, left-to-right on other machines.

A struct-declarator with no declarator, only a colon and a width, indicates an unnamed field useful for padding to conform to externally-imposed layouts. As a special case, an unnamed field with a width of 0 specifies alignment of the next field at a word boundary. The "next field" presumably is a field, not an ordinary structure member, because in the latter case the alignment would have been automatic.

The language does not restrict the types of things that are declared as fields, but implementations are not required to support any but integer fields. Moreover, even int fields may be considered to be unsigned. On the PDP-11, fields are not signed and have only integer values. In all implementations, there are no arrays of fields, and the address-of operator & may not be applied to them, so that there are no pointers to fields.

A union may be thought of as a structure all of whose members begin at offset 0 and whose size is sufficient to contain any of its members. At most one of the members can be stored in a union at any time.

A structure or union specifier of the second form, that is, one of

```
        struct identifier { struct-decl-list }
        union identifier { struct-decl-list }
```

declares the identifier to be the *structure tag* (or union tag) of the structure specified by the list. A subsequent declaration may then use the third form of specifier, one of

```
        struct identifier
        union identifier
```

Structure tags allow definition of self-referential structures; they also permit the long part of the declaration to be given once and used several times. It is illegal to declare a structure or union which contains an instance of itself, but a structure or union may contain a pointer to an instance of itself.

The names of members and tags may be the same as ordinary variables. However, names of tags and members must be mutually distinct.

Two structures may share a common initial sequence of members; that is, the same member may appear in two different structures if it has the same type in both and if all previous members are the same in both. (Actually, the compiler checks only that a name in two different structures has the same type and offset in both, but if preceding members differ the construction is nonportable.)

A simple example of a structure declaration is

```
struct tnode {
        char tword[20];
        int count;
        struct tnode *left;
        struct tnode *right;
};
```

which contains an array of 20 characters, an integer, and two pointers to similar structures. Once this declaration has been given, the declaration

```
struct tnode s, *sp;
```

declares s to be a structure of the given sort and sp to be a pointer to a structure of the given sort. With these declarations, the expression

```
sp->count
```

refers to the count field of the structure to which sp points;

```
s.left
```

refers to the left subtree pointer of the structure s; and

```
s.right->tword[0]
```

refers to the first character of the tword member of the right subtree of s.

8.6 Initialization

A declarator may specify an initial value for the identifier being declared. The initializer is preceded by =, and consists of an expression or a list of values nested in braces.

> *initializer:*
>> = *expression*
>> = { *initializer-list* }
>> = { *initializer-list* , }
>
> *initializer-list:*
>> *expression*
>> *initializer-list* , *initializer-list*
>> { *initializer-list* }

All the expressions in an initializer for a static or external variable must be constant expressions, which are described in §15, or expressions which reduce to the address of a previously declared variable, possibly offset by a constant expression. Automatic or register variables may be initialized by arbitrary expressions involving constants, and previously declared variables and functions.

Static and external variables which are not initialized are guaranteed to start off as 0; automatic and register variables which are not initialized are guaranteed to start off as garbage.

When an initializer applies to a *scalar* (a pointer or an object of arithmetic type), it consists of a single expression, perhaps in braces. The initial value of the object is taken from the expression; the same conversions as for assignment are performed.

When the declared variable is an *aggregate* (a structure or array) then the initializer consists of a brace-enclosed, comma-separated list of initializers for the members of the aggregate, written in increasing subscript or member order. If the aggregate contains subaggregates, this rule applies recursively to the members of the aggregate. If there are fewer initializers in the list than there are members of the aggregate, then the aggregate is padded with 0's. It is not permitted to initialize unions or automatic aggregates.

Braces may be elided as follows. If the initializer begins with a left brace, then the succeeding comma-separated list of initializers initializes the members of the aggregate; it is erroneous for there to be more initializers than members. If, however, the initializer does not begin with a left brace, then only enough elements from the list are taken to account for the members of the aggregate; any remaining members are left to initialize the next member of the aggregate of which the current aggregate is a part.

A final abbreviation allows a `char` array to be initialized by a string. In this case successive characters of the string initialize the members of the array.

For example,

```
int x[] = { 1, 3, 5 };
```

declares and initializes `x` as a 1-dimensional array which has three members, since no size was specified and there are three initializers.

```
float y[4][3] = {
        { 1, 3, 5 },
        { 2, 4, 6 },
        { 3, 5, 7 },
};
```

is a completely-bracketed initialization: 1, 3, and 5 initialize the first row of the array `y[0]`, namely `y[0][0]`, `y[0][1]`, and `y[0][2]`. Likewise the next two lines initialize `y[1]` and `y[2]`. The initializer ends early and therefore `y[3]` is initialized with 0. Precisely the same effect could have been achieved by

```
float y[4][3] = {
        1, 3, 5, 2, 4, 6, 3, 5, 7
};
```

The initializer for `y` begins with a left brace, but that for `y[0]` does not, therefore 3 elements from the list are used. Likewise the next three are taken successively for `y[1]` and `y[2]`. Also,

```
float y[4][3] = {
        { 1 }, { 2 }, { 3 }, { 4 }
};
```

initializes the first column of `y` (regarded as a two-dimensional array) and leaves the rest 0.

Finally,

```
char msg[] = "Syntax error on line %s\n";
```

shows a character array whose members are initialized with a string.

8.7 Type names

In two contexts (to specify type conversions explicitly by means of a cast, and as an argument of `sizeof`) it is desired to supply the name of a data type. This is accomplished using a "type name," which in essence is a declaration for an object of that type which omits the name of the object.

> *type-name:*
>   *type-specifier abstract-declarator*
>
> *abstract-declarator:*
>   *empty*
>   (*abstract-declarator*)
>   * *abstract-declarator*
>   *abstract-declarator* ()
>   *abstract-declarator* [*constant-expression*$_{opt}$]

To avoid ambiguity, in the construction

> (*abstract-declarator*)

the abstract-declarator is required to be non-empty. Under this restriction, it is possible to identify uniquely the location in the abstract-declarator where the identifier would appear if the construction were a declarator in a declaration. The named type is then the same as the type of the hypothetical identifier. For example,

```
int
int *
int *[3]
int (*)[3]
int *()
int (*)()
```

name respectively the types "integer," "pointer to integer," "array of 3 pointers to integers," "pointer to an array of 3 integers," "function returning pointer to integer," and "pointer to function returning an integer."

8.8 Typedef

Declarations whose "storage class" is typedef do not define storage, but instead define identifiers which can be used later as if they were type keywords naming fundamental or derived types.

> *typedef-name:*
>   *identifier*

Within the scope of a declaration involving typedef, each identifier appearing as part of any declarator therein become syntactically equivalent to the type keyword naming the type associated with the identifier in the way described in §8.4. For example, after

```
typedef int MILES, *KLICKSP;
typedef struct { double re, im; } complex;
```

the constructions

```
MILES distance;
extern KLICKSP metricp;
complex z, *zp;
```

are all legal declarations; the type of distance is int, that of metricp is "pointer to int," and that of z is the specified structure. zp is a pointer to such a structure.

typedef does not introduce brand new types, only synonyms for types which could be specified in another way. Thus in the example above distance is considered to have exactly the same type as any other int object.

9. Statements

Except as indicated, statements are executed in sequence.

9.1 Expression statement

Most statements are expression statements, which have the form

> *expression ;*

Usually expression statements are assignments or function calls.

9.2 Compound statement, or block

So that several statements can be used where one is expected, the compound statement (also, and equivalently, called "block") is provided:

> *compound-statement:*
>   { *declaration-list_{opt} statement-list_{opt}* }
>
> *declaration-list:*
>   *declaration*
>   *declaration declaration-list*
>
> *statement-list:*
>   *statement*
>   *statement statement-list*

If any of the identifiers in the declaration-list were previously declared, the outer declaration is pushed down for the duration of the block, after which it resumes its force.

Any initializations of `auto` or `register` variables are performed each time the block is entered at the top. It is currently possible (but a bad practice) to transfer into a block; in that case the initializations are not performed. Initializations of `static` variables are performed only once when the program begins execution. Inside a block, `extern` declarations do not reserve storage so initialization is not permitted.

9.3 Conditional statement

The two forms of the conditional statement are

> `if` (*expression*) *statement*
> `if` (*expression*) *statement* `else` *statement*

In both cases the expression is evaluated and if it is non-zero, the first substatement is executed. In the second case the second substatement is executed if the expression is 0. As usual the "else" ambiguity is resolved by connecting an `else` with the last encountered `else`-less `if`.

9.4 While statement

The `while` statement has the form

> `while` (*expression*) *statement*

The substatement is executed repeatedly so long as the value of the expression remains non-zero. The test takes place before each execution of the statement.

9.5 Do statement

The `do` statement has the form

> `do` *statement* `while` (*expression*) ;

The substatement is executed repeatedly until the value of the expression becomes zero. The test takes place after each execution of the statement.

9.6 For statement

The `for` statement has the form

> `for` (*expression-1*$_{opt}$; *expression-2*$_{opt}$; *expression-3*$_{opt}$) *statement*

This statement is equivalent to

> *expression-1* ;
> `while` (*expression-2*) {
>   *statement*
>   *expression-3* ;
> }

Thus the first expression specifies initialization for the loop; the second specifies a test, made before each iteration, such that the loop is exited when the expression becomes 0; the third expression often specifies an incrementation which is performed after each iteration.

Any or all of the expressions may be dropped. A missing *expression-2* makes the implied `while` clause equivalent to `while(1)`; other missing expressions are simply dropped from the expansion above.

9.7 Switch statement

The `switch` statement causes control to be transferred to one of several statements depending on the value of an expression. It has the form

> `switch` (*expression*) *statement*

The usual arithmetic conversion is performed on the expression, but the result must be `int`. The statement is typically compound. Any statement within the statement may be labeled with one or more case prefixes as follows:

> `case` *constant-expression* :

where the constant expression must be `int`. No two of the case constants in the same switch may have the same value. Constant expressions are precisely defined in §15.

There may also be at most one statement prefix of the form

```
        default :
```

When the switch statement is executed, its expression is evaluated and compared with each case constant. If one of the case constants is equal to the value of the expression, control is passed to the statement following the matched case prefix. If no case constant matches the expression, and if there is a default prefix, control passes to the prefixed statement. If no case matches and if there is no default then none of the statements in the switch is executed.

case and default prefixes in themselves do not alter the flow of control, which continues unimpeded across such prefixes. To exit from a switch, see break, §9.8.

Usually the statement that is the subject of a switch is compound. Declarations may appear at the head of this statement, but initializations of automatic or register variables are ineffective.

9.8 Break statement
The statement

```
        break ;
```

causes termination of the smallest enclosing while, do, for, or switch statement; control passes to the statement following the terminated statement.

9.9 Continue statement
The statement

```
        continue ;
```

causes control to pass to the loop-continuation portion of the smallest enclosing while, do, or for statement; that is to the end of the loop. More precisely, in each of the statements

```
while (...) {          do {                for (...) {
    ...                    ...                  ...
contin: ;              contin: ;           contin: ;
}                      } while (...);      }
```

a continue is equivalent to goto contin. (Following the contin: is a null statement, §9.13.)

9.10 Return statement
A function returns to its caller by means of the return statement, which has one of the forms

```
        return ;
        return expression ;
```

In the first case the returned value is undefined. In the second case, the value of the expression is returned to the caller of the function. If required, the expression is converted, as if by assignment, to the type of the function in which it appears. Flowing off the end of a function is equivalent to a return with no returned value.

9.11 Goto statement
Control may be transferred unconditionally by means of the statement

```
        goto identifier ;
```

The identifier must be a label (§9.12) located in the current function.

9.12 Labeled statement
Any statement may be preceded by label prefixes of the form

```
        identifier :
```

which serve to declare the identifier as a label. The only use of a label is as a target of a goto. The scope of a label is the current function, excluding any sub-blocks in which the same identifier has been redeclared. See §11.

9.13 Null statement

The null statement has the form

A null statement is useful to carry a label just before the } of a compound statement or to supply a null body to a looping statement such as `while`.

10. External definitions

A C program consists of a sequence of external definitions. An external definition declares an identifier to have storage class `extern` (by default) or perhaps `static`, and a specified type. The type-specifier (§8.2) may also be empty, in which case the type is taken to be `int`. The scope of external definitions persists to the end of the file in which they are declared just as the effect of declarations persists to the end of a block. The syntax of external definitions is the same as that of all declarations, except that only at this level may the code for functions be given.

10.1 External function definitions

Function definitions have the form

> *function-definition:*
>   *decl-specifiers$_{opt}$ function-declarator function-body*

The only sc-specifiers allowed among the decl-specifiers are `extern` or `static`; see §11.2 for the distinction between them. A function declarator is similar to a declarator for a "function returning ..." except that it lists the formal parameters of the function being defined.

> *function-declarator:*
>   *declarator (parameter-list$_{opt}$)*

> *parameter-list:*
>   *identifier*
>   *identifier , parameter-list*

The function-body has the form

> *function-body:*
>   *declaration-list compound-statement*

The identifiers in the parameter list, and only those identifiers, may be declared in the declaration list. Any identifiers whose type is not given are taken to be `int`. The only storage class which may be specified is `register`; if it is specified, the corresponding actual parameter will be copied, if possible, into a register at the outset of the function.

A simple example of a complete function definition is

```
int max(a, b, c)
int a, b, c;
{
      int m;

      m = (a > b) ? a : b;
      return((m > c) ? m : c);
}
```

Here `int` is the type-specifier; `max(a, b, c)` is the function-declarator; `int a, b, c;` is the declaration-list for the formal parameters; { ... } is the block giving the code for the statement.

C converts all `float` actual parameters to `double`, so formal parameters declared `float` have their declaration adjusted to read `double`. Also, since a reference to an array in any context (in particular as an actual parameter) is taken to mean a pointer to the first element of the array, declarations of formal parameters declared "array of ..." are adjusted to read "pointer to ...". Finally, because structures, unions and functions cannot be passed to a function, it is useless to declare a formal parameter to be a structure, union or function (pointers to such objects are of course permitted).

10.2 External data definitions

An external data definition has the form

> *data-definition:*
> > *declaration*

The storage class of such data may be `extern` (which is the default) or `static`, but not `auto` or `register`.

11. Scope rules

A C program need not all be compiled at the same time: the source text of the program may be kept in several files, and precompiled routines may be loaded from libraries. Communication among the functions of a program may be carried out both through explicit calls and through manipulation of external data.

Therefore, there are two kinds of scope to consider: first, what may be called the *lexical scope* of an identifier, which is essentially the region of a program during which it may be used without drawing "undefined identifier" diagnostics; and second, the scope associated with external identifiers, which is characterized by the rule that references to the same external identifier are references to the same object.

11.1 Lexical scope

The lexical scope of identifiers declared in external definitions persists from the definition through the end of the source file in which they appear. The lexical scope of identifiers which are formal parameters persists through the function with which they are associated. The lexical scope of identifiers declared at the head of blocks persists until the end of the block. The lexical scope of labels is the whole of the function in which they appear.

Because all references to the same external identifier refer to the same object (see §11.2) the compiler checks all declarations of the same external identifier for compatibility; in effect their scope is increased to the whole file in which they appear.

In all cases, however, if an identifier is explicitly declared at the head of a block, including the block constituting a function, any declaration of that identifier outside the block is suspended until the end of the block.

Remember also (§8.5) that identifiers associated with ordinary variables on the one hand and those associated with structure and union members and tags on the other form two disjoint classes which do not conflict. Members and tags follow the same scope rules as other identifiers. `typedef` names are in the same class as ordinary identifiers. They may be redeclared in inner blocks, but an explicit type must be given in the inner declaration:

```
        typedef float distance;
        ...
        (
                auto int distance;
                ...
```

The `int` must be present in the second declaration, or it would be taken to be a declaration with no declarators and type `distance`†.

11.2 Scope of externals

If a function refers to an identifier declared to be `extern`, then somewhere among the files or libraries constituting the complete program there must be an external definition for the identifier. All functions in a given program which refer to the same external identifier refer to the same object, so care must be taken that the type and size specified in the definition are compatible with those specified by each function which references the data.

The appearance of the `extern` keyword in an external definition indicates that storage for the identifiers being declared will be allocated in another file. Thus in a multi-file program, an external data definition without the `extern` specifier must appear in exactly one of the files. Any other files which wish to give an external definition for the identifier must include the `extern` in the definition. The identifier can be initialized only in the declaration where storage is allocated.

Identifiers declared `static` at the top level in external definitions are not visible in other files. Functions may be declared `static`.

---

†It is agreed that the ice is thin here.

12. Compiler control lines

The C compiler contains a preprocessor capable of macro substitution, conditional compilation, and inclusion of named files. Lines beginning with # communicate with this preprocessor. These lines have syntax independent of the rest of the language; they may appear anywhere and have effect which lasts (independent of scope) until the end of the source program file.

12.1 Token replacement

A compiler-control line of the form

> #define *identifier token-string*

(note: no trailing semicolon) causes the preprocessor to replace subsequent instances of the identifier with the given string of tokens. A line of the form

> #define *identifier* (*identifier* , ... , *identifier*) *token-string*

where there is no space between the first identifier and the (, is a macro definition with arguments. Subsequent instances of the first identifier followed by a (, a sequence of tokens delimited by commas, and a) are replaced by the token string in the definition. Each occurrence of an identifier mentioned in the formal parameter list of the definition is replaced by the corresponding token string from the call. The actual arguments in the call are token strings separated by commas; however commas in quoted strings or protected by parentheses do not separate arguments. The number of formal and actual parameters must be the same. Text inside a string or a character constant is not subject to replacement.

In both forms the replacement string is rescanned for more defined identifiers. In both forms a long definition may be continued on another line by writing \ at the end of the line to be continued.

This facility is most valuable for definition of "manifest constants," as in

```
#define TABSIZE 100

int table[TABSIZE];
```

A control line of the form

> #undef *identifier*

causes the identifier's preprocessor definition to be forgotten.

12.2 File inclusion

A compiler control line of the form

> #include "*filename*"

causes the replacement of that line by the entire contents of the file *filename*. The named file is searched for first in the directory of the original source file, and then in a sequence of standard places. Alternatively, a control line of the form

> #include <*filename*>

searches only the standard places, and not the directory of the source file.

    #include's may be nested.

12.3 Conditional compilation

A compiler control line of the form

> #if *constant-expression*

checks whether the constant expression (see §15) evaluates to non-zero. A control line of the form

> #ifdef *identifier*

checks whether the identifier is currently defined in the preprocessor; that is, whether it has been the subject of a #define control line. A control line of the form

> #ifndef *identifier*

checks whether the identifier is currently undefined in the preprocessor.

All three forms are followed by an arbitrary number of lines, possibly containing a control line

```
        #else
```

and then by a control line

```
        #endif
```

If the checked condition is true then any lines between #else and #endif are ignored. If the checked condition is false then any lines between the test and an #else or, lacking an #else, the #endif, are ignored.

These constructions may be nested.

12.4 Line control

For the benefit of other preprocessors which generate C programs, a line of the form

```
    #line constant identifier
```

causes the compiler to believe, for purposes of error diagnostics, that the line number of the next source line is given by the constant and the current input file is named by the identifier. If the identifier is absent the remembered file name does not change.

13. Implicit declarations

It is not always necessary to specify both the storage class and the type of identifiers in a declaration. The storage class is supplied by the context in external definitions and in declarations of formal parameters and structure members. In a declaration inside a function, if a storage class but no type is given, the identifier is assumed to be int; if a type but no storage class is indicated, the identifier is assumed to be auto. An exception to the latter rule is made for functions, since auto functions are meaningless (C being incapable of compiling code into the stack); if the type of an identifier is "function returning ...", it is implicitly declared to be extern.

In an expression, an identifier followed by (and not already declared is contextually declared to be "function returning int".

14. Types revisited

This section summarizes the operations which can be performed on objects of certain types.

14.1 Structures and unions

There are only two things that can be done with a structure or union: name one of its members (by means of the . operator); or take its address (by unary &). Other operations, such as assigning from or to it or passing it as a parameter, draw an error message. In the future, it is expected that these operations, but not necessarily others, will be allowed.

§7.1 says that in a direct or indirect structure reference (with . or ->) the name on the right must be a member of the structure named or pointed to by the expression on the left. To allow an escape from the typing rules, this restriction is not firmly enforced by the compiler. In fact, any lvalue is allowed before ., and that lvalue is then assumed to have the form of the structure of which the name on the right is a member. Also, the expression before a -> is required only to be a pointer or an integer. If a pointer, it is assumed to point to a structure of which the name on the right is a member. If an integer, it is taken to be the absolute address, in machine storage units, of the appropriate structure.

Such constructions are non-portable.

14.2 Functions

There are only two things that can be done with a function: call it, or take its address. If the name of a function appears in an expression not in the function-name position of a call, a pointer to the function is generated. Thus, to pass one function to another, one might say

```
    int f();
    ...
    g(f);
```

Then the definition of g might read

```
g(funcp)
int (*funcp)();
{
        ...
        (*funcp)();
        ...
}
```

Notice that f must be declared explicitly in the calling routine since its appearance in g(f) was not followed by (.

14.3 Arrays, pointers, and subscripting

Every time an identifier of array type appears in an expression, it is converted into a pointer to the first member of the array. Because of this conversion, arrays are not lvalues. By definition, the subscript operator [] is interpreted in such a way that E1[E2] is identical to *((E1)+(E2)). Because of the conversion rules which apply to +, if E1 is an array and E2 an integer, then E1[E2] refers to the E2-th member of E1. Therefore, despite its asymmetric appearance, subscripting is a commutative operation.

A consistent rule is followed in the case of multi-dimensional arrays. If E is an n-dimensional array of rank $i \times j \times \cdots \times k$, then E appearing in an expression is converted to a pointer to an $(n-1)$-dimensional array with rank $j \times \cdots \times k$. If the * operator, either explicitly or implicitly as a result of subscripting, is applied to this pointer, the result is the pointed-to $(n-1)$-dimensional array, which itself is immediately converted into a pointer.

For example, consider

```
int x[3][5];
```

Here x is a 3×5 array of integers. When x appears in an expression, it is converted to a pointer to (the first of three) 5-membered arrays of integers. In the expression x[i], which is equivalent to *(x+i), x is first converted to a pointer as described; then i is converted to the type of x, which involves multiplying i by the length the object to which the pointer points, namely 5 integer objects. The results are added and indirection applied to yield an array (of 5 integers) which in turn is converted to a pointer to the first of the integers. If there is another subscript the same argument applies again; this time the result is an integer.

It follows from all this that arrays in C are stored row-wise (last subscript varies fastest) and that the first subscript in the declaration helps determine the amount of storage consumed by an array but plays no other part in subscript calculations.

14.4 Explicit pointer conversions

Certain conversions involving pointers are permitted but have implementation-dependent aspects. They are all specified by means of an explicit type-conversion operator, §§7.2 and 8.7.

A pointer may be converted to any of the integral types large enough to hold it. Whether an int or long is required is machine dependent. The mapping function is also machine dependent, but is intended to be unsurprising to those who know the addressing structure of the machine. Details for some particular machines are given below.

An object of integral type may be explicitly converted to a pointer. The mapping always carries an integer converted from a pointer back to the same pointer, but is otherwise machine dependent.

A pointer to one type may be converted to a pointer to another type. The resulting pointer may cause addressing exceptions upon use if the subject pointer does not refer to an object suitably aligned in storage. It is guaranteed that a pointer to an object of a given size may be converted to a pointer to an object of a smaller size and back again without change.

For example, a storage-allocation routine might accept a size (in bytes) of an object to allocate, and return a char pointer; it might be used in this way.

```
extern char *alloc();
double *dp;

dp = (double *) alloc(sizeof(double));
*dp = 22.0 / 7.0;
```

alloc must ensure (in a machine-dependent way) that its return value is suitable for conversion to a pointer to double; then the *use* of the function is portable.

The pointer representation on the PDP-11 corresponds to a 16-bit integer and is measured in bytes. `chars` have no alignment requirements; everything else must have an even address.

On the Honeywell 6000, a pointer corresponds to a 36-bit integer; the word part is in the left 18 bits, and the two bits that select the character in a word just to their right. Thus `char` pointers are measured in units of 2^{16} bytes; everything else is measured in units of 2^{18} machine words. `double` quantities and aggregates containing them must lie on an even word address (0 mod 2^{19}).

The IBM 370 and the Interdata 8/32 are similar. On both, addresses are measured in bytes; elementary objects must be aligned on a boundary equal to their length, so pointers to `short` must be 0 mod 2, to `int` and `float` 0 mod 4, and to `double` 0 mod 8. Aggregates are aligned on the strictest boundary required by any of their constituents.

15. Constant expressions

In several places C requires expressions which evaluate to a constant: after `case`, as array bounds, and in initializers. In the first two cases, the expression can involve only integer constants, character constants, and `sizeof` expressions, possibly connected by the binary operators

$$+ \quad - \quad * \quad / \quad \% \quad \& \quad | \quad \hat{} \quad << \quad >> \quad == \quad != \quad < \quad > \quad <= \quad >=$$

or by the unary operators

$$- \quad \tilde{}$$

or by the ternary operator

$$?:$$

Parentheses can be used for grouping, but not for function calls.

More latitude is permitted for initializers; besides constant expressions as discussed above, one can also apply the unary `&` operator to external or static objects, and to external or static arrays subscripted with a constant expression. The unary `&` can also be applied implicitly by appearance of unsubscripted arrays and functions. The basic rule is that initializers must evaluate either to a constant or to the address of a previously declared external or static object plus or minus a constant.

16. Portability considerations

Certain parts of C are inherently machine dependent. The following list of potential trouble spots is not meant to be all-inclusive, but to point out the main ones.

Purely hardware issues like word size and the properties of floating point arithmetic and integer division have proven in practice to be not much of a problem. Other facets of the hardware are reflected in differing implementations. Some of these, particularly sign extension (converting a negative character into a negative integer) and the order in which bytes are placed in a word, are a nuisance that must be carefully watched. Most of the others are only minor problems.

The number of `register` variables that can actually be placed in registers varies from machine to machine, as does the set of valid types. Nonetheless, the compilers all do things properly for their own machine; excess or invalid `register` declarations are ignored.

Some difficulties arise only when dubious coding practices are used. It is exceedingly unwise to write programs that depend on any of these properties.

The order of evaluation of function arguments is not specified by the language. It is right to left on the PDP-11, and VAX-11, left to right on the others. The order in which side effects take place is also unspecified.

Since character constants are really objects of type `int`, multi-character character constants may be permitted. The specific implementation is very machine dependent, however, because the order in which characters are assigned to a word varies from one machine to another.

Fields are assigned to words and characters to integers right-to-left on the PDP-11 and VAX-11 and left-to-right on other machines. These differences are invisible to isolated programs which do not indulge in type punning (for example, by converting an `int` pointer to a `char` pointer and inspecting the pointed-to storage), but must be accounted for when conforming to externally-imposed storage layouts.

The language accepted by the various compilers differs in minor details. Most notably, the current PDP-11 compiler will not initialize structures containing bit-fields, and does not accept a few assignment operators in certain contexts where the value of the assignment is used.

17. Anachronisms

Since C is an evolving language, certain obsolete constructions may be found in older programs. Although most versions of the compiler support such anachronisms, ultimately they will disappear, leaving only a portability problem behind.

Earlier versions of C used the form $=op$ instead of $op=$ for assignment operators. This leads to ambiguities, typified by

```
x=-1
```

which actually decrements x since the = and the – are adjacent, but which might easily be intended to assign –1 to x.

The syntax of initializers has changed: previously, the equals sign that introduces an initializer was not present, so instead of

```
int   x      = 1;
```

one used

```
int   x      1;
```

The change was made because the initialization

```
int   f      (1+2)
```

resembles a function declaration closely enough to confuse the compilers.

18. Syntax Summary

This summary of C syntax is intended more for aiding comprehension than as an exact statement of the language.

18.1 Expressions

The basic expressions are:

> *expression:*
> > *primary*
> > * *expression*
> > & *expression*
> > – *expression*
> > ! *expression*
> > ˜ *expression*
> > ++ *lvalue*
> > –– *lvalue*
> > *lvalue* ++
> > *lvalue* ––
> > sizeof *expression*
> > (*type-name*) *expression*
> > *expression binop expression*
> > *expression* ? *expression* : *expression*
> > *lvalue asgnop expression*
> > *expression* , *expression*

> *primary:*
> > *identifier*
> > *constant*
> > *string*
> > (*expression*)
> > *primary* (*expression-list$_{opt}$*)
> > *primary* [*expression*]
> > *lvalue* . *identifier*
> > *primary* –> *identifier*

> *lvalue:*
> > *identifier*
> > *primary* [*expression*]
> > *lvalue* . *identifier*
> > *primary* –> *identifier*
> > * *expression*
> > (*lvalue*)

The primary-expression operators

> ()   []   .   ->

have highest priority and group left-to-right. The unary operators

> *   &   –   !   ˜   ++   ––   sizeof   (*type-name*)

have priority below the primary operators but higher than any binary operator, and group right-to-left. Binary operators group left-to-right; they have priority decreasing as indicated below. The conditional operator groups right to left.

binop:

```
*      /     %
+      -
>>     <<
<      >     <=      >=
==     !=
&
^
|
&&
||
?:
```

Assignment operators all have the same priority, and all group right-to-left.

asgnop:

```
=    +=   -=   *=   /=   %=   >>=   <<=   &=   ^=   |=
```

The comma operator has the lowest priority, and groups left-to-right.

18.2 Declarations

declaration:
    decl-specifiers init-declarator-list$_{opt}$;

decl-specifiers:
    type-specifier decl-specifiers$_{opt}$
    sc-specifier decl-specifiers$_{opt}$

sc-specifier:
    auto
    static
    extern
    register
    typedef

type-specifier:
    char
    short
    int
    long
    unsigned
    float
    double
    struct-or-union-specifier
    typedef-name

init-declarator-list:
    init-declarator
    init-declarator , init-declarator-list

init-declarator:
    declarator initializer$_{opt}$

declarator:
    identifier
    (declarator)
    * declarator*
    declarator ( )
    declarator [constant-expression$_{opt}$]

struct-or-union-specifier:
       struct { *struct-decl-list* }
       struct *identifier* { *struct-decl-list* }
       struct *identifier*
       union { *struct-decl-list* }
       union *identifier* { *struct-decl-list* }
       union *identifier*

struct-decl-list:
       struct-declaration
       struct-declaration struct-decl-list

struct-declaration:
       type-specifier struct-declarator-list ;

struct-declarator-list:
       struct-declarator
       struct-declarator , *struct-declarator-list*

struct-declarator:
       declarator
       declarator : *constant-expression*
       : *constant-expression*

initializer:
       = *expression*
       = { *initializer-list* }
       = { *initializer-list* , }

initializer-list:
       expression
       initializer-list , *initializer-list*
       { *initializer-list* }

type-name:
       type-specifier abstract-declarator

abstract-declarator:
       empty
       (*abstract-declarator*)
       * *abstract-declarator*
       abstract-declarator ()
       abstract-declarator [*constant-expression*$_{opt}$]

typedef-name:
       identifier

18.3 Statements

compound-statement:
       { *declaration-list*$_{opt}$ *statement-list*$_{opt}$ }

declaration-list:
       declaration
       declaration declaration-list

statement-list:
    statement
    statement statement-list

statement:
    compound-statement
    expression ;
    if (*expression*) *statement*
    if (*expression*) *statement* else *statement*
    while (*expression*) *statement*
    do *statement* while (*expression*) ;
    for (*expression-1$_{opt}$* ; *expression-2$_{opt}$* ; *expression-3$_{opt}$*) *statement*
    switch (*expression*) *statement*
    case *constant-expression* :   *statement*
    default : *statement*
    break ;
    continue ;
    return ;
    return *expression* ;
    goto *identifier* ;
    identifier : *statement*
    ;

18.4 External definitions

program:
    external-definition
    external-definition program

external-definition:
    function-definition
    data-definition

function-definition:
    type-specifier$_{opt}$ function-declarator function-body

function-declarator:
    declarator (*parameter-list$_{opt}$*)

parameter-list:
    identifier
    identifier , *parameter-list*

function-body:
    type-decl-list function-statement

function-statement:
    { *declaration-list$_{opt}$ statement-list* }

data-definition:
    extern$_{opt}$ *type-specifier$_{opt}$ init-declarator-list$_{opt}$* ;
    static$_{opt}$ *type-specifier$_{opt}$ init-declarator-list$_{opt}$* ;

18.5 Preprocessor

```
#define identifier token-string
#define identifier ( identifier , ... , identifier ) token-string
#undef identifier
#include "filename"
#include <filename>
#if constant-expression
#ifdef identifier
#ifndef identifier
#else
#endif
#line constant identifier
```

Recent Changes to C

November 15, 1978

A few extensions have been made to the C language beyond what is described in the reference document ("The C Programming Language," Kernighan and Ritchie, Prentice-Hall, 1978).

1. Structure assignment

Structures may be assigned, passed as arguments to functions, and returned by functions. The types of operands taking part must be the same. Other plausible operators, such as equality comparison, have not been implemented.

There is a subtle defect in the PDP-11 implementation of functions that return structures: if an interrupt occurs during the return sequence, and the same function is called reentrantly during the interrupt, the value returned from the first call may be corrupted. The problem can occur only in the presence of true interrupts, as in an operating system or a user program that makes significant use of signals; ordinary recursive calls are quite safe.

2. Enumeration type

There is a new data type analogous to the scalar types of Pascal. To the type-specifiers in the syntax on p. 193 of the C book add

> *enum-specifier*

with syntax

> *enum-specifier:*
>   enum { *enum-list* }
>   enum *identifier* { *enum-list* }
>   enum *identifier*

> *enum-list:*
>   *enumerator*
>   *enum-list , enumerator*

> *enumerator:*
>   *identifier*
>   *identifier = constant-expression*

The role of the identifier in the enum-specifier is entirely analogous to that of the structure tag in a struct-specifier; it names a particular enumeration. For example,

```
enum color { chartreuse, burgundy, claret, winedark };
...
enum color *cp, col;
```

makes `color` the enumeration-tag of a type describing various colors, and then declares `cp` as a pointer to an object of that type, and `col` as an object of that type.

The identifiers in the enum-list are declared as constants, and may appear wherever constants are required. If no enumerators with = appear, then the values of the constants begin at 0 and increase by 1 as the declaration is read from left to right. An enumerator with = gives the associated identifier the value indicated; subsequent identifiers continue the progression from the assigned value.

Enumeration tags and constants must all be distinct, and, unlike structure tags and members, are drawn from the same set as ordinary identifiers.

Objects of a given enumeration type are regarded as having a type distinct from objects of all other types, and *lint* flags type mismatches. In the PDP-11 implementation all enumeration variables are treated as if they were `int`.

Lint, a C Program Checker

S. C. Johnson

Bell Laboratories
Murray Hill, New Jersey 07974

ABSTRACT

Lint is a command which examines C source programs, detecting a number of bugs and obscurities. It enforces the type rules of C more strictly than the C compilers. It may also be used to enforce a number of portability restrictions involved in moving programs between different machines and/or operating systems. Another option detects a number of wasteful, or error prone, constructions which nevertheless are, strictly speaking, legal.

Lint accepts multiple input files and library specifications, and checks them for consistency.

The separation of function between *lint* and the C compilers has both historical and practical rationale. The compilers turn C programs into executable files rapidly and efficiently. This is possible in part because the compilers do not do sophisticated type checking, especially between separately compiled programs. *Lint* takes a more global, leisurely view of the program, looking much more carefully at the compatibilities.

This document discusses the use of *lint*, gives an overview of the implementation, and gives some hints on the writing of machine independent C code.

July 26, 1978

Introduction and Usage

Suppose there are two C[1] source files, *file1*.c and *file2*.c, which are ordinarily compiled and loaded together. Then the command

    lint file1.c file2.c

produces messages describing inconsistencies and inefficiencies in the programs. The program enforces the typing rules of C more strictly than the C compilers (for both historical and practical reasons) enforce them. The command

    lint −p file1.c file2.c

will produce, in addition to the above messages, additional messages which relate to the portability of the programs to other operating systems and machines. Replacing the −p by −h will produce messages about various error-prone or wasteful constructions which, strictly speaking, are not bugs. Saying −hp gets the whole works.

The next several sections describe the major messages; the document closes with sections discussing the implementation and giving suggestions for writing portable C. An appendix gives a summary of the *lint* options.

A Word About Philosophy

Many of the facts which *lint* needs may be impossible to discover. For example, whether a given function in a program ever gets called may depend on the input data. Deciding whether *exit* is ever called is equivalent to solving the famous "halting problem," known to be recursively undecidable.

Thus, most of the *lint* algorithms are a compromise. If a function is never mentioned, it can never be called. If a function is mentioned, *lint* assumes it can be called; this is not necessarily so, but in practice is quite reasonable.

Lint tries to give information with a high degree of relevance. Messages of the form "*xxx* might be a bug" are easy to generate, but are acceptable only in proportion to the fraction of real bugs they uncover. If this fraction of real bugs is too small, the messages lose their credibility and serve merely to clutter up the output, obscuring the more important messages.

Keeping these issues in mind, we now consider in more detail the classes of messages which *lint* produces.

Unused Variables and Functions

As sets of programs evolve and develop, previously used variables and arguments to functions may become unused; it is not uncommon for external variables, or even entire functions, to become unnecessary, and yet not be removed from the source. These "errors of commission" rarely cause working programs to fail, but they are a source of inefficiency, and make programs harder to understand and change. Moreover, information about such unused variables and functions can occasionally serve to discover bugs; if a function does a necessary job, and is never called, something is wrong!

Lint complains about variables and functions which are defined but not otherwise mentioned. An exception is variables which are declared through explicit **extern** statements but are never referenced; thus the statement

> extern float sin( );

will evoke no comment if *sin* is never used. Note that this agrees with the semantics of the C compiler. In some cases, these unused external declarations might be of some interest; they can be discovered by adding the −**x** flag to the *lint* invocation.

Certain styles of programming require many functions to be written with similar interfaces; frequently, some of the arguments may be unused in many of the calls. The −**v** option is available to suppress the printing of complaints about unused arguments. When −**v** is in effect, no messages are produced about unused arguments except for those arguments which are unused and also declared as register arguments; this can be considered an active (and preventable) waste of the register resources of the machine.

There is one case where information about unused, or undefined, variables is more distracting than helpful. This is when *lint* is applied to some, but not all, files out of a collection which are to be loaded together. In this case, many of the functions and variables defined may not be used, and, conversely, many functions and variables defined elsewhere may be used. The −**u** flag may be used to suppress the spurious messages which might otherwise appear.

Set/Used Information

Lint attempts to detect cases where a variable is used before it is set. This is very difficult to do well; many algorithms take a good deal of time and space, and still produce messages about perfectly valid programs. *Lint* detects local variables (automatic and register storage classes) whose first use appears physically earlier in the input file than the first assignment to the variable. It assumes that taking the address of a variable constitutes a "use," since the actual use may occur at any later time, in a data dependent fashion.

The restriction to the physical appearance of variables in the file makes the algorithm very simple and quick to implement, since the true flow of control need not be discovered. It does mean that *lint* can complain about some programs which are legal, but these programs would probably be considered bad on stylistic grounds (e.g. might contain at least two **goto**'s). Because static and external variables are initialized to 0, no meaningful information can be discovered about their uses. The algorithm deals correctly, however, with initialized automatic variables, and variables which are used in the expression which first sets them.

The set/used information also permits recognition of those local variables which are set and never used; these form a frequent source of inefficiencies, and may also be symptomatic of bugs.

Flow of Control

Lint attempts to detect unreachable portions of the programs which it processes. It will complain about unlabeled statements immediately following **goto**, **break**, **continue**, or **return** statements. An attempt is made to detect loops which can never be left at the bottom, detecting the special cases **while**(1) and **for**(;;) as infinite loops. *Lint* also complains about loops which cannot be entered at the top; some valid programs may have such loops, but at best they are bad style, at worst bugs.

Lint has an important area of blindness in the flow of control algorithm: it has no way of detecting functions which are called and never return. Thus, a call to *exit* may cause unreachable code which *lint* does not detect; the most serious effects of this are in the determination of returned function values (see the next section).

One form of unreachable statement is not usually complained about by *lint;* a **break** statement that cannot be reached causes no message. Programs generated by *yacc,*[2] and especially *lex,*[3] may have literally hundreds of unreachable **break** statements. The −**O** flag in the C compiler will often eliminate the resulting object code inefficiency. Thus, these unreached statements are of little importance, there is typically nothing the user can do about them, and the resulting messages would clutter up the *lint* output. If these messages are desired, *lint* can be invoked with the −**b** option.

Function Values

Sometimes functions return values which are never used; sometimes programs incorrectly use function "values" which have never been returned. *Lint* addresses this problem in a number of ways.

Locally, within a function definition, the appearance of both

> return(*expr*);

and

> return ;

statements is cause for alarm; *lint* will give the message

> function *name* contains return(e) and return

The most serious difficulty with this is detecting when a function return is implied by flow of control reaching the end of the function. This can be seen with a simple example:

```
f ( a ) {
        if ( a ) return ( 3 );
        g ();
        }
```

Notice that, if *a* tests false, *f* will call *g* and then return with no defined return value; this will trigger a complaint from *lint*. If *g*, like *exit*, never returns, the message will still be produced when in fact nothing is wrong.

In practice, some potentially serious bugs have been discovered by this feature; it also accounts for a substantial fraction of the "noise" messages produced by *lint*.

On a global scale, *lint* detects cases where a function returns a value, but this value is sometimes, or always, unused. When the value is always unused, it may constitute an inefficiency in the function definition. When the value is sometimes unused, it may represent bad style (e.g., not testing for error conditions).

The dual problem, using a function value when the function does not return one, is also detected. This is a serious problem. Amazingly, this bug has been observed on a couple of occasions in "working" programs; the desired function value just happened to have been computed in the function return register!

Type Checking

Lint enforces the type checking rules of C more strictly than the compilers do. The additional checking is in four major areas: across certain binary operators and implied assignments, at the structure selection operators, between the definition and uses of functions, and in the use of enumerations.

There are a number of operators which have an implied balancing between types of the operands. The assignment, conditional (?:), and relational operators have this property; the argument of a **return** statement, and expressions used in initialization also suffer similar conversions. In these operations, **char**, **short**, **int**, **long**, **unsigned**, **float**, and **double** types may be freely intermixed. The types of pointers must agree exactly, except that arrays of *x*'s can, of course, be intermixed with pointers to *x*'s.

The type checking rules also require that, in structure references, the left operand of the −> be a pointer to structure, the left operand of the . be a structure, and the right operand of these operators be a member of the structure implied by the left operand. Similar checking is done for references to unions.

Strict rules apply to function argument and return value matching. The types **float** and **double** may be freely matched, as may the types **char**, **short**, **int**, and **unsigned**. Also, pointers can be matched with the associated arrays. Aside from this, all actual arguments must agree in type with their declared counterparts.

With enumerations, checks are made that enumeration variables or members are not mixed with other types, or other enumerations, and that the only operations applied are =, initialization, ==, !=, and function arguments and return values.

Type Casts

The type cast feature in C was introduced largely as an aid to producing more portable programs. Consider the assignment

    p = 1 ;

where *p* is a character pointer. *Lint* will quite rightly complain. Now, consider the assignment

    p = (char *)1 ;

in which a cast has been used to convert the integer to a character pointer. The programmer obviously had a strong motivation for doing this, and has clearly signaled his intentions. It seems harsh for *lint* to continue to complain about this. On the other hand, if this code is moved to another machine, such code should be looked at carefully. The −c flag controls the printing of comments about casts. When −c is in effect, casts are treated as though they were assignments subject to complaint; otherwise, all legal casts are passed without comment, no matter how strange the type mixing seems to be.

Nonportable Character Use

On the PDP-11, characters are signed quantities, with a range from −128 to 127. On most of the other C implementations, characters take on only positive values. Thus, *lint* will flag certain comparisons and assignments as being illegal or nonportable. For example, the fragment

    char c;
        ...
    if((c = getchar()) < 0) ....

works on the PDP-11, but will fail on machines where characters always take on positive values. The real solution is to declare *c* an integer, since *getchar* is actually returning integer values. In any case, *lint* will say "nonportable character comparison".

A similar issue arises with bitfields; when assignments of constant values are made to bitfields, the field may be too small to hold the value. This is especially true because on some machines bitfields are considered as signed quantities. While it may seem unintuitive to consider that a two bit field declared of type **int** cannot hold the value 3, the problem disappears if the bitfield is declared to have type **unsigned**.

Assignments of longs to ints

Bugs may arise from the assignment of **long** to an **int**, which loses accuracy. This may happen in programs which have been incompletely converted to use **typedefs**. When a **typedef** variable is changed from **int** to **long**, the program can stop working because some intermediate results may be assigned to **ints**, losing accuracy. Since there are a number of legitimate reasons for assigning **longs** to **ints**, the detection of these assignments is enabled by the −a flag.

Strange Constructions

Several perfectly legal, but somewhat strange, constructions are flagged by *lint;* the messages hopefully encourage better code quality, clearer style, and may even point out bugs. The −**h** flag is used to enable these checks. For example, in the statement

```
*p++ ;
```

the * does nothing; this provokes the message "null effect" from *lint.* The program fragment

```
unsigned x ;
if( x < 0 ) ...
```

is clearly somewhat strange; the test will never succeed. Similarly, the test

```
if( x > 0 ) ...
```

is equivalent to

```
if( x != 0 )
```

which may not be the intended action. *Lint* will say "degenerate unsigned comparison" in these cases. If one says

```
if( 1 != 0 ) ....
```

lint will report "constant in conditional context", since the comparison of 1 with 0 gives a constant result.

Another construction detected by *lint* involves operator precedence. Bugs which arise from misunderstandings about the precedence of operators can be accentuated by spacing and formatting, making such bugs extremely hard to find. For example, the statements

```
if( x&077 == 0 ) ...
```

or

```
x<<2 + 40
```

probably do not do what was intended. The best solution is to parenthesize such expressions, and *lint* encourages this by an appropriate message.

Finally, when the −**h** flag is in force *lint* complains about variables which are redeclared in inner blocks in a way that conflicts with their use in outer blocks. This is legal, but is considered by many (including the author) to be bad style, usually unnecessary, and frequently a bug.

Ancient History

There are several forms of older syntax which are being officially discouraged. These fall into two classes, assignment operators and initialization.

The older forms of assignment operators (e.g., =+, =−, ...) could cause ambiguous expressions, such as

```
a =−1 ;
```

which could be taken as either

```
a =− 1 ;
```

or

```
a = −1 ;
```

The situation is especially perplexing if this kind of ambiguity arises as the result of a macro substitution. The newer, and preferred operators (+=, −=, etc.) have no such ambiguities. To spur the abandonment of the older forms, *lint* complains about these old fashioned operators.

A similar issue arises with initialization. The older language allowed

    int x 1 ;

to initialize *x* to 1. This also caused syntactic difficulties: for example,

    int x (−1) ;

looks somewhat like the beginning of a function declaration:

    int x (y) { . . .

and the compiler must read a fair ways past *x* in order to sure what the declaration really is.. Again, the problem is even more perplexing when the initializer involves a macro. The current syntax places an equals sign between the variable and the initializer:

    int x = −1 ;

This is free of any possible syntactic ambiguity.

Pointer Alignment

Certain pointer assignments may be reasonable on some machines, and illegal on others, due entirely to alignment restrictions. For example, on the PDP-11, it is reasonable to assign integer pointers to double pointers, since double precision values may begin on any integer boundary. On the Honeywell 6000, double precision values must begin on even word boundaries; thus, not all such assignments make sense. *Lint* tries to detect cases where pointers are assigned to other pointers, and such alignment problems might arise. The message "possible pointer alignment problem" results from this situation whenever either the −**p** or −**h** flags are in effect.

Multiple Uses and Side Effects

In complicated expressions, the best order in which to evaluate subexpressions may be highly machine dependent. For example, on machines (like the PDP-11) in which the stack runs backwards, function arguments will probably be best evaluated from right-to-left; on machines with a stack running forward, left-to-right seems most attractive. Function calls embedded as arguments of other functions may or may not be treated similarly to ordinary arguments. Similar issues arise with other operators which have side effects, such as the assignment operators and the increment and decrement operators.

In order that the efficiency of C on a particular machine not be unduly compromised, the C language leaves the order of evaluation of complicated expressions up to the local compiler, and, in fact, the various C compilers have considerable differences in the order in which they will evaluate complicated expressions. In particular, if any variable is changed by a side effect, and also used elsewhere in the same expression, the result is explicitly undefined.

Lint checks for the important special case where a simple scalar variable is affected. For example, the statement

    a[*i*] = *b*[*i*++] ;

will draw the complaint:

    warning: *i* evaluation order undefined

Implementation

Lint consists of two programs and a driver. The first program is a version of the Portable C Compiler[4, 5] which is the basis of the IBM 370, Honeywell 6000, and Interdata 8/32 C compilers. This compiler does lexical and syntax analysis on the input text, constructs and maintains symbol tables, and builds trees for expressions. Instead of writing an intermediate file which is passed to a code generator, as the other compilers do, *lint* produces an intermediate file which consists of lines of ascii text. Each line contains an external variable name, an encoding of the context in which it was seen (use, definition, declaration, etc.), a type specifier, and a source file name and line number. The information about variables local to a function or file is collected by accessing the symbol table, and examining the expression trees.

Comments about local problems are produced as detected. The information about external names is collected onto an intermediate file. After all the source files and library descriptions have been collected, the intermediate file is sorted to bring all information collected about a given external name together. The second, rather small, program then reads the lines from the intermediate file and compares all of the definitions, declarations, and uses for consistency.

The driver controls this process, and is also responsible for making the options available to both passes of *lint*.

Portability

C on the Honeywell and IBM systems is used, in part, to write system code for the host operating system. This means that the implementation of C tends to follow local conventions rather than adhere strictly to UNIX† system conventions. Despite these differences, many C programs have been successfully moved to GCOS and the various IBM installations with little effort. This section describes some of the differences between the implementations, and discusses the *lint* features which encourage portability.

Uninitialized external variables are treated differently in different implementations of C. Suppose two files both contain a declaration without initialization, such as

   int a ;

outside of any function. The UNIX loader will resolve these declarations, and cause only a single word of storage to be set aside for *a*. Under the GCOS and IBM implementations, this is not feasible (for various stupid reasons!) so each such declaration causes a word of storage to be set aside and called *a*. When loading or library editing takes place, this causes fatal conflicts which prevent the proper operation of the program. If *lint* is invoked with the −**p** flag, it will detect such multiple definitions.

A related difficulty comes from the amount of information retained about external names during the loading process. On the UNIX system, externally known names have seven significant characters, with the upper/lower case distinction kept. On the IBM systems, there are eight significant characters, but the case distinction is lost. On GCOS, there are only six characters, of a single case. This leads to situations where programs run on the UNIX system, but encounter loader problems on the IBM or GCOS systems. *Lint* −**p** causes all external symbols to be mapped to one case and truncated to six characters, providing a worst-case analysis.

A number of differences arise in the area of character handling: characters in the UNIX system are eight bit ascii, while they are eight bit ebcdic on the IBM, and nine bit ascii on GCOS. Moreover, character strings go from high to low bit positions ("left to right") on GCOS and IBM, and low to high ("right to left") on the PDP-11. This means that code attempting to construct strings out of character constants, or attempting to use characters as indices into arrays, must be looked at with great suspicion. *Lint* is of little help here, except to flag multi-character character constants.

Of course, the word sizes are different! This causes less trouble than might be expected, at least when moving from the UNIX system (16 bit words) to the IBM (32 bits) or GCOS (36 bits). The main problems are likely to arise in shifting or masking. C now supports a bit-field facility, which can be used to write much of this code in a reasonably portable way. Frequently, portability of such code can be enhanced by slight rearrangements in coding style. Many of the incompatibilities seem to have the flavor of writing

---

†UNIX is a Trademark of Bell Laboratories.

```
x & = 0177700 ;
```

to clear the low order six bits of *x*. This suffices on the PDP-11, but fails badly on GCOS and IBM. If the bit field feature cannot be used, the same effect can be obtained by writing

```
x & = ~ 077 ;
```

which will work on all these machines.

The right shift operator is arithmetic shift on the PDP-11, and logical shift on most other machines. To obtain a logical shift on all machines, the left operand can be typed **unsigned**. Characters are considered signed integers on the PDP-11, and unsigned on the other machines. This persistence of the sign bit may be reasonably considered a bug in the PDP-11 hardware which has infiltrated itself into the C language. If there were a good way to discover the programs which would be affected, C could be changed; in any case, *lint* is no help here.

The above discussion may have made the problem of portability seem bigger than it in fact is. The issues involved here are rarely subtle or mysterious, at least to the implementor of the program, although they can involve some work to straighten out. The most serious bar to the portability of UNIX system utilities has been the inability to mimic essential UNIX system functions on the other systems. The inability to seek to a random character position in a text file, or to establish a pipe between processes, has involved far more rewriting and debugging than any of the differences in C compilers. On the other hand, *lint* has been very helpful in moving the UNIX operating system and associated utility programs to other machines.

Shutting Lint Up

There are occasions when the programmer is smarter than *lint*. There may be valid reasons for "illegal" type casts, functions with a variable number of arguments, etc. Moreover, as specified above, the flow of control information produced by *lint* often has blind spots, causing occasional spurious messages about perfectly reasonable programs. Thus, some way of communicating with *lint*, typically to shut it up, is desirable.

The form which this mechanism should take is not at all clear. New keywords would require current and old compilers to recognize these keywords, if only to ignore them. This has both philosophical and practical problems. New preprocessor syntax suffers from similar problems.

What was finally done was to cause a number of words to be recognized by *lint* when they were embedded in comments. This required minimal preprocessor changes; the preprocessor just had to agree to pass comments through to its output, instead of deleting them as had been previously done. Thus, *lint* directives are invisible to the compilers, and the effect on systems with the older preprocessors is merely that the *lint* directives don't work.

The first directive is concerned with flow of control information; if a particular place in the program cannot be reached, but this is not apparent to *lint*, this can be asserted by the directive

```
/* NOTREACHED */
```

at the appropriate spot in the program. Similarly, if it is desired to turn off strict type checking for the next expression, the directive

```
/* NOSTRICT */
```

can be used; the situation reverts to the previous default after the next expression. The −v flag can be turned on for one function by the directive

```
/* ARGSUSED */
```

Complaints about variable number of arguments in calls to a function can be turned off by the directive

/* VARARGS */

preceding the function definition. In some cases, it is desirable to check the first several arguments, and leave the later arguments unchecked. This can be done by following the VARARGS keyword immediately with a digit giving the number of arguments which should be checked; thus,

/* VARARGS2 */

will cause the first two arguments to be checked, the others unchecked. Finally, the directive

/* LINTLIBRARY */

at the head of a file identifies this file as a library declaration file; this topic is worth a section by itself.

Library Declaration Files

Lint accepts certain library directives, such as

−ly

and tests the source files for compatibility with these libraries. This is done by accessing library description files whose names are constructed from the library directives. These files all begin with the directive

/* LINTLIBRARY */

which is followed by a series of dummy function definitions. The critical parts of these definitions are the declaration of the function return type, whether the dummy function returns a value, and the number and types of arguments to the function. The VARARGS and ARGSUSED directives can be used to specify features of the library functions.

Lint library files are processed almost exactly like ordinary source files. The only difference is that functions which are defined on a library file, but are not used on a source file, draw no complaints. *Lint* does not simulate a full library search algorithm, and complains if the source files contain a redefinition of a library routine (this is a feature!).

By default, *lint* checks the programs it is given against a standard library file, which contains descriptions of the programs which are normally loaded when a C program is run. When the **-p** flag is in effect, another file is checked containing descriptions of the standard I/O library routines which are expected to be portable across various machines. The **-n** flag can be used to suppress all library checking.

Bugs, etc.

Lint was a difficult program to write, partially because it is closely connected with matters of programming style, and partially because users usually don't notice bugs which cause *lint* to miss errors which it should have caught. (By contrast, if *lint* incorrectly complains about something that is correct, the programmer reports that immediately!)

A number of areas remain to be further developed. The checking of structures and arrays is rather inadequate; size incompatibilities go unchecked, and no attempt is made to match up structure and union declarations across files. Some stricter checking of the use of the **typedef** is clearly desirable, but what checking is appropriate, and how to carry it out, is still to be determined.

Lint shares the preprocessor with the C compiler. At some point it may be appropriate for a special version of the preprocessor to be constructed which checks for things such as unused macro definitions, macro arguments which have side effects which are not expanded at all, or are expanded more than once, etc.

The central problem with *lint* is the packaging of the information which it collects. There are many options which serve only to turn off, or slightly modify, certain features. There are pressures to add even more of these options.

In conclusion, it appears that the general notion of having two programs is a good one. The compiler concentrates on quickly and accurately turning the program text into bits which can be run; *lint* concentrates on issues of portability, style, and efficiency. *Lint* can afford to be wrong, since incorrectness and over-conservatism are merely annoying, not fatal. The compiler can be fast since it knows that *lint* will cover its flanks. Finally, the programmer can concentrate at one stage of the programming process solely on the algorithms, data structures, and correctness of the program, and then later retrofit, with the aid of *lint*, the desirable properties of universality and portability.

References

1. B. W. Kernighan and D. M. Ritchie, *The C Programming Language,* Prentice-Hall, Englewood Cliffs, New Jersey (1978).

2. S. C. Johnson, "Yacc — Yet Another Compiler-Compiler," Comp. Sci. Tech. Rep. No. 32, Bell Laboratories, Murray Hill, New Jersey (July 1975).

3. M. E. Lesk, "Lex — A Lexical Analyzer Generator," Comp. Sci. Tech. Rep. No. 39, Bell Laboratories, Murray Hill, New Jersey (October 1975).

4. S. C. Johnson and D. M. Ritchie, "UNIX Time-Sharing System: Portability of C Programs and the UNIX System," *Bell Sys. Tech. J.* 57(6) pp. 2021-2048 (1978).

5. S. C. Johnson, "A Portable Compiler: Theory and Practice," *Proc. 5th ACM Symp. on Principles of Programming Languages,* (January 1978).

Appendix: Current Lint Options

The command currently has the form

lint [−options] files... library-descriptors...

The options are

h   Perform heuristic checks

p   Perform portability checks

v   Don't report unused arguments

u   Don't report unused or undefined externals

b   Report unreachable **break** statements.

x   Report unused external declarations

a   Report assignments of **long** to **int** or shorter.

c   Complain about questionable casts

n   No library checking is done

s   Same as **h** (for historical reasons)

Make — A Program for Maintaining Computer Programs

S. I. Feldman

Bell Laboratories
Murray Hill, New Jersey 07974

ABSTRACT

In a programming project, it is easy to lose track of which files need to be reprocessed or recompiled after a change is made in some part of the source. *Make* provides a simple mechanism for maintaining up-to-date versions of programs that result from many operations on a number of files. It is possible to tell *Make* the sequence of commands that create certain files, and the list of files that require other files to be current before the operations can be done. Whenever a change is made in any part of the program, the *Make* command will create the proper files simply, correctly, and with a minimum amount of effort.

The basic operation of *Make* is to find the name of a needed target in the description, ensure that all of the files on which it depends exist and are up to date, and then create the target if it has not been modified since its generators were. The description file really defines the graph of dependencies; *Make* does a depth-first search of this graph to determine what work is really necessary.

Make also provides a simple macro substitution facility and the ability to encapsulate commands in a single file for convenient administration.

August 15, 1978

Introduction

It is common practice to divide large programs into smaller, more manageable pieces. The pieces may require quite different treatments: some may need to be run through a macro processor, some may need to be processed by a sophisticated program generator (e.g., Yacc[1] or Lex[2]). The outputs of these generators may then have to be compiled with special options and with certain definitions and declarations. The code resulting from these transformations may then need to be loaded together with certain libraries under the control of special options. Related maintenance activities involve running complicated test scripts and installing validated modules. Unfortunately, it is very easy for a programmer to forget which files depend on which others, which files have been modified recently, and the exact sequence of operations needed to make or exercise a new version of the program. After a long editing session, one may easily lose track of which files have been changed and which object modules are still valid, since a change to a declaration can obsolete a dozen other files. Forgetting to compile a routine that has been changed or that uses changed declarations will result in a program that will not work, and a bug that can be very hard to track down. On the other hand, recompiling everything in sight just to be safe is very wasteful.

The program described in this report mechanizes many of the activities of program development and maintenance. If the information on inter-file dependences and command sequences is stored in a file, the simple command

    make

is frequently sufficient to update the interesting files, regardless of the number that have been edited since the last "make". In most cases, the description file is easy to write and changes infrequently. It is usually easier to type the *make* command than to issue even one of the needed operations, so the typical cycle of program development operations becomes

    think — edit — *make* — test . . .

Make is most useful for medium-sized programming projects; it does not solve the problems of maintaining multiple source versions or of describing huge programs. *Make* was designed for use on Unix, but a version runs on GCOS.

Basic Features

The basic operation of *make* is to update a target file by ensuring that all of the files on which it depends exist and are up to date, then creating the target if it has not been modified since its dependents were. *Make* does a depth-first search of the graph of dependences. The operation of the command depends on the ability to find the date and time that a file was last modified.

To illustrate, let us consider a simple example: A program named *prog* is made by compiling and loading three C-language files x.c, y.c, and z.c with the *lS* library. By convention, the output of the C compilations will be found in files named x.o, y.o, and z.o. Assume that the files x.c and y.c share some declarations in a file named *defs*, but that z.c does not. That is, x.c and *y.c* have the line

    #include "defs"

The following text describes the relationships and operations:

    prog : x.o y.o z.o
            cc x.o y.o z.o −lS −o prog
    x.o y.o : defs

If this information were stored in a file named *makefile*, the command

    make

would perform the operations needed to recreate *prog* after any changes had been made to any of the four source files *x.c*, *y.c*, *z.c*, or *defs*.

Make operates using three sources of information: a user-supplied description file (as above), file names and "last-modified" times from the file system, and built-in rules to bridge some of the gaps. In our example, the first line says that *prog* depends on three ".o" files. Once these object files are current, the second line describes how to load them to create *prog*. The third line says that *x.o* and *y.o* depend on the file *defs*. From the file system, *make* discovers that there are three ".c" files corresponding to the needed ".o" files, and uses built-in information on how to generate an object from a source file (*i.e.,* issue a "cc −c" command).

The following long-winded description file is equivalent to the one above, but takes no advantage of *make*'s innate knowledge:

    prog : x.o y.o z.o
            cc x.o y.o z.o −lS −o prog
    x.o : x.c defs
            cc −c x.c
    y.o : y.c defs
            cc −c y.c
    z.o : z.c
            cc −c z.c

If none of the source or object files had changed since the last time *prog* was made, all of the files would be current, and the command

    make

would just announce this fact and stop. If, however, the *defs* file had been edited, *x.c* and *y.c* (but not *z.c*) would be recompiled, and then *prog* would be created from the new ".o" files. If only the file *y.c* had changed, only it would be recompiled, but it would still be necessary to reload *prog*.

If no target name is given on the *make* command line, the first target mentioned in the description is created; otherwise the specified targets are made. The command

    make x.o

would recompile *x.o* if *x.c* or *defs* had changed.

If the file exists after the commands are executed, its time of last modification is used in further decisions; otherwise the current time is used. It is often quite useful to include rules with mnemonic names and commands that do not actually produce a file with that name. These entries can take advantage of *make*'s ability to generate files and substitute macros. Thus, an entry "save" might be included to copy a certain set of files, or an entry "cleanup" might be used to throw away unneeded intermediate files. In other cases one may maintain a zero-length file purely to keep track of the time at which certain actions were performed. This technique is useful for maintaining remote archives and listings.

Make has a simple macro mechanism for substituting in dependency lines and command strings. Macros are defined by command arguments or description file lines with embedded equal signs. A macro is invoked by preceding the name by a dollar sign; macro names longer than one character must be parenthesized. The name of the macro is either the single character after the dollar sign or a name inside parentheses. The following are valid macro invocations:

        $(CFLAGS)
        $2
        $(xy)
        $Z
        $(Z)

The last two invocations are identical. $$ is a dollar sign. All of these macros are assigned values during input, as shown below. Four special macros change values during the execution of the command: $*, $@, $?, and $<. They will be discussed later. The following fragment shows the use:

        OBJECTS = x.o y.o z.o
        LIBES = −lS
        prog: $(OBJECTS)
                cc $(OBJECTS) $(LIBES) −o prog
        . . .

The command

        make

loads the three object files with the *lS* library. The command

        make "LIBES= −ll −lS"

loads them with both the Lex (''−ll'') and the Standard (''−lS'') libraries, since macro definitions on the command line override definitions in the description. (It is necessary to quote arguments with embedded blanks in UNIX† commands.)

The following sections detail the form of description files and the command line, and discuss options and built-in rules in more detail.

Description Files and Substitutions

A description file contains three types of information: macro definitions, dependency information, and executable commands. There is also a comment convention: all characters after a sharp (#) are ignored, as is the sharp itself. Blank lines and lines beginning with a sharp are totally ignored. If a non-comment line is too long, it can be continued using a backslash. If the last character of a line is a backslash, the backslash, newline, and following blanks and tabs are replaced by a single blank.

A macro definition is a line containing an equal sign not preceded by a colon or a tab. The name (string of letters and digits) to the left of the equal sign (trailing blanks and tabs are stripped) is assigned the string of characters following the equal sign (leading blanks and tabs are stripped.) The following are valid macro definitions:

---

†UNIX is a Trademark of Bell Laboratories.

```
2 = xyz
abc = −ll −ly −lS
LIBES =
```

The last definition assigns LIBES the null string. A macro that is never explicitly defined has the null string as value. Macro definitions may also appear on the *make* command line (see below).

Other lines give information about target files. The general form of an entry is:

    target1 [target2 . . .] :[:] [dependent1 . . .] [; commands] [# . . .]
    [*(tab)* commands] [# . . .]
    . . .

Items inside brackets may be omitted. Targets and dependents are strings of letters, digits, periods, and slashes. (Shell metacharacters "*" and "?" are expanded.) A command is any string of characters not including a sharp (except in quotes) or newline. Commands may appear either after a semicolon on a dependency line or on lines beginning with a tab immediately following a dependency line.

A dependency line may have either a single or a double colon. A target name may appear on more than one dependency line, but all of those lines must be of the same (single or double colon) type.

1. For the usual single-colon case, at most one of these dependency lines may have a command sequence associated with it. If the target is out of date with any of the dependents on any of the lines, and a command sequence is specified (even a null one following a semicolon or tab), it is executed; otherwise a default creation rule may be invoked.

2. In the double-colon case, a command sequence may be associated with each dependency line; if the target is out of date with any of the files on a particular line, the associated commands are executed. A built-in rule may also be executed. This detailed form is of particular value in updating archive-type files.

If a target must be created, the sequence of commands is executed. Normally, each command line is printed and then passed to a separate invocation of the Shell after substituting for macros. (The printing is suppressed in silent mode or if the command line begins with an @ sign). *Make* normally stops if any command signals an error by returning a non-zero error code. (Errors are ignored if the "−i" flags has been specified on the *make* command line, if the fake target name ".IGNORE" appears in the description file, or if the command string in the description file begins with a hyphen. Some UNIX commands return meaningless status). Because each command line is passed to a separate invocation of the Shell, care must be taken with certain commands (e.g., *cd* and Shell control commands) that have meaning only within a single Shell process; the results are forgotten before the next line is executed.

Before issuing any command, certain macros are set. $@ is set to the name of the file to be "made". $? is set to the string of names that were found to be younger than the target. If the command was generated by an implicit rule (see below), $< is the name of the related file that caused the action, and $* is the prefix shared by the current and the dependent file names.

If a file must be made but there are no explicit commands or relevant built-in rules, the commands associated with the name ".DEFAULT" are used. If there is no such name, *make* prints a message and stops.

Command Usage

The *make* command takes four kinds of arguments: macro definitions, flags, description file names, and target file names.

    make [flags] [macro definitions] [targets]

The following summary of the operation of the command explains how these arguments are interpreted.

First, all macro definition arguments (arguments with embedded equal signs) are analyzed and the assignments made. Command-line macros override corresponding definitions found in the description files.

Next, the flag arguments are examined. The permissible flags are

−i   Ignore error codes returned by invoked commands. This mode is entered if the fake target name ".IGNORE" appears in the description file.

−s   Silent mode. Do not print command lines before executing. This mode is also entered if the fake target name ".SILENT" appears in the description file.

−r   Do not use the built-in rules.

−n   No execute mode. Print commands, but do not execute them. Even lines beginning with an "@" sign are printed.

−t   Touch the target files (causing them to be up to date) rather than issue the usual commands.

−q   Question. The *make* command returns a zero or non-zero status code depending on whether the target file is or is not up to date.

−p   Print out the complete set of macro definitions and target descriptions

−d   Debug mode. Print out detailed information on files and times examined.

−f   Description file name. The next argument is assumed to be the name of a description file. A file name of "−" denotes the standard input. If there are no "−f" arguments, the file named *makefile* or *Makefile* in the current directory is read. The contents of the description files override the built-in rules if they are present).

Finally, the remaining arguments are assumed to be the names of targets to be made; they are done in left to right order. If there are no such arguments, the first name in the description files that does not begin with a period is "made".

Implicit Rules

The *make* program uses a table of interesting suffixes and a set of transformation rules to supply default dependency information and implied commands. (The Appendix describes these tables and means of overriding them.) The default suffix list is:

.o	Object file
.c	C source file
.e	Efl source file
.r	Ratfor source file
.f	Fortran source file
.s	Assembler source file
.y	Yacc-C source grammar
.yr	Yacc-Ratfor source grammar
.ye	Yacc-Efl source grammar
.l	Lex source grammar

The following diagram summarizes the default transformation paths. If there are two paths connecting a pair of suffixes, the longer one is used only if the intermediate file exists or is named in the description.

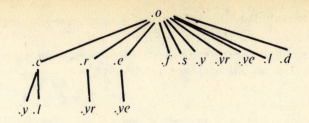

If the file *x.o* were needed and there were an *x.c* in the description or directory, it would be compiled. If there were also an *x.l*, that grammar would be run through Lex before compiling the result. However, if there were no *x.c* but there were an *x.l*, *make* would discard the intermediate C-language file and use the direct link in the graph above.

It is possible to change the names of some of the compilers used in the default, or the flag arguments with which they are invoked by knowing the macro names used. The compiler names are the macros AS, CC, RC, EC, YACC, YACCR, YACCE, and LEX. The command

>   make CC=newcc

will cause the "newcc" command to be used instead of the usual C compiler. The macros CFLAGS, RFLAGS, EFLAGS, YFLAGS, and LFLAGS may be set to cause these commands to be issued with optional flags. Thus,

>   make "CFLAGS= −O"

causes the optimizing C compiler to be used.

Example

As an example of the use of *make*, we will present the description file used to maintain the *make* command itself. The code for *make* is spread over a number of C source files and a Yacc grammar. The description file contains:

```
# Description file for the Make command
P = und −3 | opr −r2       # send to GCOS to be printed
FILES = Makefile version.c defs main.c doname.c misc.c files.c dosys.cgram.y lex.c gcos.c
OBJECTS = version.o main.o doname.o misc.o files.o dosys.o gram.o
LIBES= −lS
LINT = lint −p
CFLAGS = −O
make: $(OBJECTS)
        cc $(CFLAGS) $(OBJECTS) $(LIBES) −o make
        size make
$(OBJECTS):  defs
gram.o: lex.c
cleanup:
        -rm *.o gram.c
        -du
install:
        @size make /usr/bin/make
        cp make /usr/bin/make ; rm make
print: $(FILES)       # print recently changed files
        pr $? | $P
        touch print
test:
        make −dp | grep −v TIME > 1zap
        /usr/bin/make −dp | grep −v TIME > 2zap
        diff 1zap 2zap
        rm 1zap 2zap
lint :  dosys.c doname.c files.c main.c misc.c version.c gram.c
        $(LINT) dosys.c doname.c files.c main.c misc.c version.c gram.c
        rm gram.c
arch:
        ar uv /sys/source/s2/make.a $(FILES)
```

Make usually prints out each command before issuing it. The following output results from typing the simple command

```
make
```

in a directory containing only the source and description file:

```
cc  −c version.c
cc  −c main.c
cc  −c doname.c
cc  −c misc.c
cc  −c files.c
cc  −c dosys.c
yacc  gram.y
mv y.tab.c gram.c
cc  −c gram.c
cc  version.o main.o doname.o misc.o files.o dosys.o gram.o −lS −o make
13188+3348+3044 = 19580b = 046174b
```

Although none of the source files or grammars were mentioned by name in the description file, *make* found them using its suffix rules and issued the needed commands. The string of digits results from the "size make" command; the printing of the command line itself was suppressed by an @ sign. The @ sign on the *size* command in the description file suppressed the printing of the command, so only the sizes are written.

The last few entries in the description file are useful maintenance sequences. The "print" entry prints only the files that have been changed since the last "make print" command. A zero-length file *print* is maintained to keep track of the time of the printing; the $? macro in the command line then picks up only the names of the files changed since *print* was touched. The printed output can be sent to a different printer or to a file by changing the definition of the *P* macro:

> make print "P = opr −sp"
> *or*
> make print "P= cat >zap"

Suggestions and Warnings

The most common difficulties arise from *make*'s specific meaning of dependency. If file *x.c* has a "#include "defs"" line, then the object file *x.o* depends on *defs*; the source file *x.c* does not. (If *defs* is changed, it is not necessary to do anything to the file *x.c*, while it is necessary to recreate *x.o*.)

To discover what *make* would do, the "−n" option is very useful. The command

> make −n

orders *make* to print out the commands it would issue without actually taking the time to execute them. If a change to a file is absolutely certain to be benign (e.g., adding a new definition to an include file), the "−t" (touch) option can save a lot of time: instead of issuing a large number of superfluous recompilations, *make* updates the modification times on the affected file. Thus, the command

> make −ts

("touch silently") causes the relevant files to appear up to date. Obvious care is necessary, since this mode of operation subverts the intention of *make* and destroys all memory of the previous relationships.

The debugging flag ("−d") causes *make* to print out a very detailed description of what it is doing, including the file times. The output is verbose, and recommended only as a last resort.

Acknowledgments

I would like to thank S. C. Johnson for suggesting this approach to program maintenance control. I would like to thank S. C. Johnson and H. Gajewska for being the prime guinea pigs during development of *make*.

References

1.   S. C. Johnson, "Yacc — Yet Another Compiler-Compiler", Bell Laboratories Computing Science Technical Report #32, July 1978.

2.   M. E. Lesk, "Lex — A Lexical Analyzer Generator", Computing Science Technical Report #39, October 1975.

Appendix. Suffixes and Transformation Rules

The *make* program itself does not know what file name suffixes are interesting or how to transform a file with one suffix into a file with another suffix. This information is stored in an internal table that has the form of a description file. If the "−r" flag is used, this table is not used.

The list of suffixes is actually the dependency list for the name ".SUFFIXES"; *make* looks for a file with any of the suffixes on the list. If such a file exists, and if there is a transformation rule for that combination, *make* acts as described earlier. The transformation rule names are the concatenation of the two suffixes. The name of the rule to transform a ".*r*" file to a ".*o*" file is thus ".*r.o*". If the rule is present and no explicit command sequence has been given in the user's description files, the command sequence for the rule ".r.o" is used. If a command is generated by using one of these suffixing rules, the macro $* is given the value of the stem (everything but the suffix) of the name of the file to be made, and the macro $< is the name of the dependent that caused the action.

The order of the suffix list is significant, since it is scanned from left to right, and the first name that is formed that has both a file and a rule associated with it is used. If new names are to be appended, the user can just add an entry for ".SUFFIXES" in his own description file; the dependents will be added to the usual list. A ".SUFFIXES" line without any dependents deletes the current list. (It is necessary to clear the current list if the order of names is to be changed).

The following is an excerpt from the default rules file:

```
.SUFFIXES : .o .c .e .r .f .y .yr .ye .l .s
YACC=yacc
YACCR=yacc −r
YACCE=yacc −e
YFLAGS=
LEX=lex
LFLAGS=
CC=cc
AS=as −
CFLAGS=
RC=ec
RFLAGS=
EC=ec
EFLAGS=
FFLAGS=
.c.o :
        $(CC) $(CFLAGS) −c $<
.e.o .r.o .f.o :
        $(EC) $(RFLAGS) $(EFLAGS) $(FFLAGS) −c $<
.s.o :
        $(AS) −o $@ $<
.y.o :
        $(YACC) $(YFLAGS) $<
        $(CC) $(CFLAGS) −c y.tab.c
        rm y.tab.c
        mv y.tab.o $@
.y.c :
        $(YACC) $(YFLAGS) $<
        mv y.tab.c $@
```

UNIX Programming — Second Edition

Brian W. Kernighan

Dennis M. Ritchie

Bell Laboratories
Murray Hill, New Jersey 07974

ABSTRACT

This paper is an introduction to programming on the UNIX† system. The emphasis is on how to write programs that interface to the operating system, either directly or through the standard I/O library. The topics discussed include

- handling command arguments
- rudimentary I/O; the standard input and output
- the standard I/O library; file system access
- low-level I/O: open, read, write, close, seek
- processes: exec, fork, pipes
- signals — interrupts, etc.

There is also an appendix which describes the standard I/O library in detail.

November 12, 1978

---

†UNIX is a Trademark of Bell Laboratories.

1. INTRODUCTION

This paper describes how to write programs that interface with the UNIX operating system in a non-trivial way. This includes programs that use files by name, that use pipes, that invoke other commands as they run, or that attempt to catch interrupts and other signals during execution.

The document collects material which is scattered throughout several sections of The UNIX Programmer's Manual [1] for Version 7 UNIX. There is no attempt to be complete; only generally useful material is dealt with. It is assumed that you will be programming in C, so you must be able to read the language roughly up to the level of The C Programming Language [2]. Some of the material in sections 2 through 4 is based on topics covered more carefully there. You should also be familiar with UNIX itself at least to the level of UNIX for Beginners [3].

2. BASICS

2.1. Program Arguments

When a C program is run as a command, the arguments on the command line are made available to the function main as an argument count argc and an array argv of pointers to character strings that contain the arguments. By convention, argv[0] is the command name itself, so argc is always greater than 0.

The following program illustrates the mechanism: it simply echoes its arguments back to the terminal. (This is essentially the echo command.)

```
main(argc, argv)     /* echo arguments */
int argc;
char *argv[];
{
    int i;

    for (i = 1; i < argc; i++)
        printf("%s%c", argv[i], (i<argc-1) ? ' ' : '\n');
}
```

argv is a pointer to an array whose individual elements are pointers to arrays of characters; each is terminated by \0, so they can be treated as strings. The program starts by printing argv[1] and loops until it has printed them all.

The argument count and the arguments are parameters to main. If you want to keep them around so other routines can get at them, you must copy them to external variables.

2.2. The "Standard Input" and "Standard Output"

The simplest input mechanism is to read the "standard input," which is generally the user's terminal. The function getchar returns the next input character each time it is called. A file may be substituted for the terminal by using the < convention: if prog uses getchar, then the command line

```
prog <file
```

causes `prog` to read `file` instead of the terminal. `prog` itself need know nothing about where its input is coming from. This is also true if the input comes from another program via the pipe mechanism:

```
otherprog | prog
```

provides the standard input for `prog` from the standard output of `otherprog`.

`getchar` returns the value EOF when it encounters the end of file (or an error) on whatever you are reading. The value of EOF is normally defined to be −1, but it is unwise to take any advantage of that knowledge. As will become clear shortly, this value is automatically defined for you when you compile a program, and need not be of any concern.

Similarly, `putchar(c)` puts the character `c` on the "standard output," which is also by default the terminal. The output can be captured on a file by using >: if `prog` uses `putchar`,

```
prog >outfile
```

writes the standard output on `outfile` instead of the terminal. `outfile` is created if it doesn't exist; if it already exists, its previous contents are overwritten. And a pipe can be used:

```
prog | otherprog
```

puts the standard output of `prog` into the standard input of `otherprog`.

The function `printf`, which formats output in various ways, uses the same mechanism as `putchar` does, so calls to `printf` and `putchar` may be intermixed in any order; the output will appear in the order of the calls.

Similarly, the function `scanf` provides for formatted input conversion; it will read the standard input and break it up into strings, numbers, etc., as desired. `scanf` uses the same mechanism as `getchar`, so calls to them may also be intermixed.

Many programs read only one input and write one output; for such programs I/O with `getchar`, `putchar`, `scanf`, and `printf` may be entirely adequate, and it is almost always enough to get started. This is particularly true if the UNIX pipe facility is used to connect the output of one program to the input of the next. For example, the following program strips out all ascii control characters from its input (except for newline and tab).

```
#include <stdio.h>

main()     /* ccstrip: strip non-graphic characters */
{
    int c;
    while ((c = getchar()) != EOF)
        if ((c >= ' ' && c < 0177) || c == '\t' || c == '\n')
            putchar(c);
    exit(0);
}
```

The line

```
#include <stdio.h>
```

should appear at the beginning of each source file. It causes the C compiler to read a file (*/usr/include/stdio.h*) of standard routines and symbols that includes the definition of EOF.

If it is necessary to treat multiple files, you can use `cat` to collect the files for you:

```
cat file1 file2 ... | ccstrip >output
```

and thus avoid learning how to access files from a program. By the way, the call to `exit` at the end is not necessary to make the program work properly, but it assures that any caller of the program will see a normal termination status (conventionally 0) from the program when it completes. Section 6 discusses status returns in more detail.

3. THE STANDARD I/O LIBRARY

The "Standard I/O Library" is a collection of routines intended to provide efficient and portable I/O services for most C programs. The standard I/O library is available on each system that supports C, so programs that confine their system interactions to its facilities can be transported from one system to another essentially without change.

In this section, we will discuss the basics of the standard I/O library. The appendix contains a more complete description of its capabilities.

3.1. File Access

The programs written so far have all read the standard input and written the standard output, which we have assumed are magically pre-defined. The next step is to write a program that accesses a file that is *not* already connected to the program. One simple example is *wc*, which counts the lines, words and characters in a set of files. For instance, the command

```
wc x.c y.c
```

prints the number of lines, words and characters in `x.c` and `y.c` and the totals.

The question is how to arrange for the named files to be read — that is, how to connect the file system names to the I/O statements which actually read the data.

The rules are simple. Before it can be read or written a file has to be *opened* by the standard library function `fopen`. `fopen` takes an external name (like `x.c` or `y.c`), does some housekeeping and negotiation with the operating system, and returns an internal name which must be used in subsequent reads or writes of the file.

This internal name is actually a pointer, called a *file pointer*, to a structure which contains information about the file, such as the location of a buffer, the current character position in the buffer, whether the file is being read or written, and the like. Users don't need to know the details, because part of the standard I/O definitions obtained by including `stdio.h` is a structure definition called `FILE`. The only declaration needed for a file pointer is exemplified by

```
FILE *fp, *fopen();
```

This says that `fp` is a pointer to a `FILE`, and `fopen` returns a pointer to a `FILE`. (`FILE` is a type name, like `int`, not a structure tag.

The actual call to `fopen` in a program is

```
fp = fopen(name, mode);
```

The first argument of `fopen` is the name of the file, as a character string. The second argument is the mode, also as a character string, which indicates how you intend to use the file. The only allowable modes are read (`"r"`), write (`"w"`), or append (`"a"`).

If a file that you open for writing or appending does not exist, it is created (if possible). Opening an existing file for writing causes the old contents to be discarded. Trying to read a file that does not exist is an error, and there may be other causes of error as well (like trying to read a file when you don't have permission). If there is any error, `fopen` will return the null pointer value `NULL` (which is defined as zero in `stdio.h`).

The next thing needed is a way to read or write the file once it is open. There are several possibilities, of which `getc` and `putc` are the simplest. `getc` returns the next character from a file; it needs the file pointer to tell it what file. Thus

```
c = getc(fp)
```

places in `c` the next character from the file referred to by `fp`; it returns EOF when it reaches end of file. `putc` is the inverse of `getc`:

```
      putc(c, fp)
```

puts the character c on the file fp and returns c. getc and putc return EOF on error.

When a program is started, three files are opened automatically, and file pointers are provided for them. These files are the standard input, the standard output, and the standard error output; the corresponding file pointers are called stdin, stdout, and stderr. Normally these are all connected to the terminal, but may be redirected to files or pipes as described in Section 2.2. stdin, stdout and stderr are pre-defined in the I/O library as the standard input, output and error files; they may be used anywhere an object of type FILE * can be. They are constants, however, *not* variables, so don't try to assign to them.

With some of the preliminaries out of the way, we can now write *wc*. The basic design is one that has been found convenient for many programs: if there are command-line arguments, they are processed in order. If there are no arguments, the standard input is processed. This way the program can be used stand-alone or as part of a larger process.

```c
#include <stdio.h>

main(argc, argv)      /* wc: count lines, words, chars */
int argc;
char *argv[];
{
      int c, i, inword;
      FILE *fp, *fopen();
      long linect, wordct, charct;
      long tlinect = 0, twordct = 0, tcharct = 0;

      i = 1;
      fp = stdin;
      do {
            if (argc > 1 && (fp=fopen(argv[i], "r")) == NULL) {
                  fprintf(stderr, "wc: can't open %s\n", argv[i]);
                  continue;
            }
            linect = wordct = charct = inword = 0;
            while ((c = getc(fp)) != EOF) {
                  charct++;
                  if (c == '\n')
                        linect++;
                  if (c == ' ' || c == '\t' || c == '\n')
                        inword = 0;
                  else if (inword == 0) {
                        inword = 1;
                        wordct++;
                  }
            }
            printf("%7ld %7ld %7ld", linect, wordct, charct);
            printf(argc > 1 ? " %s\n" : "\n", argv[i]);
            fclose(fp);
            tlinect += linect;
            twordct += wordct;
            tcharct += charct;
      } while (++i < argc);
      if (argc > 2)
            printf("%7ld %7ld %7ld total\n", tlinect, twordct, tcharct);
      exit(0);
}
```

The function fprintf is identical to printf, save that the first argument is a file pointer that specifies the file to be written.

The function `fclose` is the inverse of `fopen`; it breaks the connection between the file pointer and the external name that was established by `fopen`, freeing the file pointer for another file. Since there is a limit on the number of files that a program may have open simultaneously, it's a good idea to free things when they are no longer needed. There is also another reason to call `fclose` on an output file — it flushes the buffer in which `putc` is collecting output. (`fclose` is called automatically for each open file when a program terminates normally.)

3.2. Error Handling — Stderr and Exit

`stderr` is assigned to a program in the same way that `stdin` and `stdout` are. Output written on `stderr` appears on the user's terminal even if the standard output is redirected. `wc` writes its diagnostics on `stderr` instead of `stdout` so that if one of the files can't be accessed for some reason, the message finds its way to the user's terminal instead of disappearing down a pipeline or into an output file.

The program actually signals errors in another way, using the function `exit` to terminate program execution. The argument of `exit` is available to whatever process called it (see Section 6), so the success or failure of the program can be tested by another program that uses this one as a sub-process. By convention, a return value of 0 signals that all is well; non-zero values signal abnormal situations.

`exit` itself calls `fclose` for each open output file, to flush out any buffered output, then calls a routine named `_exit`. The function `_exit` causes immediate termination without any buffer flushing; it may be called directly if desired.

3.3. Miscellaneous I/O Functions

The standard I/O library provides several other I/O functions besides those we have illustrated above.

Normally output with `putc`, etc., is buffered (except to `stderr`); to force it out immediately, use `fflush(fp)`.

`fscanf` is identical to `scanf`, except that its first argument is a file pointer (as with `fprintf`) that specifies the file from which the input comes; it returns `EOF` at end of file.

The functions `sscanf` and `sprintf` are identical to `fscanf` and `fprintf`, except that the first argument names a character string instead of a file pointer. The conversion is done from the string for `sscanf` and into it for `sprintf`.

`fgets(buf, size, fp)` copies the next line from `fp`, up to and including a newline, into `buf`; at most `size-1` characters are copied; it returns `NULL` at end of file. `fputs(buf, fp)` writes the string in `buf` onto file `fp`.

The function `ungetc(c, fp)` "pushes back" the character `c` onto the input stream `fp`; a subsequent call to `getc`, `fscanf`, etc., will encounter `c`. Only one character of pushback per file is permitted.

4. LOW-LEVEL I/O

This section describes the bottom level of I/O on the UNIX system. The lowest level of I/O in UNIX provides no buffering or any other services; it is in fact a direct entry into the operating system. You are entirely on your own, but on the other hand, you have the most control over what happens. And since the calls and usage are quite simple, this isn't as bad as it sounds.

4.1. File Descriptors

In the UNIX operating system, all input and output is done by reading or writing files, because all peripheral devices, even the user's terminal, are files in the file system. This means that a single, homogeneous interface handles all communication between a program and peripheral devices.

In the most general case, before reading or writing a file, it is necessary to inform the system of your intent to do so, a process called "opening" the file. If you are going to write on a file, it may also be necessary to create it. The system checks your right to do so (Does the file exist? Do you have permission to access it?), and if all is well, returns a small positive integer called a *file descriptor*. Whenever I/O is to be done on the file, the file descriptor is used instead of the name to identify the file. (This is roughly analogous to the use of READ(5,...) and WRITE(6,...) in Fortran.) All information about an open file is maintained by the system; the user program refers to the file only by the file descriptor.

The file pointers discussed in section 3 are similar in spirit to file descriptors, but file descriptors are more fundamental. A file pointer is a pointer to a structure that contains, among other things, the file descriptor for the file in question.

Since input and output involving the user's terminal are so common, special arrangements exist to make this convenient. When the command interpreter (the "shell") runs a program, it opens three files, with file descriptors 0, 1, and 2, called the standard input, the standard output, and the standard error output. All of these are normally connected to the terminal, so if a program reads file descriptor 0 and writes file descriptors 1 and 2, it can do terminal I/O without worrying about opening the files.

If I/O is redirected to and from files with < and >, as in

```
prog <infile >outfile
```

the shell changes the default assignments for file descriptors 0 and 1 from the terminal to the named files. Similar observations hold if the input or output is associated with a pipe. Normally file descriptor 2 remains attached to the terminal, so error messages can go there. In all cases, the file assignments are changed by the shell, not by the program. The program does not need to know where its input comes from nor where its output goes, so long as it uses file 0 for input and 1 and 2 for output.

4.2. Read and Write

All input and output is done by two functions called `read` and `write`. For both, the first argument is a file descriptor. The second argument is a buffer in your program where the data is to come from or go to. The third argument is the number of bytes to be transferred. The calls are

```
n_read = read(fd, buf, n);

n_written = write(fd, buf, n);
```

Each call returns a byte count which is the number of bytes actually transferred. On reading, the number of bytes returned may be less than the number asked for, because fewer than `n` bytes remained to be read. (When the file is a terminal, `read` normally reads only up to the next newline, which is generally less than what was requested.) A return value of zero bytes implies end of file, and −1 indicates an error of some sort. For writing, the returned value is the number of bytes actually written; it is generally an error if this isn't equal to the number supposed to be written.

The number of bytes to be read or written is quite arbitrary. The two most common values are 1, which means one character at a time ("unbuffered"), and 512, which corresponds to a physical blocksize on many peripheral devices. This latter size will be most efficient, but even character at a time I/O is not inordinately expensive.

Putting these facts together, we can write a simple program to copy its input to its output. This program will copy anything to anything, since the input and output can be redirected to any file or device.

```
#define   BUFSIZE   512  /* best size for PDP-11 UNIX */

main()    /* copy input to output */
{
      char buf[BUFSIZE];
      int  n;

      while ((n = read(0, buf, BUFSIZE)) > 0)
            write(1, buf, n);
      exit(0);
}
```

If the file size is not a multiple of BUFSIZE, some read will return a smaller number of bytes to be written by write; the next call to read after that will return zero.

It is instructive to see how read and write can be used to construct higher level routines like getchar, putchar, etc. For example, here is a version of getchar which does unbuffered input.

```
#define   CMASK      0377 /* for making char's > 0 */

getchar() /* unbuffered single character input */
{
      char c;

      return((read(0, &c, 1) > 0) ? c & CMASK : EOF);
}
```

c *must* be declared char, because read accepts a character pointer. The character being returned must be masked with 0377 to ensure that it is positive; otherwise sign extension may make it negative. (The constant 0377 is appropriate for the PDP-11 but not necessarily for other machines.)

The second version of getchar does input in big chunks, and hands out the characters one at a time.

```
#define   CMASK      0377 /* for making char's > 0 */
#define   BUFSIZE    512

getchar() /* buffered version */
{
      static char    buf[BUFSIZE];
      static char    *bufp = buf;
      static int     n = 0;

      if (n == 0) {  /* buffer is empty */
            n = read(0, buf, BUFSIZE);
            bufp = buf;
      }
      return((--n >= 0) ? *bufp++ & CMASK : EOF);
}
```

4.3. Open, Creat, Close, Unlink

Other than the default standard input, output and error files, you must explicitly open files in order to read or write them. There are two system entry points for this, open and creat [sic].

open is rather like the fopen discussed in the previous section, except that instead of returning a file pointer, it returns a file descriptor, which is just an int.

```
      int fd;

      fd = open(name, rwmode);
```

As with `fopen`, the `name` argument is a character string corresponding to the external file name. The access mode argument is different, however: `rwmode` is 0 for read, 1 for write, and 2 for read and write access. `open` returns −1 if any error occurs; otherwise it returns a valid file descriptor.

It is an error to try to `open` a file that does not exist. The entry point `creat` is provided to create new files, or to re-write old ones.

```
      fd = creat(name, pmode);
```

returns a file descriptor if it was able to create the file called `name`, and −1 if not. If the file already exists, `creat` will truncate it to zero length; it is not an error to `creat` a file that already exists.

If the file is brand new, `creat` creates it with the *protection mode* specified by the pmode argument. In the UNIX file system, there are nine bits of protection information associated with a file, controlling read, write and execute permission for the owner of the file, for the owner's group, and for all others. Thus a three-digit octal number is most convenient for specifying the permissions. For example, 0755 specifies read, write and execute permission for the owner, and read and execute permission for the group and everyone else.

To illustrate, here is a simplified version of the UNIX utility *cp*, a program which copies one file to another. (The main simplification is that our version copies only one file, and does not permit the second argument to be a directory.)

```
#define NULL 0
#define BUFSIZE 512
#define PMODE 0644 /* RW for owner, R for group, others */

main(argc, argv)     /* cp: copy f1 to f2 */
int argc;
char *argv[];
{
      int  f1, f2, n;
      char buf[BUFSIZE];

      if (argc != 3)
          error("Usage: cp from to", NULL);
      if ((f1 = open(argv[1], 0)) == -1)
          error("cp: can't open %s", argv[1]);
      if ((f2 = creat(argv[2], PMODE)) == -1)
          error("cp: can't create %s", argv[2]);

      while ((n = read(f1, buf, BUFSIZE)) > 0)
          if (write(f2, buf, n) != n)
              error("cp: write error", NULL);
      exit(0);
}

error(s1, s2)  /* print error message and die */
char *s1, *s2;
{
      printf(s1, s2);
      printf("\n");
      exit(1);
}
```

As we said earlier, there is a limit (typically 15-25) on the number of files which a program may have open simultaneously. Accordingly, any program which intends to process many files must be prepared to re-use file descriptors. The routine `close` breaks the connection between a file descriptor and an open file, and frees the file descriptor for use with some other file. Termination of a program via `exit` or return from the main program closes all open files.

The function `unlink(filename)` removes the file `filename` from the file system.

4.4. Random Access — Seek and Lseek

File I/O is normally sequential: each `read` or `write` takes place at a position in the file right after the previous one. When necessary, however, a file can be read or written in any arbitrary order. The system call `lseek` provides a way to move around in a file without actually reading or writing:

```
lseek(fd, offset, origin);
```

forces the current position in the file whose descriptor is `fd` to move to position `offset`, which is taken relative to the location specified by `origin`. Subsequent reading or writing will begin at that position. `offset` is a `long`; `fd` and `origin` are `int`'s. `origin` can be 0, 1, or 2 to specify that `offset` is to be measured from the beginning, from the current position, or from the end of the file respectively. For example, to append to a file, seek to the end before writing:

```
lseek(fd, 0L, 2);
```

To get back to the beginning ("rewind"),

```
lseek(fd, 0L, 0);
```

Notice the `0L` argument; it could also be written as `(long) 0`.

With `lseek`, it is possible to treat files more or less like large arrays, at the price of slower access. For example, the following simple function reads any number of bytes from any arbitrary place in a file.

```
get(fd, pos, buf, n) /* read n bytes from position pos */
int fd, n;
long pos;
char *buf;
{
    lseek(fd, pos, 0);   /* get to pos */
    return(read(fd, buf, n));
}
```

In pre-version 7 UNIX, the basic entry point to the I/O system is called `seek`. `seek` is identical to `lseek`, except that its `offset` argument is an `int` rather than a `long`. Accordingly, since PDP-11 integers have only 16 bits, the `offset` specified for `seek` is limited to 65,535; for this reason, `origin` values of 3, 4, 5 cause `seek` to multiply the given offset by 512 (the number of bytes in one physical block) and then interpret `origin` as if it were 0, 1, or 2 respectively. Thus to get to an arbitrary place in a large file requires two seeks, first one which selects the block, then one which has `origin` equal to 1 and moves to the desired byte within the block.

4.5. Error Processing

The routines discussed in this section, and in fact all the routines which are direct entries into the system can incur errors. Usually they indicate an error by returning a value of −1. Sometimes it is nice to know what sort of error occurred; for this purpose all these routines, when appropriate, leave an error number in the external cell `errno`. The meanings of the various error numbers are listed in the introduction to Section II of the *UNIX Programmer's Manual,* so your program can, for example, determine if an attempt to open a file failed because it did not exist or because the user lacked permission to read it. Perhaps more commonly, you may want to print out the reason for failure. The routine `perror` will print a message associated with the value of `errno`; more generally, `sys_errno` is an array of character strings which can be indexed by `errno` and printed by your program.

5. PROCESSES

It is often easier to use a program written by someone else than to invent one's own. This section describes how to execute a program from within another.

5.1. The "System" Function

The easiest way to execute a program from another is to use the standard library routine `system`. `system` takes one argument, a command string exactly as typed at the terminal (except for the newline at the end) and executes it. For instance, to time-stamp the output of a program,

```
main()
{
        system("date");
        /* rest of processing */
}
```

If the command string has to be built from pieces, the in-memory formatting capabilities of `sprintf` may be useful.

Remember than `getc` and `putc` normally buffer their input; terminal I/O will not be properly synchronized unless this buffering is defeated. For output, use `fflush`; for input, see `setbuf` in the appendix.

5.2. Low-Level Process Creation — Execl and Execv

If you're not using the standard library, or if you need finer control over what happens, you will have to construct calls to other programs using the more primitive routines that the standard library's `system` routine is based on.

The most basic operation is to execute another program *without returning*, by using the routine `execl`. To print the date as the last action of a running program, use

```
execl("/bin/date", "date", NULL);
```

The first argument to `execl` is the *file name* of the command; you have to know where it is found in the file system. The second argument is conventionally the program name (that is, the last component of the file name), but this is seldom used except as a place-holder. If the command takes arguments, they are strung out after this; the end of the list is marked by a `NULL` argument.

The `execl` call overlays the existing program with the new one, runs that, then exits. There is *no* return to the original program.

More realistically, a program might fall into two or more phases that communicate only through temporary files. Here it is natural to make the second pass simply an `execl` call from the first.

The one exception to the rule that the original program never gets control back occurs when there is an error, for example if the file can't be found or is not executable. If you don't know where `date` is located, say

```
execl("/bin/date", "date", NULL);
execl("/usr/bin/date", "date", NULL);
fprintf(stderr, "Someone stole 'date'\n");
```

A variant of `execl` called `execv` is useful when you don't know in advance how many arguments there are going to be. The call is

```
execv(filename, argp);
```

where `argp` is an array of pointers to the arguments; the last pointer in the array must be NULL so `execv` can tell where the list ends. As with `execl`, `filename` is the file in which the program is found, and `argp[0]` is the name of the program. (This arrangement is identical to the `argv` array for program arguments.)

Neither of these routines provides the niceties of normal command execution. There is no automatic search of multiple directories — you have to know precisely where the command is located. Nor do you get the expansion of metacharacters like <, >, *, ?, and [] in the argument list. If you want these, use `execl` to invoke the shell `sh`, which then does all the work. Construct a string `commandline` that contains the complete command as it would have been typed at the terminal, then say

```
execl("/bin/sh", "sh", "-c", commandline, NULL);
```

The shell is assumed to be at a fixed place, `/bin/sh`. Its argument `-c` says to treat the next argument as a whole command line, so it does just what you want. The only problem is in constructing the right information in `commandline`.

5.3. Control of Processes — Fork and Wait

So far what we've talked about isn't really all that useful by itself. Now we will show how to regain control after running a program with `execl` or `execv`. Since these routines simply overlay the new program on the old one, to save the old one requires that it first be split into two copies; one of these can be overlaid, while the other waits for the new, overlaying program to finish. The splitting is done by a routine called `fork`:

```
proc_id = fork();
```

splits the program into two copies, both of which continue to run. The only difference between the two is the value of `proc_id`, the "process id." In one of these processes (the "child"), `proc_id` is zero. In the other (the "parent"), `proc_id` is non-zero; it is the process number of the child. Thus the basic way to call, and return from, another program is

```
if (fork() == 0)
    execl("/bin/sh", "sh", "-c", cmd, NULL);        /* in child */
```

And in fact, except for handling errors, this is sufficient. The `fork` makes two copies of the program. In the child, the value returned by `fork` is zero, so it calls `execl` which does the command and then dies. In the parent, `fork` returns non-zero so it skips the `execl`. (If there is any error, `fork` returns −1).

More often, the parent wants to wait for the child to terminate before continuing itself. This can be done with the function `wait`:

```
int status;

if (fork() == 0)
    execl(...);
wait(&status);
```

This still doesn't handle any abnormal conditions, such as a failure of the `execl` or `fork`, or the possibility that there might be more than one child running simultaneously. (The `wait` returns the process id of the terminated child, if you want to check it against the value returned by `fork`.) Finally, this fragment doesn't deal with any funny behavior on the part of the child (which is reported in `status`). Still, these three lines are the heart of the standard library's `system` routine, which we'll show in a moment.

The `status` returned by `wait` encodes in its low-order eight bits the system's idea of the child's termination status; it is 0 for normal termination and non-zero to indicate various kinds of problems. The next higher eight bits are taken from the argument of the call to `exit` which caused a normal termination of the child process. It is good coding practice for all programs to return meaningful status.

When a program is called by the shell, the three file descriptors 0, 1, and 2 are set up pointing at the right files, and all other possible file descriptors are available for use. When this program calls another one, correct etiquette suggests making sure the same conditions hold. Neither `fork` nor the `exec` calls affects open files in any way. If the parent is buffering output that must come out before output from the child, the parent must flush its buffers before the `execl`. Conversely, if a caller buffers an input stream, the called program will lose any information that has been read by the caller.

5.4. Pipes

A *pipe* is an I/O channel intended for use between two cooperating processes: one process writes into the pipe, while the other reads. The system looks after buffering the data and synchronizing the two processes. Most pipes are created by the shell, as in

```
ls | pr
```

which connects the standard output of `ls` to the standard input of `pr`. Sometimes, however, it is most convenient for a process to set up its own plumbing; in this section, we will illustrate how the pipe connection is established and used.

The system call `pipe` creates a pipe. Since a pipe is used for both reading and writing, two file descriptors are returned; the actual usage is like this:

```
int   fd[2];

stat = pipe(fd);
if (stat == -1)
    /* there was an error ... */
```

`fd` is an array of two file descriptors, where `fd[0]` is the read side of the pipe and `fd[1]` is for writing. These may be used in `read`, `write` and `close` calls just like any other file descriptors.

If a process reads a pipe which is empty, it will wait until data arrives; if a process writes into a pipe which is too full, it will wait until the pipe empties somewhat. If the write side of the pipe is closed, a subsequent `read` will encounter end of file.

To illustrate the use of pipes in a realistic setting, let us write a function called `popen(cmd, mode)`, which creates a process cmd (just as `system` does), and returns a file descriptor that will either read or write that process, according to `mode`. That is, the call

```
fout = popen("pr", WRITE);
```

creates a process that executes the `pr` command; subsequent `write` calls using the file descriptor `fout` will send their data to that process through the pipe.

popen first creates the the pipe with a `pipe` system call; it then `forks` to create two copies of itself. The child decides whether it is supposed to read or write, closes the other side of the pipe, then calls the shell (via `execl`) to run the desired process. The parent likewise closes the end of the pipe it does not use. These closes are necessary to make end-of-file tests work properly. For example, if a child that intends to read fails to close the write end of the pipe, it will never see the end of the pipe file, just because there is one writer potentially active.

```
#include <stdio.h>

#define    READ 0
#define    WRITE     1
#define    tst(a, b) (mode == READ ? (b) : (a))
static     int  popen_pid;

popen(cmd, mode)
char *cmd;
int  mode;
{
      int p[2];

      if (pipe(p) < 0)
            return(NULL);
      if ((popen_pid = fork()) == 0) {
            close(tst(p[WRITE], p[READ]));
            close(tst(0, 1));
            dup(tst(p[READ], p[WRITE]));
            close(tst(p[READ], p[WRITE]));
            execl("/bin/sh", "sh", "-c", cmd, 0);
            _exit(1); /* disaster has occurred if we get here */
      }
      if (popen_pid == -1)
            return(NULL);
      close(tst(p[READ], p[WRITE]));
      return(tst(p[WRITE], p[READ]));
}
```

The sequence of closes in the child is a bit tricky. Suppose that the task is to create a child process that will read data from the parent. Then the first close closes the write side of the pipe, leaving the read side open. The lines

```
close(tst(0, 1));
dup(tst(p[READ], p[WRITE]));
```

are the conventional way to associate the pipe descriptor with the standard input of the child. The close closes file descriptor 0, that is, the standard input. dup is a system call that returns a duplicate of an already open file descriptor. File descriptors are assigned in increasing order and the first available one is returned, so the effect of the dup is to copy the file descriptor for the pipe (read side) to file descriptor 0; thus the read side of the pipe becomes the standard input. (Yes, this is a bit tricky, but it's a standard idiom.) Finally, the old read side of the pipe is closed.

A similar sequence of operations takes place when the child process is supposed to write from the parent instead of reading. You may find it a useful exercise to step through that case.

The job is not quite done, for we still need a function pclose to close the pipe created by popen. The main reason for using a separate function rather than close is that it is desirable to wait for the termination of the child process. First, the return value from pclose indicates whether the process succeeded. Equally important when a process creates several children is that only a bounded number of unwaited-for children can exist, even if some of them have terminated; performing the wait lays the child to rest. Thus:

```
#include <signal.h>

pclose(fd)        /* close pipe fd */
int fd;
{
      register r, (*hstat)(), (*istat)(), (*qstat)();
      int     status;
      extern int popen_pid;

      close(fd);
      istat = signal(SIGINT, SIG_IGN);
      qstat = signal(SIGQUIT, SIG_IGN);
      hstat = signal(SIGHUP, SIG_IGN);
      while ((r = wait(&status)) != popen_pid && r != -1);
      if (r == -1)
            status = -1;
      signal(SIGINT, istat);
      signal(SIGQUIT, qstat);
      signal(SIGHUP, hstat);
      return(status);
}
```

The calls to signal make sure that no interrupts, etc., interfere with the waiting process; this is the topic of the next section.

The routine as written has the limitation that only one pipe may be open at once, because of the single shared variable popen_pid; it really should be an array indexed by file descriptor. A popen function, with slightly different arguments and return value is available as part of the standard I/O library discussed below. As currently written, it shares the same limitation.

6. SIGNALS — INTERRUPTS AND ALL THAT

This section is concerned with how to deal gracefully with signals from the outside world (like interrupts), and with program faults. Since there's nothing very useful that can be done from within C about program faults, which arise mainly from illegal memory references or from execution of peculiar instructions, we'll discuss only the outside-world signals: *interrupt*, which is sent when the DEL character is typed; *quit*, generated by the FS character; *hangup*, caused by hanging up the phone; and *terminate*, generated by the *kill* command. When one of these events occurs, the signal is sent to *all* processes which were started from the corresponding terminal; unless other arrangements have been made, the signal terminates the process. In the *quit* case, a core image file is written for debugging purposes.

The routine which alters the default action is called signal. It has two arguments: the first specifies the signal, and the second specifies how to treat it. The first argument is just a number code, but the second is the address is either a function, or a somewhat strange code that requests that the signal either be ignored, or that it be given the default action. The include file signal.h gives names for the various arguments, and should always be included when signals are used. Thus

```
#include <signal.h>
 ...
signal(SIGINT, SIG_IGN);
```

causes interrupts to be ignored, while

```
signal(SIGINT, SIG_DFL);
```

restores the default action of process termination. In all cases, signal returns the previous value of the signal. The second argument to signal may instead be the name of a function (which has to be declared explicitly if the compiler hasn't seen it already). In this case, the named routine will be called when the signal occurs. Most commonly this facility is used to allow the program to clean up unfinished business before terminating, for example to delete a temporary file:

```
#include <signal.h>

main()
{
    int onintr();

    if (signal(SIGINT, SIG_IGN) != SIG_IGN)
        signal(SIGINT, onintr);

    /* Process ... */

    exit(0);
}

onintr()
{
    unlink(tempfile);
    exit(1);
}
```

Why the test and the double call to `signal`? Recall that signals like interrupt are sent to *all* processes started from a particular terminal. Accordingly, when a program is to be run non-interactively (started by &), the shell turns off interrupts for it so it won't be stopped by interrupts intended for foreground processes. If this program began by announcing that all interrupts were to be sent to the `onintr` routine regardless, that would undo the shell's effort to protect it when run in the background.

The solution, shown above, is to test the state of interrupt handling, and to continue to ignore interrupts if they are already being ignored. The code as written depends on the fact that `signal` returns the previous state of a particular signal. If signals were already being ignored, the process should continue to ignore them; otherwise, they should be caught.

A more sophisticated program may wish to intercept an interrupt and interpret it as a request to stop what it is doing and return to its own command-processing loop. Think of a text editor: interrupting a long printout should not cause it to terminate and lose the work already done. The outline of the code for this case is probably best written like this:

```
#include <signal.h>
#include <setjmp.h>
jmp_buf    sjbuf;

main()
{
    int (*istat)(), onintr();

    istat = signal(SIGINT, SIG_IGN);   /* save original status */
    setjmp(sjbuf); /* save current stack position */
    if (istat != SIG_IGN)
        signal(SIGINT, onintr);

    /* main processing loop */
}
```

```
onintr()
{
        printf("\nInterrupt\n");
        longjmp(sjbuf);       /* return to saved state */
}
```

The include file `setjmp.h` declares the type `jmp_buf` an object in which the state can be saved. `sjbuf` is such an object; it is an array of some sort. The `setjmp` routine then saves the state of things. When an interrupt occurs, a call is forced to the `onintr` routine, which can print a message, set flags, or whatever. `longjmp` takes as argument an object stored into by `setjmp`, and restores control to the location after the call to `setjmp`, so control (and the stack level) will pop back to the place in the main routine where the signal is set up and the main loop entered. Notice, by the way, that the signal gets set again after an interrupt occurs. This is necessary; most signals are automatically reset to their default action when they occur.

Some programs that want to detect signals simply can't be stopped at an arbitrary point, for example in the middle of updating a linked list. If the routine called on occurrence of a signal sets a flag and then returns instead of calling `exit` or `longjmp`, execution will continue at the exact point it was interrupted. The interrupt flag can then be tested later.

There is one difficulty associated with this approach. Suppose the program is reading the terminal when the interrupt is sent. The specified routine is duly called; it sets its flag and returns. If it were really true, as we said above, that "execution resumes at the exact point it was interrupted," the program would continue reading the terminal until the user typed another line. This behavior might well be confusing, since the user might not know that the program is reading; he presumably would prefer to have the signal take effect instantly. The method chosen to resolve this difficulty is to terminate the terminal read when execution resumes after the signal, returning an error code which indicates what happened.

Thus programs which catch and resume execution after signals should be prepared for "errors" which are caused by interrupted system calls. (The ones to watch out for are reads from a terminal, `wait`, and `pause`.) A program whose `onintr` program just sets `intflag`, resets the interrupt signal, and returns, should usually include code like the following when it reads the standard input:

```
if (getchar() == EOF)
    if (intflag)
        /* EOF caused by interrupt */
    else
        /* true end-of-file */
```

A final subtlety to keep in mind becomes important when signal-catching is combined with execution of other programs. Suppose a program catches interrupts, and also includes a method (like "!" in the editor) whereby other programs can be executed. Then the code should look something like this:

```
if (fork() == 0)
    execl(...);
signal(SIGINT, SIG_IGN); /* ignore interrupts */
wait(&status); /* until the child is done */
signal(SIGINT, onintr);  /* restore interrupts */
```

Why is this? Again, it's not obvious but not really difficult. Suppose the program you call catches its own interrupts. If you interrupt the subprogram, it will get the signal and return to its main loop, and probably read your terminal. But the calling program will also pop out of its wait for the subprogram and read your terminal. Having two processes reading your terminal is very unfortunate, since the system figuratively flips a coin to decide who should get each line of input. A simple way out is to have the parent program ignore interrupts until the child is done. This reasoning is reflected in the standard I/O library function `system`:

```
#include <signal.h>

system(s) /* run command string s */
char *s;
{
    int status, pid, w;
    register int (*istat)(), (*qstat)();

    if ((pid = fork()) == 0) {
        execl("/bin/sh", "sh", "-c", s, 0);
        _exit(127);
    }
    istat = signal(SIGINT, SIG_IGN);
    qstat = signal(SIGQUIT, SIG_IGN);
    while ((w = wait(&status)) != pid && w != -1)
        ;
    if (w == -1)
        status = -1;
    signal(SIGINT, istat);
    signal(SIGQUIT, qstat);
    return(status);
}
```

As an aside on declarations, the function signal obviously has a rather strange second argument. It is in fact a pointer to a function delivering an integer, and this is also the type of the signal routine itself. The two values SIG_IGN and SIG_DFL have the right type, but are chosen so they coincide with no possible actual functions. For the enthusiast, here is how they are defined for the PDP-11; the definitions should be sufficiently ugly and nonportable to encourage use of the include file.

```
#define   SIG_DFL   (int (*)())0
#define   SIG_IGN   (int (*)())1
```

References

[1] K. L. Thompson and D. M. Ritchie, *The UNIX Programmer's Manual*, Bell Laboratories, 1978.

[2] B. W. Kernighan and D. M. Ritchie, *The C Programming Language*, Prentice-Hall, Inc., 1978.

[3] B. W. Kernighan, "UNIX for Beginners — Second Edition." Bell Laboratories, 1978.

Appendix — The Standard I/O Library

D. M. Ritchie

Bell Laboratories
Murray Hill, New Jersey 07974

The standard I/O library was designed with the following goals in mind.

1. It must be as efficient as possible, both in time and in space, so that there will be no hesitation in using it no matter how critical the application.

2. It must be simple to use, and also free of the magic numbers and mysterious calls whose use mars the understandability and portability of many programs using older packages.

3. The interface provided should be applicable on all machines, whether or not the programs which implement it are directly portable to other systems, or to machines other than the PDP-11 running a version of UNIX.

1. General Usage

Each program using the library must have the line

```
#include <stdio.h>
```

which defines certain macros and variables. The routines are in the normal C library, so no special library argument is needed for loading. All names in the include file intended only for internal use begin with an underscore _ to reduce the possibility of collision with a user name. The names intended to be visible outside the package are

stdin   The name of the standard input file

stdout   The name of the standard output file

stderr   The name of the standard error file

EOF   is actually −1, and is the value returned by the read routines on end-of-file or error.

NULL   is a notation for the null pointer, returned by pointer-valued functions to indicate an error

FILE   expands to struct _iob and is a useful shorthand when declaring pointers to streams.

BUFSIZ   is a number (viz. 512) of the size suitable for an I/O buffer supplied by the user. See setbuf, below.

getc, getchar, putc, putchar, feof, ferror, fileno
         are defined as macros. Their actions are described below; they are mentioned here to point out that it is not possible to redeclare them and that they are not actually functions; thus, for example, they may not have breakpoints set on them.

The routines in this package offer the convenience of automatic buffer allocation and output flushing where appropriate. The names stdin, stdout, and stderr are in effect constants and may not be assigned to.

2. Calls

FILE *fopen(filename, type) char *filename, *type;
         opens the file and, if needed, allocates a buffer for it. filename is a character string specifying the name. type is a character string (not a single character). It may be "r", "w", or "a" to indicate intent to read, write, or append. The value returned is a file pointer. If it is NULL the attempt to open failed.

FILE *freopen(filename, type, ioptr) char *filename, *type; FILE *ioptr;

The stream named by `ioptr` is closed, if necessary, and then reopened as if by `fopen`. If the attempt to open fails, `NULL` is returned, otherwise `ioptr`, which will now refer to the new file. Often the reopened stream is `stdin` or `stdout`.

`int getc(ioptr) FILE *ioptr;`
    returns the next character from the stream named by `ioptr`, which is a pointer to a file such as returned by `fopen`, or the name `stdin`. The integer `EOF` is returned on end-of-file or when an error occurs. The null character `\0` is a legal character.

`int fgetc(ioptr) FILE *ioptr;`
    acts like `getc` but is a genuine function, not a macro, so it can be pointed to, passed as an argument, etc.

`putc(c, ioptr) FILE *ioptr;`
    `putc` writes the character `c` on the output stream named by `ioptr`, which is a value returned from `fopen` or perhaps `stdout` or `stderr`. The character is returned as value, but `EOF` is returned on error.

`fputc(c, ioptr) FILE *ioptr;`
    acts like `putc` but is a genuine function, not a macro.

`fclose(ioptr) FILE *ioptr;`
    The file corresponding to `ioptr` is closed after any buffers are emptied. A buffer allocated by the I/O system is freed. `fclose` is automatic on normal termination of the program.

`fflush(ioptr) FILE *ioptr;`
    Any buffered information on the (output) stream named by `ioptr` is written out. Output files are normally buffered if and only if they are not directed to the terminal; however, `stderr` always starts off unbuffered and remains so unless `setbuf` is used, or unless it is reopened.

`exit(errcode);`
    terminates the process and returns its argument as status to the parent. This is a special version of the routine which calls `fflush` for each output file. To terminate without flushing, use `_exit`.

`feof(ioptr) FILE *ioptr;`
    returns non-zero when end-of-file has occurred on the specified input stream.

`ferror(ioptr) FILE *ioptr;`
    returns non-zero when an error has occurred while reading or writing the named stream. The error indication lasts until the file has been closed.

`getchar();`
    is identical to `getc(stdin)`.

`putchar(c);`
    is identical to `putc(c, stdout)`.

`char *fgets(s, n, ioptr) char *s; FILE *ioptr;`
    reads up to n−1 characters from the stream `ioptr` into the character pointer `s`. The read terminates with a newline character. The newline character is placed in the buffer followed by a null character. `fgets` returns the first argument, or `NULL` if error or end-of-file occurred.

`fputs(s, ioptr) char *s; FILE *ioptr;`
    writes the null-terminated string (character array) `s` on the stream `ioptr`. No newline is appended. No value is returned.

`ungetc(c, ioptr) FILE *ioptr;`

The argument character c is pushed back on the input stream named by ioptr. Only one character may be pushed back.

```
printf(format, a1, ...) char *format;
fprintf(ioptr, format, a1, ...) FILE *ioptr; char *format;
sprintf(s, format, a1, ...)char *s, *format;
```
printf writes on the standard output. fprintf writes on the named output stream. sprintf puts characters in the character array (string) named by s. The specifications are as described in section printf(3) of the *UNIX Programmer's Manual.*

```
scanf(format, a1, ...) char *format;
fscanf(ioptr, format, a1, ...) FILE *ioptr; char *format;
sscanf(s, format, a1, ...) char *s, *format;
```
scanf reads from the standard input. fscanf reads from the named input stream. sscanf reads from the character string supplied as s. scanf reads characters, interprets them according to a format, and stores the results in its arguments. Each routine expects as arguments a control string format, and a set of arguments, *each of which must be a pointer,* indicating where the converted input should be stored.

scanf returns as its value the number of successfully matched and assigned input items. This can be used to decide how many input items were found. On end of file, EOF is returned; note that this is different from 0, which means that the next input character does not match what was called for in the control string.

```
fread(ptr, sizeof(*ptr), nitems, ioptr) FILE *ioptr;
```
reads nitems of data beginning at ptr from file ioptr. No advance notification that binary I/O is being done is required; when, for portability reasons, it becomes required, it will be done by adding an additional character to the mode-string on the fopen call.

```
fwrite(ptr, sizeof(*ptr), nitems, ioptr) FILE *ioptr;
```
Like fread, but in the other direction.

```
rewind(ioptr) FILE *ioptr;
```
rewinds the stream named by ioptr. It is not very useful except on input, since a rewound output file is still open only for output.

```
system(string) char *string;
```
The string is executed by the shell as if typed at the terminal.

```
getw(ioptr) FILE *ioptr;
```
returns the next word from the input stream named by ioptr. EOF is returned on end-of-file or error, but since this a perfectly good integer feof and ferror should be used. A "word" is 16 bits on the PDP-11.

```
putw(w, ioptr) FILE *ioptr;
```
writes the integer w on the named output stream.

```
setbuf(ioptr, buf) FILE *ioptr; char *buf;
```
setbuf may be used after a stream has been opened but before I/O has started. If buf is NULL, the stream will be unbuffered. Otherwise the buffer supplied will be used. It must be a character array of sufficient size:

```
char buf[BUFSIZ];
```

```
fileno(ioptr) FILE *ioptr;
```
returns the integer file descriptor associated with the file.

```
fseek(ioptr, offset, ptrname) FILE *ioptr; long offset;
```
The location of the next byte in the stream named by ioptr is adjusted. offset is a long integer. If ptrname is 0, the offset is measured from the beginning of the file; if ptrname is 1, the offset is measured from the current read or write pointer; if ptrname is 2, the offset is measured from the end of the file. The routine accounts properly for any buffering. (When

this routine is used on non-UNIX systems, the offset must be a value returned from `ftell` and the ptrname must be 0).

`long ftell(ioptr) FILE *ioptr;`
The byte offset, measured from the beginning of the file, associated with the named stream is returned. Any buffering is properly accounted for. (On non-UNIX systems the value of this call is useful only for handing to `fseek`, so as to position the file to the same place it was when `ftell` was called.)

`getpw(uid, buf) char *buf;`
The password file is searched for the given integer user ID. If an appropriate line is found, it is copied into the character array `buf`, and 0 is returned. If no line is found corresponding to the user ID then 1 is returned.

`char *malloc(num);`
allocates `num` bytes. The pointer returned is sufficiently well aligned to be usable for any purpose. NULL is returned if no space is available.

`char *calloc(num, size);`
allocates space for `num` items each of size `size`. The space is guaranteed to be set to 0 and the pointer is sufficiently well aligned to be usable for any purpose. NULL is returned if no space is available .

`cfree(ptr) char *ptr;`
Space is returned to the pool used by `calloc`. Disorder can be expected if the pointer was not obtained from `calloc`.

The following are macros whose definitions may be obtained by including `<ctype.h>`.

`isalpha(c)` returns non-zero if the argument is alphabetic.

`isupper(c)` returns non-zero if the argument is upper-case alphabetic.

`islower(c)` returns non-zero if the argument is lower-case alphabetic.

`isdigit(c)` returns non-zero if the argument is a digit.

`isspace(c)` returns non-zero if the argument is a spacing character: tab, newline, carriage return, vertical tab, form feed, space.

`ispunct(c)` returns non-zero if the argument is any punctuation character, i.e., not a space, letter, digit or control character.

`isalnum(c)` returns non-zero if the argument is a letter or a digit.

`isprint(c)` returns non-zero if the argument is printable — a letter, digit, or punctuation character.

`iscntrl(c)` returns non-zero if the argument is a control character.

`isascii(c)` returns non-zero if the argument is an ascii character, i.e., less than octal 0200.

`toupper(c)` returns the upper-case character corresponding to the lower-case letter `c`.

`tolower(c)` returns the lower-case character corresponding to the upper-case letter `c`.

A Tutorial Introduction to ADB

J. F. Maranzano

S. R. Bourne

Bell Laboratories
Murray Hill, New Jersey 07974

ABSTRACT

Debugging tools generally provide a wealth of information about the inner workings of programs. These tools have been available on UNIX† to allow users to examine "core" files that result from aborted programs. A new debugging program, ADB, provides enhanced capabilities to examine "core" and other program files in a variety of formats, run programs with embedded breakpoints and patch files.

ADB is an indispensable but complex tool for debugging crashed systems and/or programs. This document provides an introduction to ADB with examples of its use. It explains the various formatting options, techniques for debugging C programs, examples of printing file system information and patching.

May 5, 1977

---

†UNIX is a Trademark of Bell Laboratories.

1. Introduction

ADB is a new debugging program that is available on UNIX. It provides capabilities to look at "core" files resulting from aborted programs, print output in a variety of formats, patch files, and run programs with embedded breakpoints. This document provides examples of the more useful features of ADB. The reader is expected to be familiar with the basic commands on UNIX† with the C language, and with References 1, 2 and 3.

2. A Quick Survey

2.1. Invocation

ADB is invoked as:

adb objfile corefile

where *objfile* is an executable UNIX file and *corefile* is a core image file. Many times this will look like:

adb a.out core

or more simply:

adb

where the defaults are *a.out* and *core* respectively. The filename minus (−) means ignore this argument as in:

adb − core

ADB has requests for examining locations in either file. The **?** request examines the contents of *objfile,* the **/** request examines the *corefile.* The general form of these requests is:

address ? format

or

address / format

2.2. Current Address

ADB maintains a current address, called dot, similar in function to the current pointer in the UNIX editor. When an address is entered, the current address is set to that location, so that:

0126?i

---

†UNIX is a Trademark of Bell Laboratories.

sets dot to octal 126 and prints the instruction at that address. The request:

.,10/d

prints 10 decimal numbers starting at dot. Dot ends up referring to the address of the last item printed. When used with the ? or / requests, the current address can be advanced by typing newline; it can be decremented by typing ˆ.

Addresses are represented by expressions. Expressions are made up from decimal, octal, and hexadecimal integers, and symbols from the program under test. These may be combined with the operators +, −, *, % (integer division), & (bitwise and), | (bitwise inclusive or), # (round up to the next multiple), and ˜ (not). (All arithmetic within ADB is 32 bits.) When typing a symbolic address for a C program, the user can type *name* or *_name;* ADB will recognize both forms.

2.3. Formats

To print data, a user specifies a collection of letters and characters that describe the format of the printout. Formats are "remembered" in the sense that typing a request without one will cause the new printout to appear in the previous format. The following are the most commonly used format letters.

b	one byte in octal
c	one byte as a character
o	one word in octal
d	one word in decimal
f	two words in floating point
i	PDP 11 instruction
s	a null terminated character string
a	the value of dot
u	one word as unsigned integer
n	print a newline
r	print a blank space
ˆ	backup dot

(Format letters are also available for "long" values, for example, 'D' for long decimal, and 'F' for double floating point.) For other formats see the ADB manual.

2.4. General Request Meanings

The general form of a request is:

address,count command modifier

which sets 'dot' to *address* and executes the command *count* times.

The following table illustrates some general ADB command meanings:

Command	Meaning
?	Print contents from *a.out* file
/	Print contents from *core* file
=	Print value of "dot"
:	Breakpoint control
$	Miscellaneous requests
;	Request separator
!	Escape to shell

ADB catches signals, so a user cannot use a quit signal to exit from ADB. The request $q or $Q (or cntl-D) must be used to exit from ADB.

3. Debugging C Programs

3.1. Debugging A Core Image

Consider the C program in Figure 1. The program is used to illustrate a common error made by C programmers. The object of the program is to change the lower case "t" to upper case in the string pointed to by *charp* and then write the character string to the file indicated by argument 1. The bug shown is that the character "T" is stored in the pointer *charp* instead of the string pointed to by *charp*. Executing the program produces a core file because of an out of bounds memory reference.

ADB is invoked by:

adb a.out core

The first debugging request:

$c

is used to give a C backtrace through the subroutines called. As shown in Figure 2 only one function (*main*) was called and the arguments *argc* and *argv* have octal values 02 and 0177762 respectively. Both of these values look reasonable; 02 = two arguments, 0177762 = address on stack of parameter vector.
The next request:

$C

is used to give a C backtrace plus an interpretation of all the local variables in each function and their values in octal. The value of the variable *cc* looks incorrect since *cc* was declared as a character.

The next request:

$r

prints out the registers including the program counter and an interpretation of the instruction at that location.

The request:

$e

prints out the values of all external variables.

A map exists for each file handled by ADB. The map for the *a.out* file is referenced by **?** whereas the map for *core* file is referenced by **/**. Furthermore, a good rule of thumb is to use **?** for instructions and **/** for data when looking at programs. To print out information about the maps type:

$m

This produces a report of the contents of the maps. More about these maps later.

In our example, it is useful to see the contents of the string pointed to by *charp*. This is done by:

*charp/s

which says use *charp* as a pointer in the *core* file and print the information as a character string. This printout clearly shows that the character buffer was incorrectly overwritten and helps identify the error. Printing the locations around *charp* shows that the buffer is unchanged but that the pointer is destroyed. Using ADB similarly, we could print information about the arguments to a function. The request:

main.argc/d

prints the decimal *core* image value of the argument *argc* in the function *main*.

The request:

*main.argv,3/o

prints the octal values of the three consecutive cells pointed to by *argv* in the function *main*. Note that these values are the addresses of the arguments to main. Therefore:

0177770/s

prints the ASCII value of the first argument. Another way to print this value would have been

*"/s

The " means ditto which remembers the last address typed, in this case *main.argc* ; the * instructs ADB to use the address field of the *core* file as a pointer.

The request:

. = o

prints the current address (not its contents) in octal which has been set to the address of the first argument. The current address, dot, is used by ADB to "remember" its current location. It allows the user to reference locations relative to the current address, for example:

. − 10/d

3.2. Multiple Functions

Consider the C program illustrated in Figure 3. This program calls functions *f*, *g*, and *h* until the stack is exhausted and a core image is produced.

Again you can enter the debugger via:

adb

which assumes the names *a.out* and *core* for the executable file and core image file respectively. The request:

$c

will fill a page of backtrace references to *f*, *g*, and *h*. Figure 4 shows an abbreviated list (typing *DEL* will terminate the output and bring you back to ADB request level).

The request:

,5$C

prints the five most recent activations.

Notice that each function (*f,g,h*) has a counter of the number of times it was called.

The request:

fcnt/d

prints the decimal value of the counter for the function *f*. Similarly *gcnt* and *hcnt* could be printed. To print the value of an automatic variable, for example the decimal value of *x* in the last call of the function *h*, type:

h.x/d

It is currently not possible in the exported version to print stack frames other than the most recent activation of a function. Therefore, a user can print everything with $C or the occurrence of a variable in the most recent call of a function. It is possible with the $C request, however, to print the stack frame starting at some address as **address$C.**

3.3. Setting Breakpoints

Consider the C program in Figure 5. This program, which changes tabs into blanks, is adapted from *Software Tools* by Kernighan and Plauger, pp. 18-27.

We will run this program under the control of ADB (see Figure 6a) by:

>   **adb a.out** −

Breakpoints are set in the program as:

>   **address:b [request]**

The requests:

>   **settab + 4:b**
>   **fopen + 4:b**
>   **getc + 4:b**
>   **tabpos + 4:b**

set breakpoints at the start of these functions. C does not generate statement labels. Therefore it is currently not possible to plant breakpoints at locations other than function entry points without a knowledge of the code generated by the C compiler. The above addresses are entered as **symbol + 4** so that they will appear in any C backtrace since the first instruction of each function is a call to the C save routine (*csv*). Note that some of the functions are from the C library.

To print the location of breakpoints one types:

>   **$b**

The display indicates a *count* field. A breakpoint is bypassed *count* − *1* times before causing a stop. The *command* field indicates the ADB requests to be executed each time the breakpoint is encountered. In our example no *command* fields are present.

By displaying the original instructions at the function *settab* we see that the breakpoint is set after the jsr to the C save routine. We can display the instructions using the ADB request:

>   **settab,5?ia**

This request displays five instructions starting at *settab* with the addresses of each location displayed. Another variation is:

>   **settab,5?i**

which displays the instructions with only the starting address.

Notice that we accessed the addresses from the *a.out* file with the **?** command. In general when asking for a printout of multiple items, ADB will advance the current address the number of bytes necessary to satisfy the request; in the above example five instructions were displayed and the current address was advanced 18 (decimal) bytes.

To run the program one simply types:

>   **:r**

To delete a breakpoint, for instance the entry to the function *settab*, one types:

>   **settab + 4:d**

To continue execution of the program from the breakpoint type:

>   **:c**

Once the program has stopped (in this case at the breakpoint for *fopen*), ADB requests can be used to display the contents of memory. For example:

>   **$C**

to display a stack trace, or:

tabs,3/8o

to print three lines of 8 locations each from the array called *tabs*. By this time (at location *fopen)* in the C program, *settab* has been called and should have set a one in every eighth location of *tabs*.

3.4. Advanced Breakpoint Usage

We continue execution of the program with:

:c

See Figure 6b. *Getc* is called three times and the contents of the variable *c* in the function *main* are displayed each time. The single character on the left hand edge is the output from the C program. On the third occurrence of *getc* the program stops. We can look at the full buffer of characters by typing:

ibuf+6/20c

When we continue the program with:

:c

we hit our first breakpoint at *tabpos* since there is a tab following the "This" word of the data.

Several breakpoints of *tabpos* will occur until the program has changed the tab into equivalent blanks. Since we feel that *tabpos* is working, we can remove the breakpoint at that location by:

tabpos+4:d

If the program is continued with:

:c

it resumes normal execution after ADB prints the message

a.out:running

The UNIX quit and interrupt signals act on ADB itself rather than on the program being debugged. If such a signal occurs then the program being debugged is stopped and control is returned to ADB. The signal is saved by ADB and is passed on to the test program if:

:c

is typed. This can be useful when testing interrupt handling routines. The signal is not passed on to the test program if:

:c 0

is typed.

Now let us reset the breakpoint at *settab* and display the instructions located there when we reach the breakpoint. This is accomplished by:

settab+4:b settab,5?ia *

It is also possible to execute the ADB requests for each occurrence of the breakpoint but only

---

* Owing to a bug in early versions of ADB (including the version distributed in Generic 3 UNIX) these statements must be written as:

```
            settab+4:b        settab,5?ia;0
            getc+4,3:b        main.c?C;0
            settab+4:b        settab,5?ia; ptab/o;0
```
Note that ;0 will set dot to zero and stop at the breakpoint.

stop after the third occurrence by typing:

      getc+4,3:b main.c?C *

This request will print the local variable *c* in the function *main* at each occurrence of the breakpoint. The semicolon is used to separate multiple ADB requests on a single line.

Warning: setting a breakpoint causes the value of dot to be changed; executing the program under ADB does not change dot. Therefore:

      settab+4:b .,5?ia
      fopen+4:b

will print the last thing dot was set to (in the example *fopen+4*) *not* the current location (*settab+4*) at which the program is executing.

A breakpoint can be overwritten without first deleting the old breakpoint. For example:

      settab+4:b settab,5?ia; ptab/o *

could be entered after typing the above requests.

Now the display of breakpoints:

      $b

shows the above request for the *settab* breakpoint. When the breakpoint at *settab* is encountered the ADB requests are executed. Note that the location at *settab+4* has been changed to plant the breakpoint; all the other locations match their original value.

Using the functions, *f, g* and *h* shown in Figure 3, we can follow the execution of each function by planting non-stopping breakpoints. We call ADB with the executable program of Figure 3 as follows:

      adb ex3 −

Suppose we enter the following breakpoints:

      h+4:b   **hcnt/d; h.hi/; h.hr/**
      g+4:b   **gcnt/d; g.gi/; g.gr/**
      f+4:b   **fcnt/d; f.fi/; f.fr/**
      :r

Each request line indicates that the variables are printed in decimal (by the specification **d**). Since the format is not changed, the **d** can be left off all but the first request.

The output in Figure 7 illustrates two points. First, the ADB requests in the breakpoint line are not examined until the program under test is run. That means any errors in those ADB requests is not detected until run time. At the location of the error ADB stops running the program.

The second point is the way ADB handles register variables. ADB uses the symbol table to address variables. Register variables, like *f.fr* above, have pointers to uninitialized places on the stack. Therefore the message "symbol not found".

Another way of getting at the data in this example is to print the variables used in the call as:

      f+4:b   **fcnt/d; f.a/; f.b/; f.fi/**
      g+4:b   **gcnt/d; g.p/; g.q/; g.gi/**
      :c

The operator / was used instead of ? to read values from the *core* file. The output for each function, as shown in Figure 7, has the same format. For the function *f*, for example, it shows the name and value of the *external* variable *fcnt*. It also shows the address on the stack and value of the variables *a, b* and *fi*.

Notice that the addresses on the stack will continue to decrease until no address space is left for program execution at which time (after many pages of output) the program under test aborts. A display with names would be produced by requests like the following:

f+4:b   fcnt/d; f.a/"a="d; f.b/"b="d; f.fi/"fi="d

In this format the quoted string is printed literally and the **d** produces a decimal display of the variables. The results are shown in Figure 7.

3.5. Other Breakpoint Facilities

- Arguments and change of standard input and output are passed to a program as:

  :r arg1 arg2 ... <infile >outfile

  This request kills any existing program under test and starts the *a.out* afresh.

- The program being debugged can be single stepped by:

  :s

  If necessary, this request will start up the program being debugged and stop after executing the first instruction.

- ADB allows a program to be entered at a specific address by typing:

  address:r

- The count field can be used to skip the first *n* breakpoints as:

  ,n:r

  The request:

  ,n:c

  may also be used for skipping the first *n* breakpoints when continuing a program.

- A program can be continued at an address different from the breakpoint by:

  address:c

- The program being debugged runs as a separate process and can be killed by:

  :k

4. Maps

UNIX supports several executable file formats. These are used to tell the loader how to load the program file. File type 407 is the most common and is generated by a C compiler invocation such as **cc pgm.c**. A 410 file is produced by a C compiler command of the form **cc -n pgm.c**, whereas a 411 file is produced by **cc -i pgm.c**. ADB interprets these different file formats and provides access to the different segments through a set of maps (see Figure 8). To print the maps type:

  $m

In 407 files, both text (instructions) and data are intermixed. This makes it impossible for ADB to differentiate data from instructions and some of the printed symbolic addresses look incorrect; for example, printing data addresses as offsets from routines.

In 410 files (shared text), the instructions are separated from data and **?*** accesses the data part of the *a.out* file. The **?*** request tells ADB to use the second part of the map in the *a.out* file. Accessing data in the *core* file shows the data after it was modified by the execution of the program. Notice also that the data segment may have grown during program execution.

In 411 files (separated I & D space), the instructions and data are also separated. However, in this case, since data is mapped through a separate set of segmentation registers, the base of the data segment is also relative to address zero. In this case since the addresses overlap it is necessary to use the **?*** operator to access the data space of the *a.out* file. In both 410 and 411 files the corresponding core file does not contain the program text.

Figure 9 shows the display of three maps for the same program linked as a 407, 410, 411 respectively. The b, e, and f fields are used by ADB to map addresses into file addresses. The "f1" field is the length of the header at the beginning of the file (020 bytes for an *a.out* file and 02000 bytes for a *core* file). The "f2" field is the displacement from the beginning of the file to the data. For a 407 file with mixed text and data this is the same as the length of the header; for 410 and 411 files this is the length of the header plus the size of the text portion.

The "b" and "e" fields are the starting and ending locations for a segment. Given an address, A, the location in the file (either *a.out* or *core*) is calculated as:

$$b1 \leqslant A \leqslant e1 \Rightarrow \text{file address} = (A - b1) + f1$$
$$b2 \leqslant A \leqslant e2 \Rightarrow \text{file address} = (A - b2) + f2$$

A user can access locations by using the ADB defined variables. The **$v** request prints the variables initialized by ADB:

b	**base address of data segment**
d	**length of the data segment**
s	**length of the stack**
t	**length of the text**
m	**execution type (407,410,411)**

In Figure 9 those variables not present are zero. Use can be made of these variables by expressions such as:

      <b

in the address field. Similarly the value of the variable can be changed by an assignment request such as:

      02000>b

that sets **b** to octal 2000. These variables are useful to know if the file under examination is an executable or *core* image file.

ADB reads the header of the *core* image file to find the values for these variables. If the second file specified does not seem to be a *core* file, or if it is missing then the header of the executable file is used instead.

5. Advanced Usage

It is possible with ADB to combine formatting requests to provide elaborate displays. Below are several examples.

5.1. Formatted dump

The line:

      <b,−1/4o4^8Cn

prints 4 octal words followed by their ASCII interpretation from the data space of the core image file. Broken down, the various request pieces mean:

      <b   The base address of the data segment.

<b,−1   Print from the base address to the end of file. A negative count is used here and elsewhere to loop indefinitely or until some error condition (like end of file) is detected.

The format **4o4^8Cn** is broken down as follows:

4o   Print 4 octal locations.

4^   Backup the current address 4 locations (to the original start of the field).

8C   Print 8 consecutive characters using an escape convention; each character in the range 0 to 037 is printed as @ followed by the corresponding character in the range 0140 to 0177. An @ is printed as @@.

n   Print a newline.

The request:

    <b,<d/4o4^8Cn

could have been used instead to allow the printing to stop at the end of the data segment (<d provides the data segment size in bytes).

The formatting requests can be combined with ADB's ability to read in a script to produce a core image dump script. ADB is invoked as:

    adb a.out core < dump

to read in a script file, *dump*, of requests. An example of such a script is:

```
120$w
4095$s
$v
=3n
$m
=3n"C Stack Backtrace"
$C
=3n"C External Variables"
$e
=3n"Registers"
$r
0$s
=3n"Data Segment"
<b,−1/8ona
```

The request **120$w** sets the width of the output to 120 characters (normally, the width is 80 characters). ADB attempts to print addresses as:

    symbol + offset

The request **4095$s** increases the maximum permissible offset to the nearest symbolic address from 255 (default) to 4095. The request = can be used to print literal strings. Thus, headings are provided in this *dump* program with requests of the form:

    =3n"C Stack Backtrace"

that spaces three lines and prints the literal string. The request **$v** prints all non-zero ADB variables (see Figure 8). The request **0$s** sets the maximum offset for symbol matches to zero thus suppressing the printing of symbolic labels in favor of octal values. Note that this is only done for the printing of the data segment. The request:

> < b, − 1/8ona

prints a dump from the base of the data segment to the end of file with an octal address field and eight octal numbers per line.

Figure 11 shows the results of some formatting requests on the C program of Figure 10.

5.2. Directory Dump

As another illustration (Figure 12) consider a set of requests to dump the contents of a directory (which is made up of an integer *inumber* followed by a 14 character name):

> **adb dir −**
> **=n8t"Inum"8t"Name"**
> **0, − 1? u8t14cn**

In this example, the **u** prints the *inumber* as an unsigned decimal integer, the **8t** means that ADB will space to the next multiple of 8 on the output line, and the **14c** prints the 14 character file name.

5.3. Ilist Dump

Similarly the contents of the *ilist* of a file system, (e.g. /dev/src, on UNIX systems distributed by the UNIX Support Group; see UNIX Programmer's Manual Section V) could be dumped with the following set of requests:

> **adb /dev/src −**
> **02000>b**
> **?m <b**
> **< b, − 1?"flags"8ton"links,uid,gid"8t3bn",size"8tbrdn"addr"8t8un"times"8t2Y2na**

In this example the value of the base for the map was changed to 02000 (by saying **?m<b**) since that is the start of an *ilist* within a file system. An artifice (**brd** above) was used to print the 24 bit size field as a byte, a space, and a decimal integer. The last access time and last modify time are printed with the **2Y** operator. Figure 12 shows portions of these requests as applied to a directory and file system.

5.4. Converting values

ADB may be used to convert values from one representation to another. For example:

> **072 = odx**

will print

> **072   58   #3a**

which is the octal, decimal and hexadecimal representations of 072 (octal). The format is remembered so that typing subsequent numbers will print them in the given formats. Character values may be converted similarly, for example:

> **'a' = co**

prints

> **a   0141**

It may also be used to evaluate expressions but be warned that all binary operators have the same precedence which is lower than that for unary operators.

6. Patching

Patching files with ADB is accomplished with the *write*, w or W, request (which is not like the *ed* editor write command). This is often used in conjunction with the *locate*, l or L request. In general, the request syntax for l and w are similar as follows:

>   ?l value

The request l is used to match on two bytes, L is used for four bytes. The request w is used to write two bytes, whereas W writes four bytes. The **value** field in either *locate* or *write* requests is an expression. Therefore, decimal and octal numbers, or character strings are supported.

In order to modify a file, ADB must be called as:

>   adb −w file1 file2

When called with this option, *file1* and *file2* are created if necessary and opened for both reading and writing.

For example, consider the C program shown in Figure 10. We can change the word "This" to "The " in the executable file for this program, *ex7*, by using the following requests:

>   adb −w ex7 −
>   ?l 'Th'
>   ?W 'The '

The request ?l starts at dot and stops at the first match of "Th" having set dot to the address of the location found. Note the use of ? to write to the *a.out* file. The form ?* would have been used for a 411 file.

More frequently the request will be typed as:

>   ?l 'Th'; ?s

and locates the first occurrence of "Th" and print the entire string. Execution of this ADB request will set dot to the address of the "Th" characters.

As another example of the utility of the patching facility, consider a C program that has an internal logic flag. The flag could be set by the user through ADB and the program run. For example:

>   adb a.out −
>   :s arg1 arg2
>   flag/w 1
>   :c

The :s request is normally used to single step through a process or start a process in single step mode. In this case it starts *a.out* as a subprocess with arguments **arg1** and **arg2**. If there is a subprocess running ADB writes to it rather than to the file so the w request causes *flag* to be changed in the memory of the subprocess.

7. Anomalies

Below is a list of some strange things that users should be aware of.

1. Function calls and arguments are put on the stack by the C save routine. Putting breakpoints at the entry point to routines means that the function appears not to have been called when the breakpoint occurs.

2. When printing addresses, ADB uses either text or data symbols from the *a.out* file. This sometimes causes unexpected symbol names to be printed with data (e.g. *savr5+022*). This does not happen if ? is used for text (instructions) and / for data.

3.   ADB cannot handle C register variables in the most recently activated function.

8. Acknowledgements

The authors are grateful for the thoughtful comments on how to organize this document from R. B. Brandt, E. N. Pinson and B. A. Tague. D. M. Ritchie made the system changes necessary to accommodate tracing within ADB. He also participated in discussions during the writing of ADB. His earlier work with DB and CDB led to many of the features found in ADB.

9. References

1.   D. M. Ritchie and K. Thompson, "The UNIX Time-Sharing System," CACM, July, 1974.

2.   B. W. Kernighan and D. M. Ritchie, *The C Programming Language,* Prentice-Hall, 1978.

3.   K. Thompson and D. M. Ritchie, UNIX Programmer's Manual - 7th Edition, 1978.

4.   B. W. Kernighan and P. J. Plauger, *Software Tools,* Addison-Wesley, 1976.

Figure 1: C program with pointer bug

```
struct buf {
        int fildes;
        int nleft;
        char *nextp;
        char buff[512];
        }bb;
struct buf *obuf;

char *charp "this is a sentence.";

main(argc,argv)
int argc;
char **argv;
{
        char     cc;

        if(argc < 2) {
                printf("Input file missing\n");
                exit(8);
        }

        if((fcreat(argv[1],obuf)) < 0){
                printf("%s : not found\n", argv[1]);
                exit(8);
        }
        charp = 'T';
printf("debug 1 %s\n",charp);
        while(cc=  *charp++)
                putc(cc,obuf);
        fflush(obuf);
}
```

Figure 2: ADB output for C program of Figure 1

```
adb a.out core
$c
~main(02,0177762)
$C
~main(02,0177762)
        argc:       02
        argv:       0177762
        cc:         02124
$r
ps      0170010
pc      0204        ~main+0152
sp      0177740
r5      0177752
r4      01
r3      0
r2      0
r1      0
r0      0124
~main+0152:     mov     _obuf,(sp)
$e
savr5:      0
_obuf:      0
_charp:     0124
_errno:     0
_fout:      0
$m
text map    `ex1´
b1 = 0              e1  = 02360           f1 = 020
b2 = 0              e2  = 02360           f2 = 020
data map    `core1´
b1 = 0              e1  = 03500           f1 = 02000
b2 = 0175400       e2  = 0200000         f2 = 05500
*charp/s
0124:           TTTTTTTTTTTTTTTTTTTTTTTTTTTTTTTTTTTTTTTTLx        Nh@x&_
~
charp/s
_charp:         T

_charp+02:      this is a sentence.

_charp+026:     Input file missing
main.argc/d
0177756:        2
*main.argv/3o
0177762:        0177770 0177776 0177777
0177770/s
0177770:        a.out
*main.argv/3o
0177762:        0177770 0177776 0177777
*"/s
0177770:        a.out
 .=o
                0177770
 .-10/d
0177756:        2
$q
```

Figure 3: Multiple function C program for stack trace illustration

```
int         fcnt,gcnt,hcnt;
h(x,y)
{
        int hi; register int hr;
        hi = x+1;
        hr = x−y+1;
        hcnt++ ;
        hj:
        f(hr,hi);
}

g(p,q)
{
        int gi; register int gr;
        gi = q−p;
        gr = q−p+1;
        gcnt++ ;
        gj:
        h(gr,gi);
}

f(a,b)
{
        int fi; register int fr;
        fi = a+2*b;
        fr = a+b;
        fcnt++ ;
        fj:
        g(fr,fi);
}

main()
{
        f(1,1);
}
```

Figure 4:   ADB output for C program of Figure 3

```
adb
$c
‾h(04452,04451)
‾g(04453,011124)
‾f(02,04451)
‾h(04450,04447)
‾g(04451,011120)
‾f(02,04447)
‾h(04446,04445)
‾g(04447,011114)
‾f(02,04445)
‾h(04444,04443)
HIT DEL KEY
adb
,5$C
‾h(04452,04451)
                x:          04452
                y:          04451
                hi:         ?
‾g(04453,011124)
                p:          04453
                q:          011124
                gi:         04451
                gr:         ?
‾f(02,04451)
                a:          02
                b:          04451
                fi:         011124
                fr:         04453
‾h(04450,04447)
                x:          04450
                y:          04447
                hi:         04451
                hr:         02
‾g(04451,011120)
                p:          04451
                q:          011120
                gi:         04447
                gr:         04450
fcnt/d
_fcnt:          1173
gcnt/d
_gcnt:          1173
hcnt/d
_hcnt:          1172
h.x/d
022004:         2346
$q
```

Figure 5: C program to decode tabs

```
#define MAXLINE        80
#define YES            1
#define NO             0
#define TABSP          8

char    input[] "data";
char    ibuf[518];
int     tabs[MAXLINE];

main()
{
        int col, *ptab;
        char c;

        ptab = tabs;
        settab(ptab);      /*Set initial tab stops */
        col = 1;
        if(fopen(input,ibuf) < 0) {
                printf("%s : not found\n",input);
                exit(8);
        }
        while((c = getc(ibuf)) != -1) {
                switch(c) {
                        case '\t': /* TAB */
                                while(tabpos(col) != YES) {
                                        putchar(' ');      /* put BLANK */
                                        col++ ;
                                }
                                break;
                        case '\n':/*NEWLINE */
                                putchar('\n');
                                col = 1;
                                break;
                        default:
                                putchar(c);
                                col++ ;
                }
        }
}

/* Tabpos return YES if col is a tab stop */
tabpos(col)
int col;
{
        if(col > MAXLINE)
                return(YES);
        else
                return(tabs[col]);
}

/* Settab - Set initial tab stops */
settab(tabp)
int *tabp;
{
        int i;
        for(i = 0; i <= MAXLINE; i++)
                (i%TABSP) ? (tabs[i] = NO) : (tabs[i] = YES);
}
```

Figure 6a: ADB output for C program of Figure 5

```
adb a.out —
settab+4:b
fopen+4:b
getc+4:b
tabpos+4:b
$b
breakpoints
count    bkpt               command
1        ˜tabpos+04
1        _getc+04
1        _fopen+04
1        ˜settab+04
settab,5?ia
˜settab:          jsr      r5,csv
˜settab+04:       tst      —(sp)
˜settab+06:       clr      0177770(r5)
˜settab+012:      cmp      $0120,0177770(r5)
˜settab+020:      blt      ˜settab+076
˜settab+022:
settab,5?i
˜settab:          jsr      r5,csv
                  tst      —(sp)
                  clr      0177770(r5)
                  cmp      $0120,0177770(r5)
                  blt      ˜settab+076
:r
a.out: running
breakpoint        ˜settab+04:    tst      —(sp)
settab+4:d
:c
a.out: running
breakpoint        _fopen+04:     mov      04(r5),nulstr+012
$C
_fopen(02302,02472)
˜main(01,0177770)
        col:      01
        c:        0
        ptab:     03500
tabs,3/8o
03500:        01    0    0    0    0    0    0    0
              01    0    0    0    0    0    0    0
              01    0    0    0    0    0    0    0
```

Figure 6b: ADB output for C program of Figure 5

```
:c
a.out: running
breakpoint          _getc+04:        mov     04(r5),r1
ibuf+6/20c
__cleanu+0202:             This     is      a test    of
:c
a.out: running
breakpoint          ~tabpos+04:      cmp     $0120,04(r5)
tabpos+4:d
settab+4:b  settab,5?ia
settab+4:b  settab,5?ia;  0
getc+4,3:b  main.c?C;  0
settab+4:b  settab,5?ia;  ptab/o;  0
$b
breakpoints
count   bkpt               command
1          ~tabpos+04
3          _getc+04         main.c?C;0
1          _fopen+04
1          ~settab+04       settab,5?ia;ptab?o;0
~settab:          jsr     r5,csv
~settab+04:       bpt
~settab+06:       clr     0177770(r5)
~settab+012:      cmp     $0120,0177770(r5)
~settab+020:      blt     ~settab+076
~settab+022:
0177766:          0177770
0177744:          @`
T0177744:         T
h0177744:         h
i0177744:         i
s0177744:         s
```

Figure 7: ADB output for C program with breakpoints

```
adb ex3 —
h+4:b hcnt/d; h.hi/; h.hr/
g+4:b gcnt/d; g.gi/; g.gr/
f+4:b fcnt/d; f.fi/; f.fr/
:r
ex3: running
_fcnt:          0
0177732:       214
symbol not found
f+4:b fcnt/d; f.a/; f.b/; f.fi
g+4:b gcnt/d; g.p/; g.q/; g.gi
h+4:b hcnt/d; h.x/; h.y/; h.hi
:c
ex3: running
_fcnt:          0
0177746:        1
0177750:        1
0177732:       214
_gcnt:          0
0177726:        2
0177730:        3
0177712:       214
_hcnt:          0
0177706:        2
0177710:        1
0177672:       214
_fcnt:          1
0177666:        2
0177670:        3
0177652:       214
_gcnt:          1
0177646:        5
0177650:        8
0177632:       214
HIT DEL
f+4:b fcnt/d; f.a/"a = "d; f.b/"b = "d; f.fi/"fi = "d
g+4:b gcnt/d; g.p/"p = "d; g.q/"q = "d; g.gi/"gi = "d
h+4:b hcnt/d; h.x/"x = "d; h.y/"h = "d; h.hi/"hi = "d
:r
ex3: running
_fcnt:          0
0177746:        a = 1
0177750:        b = 1
0177732:        fi = 214
_gcnt:          0
0177726:        p = 2
0177730:        q = 3
0177712:        gi = 214
_hcnt:          0
0177706:        x = 2
0177710:        y = 1
0177672:        hi = 214
_fcnt:          1
0177666:        a = 2
0177670:        b = 3
0177652:        fi = 214
HIT DEL
$q
```

Figure 8: ADB address maps

407 files

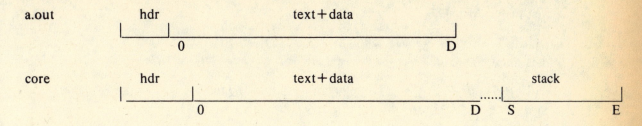

410 files (shared text)

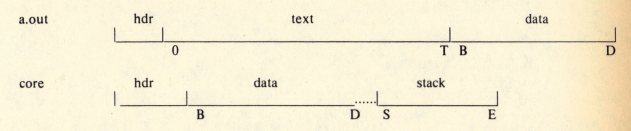

411 files (separated I and D space)

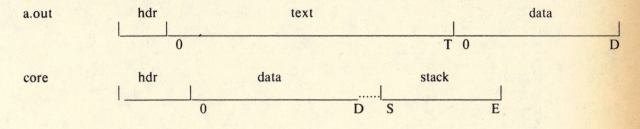

The following *adb* variables are set.

		407	410	411
b	base of data	0	B	0
d	length of data	D	D−B	D
s	length of stack	S	S	S
t	length of text	0	T	T

Figure 9: ADB output for maps

```
adb map407 core407
$m
text map    `map407´
b1 = 0              e1      = 0256        f1 = 020
b2 = 0              e2      = 0256        f2 = 020
data map    `core407´
b1 = 0              e1      = 0300        f1 = 02000
b2 = 0175400        e2      = 0200000     f2 = 02300
$v
variables
d = 0300
m = 0407
s = 02400
$q


adb map410 core410
$m
text map    `map410´
b1 = 0              e1      = 0200          f1 = 020
b2 = 020000         e2      = 020116   f2 = 0220
data map    `core410´
b1 = 020000         e1      = 020200   f1 = 02000
b2 = 0175400        e2      = 0200000     f2 = 02200
$v
variables
b = 020000
d = 0200
m = 0410
s = 02400
t = 0200
$q


adb map411 core411
$m
text map    `map411´
b1 = 0              e1      = 0200        f1 = 020
b2 = 0              e2      = 0116        f2 = 0220
data map    `core411´
b1 = 0              e1      = 0200        f1 = 02000
b2 = 0175400        e2      = 0200000     f2 = 02200
$v
variables
d = 0200
m = 0411
s = 02400
t = 0200
$q
```

Figure 10:   Simple C program for illustrating formatting and patching

```
char      str1[]     "This is a character string";
int       one        1;
int       number 456;
long      lnum    1234;
float     fpt        1.25;
char      str2[]     "This is the second character string";
main()
{
          one = 2;
}
```

Figure 11: ADB output illustrating fancy formats

```
adb map410 core410
<b,-1/8ona
020000:            0      064124     071551     064440     020163     020141     064143     071141
_str1+016: 061541      062564     020162     072163     064562     063556     0      02

_number:
_number:   0710 0      02322040240     0      064124     071551     064440
_str2+06:  020163      064164     020145     062563     067543     062156     061440     060550
_str2+026: 060562      072143     071145     071440     071164     067151     0147 0
savr5+02: 0      0      0      0      0      0      0      0

<b,20/4o4^8Cn
020000:            0      064124     071551     064440     @`@`This i
           020163     020141     064143     071141     s a char
           061541     062564     020162     072163     acter st
           064562     063556     0      02      ring@`@`@b@`
 number:   0710 0      02322040240     H@a@`@`R@d @@
           0      064124     071551     064440     @`@`This i
           020163     064164     020145     062563     s the se
           067543     062156     061440     060550     cond cha
           060562     072143     071145     071440     racter s
           071164     067151     0147 0      tring@`@`@`
           0      0      0      0      @`@`@`@`@`@`@`@`
           0      0      0      0      @`@`@`@`@`@`@`@`
data address not found
<b,20/4o4^8t8cna
020000:            0      064124     071551     064440             This i
_str1+06:  020163     020141     064143     071141     s a char
_str1+016: 061541     062564     020162     072163     acter st
_str1+026: 064562     063556     0      02             ring

_number:
_number:   0710 0      02322040240             HR
_fpt+02:   0      064124     071551     064440             This i
_str2+06:  020163     064164     020145     062563     s the se
_str2+016: 067543     062156     061440     060550     .cond cha
_str2+026: 060562     072143     071145     071440     racter s
_str2+036: 071164     067151     0147 0             tring
savr5+02: 0      0      0      0
savr5+012: 0      0      0      0
data address not found
<b,10/2b8t^2cn
020000:            0      0

_str1:     0124  0150      Th
           0151  0163      is
           040   0151      i
           0163  040       s
           0141  040       a
           0143  0150      ch
           0141  0162      ar
           0141  0143      ac
           0164  0145      te

$Q
```

Figure 12:   Directory and inode dumps
adb dir −
=nt"Inode"t"Name"
0,−1?ut14cn


```
          Inode     Name
0:        652  .
          82   ..
          5971 cap.c
          5323 cap
          0    pp
```


adb /dev/src −
02000>b
?m<b
```
new map      `/dev/src`
b1 = 02000        e1      = 0100000000   f1 = 0
b2 = 0            e2      = 0            f2 = 0
```
$v
```
variables
b = 02000
```
<b,−1?"flags"8ton"links,uid,gid"8t3bn"size"8tbrdn"addr"8t8un"times"8t2Y2na
```
02000:          flags 073145
          links,uid,gid     0163 0164 0141
          size  0162 10356
          addr 28770      8236 25956      27766      25455      8236 25956      25206
          times1976 Feb 5 08:34:56  1975 Dec 28 10:55:15

02040:          flags 024555
          links,uid,gid     012   0163 0164
          size  0162 25461
          addr 8308 30050      8294 25130      15216      26890      29806      10784
          times1976 Aug 17 12:16:51 1976 Aug 17 12:16:51

02100:          flags 05173
          links,uid,gid     011   0162 0145
          size  0147 29545
          addr 25972      8306 28265      8308 25642      15216      2314 25970
          times1977 Apr 2 08:58:01  1977 Feb 5 10:21:44
```

ADB Summary

Command Summary

a) formatted printing

? *format*   print from *a.out* file according to *format*

/ *format*   print from *core* file according to *format*

= *format* print the value of *dot*

?w expr   write expression into *a.out* file

/w expr   write expression into *core* file

?l expr   locate expression in *a.out* file

b) breakpoint and program control

:b   set breakpoint at *dot*
:c   continue running program
:d   delete breakpoint
:k   kill the program being debugged
:r   run *a.out* file under ADB control
:s   single step

c) miscellaneous printing

$b   print current breakpoints
$c   C stack trace
$e   external variables
$f   floating registers
$m   print ADB segment maps
$q   exit from ADB
$r   general registers
$s   set offset for symbol match
$v   print ADB variables
$w   set output line width

d) calling the shell

!   call *shell* to read rest of line

e) assignment to variables

> *name*   assign dot to variable or register *name*

Format Summary

a	the value of dot
b	one byte in octal
c	one byte as a character
d	one word in decimal
f	two words in floating point
i	PDP 11 instruction
o	one word in octal
n	print a newline
r	print a blank space
s	a null terminated character string
n t	move to next *n* space tab
u	one word as unsigned integer
x	hexadecimal
Y	date
^	backup dot
"..."	print string

Expression Summary

a) expression components

decimal integer	e.g. 256
octal integer	e.g. 0277
hexadecimal	e.g. #ff
symbols	e.g. flag _main main.argc
variables	e.g. <b
registers	e.g. <pc <r0
(expression)	expression grouping

b) dyadic operators

+	add
−	subtract
*	multiply
%	integer division
&	bitwise and
|	bitwise or
#	round up to the next multiple

c) monadic operators

~	not
*	contents of location
−	integer negate

SUPPORTING TOOLS
AND LANGUAGES

Yacc: Yet Another Compiler-Compiler

Stephen C. Johnson

Bell Laboratories
Murray Hill, New Jersey 07974

ABSTRACT

Computer program input generally has some structure; in fact, every computer program that does input can be thought of as defining an "input language" which it accepts. An input language may be as complex as a programming language, or as simple as a sequence of numbers. Unfortunately, usual input facilities are limited, difficult to use, and often are lax about checking their inputs for validity.

Yacc provides a general tool for describing the input to a computer program. The Yacc user specifies the structures of his input, together with code to be invoked as each such structure is recognized. Yacc turns such a specification into a subroutine that handles the input process; frequently, it is convenient and appropriate to have most of the flow of control in the user's application handled by this subroutine.

The input subroutine produced by Yacc calls a user-supplied routine to return the next basic input item. Thus, the user can specify his input in terms of individual input characters, or in terms of higher level constructs such as names and numbers. The user-supplied routine may also handle idiomatic features such as comment and continuation conventions, which typically defy easy grammatical specification.

Yacc is written in portable C. The class of specifications accepted is a very general one: LALR(1) grammars with disambiguating rules.

In addition to compilers for C, APL, Pascal, RATFOR, etc., Yacc has also been used for less conventional languages, including a phototypesetter language, several desk calculator languages, a document retrieval system, and a Fortran debugging system.

July 31, 1978

0: Introduction

Yacc provides a general tool for imposing structure on the input to a computer program. The Yacc user prepares a specification of the input process; this includes rules describing the input structure, code to be invoked when these rules are recognized, and a low-level routine to do the basic input. Yacc then generates a function to control the input process. This function, called a *parser*, calls the user-supplied low-level input routine (the *lexical analyzer*) to pick up the basic items (called *tokens*) from the input stream. These tokens are organized according to the input structure rules, called *grammar rules*; when one of these rules has been recognized, then user code supplied for this rule, an *action*, is invoked; actions have the ability to return values and make use of the values of other actions.

Yacc is written in a portable dialect of C[1] and the actions, and output subroutine, are in C as well. Moreover, many of the syntactic conventions of Yacc follow C.

The heart of the input specification is a collection of grammar rules. Each rule describes an allowable structure and gives it a name. For example, one grammar rule might be

    date : month_name day ´,´ year ;

Here, *date*, *month_name*, *day*, and *year* represent structures of interest in the input process; presumably, *month_name*, *day*, and *year* are defined elsewhere. The comma "," is enclosed in single quotes; this implies that the comma is to appear literally in the input. The colon and semicolon merely serve as punctuation in the rule, and have no significance in controlling the input. Thus, with proper definitions, the input

    July 4, 1776

might be matched by the above rule.

An important part of the input process is carried out by the lexical analyzer. This user routine reads the input stream, recognizing the lower level structures, and communicates these tokens to the parser. For historical reasons, a structure recognized by the lexical analyzer is called a *terminal symbol*, while the structure recognized by the parser is called a *nonterminal symbol*. To avoid confusion, terminal symbols will usually be referred to as *tokens*.

There is considerable leeway in deciding whether to recognize structures using the lexical analyzer or grammar rules. For example, the rules

    month_name : ´J´ ´a´ ´n´ ;
    month_name : ´F´ ´e´ ´b´ ;

    . . .

    month_name : ´D´ ´e´ ´c´ ;

might be used in the above example. The lexical analyzer would only need to recognize individual letters, and *month_name* would be a nonterminal symbol. Such low-level rules tend to waste time and space, and may complicate the specification beyond Yacc's ability to deal with it. Usually, the lexical analyzer would recognize the month names, and return an indication that a *month_name* was seen; in this case, *month_name* would be a token.

Literal characters such as '','' must also be passed through the lexical analyzer, and are also considered tokens.

Specification files are very flexible. It is realively easy to add to the above example the rule

     date : month ´/´ day ´/´ year ;

allowing

     7 / 4 / 1776

as a synonym for

     July 4, 1776

In most cases, this new rule could be ''slipped in'' to a working system with minimal effort, and little danger of disrupting existing input.

The input being read may not conform to the specifications. These input errors are detected as early as is theoretically possible with a left-to-right scan; thus, not only is the chance of reading and computing with bad input data substantially reduced, but the bad data can usually be quickly found. Error handling, provided as part of the input specifications, permits the reentry of bad data, or the continuation of the input process after skipping over the bad data.

In some cases, Yacc fails to produce a parser when given a set of specifications. For example, the specifications may be self contradictory, or they may require a more powerful recognition mechanism than that available to Yacc. The former cases represent design errors; the latter cases can often be corrected by making the lexical analyzer more powerful, or by rewriting some of the grammar rules. While Yacc cannot handle all possible specifications, its power compares favorably with similar systems; moreover, the constructions which are difficult for Yacc to handle are also frequently difficult for human beings to handle. Some users have reported that the discipline of formulating valid Yacc specifications for their input revealed errors of conception or design early in the program development.

The theory underlying Yacc has been described elsewhere.[2,3,4] Yacc has been extensively used in numerous practical applications, including *lint*,[5] the Portable C Compiler,[6] and a system for typesetting mathematics.[7]

The next several sections describe the basic process of preparing a Yacc specification; Section 1 describes the preparation of grammar rules, Section 2 the preparation of the user supplied actions associated with these rules, and Section 3 the preparation of lexical analyzers. Section 4 describes the operation of the parser. Section 5 discusses various reasons why Yacc may be unable to produce a parser from a specification, and what to do about it. Section 6 describes a simple mechanism for handling operator precedences in arithmetic expressions. Section 7 discusses error detection and recovery. Section 8 discusses the operating environment and special features of the parsers Yacc produces. Section 9 gives some suggestions which should improve the style and efficiency of the specifications. Section 10 discusses some advanced topics, and Section 11 gives acknowledgements. Appendix A has a brief example, and Appendix B gives a summary of the Yacc input syntax. Appendix C gives an example using some of the more advanced features of Yacc, and, finally, Appendix D describes mechanisms and syntax no longer actively supported, but provided for historical continuity with older versions of Yacc.

1: Basic Specifications

Names refer to either tokens or nonterminal symbols. Yacc requires token names to be declared as such. In addition, for reasons discussed in Section 3, it is often desirable to include the lexical analyzer as part of the specification file; it may be useful to include other programs as well. Thus, every specification file consists of three sections: the *declarations*, *(grammar) rules*, and *programs*. The sections are separated by double percent "%%" marks. (The percent "%" is generally used in Yacc specifications as an escape character.)

In other words, a full specification file looks like

```
declarations
%%
rules
%%
programs
```

The declaration section may be empty. Moreover, if the programs section is omitted, the second %% mark may be omitted also; thus, the smallest legal Yacc specification is

```
%%
rules
```

Blanks, tabs, and newlines are ignored except that they may not appear in names or multi-character reserved symbols. Comments may appear wherever a name is legal; they are enclosed in /* . . . */, as in C and PL/I.

The rules section is made up of one or more grammar rules. A grammar rule has the form:

```
A : BODY ;
```

A represents a nonterminal name, and BODY represents a sequence of zero or more names and literals. The colon and the semicolon are Yacc punctuation.

Names may be of arbitrary length, and may be made up of letters, dot ".", underscore "_", and non-initial digits. Upper and lower case letters are distinct. The names used in the body of a grammar rule may represent tokens or nonterminal symbols.

A literal consists of a character enclosed in single quotes "''". As in C, the backslash "\" is an escape character within literals, and all the C escapes are recognized. Thus

'\n'	newline
'\r'	return
'\''	single quote "'"
'\\'	backslash "\"
'\t'	tab
'\b'	backspace
'\f'	form feed
'\xxx'	"xxx" in octal

For a number of technical reasons, the NUL character ('\0' or 0) should never be used in grammar rules.

If there are several grammar rules with the same left hand side, the vertical bar "|" can be used to avoid rewriting the left hand side. In addition, the semicolon at the end of a rule can be dropped before a vertical bar. Thus the grammar rules

```
A    :    B C D ;
A    :    E F ;
A    :    G ;
```

can be given to Yacc as

```
A    :    B C D
     |    E F
     |    G
     ;
```

It is not necessary that all grammar rules with the same left side appear together in the grammar rules section, although it makes the input much more readable, and easier to change.

If a nonterminal symbol matches the empty string, this can be indicated in the obvious way:

        empty :   ;

Names representing tokens must be declared; this is most simply done by writing

        %token   name1 name2 . . .

in the declarations section. (See Sections 3 , 5, and 6 for much more discussion). Every name not defined in the declarations section is assumed to represent a nonterminal symbol. Every nonterminal symbol must appear on the left side of at least one rule.

Of all the nonterminal symbols, one, called the *start symbol*, has particular importance. The parser is designed to recognize the start symbol; thus, this symbol represents the largest, most general structure described by the grammar rules. By default, the start symbol is taken to be the left hand side of the first grammar rule in the rules section. It is possible, and in fact desirable, to declare the start symbol explicitly in the declarations section using the %start keyword:

        %start   symbol

The end of the input to the parser is signaled by a special token, called the *endmarker*. If the tokens up to, but not including, the endmarker form a structure which matches the start symbol, the parser function returns to its caller after the endmarker is seen; it *accepts* the input. If the endmarker is seen in any other context, it is an error.

It is the job of the user-supplied lexical analyzer to return the endmarker when appropriate; see section 3, below. Usually the endmarker represents some reasonably obvious I/O status, such as "end-of-file" or "end-of-record".

2: Actions

With each grammar rule, the user may associate actions to be performed each time the rule is recognized in the input process. These actions may return values, and may obtain the values returned by previous actions. Moreover, the lexical analyzer can return values for tokens, if desired.

An action is an arbitrary C statement, and as such can do input and output, call subprograms, and alter external vectors and variables. An action is specified by one or more statements, enclosed in curly braces "{" and "}". For example,

        A   :   '(' B ')'
                        {   hello(1, "abc"); }

and

        XXX   :   YYY ZZZ
                        {   printf("a message\n");
                                flag = 25; }

are grammar rules with actions.

To facilitate easy communication between the actions and the parser, the action statements are altered slightly. The symbol "dollar sign" "$" is used as a signal to Yacc in this context.

To return a value, the action normally sets the pseudo-variable "$$" to some value. For example, an action that does nothing but return the value 1 is

```
{ $$ = 1; }
```

To obtain the values returned by previous actions and the lexical analyzer, the action may use the pseudo-variables $1, $2, . . ., which refer to the values returned by the components of the right side of a rule, reading from left to right. Thus, if the rule is

```
A    :       B C D ;
```

for example, then $2 has the value returned by C, and $3 the value returned by D.

As a more concrete example, consider the rule

```
expr   :        '(' expr ')' ;
```

The value returned by this rule is usually the value of the *expr* in parentheses. This can be indicated by

```
expr   :        '(' expr ')'          { $$ = $2 ; }
```

By default, the value of a rule is the value of the first element in it ($1). Thus, grammar rules of the form

```
A    :      B ;
```

frequently need not have an explicit action.

In the examples above, all the actions came at the end of their rules. Sometimes, it is desirable to get control before a rule is fully parsed. Yacc permits an action to be written in the middle of a rule as well as at the end. This rule is assumed to return a value, accessible through the usual mechanism by the actions to the right of it. In turn, it may access the values returned by the symbols to its left. Thus, in the rule

```
A    :        B
                     { $$ = 1; }
              C
                     {  x = $2;   y = $3; }
         ;
```

the effect is to set *x* to 1, and *y* to the value returned by C.

Actions that do not terminate a rule are actually handled by Yacc by manufacturing a new nonterminal symbol name, and a new rule matching this name to the empty string. The interior action is the action triggered off by recognizing this added rule. Yacc actually treats the above example as if it had been written:

```
$ACT :        /* empty */
                     { $$ = 1; }
         ;

A    :        B $ACT C
                     {  x = $2;   y = $3; }
         ;
```

In many applications, output is not done directly by the actions; rather, a data structure, such as a parse tree, is constructed in memory, and transformations are applied to it before output is generated. Parse trees are particularly easy to construct, given routines to build and maintain the tree structure desired. For example, suppose there is a C function *node*, written so that the call

```
node( L, n1, n2 )
```

creates a node with label L, and descendants n1 and n2, and returns the index of the newly created node. Then parse tree can be built by supplying actions such as:

```
expr    :        expr '+' expr
                    { $$ = node('+', $1, $3 ); }
```

in the specification.

The user may define other variables to be used by the actions. Declarations and definitions can appear in the declarations section, enclosed in the marks "%{" and "%}". These declarations and definitions have global scope, so they are known to the action statements and the lexical analyzer. For example,

```
%{   int variable = 0;   %}
```

could be placed in the declarations section, making *variable* accessible to all of the actions. The Yacc parser uses only names beginning in "yy"; the user should avoid such names.

In these examples, all the values are integers: a discussion of values of other types will be found in Section 10.

3: Lexical Analysis

The user must supply a lexical analyzer to read the input stream and communicate tokens (with values, if desired) to the parser. The lexical analyzer is an integer-valued function called *yylex*. The function returns an integer, the *token number*, representing the kind of token read. If there is a value associated with that token, it should be assigned to the external variable *yylval*.

The parser and the lexical analyzer must agree on these token numbers in order for communication between them to take place. The numbers may be chosen by Yacc, or chosen by the user. In either case, the "# define" mechanism of C is used to allow the lexical analyzer to return these numbers symbolically. For example, suppose that the token name DIGIT has been defined in the declarations section of the Yacc specification file. The relevant portion of the lexical analyzer might look like:

```
yylex(){
        extern int yylval;
        int c;
        . . .
        c = getchar();
        . . .
        switch( c ) {
            . . .
        case '0':
        case '1':
            . . .
        case '9':
                yylval = c − '0';
                return( DIGIT );
                . . .
            }
        . . .
```

The intent is to return a token number of DIGIT, and a value equal to the numerical value of the digit. Provided that the lexical analyzer code is placed in the programs section of the specification file, the identifier DIGIT will be defined as the token number associated with the token DIGIT.

This mechanism leads to clear, easily modified lexical analyzers; the only pitfall is the need to avoid using any token names in the grammar that are reserved or significant in C or the parser; for example, the use of token names *if* or *while* will almost certainly cause severe difficulties when the lexical analyzer is compiled. The token name *error* is reserved for error handling, and should not be used naively (see Section 7).

As mentioned above, the token numbers may be chosen by Yacc or by the user. In the default situation, the numbers are chosen by Yacc. The default token number for a literal character is the numerical value of the character in the local character set. Other names are assigned token numbers starting at 257.

To assign a token number to a token (including literals), the first appearance of the token name or literal *in the declarations section* can be immediately followed by a nonnegative integer. This integer is taken to be the token number of the name or literal. Names and literals not defined by this mechanism retain their default definition. It is important that all token numbers be distinct.

For historical reasons, the endmarker must have token number 0 or negative. This token number cannot be redefined by the user; thus, all lexical analyzers should be prepared to return 0 or negative as a token number upon reaching the end of their input.

A very useful tool for constructing lexical analyzers is the *Lex* program developed by Mike Lesk.[8] These lexical analyzers are designed to work in close harmony with Yacc parsers. The specifications for these lexical analyzers use regular expressions instead of grammar rules. Lex can be easily used to produce quite complicated lexical analyzers, but there remain some languages (such as FORTRAN) which do not fit any theoretical framework, and whose lexical analyzers must be crafted by hand.

4: How the Parser Works

Yacc turns the specification file into a C program, which parses the input according to the specification given. The algorithm used to go from the specification to the parser is complex, and will not be discussed here (see the references for more information). The parser itself, however, is relatively simple, and understanding how it works, while not strictly necessary, will nevertheless make treatment of error recovery and ambiguities much more comprehensible.

The parser produced by Yacc consists of a finite state machine with a stack. The parser is also capable of reading and remembering the next input token (called the *lookahead* token). The *current state* is always the one on the top of the stack. The states of the finite state machine are given small integer labels; initially, the machine is in state 0, the stack contains only state 0, and no lookahead token has been read.

The machine has only four actions available to it, called *shift*, *reduce*, *accept*, and *error*. A move of the parser is done as follows:

1. Based on its current state, the parser decides whether it needs a lookahead token to decide what action should be done; if it needs one, and does not have one, it calls *yylex* to obtain the next token.

2. Using the current state, and the lookahead token if needed, the parser decides on its next action, and carries it out. This may result in states being pushed onto the stack, or popped off of the stack, and in the lookahead token being processed or left alone.

The *shift* action is the most common action the parser takes. Whenever a shift action is taken, there is always a lookahead token. For example, in state 56 there may be an action:

IF   shift 34

which says, in state 56, if the lookahead token is IF, the current state (56) is pushed down on the stack, and state 34 becomes the current state (on the top of the stack). The lookahead token is cleared.

The *reduce* action keeps the stack from growing without bounds. Reduce actions are appropriate when the parser has seen the right hand side of a grammar rule, and is prepared to announce that it has seen an instance of the rule, replacing the right hand side by the left hand side. It may be necessary to consult the lookahead token to decide whether to reduce, but usually it is not; in fact, the default action (represented by a ".") is often a reduce action.

Reduce actions are associated with individual grammar rules. Grammar rules are also given small integer numbers, leading to some confusion. The action

.   reduce 18

refers to *grammar rule* 18, while the action

IF   shift 34

refers to *state* 34.

Suppose the rule being reduced is

A   :   x y z   ;

The reduce action depends on the left hand symbol (A in this case), and the number of symbols on the right hand side (three in this case). To reduce, first pop off the top three states from the stack (In general, the number of states popped equals the number of symbols on the right side of the rule). In effect, these states were the ones put on the stack while recognizing x, y, and z, and no longer serve any useful purpose. After popping these states, a state is uncovered which was the state the parser was in before beginning to process the rule. Using this uncovered state, and the symbol on the left side of the rule, perform what is in effect a shift of A. A new state is obtained, pushed onto the stack, and parsing continues. There are significant differences between the processing of the left hand symbol and an ordinary shift of a token, however, so this action is called a *goto* action. In particular, the lookahead token is cleared by a shift, and is not affected by a goto. In any case, the uncovered state contains an entry such as:

A   goto 20

causing state 20 to be pushed onto the stack, and become the current state.

In effect, the reduce action "turns back the clock" in the parse, popping the states off the stack to go back to the state where the right hand side of the rule was first seen. The parser then behaves as if it had seen the left side at that time. If the right hand side of the rule is empty, no states are popped off of the stack: the uncovered state is in fact the current state.

The reduce action is also important in the treatment of user-supplied actions and values. When a rule is reduced, the code supplied with the rule is executed before the stack is adjusted. In addition to the stack holding the states, another stack, running in parallel with it, holds the values returned from the lexical analyzer and the actions. When a shift takes place, the external variable *yylval* is copied onto the value stack. After the return from the user code, the reduction is carried out. When the *goto* action is done, the external variable *yyval* is copied onto the value stack. The pseudo-variables $1, $2, etc., refer to the value stack.

The other two parser actions are conceptually much simpler. The *accept* action indicates that the entire input has been seen and that it matches the specification. This action appears only when the lookahead token is the endmarker, and indicates that the parser has successfully done its job. The *error* action, on the other hand, represents a place where the parser can no longer continue parsing according to the specification. The input tokens it has seen, together with the lookahead token, cannot be followed by anything that would result in a legal input. The parser reports an error, and attempts to recover the situation and resume parsing: the error recovery (as opposed to the detection of error) will be covered in Section 7.

It is time for an example! Consider the specification

```
%token  DING  DONG  DELL
%%
rhyme   :       sound  place
        ;
sound   :       DING  DONG
        ;
place   :       DELL
        ;
```

When Yacc is invoked with the −v option, a file called *y.output* is produced, with a human-readable description of the parser. The *y.output* file corresponding to the above grammar (with some statistics stripped off the end) is:

state 0

    $accept : _rhyme $end

    DING shift 3
    . error

    rhyme goto 1
    sound goto 2

state 1

    $accept : rhyme_$end

    $end accept
    . error

state 2

    rhyme : sound_place

    DELL shift 5
    . error

    place   goto 4

state 3

    sound : DING_DONG

    DONG shift 6
    . error

state 4

    rhyme : sound place_   (1)

    . reduce 1

state 5

    place : DELL_   (3)

    . reduce 3

state 6

    sound : DING DONG_   (2)

    . reduce 2

Notice that, in addition to the actions for each state, there is a description of the parsing rules being processed in each state. The _ character is used to indicate what has been seen, and what is yet to come, in each rule. Suppose the input is

DING DONG DELL

It is instructive to follow the steps of the parser while processing this input.

Initially, the current state is state 0. The parser needs to refer to the input in order to decide between the actions available in state 0, so the first token, *DING*, is read, becoming the lookahead token. The action in state 0 on *DING* is is "shift 3", so state 3 is pushed onto the stack, and the lookahead token is cleared. State 3 becomes the current state. The next token, *DONG*, is read, becoming the lookahead token. The action in state 3 on the token *DONG* is "shift 6", so state 6 is pushed onto the stack, and the lookahead is cleared. The stack now contains 0, 3, and 6. In state 6, without even consulting the lookahead, the parser reduces by rule 2.

> sound : DING DONG

This rule has two symbols on the right hand side, so two states, 6 and 3, are popped off of the stack, uncovering state 0. Consulting the description of state 0, looking for a goto on *sound*,

> sound goto 2

is obtained; thus state 2 is pushed onto the stack, becoming the current state.

In state 2, the next token, *DELL*, must be read. The action is "shift 5", so state 5 is pushed onto the stack, which now has 0, 2, and 5 on it, and the lookahead token is cleared. In state 5, the only action is to reduce by rule 3. This has one symbol on the right hand side, so one state, 5, is popped off, and state 2 is uncovered. The goto in state 2 on *place*, the left side of rule 3, is state 4. Now, the stack contains 0, 2, and 4. In state 4, the only action is to reduce by rule 1. There are two symbols on the right, so the top two states are popped off, uncovering state 0 again. In state 0, there is a goto on *rhyme* causing the parser to enter state 1. In state 1, the input is read; the endmarker is obtained, indicated by "$end" in the *y.output* file. The action in state 1 when the endmarker is seen is to accept, successfully ending the parse.

The reader is urged to consider how the parser works when confronted with such incorrect strings as *DING DONG DONG*, *DING DONG*, *DING DONG DELL DELL*, etc. A few minutes spend with this and other simple examples will probably be repaid when problems arise in more complicated contexts.

5: Ambiguity and Conflicts

A set of grammar rules is *ambiguous* if there is some input string that can be structured in two or more different ways. For example, the grammar rule

> expr   :   expr '−' expr

is a natural way of expressing the fact that one way of forming an arithmetic expression is to put two other expressions together with a minus sign between them. Unfortunately, this grammar rule does not completely specify the way that all complex inputs should be structured. For example, if the input is

> expr − expr − expr

the rule allows this input to be structured as either

> (expr − expr) − expr

or as

> expr − (expr − expr)

(The first is called *left association*, the second *right association*).

Yacc detects such ambiguities when it is attempting to build the parser. It is instructive to consider the problem that confronts the parser when it is given an input such as

> expr − expr − expr

When the parser has read the second expr, the input that it has seen:

> expr − expr

matches the right side of the grammar rule above. The parser could *reduce* the input by applying this rule; after applying the rule; the input is reduced to *expr*(the left side of the rule). The parser would then read the final part of the input:

> — expr

and again reduce. The effect of this is to take the left associative interpretation.

Alternatively, when the parser has seen

> expr — expr

it could defer the immediate application of the rule, and continue reading the input until it had seen

> expr — expr — expr

It could then apply the rule to the rightmost three symbols, reducing them to *expr* and leaving

> expr — expr

Now the rule can be reduced once more; the effect is to take the right associative interpretation. Thus, having read

> expr — expr

the parser can do two legal things, a shift or a reduction, and has no way of deciding between them. This is called a *shift / reduce conflict*. It may also happen that the parser has a choice of two legal reductions; this is called a *reduce / reduce conflict*. Note that there are never any "Shift/shift" conflicts.

When there are shift/reduce or reduce/reduce conflicts, Yacc still produces a parser. It does this by selecting one of the valid steps wherever it has a choice. A rule describing which choice to make in a given situation is called a *disambiguating rule*.

Yacc invokes two disambiguating rules by default:

1. In a shift/reduce conflict, the default is to do the shift.
2. In a reduce/reduce conflict, the default is to reduce by the *earlier* grammar rule (in the input sequence).

Rule 1 implies that reductions are deferred whenever there is a choice, in favor of shifts. Rule 2 gives the user rather crude control over the behavior of the parser in this situation, but reduce/reduce conflicts should be avoided whenever possible.

Conflicts may arise because of mistakes in input or logic, or because the grammar rules, while consistent, require a more complex parser than Yacc can construct. The use of actions within rules can also cause conflicts, if the action must be done before the parser can be sure which rule is being recognized. In these cases, the application of disambiguating rules is inappropriate, and leads to an incorrect parser. For this reason, Yacc always reports the number of shift/reduce and reduce/reduce conflicts resolved by Rule 1 and Rule 2.

In general, whenever it is possible to apply disambiguating rules to produce a correct parser, it is also possible to rewrite the grammar rules so that the same inputs are read but there are no conflicts. For this reason, most previous parser generators have considered conflicts to be fatal errors. Our experience has suggested that this rewriting is somewhat unnatural, and produces slower parsers; thus, Yacc will produce parsers even in the presence of conflicts.

As an example of the power of disambiguating rules, consider a fragment from a programming language involving an "if-then-else" construction:

```
stat    :       IF '(' cond ')' stat
        |       IF '(' cond ')' stat ELSE stat
        ;
```

In these rules, *IF* and *ELSE* are tokens, *cond* is a nonterminal symbol describing conditional (logical) expressions, and *stat* is a nonterminal symbol describing statements. The first rule will be called the *simple-if* rule, and the second the *if-else* rule.

These two rules form an ambiguous construction, since input of the form

    IF (C1) IF (C2) S1 ELSE S2

can be structured according to these rules in two ways:

    IF (C1) {
         IF (C2) S1
         }
    ELSE S2

or

    IF (C1) {
         IF (C2) S1
         ELSE S2
         }

The second interpretation is the one given in most programming languages having this construct. Each *ELSE* is associated with the last preceding "un-*ELSE*'d" *IF*. In this example, consider the situation where the parser has seen

    IF (C1) IF (C2) S1

and is looking at the *ELSE*. It can immediately reduce by the simple-if rule to get

    IF (C1) stat

and then read the remaining input,

    ELSE S2

and reduce

    IF (C1) stat ELSE S2

by the if-else rule. This leads to the first of the above groupings of the input.

On the other hand, the *ELSE* may be shifted, *S2* read, and then the right hand portion of

    IF (C1) IF (C2) S1 ELSE S2

can be reduced by the if-else rule to get

    IF (C1) stat

which can be reduced by the simple-if rule. This leads to the second of the above groupings of the input, which is usually desired.

Once again the parser can do two valid things — there is a shift/reduce conflict. The application of disambiguating rule 1 tells the parser to shift in this case, which leads to the desired grouping.

This shift/reduce conflict arises only when there is a particular current input symbol, *ELSE*, and particular inputs already seen, such as

    IF (C1) IF (C2) S1

In general, there may be many conflicts, and each one will be associated with an input symbol and a set of previously read inputs. The previously read inputs are characterized by the state of the parser.

The conflict messages of Yacc are best understood by examining the verbose (−v) option output file. For example, the output corresponding to the above conflict state might be:

23: shift/reduce conflict (shift 45, reduce 18) on ELSE

state 23

        stat : IF (cond) stat_   (18)
        stat : IF (cond) stat_ELSE stat

    ELSE   shift 45
            reduce 18

The first line describes the conflict, giving the state and the input symbol. The ordinary state description follows, giving the grammar rules active in the state, and the parser actions. Recall that the underline marks the portion of the grammar rules which has been seen. Thus in the example, in state 23 the parser has seen input corresponding to

        IF (cond) stat

and the two grammar rules shown are active at this time. The parser can do two possible things. If the input symbol is *ELSE*, it is possible to shift into state 45. State 45 will have, as part of its description, the line

        stat : IF (cond) stat ELSE_stat

since the *ELSE* will have been shifted in this state. Back in state 23, the alternative action, described by ".", is to be done if the input symbol is not mentioned explicitly in the above actions; thus, in this case, if the input symbol is not *ELSE*, the parser reduces by grammar rule 18:

        stat : IF ´(´ cond ´)´ stat

Once again, notice that the numbers following "shift" commands refer to other states, while the numbers following "reduce" commands refer to grammar rule numbers. In the *y.output* file, the rule numbers are printed after those rules which can be reduced. In most one states, there will be at most reduce action possible in the state, and this will be the default command. The user who encounters unexpected shift/reduce conflicts will probably want to look at the verbose output to decide whether the default actions are appropriate. In really tough cases, the user might need to know more about the behavior and construction of the parser than can be covered here. In this case, one of the theoretical references[2, 3, 4] might be consulted; the services of a local guru might also be appropriate.

6: Precedence

There is one common situation where the rules given above for resolving conflicts are not sufficient; this is in the parsing of arithmetic expressions. Most of the commonly used constructions for arithmetic expressions can be naturally described by the notion of *precedence* levels for operators, together with information about left or right associativity. It turns out that ambiguous grammars with appropriate disambiguating rules can be used to create parsers that are faster and easier to write than parsers constructed from unambiguous grammars. The basic notion is to write grammar rules of the form

        expr : expr OP expr

and

        expr : UNARY expr

for all binary and unary operators desired. This creates a very ambiguous grammar, with many parsing conflicts. As disambiguating rules, the user specifies the precedence, or binding strength, of all the operators, and the associativity of the binary operators. This information is sufficient to allow Yacc to resolve the parsing conflicts in accordance with these rules, and construct a parser that realizes the desired precedences and associativities.

The precedences and associativities are attached to tokens in the declarations section. This is done by a series of lines beginning with a Yacc keyword: %left, %right, or %nonassoc, followed by a list of tokens. All of the tokens on the same line are assumed to have the same precedence level and associativity; the lines are listed in order of increasing precedence or binding strength. Thus,

```
%left '+' '−'
%left '*' '/'
```

describes the precedence and associativity of the four arithmetic operators. Plus and minus are left associative, and have lower precedence than star and slash, which are also left associative. The keyword %right is used to describe right associative operators, and the keyword %nonassoc is used to describe operators, like the operator .LT. in Fortran, that may not associate with themselves; thus,

```
A .LT. B .LT. C
```

is illegal in Fortran, and such an operator would be described with the keyword %nonassoc in Yacc. As an example of the behavior of these declarations, the description

```
%right '='
%left '+' '−'
%left '*' '/'


%%

expr    :        expr '=' expr
        |        expr '+' expr
        |        expr '−' expr
        |        expr '*' expr
        |        expr '/' expr
        |        NAME
        ;
```

might be used to structure the input

```
a = b = c*d − e − f*g
```

as follows:

```
a = ( b = ( ((c*d)−e) − (f*g) ) )
```

When this mechanism is used, unary operators must, in general, be given a precedence. Sometimes a unary operator and a binary operator have the same symbolic representation, but different precedences. An example is unary and binary '−'; unary minus may be given the same strength as multiplication, or even higher, while binary minus has a lower strength than multiplication. The keyword, %prec, changes the precedence level associated with a particular grammar rule. %prec appears immediately after the body of the grammar rule, before the action or closing semicolon, and is followed by a token name or literal. It causes the precedence of the grammar rule to become that of the following token name or literal. For example, to make unary minus have the same precedence as multiplication the rules might resemble:

```
%left  '+'  '−'
%left  '*'  '/'

%%

expr    :       expr  '+'  expr
        |       expr  '−'  expr
        |       expr  '*'  expr
        |       expr  '/'  expr
        |       '−'  expr     %prec  '*'
        |       NAME
        ;
```

A token declared by %left, %right, and %nonassoc need not be, but may be, declared by %token as well.

The precedences and associativities are used by Yacc to resolve parsing conflicts; they give rise to disambiguating rules. Formally, the rules work as follows:

1. The precedences and associativities are recorded for those tokens and literals that have them.

2. A precedence and associativity is associated with each grammar rule; it is the precedence and associativity of the last token or literal in the body of the rule. If the %prec construction is used, it overrides this default. Some grammar rules may have no precedence and associativity associated with them.

3. When there is a reduce/reduce conflict, or there is a shift/reduce conflict and either the input symbol or the grammar rule has no precedence and associativity, then the two disambiguating rules given at the beginning of the section are used, and the conflicts are reported.

4. If there is a shift/reduce conflict, and both the grammar rule and the input character have precedence and associativity associated with them, then the conflict is resolved in favor of the action (shift or reduce) associated with the higher precedence. If the precedences are the same, then the associativity is used; left associative implies reduce, right associative implies shift, and nonassociating implies error.

Conflicts resolved by precedence are not counted in the number of shift/reduce and reduce/reduce conflicts reported by Yacc. This means that mistakes in the specification of precedences may disguise errors in the input grammar; it is a good idea to be sparing with precedences, and use them in an essentially "cookbook" fashion, until some experience has been gained. The *y.output* file is very useful in deciding whether the parser is actually doing what was intended.

7: Error Handling

Error handling is an extremely difficult area, and many of the problems are semantic ones. When an error is found, for example, it may be necessary to reclaim parse tree storage, delete or alter symbol table entries, and, typically, set switches to avoid generating any further output.

It is seldom acceptable to stop all processing when an error is found; it is more useful to continue scanning the input to find further syntax errors. This leads to the problem of getting the parser "restarted" after an error. A general class of algorithms to do this involves discarding a number of tokens from the input string, and attempting to adjust the parser so that input can continue.

To allow the user some control over this process, Yacc provides a simple, but reasonably general, feature. The token name "error" is reserved for error handling. This name can be used in grammar rules; in effect, it suggests places where errors are expected, and recovery might take place. The parser pops its stack until it enters a state where the token "error" is legal. It then behaves as if the token "error" were the current lookahead token, and performs the action encountered. The lookahead token is then reset to the token that caused the error. If no special error rules have been specified, the processing halts when an error is detected.

In order to prevent a cascade of error messages, the parser, after detecting an error, remains in error state until three tokens have been successfully read and shifted. If an error is detected when the parser is already in error state, no message is given, and the input token is quietly deleted.

As an example, a rule of the form

        stat   :   error

would, in effect, mean that on a syntax error the parser would attempt to skip over the statement in which the error was seen. More precisely, the parser will scan ahead, looking for three tokens that might legally follow a statement, and start processing at the first of these; if the beginnings of statements are not sufficiently distinctive, it may make a false start in the middle of a statement, and end up reporting a second error where there is in fact no error.

Actions may be used with these special error rules. These actions might attempt to reinitialize tables, reclaim symbol table space, etc.

Error rules such as the above are very general, but difficult to control. Somewhat easier are rules such as

        stat   :   error ';'

Here, when there is an error, the parser attempts to skip over the statement, but will do so by skipping to the next ';'. All tokens after the error and before the next ';' cannot be shifted, and are discarded. When the ';' is seen, this rule will be reduced, and any "cleanup" action associated with it performed.

Another form of error rule arises in interactive applications, where it may be desirable to permit a line to be reentered after an error. A possible error rule might be

        input   :   error '\n' { printf("Reenter last line: "); } input
                         { $$ = $4; }

There is one potential difficulty with this approach; the parser must correctly process three input tokens before it admits that it has correctly resynchronized after the error. If the reentered line contains an error in the first two tokens, the parser deletes the offending tokens, and gives no message; this is clearly unacceptable. For this reason, there is a mechanism that can be used to force the parser to believe that an error has been fully recovered from. The statement

        yyerrok ;

in an action resets the parser to its normal mode. The last example is better written

        input   :   error '\n'
                         {   yyerrok;
                                  printf("Reenter last line: ");   }
                 input
                         { $$ = $4; }
                 ;

As mentioned above, the token seen immediately after the "error" symbol is the input token at which the error was discovered. Sometimes, this is inappropriate; for example, an error recovery action might take upon itself the job of finding the correct place to resume input. In this case, the previous lookahead token must be cleared. The statement

        yyclearin ;

in an action will have this effect. For example, suppose the action after error were to call some sophisticated resynchronization routine, supplied by the user, that attempted to advance the input to the beginning of the next valid statement. After this routine was called, the next token returned by yylex would presumably be the first token in a legal statement; the old, illegal token must be discarded, and the error state reset. This could be done by a rule like

```
stat    :    error
        {       resynch();
                yyerrok ;
                yyclearin ;   }

        ;
```

These mechanisms are admittedly crude, but do allow for a simple, fairly effective recovery of the parser from many errors; moreover, the user can get control to deal with the error actions required by other portions of the program.

8: The Yacc Environment

When the user inputs a specification to Yacc, the output is a file of C programs, called *y.tab.c* on most systems (due to local file system conventions, the names may differ from installation to installation). The function produced by Yacc is called *yyparse*; it is an integer valued function. When it is called, it in turn repeatedly calls *yylex*, the lexical analyzer supplied by the user (see Section 3) to obtain input tokens. Eventually, either an error is detected, in which case (if no error recovery is possible) *yyparse* returns the value 1, or the lexical analyzer returns the endmarker token and the parser accepts. In this case, *yyparse* returns the value 0.

The user must provide a certain amount of environment for this parser in order to obtain a working program. For example, as with every C program, a program called *main* must be defined, that eventually calls *yyparse*. In addition, a routine called *yyerror* prints a message when a syntax error is detected.

These two routines must be supplied in one form or another by the user. To ease the initial effort of using Yacc, a library has been provided with default versions of *main* and *yyerror*. The name of this library is system dependent; on many systems the library is accessed by a −ly argument to the loader. To show the triviality of these default programs, the source is given below:

```
main(){
        return( yyparse() );
        }
```

and

```
# include <stdio.h>

yyerror(s) char *s; {
        fprintf( stderr, "%s\n", s );
        }
```

The argument to *yyerror* is a string containing an error message, usually the string "syntax error". The average application will want to do better than this. Ordinarily, the program should keep track of the input line number, and print it along with the message when a syntax error is detected. The external integer variable *yychar* contains the lookahead token number at the time the error was detected; this may be of some interest in giving better diagnostics. Since the *main* program is probably supplied by the user (to read arguments, etc.) the Yacc library is useful only in small projects, or in the earliest stages of larger ones.

The external integer variable *yydebug* is normally set to 0. If it is set to a nonzero value, the parser will output a verbose description of its actions, including a discussion of which input symbols have been read, and what the parser actions are. Depending on the operating environment, it may be possible to set this variable by using a debugging system.

9: Hints for Preparing Specifications

This section contains miscellaneous hints on preparing efficient, easy to change, and clear specifications. The individual subsections are more or less independent.

Input Style

It is difficult to provide rules with substantial actions and still have a readable specification file. The following style hints owe much to Brian Kernighan.

a.   Use all capital letters for token names, all lower case letters for nonterminal names. This rule comes under the heading of "knowing who to blame when things go wrong."

b.   Put grammar rules and actions on separate lines. This allows either to be changed without an automatic need to change the other.

c.   Put all rules with the same left hand side together. Put the left hand side in only once, and let all following rules begin with a vertical bar.

d.   Put a semicolon only after the last rule with a given left hand side, and put the semicolon on a separate line. This allows new rules to be easily added.

e.   Indent rule bodies by two tab stops, and action bodies by three tab stops.

The example in Appendix A is written following this style, as are the examples in the text of this paper (where space permits). The user must make up his own mind about these stylistic questions; the central problem, however, is to make the rules visible through the morass of action code.

Left Recursion

The algorithm used by the Yacc parser encourages so called "left recursive" grammar rules: rules of the form

```
name    :       name rest_of_rule ;
```

These rules frequently arise when writing specifications of sequences and lists:

```
list    :       item
        |       list ',' item
        ;
```

and

```
seq     :       item
        |       seq  item
        ;
```

In each of these cases, the first rule will be reduced for the first item only, and the second rule will be reduced for the second and all succeeding items.

With right recursive rules, such as

```
seq     :       item
        |       item  seq
        ;
```

the parser would be a bit bigger, and the items would be seen, and reduced, from right to left. More seriously, an internal stack in the parser would be in danger of overflowing if a very long sequence were read. Thus, the user should use left recursion wherever reasonable.

It is worth considering whether a sequence with zero elements has any meaning, and if so, consider writing the sequence specification with an empty rule:

```
seq    :      /* empty */
       |      seq  item
       ;
```

Once again, the first rule would always be reduced exactly once, before the first item was read, and then the second rule would be reduced once for each item read. Permitting empty sequences often leads to increased generality. However, conflicts might arise if Yacc is asked to decide which empty sequence it has seen, when it hasn't seen enough to know!

Lexical Tie-ins

Some lexical decisions depend on context. For example, the lexical analyzer might want to delete blanks normally, but not within quoted strings. Or names might be entered into a symbol table in declarations, but not in expressions.

One way of handling this situation is to create a global flag that is examined by the lexical analyzer, and set by actions. For example, suppose a program consists of 0 or more declarations, followed by 0 or more statements. Consider:

```
%{
        int dflag;
%}
  ... other declarations ...

%%

prog   :      decls  stats
       ;

decls  :      /* empty */
                     {      dflag = 1;  }
       |      decls  declaration
       ;

stats  :      /* empty */
                     {      dflag = 0;  }
       |      stats  statement
       ;

       ... other rules ...
```

The flag *dflag* is now 0 when reading statements, and 1 when reading declarations, *except for the first token in the first statement*. This token must be seen by the parser before it can tell that the declaration section has ended and the statements have begun. In many cases, this single token exception does not affect the lexical scan.

This kind of "backdoor" approach can be elaborated to a noxious degree. Nevertheless, it represents a way of doing some things that are difficult, if not impossible, to do otherwise.

Reserved Words

Some programming languages permit the user to use words like "if", which are normally reserved, as label or variable names, provided that such use does not conflict with the legal use of these names in the programming language. This is extremely hard to do in the framework of Yacc; it is difficult to pass information to the lexical analyzer telling it "this instance of 'if' is a keyword, and that instance is a variable". The user can make a stab at it, using the mechanism described in the last subsection, but it is difficult.

A number of ways of making this easier are under advisement. Until then, it is better that the keywords be *reserved*; that is, be forbidden for use as variable names. There are powerful stylistic reasons for preferring this, anyway.

10: Advanced Topics

This section discusses a number of advanced features of Yacc.

Simulating Error and Accept in Actions

The parsing actions of error and accept can be simulated in an action by use of macros YYACCEPT and YYERROR. YYACCEPT causes *yyparse* to return the value 0; YYERROR causes the parser to behave as if the current input symbol had been a syntax error; *yyerror* is called, and error recovery takes place. These mechanisms can be used to simulate parsers with multiple endmarkers or context-sensitive syntax checking.

Accessing Values in Enclosing Rules.

An action may refer to values returned by actions to the left of the current rule. The mechanism is simply the same as with ordinary actions, a dollar sign followed by a digit, but in this case the digit may be 0 or negative. Consider

```
sent    :       adj noun verb adj noun
                        { look at the sentence . . . }
        ;

adj     :       THE             {       $$ = THE; }
        |       YOUNG           {       $$ = YOUNG; }
        . . .
        ;

noun    :       DOG
                        {       $$ = DOG; }
        |       CRONE
                        {       if( $0 == YOUNG ){
                                    printf( "what?\n" );
                                }
                        $$ = CRONE;
                        }
        ;
        . . .
```

In the action following the word CRONE, a check is made that the preceding token shifted was not YOUNG. Obviously, this is only possible when a great deal is known about what might precede the symbol *noun* in the input. There is also a distinctly unstructured flavor about this. Nevertheless, at times this mechanism will save a great deal of trouble, especially when a few combinations are to be excluded from an otherwise regular structure.

Support for Arbitrary Value Types

By default, the values returned by actions and the lexical analyzer are integers. Yacc can also support values of other types, including structures. In addition, Yacc keeps track of the types, and inserts appropriate union member names so that the resulting parser will be strictly type checked. The Yacc value stack (see Section 4) is declared to be a *union* of the various types of values desired. The user declares the union, and associates union member names to each token and nonterminal symbol having a value. When the value is referenced through a $$ or $n construction, Yacc will automatically insert the appropriate union name, so that no unwanted conversions will take place. In addition, type checking commands such as *Lint* [5] will be far more silent.

There are three mechanisms used to provide for this typing. First, there is a way of defining the union; this must be done by the user since other programs, notably the lexical analyzer, must know about the union member names. Second, there is a way of associating a union member name with tokens and nonterminals. Finally, there is a mechanism for describing the type of those few values where Yacc can not easily determine the type.

To declare the union, the user includes in the declaration section:

```
%union  {
        body of union ...
        }
```

This declares the Yacc value stack, and the external variables *yylval* and *yyval*, to have type equal to this union. If Yacc was invoked with the **−d** option, the union declaration is copied onto the *y.tab.h* file. Alternatively, the union may be declared in a header file, and a typedef used to define the variable YYSTYPE to represent this union. Thus, the header file might also have said:

```
typedef union {
        body of union ...
        } YYSTYPE;
```

The header file must be included in the declarations section, by use of %{ and %}.

Once YYSTYPE is defined, the union member names must be associated with the various terminal and nonterminal names. The construction

```
< name >
```

is used to indicate a union member name. If this follows one of the keywords %token, %left, %right, and %nonassoc, the union member name is associated with the tokens listed. Thus, saying

```
%left  <optype>  ′+′ ′−′
```

will cause any reference to values returned by these two tokens to be tagged with the union member name *optype*. Another keyword, %type, is used similarly to associate union member names with nonterminals. Thus, one might say

```
%type  <nodetype>  expr  stat
```

There remain a couple of cases where these mechanisms are insufficient. If there is an action within a rule, the value returned by this action has no *a priori* type. Similarly, reference to left context values (such as $0 − see the previous subsection) leaves Yacc with no easy way of knowing the type. In this case, a type can be imposed on the reference by inserting a union member name, between < and >, immediately after the first $. An example of this usage is

```
rule    :       aaa  { $<intval>$  =  3; } bbb
                {        fun( $<intval>2, $<other>0 );  }
        ;
```

This syntax has little to recommend it, but the situation arises rarely.

A sample specification is given in Appendix C. The facilities in this subsection are not triggered until they are used: in particular, the use of %type will turn on these mechanisms. When they are used, there is a fairly strict level of checking. For example, use of $n or $$ to refer to something with no defined type is diagnosed. If these facilities are not triggered, the Yacc value stack is used to hold *int's*, as was true historically.

11: Acknowledgements

Yacc owes much to a most stimulating collection of users, who have goaded me beyond my inclination, and frequently beyond my ability, in their endless search for "one more feature". Their irritating unwillingness to learn how to do things my way has usually led to my doing things their way; most of the time, they have been right. B. W. Kernighan, P. J. Plauger, S. I. Feldman, C. Imagna, M. E. Lesk, and A. Snyder will recognize some of their ideas in the current version of Yacc. C. B. Haley contributed to the error recovery algorithm. D. M. Ritchie, B. W. Kernighan, and M. O. Harris helped translate this document into English. Al Aho also deserves special credit for bringing the mountain to Mohammed, and other favors.

References

1. B. W. Kernighan and D. M. Ritchie, *The C Programming Language,* Prentice-Hall, Englewood Cliffs, New Jersey (1978).

2. A. V. Aho and S. C. Johnson, "LR Parsing," *Comp. Surveys* **6**(2) pp. 99-124 (June 1974).

3. A. V. Aho, S. C. Johnson, and J. D. Ullman, "Deterministic Parsing of Ambiguous Grammars," *Comm. Assoc. Comp. Mach.* **18**(8) pp. 441-452 (August 1975).

4. A. V. Aho and J. D. Ullman, *Principles of Compiler Design,* Addison-Wesley, Reading, Mass. (1977).

5. S. C. Johnson, "Lint, a C Program Checker," Comp. Sci. Tech. Rep. No. 65 (December 1977).

6. S. C. Johnson, "A Portable Compiler: Theory and Practice," *Proc. 5th ACM Symp. on Principles of Programming Languages*, (January 1978).

7. B. W. Kernighan and L. L. Cherry, "A System for Typesetting Mathematics," *Comm. Assoc. Comp. Mach.* **18** pp. 151-157 (March 1975).

8. M. E. Lesk, "Lex — A Lexical Analyzer Generator," Comp. Sci. Tech. Rep. No. 39, Bell Laboratories, Murray Hill, New Jersey (October 1975).

Appendix A: A Simple Example

This example gives the complete Yacc specification for a small desk calculator; the desk calculator has 26 registers, labeled "a" through "z", and accepts arithmetic expressions made up of the operators +, −, *, /, % (mod operator), & (bitwise and), | (bitwise or), and assignment. If an expression at the top level is an assignment, the value is not printed; otherwise it is. As in C, an integer that begins with 0 (zero) is assumed to be octal; otherwise, it is assumed to be decimal.

As an example of a Yacc specification, the desk calculator does a reasonable job of showing how precedences and ambiguities are used, and demonstrating simple error recovery. The major oversimplifications are that the lexical analysis phase is much simpler than for most applications, and the output is produced immediately, line by line. Note the way that decimal and octal integers are read in by the grammar rules; This job is probably better done by the lexical analyzer.

```
%{
# include <stdio.h>
# include <ctype.h>

int regs[26];
int base;

%}

%start list

%token DIGIT LETTER

%left '|'
%left '&'
%left '+' '−'
%left '*' '/' '%'
%left UMINUS      /* supplies precedence for unary minus */

%%      /* beginning of rules section */

list    :       /* empty */
        |       list stat '\n'
        |       list error '\n'
                {       yyerrok; }
        ;

stat    :       expr
                {       printf( "%d\n", $1 ); }
        |       LETTER '=' expr
                {       regs[$1]  =  $3; }
        ;

expr    :       '(' expr ')'
                {       $$  =  $2; }
        |       expr '+' expr
                {       $$  =  $1  +  $3; }
        |       expr '−' expr
                {       $$  =  $1  −  $3; }
```

```
       |      expr '*' expr
                   {        $$  =  $1 * $3; }
       |      expr '/' expr
                   {        $$  =  $1 / $3; }
       |      expr '%' expr
                   {        $$  =  $1 % $3; }
       |      expr '&' expr
                   {        $$  =  $1 & $3; }
       |      expr '|' expr
                   {        $$  =  $1 | $3; }
       |      '−' expr        %prec  UMINUS
                   {        $$  =  − $2; }
       |      LETTER
                   {        $$  =  regs[$1]; }
       |      number
       ;

number:       DIGIT
                   {        $$ = $1;   base  =  ($1==0) ? 8 : 10; }
       |      number DIGIT
                   {        $$  =  base * $1  +  $2; }
       ;

%%    /* start of programs */

yylex() {                   /* lexical analysis routine */
        /* returns LETTER for a lower case letter, yylval = 0 through 25 */
        /* return DIGIT for a digit, yylval = 0 through 9 */
        /* all other characters are returned immediately */

      int  c;

      while( (c=getchar()) == ' ' ) {/* skip blanks */ }

      /* c is now nonblank */

      if( islower( c ) ) {
            yylval  =  c − 'a';
            return ( LETTER );
            }
      if( isdigit( c ) ) {
            yylval  =  c − '0';
            return( DIGIT );
            }
      return( c );
      }
```

Appendix B: Yacc Input Syntax

This Appendix has a description of the Yacc input syntax, as a Yacc specification. Context dependencies, etc., are not considered. Ironically, the Yacc input specification language is most naturally specified as an LR(2) grammar; the sticky part comes when an identifier is seen in a rule, immediately following an action. If this identifier is followed by a colon, it is the start of the next rule; otherwise it is a continuation of the current rule, which just happens to have an action embedded in it. As implemented, the lexical analyzer looks ahead after seeing an identifier, and decide whether the next token (skipping blanks, newlines, comments, etc.) is a colon. If so, it returns the token C_IDENTIFIER. Otherwise, it returns IDENTIFIER. Literals (quoted strings) are also returned as IDENTIFIERS, but never as part of C_IDENTIFIERs.

```
            /* grammar for the input to Yacc */

            /* basic entities */
%token  IDENTIFIER      /* includes identifiers  and literals */
%token  C_IDENTIFIER    /*  identifier (but not literal) followed by colon  */
%token  NUMBER              /*  [0-9]+  */

            /* reserved words:  %type => TYPE, %left => LEFT, etc. */

%token  LEFT RIGHT NONASSOC TOKEN PREC TYPE START UNION

%token  MARK /* the %% mark */
%token  LCURL /* the %{ mark */
%token  RCURL /* the %} mark */

            /* ascii character literals stand for themselves */

%start   spec

%%

spec     :          defs MARK rules tail
         ;

tail     :          MARK {  In this action, eat up the rest of the file  }
         |          /* empty: the second MARK is optional */
         ;

defs     :          /* empty */
         |          defs def
         ;

def      :          START IDENTIFIER
         |          UNION { Copy union definition to output }
         |          LCURL { Copy C code to output file } RCURL
         |          ndefs rword tag nlist
         ;

rword    :          TOKEN
         |          LEFT
         |          RIGHT
```

```
          |           NONASSOC
          |           TYPE
          ;


tag       :           /* empty: union tag is optional */
          |           '<' IDENTIFIER '>'
          ;


nlist     :           nmno
          |           nlist nmno
          |           nlist ',' nmno
          ;


nmno      :           IDENTIFIER              /* NOTE: literal illegal with %type */
          |           IDENTIFIER NUMBER       /* NOTE: illegal with %type */
          ;


          /* rules section */


rules     :           C_IDENTIFIER rbody prec
          |           rules rule
          ;


rule      :           C_IDENTIFIER rbody prec
          |           '|' rbody prec
          ;


rbody     :           /* empty */
          |           rbody IDENTIFIER
          |           rbody act
          ;


act       :           '{' { Copy action, translate $$, etc. } '}'
          ;


prec      :           /* empty */
          |           PREC IDENTIFIER
          |           PREC IDENTIFIER act
          |           prec ';'
          ;
```

Appendix C: An Advanced Example

This Appendix gives an example of a grammar using some of the advanced features discussed in Section 10. The desk calculator example in Appendix A is modified to provide a desk calculator that does floating point interval arithmetic. The calculator understands floating point constants, the arithmetic operations +, −, *, /, unary −, and = (assignment), and has 26 floating point variables, "a" through "z". Moreover, it also understands *intervals*, written

$$(x , y)$$

where *x* is less than or equal to *y*. There are 26 interval valued variables "A" through "Z" that may also be used. The usage is similar to that in Appendix A; assignments return no value, and print nothing, while expressions print the (floating or interval) value.

This example explores a number of interesting features of Yacc and C. Intervals are represented by a structure, consisting of the left and right endpoint values, stored as *double*'s. This structure is given a type name, INTERVAL, by using *typedef*. The Yacc value stack can also contain floating point scalars, and integers (used to index into the arrays holding the variable values). Notice that this entire strategy depends strongly on being able to assign structures and unions in C. In fact, many of the actions call functions that return structures as well.

It is also worth noting the use of YYERROR to handle error conditions: division by an interval containing 0, and an interval presented in the wrong order. In effect, the error recovery mechanism of Yacc is used to throw away the rest of the offending line.

In addition to the mixing of types on the value stack, this grammar also demonstrates an interesting use of syntax to keep track of the type (e.g. scalar or interval) of intermediate expressions. Note that a scalar can be automatically promoted to an interval if the context demands an interval value. This causes a large number of conflicts when the grammar is run through Yacc: 18 Shift/Reduce and 26 Reduce/Reduce. The problem can be seen by looking at the two input lines:

$$2.5 + (3.5 − 4.)$$

and

$$2.5 + (3.5 , 4.)$$

Notice that the 2.5 is to be used in an interval valued expression in the second example, but this fact is not known until the "," is read; by this time, 2.5 is finished, and the parser cannot go back and change its mind. More generally, it might be necessary to look ahead an arbitrary number of tokens to decide whether to convert a scalar to an interval. This problem is evaded by having two rules for each binary interval valued operator: one when the left operand is a scalar, and one when the left operand is an interval. In the second case, the right operand must be an interval, so the conversion will be applied automatically. Despite this evasion, there are still many cases where the conversion may be applied or not, leading to the above conflicts. They are resolved by listing the rules that yield scalars first in the specification file; in this way, the conflicts will be resolved in the direction of keeping scalar valued expressions scalar valued until they are forced to become intervals.

This way of handling multiple types is very instructive, but not very general. If there were many kinds of expression types, instead of just two, the number of rules needed would increase dramatically, and the conflicts even more dramatically. Thus, while this example is instructive, it is better practice in a more normal programming language environment to keep the type information as part of the value, and not as part of the grammar.

Finally, a word about the lexical analysis. The only unusual feature is the treatment of floating point constants. The C library routine *atof* is used to do the actual conversion from a character string to a double precision value. If the lexical analyzer detects an error, it responds by returning a token that is illegal in the grammar, provoking a syntax error in the parser, and thence error recovery.

```
%{

# include <stdio.h>
# include <ctype.h>

typedef struct interval {
        double lo, hi;
        } INTERVAL;

INTERVAL vmul(), vdiv();

double atof();

double dreg[ 26 ];
INTERVAL vreg[ 26 ];

%}

%start   lines

%union   {
        int ival;
        double dval;
        INTERVAL vval;
        }

%token <ival> DREG VREG        /* indices into dreg, vreg arrays */

%token <dval> CONST            /* floating point constant */

%type <dval> dexp          /* expression */

%type <vval> vexp          /* interval expression */

        /* precedence information about the operators */

%left   '+' '-'
%left   '*' '/'
%left   UMINUS        /* precedence for unary minus */

%%

lines   :       /* empty */
        |       lines line
        ;

line    :       dexp '\n'
                        {       printf( "%15.8f\n", $1 ); }
        |       vexp '\n'
                        {       printf( "(%15.8f , %15.8f )\n", $1.lo, $1.hi ); }
        |       DREG '=' dexp '\n'
                        {       dreg[$1] = $3; }
        |       VREG '=' vexp '\n'
```

```
                        {           vreg[$1]  =  $3; }
        |       error '\n'
                        {           yyerrok; }
        ;


dexp    :       CONST
        |       DREG
                        {           $$  =  dreg[$1]; }
        |       dexp '+' dexp
                        {           $$  =  $1  +  $3; }
        |       dexp '−' dexp
                        {           $$  =  $1  −  $3; }
        |       dexp '*' dexp
                        {           $$  =  $1  *  $3; }
        |       dexp '/' dexp
                        {           $$  =  $1  /  $3; }
        |       '−' dexp        %prec UMINUS
                        {           $$  =  − $2; }
        |       '(' dexp ')'
                        {           $$  =  $2; }
        ;


vexp    :       dexp
                        {           $$.hi  =  $$.lo  =  $1; }
        |       '(' dexp ',' dexp ')'
                        {
                        $$.lo  =  $2;
                        $$.hi  =  $4;
                        if( $$.lo  >  $$.hi ){
                                printf( "interval  out  of  order\n" );
                                YYERROR;
                                }
                        }
        |       VREG
                        {           $$  =  vreg[$1];   }
        |       vexp '+' vexp
                        {           $$.hi  =  $1.hi  +  $3.hi;
                                    $$.lo  =  $1.lo  +  $3.lo;   }
        |       dexp '+' vexp
                        {           $$.hi  =  $1  +  $3.hi;
                                    $$.lo  =  $1  +  $3.lo;    }
        |       vexp '−' vexp
                        {           $$.hi  =  $1.hi  −  $3.lo;
                                    $$.lo  =  $1.lo  −  $3.hi;    }
        |       dexp '−' vexp
                        {           $$.hi  =  $1  −  $3.lo;
                                    $$.lo  =  $1  −  $3.hi;    }
        |       vexp '*' vexp
                        {           $$  =  vmul( $1.lo, $1.hi, $3 ); }
        |       dexp '*' vexp
                        {           $$  =  vmul( $1, $1, $3 ); }
        |       vexp '/' vexp
                        {           if( dcheck( $3 ) ) YYERROR;
                                    $$  =  vdiv( $1.lo, $1.hi, $3 ); }
```

```
        |       dexp '/' vexp
                        {       if( dcheck( $3 ) ) YYERROR;
                                $$ = vdiv( $1, $1, $3 ); }
        |       '−' vexp        %prec UMINUS
                        {       $$.hi = −$2.lo;    $$.lo = −$2.hi;  }
        |       '(' vexp ')'
                        {       $$ = $2; }
        ;

%%

# define BSZ 50        /* buffer size for floating point numbers */

        /* lexical analysis */

yylex(){
        register c;

        while( (c=getchar()) == ' ' ){ /* skip over blanks */ }

        if( isupper( c ) ){
                yylval.ival = c − 'A';
                return( VREG );
                }
        if( islower( c ) ){
                yylval.ival = c − 'a';
                return( DREG );
                }

        if( isdigit( c ) || c=='.' ){
                /* gobble up digits, points, exponents */

                char buf[BSZ+1], *cp = buf;
                int dot = 0, exp = 0;

                for( ; (cp−buf)<BSZ ; ++cp,c=getchar() ){

                        *cp = c;
                        if( isdigit( c ) ) continue;
                        if( c == '.' ){
                                if( dot++ || exp ) return( '.' );   /* will cause syntax error */
                                continue;
                                }

                        if( c == 'e' ){
                                if( exp++ ) return( 'e' );   /* will cause syntax error */
                                continue;
                                }

                        /* end of number */
                        break;
                        }
                *cp = '\0';
                if( (cp−buf) >= BSZ ) printf( "constant too long: truncated\n" );
```

```
                  else ungetc( c, stdin );   /* push back last char read */
                  yylval.dval = atof( buf );
                  return( CONST );
                  }
            return( c );
            }

INTERVAL hilo( a, b, c, d ) double a, b, c, d; {
      /* returns the smallest interval containing a, b, c, and d */
      /* used by *, / routines */
      INTERVAL v;

      if( a>b ) { v.hi = a;   v.lo = b; }
      else { v.hi = b;   v.lo = a; }

      if( c>d ) {
            if( c>v.hi ) v.hi = c;
            if( d<v.lo ) v.lo = d;
            }
      else {
            if( d>v.hi ) v.hi = d;
            if( c<v.lo ) v.lo = c;
            }
      return( v );
      }

INTERVAL vmul( a, b, v ) double a, b;   INTERVAL v; {
      return( hilo( a*v.hi, a*v.lo, b*v.hi, b*v.lo ) );
      }

dcheck( v ) INTERVAL v; {
      if( v.hi >= 0. && v.lo <= 0. ){
            printf( "divisor interval contains 0.\n" );
            return( 1 );
            }
      return( 0 );
      }

INTERVAL vdiv( a, b, v ) double a, b;   INTERVAL v; {
      return( hilo( a/v.hi, a/v.lo, b/v.hi, b/v.lo ) );
      }
```

Appendix D: Old Features Supported but not Encouraged

This Appendix mentions synonyms and features which are supported for historical continuity, but, for various reasons, are not encouraged.

1.   Literals may also be delimited by double quotes ''"''.

2.   Literals may be more than one character long. If all the characters are alphabetic, numeric, or _, the type number of the literal is defined, just as if the literal did not have the quotes around it. Otherwise, it is difficult to find the value for such literals.

   The use of multi-character literals is likely to mislead those unfamiliar with Yacc, since it suggests that Yacc is doing a job which must be actually done by the lexical analyzer.

3.   Most places where % is legal, backslash ''\'' may be used. In particular, \\ is the same as %%, \left the same as %left, etc.

4.   There are a number of other synonyms:

   %< is the same as %left
   %> is the same as %right
   %binary and %2 are the same as %nonassoc
   %0 and %term are the same as %token
   %= is the same as %prec

5.   Actions may also have the form

   ={ ... }

   and the curly braces can be dropped if the action is a single C statement.

6.   C code between %{ and %} used to be permitted at the head of the rules section, as well as in the declaration section.

Lex - A Lexical Analyzer Generator

M. E. Lesk and E. Schmidt

Bell Laboratories
Murray Hill, New Jersey 07974

Lex helps write programs whose control flow is directed by instances of regular expressions in the input stream. It is well suited for editor-script type transformations and for segmenting input in preparation for a parsing routine.

Lex source is a table of regular expressions and corresponding program fragments. The table is translated to a program which reads an input stream, copying it to an output stream and partitioning the input into strings which match the given expressions. As each such string is recognized the corresponding program fragment is executed. The recognition of the expressions is performed by a deterministic finite automaton generated by Lex. The program fragments written by the user are executed in the order in which the corresponding regular expressions occur in the input stream.

The lexical analysis programs written with Lex accept ambiguous specifications and choose the longest match possible at each input point. If necessary, substantial lookahead is performed on the input, but the input stream will be backed up to the end of the current partition, so that the user has general freedom to manipulate it.

Lex can be used to generate analyzers in either C or Ratfor, a language which can be translated automatically to portable Fortran. It is available on the PDP-11 UNIX, Honeywell GCOS, and IBM OS systems. Lex is designed to simplify interfacing with Yacc, for those with access to this compiler-compiler system.

Contents

1. Introduction.
2. Lex Source.
3. Lex Regular Expressions.
4. Lex Actions.
5. Ambiguous Source Rules.
6. Lex Source Definitions.
7. Usage.
8. Lex and Yacc.
9. Examples.
10. Left Context Sensitivity.
11. Character Set.
12. Summary of Source Format.
13. Caveats and Bugs.
14. Acknowledgments.
15. References.

1 Introduction.

Lex is a program generator designed for lexical processing of character input streams. It accepts a high-level, problem oriented specification for character string matching, and produces a program in a general purpose language which recognizes regular expressions. The regular expressions are specified by the user in the source specifications given to Lex. The Lex written code recognizes these expressions in an input stream and partitions the input stream into strings matching the expressions. At the boundaries between strings program sections provided by the user are executed. The Lex source file associates the regular expressions and the program fragments. As each expression appears in the input to the program written by Lex, the corresponding fragment is executed.

The user supplies the additional code beyond expression matching needed to complete his tasks, possibly including code written by other generators. The program that recognizes the expressions is generated in the general purpose programming language employed for the user's program fragments. Thus, a high level expression language is provided to write the string expressions to be matched while the user's freedom to write actions is unimpaired. This avoids forcing the user who wishes to use a string manipulation language for input analysis to

Source → [Lex] → yylex

Input → [yylex] → Output

An overview of Lex

Figure 1

write processing programs in the same and often inappropriate string handling language.

Lex is not a complete language, but rather a generator representing a new language feature which can be added to different programming languages, called "host languages." Just as general purpose languages can produce code to run on different computer hardware, Lex can write code in different host languages. The host language is used for the output code generated by Lex and also for the program fragments added by the user. Compatible run-time libraries for the different host languages are also provided. This makes Lex adaptable to different environments and different users. Each application may be directed to the combination of hardware and host language appropriate to the task, the user's background, and the properties of local implementations. At present there are only two host languages, C[1] and Fortran (in the form of the Ratfor language[2]). 'Lex itself exists on UNIX, GCOS, and OS/370; but the code generated by Lex may be taken anywhere the appropriate compilers exist.

Lex turns the user's expressions and actions (called *source* in this memo) into the host general-purpose language; the generated program is named *yylex*. The *yylex* program will recognize expressions in a stream (called *input* in this memo) and perform the specified actions for each expression as it is detected. See Figure 1.

For a trivial example, consider a program to delete from the input all blanks or tabs at the ends of lines.

```
%%
[ \t]+$   ;
```

is all that is required. The program contains a %% delimiter to mark the beginning of the rules, and one rule.

This rule contains a regular expression which matches one or more instances of the characters blank or tab (written \t for visibility, in accordance with the C language convention) just prior to the end of a line. The brackets indicate the character class made of blank and tab; the + indicates "one or more ..."; and the $ indicates "end of line," as in QED. No action is specified, so the program generated by Lex (yylex) will ignore these characters. Everything else will be copied. To change any remaining string of blanks or tabs to a single blank, add another rule:

```
%%
[ \t]+$    ;
[ \t]+     printf(" ");
```

The finite automaton generated for this source will scan for both rules at once, observing at the termination of the string of blanks or tabs whether or not there is a newline character, and executing the desired rule action. The first rule matches all strings of blanks or tabs at the end of lines, and the second rule all remaining strings of blanks or tabs.

Lex can be used alone for simple transformations, or for analysis and statistics gathering on a lexical level. Lex can also be used with a parser generator to perform the lexical analysis phase; it is particularly easy to interface Lex and Yacc [3]. Lex programs recognize only regular expressions; Yacc writes parsers that accept a large class of context free grammars, but require a lower level analyzer to recognize input tokens. Thus, a combination of Lex and Yacc is often appropriate. When used as a preprocessor for a later parser generator, Lex is used to partition the input stream, and the parser generator assigns structure to the resulting pieces. The flow of control in such a case (which might be the first half of a compiler, for example) is shown in Figure 2. Additional programs, written by other generators or by hand, can be added easily to programs written by Lex. Yacc users will realize that the name *yylex* is what Yacc expects its lexical analyzer to be named, so that the use of this name by Lex simplifies interfacing.

Lex generates a deterministic finite automaton from the regular expressions in the source [4]. The automaton is interpreted, rather than compiled, in order to save space. The result is still a fast analyzer. In particular, the time

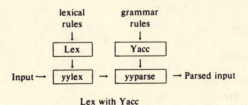

Lex with Yacc

Figure 2

taken by a Lex program to recognize and partition an input stream is proportional to the length of the input. The number of Lex rules or the complexity of the rules is not important in determining speed, unless rules which include forward context require a significant amount of rescanning. What does increase with the number and complexity of rules is the size of the finite automaton, and therefore the size of the program generated by Lex.

In the program written by Lex, the user's fragments (representing the *actions* to be performed as each regular expression is found) are gathered as cases of a switch (in C) or branches of a computed GOTO (in Ratfor). The automaton interpreter directs the control flow. Opportunity is provided for the user to insert either declarations or additional statements in the routine containing the actions, or to add subroutines outside this action routine.

Lex is not limited to source which can be interpreted on the basis of one character lookahead. For example, if there are two rules, one looking for *ab* and another for *abcdefg*, and the input stream is *abcdefh*, Lex will recognize *ab* and leave the input pointer just before *cd*. . . Such backup is more costly than the processing of simpler languages.

2 Lex Source.

The general format of Lex source is:

```
{definitions}
%%
{rules}
%%
{user subroutines}
```

where the definitions and the user subroutines are often omitted. The second %% is optional, but the first is required to mark the beginning of the rules. The absolute minimum Lex program is thus

```
%%
```

(no definitions, no rules) which translates into a program which copies the input to the output unchanged.

In the outline of Lex programs shown above, the *rules* represent the user's control decisions; they are a table, in which the left column contains *regular expressions* (see section 3) and the right column contains *actions*, program fragments to be executed when the expressions are recognized. Thus an individual rule might appear

```
integer    printf("found keyword INT");
```

to look for the string *integer* in the input stream and print the message "found keyword INT" whenever it appears. In this example the host procedural language is C and the C library function *printf* is used to print the string. The end of the expression is indicated by the first blank or tab character. If the action is merely a single C expression, it can just be given on the right side of the line; if it is compound, or takes more than a line, it should be enclosed in braces. As a slightly more useful example, suppose it is desired to change a number of words from British to American spelling. Lex rules such as

```
colour      printf("color");
mechanise   printf("mechanize");
petrol      printf("gas");
```

would be a start. These rules are not quite enough, since the word *petroleum* would become *gaseum*, a way of dealing with this will be described later.

3 Lex Regular Expressions.

The definitions of regular expressions are very similar to those in QED [5]. A regular expression specifies a set of strings to be matched. It contains text characters (which match the corresponding characters in the strings being compared) and operator characters (which specify repetitions, choices, and other features). The letters of the alphabet and the digits are always text characters; thus the regular expression

```
integer
```

matches the string *integer* wherever it appears and the expression

```
a57D
```

looks for the string *a57D*.

Operators. The operator characters are

```
" \ [ ] ^ - ? . * + | ( ) $ / { } % < >
```

and if they are to be used as text characters, an escape should be used. The quotation mark operator (") indicates that whatever is contained between a pair of quotes is to be taken as text characters. Thus

```
xyz"++"
```

matches the string *xyz++* when it appears. Note that a part of a string may be quoted. It is harmless but unnecessary to quote an ordinary text character; the expression

```
"xyz++"
```

is the same as the one above. Thus by quoting every non-alphanumeric character being used as a text character, the user can avoid remembering the list above of current operator characters, and is safe should further extensions to Lex lengthen the list.

An operator character may also be turned into a text character by preceding it with \ as in

```
xyz\+\+
```

which is another, less readable, equivalent of the above

expressions. Another use of the quoting mechanism is to get a blank into an expression; normally, as explained above, blanks or tabs end a rule. Any blank character not contained within [] (see below) must be quoted. Several normal C escapes with \ are recognized: \n is newline, \t is tab, and \b is backspace. To enter \ itself, use \\. Since newline is illegal in an expression, \n must be used; it is not required to escape tab and backspace. Every character but blank, tab, newline and the list above is always a text character.

Character classes. Classes of characters can be specified using the operator pair []. The construction *[ab]* matches a single character, which may be *a*, *b*, or *c*. Within square brackets, most operator meanings are ignored. Only three characters are special: these are \ — and ˆ. The − character indicates ranges. For example,

$$[a-z0-9<>\_]$$

indicates the character class containing all the lower case letters, the digits, the angle brackets, and underline. Ranges may be given in either order. Using − between any pair of characters which are not both upper case letters, both lower case letters, or both digits is implementation dependent and will get a warning message. (E.g., [0-z] in ASCII is many more characters than it is in EBCDIC). If it is desired to include the character − in a character class, it should be first or last; thus

$$[-+0-9]$$

matches all the digits and the two signs.

In character classes, the ˆ operator must appear as the first character after the left bracket; it indicates that the resulting string is to be complemented with respect to the computer character set. Thus

$$[\hat{}abc]$$

matches all characters except a, b, or c, including all special or control characters; or

$$[\hat{}a-zA-Z]$$

is any character which is not a letter. The \ character provides the usual escapes within character class brackets.

Arbitrary character. To match almost any character, the operator character

.

is the class of all characters except newline. Escaping into octal is possible although non-portable:

$$[\backslash40-\backslash176]$$

matches all printable characters in the ASCII character set, from octal 40 (blank) to octal 176 (tilde).

Optional expressions. The operator *?* indicates an optional element of an expression. Thus

$$ab?c$$

matches either *ac* or *abc*.

Repeated expressions. Repetitions of classes are indicated by the operators ∗ and +.

$$a*$$

is any number of consecutive *a* characters, including zero; while

$$a+$$

is one or more instances of *a*. For example,

$$[a-z]+$$

is all strings of lower case letters. And

$$[A-Za-z][A-Za-z0-9]*$$

indicates all alphanumeric strings with a leading alphabetic character. This is a typical expression for recognizing identifiers in computer languages.

Alternation and Grouping. The operator | indicates alternation:

$$(ab|cd)$$

matches either *ab* or *cd*. Note that parentheses are used for grouping, although they are not necessary on the outside level;

$$ab|cd$$

would have sufficed. Parentheses can be used for more complex expressions:

$$(ab|cd+)?(ef)*$$

matches such strings as *abefef*, *efefef*, *cdef*, or *cddd*; but not *abc*, *abcd*, or *abcdef*.

Context sensitivity. Lex will recognize a small amount of surrounding context. The two simplest operators for this are ˆ and *$*. If the first character of an expression is ˆ, the expression will only be matched at the beginning of a line (after a newline character, or at the beginning of the input stream). This can never conflict with the other meaning of ˆ, complementation of character classes, since that only applies within the [] operators. If the very last character is *$*, the expression will only be matched at the end of a line (when immediately followed by newline). The latter operator is a special case of the / operator character, which indicates trailing context. The expression

$$ab/cd$$

matches the string *ab*, but only if followed by *cd*. Thus

ab$

is the same as

ab/\n

Left context is handled in Lex by *start conditions* as explained in section 10. If a rule is only to be executed when the Lex automaton interpreter is in start condition *x*, the rule should be prefixed by

<x>

using the angle bracket operator characters. If we considered ''being at the beginning of a line'' to be start condition *ONE*, then the ˆ operator would be equivalent to

<ONE>

Start conditions are explained more fully later.

Repetitions and Definitions. The operators {} specify either repetitions (if they enclose numbers) or definition expansion (if they enclose a name). For example

{digit}

looks for a predefined string named *digit* and inserts it at that point in the expression. The definitions are given in the first part of the Lex input, before the rules. In contrast,

a{1,5}

looks for 1 to 5 occurrences of *a*.

Finally, initial % is special, being the separator for Lex source segments.

4 Lex Actions.

When an expression written as above is matched, Lex executes the corresponding action. This section describes some features of Lex which aid in writing actions. Note that there is a default action, which consists of copying the input to the output. This is performed on all strings not otherwise matched. Thus the Lex user who wishes to absorb the entire input, without producing any output, must provide rules to match everything. When Lex is being used with Yacc, this is the normal situation. One may consider that actions are what is done instead of copying the input to the output; thus, in general, a rule which merely copies can be omitted. Also, a character combination which is omitted from the rules and which appears as input is likely to be printed on the output, thus calling attention to the gap in the rules.

One of the simplest things that can be done is to ignore the input. Specifying a C null statement, *;* as an action causes this result. A frequent rule is

[\t\n]   ;

which causes the three spacing characters (blank, tab, and newline) to be ignored.

Another easy way to avoid writing actions is the action character |, which indicates that the action for this rule is the action for the next rule. The previous example could also have been written

```
" "
"\t"
"\n"
```

with the same result, although in different style. The quotes around \n and \t are not required.

In more complex actions, the user will often want to know the actual text that matched some expression like *[a−z]+*. Lex leaves this text in an external character array named *yytext*. Thus, to print the name found, a rule like

[a-z]+   printf("%s", yytext);

will print the string in *yytext*. The C function *printf* accepts a format argument and data to be printed; in this case, the format is ''print string'' (% indicating data conversion, and *s* indicating string type), and the data are the characters in *yytext*. So this just places the matched string on the output. This action is so common that it may be written as ECHO:

[a-z]+   ECHO;

is the same as the above. Since the default action is just to print the characters found, one might ask why give a rule, like this one, which merely specifies the default action? Such rules are often required to avoid matching some other rule which is not desired. For example, if there is a rule which matches *read* it will normally match the instances of *read* contained in *bread* or *readjust*, to avoid this, a rule of the form *[a−z]+* is needed. This is explained further below.

Sometimes it is more convenient to know the end of what has been found; hence Lex also provides a count *yyleng* of the number of characters matched. To count both the number of words and the number of characters in words in the input, the user might write

[a-zA-Z]+   {words++; chars += yyleng;}

which accumulates in *chars* the number of characters in the words recognized. The last character in the string matched can be accessed by

yytext[yyleng-1]

in C or

yytext(yyleng)

in Ratfor.

Occasionally, a Lex action may decide that a rule has not recognized the correct span of characters. Two routines are provided to aid with this situation. First, *yymore()* can be called to indicate that the next input expression recognized is to be tacked on to the end of this input. Normally, the next input string would overwrite the current entry in *yytext*. Second, *yyless (n)* may be called to indicate that not all the characters matched by the currently successful expression are wanted right now. The argument *n* indicates the number of characters in *yytext* to be retained. Further characters previously matched are returned to the input. This provides the same sort of lookahead offered by the / operator, but in a different form.

Example: Consider a language which defines a string as a set of characters between quotation (") marks, and provides that to include a " in a string it must be preceded by a \. The regular expression which matches that is somewhat confusing, so that it might be preferable to write

```
\"[^"]*    {
           if (yytext[yyleng-1] == '\\')
               yymore();
           else
               ... normal user processing
           }
```

which will, when faced with a string such as *"abc\"def"* first match the five characters *"abc*; then the call to *yymore()* will cause the next part of the string, *"def*, to be tacked on the end. Note that the final quote terminating the string should be picked up in the code labeled "normal processing".

The function *yyless()* might be used to reprocess text in various circumstances. Consider the C problem of distinguishing the ambiguity of "=−a". Suppose it is desired to treat this as "=− a" but print a message. A rule might be

```
=−[a-zA-Z]    {
              printf("Operator (=−) ambiguous\n");
              yyless(yyleng-1);
              ... action for =− ...
              }
```

which prints a message, returns the letter after the operator to the input stream, and treats the operator as "=−". Alternatively it might be desired to treat this as "= −a". To do this, just return the minus sign as well as the letter to the input:

```
=−[a-zA-Z]    {
              printf("Operator (=−) ambiguous\n");
              yyless(yyleng-2);
              ... action for = ...
              }
```

will perform the other interpretation. Note that the expressions for the two cases might more easily be written

$$=−/[A\text{-}Za\text{-}z]$$

in the first case and

$$=/\text{-}[A\text{-}Za\text{-}z]$$

in the second; no backup would be required in the rule action. It is not necessary to recognize the whole identifier to observe the ambiguity. The possibility of "=−3", however, makes

$$=−/[^{\hat{}} \text{\t\n}]$$

a still better rule.

In addition to these routines, Lex also permits access to the I/O routines it uses. They are:

1) *input()* which returns the next input character;
2) *output(c)* which writes the character *c* on the output; and
3) *unput(c)* pushes the character *c* back onto the input stream to be read later by *input()*.

By default these routines are provided as macro definitions, but the user can override them and supply private versions. There is another important routine in Ratfor, named *lexshf*, which is described below under "Character Set". These routines define the relationship between external files and internal characters, and must all be retained or modified consistently. They may be redefined, to cause input or output to be transmitted to or from strange places, including other programs or internal memory; but the character set used must be consistent in all routines; a value of zero returned by *input* must mean end of file; and the relationship between *unput* and *input* must be retained or the Lex lookahead will not work. Lex does not look ahead at all if it does not have to, but every rule ending in + * ? or $ or containing / implies lookahead. Lookahead is also necessary to match an expression that is a prefix of another expression. See below for a discussion of the character set used by Lex. The standard Lex library imposes a 100 character limit on backup.

Another Lex library routine that the user will sometimes want to redefine is *yywrap()* which is called whenever Lex reaches an end-of-file. If *yywrap* returns a 1, Lex continues with the normal wrapup on end of input. Sometimes, however, it is convenient to arrange for more input to arrive from a new source. In this case, the user should provide a *yywrap* which arranges for new input and returns 0. This instructs Lex to continue processing. The default *yywrap* always returns 1.

This routine is also a convenient place to print tables, summaries, etc. at the end of a program. Note that it is not possible to write a normal rule which recognizes end-of-file; the only access to this condition is through *yywrap*. In fact, unless a private version of *input()* is supplied a file containing nulls cannot be handled, since a value of 0 returned by *input* is taken to be end-of-file.

In Ratfor all of the standard I/O library routines, *input, output*, *unput*, *yywrap*, and *lexshf*, are defined as integer functions. This requires *input* and *yywrap* to be called with arguments. One dummy argument is supplied and ignored.

5 Ambiguous Source Rules.

Lex can handle ambiguous specifications. When more than one expression can match the current input, Lex chooses as follows:

1) The longest match is preferred.
2) Among rules which matched the same number of characters, the rule given first is preferred.

Thus, suppose the rules

```
integer    keyword action ...;
[a-z]+     identifier action ...;
```

to be given in that order. If the input is *integers*, it is taken as an identifier, because *[a-z]+* matches 8 characters while *integer* matches only 7. If the input is *integer*, both rules match 7 characters, and the keyword rule is selected because it was given first. Anything shorter (e.g. *int*) will not match the expression *integer* and so the identifier interpretation is used.

The principle of preferring the longest match makes rules containing expressions like .* dangerous. For example,

```
'.*'
```

might seem a good way of recognizing a string in single quotes. But it is an invitation for the program to read far ahead, looking for a distant single quote. Presented with the input

```
'first' quoted string here, 'second' here
```

the above expression will match

```
'first' quoted string here, 'second'
```

which is probably not what was wanted. A better rule is of the form

```
'[^\n]*'
```

which, on the above input, will stop after *'first'*. The consequences of errors like this are mitigated by the fact that the . operator will not match newline. Thus expressions like .* stop on the current line. Don't try to defeat this with expressions like [.\n]+ or equivalents; the Lex generated program will try to read the entire input file, causing internal buffer overflows.

Note that Lex is normally partitioning the input stream, not searching for all possible matches of each expression. This means that each character is accounted for once and only once. For example, suppose it is desired to count occurrences of both *she* and *he* in an input text. Some

Lex rules to do this might be

```
she    s++;
he     h++;
\n     |
.      ;
```

where the last two rules ignore everything besides *he* and *she*. Remember that . does not include newline. Since *she* includes *he*, Lex will normally **not** recognize the instances of *he* included in *she*, since once it has passed a *she* those characters are gone.

Sometimes the user would like to override this choice. The action REJECT means "go do the next alternative." It causes whatever rule was second choice after the current rule to be executed. The position of the input pointer is adjusted accordingly. Suppose the user really wants to count the included instances of *he*:

```
she    {s++; REJECT;}
he     {h++; REJECT;}
\n     |
.      ;
```

these rules are one way of changing the previous example to do just that. After counting each expression, it is rejected; whenever appropriate, the other expression will then be counted. In this example, of course, the user could note that *she* includes *he* but not vice versa, and omit the REJECT action on *he*, in other cases, however, it would not be possible a priori to tell which input characters were in both classes.

Consider the two rules

```
a[bc]+    { ... ; REJECT;}
a[cd]+    { ... ; REJECT;}
```

If the input is *ab*, only the first rule matches, and on *ad* only the second matches. The input string *accb* matches the first rule for four characters and then the second rule for three characters. In contrast, the input *accd* agrees with the second rule for four characters and then the first rule for three.

In general, REJECT is useful whenever the purpose of Lex is not to partition the input stream but to detect all examples of some items in the input, and the instances of these items may overlap or include each other. Suppose a digram table of the input is desired; normally the digrams overlap, that is the word *the* is considered to contain both *th* and *he*. Assuming a two-dimensional array named *digram* to be incremented, the appropriate source is

```
%%
[a-z][a-z]    {digram[yytext[0]][yytext[1]]++; REJECT;}
\n            ;
```

where the REJECT is necessary to pick up a letter pair beginning at every character, rather than at every other character.

6 Lex Source Definitions.

Remember the format of the Lex source:

```
{definitions}
%%
{rules}
%%
{user routines}
```

So far only the rules have been described. The user needs additional options, though, to define variables for use in his program and for use by Lex. These can go either in the definitions section or in the rules section.

Remember that Lex is turning the rules into a program. Any source not intercepted by Lex is copied into the generated program. There are three classes of such things.

1) Any line which is not part of a Lex rule or action which begins with a blank or tab is copied into the Lex generated program. Such source input prior to the first %% delimiter will be external to any function in the code; if it appears immediately after the first %%, it appears in an appropriate place for declarations in the function written by Lex which contains the actions. This material must look like program fragments, and should precede the first Lex rule.

As a side effect of the above, lines which begin with a blank or tab, and which contain a comment, are passed through to the generated program. This can be used to include comments in either the Lex source or the generated code. The comments should follow the host language convention.

2) Anything included between lines containing only %{ and %} is copied out as above. The delimiters are discarded. This format permits entering text like preprocessor statements that must begin in column 1, or copying lines that do not look like programs.

3) Anything after the third %% delimiter, regardless of formats, etc., is copied out after the Lex output.

Definitions intended for Lex are given before the first %% delimiter. Any line in this section not contained between %{ and %}, and begining in column 1, is assumed to define Lex substitution strings. The format of such lines is

name translation

and it causes the string given as a translation to be associated with the name. The name and translation must be separated by at least one blank or tab, and the name must begin with a letter. The translation can then be called out by the {name} syntax in a rule. Using {D} for the digits and {E} for an exponent field, for example, might abbreviate rules to recognize numbers:

```
D                 [0-9]
E                 [TEde][-+]?{D}+
%%
{D}+              printf("integer");
{D}+"."{D}*({E})?  |
{D}*"."{D}+({E})?  |
{D}+{E}
```

Note the first two rules for real numbers; both require a decimal point and contain an optional exponent field, but the first requires at least one digit before the decimal point and the second requires at least one digit after the decimal point. To correctly handle the problem posed by a Fortran expression such as *35.EQ.I*, which does not contain a real number, a context-sensitive rule such as

```
[0-9]+/"."EQ    printf("integer");
```

could be used in addition to the normal rule for integers.

The definitions section may also contain other commands, including the selection of a host language, a character set table, a list of start conditions, or adjustments to the default size of arrays within Lex itself for larger source programs. These possibilities are discussed below under "Summary of Source Format," section 12.

7 Usage.

There are two steps in compiling a Lex source program. First, the Lex source must be turned into a generated program in the host general purpose language. Then this program must be compiled and loaded, usually with a library of Lex subroutines. The generated program is on a file named *lex.yy.c* for a C host language source and *lex.yy.r* for a Ratfor host environment. There are two I/O libraries, one for C defined in terms of the C standard library [6], and the other defined in terms of Ratfor. To indicate that a Lex source file is intended to be used with the Ratfor host language, make the first line of the file *%R*.

The C programs generated by Lex are slightly different on OS/370, because the OS compiler is less powerful than the UNIX or GCOS compilers, and does less at compile time. C programs generated on GCOS and UNIX are the same. The C host language is default, but may be explicitly requested by making the first line of the source file *%C*.

The Ratfor generated by Lex is the same on all systems, but can not be compiled directly on TSO. See below for instructions. The Ratfor I/O library, however, varies slightly because the different Fortrans disagree on the method of indicating end-of-input and the name of the library routine for logical AND. The Ratfor I/O library, dependent on Fortran character I/O, is quite slow. In particular it reads all input lines as 80A1 format; this will truncate any longer line, discarding your data, and pads any shorter line with blanks. The library version of *input* removes the padding (including any trailing blanks from the original input) before processing. Each source file using a Ratfor host should begin with the "%R" command.

UNIX. The libraries are accessed by the loader flags *-llc* for C and *-llr* for Ratfor; the C name may be abbreviated to *-ll.* So an appropriate set of commands is

C Host	Ratfor Host
lex source	lex source
cc lex.yy.c -ll -lS	rc -2 lex.yy.r -llr

The resulting program is placed on the usual file *a.out* for later execution. To use Lex with Yacc see below. Although the default Lex I/O routines use the C standard library, the Lex automata themselves do not do so; if private versions of *input, output* and *unput* are given, the library can be avoided. Note the "-2" option in the Ratfor compile command; this requests the larger version of the compiler, a useful precaution.

GCOS. The Lex commands on GCOS are stored in the "." library. The appropriate command sequences are:

C Host	Ratfor Host
./lex source	./lex source
./cc lex.yy.c ./lexclib h=	./rc a= lex.yy.r ./lexrlib h=

The resulting program is placed on the usual file *.program* for later execution (as indicated by the "h=" option); it may be copied to a permanent file if desired. Note the "a=" option in the Ratfor compile command; this indicates that the Fortran compiler is to run in ASCII mode.

TSO. Lex is just barely available on TSO. Restrictions imposed by the compilers which must be used with its output make it rather inconvenient. To use the C version, type

    exec 'dot.lex.clist(lex)' 'sourcename'
    exec 'dot.lex.clist(cload)' 'libraryname membername'

The first command analyzes the source file and writes a C program on file *lex.yy.text.* The second command runs this file through the C compiler and links it with the Lex C library (stored on 'hr289.lcl.load') placing the object program in your file *libraryname.LOAD(membername)* as a completely linked load module. The compiling command uses a special version of the C compiler command on TSO which provides an unusually large intermediate assembler file to compensate for the unusual bulk of C-compiled Lex programs on the OS system. Even so, almost any Lex source program is too big to compile, and must be split.

The same Lex command will compile Ratfor Lex programs, leaving a file *lex.yy.rat* instead of *lex.yy.text* in your directory. The Ratfor program must be edited, however, to compensate for peculiarities of IBM Ratfor. A command sequence to do this, and then compile and load, is available. The full commands are:

    exec 'dot.lex.clist(lex)' 'sourcename'

    exec 'dot.lex.clist(rload)' 'libraryname membername'

with the same overall effect as the C language commands. However, the Ratfor commands will run in a 150K byte partition, while the C commands require 250K bytes to operate.

The steps involved in processing the generated Ratfor program are:

a. Edit the Ratfor program.
1. Remove all tabs.
2. Change all lower case letters to upper case letters.
3. Convert the file to an 80-column card image file.
b. Process the Ratfor through the Ratfor preprocessor to get Fortran code.
c. Compile the Fortran.
d. Load with the libraries 'hr289.lrl.load' and 'sys1.fortlib'.

The final load module will only read input in 80-character fixed length records. *Warning:* Work is in progress on the IBM C compiler, and Lex and its availability on the IBM 370 are subject to change without notice.

8 Lex and Yacc.

If you want to use Lex with Yacc, note that what Lex writes is a program named *yylex()*, the name required by Yacc for its analyzer. Normally, the default main program on the Lex library calls this routine, but if Yacc is loaded, and its main program is used, Yacc will call *yylex()*. In this case each Lex rule should end with

    return(token);

where the appropriate token value is returned. An easy way to get access to Yacc's names for tokens is to compile the Lex output file as part of the Yacc output file by placing the line

    # include "lex.yy.c"

in the last section of Yacc input. Supposing the grammar to be named "good" and the lexical rules to be named "better" the UNIX command sequence can just be:

    yacc good
    lex better
    cc y.tab.c -ly -ll -lS

The Yacc library (-ly) should be loaded before the Lex library, to obtain a main program which invokes the Yacc parser. The generations of Lex and Yacc programs can be done in either order.

9 Examples.

As a trivial problem, consider copying an input file while adding 3 to every positive number divisible by 7. Here is a suitable Lex source program

```
%%
                int k;
[0-9]+      {
            scanf(-1, yytext, "%d", &k);
            if (k%7 == 0)
                printf("%d", k+3);
            else
                printf("%d",k);
            }
```

to do just that. The rule [0-9]+ recognizes strings of digits; *scanf* converts the digits to binary and stores the result in *k*. The operator % (remainder) is used to check whether *k* is divisible by 7; if it is, it is incremented by 3 as it is written out. It may be objected that this program will alter such input items as *49.63* or *X7*. Furthermore, it increments the absolute value of all negative numbers divisible by 7. To avoid this, just add a few more rules after the active one, as here:

```
%%
                    int k;
-?[0-9]+        {
                scanf(-1, yytext, "%d", &k);
                printf("%d", k%7 == 0 ? k+3 : k);
                }
-?[0-9.]+          ECHO;
[A-Za-z][A-Za-z0-9]+    ECHO;
```

Numerical strings containing a "." or preceded by a letter will be picked up by one of the last two rules, and not changed. The *if-else* has been replaced by a C conditional expression to save space; the form *a?b:c* means "if *a* then *b* else *c*".

For an example of statistics gathering, here is a program which histograms the lengths of words, where a word is defined as a string of letters.

```
            int lengs[100];
%%
[a-z]+      lengs[yyleng]++;
.           |
\n          ;
%%
yywrap()
{
int i;
printf("Length  No. words\n");
for(i=0; i<100; i++)
    if (lengs[i] > 0)
        printf("%5d%10d\n",i,lengs[i]);
return(1);
}
```

This program accumulates the histogram, while producing no output. At the end of the input it prints the table. The final statement *return(1);* indicates that Lex is to perform wrapup. If *yywrap* returns zero (false) it implies that further input is available and the program is to continue reading and processing. To provide a *yywrap* that never returns true causes an infinite loop.

As a larger example, here are some parts of a program written by N. L. Schryer to convert double precision Fortran to single precision Fortran. Because Fortran does not distinguish upper and lower case letters, this routine begins by defining a set of classes including both cases of each letter:

```
a   [aA]
b   [bB]
c   [cC]
...
z   [zZ]
```

An additional class recognizes white space:

```
W   [ \t]*
```

The first rule changes "double precision" to "real", or "DOUBLE PRECISION" to "REAL".

```
{d}{o}{u}{b}{l}{e}{W}{p}{r}{e}{c}{i}{s}{i}{o}{n} {
    printf(yytext[0]=='d'? "real" : "REAL");
    }
```

Care is taken throughout this program to preserve the case (upper or lower) of the original program. The conditional operator is used to select the proper form of the keyword. The next rule copies continuation card indications to avoid confusing them with constants:

```
^"     "[^ 0]   ECHO;
```

In the regular expression, the quotes surround the blanks. It is interpreted as "beginning of line, then five blanks, then anything but blank or zero." Note the two different meanings of ^. There follow some rules to change double precision constants to ordinary floating constants.

```
[0-9]+{W}{d}{W}[+-]?{W}[0-9]+     |
[0-9]+{W}"."{W}{d}{W}[+-]?{W}[0-9]+     |
"."{W}[0-9]+{W}{d}{W}[+-]?{W}[0-9]+     {
    /* convert constants */
    for(p=yytext; *p != 0; p++)
        {
        if (*p == 'd' | *p == 'D')
            *p =+ 'e'- 'd';
        ECHO;
        }
```

After the floating point constant is recognized, it is scanned by the *for* loop to find the letter *d* or *D*. The program than adds *'e'-'d'*, which converts it to the next letter of the alphabet. The modified constant, now single-precision, is written out again. There follow a series of names which must be respelled to remove their initial *d*. By using the array *yytext* the same action suffices for all the names (only a sample of a rather long list is given here).

```
{d}{s}{i}{n}        |
{d}{c}{o}{s}        |
{d}{s}{q}{r}{t}     |
{d}{a}{t}{a}{n}     |
...
{d}{f}{l}{o}{a}{t}    printf("%s",yytext+1);
```

Another list of names must have initial *d* changed to initial *a*:

```
{d}{l}{o}{g}         |
{d}{l}{o}{g}10       |
{d}{m}{i}{n}1        |
{d}{m}{a}{x}1        {
                     yytext[0] =+ 'a' - 'd';
                     ECHO;
                     }
```

And one routine must have initial *d* changed to initial *r*:

```
{d}1{m}{a}{c}{h}     {yytext[0] =+ 'r' - 'd';
```

To avoid such names as *dsinx* being detected as instances of *dsin*, some final rules pick up longer words as identifiers and copy some surviving characters:

```
[A-Za-z][A-Za-z0-9]*   |
[0-9]+                 |
\n                     |
                       ECHO;
```

Note that this program is not complete; it does not deal with the spacing problems in Fortran or with the use of keywords as identifiers.

10 Left Context Sensitivity.

Sometimes it is desirable to have several sets of lexical rules to be applied at different times in the input. For example, a compiler preprocessor might distinguish preprocessor statements and analyze them differently from ordinary statements. This requires sensitivity to prior context, and there are several ways of handling such problems. The ^ operator, for example, is a prior context operator, recognizing immediately preceding left context just as *$* recognizes immediately following right context. Adjacent left context could be extended, to produce a facility similar to that for adjacent right context, but it is unlikely to be as useful, since often the relevant left context appeared some time earlier, such as at the beginning of a line.

This section describes three means of dealing with different environments: a simple use of flags, when only a few rules change from one environment to another, the use of *start conditions* on rules, and the possibility of making multiple lexical analyzers all run together. In each case, there are rules which recognize the need to change the environment in which the following input text is analyzed, and set some parameter to reflect the change. This may be a flag explicitly tested by the user's action code; such a flag is the simplest way of dealing with the problem, since Lex is not involved at all. It may be more convenient, however, to have Lex remember the flags as initial conditions on the rules. Any rule may be associated with a start condition. It will only be recognized when Lex is in that start condition. The current start condition may be changed at any time. Finally, if the sets of rules for the different environments are very dissimilar, clarity may be best achieved by writing several distinct lexical analyzers, and switching from one to another as desired.

Consider the following problem: copy the input to the output, changing the word *magic* to *first* on every line which began with the letter *a*, changing *magic* to *second* on every line which began with the letter *b*, and changing *magic* to *third* on every line which began with the letter *c*. All other words and all other lines are left unchanged.

These rules are so simple that the easiest way to do this job is with a flag:

```
           int flag;
%%
^a         {flag = 'a'; ECHO;}
^b         {flag = 'b'; ECHO;}
^c         {flag = 'c'; ECHO;}
\n         {flag = 0 ; ECHO;}
magic      {
           switch (flag)
           {
           case 'a': printf("first"); break;
           case 'b': printf("second"); break;
           case 'c': printf("third"); break;
           default: ECHO; break;
           }
           }
```

should be adequate.

To handle the same problem with start conditions, each start condition must be introduced to Lex in the definitions section with a line reading

         %Start   name1 name2 ...

where the conditions may be named in any order. The word *Start* may be abbreviated to *s* or *S*. The conditions may be referenced at the head of a rule with the < > brackets:

         <name1>expression

is a rule which is only recognized when Lex is in the start condition *name1*. To enter a start condition, execute the action statement

         BEGIN name1;

which changes the start condition to *name1*. To resume the normal state,

BEGIN 0;

resets the initial condition of the Lex automaton interpreter. A rule may be active in several start conditions:

<name1,name2,name3>

is a legal prefix. Any rule not beginning with the <> prefix operator is always active.

The same example as before can be written:

```
%START AA BB CC
%%
^a                    {ECHO; BEGIN AA;}
^b                    {ECHO; BEGIN BB;}
^c                    {ECHO; BEGIN CC;}
\n                    {ECHO; BEGIN 0;}
<AA>magic             printf("first");
<BB>magic             printf("second");
<CC>magic             printf("third");
```

where the logic is exactly the same as in the previous method of handling the problem, but Lex does the work rather than the user's code.

11 Character Set.

The programs generated by Lex handle character I/O only through the routines *input, output,* and *unput.* Thus the character representation provided in these routines is accepted by Lex and employed to return values in *yytext.* For internal use a character is represented as a small integer which, if the standard library is used, has a value equal to the integer value of the bit pattern representing the character on the host computer. In C, the I/O routines are assumed to deal directly in this representation. In Ratfor, it is anticipated that many users will prefer left-adjusted rather than right-adjusted characters; thus the routine *lexshf* is called to change the representation delivered by *input* into a right-adjusted integer. If the user changes the I/O library, the routine *lexshf* should also be changed to a compatible version. The Ratfor library I/O system is arranged to represent the letter *a* as in the Fortran value *1Ha* while in C the letter *a* is represented as the character constant *'a'.* If this interpretation is changed, by providing I/O routines which translate the characters, Lex must be told about it, by giving a translation table. This table must be in the definitions section, and must be bracketed by lines containing only "%T". The table contains lines of the form

{integer} {character string}

which indicate the value associated with each character. Thus the next example maps the lower and upper case letters together into the integers 1 through 26, newline into 27, + and - into 28 and 29, and the digits into 30 through 39. Note the escape for newline. If a table is supplied, every character that is to appear either in the

```
%T
    1       Aa
    2       Bb
    ...
   26       Zz
   27       \n
   28       +
   29       -
   30       0
   31       1
    ...
   39       9
%T
```

Sample character table.

rules or in any valid input must be included in the table. No character may be assigned the number 0, and no character may be assigned a bigger number than the size of the hardware character set.

It is not likely that C users will wish to use the character table feature; but for Fortran portability it may be essential.

Although the contents of the Lex Ratfor library routines for input and output run almost unmodified on UNIX, GCOS, and OS/370, they are not really machine independent, and would not work with CDC or Burroughs Fortran compilers. The user is of course welcome to replace *input, output, unput* and *lexshf* but to replace them by completely portable Fortran routines is likely to cause a substantial decrease in the speed of Lex Ratfor programs. A simple way to produce portable routines would be to leave *input* and *output* as routines that read with 80A1 format, but replace *lexshf* by a table lookup routine.

12 Summary of Source Format.

The general form of a Lex source file is:

```
{definitions}
%%
{rules}
%%
{user subroutines}
```

The definitions section contains a combination of

1) Definitions, in the form "name space translation".

2) Included code, in the form "space code".

3) Included code, in the form

```
%{
code
%}
```

4)   Start conditions, given in the form

%S name1 name2 ...

5)   Character set tables, in the form

%T
number space character-string
...
%T

6)   'A language specifier, which must also precede any rules or included code, in the form ''%C'' for C or ''%R'' for Ratfor.

7)   Changes to internal array sizes, in the form

%*x*   *nnn*

where *nnn* is a decimal integer representing an array size and *x* selects the parameter as follows:

Letter	Parameter
p	positions
n	states
e	tree nodes
a	transitions
k	packed character classes
o	output array size

Lines in the rules section have the form ''expression action'' where the action may be continued on succeeding lines by using braces to delimit it.

Regular expressions in Lex use the following operators:

x	the character "x"
"x"	an "x", even if x is an operator.
\x	an "x", even if x is an operator.
[xy]	the character x or y.
[x-z]	the characters x, y or z.
[^x]	any character but x.
.	any character but newline.
^x	an x at the beginning of a line.
<y>x	an x when Lex is in start condition y.
x$	an x at the end of a line.
x?	an optional x.
x*	0,1,2, ... instances of x.
x+	1,2,3, ... instances of x.
x|y	an x or a y.
(x)	an x.
x/y	an x but only if followed by y.
{xx}	the translation of xx from the definitions section.
x{m,n}	*m* through *n* occurrences of x

13 Caveats and Bugs.

There are pathological expressions which produce exponential growth of the tables when converted to deterministic machines; fortunately, they are rare.

REJECT does not rescan the input; instead it remembers the results of the previous scan. This means that if a rule with trailing context is found, and REJECT executed, the user must not have used *unput* to change the characters forthcoming from the input stream. This is the only restriction on the user's ability to manipulate the not-yet-processed input.

TSO Lex is an older version. Among the non-supported features are REJECT, start conditions, or variable length trailing context, And any significant Lex source is too big for the IBM C compiler when translated.

14 Acknowledgments.

As should be obvious from the above, the outside of Lex is patterned on Yacc and the inside on Aho's string matching routines. Therefore, both S. C. Johnson and A. V. Aho are really originators of much of Lex, as well as debuggers of it. Many thanks are due to both.

The code of the current version of Lex was designed, written, and debugged by Eric Schmidt.

15 References.

1.   B. W. Kernighan and D. M. Ritchie, *The C Programming Language,* Prentice-Hall, N. J. (1978).

2.   B. W. Kernighan, *Ratfor: A Preprocessor for a Rational Fortran,* Software — Practice and Experience, **5**, pp. 395-496 (1975).

3.   S. C. Johnson, *Yacc: Yet Another Compiler Compiler,* Computing Science Technical Report No. 32, 1975, Bell Laboratories, Murray Hill, NJ 07974.

4.   A. V. Aho and M. J. Corasick, *Efficient String Matching: An Aid to Bibliographic Search,* Comm. ACM **18**, 333-340 (1975).

5.   B. W. Kernighan, D. M. Ritchie and K. L. Thompson, *QED Text Editor,* Computing Science Technical Report No. 5, 1972, Bell Laboratories, Murray Hill, NJ 07974.

6.   D. M. Ritchie, private communication. See also M. E. Lesk, *The Portable C Library,* Computing Science Technical Report No. 31, Bell Laboratories, Murray Hill, NJ 07974.

A Portable Fortran 77 Compiler

S. I. Feldman

P. J. Weinberger

Bell Laboratories
Murray Hill, New Jersey 07974

ABSTRACT

The Fortran language has just been revised. The new language, known as Fortran 77, became an official American National Standard on April 3, 1978. We report here on a compiler and run-time system for the new extended language. This is believed to be the first complete Fortran 77 system to be implemented. This compiler is designed to be portable, to be correct and complete, and to generate code compatible with calling sequences produced by C compilers. In particular, this Fortran is quite usable on UNIX† systems. In this paper, we describe the language compiled, interfaces between procedures, and file formats assumed by the I/O system. An appendix describes the Fortran 77 language.

1 August 1978

---

†UNIX is a Trademark of Bell Laboratories.

1. INTRODUCTION

The Fortran language has just been revised. The new language, known as Fortran 77, became an official American National Standard [1] on April 3, 1978. for the language, known as Fortran 77, is about to be published. Fortran 77 supplants 1966 Standard Fortran [2]. We report here on a compiler and run-time system for the new extended language. The compiler and computation library were written by SIF, the I/O system by PJW. We believe ours to be the first complete Fortran 77 system to be implemented. This compiler is designed to be portable to a number of different machines, to be correct and complete, and to generate code compatible with calling sequences produced by compilers for the C language [3]. In particular, it is in use on UNIX† systems. Two families of C compilers are in use at Bell Laboratories, those based on D. M. Ritchie's PDP-11 compiler[4] and those based on S. C. Johnson's portable C compiler [5]. This Fortran compiler can drive the second passes of either family. In this paper, we describe the language compiled, interfaces between procedures, and file formats assumed by the I/O system. We will describe implementation details in companion papers.

1.1. Usage

At present, versions of the compiler run on and compile for the PDP-11, the VAX-11/780, and the Interdata 8/32 UNIX systems. The command to run the compiler is

$$f77 \quad flags \quad file \dots$$

f77 is a general-purpose command for compiling and loading Fortran and Fortran-related files. EFL [6] and Ratfor [7] source files will be preprocessed before being presented to the Fortran compiler. C and assembler source files will be compiled by the appropriate programs. Object files will be loaded. (The **f77** and **cc** commands cause slightly different loading sequences to be generated, since Fortran programs need a few extra libraries and a different startup routine than do C programs.) The following file name suffixes are understood:

.f	Fortran source file
.e	EFL source file
.r	Ratfor source file
.c	C source file
.s	Assembler source file
.o	Object file

The following flags are understood:

−S Generate assembler output for each source file, but do not assemble it. Assem-

---

†UNIX is a Trademark of Bell Laboratories.

bler output for a source file **x.f, x.e, x.r,** or **x.c** is put on file **x.s.**

−c	Compile but do not load. Output for **x.f, x.e, x.r, x.c,** or **x.s** is put on file **x.o.**
−m	Apply the M4 macro preprocessor to each EFL or Ratfor source file before using the appropriate compiler.
−f	Apply the EFL or Ratfor processor to all relevant files, and leave the output from **x.e** or **x.r** on **x.f.** Do not compile the resulting Fortran program.
−p	Generate code to produce usage profiles.
−o *f*	Put executable module on file *f.* (Default is **a.out**).
−w	Suppress all warning messages.
−w66	Suppress warnings about Fortran 66 features used.
−O	Invoke the C object code optimizer.
−C	Compile code the checks that subscripts are within array bounds.
−onetrip	Compile code that performs every **do** loop at least once. (see Section 2.10).
−U	Do not convert upper case letters to lower case. The default is to convert Fortran programs to lower case.
−u	Make the default type of a variable **undefined.** (see Section 2.3).
−I2	On machines which support short integers, make the default integer constants and variables short. (**−I4** is the standard value of this option). (see Section 2.14). All logical quantities will be short.
−E	The remaining characters in the argument are used as an EFL flag argument.
−R	The remaining characters in the argument are used as a Ratfor flag argument.
−F	Ratfor and and EFL source programs are pre-processed into Fortran files, but those files are not compiled or removed.

Other flags, all library names (arguments beginning −l), and any names not ending with one of the understood suffixes are passed to the loader.

1.2. Documentation Conventions

In running text, we write Fortran keywords and other literal strings in boldface lower case. Examples will be presented in lightface lower case. Names representing a class of values will be printed in italics.

1.3. Implementation Strategy

The compiler and library are written entirely in C. The compiler generates C compiler intermediate code. Since there are C compilers running on a variety of machines, relatively small changes will make this Fortran compiler generate code for any of them. Furthermore, this approach guarantees that the resulting programs are compatible with C usage. The runtime computational library is complete. The mathematical functions are computed to at least 63 bit precision. The runtime I/O library makes use of D. M. Ritchie's Standard C I/O package [8] for transferring data. With the few exceptions described below, only documented calls are used, so it should be relatively easy to modify to run on other operating systems.

2. LANGUAGE EXTENSIONS

Fortran 77 includes almost all of Fortran 66 as a subset. We describe the differences briefly in the Appendix. The most important additions are a character string data type, file-oriented input/output statements, and random access I/O. Also, the language has been cleaned up considerably.

In addition to implementing the language specified in the new Standard, our compiler implements a few extensions described in this section. Most are useful additions to the language. The remainder are extensions to make it easier to communicate with C procedures or to permit compilation of old (1966 Standard) programs.

2.1. Double Complex Data Type

The new type **double complex** is defined. Each datum is represented by a pair of double precision real variables. A double complex version of every **complex** built-in function is provided. The specific function names begin with **z** instead of **c**.

2.2. Internal Files

The Fortran 77 standard introduces "internal files" (memory arrays), but restricts their use to formatted sequential I/O statements. Our I/O system also permits internal files to be used in direct and unformatted reads and writes.

2.3. Implicit Undefined statement

Fortran 66 has a fixed rule that the type of a variable that does not appear in a type statement is **integer** if its first letter is **i, j, k, l, m** or **n**, and **real** otherwise. Fortran 77 has an **implicit** statement for overriding this rule. As an aid to good programming practice, we permit an additional type, **undefined.** The statement

        implicit undefined(a-z)

turns off the automatic data typing mechanism, and the compiler will issue a diagnostic for each variable that is used but does not appear in a type statement. Specifying the −**u** compiler flag is equivalent to beginning each procedure with this statement.

2.4. Recursion

Procedures may call themselves, directly or through a chain of other procedures.

2.5. Automatic Storage

Two new keywords are recognized, **static** and **automatic.** These keywords may appear as "types" in type statements and in **implicit** statements. Local variables are static by default; there is exactly one copy of the datum, and its value is retained between calls. There is one copy of each variable declared **automatic** for each invocation of the procedure. Automatic variables may not appear in **equivalence, data,** or **save** statements.

2.6. Source Input Format

The Standard expects input to the compiler to be in 72 column format: except in comment lines, the first five characters are the statement number, the next is the continuation character, and the next sixty-six are the body of the line. (If there are fewer than seventy-two characters on a line, the compiler pads it with blanks; characters after the seventy-second are ignored).

In order to make it easier to type Fortran programs, our compiler also accepts input in variable length lines. An ampersand ("&") in the first position of a line indicates a continuation line; the remaining characters form the body of the line. A tab character in one of the first six positions of a line signals the end of the statement number and continuation part of the line; the remaining characters form the body of the line. A tab elsewhere on the line is treated as another kind of blank by the compiler.

In the Standard, there are only 26 letters — Fortran is a one-case language. Consistent with ordinary UNIX system usage, our compiler expects lower case input. By default, the compiler converts all upper case characters to lower case except those inside character constants. However, if the −**U** compiler flag is specified, upper case letters are not transformed. In this mode, it is possible to specify external names with upper case letters in them, and to have distinct variables differing only in case. Regardless of the setting of the flag, keywords will only be recognized in lower case.

2.7. Include Statement

The statement

>   include 'stuff'

is replaced by the contents of the file **stuff**. **include**s may be nested to a reasonable depth, currently ten.

2.8. Binary Initialization Constants

A **logical, real,** or **integer** variable may be initialized in a **data** statement by a binary constant, denoted by a letter followed by a quoted string. If the letter is **b**, the string is binary, and only zeroes and ones are permitted. If the letter is **o**, the string is octal, with digits $0-7$. If the letter is **z** or **x**, the string is hexadecimal, with digits $0-9$, **a–f**. Thus, the statements

>   integer a(3)
>   data a / b'1010', o'12', z'a' /

initialize all three elements of **a** to ten.

2.9. Character Strings

For compatibility with C usage, the following backslash escapes are recognized:

\n	newline
\t	tab
\b	backspace
\f	form feed
\0	null
\'	apostrophe (does not terminate a string)
\"	quotation mark (does not terminate a string)
\\	\
\x	x, where x is any other character

Fortran 77 only has one quoting character, the apostrophe. Our compiler and I/O system recognize both the apostrophe (') and the double-quote ("). If a string begins with one variety of quote mark, the other may be embedded within it without using the repeated quote or backslash escapes.

Every unequivalenced scalar local character variable and every character string constant is aligned on an **integer** word boundary. Each character string constant appearing outside a **data** statement is followed by a null character to ease communication with C routines.

2.10. Hollerith

Fortran 77 does not have the old Hollerith (n**h**) notation, though the new Standard recommends implementing the old Hollerith feature in order to improve compatibility with old programs. In our compiler, Hollerith data may be used in place of character string constants, and may also be used to initialize non-character variables in **data** statements.

2.11. Equivalence Statements

As a very special and peculiar case, Fortran 66 permits an element of a multiply-dimensioned array to be represented by a singly-subscripted reference in **equivalence** statements. Fortran 77 does not permit this usage, since subscript lower bounds may now be different from 1. Our compiler permits single subscripts in **equivalence** statements, under the interpretation that all missing subscripts are equal to 1. A warning message is printed for each such incomplete subscript.

2.12. One-Trip DO Loops

The Fortran 77 Standard requires that the range of a **do** loop not be performed if the initial value is already past the limit value, as in

> do 10 i = 2, 1

The 1966 Standard stated that the effect of such a statement was undefined, but it was common practice that the range of a **do** loop would be performed at least once. In order to accommodate old programs, though they were in violation of the 1966 Standard, the −**onetrip** compiler flag causes non-standard loops to be generated.

2.13. Commas in Formatted Input

The I/O system attempts to be more lenient than the Standard when it seems worthwhile. When doing a formatted read of non-character variables, commas may be used as value separators in the input record, overriding the field lengths given in the format statement. Thus, the format

> (i10, f20.10, i4)

will read the record

> −345,.05e−3,12

correctly.

2.14. Short Integers

On machines that support halfword integers, the compiler accepts declarations of type **integer∗2**. (Ordinary integers follow the Fortran rules about occupying the same space as a REAL variable; they are assumed to be of C type **long int**; halfword integers are of C type **short int**.) An expression involving only objects of type **integer∗2** is of that type. Generic functions return short or long integers depending on the actual types of their arguments. If a procedure is compiled using the −**I2** flag, all small integer constants will be of type **integer∗2**. If the precision of an integer-valued intrinsic function is not determined by the generic function rules, one will be chosen that returns the prevailing length (**integer∗2** when the −**I2** command flag is in effect). When the −**I2** option is in effect, all quantities of type **logical** will be short. Note that these short integer and logical quantities do not obey the standard rules for storage association.

2.15. Additional Intrinsic Functions

This compiler supports all of the intrinsic functions specified in the Fortran 77 Standard. In addition, there are functions for performing bitwise Boolean operations (**or, and, xor,** and **not)** and for accessing the UNIX command arguments (**getarg** and **iargc**).

3. VIOLATIONS OF THE STANDARD

We know only thre ways in which our Fortran system violates the new standard:

3.1. Double Precision Alignment

The Fortran standards (both 1966 and 1977) permit **common** or **equivalence** statements to force a double precision quantity onto an odd word boundary, as in the following example:

> real a(4)
> double precision b,c
>
> equivalence (a(1),b), (a(4),c)

Some machines (e.g., Honeywell 6000, IBM 360) require that double precision quantities be on double word boundaries; other machines (e.g., IBM 370), run inefficiently if this alignment rule is not observed. It is possible to tell which equivalenced and common variables suffer from a forced odd alignment, but every double precision argument would have to be assumed on a bad boundary. To load such a quantity on some machines, it would be necessary to use separate operations to move the upper and lower halves into the halves of an aligned temporary, then to load that double precision temporary; the reverse would be needed to store a result. We have chosen to require that all double precision real and complex quantities fall on even word boundaries on machines with corresponding hardware requirements, and to issue a diagnostic if the source code demands a violation of the rule.

3.2. Dummy Procedure Arguments

If any argument of a procedure is of type character, all dummy procedure arguments of that procedure must be declared in an **external** statement. This requirement arises as a subtle corollary of the way we represent character string arguments and of the one-pass nature of the compiler. A warning is printed if a dummy procedure is not declared **external**. Code is correct if there are no **character** arguments.

3.3. T and TL Formats

The implementation of the **t** (absolute tab) and **tl** (leftward tab) format codes is defective. These codes allow rereading or rewriting part of the record which has already been processed. (Section 6.3.2 in the Appendix.) The implementation uses seeks, so if the unit is not one which allows seeks, such as a terminal, the program is in error. (People who can make a case for using **tl** should let us know.) A benefit of the implementation chosen is that there is no upper limit on the length of a record, nor is it necessary to predeclare any record lengths except where specifically required by Fortran or the operating system.

4. INTER-PROCEDURE INTERFACE

To be able to write C procedures that call or are called by Fortran procedures, it is necessary to know the conventions for procedure names, data representation, return values, and argument lists that the compiled code obeys.

4.1. Procedure Names

On UNIX systems, the name of a common block or a Fortran procedure has an underscore appended to it by the compiler to distinguish it from a C procedure or external variable with the same user-assigned name. Fortran library procedure names have embedded underscores to avoid clashes with user-assigned subroutine names.

4.2. Data Representations

The following is a table of corresponding Fortran and C declarations:

Fortran	C
integer*2 x	short int x;
integer x	long int x;
logical x	long int x;
real x	float x;
double precision x	double x;
complex x	struct { float r, i; } x;
double complex x	struct { double dr, di; } x;
character*6 x	char x[6];

(By the rules of Fortran, **integer, logical,** and **real** data occupy the same amount of memory).

4.3. Return Values

A function of type **integer, logical, real,** or **double precision** declared as a C function that returns the corresponding type. A **complex** or **double complex** function is equivalent to a C routine with an additional initial argument that points to the place where the return value is to be stored. Thus,

    complex function f(. . .)

is equivalent to

    f_(temp, . . .)
    struct { float r, i; } *temp;
      . . .

A character-valued function is equivalent to a C routine with two extra initial arguments: a data address and a length. Thus,

    character*15 function g(. . .)

is equivalent to

    g_(result, length, . . .)
    char result[ ];
    long int length;
      . . .

and could be invoked in C by

    char chars[15];
      . . .
    g_(chars, 15L, . . .);

Subroutines are invoked as if they were **integer**-valued functions whose value specifies which alternate return to use. Alternate return arguments (statement labels) are not passed to the function, but are used to do an indexed branch in the calling procedure. (If the subroutine has no entry points with alternate return arguments, the returned value is undefined.) The statement

    call nret(*1, *2, *3)

is treated exactly as if it were the computed **goto**

    goto (1, 2, 3), nret( )

4.4. Argument Lists

All Fortran arguments are passed by address. In addition, for every argument that is of type character or that is a dummy procedure, an argument giving the length of the value is passed. (The string lengths are **long int** quantities passed by value). The order of arguments is then:

> Extra arguments for complex and character functions
> Address for each datum or function
> A **long int** for each character or procedure argument

Thus, the call in

```
external f
character*7 s
integer b(3)
   . . .
call sam(f, b(2), s)
```

is equivalent to that in

```
int f();
char s[7];
long int b[3];
   . . .
sam_(f, &b[1], s, 0L, 7L);
```

Note that the first element of a C array always has subscript zero, but Fortran arrays begin at 1 by default. Fortran arrays are stored in column-major order, C arrays are stored in row-major order.

5. FILE FORMATS

5.1. Structure of Fortran Files

Fortran requires four kinds of external files: sequential formatted and unformatted, and direct formatted and unformatted. On UNIX systems, these are all implemented as ordinary files which are assumed to have the proper internal structure.

Fortran I/O is based on "records". When a direct file is opened in a Fortran program, the record length of the records must be given, and this is used by the Fortran I/O system to make the file look as if it is made up of records of the given length. In the special case that the record length is given as 1, the files are not considered to be divided into records, but are treated as byte-addressable byte strings; that is, as ordinary UNIX file system files. (A read or write request on such a file keeps consuming bytes until satisfied, rather than being restricted to a single record.)

The peculiar requirements on sequential unformatted files make it unlikely that they will ever be read or written by any means except Fortran I/O statements. Each record is preceded and followed by an integer containing the record's length in bytes.

The Fortran I/O system breaks sequential formatted files into records while reading by using each newline as a record separator. The result of reading off the end of a record is undefined according to the Standard. The I/O system is permissive and treats the record as being extended by blanks. On output, the I/O system will write a newline at the end of each record. It is also possible for programs to write newlines for themselves. This is an error, but the only effect will be that the single record the user thought he wrote will be treated as more than one record when being read or backspaced over.

5.2. Portability Considerations

The Fortran I/O system uses only the facilities of the standard C I/O library, a widely available and fairly portable package, with the following two nonstandard features: The I/O system needs to know whether a file can be used for direct I/O, and whether or not it is possible to backspace. Both of these facilities are implemented using the **fseek** routine, so there is a routine **canseek** which determines if **fseek** will have the desired effect. Also, the **inquire** statement provides the user with the ability to find out if two files are the same, and to get the name of an already opened file in a form which would enable the program to reopen it. (The UNIX operating system implementation attempts to determine the full pathname.) Therefore there are two routines which depend on facilities of the operating system to provide these two services. In any case, the I/O system runs on the PDP-11, VAX-11/780, and Interdata 8/32 UNIX systems.

5.3. Pre-Connected Files and File Positions

Units 5, 6, and 0 are preconnected when the program starts. Unit 5 is connected to the standard input, unit 6 is connected to the standard output, and unit 0 is connected to the standard error unit. All are connected for sequential formatted I/O.

All the other units are also preconnected when execution begins. Unit n is connected to a file named **fort.**n. These files need not exist, nor will they be created unless their units are used without first executing an **open**. The default connection is for sequential formatted I/O.

The Standard does not specify where a file which has been explicitly **open**ed for sequential I/O is initially positioned. In fact, the I/O system attempts to position the file at the end, so a **write** will append to the file and a **read** will result in an end-of-file indication. To position a file to its beginning, use a **rewind** statement. The preconnected units 0, 5, and 6 are positioned as they come from the program's parent process.

REFERENCES

1. *Sigplan Notices* **11**, No.3 (1976), as amended in X3J3 internal documents through "/90.1".

2. *USA Standard FORTRAN, USAS X3.9-1966*, New York: United States of America Standards Institute, March 7, 1966. Clarified in *Comm. ACM* **12**, 289 (1969) and *Comm. ACM* **14**, 628 (1971).

3. B. W. Kernighan and D. M. Ritchie, *The C Programming Language,* Englewood Cliffs: Prentice-Hall (1978).

4. D. M. Ritchie, private communication.

5. S. C. Johnson, "A Portable Compiler: Theory and Practice", Proc. 5th ACM Symp. on Principles of Programming Languages (January 1978).

6. S. I. Feldman, "An Informal Description of EFL", internal memorandum.

7. B. W. Kernighan, "RATFOR — A Preprocessor for a Rational Fortran", *Bell Laboratories Computing Science Technical Report #55,* (January 1977).

8. D. M. Ritchie, private communication.

APPENDIX. Differences Between Fortran 66 and Fortran 77

The following is a very brief description of the differences between the 1966 [2] and the 1977 [1] Standard languages. We assume that the reader is familiar with Fortran 66. We do not pretend to be complete, precise, or unbiased, but plan to describe what we feel are the most important aspects of the new language. At present the only current information on the 1977 Standard is in publications of the X3J3 Subcommittee of the American National Standards Institute. The following information is from the "/92" document. This draft Standard is written in English rather than a meta-language, but it is forbidding and legalistic. No tutorials or textbooks are available yet.

1. Features Deleted from Fortran 66

1.1. Hollerith

All notions of "Hollerith" (nh) as data have been officially removed, although our compiler, like almost all in the foreseeable future, will continue to support this archaism.

1.2. Extended Range

In Fortran 66, under a set of very restrictive and rarely-understood conditions, it is permissible to jump out of the range of a **do** loop, then jump back into it. Extended range has been removed in the Fortran 77 language. The restrictions are so special, and the implementation of extended range is so unreliable in many compilers, that this change really counts as no loss.

2. Program Form

2.1. Blank Lines

Completely blank lines are now legal comment lines.

2.2. Program and Block Data Statements

A main program may now begin with a statement that gives that program an external name:

        program work

Block data procedures may also have names.

        block data stuff

There is now a rule that only *one* unnamed block data procedure may appear in a program. (This rule is not enforced by our system.) The Standard does not specify the effect of the program and block data names, but they are clearly intended to aid conventional loaders.

2.3. ENTRY Statement

Multiple entry points are now legal. Subroutine and function subprograms may have additional entry points, declared by an **entry** statement with an optional argument list.

        entry extra(a, b, c)

Execution begins at the first statement following the **entry** line. All variable declarations must precede all executable statements in the procedure. If the procedure begins with a **subroutine** statement, all entry points are subroutine names. If it begins with a **function** statement, each entry is a function entry point, with type determined by the type declared for the entry name. If any entry is a character-valued function, then all entries must be. In a function, an entry name of the same type as that where control entered must be assigned a value. Arguments do not retain their values between calls. (The ancient trick of calling one entry point with a large number of arguments to cause the procedure to "remember" the locations of those arguments, then invoking an entry with just a few arguments for later calculation, is still illegal. Furthermore, the trick doesn't work in our implementation, since arguments are not kept in static storage.)

2.4. DO Loops

do variables and range parameters may now be of integer, real, or double precision types. (The use of floating point **do** variables is very dangerous because of the possibility of unexpected roundoff, and we strongly recommend against their use). The action of the **do** statement is now defined for all values of the **do** parameters. The statement

do 10 i = l, u, d

performs $\max(0, \lfloor (u-l)/d \rfloor)$ iterations. The **do** variable has a predictable value when exiting a loop: the value at the time a **goto** or **return** terminates the loop; otherwise the value that failed the limit test.

2.5. Alternate Returns

In a **subroutine** or subroutine **entry** statement, some of the arguments may be noted by an asterisk, as in

subroutine s(a, *, b, *)

The meaning of the "alternate returns" is described in section 5.2 of the Appendix.

3. Declarations

3.1. CHARACTER Data Type

One of the biggest improvements to the language is the addition of a character-string data type. Local and common character variables must have a length denoted by a constant expression:

character*17 a, b(3,4)
character*(6+3) c

If the length is omitted entirely, it is assumed equal to 1. A character string argument may have a constant length, or the length may be declared to be the same as that of the corresponding actual argument at run time by a statement like

character*(*) a

(There is an intrinsic function **len** that returns the actual length of a character string). Character arrays and common blocks containing character variables must be packed: in an array of character variables, the first character of one element must follow the last character of the preceding element, without holes.

3.2. IMPLICIT Statement

The traditional implied declaration rules still hold: a variable whose name begins with **i, j, k, l, m,** or **n** is of type **integer,** other variables are of type **real,** unless otherwise declared. This general rule may be overridden with an **implicit** statement:

implicit real(a-c,g), complex(w-z), character*(17) (s)

declares that variables whose name begins with an **a ,b, c,** or **g** are **real,** those beginning with **w, x, y,** or **z** are assumed **complex,** and so on. It is still poor practice to depend on implicit typing, but this statement is an industry standard.

3.3. PARAMETER Statement

It is now possible to give a constant a symbolic name, as in

> parameter (x=17, y=x/3, pi=3.14159d0, s='hello')

The type of each parameter name is governed by the same implicit and explicit rules as for a variable. The right side of each equal sign must be a constant expression (an expression made up of constants, operators, and already defined parameters).

3.4. Array Declarations

Arrays may now have as many as seven dimensions. (Only three were permitted in 1966). The lower bound of each dimension may be declared to be other than 1 by using a colon. Furthermore, an adjustable array bound may be an integer expression involving constants, arguments, and variables in **common.**

> real a(−5:3, 7, m:n), b(n+1:2*n)

The upper bound on the last dimension of an array argument may be denoted by an asterisk to indicate that the upper bound is not specified:

> integer a(5, *), b(*), c(0:1, −2:*)

3.5. SAVE Statement

A poorly known rule of Fortran 66 is that local variables in a procedure do not necessarily retain their values between invocations of that procedure. At any instant in the execution of a program, if a common block is declared neither in the currently executing procedure nor in any of the procedures in the chain of callers, all of the variables in that common block also become undefined. (The only exceptions are variables that have been defined in a **data** statement and never changed). These rules permit overlay and stack implementations for the affected variables. Fortran 77 permits one to specify that certain variables and common blocks are to retain their values between invocations. The declaration

> save a, /b/, c

leaves the values of the variables **a** and **c** and all of the contents of common block **b** unaffected by a return. The simple declaration

> save

has this effect on all variables and common blocks in the procedure. A common block must be **saved** in every procedure in which it is declared if the desired effect is to occur.

3.6. INTRINSIC Statement

All of the functions specified in the Standard are in a single category, "intrinsic functions", rather than being divided into "intrinsic" and "basic external" functions. If an intrinsic function is to be passed to another procedure, it must be declared **intrinsic.** Declaring it **external** (as in Fortran 66) causes a function other than the built-in one to be passed.

4. Expressions

4.1. Character Constants

Character string constants are marked by strings surrounded by apostrophes. If an apostrophe is to be included in a constant, it is repeated:

> 'abc'
> 'ain''t'

There are no null (zero-length) character strings in Fortran 77. Our compiler has two different quotation marks, " ' " and " " ". (See Section 2.9 in the main text.)

4.2. Concatenation

One new operator has been added, character string concatenation, marked by a double slash ("//"). The result of a concatenation is the string containing the characters of the left operand followed by the characters of the right operand. The strings

> 'ab' // 'cd'
> 'abcd'

are equal. The strings being concatenated must be of constant length in all concatenations that are not the right sides of assignments. (The only concatenation expressions in which a character string declared adjustable with a "*(*)" modifier or a substring denotation with nonconstant position values may appear are the right sides of assignments).

4.3. Character String Assignment

The left and right sides of a character assignment may not share storage. (The assumed implementation of character assignment is to copy characters from the right to the left side.) If the left side is longer than the right, it is padded with blanks. If the left side is shorter than the right, trailing characters are discarded.

4.4. Substrings

It is possible to extract a substring of a character variable or character array element, using the colon notation:

> a(i, j) (m:n)

is the string of $(n-m+1)$ characters beginning at the mth character of the character array element a_{ij}. Results are undefined unless $m \leqslant n$. Substrings may be used on the left sides of assignments and as procedure actual arguments.

4.5. Exponentiation

It is now permissible to raise real quantities to complex powers, or complex quantities to real or complex powers. (The principal part of the logarithm is used). Also, multiple exponentiation is now defined:

> a**b**c = a ** (b**c)

4.6. Relaxation of Restrictions

Mixed mode expressions are now permitted. (For instance, it is permissible to combine integer and complex quantities in an expression.)

Constant expressions are permitted where a constant is allowed, except in **data** statements. (A constant expression is made up of explicit constants and **parameters** and the Fortran operators, except for exponentiation to a floating-point power). An adjustable dimension may now be an integer expression involving constants, arguments, and variables in B common..

Subscripts may now be general integer expressions; the old $cv \pm c'$ rules have been removed. **do** loop bounds may be general integer, real, or double precision expressions. Computed **goto** expressions and I/O unit numbers may be general integer expressions.

5. Executable Statements

5.1. IF-THEN-ELSE

At last, the if-then-else branching structure has been added to Fortran. It is called a "Block If". A Block If begins with a statement of the form

    if (. . .) then

and ends with an

    end if

statement. Two other new statements may appear in a Block If. There may be several

    else if(. . .) then

statements, followed by at most one

    else

statement. If the logical expression in the Block If statement is true, the statements following it up to the next **elseif, else,** or **endif** are executed. Otherwise, the next **elseif** statement in the group is executed. If none of the **elseif** conditions are true, control passes to the statements following the **else** statement, if any. (The **else** must follow all **elseifs** in a Block If. Of course, there may be Block Ifs embedded inside of other Block If structures). A case construct may be rendered

    if (s .eq. 'ab') then
      . . .
    else if (s .eq. 'cd') then
      . . .
    else
      . . .
    end if

5.2. Alternate Returns

Some of the arguments of a subroutine call may be statement labels preceded by an asterisk, as in

    call joe(j, *10, m, *2)

A **return** statement may have an integer expression, such as

    return k

If the entry point has n alternate return (asterisk) arguments and if $1 \leqslant k \leqslant n$, the return is followed by a branch to the corresponding statement label; otherwise the usual return to the statement following the **call** is executed.

6. Input/Output

6.1. Format Variables

A format may be the value of a character expression (constant or otherwise), or be stored in a character array, as in

    write(6, '(i5)') x

6.2. END=, ERR=, and IOSTAT= Clauses

A **read** or **write** statement may contain **end=**, **err=**, and **iostat=** clauses, as in

        write(6, 101, err=20, iostat=a(4))
        read(5, 101, err=20, end=30, iostat=x)

Here 5 and 6 are the *units* on which the I/O is done, 101 is the statement number of the associated format, 20 and 30 are statement numbers, and **a** and **x** are integers. If an error occurs during I/O, control returns to the program at statement 20. If the end of the file is reached, control returns to the program at statement 30. In any case, the variable referred to in the **iostat=** clause is given a value when the I/O statement finishes. (Yes, the value is assigned to the name on the right side of the equal sign.) This value is zero if all went well, negative for end of file, and some positive value for errors.

6.3. Formatted I/O

6.3.1. Character Constants

Character constants in formats are copied literally to the output. Character constants cannot be read into.

        write(6,'(i2," isn""t ",i1)') 7, 4

produces

        7 isn't 4

Here the format is the character constant

        (i2,' isn"t ',i1)

and the character constant

        isn't

is copied into the output.

6.3.2. Positional Editing Codes

t, tl, tr, and **x** codes control where the next character is in the record. **tr** *n* or *n***x** specifies that the next character is *n* to the right of the current position. **tl** *n* specifies that the next character is *n* to the left of the current position, allowing parts of the record to be reconsidered. **t** *n* says that the next character is to be character number *n* in the record. (See section 3.4 in the main text.)

6.3.3. Colon

A colon in the format terminates the I/O operation if there are no more data items in the I/O list, otherwise it has no effect. In the fragment

        x='("hello", :, " there", i4)'
        write(6, x) 12
        write(6, x)

the first **write** statement prints **hello there 12**, while the second only prints **hello**.

6.3.4. Optional Plus Signs

According to the Standard, each implementation has the option of putting plus signs in front of non-negative numeric output. The **sp** format code may be used to make the optional plus signs actually appear for all subsequent items while the format is active. The **ss** format code guarantees that the I/O system will not insert the optional plus signs, and the **s** format code restores the default behavior of the I/O system. (Since we never put out optional plus signs, **ss** and **s** codes have the same effect in our implementation.)

6.3.5. Blanks on Input

Blanks in numeric input fields, other than leading blanks will be ignored following a **bn** code in a format statement, and will be treated as zeros following a **bz** code in a format statement. The default for a unit may be changed by using the **open** statement. (Blanks are ignored by default.)

6.3.6. Unrepresentable Values

The Standard requires that if a numeric item cannot be represented in the form required by a format code, the output field must be filled with asterisks. (We think this should have been an option.)

6.3.7. Iw.m

There is a new integer output code, **i**$w.m$. It is the same as **i**w, except that there will be at least m digits in the output field, including, if necessary, leading zeros. The case **i**$w.0$ is special, in that if the value being printed is 0, the output field is entirely blank. **i**$w.1$ is the same as **i**w.

6.3.8. Floating Point

On input, exponents may start with the letter **E, D, e,** or **d.** All have the same meaning. On output we always use **e.** The **e** and **d** format codes also have identical meanings. A leading zero before the decimal point in **e** output without a scale factor is optional with the implementation. (We do not print it.) There is a **g**$w.d$ format code which is the same as **e**$w.d$ and **f**$w.d$ on input, but which chooses **f** or **e** formats for output depending. on the size of the number and of d.

6.3.9. "A" Format Code

A codes are used for character values. **a**w use a field width of w, while a plain **a** uses the length of the character item.

6.4. Standard Units

There are default formatted input and output units. The statement

        read 10, a, b

reads from the standard unit using format statement 10. The default unit may be explicitly specified by an asterisk, as in

        read(*, 10) a,b

Similarly, the standard output units is specified by a **print** statement or an asterisk unit:

        print 10
        write(*, 10)

6.5. List-Directed Formatting

List-directed I/O is a kind of free form input for sequential I/O. It is invoked by using an asterisk as the format identifier, as in

        read(6, *) a,b,c

On input, values are separated by strings of blanks and possibly a comma. Values, except for character strings, cannot contain blanks. End of record counts as a blank, except in character strings, where it is ignored. Complex constants are given as two real constants separated by a comma and enclosed in parentheses. A null input field, such as between two consecutive commas, means the corresponding variable in the I/O list is not changed. Values may be preceded by repetition counts, as in

        4*(3.,2.) 2*, 4*'hello'

which stands for 4 complex constants, 2 null values, and 4 string constants.

For output, suitable formats are chosen for each item. The values of character strings are printed; they are not enclosed in quotes, so they cannot be read back using list-directed input.

6.6. Direct I/O

A file connected for direct access consists of a set of equal-sized records each of which is uniquely identified by a positive integer. The records may be written or read in any order, using direct access I/O statements.

Direct access **read** and **write** statements have an extra argument, **rec=**, which gives the record number to be read or written.

        read(2, rec=13, err=20) (a(i), i=1, 203)

reads the thirteenth record into the array **a.**

The size of the records must be given by an **open** statement (see below). Direct access files may be connected for either formatted or unformatted I/O.

6.7. Internal Files

Internal files are character string objects, such as variables or substrings, or arrays of type character. In the former cases there is only a single record in the file, in the latter case each array element is a record. The Standard includes only sequential formatted I/O on internal files. (I/O is not a very precise term to use here, but internal files are dealt with using **read** and **write**). There is no list-directed I/O on internal files. Internal files are used by giving the name of the character object in place of the unit number, as in

        character*80 x
        read(5,"(a)") x
        read(x,"(i3,i4)") n1,n2

which reads a card image into **x** and then reads two integers from the front of it. A sequential **read** or **write** always starts at the beginning of an internal file.

(We also support a compatible extension, direct I/O on internal files. This is like direct I/O on external files, except that the number of records in the file cannot be changed.)

6.8. OPEN, CLOSE, and INQUIRE Statements

These statements are used to connect and disconnect units and files, and to gather information about units and files.

6.8.1. OPEN

The **open** statement is used to connect a file with a unit, or to alter some properties of the connection. The following is a minimal example.

        open(1, file='fort.junk')

open takes a variety of arguments with meanings described below.

unit= a small non-negative integer which is the unit to which the file is to be connected. We allow, at the time of this writing, 0 through 9. If this parameter is the first one in the **open** statement, the **unit=** can be omitted.

iostat= is the same as in **read** or **write**.

err= is the same as in **read** or **write**.

file= a character expression, which when stripped of trailing blanks, is the name of the file to be connected to the unit. The filename should not be given if the **status=scratch**.

status= one of **old, new, scratch**, or **unknown**. If this parameter is not given, **unknown** is assumed. If **scratch** is given, a temporary file will be created. Temporary files are destroyed at the end of execution. If **new** is given, the file will be created if it doesn't exist, or truncated if it does. The meaning of **unknown** is processor dependent; our system treats it as synonymous with **old**.

access= **sequential** or **direct**, depending on whether the file is to be opened for sequential or direct I/O.

form= **formatted** or **unformatted**.

recl= a positive integer specifying the record length of the direct access file being opened. We measure all record lengths in bytes. On UNIX systems a record length of 1 has the special meaning explained in section 5.1 of the text.

blank= **null** or **zero**. This parameter has meaning only for formatted I/O. The default value is **null**. **zero** means that blanks, other than leading blanks, in numeric input fields are to be treated as zeros.

Opening a new file on a unit which is already connected has the effect of first closing the old file.

6.8.2. CLOSE

close severs the connection between a unit and a file. The unit number must be given. The optional parameters are **iostat=** and **err=** with their usual meanings, and **status=** either **keep** or **delete**. Scratch files cannot be kept, otherwise **keep** is the default. **delete** means the file will be removed. A simple example is

        close(3, err=17)

6.8.3. INQUIRE

The **inquire** statement gives information about a unit ("inquire by unit") or a file ("inquire by file"). Simple examples are:

        inquire(unit=3, namexx)
        inquire(file='junk', number=n, exist=l)

file= a character variable specifies the file the **inquire** is about. Trailing blanks in the file name are ignored.

unit= an integer variable specifies the unit the **inquire** is about. Exactly one of **file=** or **unit=** must be used.

iostat=, err= are as before.

exist= a logical variable. The logical variable is set to **.true.** if the file or unit exists and is set to **.false.** otherwise.

opened= a logical variable. The logical variable is set to **.true.** if the file is connected to a unit or if the unit is connected to a file, and it is set to **.false.** otherwise.

number= an integer variable to which is assigned the number of the unit connected to the file, if any.

named= a logical variable to which is assigned **.true.** if the file has a name, or **.false.** otherwise.

name= a character variable to which is assigned the name of the file (inquire by file) or the name of the file connected to the unit (inquire by unit). The name will be the full name of the file.

access= a character variable to which will be assigned the value 'sequential' if the connection is for sequential I/O, 'direct' if the connection is for direct I/O. The value becomes undefined if there is no connection.

sequential= a character variable to which is assigned the value 'yes' if the file could be connected for sequential I/O, 'no' if the file could not be connected for sequential I/O, and 'unknown' if we can't tell.

direct= a character variable to which is assigned the value 'yes' if the file could be connected for direct I/O, 'no' if the file could not be connected for direct I/O, and 'unknown' if we can't tell.

form= a character variable to which is assigned the value 'formatted' if the file is connected for formatted I/O, or 'unformatted' if the file is connected for unformatted I/O.

formatted= a character variable to which is assigned the value 'yes' if the file could be connected for formatted I/O, 'no' if the file could not be connected for formatted I/O, and 'unknown' if we can't tell.

unformatted= a character variable to which is assigned the value 'yes' if the file could be connected for unformatted I/O, 'no' if the file could not be connected for unformatted I/O, and 'unknown' if we can't tell.

recl= an integer variable to which is assigned the record length of the records in the file if the file is connected for direct access.

nextrec= an integer variable to which is assigned one more than the number of the the last record read from a file connected for direct access.

blank= a character variable to which is assigned the value 'null' if null blank control is in effect for the file connected for formatted I/O, 'zero' if blanks are being converted to zeros and the file is connected for formatted I/O.

The gentle reader will remember that the people who wrote the standard probably weren't thinking of his needs. Here is an example. The declarations are omitted.

        open(1, file="/dev/console")

On a UNIX system this statement opens the console for formatted sequential I/O. An **inquire** statement for either unit 1 or file "/dev/console" would reveal that the file exists, is connected to unit 1, has a name, namely "/dev/console", is opened for sequential I/O, could be connected for sequential I/O, could not be connected for direct I/O (can't seek), is connected for formatted I/O, could be connected for formatted I/O, could not be connected for unformatted I/O (can't seek), has neither a record length nor a next record number, and is ignoring blanks in numeric fields.

In the UNIX system environment, the only way to discover what permissions you have for a file is to open it and try to read and write it. The **err=** parameter will return system error numbers. The **inquire** statement does not give a way of determining permissions.

RATFOR — A Preprocessor for a Rational Fortran

Brian W. Kernighan

Bell Laboratories
Murray Hill, New Jersey 07974

ABSTRACT

Although Fortran is not a pleasant language to use, it does have the advantages of universality and (usually) relative efficiency. The Ratfor language attempts to conceal the main deficiencies of Fortran while retaining its desirable qualities, by providing decent control flow statements:

- statement grouping
- **if-else** and **switch** for decision-making
- **while**, **for**, **do**, and **repeat-until** for looping
- **break** and **next** for controlling loop exits

and some "syntactic sugar":

- free form input (multiple statements/line, automatic continuation)
- unobtrusive comment convention
- translation of $>$, $>=$, etc., into .GT., .GE., etc.
- **return**(expression) statement for functions
- **define** statement for symbolic parameters
- **include** statement for including source files

Ratfor is implemented as a preprocessor which translates this language into Fortran.

Once the control flow and cosmetic deficiencies of Fortran are hidden, the resulting language is remarkably pleasant to use. Ratfor programs are markedly easier to write, and to read, and thus easier to debug, maintain and modify than their Fortran equivalents.

It is readily possible to write Ratfor programs which are portable to other env ironments. Ratfor is written in itself in this way, so it is also portable; versions of Ratfor are now running on at least two dozen different types of computers at over five hundred locations.

This paper discusses design criteria for a Fortran preprocessor, the Ratfor language and its implementation, and user experience.

1. INTRODUCTION

Most programmers will agree that Fortran is an unpleasant language to program in, yet there are many occasions when they are forced to use it. For example, Fortran is often the only language thoroughly supported on the local computer. Indeed, it is the closest thing to a universal programming language currently available: with care it is possible to write large, truly portable Fortran programs[1]. Finally, Fortran is often the most "efficient" language available, particularly for programs requiring much computation.

But Fortran *is* unpleasant. Perhaps the worst deficiency is in the control flow statements — conditional branches and loops — which express the logic of the program. The conditional statements in Fortran are primitive. The Arithmetic IF forces the user into at least two statement numbers and two (implied) GOTO's; it leads to unintelligible code, and is eschewed by good programmers. The Logical IF is better, in that the test part can be stated clearly, but hopelessly restrictive because the statement that follows the IF can only be one Fortran statement (with some *further* restrictions!). And of course there can be no ELSE part to a Fortran IF: there is no way to specify an alternative action if the IF is not satisfied.

The Fortran DO restricts the user to going forward in an arithmetic progression. It is fine for "1 to N in steps of 1 (or 2 or ...)", but there is no direct way to go backwards, or even (in ANSI Fortran[2]) to go from 1 to N−1. And of course the DO is useless if one's problem doesn't map into an arithmetic progression.

The result of these failings is that Fortran programs must be written with numerous labels and branches. The resulting code is particularly difficult to read and understand, and thus hard to debug and modify.

When one is faced with an unpleasant language, a useful technique is to define a new language that overcomes the deficiencies, and to translate it into the unpleasant one with a preprocessor. This is the approach taken with Ratfor. (The preprocessor idea is of course not new, and preprocessors for Fortran are especially popular today. A recent listing [3] of preprocessors shows more than 50, of which at least half a dozen are widely available.)

2. LANGUAGE DESCRIPTION

Design

Ratfor attempts to retain the merits of Fortran (universality, portability, efficiency) while hiding the worst Fortran inadequacies. The language *is* Fortran except for two aspects. First, since control flow is central to any program, regardless of the specific application, the primary task of Ratfor is to conceal this part of Fortran from the user, by providing decent control flow structures. These structures are sufficient and comfortable for structured programming in the narrow sense of programming without GOTO's. Second, since the preprocessor must examine an entire program to translate the control structure, it is possible at the same time to clean up many of the "cosmetic" deficiencies of Fortran, and thus provide a language which is easier and more pleasant to read and write.

Beyond these two aspects — control flow and cosmetics — Ratfor does nothing about the host of other weaknesses of Fortran. Although it would be straightforward to extend it to provide character strings, for example, they are not needed by everyone, and of course the preprocessor would be harder to implement. Throughout, the design principle which has determined what should be in Ratfor and what should not has been *Ratfor doesn't know any Fortran.* Any language feature which would require

---

This paper is a revised and expanded version of oe published in *Software—Practice and Experience,* October 1975. The Ratfor described here is the one in use on UNIX and GCOS at Bell Laboratories, Murray Hill, N. J.

that Ratfor really understand Fortran has been omitted. We will return to this point in the section on implementation.

Even within the confines of control flow and cosmetics, we have attempted to be selective in what features to provide. The intent has been to provide a small set of the most useful constructs, rather than to throw in everything that has ever been thought useful by someone.

The rest of this section contains an informal description of the Ratfor language. The control flow aspects will be quite familiar to readers used to languages like Algol, PL/I, Pascal, etc., and the cosmetic changes are equally straightforward. We shall concentrate on showing what the language looks like.

Statement Grouping

Fortran provides no way to group statements together, short of making them into a subroutine. The standard construction "if a condition is true, do this group of things," for example,

```
if (x > 100)
    { call error("x>100"); err = 1; return }
```

cannot be written directly in Fortran. Instead a programmer is forced to translate this relatively clear thought into murky Fortran, by stating the negative condition and branching around the group of statements:

```
        if (x .le. 100) goto 10
            call error(5hx>100)
            err = 1
            return
10      ...
```

When the program doesn't work, or when it must be modified, this must be translated back into a clearer form before one can be sure what it does.

Ratfor eliminates this error-prone and confusing back-and-forth translation; the first form *is* the way the computation is written in Ratfor. A group of statements can be treated as a unit by enclosing them in the braces { and }. This is true throughout the language: wherever a single Ratfor statement can be used, there can be several enclosed in braces. (Braces seem clearer and less obtrusive than **begin** and **end** or **do** and **end**, and of course **do** and **end** already have Fortran meanings.)

Cosmetics contribute to the readability of code, and thus to its understandability. The character ">" is clearer than ".GT.", so Ratfor translates it appropriately, along with several other similar shorthands. Although many Fortran compilers permit character strings in quotes

(like "x>100"), quotes are not allowed in ANSI Fortran, so Ratfor converts it into the right number of **H**'s: computers count better than people do.

Ratfor is a free-form language: statements may appear anywhere on a line, and several may appear on one line if they are separated by semi-colons. The example above could also be written as

```
if (x > 100) {
        call error("x>100")
        err = 1
        return
}
```

In this case, no semicolon is needed at the end of each line because Ratfor assumes there is one statement per line unless told otherwise.

Of course, if the statement that follows the **if** is a single statement (Ratfor or otherwise), no braces are needed:

```
if (y <= 0.0 & z <= 0.0)
        write(6, 20) y, z
```

No continuation need be indicated because the statement is clearly not finished on the first line. In general Ratfor continues lines when it seems obvious that they are not yet done. (The continuation convention is discussed in detail later.)

Although a free-form language permits wide latitude in formatting styles, it is wise to pick one that is readable, then stick to it. In particular, proper indentation is vital, to make the logical structure of the program obvious to the reader.

The "else" Clause

Ratfor provides an **else** statement to handle the construction "if a condition is true, do this thing, *otherwise* do that thing."

```
if (a <= b)
        { sw = 0; write(6, 1) a, b }
else
        { sw = 1; write(6, 1) b, a }
```

This writes out the smaller of **a** and **b**, then the larger, and sets **sw** appropriately.

The Fortran equivalent of this code is circuitous indeed:

```
            if (a .gt. b) goto 10
                    sw = 0
                    write(6, 1) a, b
                    goto 20
    10      sw = 1
            write(6, 1) b, a
    20          ...
```

This is a mechanical translation; shorter forms exist, as they do for many similar situations. But all translations suffer from the same problem: since they are translations, they are less clear and understandable than code that is not a translation. To understand the Fortran version, one must scan the entire program to make sure that no other statement branches to statements 10 or 20 before one knows that indeed this is an **if-else** construction. With the Ratfor version, there is no question about how one gets to the parts of the statement. The **if-else** is a single unit, which can be read, understood, and ignored if not relevant. The program says what it means.

As before, if the statement following an **if** or an **else** is a single statement, no braces are needed:

```
    if (a <= b)
            sw = 0
    else
            sw = 1
```

The syntax of the **if** statement is

```
    if (legal Fortran condition)
            Ratfor statement
    else
            Ratfor statement
```

where the **else** part is optional. The *legal Fortran condition* is anything that can legally go into a Fortran Logical IF. Ratfor does not check this clause, since it does not know enough Fortran to know what is permitted. The *Ratfor statement* is any Ratfor or Fortran statement, or any collection of them in braces.

Nested if's

Since the statement that follows an **if** or an **else** can be any Ratfor statement, this leads immediately to the possibility of another **if** or **else**. As a useful example, consider this problem: the variable **f** is to be set to −1 if **x** is less than zero, to +1 if **x** is greater than 100, and to 0 otherwise. Then in Ratfor, we write

```
    if (x < 0)
            f = −1
    else if (x > 100)
            f = +1
    else
            f = 0
```

Here the statement after the first **else** is another **if-else**. Logically it is just a single statement, although it is rather complicated.

This code says what it means. Any version written in straight Fortran will necessarily be indirect because Fortran does not let you say what you mean. And as always, clever shortcuts may turn out to be too clever to understand a year from now.

Following an **else** with an **if** is one way to write a multi-way branch in Ratfor. In general the structure

```
    if (...)
            − − −
    else if (...)
            − − −
    else if (...)
            − − −
        ...
    else
            − − −
```

provides a way to specify the choice of exactly one of several alternatives. (Ratfor also provides a **switch** statement which does the same job in certain special cases; in more general situations, we have to make do with spare parts.) The tests are laid out in sequence, and each one is followed by the code associated with it. Read down the list of decisions until one is found that is satisfied. The code associated with this condition is executed, and then the entire structure is finished. The trailing **else** part handles the "default" case, where none of the other conditions apply. If there is no default action, this final **else** part is omitted:

```
    if (x < 0)
            x = 0
    else if (x > 100)
            x = 100
```

if-else ambiguity

There is one thing to notice about complicated structures involving nested **if**'s and **else**'s. Consider

```
if (x > 0)
        if (y > 0)
                write(6, 1) x, y
        else
                write(6, 2) y
```

There are two **if**'s and only one **else**. Which **if** does the **else** go with?

This is a genuine ambiguity in Ratfor, as it is in many other programming languages. The ambiguity is resolved in Ratfor (as elsewhere) by saying that in such cases the **else** goes with the closest previous un-**else**'ed **if**. Thus in this case, the **else** goes with the inner **if**, as we have indicated by the indentation.

It is a wise practice to resolve such cases by explicit braces, just to make your intent clear. In the case above, we would write

```
if (x > 0) {
        if (y > 0)
                write(6, 1) x, y
        else
                write(6, 2) y
}
```

which does not change the meaning, but leaves no doubt in the reader's mind. If we want the other association, we *must* write

```
if (x > 0) {
        if (y > 0)
                write(6, 1) x, y
}
else
        write(6, 2) y
```

The "switch" Statement

The **switch** statement provides a clean way to express multi-way branches which branch on the value of some integer-valued expression. The syntax is

```
switch (expression) {

        case expr1 :
                statements
        case expr2, expr3 :
                statements
        ...

        default:
                statements

}
```

Each **case** is followed by a list of comma-separated integer expressions. The *expression* inside **switch** is compared against the case expressions *expr1, expr2,* and so on in turn until one matches, at which time the statements following that **case** are executed. If no cases match *expression,* and there is a **default** section, the

statements with it are done; if there is no **default**, nothing is done. In all situations, as soon as some block of statements is executed, the entire **switch** is exited immediately. (Readers familiar with C[4] should beware that this behavior is not the same as the C **switch**.)

The "do" Statement

The **do** statement in Ratfor is quite similar to the DO statement in Fortran, except that it uses no statement number. The statement number, after all, serves only to mark the end of the DO, and this can be done just as easily with braces. Thus

```
do i = 1, n {
        x(i) = 0.0
        y(i) = 0.0
        z(i) = 0.0
}
```

is the same as

```
do 10 i = 1, n
        x(i) = 0.0
        y(i) = 0.0
        z(i) = 0.0
10      continue
```

The syntax is:

> do *legal-Fortran-DO-text*
> *Ratfor statement*

The part that follows the keyword **do** has to be something that can legally go into a Fortran DO statement. Thus if a local version of Fortran allows DO limits to be expressions (which is not currently permitted in ANSI Fortran), they can be used in a Ratfor **do**.

The *Ratfor statement* part will often be enclosed in braces, but as with the **if**, a single statement need not have braces around it. This code sets an array to zero:

```
do i = 1, n
        x(i) = 0.0
```

Slightly more complicated,

```
do i = 1, n
        do j = 1, n
                m(i, j) = 0
```

sets the entire array **m** to zero, and

```
do i = 1, n
     do j = 1, n
          if (i < j)
               m(i, j) = -1
          else if (i == j)
               m(i, j) = 0
          else
               m(i, j) = +1
```

sets the upper triangle of **m** to -1, the diagonal to zero, and the lower triangle to $+1$. (The operator $==$ is "equals", that is, ".EQ.".) In each case, the statement that follows the **do** is logically a *single* statement, even though complicated, and thus needs no braces.

"break" and "next"

Ratfor provides a statement for leaving a loop early, and one for beginning the next iteration. **break** causes an immediate exit from the **do**; in effect it is a branch to the statement *after* the **do**. **next** is a branch to the bottom of the loop, so it causes the next iteration to be done. For example, this code skips over negative values in an array:

```
do i = 1, n {
     if (x(i) < 0.0)
          next
     process positive element
}
```

break and **next** also work in the other Ratfor looping constructions that we will talk about in the next few sections.

break and **next** can be followed by an integer to indicate breaking or iterating that level of enclosing loop; thus

```
break 2
```

exits from two levels of enclosing loops, and **break 1** is equivalent to **break**. **next 2** iterates the second enclosing loop. (Realistically, multi-level **break**'s and **next**'s are not likely to be much used because they lead to code that is hard to understand and somewhat risky to change.)

The "while" Statement

One of the problems with the Fortran DO statement is that it generally insists upon being done once, regardless of its limits. If a loop begins

```
DO I = 2, 1
```

this will typically be done once with **I** set to 2, even though common sense would suggest that perhaps it shouldn't be. Of course a Ratfor **do** can easily be preceded by a test

```
if (j <= k)
     do i = j, k {
          - - -
     }
```

but this has to be a conscious act, and is often overlooked by programmers.

A more serious problem with the DO statement is that it encourages that a program be written in terms of an arithmetic progression with small positive steps, even though that may not be the best way to write it. If code has to be contorted to fit the requirements imposed by the Fortran DO, it is that much harder to write and understand.

To overcome these difficulties, Ratfor provides a **while** statement, which is simply a loop: "while some condition is true, repeat this group of statements". It has no preconceptions about why one is looping. For example, this routine to compute sin(x) by the Maclaurin series combines two termination criteria.

```
real function sin(x, e)
     # returns sin(x) to accuracy e, by
     # sin(x) = x - x**3/3! + x**5/5! - ...

     sin = x
     term = x

     i = 3
     while (abs(term) > e & i < 100) {
          term = -term * x**2 / float(i*(i-1))
          sin = sin + term
          i = i + 2
     }

     return
     end
```

Notice that if the routine is entered with **term** already smaller than **e**, the loop will be done *zero times*, that is, no attempt will be made to compute **x**∗∗**3** and thus a potential underflow is avoided. Since the test is made at the top of a **while** loop instead of the bottom, a special case disappears — the code works at one of its boundaries. (The test **i**<**100** is the other boundary — making sure the routine stops after some maximum number of iterations.)

As an aside, a sharp character "#" in a line marks the beginning of a comment; the rest of the line is comment. Comments and code can co-exist on the same line — one can make marginal remarks, which is not possible with Fortran's "C in column 1" convention. Blank lines are also permitted anywhere (they are not in Fortran); they should be used to emphasize the natural divisions of a program.

The syntax of the **while** statement is

while (*legal Fortran condition*)
   Ratfor statement

As with the **if**, *legal Fortran condition* is something that can go into a Fortran Logical IF, and *Ratfor statement* is a single statement, which may be multiple statements in braces.

   The **while** encourages a style of coding not normally practiced by Fortran programmers. For example, suppose **nextch** is a function which returns the next input character both as a function value and in its argument. Then a loop to find the first non-blank character is just

   while (nextch(ich) == iblank)
      ;

A semicolon by itself is a null statement, which is necessary here to mark the end of the **while**; if it were not present, the **while** would control the next statement. When the loop is broken, **ich** contains the first non-blank. Of course the same code can be written in Fortran as

100   if (nextch(ich) .eq. iblank) goto 100

but many Fortran programmers (and a few compilers) believe this line is illegal. The language at one's disposal strongly influences how one thinks about a problem.

The "for" Statement

   The **for** statement is another Ratfor loop, which attempts to carry the separation of loop-body from reason-for-looping a step further than the **while**. A **for** statement allows explicit initialization and increment steps as part of the statement. For example, a DO loop is just

   for (i = 1; i <= n; i = i + 1) ...

This is equivalent to

i = 1
while (i <= n) {
   ...
   i = i + 1
}

The initialization and increment of **i** have been moved into the **for** statement, making it easier to see at a glance what controls the loop.

   The **for** and **while** versions have the advantage that they will be done zero times if **n** is less than 1; this is not true of the **do**.

   The loop of the sine routine in the previous section can be re-written with a **for** as

for (i=3; abs(term) > e & i < 100; i=i+2) {
   term = −term * x**2 / float(i*(i−1))
   sin = sin + term
}

   The syntax of the **for** statement is

for (*init* ; *condition* ; *increment*)
   Ratfor statement

init is any single Fortran statement, which gets done once before the loop begins. *increment* is any single Fortran statement, which gets done at the end of each pass through the loop, before the test. *condition* is again anything that is legal in a logical IF. Any of *init, condition,* and *increment* may be omitted, although the semicolons *must* always be present. A non-existent *condition* is treated as always true, so **for(;;)** is an indefinite repeat. (But see the **repeat-until** in the next section.)

   The **for** statement is particularly useful for backward loops, chaining along lists, loops that might be done zero times, and similar things which are hard to express with a DO statement, and obscure to write out with IF's and GOTO's. For example, here is a backwards DO loop to find the last non-blank character on a card:

for (i = 80; i > 0; i = i − 1)
   if (card(i) != blank)
      break

("!=" is the same as ".NE."). The code scans the columns from 80 through to 1. If a non-blank is found, the loop is immediately broken. (**break** and **next** work in **for**'s and **while**'s just as in **do**'s). If **i** reaches zero, the card is all blank.

   This code is rather nasty to write with a regular Fortran DO, since the loop must go forward, and we must explicitly set up proper conditions when we fall out of the loop. (Forgetting this is a common error.) Thus:

DO 10 J = 1, 80
   I = 81 − J
   IF (CARD(I) .NE. BLANK) GO TO 11
10   CONTINUE
   I = 0
11   ...

The version that uses the **for** handles the termination condition properly for free; **i** *is* zero when we fall out of the **for** loop.

   The increment in a **for** need not be an arithmetic progression; the following program walks along a list (stored in an integer array **ptr**) until a zero pointer is found, adding up elements from a parallel array of values:

```
        sum = 0.0
        for (i = first; i > 0; i = ptr(i))
                sum = sum + value(i)
```

Notice that the code works correctly if the list is empty. Again, placing the test at the top of a loop instead of the bottom eliminates a potential boundary error.

The "repeat-until" statement

In spite of the dire warnings, there are times when one really needs a loop that tests at the bottom after one pass through. This service is provided by the **repeat-until**:

```
        repeat
                Ratfor statement
        until (legal Fortran condition)
```

The *Ratfor statement* part is done once, then the condition is evaluated. If it is true, the loop is exited; if it is false, another pass is made.

The **until** part is optional, so a bare **repeat** is the cleanest way to specify an infinite loop. Of course such a loop must ultimately be broken by some transfer of control such as **stop**, **return**, or **break**, or an implicit stop such as running out of input with a READ statement.

As a matter of observed fact[8], the **repeat-until** statement is *much* less used than the other looping constructions; in particular, it is typically outnumbered ten to one by **for** and **while**. Be cautious about using it, for loops that test only at the bottom often don't handle null cases well.

More on break and next

break exits immediately from **do**, **while**, **for**, and **repeat-until**. **next** goes to the test part of **do**, **while** and **repeat-until**, and to the increment step of a **for**.

"return" Statement

The standard Fortran mechanism for returning a value from a function uses the name of the function as a variable which can be assigned to; the last value stored in it is the function value upon return. For example, here is a routine **equal** which returns 1 if two arrays are identical, and zero if they differ. The array ends are marked by the special value −1.

```
# equal _ compare str1 to str2;
#     return 1 if equal, 0 if not
      integer function equal(str1, str2)
      integer str1(100), str2(100)
      integer i

      for (i = 1; str1(i) == str2(i); i = i + 1)
          if (str1(i) == −1) {
                  equal = 1
                  return
          }
      equal = 0
      return
      end
```

In many languages (e.g., PL/I) one instead says

```
        return (expression)
```

to return a value from a function. Since this is often clearer, Ratfor provides such a **return** statement — in a function **F**, **return**(expression) is equivalent to

```
        { F = expression; return }
```

For example, here is **equal** again:

```
# equal _ compare str1 to str2;
#     return 1 if equal, 0 if not
      integer function equal(str1, str2)
      integer str1(100), str2(100)
      integer i

      for (i = 1; str1(i) == str2(i); i = i + 1)
          if (str1(i) == −1)
                  return(1)
      return(0)
      end
```

If there is no parenthesized expression after **return**, a normal RETURN is made. (Another version of **equal** is presented shortly.)

Cosmetics

As we said above, the visual appearance of a language has a substantial effect on how easy it is to read and understand programs. Accordingly, Ratfor provides a number of cosmetic facilities which may be used to make programs more readable.

Free-form Input

Statements can be placed anywhere on a line; long statements are continued automatically, as are long conditions in **if**, **while**, **for**, and **until**. Blank lines are ignored. Multiple statements may appear on one line, if they are separated by semicolons. No semicolon is needed at the end of a line, if Ratfor can make some reasonable guess about whether the statement ends there. Lines ending with any of the characters

$$= \quad + \quad - \quad * \quad , \quad | \quad \& \quad (\quad \_$$

are assumed to be continued on the next line. Underscores are discarded wherever they occur; all others remain as part of the statement.

Any statement that begins with an all-numeric field is assumed to be a Fortran label, and placed in columns 1-5 upon output. Thus

```
write(6, 100); 100 format("hello")
```

is converted into

```
      write(6, 100)
100   format(5hhello)
```

Translation Services

Text enclosed in matching single or double quotes is converted to **nH...** but is otherwise unaltered (except for formatting — it may get split across card boundaries during the reformatting process). Within quoted strings, the backslash '\' serves as an escape character: the next character is taken literally. This provides a way to get quotes (and of course the backslash itself) into quoted strings:

```
"\\\'"
```

is a string containing a backslash and an apostrophe. (This is *not* the standard convention of doubled quotes, but it is easier to use and more general.)

Any line that begins with the character '%' is left absolutely unaltered except for stripping off the '%' and moving the line one position to the left. This is useful for inserting control cards, and other things that should not be transmogrified (like an existing Fortran program). Use '%' only for ordinary statements, not for the condition parts of **if**, **while**, etc., or the output may come out in an unexpected place.

The following character translations are made, except within single or double quotes or on a line beginning with a '%'.

==	.eq.	!=	.ne.
>	.gt.	>=	.ge.
<	.lt.	<=	.le.
&	.and.			.or.
!	.not.	¬	.not.

In addition, the following translations are provided for input devices with restricted character sets.

[	{	]	}
$(	{	$)	}

"define" Statement

Any string of alphanumeric characters can be defined as a name; thereafter, whenever that name occurs in the input (delimited by non-alphanumerics) it is replaced by the rest of the definition line. (Comments and trailing white spaces are stripped off). A defined name can be arbitrarily long, and must begin with a letter.

define is typically used to create symbolic parameters:

```
define ROWS 100
define COLS  50

dimension a(ROWS), b(ROWS, COLS)

    if (i > ROWS | j > COLS) ...
```

Alternately, definitions may be written as

```
define(ROWS, 100)
```

In this case, the defining text is everything after the comma up to the balancing right parenthesis; this allows multi-line definitions.

It is generally a wise practice to use symbolic parameters for most constants, to help make clear the function of what would otherwise be mysterious numbers. As an example, here is the routine **equal** again, this time with symbolic constants.

```
define    YES      1
define    NO       0
define    EOS     −1
define    ARB     100

# equal _ compare str1 to str2;
#    return YES if equal, NO if not
    integer function equal(str1, str2)
    integer str1(ARB), str2(ARB)
    integer i

    for (i = 1; str1(i) == str2(i); i = i + 1)
        if (str1(i) == EOS)
            return(YES)
    return(NO)
    end
```

"include" Statement

The statement

```
include file
```

inserts the file found on input stream *file* into the Ratfor input in place of the **include** statement. The standard usage is to place COMMON blocks on a file, and **include** that file whenever a copy is needed:

```
subroutine x
    include commonblocks
    ...
    end

suroutine y
    include commonblocks
    ...
    end
```

This ensures that all copies of the COMMON blocks are identical

Pitfalls, Botches, Blemishes and other Failings

Ratfor catches certain syntax errors, such as missing braces, **else** clauses without an **if**, and most errors involving missing parentheses in statements. Beyond that, since Ratfor knows no Fortran, any errors you make will be reported by the Fortran compiler, so you will from time to time have to relate a Fortran diagnostic back to the Ratfor source.

Keywords are reserved — using **if**, **else**, etc., as variable names will typically wreak havoc. Don't leave spaces in keywords. Don't use the Arithmetic IF.

The Fortran **nH** convention is not recognized anywhere by Ratfor; use quotes instead.

3. IMPLEMENTATION

Ratfor was originally written in C[4] on the UNIX operating system[5]. The language is specified by a context free grammar and the compiler constructed using the YACC compiler-compiler[6].

The Ratfor grammar is simple and straightforward, being essentially

```
prog  : stat
      | prog   stat
stat  : if (...) stat
      | if (...) stat else stat
      | while (...) stat
      | for (...; ...; ...) stat
      | do ... stat
      | repeat stat
      | repeat stat until (...)
      | switch (...) { case ...: prog ...
                       default: prog }
      | return
      | break
      | next
      | digits   stat
      | { prog }
      | anything unrecognizable
```

The observation that Ratfor knows no Fortran follows directly from the rule that says a statement is "anything unrecognizable". In fact most of Fortran falls into this category, since any statement that does not begin with one of the keywords is by definition "unrecognizable."

Code generation is also simple. If the first thing on a source line is not a keyword (like **if**, **else**, etc.) the entire statement is simply copied to the output with appropriate character translation and formatting. (Leading digits are treated as a label.) Keywords cause only slightly more complicated actions. For example, when **if** is recognized, two consecutive labels L and L+1 are generated and the value of L is stacked. The condition is then isolated, and the code

```
if (.not. (condition)) goto L
```

is output. The *statement* part of the **if** is then translated. When the end of the statement is encountered (which may be some distance away and include nested **if**'s, of course), the code

```
L       continue
```

is generated, unless there is an **else** clause, in which case the code is

```
        goto L+1
L       continue
```

In this latter case, the code

```
L+1     continue
```

is produced after the *statement* part of the **else**. Code generation for the various loops is equally simple.

One might argue that more care should be taken in code generation. For example, if there is no trailing **else**,

```
if (i > 0) x = a
```

should be left alone, not converted into

```
        if (.not. (i .gt. 0)) goto 100
        x = a
100     continue
```

But what are optimizing compilers for, if not to improve code? It is a rare program indeed where this kind of "inefficiency" will make even a measurable difference. In the few cases where it is important, the offending lines can be protected by '%'.

The use of a compiler-compiler is definitely the preferred method of software development. The language is well-defined, with few syntactic irregularities. Implementation is quite simple; the original construction took under a week. The language is sufficiently simple, however, that an *ad hoc* recognizer can be readily constructed to do the same job if no compiler-compiler is available.

The C version of Ratfor is used on UNIX and on the Honeywell GCOS systems. C compilers are not as widely available as Fortran, however, so there is also a Ratfor written in itself and originally bootstrapped with the C version. The Ratfor version was written so as to translate into the portable subset of Fortran described in [1], so it is portable, having been run essentially without change on at least twelve distinct machines. (The main restrictions of the portable subset are: only one character per machine word; subscripts in the form $c*v\pm c$; avoiding expressions in places like DO loops; consistency in subroutine argument usage, and in COMMON declarations. Ratfor itself will not gratuitously generate non-standard Fortran.)

The Ratfor version is about 1500 lines of Ratfor (compared to about 1000 lines of C); this compiles into 2500 lines of Fortran. This expansion ratio is somewhat higher than average, since the compiled code contains unnecessary occurrences of COMMON declarations. The execution time of the Ratfor version is dominated by two routines that read and write cards. Clearly these routines could be replaced by machine coded local versions; unless this is done, the efficiency of other parts of the translation process is largely irrelevant.

4. EXPERIENCE

Good Things

"It's so much better than Fortran" is the most common response of users when asked how well Ratfor meets their needs. Although cynics might consider this to be vacuous, it does seem to be true that decent control flow and cosmetics converts Fortran from a bad language into quite a reasonable one, assuming that Fortran data structures are adequate for the task at hand.

Although there are no quantitative results, users feel that coding in Ratfor is at least twice as fast as in Fortran. More important, debugging and subsequent revision are much faster than in Fortran. Partly this is simply because the code can be *read*. The looping statements which test at the top instead of the bottom seem to elim-

inate or at least reduce the occurrence of a wide class of boundary errors. And of course it is easy to do structured programming in Ratfor; this self-discipline also contributes markedly to reliability.

One interesting and encouraging fact is that programs written in Ratfor tend to be as readable as programs written in more modern languages like Pascal. Once one is freed from the shackles of Fortran's clerical detail and rigid input format, it is easy to write code that is readable, even esthetically pleasing. For example, here is a Ratfor implementation of the linear table search discussed by Knuth [7]:

```
A(m+1) = x
for (i = 1; A(i) != x; i = i + 1)
    ;
if (i > m) {
    m = i
    B(i) = 1
}
else
    B(i) = B(i) + 1
```

A large corpus (5400 lines) of Ratfor, including a subset of the Ratfor preprocessor itself, can be found in [8].

Bad Things

The biggest single problem is that many Fortran syntax errors are not detected by Ratfor but by the local Fortran compiler. The compiler then prints a message in terms of the generated Fortran, and in a few cases this may be difficult to relate back to the offending Ratfor line, especially if the implementation conceals the generated Fortran. This problem could be dealt with by tagging each generated line with some indication of the source line that created it, but this is inherently implementation-dependent, so no action has yet been taken. Error message interpretation is actually not so arduous as might be thought. Since Ratfor generates no variables, only a simple pattern of IF's and GOTO's, data-related errors like missing DIMENSION statements are easy to find in the Fortran. Furthermore, there has been a steady improvement in Ratfor's ability to catch trivial syntactic errors like unbalanced parentheses and quotes.

There are a number of implementation weaknesses that are a nuisance, especially to new users. For example, keywords are reserved. This rarely makes any difference, except for those hardy souls who want to use an Arithmetic IF. A few standard Fortran constructions are not accepted by Ratfor, and this is perceived as a problem by users with a large corpus of existing Fortran programs. Protecting every line with a

'%' is not really a complete solution, although it serves as a stop-gap. The best long-term solution is provided by the program Struct [9], which converts arbitrary Fortran programs into Ratfor.

Users who export programs often complain that the generated Fortran is "unreadable" because it is not tastefully formatted and contains extraneous CONTINUE statements. To some extent this can be ameliorated (Ratfor now has an option to copy Ratfor comments into the generated Fortran), but it has always seemed that effort is better spent on the input language than on the output esthetics.

One final problem is partly attributable to success — since Ratfor is relatively easy to modify, there are now several dialects of Ratfor. Fortunately, so far most of the differences are in character set, or in invisible aspects like code generation.

5. CONCLUSIONS

Ratfor demonstrates that with modest effort it is possible to convert Fortran from a bad language into quite a good one. A preprocessor is clearly a useful way to extend or ameliorate the facilities of a base language.

When designing a language, it is important to concentrate on the essential requirement of providing the user with the best language possible for a given effort. One must avoid throwing in "features" — things which the user may trivially construct within the existing framework.

One must also avoid getting sidetracked on irrelevancies. For instance it seems pointless for Ratfor to prepare a neatly formatted listing of either its input or its output. The user is presumably capable of the self-discipline required to prepare neat input that reflects his thoughts. It is much more important that the language provide free-form input so he *can* format it neatly. No one should read the output anyway except in the most dire circumstances.

Acknowledgements

C. A. R. Hoare once said that "One thing [the language designer] should not do is to include untried ideas of his own." Ratfor follows this precept very closely — everything in it has been stolen from someone else. Most of the control flow structures are taken directly from the language C[4] developed by Dennis Ritchie; the comment and continuation conventions are adapted from Altran[10].

I am grateful to Stuart Feldman, whose patient simulation of an innocent user during the early days of Ratfor led to several design improvements and the eradication of bugs. He

also translated the C parse-tables and YACC parser into Fortran for the first Ratfor version of Ratfor.

References

[1] B. G. Ryder, "The PFORT Verifier," *Software—Practice & Experience,* October 1974.

[2] American National Standard Fortran. American National Standards Institute, New York, 1966.

[3] *For-word: Fortran Development Newsletter,* August 1975.

[4] B. W. Kernighan and D. M. Ritchie, *The C Programming Language,* Prentice-Hall, Inc., 1978.

[5] D. M. Ritchie and K. L. Thompson, "The UNIX Time-sharing System." *CACM,* July 1974.

[6] S. C. Johnson, "YACC — Yet Another Compiler-Compiler." Bell Laboratories Computing Science Technical Report #32, 1978.

[7] D. E. Knuth, "Structured Programming with goto Statements." *Computing Surveys,* December 1974.

[8] B. W. Kernighan and P. J. Plauger, *Software Tools,* Addison-Wesley, 1976.

[9] B. S. Baker, "Struct — A Program which Structures Fortran", Bell Laboratories internal memorandum, December 1975.

[10] A. D. Hall, "The Altran System for Rational Function Manipulation — A Survey." *CACM,* August 1971.

The M4 Macro Processor

Brian W. Kernighan

Dennis M. Ritchie

Bell Laboratories
Murray Hill, New Jersey 07974

ABSTRACT

M4 is a macro processor available on UNIX† and GCOS. Its primary use has been as a front end for Ratfor for those cases where parameterless macros are not adequately powerful. It has also been used for languages as disparate as C and Cobol. M4 is particularly suited for functional languages like Fortran, PL/I and C since macros are specified in a functional notation.

M4 provides features seldom found even in much larger macro processors, including

- arguments
- condition testing
- arithmetic capabilities
- string and substring functions
- file manipulation

This paper is a user's manual for M4.

July 1, 1977

---

†UNIX is a Trademark of Bell Laboratories.

Introduction

A macro processor is a useful way to enhance a programming language, to make it more palatable or more readable, or to tailor it to a particular application. The **#define** statement in C and the analogous **define** in Ratfor are examples of the basic facility provided by any macro processor — replacement of text by other text.

The M4 macro processor is an extension of a macro processor called M3 which was written by D. M. Ritchie for the AP-3 minicomputer; M3 was in turn based on a macro processor implemented for [1]. Readers unfamiliar with the basic ideas of macro processing may wish to read some of the discussion there.

M4 is a suitable front end for Ratfor and C, and has also been used successfully with Cobol. Besides the straightforward replacement of one string of text by another, it provides macros with arguments, conditional macro expansion, arithmetic, file manipulation, and some specialized string processing functions.

The basic operation of M4 is to copy its input to its output. As the input is read, however, each alphanumeric "token" (that is, string of letters and digits) is checked. If it is the name of a macro, then the name of the macro is replaced by its defining text, and the resulting string is pushed back onto the input to be rescanned. Macros may be called with arguments, in which case the arguments are collected and substituted into the right places in the defining text before it is rescanned.

M4 provides a collection of about twenty built-in macros which perform various useful operations; in addition, the user can define new macros. Built-ins and user-defined macros work exactly the same way, except that some of the built-in macros have side effects on the state of the process.

Usage

On UNIX, use

m4 [files]

Each argument file is processed in order; if there are no arguments, or if an argument is `-`, the standard input is read at that point. The processed text is written on the standard output, which may be captured for subsequent processing with

m4 [files] >outputfile

On GCOS, usage is identical, but the program is called **./m4**.

Defining Macros

The primary built-in function of M4 is **define**, which is used to define new macros. The input

define(name, stuff)

causes the string **name** to be defined as **stuff**. All subsequent occurrences of **name** will be replaced by **stuff**. **name** must be alphanumeric and must begin with a letter (the underscore _ counts as a letter). **stuff** is any text that contains balanced parentheses; it may stretch over multiple lines.

Thus, as a typical example,

define(N, 100)

...

if (i > N)

defines N to be 100, and uses this "symbolic

constant'' in a later **if** statement.

The left parenthesis must immediately follow the word **define**, to signal that **define** has arguments. If a macro or built-in name is not followed immediately by `(', it is assumed to have no arguments. This is the situation for **N** above; it is actually a macro with no arguments, and thus when it is used there need be no (...) following it.

You should also notice that a macro name is only recognized as such if it appears surrounded by non-alphanumerics. For example, in

define(N, 100)

...

if (NNN > 100)

the variable NNN is absolutely unrelated to the defined macro **N**, even though it contains a lot of **N**'s.

Things may be defined in terms of other things. For example,

define(N, 100)
define(M, N)

defines both **M** and **N** to be 100.

What happens if **N** is redefined? Or, to say it another way, is **M** defined as **N** or as 100? In M4, the latter is true — **M** is 100, so even if **N** subsequently changes, **M** does not.

This behavior arises because M4 expands macro names into their defining text as soon as it possibly can. Here, that means that when the string **N** is seen as the arguments of **define** are being collected, it is immediately replaced by 100; it's just as if you had said

define(M, 100)

in the first place.

If this isn't what you really want, there are two ways out of it. The first, which is specific to this situation, is to interchange the order of the definitions:

define(M, N)
define(N, 100)

Now **M** is defined to be the string **N**, so when you ask for **M** later, you'll always get the value of **N** at that time (because the **M** will be replaced by **N** which will be replaced by 100).

Quoting

The more general solution is to delay the expansion of the arguments of **define** by *quoting* them. Any text surrounded by the single quotes ` and ´ is not expanded immediately, but has the quotes stripped off. If you say

define(N, 100)
define(M, `N´)

the quotes around the N are stripped off as the argument is being collected, but they have served their purpose, and M is defined as the string N, not 100. The general rule is that M4 always strips off one level of single quotes whenever it evaluates something. This is true even outside of macros. If you want the word **define** to appear in the output, you have to quote it in the input, as in

`define´ = 1;

As another instance of the same thing, which is a bit more surprising, consider redefining N:

define(N, 100)
...
define(N, 200)

Perhaps regrettably, the N in the second definition is evaluated as soon as it's seen; that is, it is replaced by 100, so it's as if you had written

define(100, 200)

This statement is ignored by M4, since you can only define things that look like names, but it obviously doesn't have the effect you wanted. To really redefine N, you must delay the evaluation by quoting:

define(N, 100)
...
define(`N´, 200)

In M4, it is often wise to quote the first argument of a macro.

If ` and ´ are not convenient for some reason, the quote characters can be changed with the built-in **changequote**:

changequote([,])

makes the new quote characters the left and right brackets. You can restore the original characters with just

changequote

There are two additional built-ins related to **define**. **undefine** removes the definition of some macro or built-in:

undefine(`N´)

removes the definition of N. (Why are the quotes absolutely necessary?) Built-ins can be removed with **undefine**, as in

undefine(`define´)

but once you remove one, you can never get it back.

The built-in **ifdef** provides a way to determine if a macro is currently defined. In particular, M4 has pre-defined the names **unix** and **gcos** on the corresponding systems, so you can tell which one you're using:

ifdef(`unix´, `define(wordsize,16)´)
ifdef(`gcos´, `define(wordsize,36)´)

makes a definition appropriate for the particular machine. Don't forget the quotes!

ifdef actually permits three arguments; if the name is undefined, the value of **ifdef** is then the third argument, as in

ifdef(`unix´, on UNIX, not on UNIX)

Arguments

So far we have discussed the simplest form of macro processing — replacing one string by another (fixed) string. User-defined macros may also have arguments, so different invocations can have different results. Within the replacement text for a macro (the second argument of its **define**) any occurrence of **$n** will be replaced by the nth argument when the macro is actually used. Thus, the macro **bump**, defined as

define(bump, $1 = $1 + 1)

generates code to increment its argument by 1:

bump(x)

is

x = x + 1

A macro can have as many arguments as you want, but only the first nine are accessible, through **$1** to **$9**. (The macro name itself is **$0**, although that is less commonly used.) Arguments that are not supplied are replaced by null strings, so we can define a macro **cat** which simply concatenates its arguments, like this:

define(cat, $1$2$3$4$5$6$7$8$9)

Thus

cat(x, y, z)

is equivalent to

xyz

$4 through **$9** are null, since no corresponding arguments were provided.

Leading unquoted blanks, tabs, or newlines that occur during argument collection are discarded. All other white space is retained. Thus

define(a,   b   c)

defines **a** to be **b   c**.

Arguments are separated by commas, but parentheses are counted properly, so a comma "protected" by parentheses does not terminate an argument. That is, in

define(a, (b,c))

there are only two arguments; the second is literally **(b,c)**. And of course a bare comma or parenthesis can be inserted by quoting it.

Arithmetic Built-ins

M4 provides two built-in functions for doing arithmetic on integers (only). The simplest is **incr**, which increments its numeric argument by 1. Thus to handle the common programming situation where you want a variable to be defined as "one more than N", write

define(N, 100)
define(N1, `incr(N)´)

Then **N1** is defined as one more than the current value of **N**.

The more general mechanism for arithmetic is a built-in called **eval**, which is capable of arbitrary arithmetic on integers. It provides the operators (in decreasing order of precedence)

unary + and −
** or ^   (exponentiation)
* / % (modulus)
+ −
== != < <= > >=
!   (not)
& or &&   (logical and)
| or || (logical or)

Parentheses may be used to group operations where needed. All the operands of an expression given to **eval** must ultimately be numeric. The numeric value of a true relation (like $1 > 0$) is 1, and false is 0. The precision in **eval** is 32 bits on UNIX and 36 bits on GCOS.

As a simple example, suppose we want **M** to be $2**N+1$. Then

define(N, 3)
define(M, `eval(2**N+1)')

As a matter of principle, it is advisable to quote the defining text for a macro unless it is very simple indeed (say just a number); it usually gives the result you want, and is a good habit to get into.

File Manipulation

You can include a new file in the input at any time by the built-in function **include**:

include(filename)

inserts the contents of **filename** in place of the **include** command. The contents of the file is often a set of definitions. The value of **include** (that is, its replacement text) is the contents of the file; this can be captured in definitions, etc.

It is a fatal error if the file named in **include** cannot be accessed. To get some control over this situation, the alternate form **sinclude** can be used; **sinclude** ("silent include") says nothing and continues if it can't access the file.

It is also possible to divert the output of M4 to temporary files during processing, and output the collected material upon command. M4 maintains nine of these diversions, numbered 1 through 9. If you say

divert(n)

all subsequent output is put onto the end of a temporary file referred to as **n**. Diverting to this file is stopped by another **divert** command; in particular, **divert** or **divert(0)** resumes the normal output process.

Diverted text is normally output all at once at the end of processing, with the diversions output in numeric order. It is possible, however, to bring back diversions at any time, that is, to append them to the current diversion.

undivert

brings back all diversions in numeric order, and **undivert** with arguments brings back the selected diversions in the order given. The act of undiverting discards the diverted stuff, as does diverting into a diversion whose number is not between 0 and 9 inclusive.

The value of **undivert** is *not* the diverted stuff. Furthermore, the diverted material is *not* rescanned for macros.

The built-in **divnum** returns the number of the currently active diversion. This is zero during normal processing.

System Command

You can run any program in the local operating system with the **syscmd** built-in. For example,

syscmd(date)

on UNIX runs the **date** command. Normally **syscmd** would be used to create a file for a subsequent **include**.

To facilitate making unique file names, the built-in **maketemp** is provided, with specifications identical to the system function *mktemp:* a string of XXXXX in the argument is replaced by the process id of the current process.

Conditionals

There is a built-in called **ifelse** which enables you to perform arbitrary conditional testing. In the simplest form,

ifelse(a, b, c, d)

compares the two strings **a** and **b**. If these are identical, **ifelse** returns the string **c**; otherwise it returns **d**. Thus we might define a macro called **compare** which compares two strings and returns "yes" or "no" if they are the same or different.

define(compare, `ifelse($1, $2, yes, no)´)

Note the quotes, which prevent too-early evaluation of **ifelse**.

If the fourth argument is missing, it is treated as empty.

ifelse can actually have any number of arguments, and thus provides a limited form of multi-way decision capability. In the input

ifelse(a, b, c, d, e, f, g)

if the string **a** matches the string **b**, the result is **c**. Otherwise, if **d** is the same as **e**, the result is **f**. Otherwise the result is **g**. If the final argument is omitted, the result is null, so

ifelse(a, b, c)

is **c** if **a** matches **b**, and null otherwise.

String Manipulation

The built-in **len** returns the length of the string that makes up its argument. Thus

len(abcdef)

is 6, and **len((a,b))** is 5.

The built-in **substr** can be used to produce substrings of strings. **substr(s, i, n)** returns the substring of **s** that starts at the ith position (origin zero), and is **n** characters long. If **n** is omitted, the rest of the string is returned, so

substr(`now is the time´, 1)

is

ow is the time

If **i** or **n** are out of range, various sensible things happen.

index(s1, s2) returns the index (position) in **s1** where the string **s2** occurs, or −1 if it doesn't occur. As with **substr**, the origin for strings is 0.

The built-in **translit** performs character transliteration.

translit(s, f, t)

modifies **s** by replacing any character found in **f** by the corresponding character of **t**. That is,

translit(s, aeiou, 12345)

replaces the vowels by the corresponding digits. If **t** is shorter than **f**, characters which don't have an entry in **t** are deleted; as a limiting case, if **t** is not present at all, characters from **f** are deleted from **s**. So

translit(s, aeiou)

deletes vowels from **s**.

There is also a built-in called **dnl** which deletes all characters that follow it up to and including the next newline; it is useful mainly for throwing away empty lines that otherwise tend to clutter up M4 output. For example, if you say

define(N, 100)
define(M, 200)
define(L, 300)

the newline at the end of each line is not part of the definition, so it is copied into the output, where it may not be wanted. If you add **dnl** to each of these lines, the newlines will disappear.

Another way to achieve this, due to J. E. Weythman, is

divert(−1)
    define(...)
    ...
divert

Printing

The built-in **errprint** writes its arguments out on the standard error file. Thus you can say

errprint(`fatal error´)

dumpdef is a debugging aid which dumps the current definitions of defined terms. If there are no arguments, you get everything; otherwise you get the ones you name as arguments. Don't forget to quote the names!

Summary of Built-ins

Each entry is preceded by the page number where it is described.

3   changequote(L, R)
1   define(name, replacement)
4   divert(number)
4   divnum
5   dnl
5   dumpdef(`name', `name', ...)
5   errprint(s, s, ...)
4   eval(numeric expression)
3   ifdef(`name', this if true, this if false)
5   ifelse(a, b, c, d)
4   include(file)
3   incr(number)
5   index(s1, s2)
5   len(string)
4   maketemp(...XXXXX...)
4   sinclude(file)
5   substr(string, position, number)
4   syscmd(s)
5   translit(str, from, to)
3   undefine(`name')
4   undivert(number,number,...)

Acknowledgements

We are indebted to Rick Becker, John Chambers, Doug McIlroy, and especially Jim Weythman, whose pioneering use of M4 has led to several valuable improvements. We are also deeply grateful to Weythman for several substantial contributions to the code.

References

[1]   B. W. Kernighan and P. J. Plauger, *Software Tools,* Addison-Wesley, Inc., 1976.

SED — A Non-interactive Text Editor

Lee E. McMahon

Bell Laboratories
Murray Hill, New Jersey 07974

ABSTRACT

Sed is a non-interactive context editor that runs on the UNIX† operating system. *Sed* is designed to be especially useful in three cases:

1) To edit files too large for comfortable interactive editing;
2) To edit any size file when the sequence of editing commands is too complicated to be comfortably typed in interactive mode.
3) To perform multiple 'global' editing functions efficiently in one pass through the input.

This memorandum constitutes a manual for users of *sed*.

August 15, 1978

---

†UNIX is a Trademark of Bell Laboratories.

Introduction

Sed is a non-interactive context editor designed to be especially useful in three cases:

1) To edit files too large for comfortable interactive editing;
2) To edit any size file when the sequence of editing commands is too complicated to be comfortably typed in interactive mode;
3) To perform multiple 'global' editing functions efficiently in one pass through the input.

Since only a few lines of the input reside in core at one time, and no temporary files are used, the effective size of file that can be edited is limited only by the requirement that the input and output fit simultaneously into available secondary storage.

Complicated editing scripts can be created separately and given to *sed* as a command file. For complex edits, this saves considerable typing, and its attendant errors. *Sed* running from a command file is much more efficient than any interactive editor known to the author, even if that editor can be driven by a pre-written script.

The principal loss of functions compared to an interactive editor are lack of relative addressing (because of the line-at-a-time operation), and lack of immediate verification that a command has done what was intended.

Sed is a lineal descendant of the UNIX editor, *ed*. Because of the differences between interactive and non-interactive operation, considerable changes have been made between *ed* and *sed*; even confirmed users of *ed* will frequently be surprised (and probably chagrined), if they rashly use *sed* without reading Sections 2 and 3 of this document. The most striking family resemblance between the two editors is in the class of patterns ('regular expressions') they recognize; the code for matching patterns is copied almost verbatim from the code for *ed*, and the description of regular expressions in Section 2 is copied almost verbatim from the UNIX Programmer's Manual[1]. (Both code and description were written by Dennis M. Ritchie.)

1. Overall Operation

Sed by default copies the standard input to the standard output, perhaps performing one or more editing commands on each line before writing it to the output. This behavior may be modified by flags on the command line; see Section 1.1 below.

The general format of an editing command is:

[address1,address2] [function] [arguments]

One or both addresses may be omitted; the format of addresses is given in Section 2. Any number of blanks or tabs may separate the addresses from the function. The function must be present; the available commands are discussed in Section 3. The arguments may be required or optional, according to which function is given; again, they are discussed in Section 3 under each individual function.

Tab characters and spaces at the beginning of lines are ignored.

1.1. Command-line Flags

Three flags are recognized on the command line:

-   **-n:** tells *sed* not to copy all lines, but only those specified by *p* functions or *p* flags after *s* functions (see Section 3.3);
-   **-e:** tells *sed* to take the next argument as an editing command;
-   **-f:** tells *sed* to take the next argument as a file name; the file should contain editing commands, one to a line.

1.2. Order of Application of Editing Commands

Before any editing is done (in fact, before any input file is even opened), all the editing commands are compiled into a form which will be moderately efficient during the execution phase (when the commands are actually applied to lines of the input file). The commands are compiled in the order in which they are encountered; this is generally the order in which they will be attempted at execution time. The commands are applied one at a time; the input to each command is the output of all preceding commands.

The default linear order of application of editing commands can be changed by the flow-of-control commands, *t* and *b* (see Section 3). Even when the order of application is changed by these commands, it is still true that the input line to any command is the output of any previously applied command.

1.3. Pattern-space

The range of pattern matches is called the pattern space. Ordinarily, the pattern space is one line of the input text, but more than one line can be read into the pattern space by using the *N* command (Section 3.6.).

1.4. Examples

Examples are scattered throughout the text. Except where otherwise noted, the examples all assume the following input text:

        In Xanadu did Kubla Khan
        A stately pleasure dome decree:
        Where Alph, the sacred river, ran
        Through caverns measureless to man
        Down to a sunless sea.

(In no case is the output of the *sed* commands to be considered an improvement on Coleridge.)

Example:

The command

        2q

will quit after copying the first two lines of the input. The output will be:

        In Xanadu did Kubla Khan
        A stately pleasure dome decree:

2. ADDRESSES: Selecting lines for editing

Lines in the input file(s) to which editing commands are to be applied can be selected by addresses. Addresses may be either line numbers or context addresses.

The application of a group of commands can be controlled by one address (or address-pair) by grouping the commands with curly braces ('{ }') (Sec. 3.6.).

2.1. Line-number Addresses

A line number is a decimal integer. As each line is read from the input, a line-number counter is incremented; a line-number address matches (selects) the input line which causes the internal counter to equal the address line-number. The counter runs cumulatively through multiple input files; it is not reset when a new input file is opened.

As a special case, the character $ matches the last line of the last input file.

2.2. Context Addresses

A context address is a pattern ('regular expression') enclosed in slashes ('/'). The regular expressions recognized by *sed* are constructed as follows:

1) An ordinary character (not one of those discussed below) is a regular expression, and matches that character.

2) A circumflex '^' at the beginning of a regular expression matches the null character at the beginning of a line.

3) A dollar-sign '$' at the end of a regular expression matches the null character at the end of a line.

4) The characters '\n' match an imbedded newline character, but not the newline at the end of the pattern space.

5) A period '.' matches any character except the terminal newline of the pattern space.

6) A regular expression followed by an asterisk '*' matches any number (including 0) of adjacent occurrences of the regular expression it follows.

7) A string of characters in square brackets '[ ]' matches any character in the string, and no others. If, however, the first character of the string is circumflex '^', the regular expression matches any character *except* the characters in the string and the terminal newline of the pattern space.

8) A concatenation of regular expressions is a regular expression which matches the concatenation of strings matched by the components of the regular expression.

9) A regular expression between the sequences '\(' and '\)' is identical in effect to the unadorned regular expression, but has side-effects which are described under the s command below and specification 10) immediately below.

10) The expression '\d' means the same string of characters matched by an expression enclosed in '\(' and '\)' earlier in the same pattern. Here d is a single digit; the string specified is that beginning with the dth occurrence of '\(' counting from the left. For example, the expression '^\(.*\)\1' matches a line beginning with two repeated occurrences of the same string.

11) The null regular expression standing alone (e.g., '//') is equivalent to the last regular expression compiled.

To use one of the special characters (^ $. * [ ] \ /) as a literal (to match an occurrence of itself in the input), precede the special character by a backslash '\'.

For a context address to 'match' the input requires that the whole pattern within the address match some portion of the pattern space.

2.3. Number of Addresses

The commands in the next section can have 0, 1, or 2 addresses. Under each command the maximum number of allowed addresses is given. For a command to have more addresses than the maximum allowed is considered an error.

If a command has no addresses, it is applied to every line in the input.

If a command has one address, it is applied to all lines which match that address.

If a command has two addresses, it is applied to the first line which matches the first address, and to all subsequent lines until (and including) the first subsequent line which matches the second address. Then an attempt is made on subsequent lines to again match the first address, and the process is repeated.

Two addresses are separated by a comma.

Examples:

/an/	matches lines 1, 3, 4 in our sample text
/an.*an/	matches line 1
/ˆan/	matches no lines
/./	matches all lines
/\./	matches line 5
/r*an/	matches lines 1,3, 4 (number = zero!)
/\(an\).*\1/	matches line 1

3. FUNCTIONS

All functions are named by a single character. In the following summary, the maximum number of allowable addresses is given enclosed in parentheses, then the single character function name, possible arguments enclosed in angles (< >), an expanded English translation of the single-character name, and finally a description of what each function does. The angles around the arguments are *not* part of the argument, and should not be typed in actual editing commands.

3.1. Whole-line Oriented Functions

(2)d -- delete lines

> The *d* function deletes from the file (does not write to the output) all those lines matched by its address(es).

> It also has the side effect that no further commands are attempted on the corpse of a deleted line; as soon as the *d* function is executed, a new line is read from the input, and the list of editing commands is re-started from the beginning on the new line.

(2)n -- next line

> The *n* function reads the next line from the input, replacing the current line. The current line is written to the output if it should be. The list of editing commands is continued following the *n* command.

(1)a\
<text> -- append lines

> The *a* function causes the argument <text> to be written to the output after the line matched by its address. The *a* command is inherently multi-line; *a* must appear at the end of a line, and <text> may contain any number of lines. To preserve the one-command-to-a-line fiction, the interior newlines must be hidden by a backslash character ('\') immediately preceding the newline. The <text> argument is terminated by the first unhidden newline (the first one not immediately preceded by backslash).

> Once an *a* function is successfully executed, <text> will be written to the output regardless of what later commands do to the line which triggered it. The triggering line may be deleted entirely; <text> will still be written to the output.

> The <text> is not scanned for address matches, and no editing commands are attempted on it. It does not cause any change in the line-number counter.

(1)i\
<text> -- insert lines

The *i* function behaves identically to the *a* function, except that <text> is written to the output *before* the matched line. All other comments about the *a* function apply to the *i* function as well.

(2)c\
<text> -- change lines

The *c* function deletes the lines selected by its address(es), and replaces them with the lines in <text>. Like *a* and *i*, *c* must be followed by a newline hidden by a backslash; and interior new lines in <text> must be hidden by backslashes.

The *c* command may have two addresses, and therefore select a range of lines. If it does, all the lines in the range are deleted, but only one copy of <text> is written to the output, *not* one copy per line deleted. As with *a* and *i*, <text> is not scanned for address matches, and no editing commands are attempted on it. It does not change the line-number counter.

After a line has been deleted by a *c* function, no further commands are attempted on the corpse.

If text is appended after a line by *a* or *r* functions, and the line is subsequently changed, the text inserted by the *c* function will be placed *before* the text of the *a* or *r* functions. (The *r* function is described in Section 3.4.)

Note: Within the text put in the output by these functions, leading blanks and tabs will disappear, as always in *sed* commands. To get leading blanks and tabs into the output, precede the first desired blank or tab by a backslash; the backslash will not appear in the output.

Example:

The list of editing commands:

```
n
a\
XXXX
d
```

applied to our standard input, produces:

```
In Xanadu did Kubhla Khan
XXXX
Where Alph, the sacred river, ran
XXXX
Down to a sunless sea.
```

In this particular case, the same effect would be produced by either of the two following command lists:

```
n          n
i\         c\
XXXX       XXXX
d
```

3.2. Substitute Function

One very important function changes parts of lines selected by a context search within the line.

(2)s<pattern><replacement><flags> -- substitute

The *s* function replaces *part* of a line (selected by <pattern>) with <replacement>. It can best be read:

Substitute for <pattern>, <replacement>

The <pattern> argument contains a pattern, exactly like the patterns in addresses (see 2.2 above). The only difference between <pattern> and a context address is that the context address must be delimited by slash ('/') characters; <pattern> may be delimited by any character other than space or newline.

By default, only the first string matched by <pattern> is replaced, but see the *g* flag below.

The <replacement> argument begins immediately after the second delimiting character of <pattern>, and must be followed immediately by another instance of the delimiting character. (Thus there are exactly *three* instances of the delimiting character.)

The <replacement> is not a pattern, and the characters which are special in patterns do not have special meaning in <replacement>. Instead, other characters are special:

> &   is replaced by the string matched by <pattern>
>
> *d* (where *d* is a single digit) is replaced by the *d*th substring matched by parts of <pattern> enclosed in '\\(' and '\\)'. If nested substrings occur in <pattern>, the *d*th is determined by counting opening delimiters ('\\(').
>
> As in patterns, special characters may be made literal by preceding them with backslash ('\\').

The <flags> argument may contain the following flags:

> g -- substitute <replacement> for all (non-overlapping) instances of <pattern> in the line. After a successful substitution, the scan for the next instance of <pattern> begins just after the end of the inserted characters; characters put into the line from <replacement> are not rescanned.
>
> p -- print the line if a successful replacement was done. The *p* flag causes the line to be written to the output if and only if a substitution was actually made by the *s* function. Notice that if several *s* functions, each followed by a *p* flag, successfully substitute in the same input line, multiple copies of the line will be written to the output: one for each successful substitution.
>
> w <filename> -- write the line to a file if a successful replacement was done. The *w* flag causes lines which are actually substituted by the *s* function to be written to a file named by <filename>. If <filename> exists before *sed* is run, it is overwritten; if not, it is created.
>
> A single space must separate *w* and <filename>.
>
> The possibilities of multiple, somewhat different copies of one input line being written are the same as for *p*.
>
> A maximum of 10 different file names may be mentioned after *w* flags and *w* functions (see below), combined.

Examples:

The following command, applied to our standard input,

> s/to/by/w changes

produces, on the standard output:

> In Xanadu did Kubhla Khan
> A stately pleasure dome decree:
> Where Alph, the sacred river, ran
> Through caverns measureless by man
> Down by a sunless sea.

and, on the file 'changes':

> Through caverns measureless by man
> Down by a sunless sea.

If the nocopy option is in effect, the command:

> s/[.,;?:]/*P&*/gp

produces:

> A stately pleasure dome decree*P:*
> Where Alph*P,* the sacred river*P,* ran
> Down to a sunless sea*P.*

Finally, to illustrate the effect of the g flag, the command:

> /X/s/an/AN/p

produces (assuming nocopy mode):

> In XANadu did Kubhla Khan

and the command:

> /X/s/an/AN/gp

produces:

> In XANadu did Kubhla KhAN

3.3. Input-output Functions

(2)p -- print

> The print function writes the addressed lines to the standard output file. They are written at the time the p function is encountered, regardless of what succeeding editing commands may do to the lines.

(2)w <filename> -- write on <filename>

> The write function writes the addressed lines to the file named by <filename>. If the file previously existed, it is overwritten; if not, it is created. The lines are written exactly as they exist when the write function is encountered for each line, regardless of what subsequent editing commands may do to them.

> Exactly one space must separate the w and <filename>.

> A maximum of ten different files may be mentioned in write functions and w flags after s functions, combined.

(1)r <filename> -- read the contents of a file

> The read function reads the contents of <filename>, and appends them after the line matched by the address. The file is read and appended regardless of what subsequent editing commands do to the line which matched its address. If r and a functions are executed on the same line, the text from the a

functions and the *r* functions is written to the output in the order that the functions are executed.

Exactly one space must separate the *r* and <filename>. If a file mentioned by a *r* function cannot be opened, it is considered a null file, not an error, and no diagnostic is given.

NOTE: Since there is a limit to the number of files that can be opened simultaneously, care should be taken that no more than ten files be mentioned in *w* functions or flags; that number is reduced by one if any *r* functions are present. (Only one read file is open at one time.)

Examples

Assume that the file 'note1' has the following contents:

> Note: Kubla Khan (more properly Kublai Khan; 1216-1294) was the grandson and most eminent successor of Genghiz (Chingiz) Khan, and founder of the Mongol dynasty in China.

Then the following command:

/Kubla/r note1

produces:

> In Xanadu did Kubla Khan
> > Note: Kubla Khan (more properly Kublai Khan; 1216-1294) was the grandson and most eminent successor of Genghiz (Chingiz) Khan, and founder of the Mongol dynasty in China.
>
> A stately pleasure dome decree:
> Where Alph, the sacred river, ran
> Through caverns measureless to man
> Down to a sunless sea.

3.4. Multiple Input-line Functions

Three functions, all spelled with capital letters, deal specially with pattern spaces containing imbedded newlines; they are intended principally to provide pattern matches across lines in the input.

(2)N -- Next line

> The next input line is appended to the current line in the pattern space; the two input lines are separated by an imbedded newline. Pattern matches may extend across the imbedded newline(s).

(2)D -- Delete first part of the pattern space

> Delete up to and including the first newline character in the current pattern space. If the pattern space becomes empty (the only newline was the terminal newline), read another line from the input. In any case, begin the list of editing commands again from its beginning.

(2)P -- Print first part of the pattern space

> Print up to and including the first newline in the pattern space.

The *P* and *D* functions are equivalent to their lower-case counterparts if there are no imbedded newlines in the pattern space.

3.5. Hold and Get Functions

Four functions save and retrieve part of the input for possible later use.

>   (2)h -- hold pattern space
>
>>   The *h* functions copies the contents of the pattern space into a hold area (destroying the previous contents of the hold area).
>
>   (2)H -- Hold pattern space
>
>>   The *H* function appends the contents of the pattern space to the contents of the hold area; the former and new contents are separated by a newline.
>
>   (2)g -- get contents of hold area
>
>>   The *g* function copies the contents of the hold area into the pattern space (destroying the previous contents of the pattern space).
>
>   (2)G -- Get contents of hold area
>
>>   The *G* function appends the contents of the hold area to the contents of the pattern space; the former and new contents are separated by a newline.
>
>   (2)x -- exchange
>
>>   The exchange command interchanges the contents of the pattern space and the hold area.

Example

The commands

```
1h
1s/ did.*//
1x
G
s/\n/ :/
```

applied to our standard example, produce:

```
In Xanadu did Kubla Khan  :In Xanadu
A stately pleasure dome decree:  :In Xanadu
Where Alph, the sacred river, ran  :In Xanadu
Through caverns measureless to man  :In Xanadu
Down to a sunless sea.  :In Xanadu
```

3.6. Flow-of-Control Functions

These functions do no editing on the input lines, but control the application of functions to the lines selected by the address part.

>   (2)! -- Don't
>
>>   The *Don't* command causes the next command (written on the same line), to be applied to all and only those input lines *not* selected by the adress part.
>
>   (2){ -- Grouping
>
>>   The grouping command '{' causes the next set of commands to be applied (or not applied) as a block to the input lines selected by the addresses of the grouping command. The first of the commands under control of the grouping may appear on the same line as the '{' or on the next line.

The group of commands is terminated by a matching '}' standing on a line by itself.

Groups can be nested.

(0):<label> -- place a label

The label function marks a place in the list of editing commands which may be referred to by *b* and *t* functions. The <label> may be any sequence of eight or fewer characters; if two different colon functions have identical labels, a compile time diagnostic will be generated, and no execution attempted.

(2)b<label> -- branch to label

The branch function causes the sequence of editing commands being applied to the current input line to be restarted immediately after the place where a colon function with the same <label> was encountered. If no colon function with the same label can be found after all the editing commands have been compiled, a compile time diagnostic is produced, and no execution is attempted.

A *b* function with no <label> is taken to be a branch to the end of the list of editing commands; whatever should be done with the current input line is done, and another input line is read; the list of editing commands is restarted from the beginning on the new line.

(2)t<label> -- test substitutions

The *t* function tests whether *any* successful substitutions have been made on the current input line; if so, it branches to <label>; if not, it does nothing. The flag which indicates that a successful substitution has been executed is reset by:

  1) reading a new input line, or
  2) executing a *t* function.

3.7. Miscellaneous Functions

(1)= -- equals

The = function writes to the standard output the line number of the line matched by its address.

(1)q -- quit

The *q* function causes the current line to be written to the output (if it should be), any appended or read text to be written, and execution to be terminated.

Reference

[1] Ken Thompson and Dennis M. Ritchie, *The UNIX Programmer's Manual.* Bell Laboratories, 1978.

Awk — A Pattern Scanning and Processing Language
(Second Edition)

Alfred V. Aho

Brian W. Kernighan

Peter J. Weinberger

Bell Laboratories
Murray Hill, New Jersey 07974

ABSTRACT

Awk is a programming language whose basic operation is to search a set of files for patterns, and to perform specified actions upon lines or fields of lines which contain instances of those patterns. *Awk* makes certain data selection and transformation operations easy to express; for example, the *awk* program

$$\text{length} > 72$$

prints all input lines whose length exceeds 72 characters; the program

$$\text{NF} \% 2 == 0$$

prints all lines with an even number of fields; and the program

$$\{ \ \$1 = \log(\$1); \ \text{print} \ \}$$

replaces the first field of each line by its logarithm.

Awk patterns may include arbitrary boolean combinations of regular expressions and of relational operators on strings, numbers, fields, variables, and array elements. Actions may include the same pattern-matching constructions as in patterns, as well as arithmetic and string expressions and assignments, **if-else**, **while**, **for** statements, and multiple output streams.

This report contains a user's guide, a discussion of the design and implementation of *awk*, and some timing statistics.

September 1, 1978

1. Introduction

Awk is a programming language designed to make many common information retrieval and text manipulation tasks easy to state and to perform.

The basic operation of *awk* is to scan a set of input lines in order, searching for lines which match any of a set of patterns which the user has specified. For each pattern, an action can be specified; this action will be performed on each line that matches the pattern.

Readers familiar with the UNIX† program *grep*[1] will recognize the approach, although in *awk* the patterns may be more general than in *grep*, and the actions allowed are more involved than merely printing the matching line. For example, the *awk* program

```
{print $3, $2}
```

prints the third and second columns of a table in that order. The program

```
$2 ~ /A|B|C/
```

prints all input lines with an A, B, or C in the second field. The program

```
$1 != prev   { print; prev = $1 }
```

prints all lines in which the first field is different from the previous first field.

1.1. Usage

The command

```
awk   program   [files]
```

executes the *awk* commands in the string program on the set of named files, or on the standard input if there are no files. The statements can also be placed in a file pfile, and executed by the command

---

†UNIX is a Trademark of Bell Laboratories.

```
awk   −f pfile   [files]
```

1.2. Program Structure

An *awk* program is a sequence of statements of the form:

> *pattern*   { *action* }
> *pattern*   { *action* }
> ...

Each line of input is matched against each of the patterns in turn. For each pattern that matches, the associated action is executed. When all the patterns have been tested, the next line is fetched and the matching starts over.

Either the pattern or the action may be left out, but not both. If there is no action for a pattern, the matching line is simply copied to the output. (Thus a line which matches several patterns can be printed several times.) If there is no pattern for an action, then the action is performed for every input line. A line which matches no pattern is ignored.

Since patterns and actions are both optional, actions must be enclosed in braces to distinguish them from patterns.

1.3. Records and Fields

Awk input is divided into "records" terminated by a record separator. The default record separator is a newline, so by default *awk* processes its input a line at a time. The number of the current record is available in a variable named NR.

Each input record is considered to be divided into "fields." Fields are normally separated by white space — blanks or tabs — but the input field separator may be changed, as described below. Fields are referred to as $1, $2, and so forth, where $1 is the first field, and $0 is the whole input record itself. Fields may be assigned to. The number of fields in the current record is available in a variable named **NF**.

The variables **FS** and **RS** refer to the input field and record separators; they may be changed at any time to any single character. The optional command-line argument $-Fc$ may also be used to set **FS** to the character c.

If the record separator is empty, an empty input line is taken as the record separator, and blanks, tabs and newlines are treated as field separators.

The variable **FILENAME** contains the name of the current input file.

1.4. Printing

An action may have no pattern, in which case the action is executed for all lines. The simplest action is to print some or all of a record; this is accomplished by the *awk* command **print**. The *awk* program

    { print }

prints each record, thus copying the input to the output intact. More useful is to print a field or fields from each record. For instance,

    print $2, $1

prints the first two fields in reverse order. Items separated by a comma in the print statement will be separated by the current output field separator when output. Items not separated by commas will be concatenated, so

    print $1 $2

runs the first and second fields together.

The predefined variables **NF** and **NR** can be used; for example

    { print NR, NF, $0 }

prints each record preceded by the record number and the number of fields.

Output may be diverted to multiple files; the program

    { print $1 >"foo1"; print $2 >"foo2" }

writes the first field, $1, on the file **foo1**, and the second field on file **foo2**. The >> notation can also be used:

    print $1 >>"foo"

appends the output to the file **foo**. (In each case, the output files are created if necessary.) The file name can be a variable or a field as well as a constant; for example,

    print $1 >$2

uses the contents of field 2 as a file name.

Naturally there is a limit on the number of output files; currently it is 10.

Similarly, output can be piped into another process (on UNIX only); for instance,

    print | "mail bwk"

mails the output to **bwk**.

The variables **OFS** and **ORS** may be used to change the current output field separator and output record separator. The output record separator is appended to the output of the **print** statement.

Awk also provides the **printf** statement for output formatting:

    printf format expr, expr, ...

formats the expressions in the list according to the specification in **format** and prints them. For example,

    printf "%8.2f %10ld\n", $1, $2

prints $1 as a floating point number 8 digits wide, with two after the decimal point, and $2 as a 10-digit long decimal number, followed by a newline. No output separators are produced automatically; you must add them yourself, as in this example. The version of **printf** is identical to that used with C.[2]

2. Patterns

A pattern in front of an action acts as a selector that determines whether the action is to be executed. A variety of expressions may be used as patterns: regular expressions, arithmetic relational expressions, string-valued expressions, and arbitrary boolean combinations of these.

2.1. BEGIN and END

The special pattern **BEGIN** matches the beginning of the input, before the first record is read. The pattern **END** matches the end of the input, after the last record has been processed. **BEGIN** and **END** thus provide a way to gain control before and after processing, for initialization and wrapup.

As an example, the field separator can be set to a colon by

    BEGIN   { FS = ":" }
    ... *rest of program* ...

Or the input lines may be counted by

    END { print NR }

If **BEGIN** is present, it must be the first pattern; **END** must be the last if used.

2.2. Regular Expressions

The simplest regular expression is a literal string of characters enclosed in slashes, like

    /smith/

This is actually a complete *awk* program which will print all lines which contain any occurrence of the name "smith". If a line contains "smith" as part of a larger word, it will also be printed, as in

    blacksmithing

Awk regular expressions include the regular expression forms found in the UNIX text editor *ed*[1] and *grep* (without back-referencing). In addition, *awk* allows parentheses for grouping, | for alternatives, + for "one or more", and ? for "zero or one", all as in *lex*. Character classes may be abbreviated: [a−zA−Z0−9] is the set of all letters and digits. As an example, the *awk* program

    /[Aa]ho|[Ww]einberger|[Kk]ernighan/

will print all lines which contain any of the names "Aho," "Weinberger" or "Kernighan," whether capitalized or not.

Regular expressions (with the extensions listed above) must be enclosed in slashes, just as in *ed* and *sed*. Within a regular expression, blanks and the regular expression metacharacters are significant. To turn of the magic meaning of one of the regular expression characters, precede it with a backslash. An example is the pattern

    /\/.*\//

which matches any string of characters enclosed in slashes.

One can also specify that any field or variable matches a regular expression (or does not match it) with the operators ∼ and !∼. The program

    $1 ∼ /[jJ]ohn/

prints all lines where the first field matches "john" or "John." Notice that this will also match "Johnson", "St. Johnsbury", and so on. To restrict it to exactly [jJ]ohn, use

    $1 ∼ /^[jJ]ohn$/

The caret ^ refers to the beginning of a line or field; the dollar sign $ refers to the end.

2.3. Relational Expressions

An *awk* pattern can be a relational expression involving the usual relational operators <, <=, ==, !=, >=, and >. An example is

    $2 > $1 + 100

which selects lines where the second field is at least 100 greater than the first field. Similarly,

    NF % 2 == 0

prints lines with an even number of fields.

In relational tests, if neither operand is numeric, a string comparison is made; otherwise it is numeric. Thus,

    $1 >= "s"

selects lines that begin with an s, t, u, etc. In the absence of any other information, fields are treated as strings, so the program

    $1 > $2

will perform a string comparison.

2.4. Combinations of Patterns

A pattern can be any boolean combination of patterns, using the operators || (or), && (and), and ! (not). For example,

    $1 >= "s" && $1 < "t" && $1 != "smith"

selects lines where the first field begins with "s", but is not "smith". && and || guarantee that their operands will be evaluated from left to right; evaluation stops as soon as the truth or falsehood is determined.

2.5. Pattern Ranges

The "pattern" that selects an action may also consist of two patterns separated by a comma, as in

    pat1, pat2   { ... }

In this case, the action is performed for each line between an occurrence of **pat1** and the next occurrence of **pat2** (inclusive). For example,

    /start/, /stop/

prints all lines between **start** and **stop**, while

    NR == 100, NR == 200 { ... }

does the action for lines 100 through 200 of the input.

3. Actions

An *awk* action is a sequence of action statements terminated by newlines or semicolons. These action statements can be used to do a variety of bookkeeping and string manipulating tasks.

3.1. Built-in Functions

Awk provides a "length" function to compute the length of a string of characters. This program prints each record, preceded by its length:

```
{print length, $0}
```

length by itself is a "pseudo-variable" which yields the length of the current record; length(argument) is a function which yields the length of its argument, as in the equivalent

```
{print length($0), $0}
```

The argument may be any expression.

Awk also provides the arithmetic functions sqrt, log, exp, and int, for square root, base *e* logarithm, exponential, and integer part of their respective arguments.

The name of one of these built-in functions, without argument or parentheses, stands for the value of the function on the whole record. The program

```
length < 10 || length > 20
```

prints lines whose length is less than 10 or greater than 20.

The function substr(s, m, n) produces the substring of s that begins at position m (origin 1) and is at most n characters long. If n is omitted, the substring goes to the end of s. The function index(s1, s2) returns the position where the string s2 occurs in s1, or zero if it does not.

The function sprintf(f, e1, e2, ...) produces the value of the expressions e1, e2, etc., in the printf format specified by f. Thus, for example,

```
x = sprintf("%8.2f %10ld", $1, $2)
```

sets x to the string produced by formatting the values of $1 and $2.

3.2. Variables, Expressions, and Assignments

Awk variables take on numeric (floating point) or string values according to context. For example, in

```
x = 1
```

x is clearly a number, while in

```
x = "smith"
```

it is clearly a string. Strings are converted to numbers and vice versa whenever context demands it. For instance,

```
x = "3" + "4"
```

assigns 7 to x. Strings which cannot be interpreted as numbers in a numerical context will generally have numeric value zero, but it is unwise to count on this behavior.

By default, variables (other than built-ins) are initialized to the null string, which has numerical value zero; this eliminates the need for most BEGIN sections. For example, the sums of the first two fields can be computed by

```
      { s1 += $1; s2 += $2 }
END { print s1, s2 }
```

Arithmetic is done internally in floating point. The arithmetic operators are +, −, *, /, and % (mod). The C increment ++ and decrement −− operators are also available, and so are the assignment operators +=, −=, *=, /=, and %=. These operators may all be used in expressions.

3.3. Field Variables

Fields in *awk* share essentially all of the properties of variables — they may be used in arithmetic or string operations, and may be assigned to. Thus one can replace the first field with a sequence number like this:

```
{ $1 = NR; print }
```

or accumulate two fields into a third, like this:

```
{ $1 = $2 + $3; print $0 }
```

or assign a string to a field:

```
{ if ($3 > 1000)
      $3 = "too big"
   print
}
```

which replaces the third field by "too big" when it is, and in any case prints the record.

Field references may be numerical expressions, as in

```
{ print $i, $(i+1), $(i+n) }
```

Whether a field is deemed numeric or string depends on context; in ambiguous cases like

```
if ($1 == $2) ...
```

fields are treated as strings.

Each input line is split into fields automatically as necessary. It is also possible to split any variable or string into fields:

```
n = split(s, array, sep)
```

splits the the string s into array[1], ..., array[n]. The number of elements found is returned. If the sep argument is provided, it is used as the field separator; otherwise FS is used as the separator.

3.4. String Concatenation

Strings may be concatenated. For example

```
length($1 $2 $3)
```

returns the length of the first three fields. Or in a print statement,

```
print $1 " is " $2
```

prints the two fields separated by " is ". Variables and numeric expressions may also appear in concatenations.

3.5. Arrays

Array elements are not declared; they spring into existence by being mentioned. Subscripts may have *any* non-null value, including non-numeric strings. As an example of a conventional numeric subscript, the statement

```
x[NR] = $0
```

assigns the current input record to the NR-th element of the array x. In fact, it is possible in principle (though perhaps slow) to process the entire input in a random order with the *awk* program

```
{ x[NR] = $0 }
END { ... program ... }
```

The first action merely records each input line in the array x.

Array elements may be named by non-numeric values, which gives *awk* a capability rather like the associative memory of Snobol tables. Suppose the input contains fields with values like apple, orange, etc. Then the program

```
/apple/   { x["apple"]++ }
/orange/  { x["orange"]++ }
END       { print x["apple"], x["orange"] }
```

increments counts for the named array elements, and prints them at the end of the input.

3.6. Flow-of-Control Statements

Awk provides the basic flow-of-control statements if-else, while, for, and statement grouping with braces, as in C. We showed the if statement in section 3.3 without describing it. The condition in parentheses is evaluated; if it is true, the statement following the if is done. The else part is optional.

The while statement is exactly like that of C. For example, to print all input fields one per line,

```
i = 1
while (i <= NF) {
    print $i
    ++i
}
```

The for statement is also exactly that of C:

```
for (i = 1; i <= NF; i++)
    print $i
```

does the same job as the while statement above.

There is an alternate form of the for statement which is suited for accessing the elements of an associative array:

```
for (i in array)
    statement
```

does *statement* with i set in turn to each element of array. The elements are accessed in an apparently random order. Chaos will ensue if i is altered, or if any new elements are accessed during the loop.

The expression in the condition part of an if, while or for can include relational operators like <, <=, >, >=, == ("is equal to"), and != ("not equal to"); regular expression matches with the match operators ~ and !~; the logical operators ||, &&, and !; and of course parentheses for grouping.

The break statement causes an immediate exit from an enclosing while or for; the continue statement causes the next iteration to begin.

The statement next causes *awk* to skip immediately to the next record and begin scanning the patterns from the top. The statement exit causes the program to behave as if the end of the input had occurred.

Comments may be placed in *awk* programs; they begin with the character # and end with the end of the line, as in

```
print x, y # this is a comment
```

4. Design

The UNIX system already provides several programs that operate by passing input through a selection mechanism. *Grep*, the first and simplest, merely prints all lines which match a single specified pattern. *Egrep* provides more general patterns, i.e., regular expressions in full generality; *fgrep* searches for a set of keywords with a particularly fast algorithm. *Sed*[1] provides most of the editing facilities of the editor *ed*, applied to a stream of input. None of these programs provides numeric capabilities, logical relations, or variables.

Lex[3] provides general regular expression recognition capabilities, and, by serving as a C program generator, is essentially open-ended in its capabilities. The use of *lex*, however, requires a knowledge of C programming, and a *lex* program must be compiled and loaded before use, which discourages its use for one-shot applications.

Awk is an attempt to fill in another part of the matrix of possibilities. It provides general regular expression capabilities and an implicit input/output loop. But it also provides convenient numeric processing, variables, more general selection, and control flow in the actions. It does not require compilation or a knowledge of C. Finally, *awk* provides a convenient way to access fields within lines; it is unique in this respect.

Awk also tries to integrate strings and numbers completely, by treating all quantities as both string and numeric, deciding which representation is appropriate as late as possible. In most cases the user can simply ignore the differences.

Most of the effort in developing *awk* went into deciding what *awk* should or should not do (for instance, it doesn't do string substitution) and what the syntax should be (no explicit operator for concatenation) rather than on writing or debugging the code. We have tried to make the syntax powerful but easy to use and well adapted to scanning files. For example, the absence of declarations and implicit initializations, while probably a bad idea for a general-purpose programming language, is desirable in a language that is meant to be used for tiny programs that may even be composed on the command line.

In practice, *awk* usage seems to fall into two broad categories. One is what might be called "report generation" — processing an input to extract counts, sums, sub-totals, etc. This also includes the writing of trivial data validation programs, such as verifying that a field contains only numeric information or that certain delimiters are properly balanced. The combination of textual and numeric processing is invaluable here.

A second area of use is as a data transformer, converting data from the form produced by one program into that expected by another. The simplest examples merely select fields, perhaps with rearrangements.

5. Implementation

The actual implementation of *awk* uses the language development tools available on the UNIX operating system. The grammar is specified with *yacc*;[4] the lexical analysis is done by *lex*; the regular expression recognizers are deterministic finite automata constructed directly from the expressions. An *awk* program is translated into a parse tree which is then directly executed by a simple interpreter.

Awk was designed for ease of use rather than processing speed; the delayed evaluation of variable types and the necessity to break input into fields makes high speed difficult to achieve in any case. Nonetheless, the program has not proven to be unworkably slow.

Table I below shows the execution (user + system) time on a PDP-11/70 of the UNIX programs *wc*, *grep*, *egrep*, *fgrep*, *sed*, *lex*, and *awk* on the following simple tasks:

1. count the number of lines.

2. print all lines containing "doug".

3. print all lines containing "doug", "ken" or "dmr".

4. print the third field of each line.

5. print the third and second fields of each line, in that order.

6. append all lines containing "doug", "ken", and "dmr" to files "jdoug", "jken", and "jdmr", respectively.

7. print each line prefixed by "line-number : ".

8. sum the fourth column of a table.

The program *wc* merely counts words, lines and characters in its input; we have already mentioned the others. In all cases the input was a file containing 10,000 lines as created by the command *ls* −*l*; each line has the form

```
−rw−rw−rw−  1 ava 123 Oct 15 17:05 xxx
```

The total length of this input is 452,960 characters. Times for *lex* do not include compile or load.

As might be expected, *awk* is not as fast as the specialized tools *wc*, *sed*, or the programs in the *grep* family, but is faster than the more general tool *lex*. In all cases, the tasks were about as easy to express as *awk* programs as programs in these other languages; tasks involving fields were considerably easier to express as *awk* programs. Some of the test programs are shown in *awk*, *sed* and *lex*.

References

1.   K. Thompson and D. M. Ritchie, *UNIX Programmer's Manual,* Bell Laboratories (May 1975). Sixth Edition

2.   B. W. Kernighan and D. M. Ritchie, *The C Programming Language,* Prentice-Hall, Englewood Cliffs, New Jersey (1978).

3.   M. E. Lesk, "Lex — A Lexical Analyzer Generator," Comp. Sci. Tech. Rep. No. 39, Bell Laboratories, Murray Hill, New Jersey (October 1975).

4.   S. C. Johnson, "Yacc — Yet Another Compiler-Compiler," Comp. Sci. Tech. Rep. No. 32, Bell Laboratories, Murray Hill, New Jersey (July 1975).

Program	Task							
	1	2	3	4	5	6	7	8
wc	8.6							
grep	11.7	13.1						
egrep	6.2	11.5	11.6					
fgrep	7.7	13.8	16.1					
sed	10.2	11.6	15.8	29.0	30.5	16.1		
lex	65.1	150.1	144.2	67.7	70.3	104.0	81.7	92.8
awk	15.0	25.6	29.9	33.3	38.9	46.4	71.4	31.1

Table I. Execution Times of Programs. (Times are in sec.)

The programs for some of these jobs are shown below. The *lex* programs are generally too long to show.

AWK:

1. END {print NR}

2. /doug/

3. /ken|doug|dmr/

4. {print $3}

5. {print $3, $2}

6. /ken/   {print >"jken"}
    /doug/   {print >"jdoug"}
    /dmr/   {print >"jdmr"}

7. {print NR ": " $0}

8.   {sum = sum + $4}
    END {print sum}

SED:

1. $=

2. /doug/p

3. /doug/p
    /doug/d
    /ken/p
    /ken/d
    /dmr/p
    /dmr/d

4. /[^]* [ ]*[^]* [ ]*\([^]*\) .*/s//\1/p

5. /[^]* [ ]*\([^]*\) [ ]*\([^]*\) .*/s//\2 \1/p

6. /ken/w jken
    /doug/w jdoug
    /dmr/w jdmr

LEX:

1.  ```
    %{
    int i;
    %}
    %%
    \n   i++;
    .    ;
    %%
    yywrap() {
         printf("%d\n", i);
    }
    ```

2.  ```
    %%
    ^.*doug.*$     printf("%s\n", yytext);
    .    ;
    \n   ;
    ```

DC − An Interactive Desk Calculator

Robert Morris

Lorinda Cherry

Bell Laboratories
Murray Hill, New Jersey 07974

ABSTRACT

DC is an interactive desk calculator program implemented on the UNIX†
time-sharing system to do arbitrary-precision integer arithmetic. It has provision for manipulating scaled fixed-point numbers and for input and output in
bases other than decimal.

The size of numbers that can be manipulated is limited only by available
core storage. On typical implementations of UNIX, the size of numbers that can
be handled varies from several hundred digits on the smallest systems to
several thousand on the largest.

November 15, 1978

---

†UNIX is a Trademark of Bell Laboratories.

DC is an arbitrary precision arithmetic package implemented on the UNIX† time-sharing system in the form of an interactive desk calculator. It works like a stacking calculator using reverse Polish notation. Ordinarily DC operates on decimal integers, but one may specify an input base, output base, and a number of fractional digits to be maintained.

A language called BC [1] has been developed which accepts programs written in the familiar style of higher-level programming languages and compiles output which is interpreted by DC. Some of the commands described below were designed for the compiler interface and are not easy for a human user to manipulate.

Numbers that are typed into DC are put on a push-down stack. DC commands work by taking the top number or two off the stack, performing the desired operation, and pushing the result on the stack. If an argument is given, input is taken from that file until its end, then from the standard input.

SYNOPTIC DESCRIPTION

Here we describe the DC commands that are intended for use by people. The additional commands that are intended to be invoked by compiled output are described in the detailed description.

Any number of commands are permitted on a line. Blanks and new-line characters are ignored except within numbers and in places where a register name is expected.

The following constructions are recognized:

number

The value of the number is pushed onto the main stack. A number is an unbroken string of the digits 0-9 and the capital letters $A-F$ which are treated as digits with values $10-15$ respectively. The number may be preceded by an underscore to input a negative number. Numbers may contain decimal points.

+ − * % ^

The top two values on the stack are added $(+)$, subtracted $(-)$, multiplied $(*)$, divided $(/)$, remaindered $(\%)$, or exponentiated $(\hat{\ })$. The two entries are popped off the stack; the result is pushed on the stack in their place. The result of a division is an integer truncated toward zero. See the detailed description below for the treatment of numbers with decimal points. An exponent must not have any digits after the decimal point.

---

†UNIX is a Trademark of Bell Laboratories.

s*x*

> The top of the main stack is popped and stored into a register named *x*, where *x* may be any character. If the **s** is capitalized, *x* is treated as a stack and the value is pushed onto it. Any character, even blank or new-line, is a valid register name.

l*x*

> The value in register *x* is pushed onto the stack. The register *x* is not altered. If the **l** is capitalized, register *x* is treated as a stack and its top value is popped onto the main stack.

All registers start with empty value which is treated as a zero by the command **l** and is treated as an error by the command **L**.

d

> The top value on the stack is duplicated.

p

> The top value on the stack is printed. The top value remains unchanged.

f

> All values on the stack and in registers are printed.

x

> treats the top element of the stack as a character string, removes it from the stack, and executes it as a string of DC commands.

[...]

> puts the bracketed character string onto the top of the stack.

q

> exits the program. If executing a string, the recursion level is popped by two. If **q** is capitalized, the top value on the stack is popped and the string execution level is popped by that value.

<*x* **>***x* **=***x* **!<***x* **!>***x* **!=***x*

> The top two elements of the stack are popped and compared. Register *x* is executed if they obey the stated relation. Exclamation point is negation.

v

> replaces the top element on the stack by its square root. The square root of an integer is truncated to an integer. For the treatment of numbers with decimal points, see the detailed description below.

!

> interprets the rest of the line as a UNIX command. Control returns to DC when the UNIX command terminates.

c

> All values on the stack are popped; the stack becomes empty.

i

The top value on the stack is popped and used as the number radix for further input. If **i** is capitalized, the value of the input base is pushed onto the stack. No mechanism has been provided for the input of arbitrary numbers in bases less than 1 or greater than 16.

o

The top value on the stack is popped and used as the number radix for further output. If **o** is capitalized, the value of the output base is pushed onto the stack.

k

The top of the stack is popped, and that value is used as a scale factor that influences the number of decimal places that are maintained during multiplication, division, and exponentiation. The scale factor must be greater than or equal to zero and less than 100. If **k** is capitalized, the value of the scale factor is pushed onto the stack.

z

The value of the stack level is pushed onto the stack.

?

A line of input is taken from the input source (usually the console) and executed.

DETAILED DESCRIPTION

Internal Representation of Numbers

Numbers are stored internally using a dynamic storage allocator. Numbers are kept in the form of a string of digits to the base 100 stored one digit per byte (centennial digits). The string is stored with the low-order digit at the beginning of the string. For example, the representation of 157 is 57,1. After any arithmetic operation on a number, care is taken that all digits are in the range $0-99$ and that the number has no leading zeros. The number zero is represented by the empty string.

Negative numbers are represented in the 100's complement notation, which is analogous to two's complement notation for binary numbers. The high order digit of a negative number is always -1 and all other digits are in the range $0-99$. The digit preceding the high order -1 digit is never a 99. The representation of -157 is $43,98,-1$. We shall call this the canonical form of a number. The advantage of this kind of representation of negative numbers is ease of addition. When addition is performed digit by digit, the result is formally correct. The result need only be modified, if necessary, to put it into canonical form.

Because the largest valid digit is 99 and the byte can hold numbers twice that large, addition can be carried out and the handling of carries done later when that is convenient, as it sometimes is.

An additional byte is stored with each number beyond the high order digit to indicate the number of assumed decimal digits after the decimal point. The representation of .001 is 1,*3* where the scale has been italicized to emphasize the fact that it is not the high order digit. The value of this extra byte is called the **scale factor** of the number.

The Allocator

DC uses a dynamic string storage allocator for all of its internal storage. All reading and writing of numbers internally is done through the allocator. Associated with each string in the allocator is a four-word header containing pointers to the beginning of the string, the end of the string, the next place to write, and the next place to read. Communication between the allocator and DC is done via pointers to these headers.

The allocator initially has one large string on a list of free strings. All headers except the one pointing to this string are on a list of free headers. Requests for strings are made by size. The size of the string actually supplied is the next higher power of 2. When a request for a string is made, the allocator first checks the free list to see if there is a string of the desired size. If none is found, the allocator finds the next larger free string and splits it repeatedly until it has a string of the right size. Left-over strings are put on the free list. If there are no larger strings, the allocator tries to coalesce smaller free strings into larger ones. Since all strings are the result of splitting large strings, each string has a neighbor that is next to it in core and, if free, can be combined with it to make a string twice as long. This is an implementation of the 'buddy system' of allocation described in [2].

Failing to find a string of the proper length after coalescing, the allocator asks the system for more space. The amount of space on the system is the only limitation on the size and number of strings in DC. If at any time in the process of trying to allocate a string, the allocator runs out of headers, it also asks the system for more space.

There are routines in the allocator for reading, writing, copying, rewinding, forward-spacing, and backspacing strings. All string manipulation is done using these routines.

The reading and writing routines increment the read pointer or write pointer so that the characters of a string are read or written in succession by a series of read or write calls. The write pointer is interpreted as the end of the information-containing portion of a string and a call to read beyond that point returns an end-of-string indication. An attempt to write beyond the end of a string causes the allocator to allocate a larger space and then copy the old string into the larger block.

Internal Arithmetic

All arithmetic operations are done on integers. The operands (or operand) needed for the operation are popped from the main stack and their scale factors stripped off. Zeros are added or digits removed as necessary to get a properly scaled result from the internal arithmetic routine. For example, if the scale of the operands is different and decimal alignment is required, as it is for addition, zeros are appended to the operand with the smaller scale. After performing the required arithmetic operation, the proper scale factor is appended to the end of the number before it is pushed on the stack.

A register called **scale** plays a part in the results of most arithmetic operations. **scale** is the bound on the number of decimal places retained in arithmetic computations. **scale** may be set to the number on the top of the stack truncated to an integer with the **k** command. **K** may be used to push the value of **scale** on the stack. **scale** must be greater than or equal to 0 and less than 100. The descriptions of the individual arithmetic operations will include the exact effect of **scale** on the computations.

Addition and Subtraction

The scales of the two numbers are compared and trailing zeros are supplied to the number with the lower scale to give both numbers the same scale. The number with the smaller scale is multiplied by 10 if the difference of the scales is odd. The scale of the result is then set to the larger of the scales of the two operands.

Subtraction is performed by negating the number to be subtracted and proceeding as in addition.

Finally, the addition is performed digit by digit from the low order end of the number. The carries are propagated in the usual way. The resulting number is brought into canonical form, which may require stripping of leading zeros, or for negative numbers replacing the high-order configuration $99, -1$ by the digit -1. In any case, digits which are not in the range $0-99$ must be brought into that range, propagating any carries or borrows that result.

Multiplication

The scales are removed from the two operands and saved. The operands are both made positive. Then multiplication is performed in a digit by digit manner that exactly mimics the hand method of multiplying. The first number is multiplied by each digit of the second number, beginning with its low order digit. The intermediate products are accumulated into a partial sum which becomes the final product. The product is put into the canonical form and its sign is computed from the signs of the original operands.

The scale of the result is set equal to the sum of the scales of the two operands. If that scale is larger than the internal register **scale** and also larger than both of the scales of the two operands, then the scale of the result is set equal to the largest of these three last quantities.

Division

The scales are removed from the two operands. Zeros are appended or digits removed from the dividend to make the scale of the result of the integer division equal to the internal quantity **scale**. The signs are removed and saved.

Division is performed much as it would be done by hand. The difference of the lengths of the two numbers is computed. If the divisor is longer than the dividend, zero is returned. Otherwise the top digit of the divisor is divided into the top two digits of the dividend. The result is used as the first (high-order) digit of the quotient. It may turn out be one unit too low, but if it is, the next trial quotient will be larger than 99 and this will be adjusted at the end of the process. The trial digit is multiplied by the divisor and the result subtracted from the dividend and the process is repeated to get additional quotient digits until the remaining dividend is smaller than the divisor. At the end, the digits of the quotient are put into the canonical form, with propagation of carry as needed. The sign is set from the sign of the operands.

Remainder

The division routine is called and division is performed exactly as described. The quantity returned is the remains of the dividend at the end of the divide process. Since division truncates toward zero, remainders have the same sign as the dividend. The scale of the remainder is set to the maximum of the scale of the dividend and the scale of the quotient plus the scale of the divisor.

Square Root

The scale is stripped from the operand. Zeros are added if necessary to make the integer result have a scale that is the larger of the internal quantity **scale** and the scale of the operand.

The method used to compute sqrt(y) is Newton's method with successive approximations by the rule

$$x_{n+1} = \tfrac{1}{2}(x_n + \frac{y}{x_n})$$

The initial guess is found by taking the integer square root of the top two digits.

Exponentiation

Only exponents with zero scale factor are handled. If the exponent is zero, then the result is 1. If the exponent is negative, then it is made positive and the base is divided into one. The scale of the base is removed.

The integer exponent is viewed as a binary number. The base is repeatedly squared and the result is obtained as a product of those powers of the base that correspond to the positions of the one-bits in the binary representation of the exponent. Enough digits of the result are removed to make the scale of the result the same as if the indicated multiplication had been performed.

Input Conversion and Base

Numbers are converted to the internal representation as they are read in. The scale stored with a number is simply the number of fractional digits input. Negative numbers are indicated by preceding the number with a _. The hexadecimal digits A−F correspond to the numbers 10−15 regardless of input base. The **i** command can be used to change the base of the input numbers. This command pops the stack, truncates the resulting number to an integer, and uses it as the input base for all further input. The input base is initialized to 10 but may, for example be changed to 8 or 16 to do octal or hexadecimal to decimal conversions. The command **I** will push the value of the input base on the stack.

Output Commands

The command **p** causes the top of the stack to be printed. It does not remove the top of the stack. All of the stack and internal registers can be output by typing the command **f**. The **o** command can be used to change the output base. This command uses the top of the stack, truncated to an integer as the base for all further output. The output base in initialized to 10. It will work correctly for any base. The command **O** pushes the value of the output base on the stack.

Output Format and Base

The input and output bases only affect the interpretation of numbers on input and output; they have no effect on arithmetic computations. Large numbers are output with 70 characters per line; a \ indicates a continued line. All choices of input and output bases work correctly, although not all are useful. A particularly useful output base is 100000, which has the effect of grouping digits in fives. Bases of 8 and 16 can be used for decimal-octal or decimal-hexadecimal conversions.

Internal Registers

Numbers or strings may be stored in internal registers or loaded on the stack from registers with the commands **s** and **l**. The command **s**x pops the top of the stack and stores the result in register **x**. x can be any character. **l**x puts the contents of register **x** on the top of the stack. The **l** command has no effect on the contents of register x. The **s** command, however, is destructive.

Stack Commands

The command **c** clears the stack. The command **d** pushes a duplicate of the number on the top of the stack on the stack. The command **z** pushes the stack size on the stack. The command **X** replaces the number on the top of the stack with its scale factor. The command **Z** replaces the top of the stack with its length.

Subroutine Definitions and Calls

Enclosing a string in [] pushes the ascii string on the stack. The **q** command quits or in executing a string, pops the recursion levels by two.

Internal Registers − Programming DC

The load and store commands together with [] to store strings, **x** to execute and the testing commands '<', '>', '=', '!<', '!>', '!=' can be used to program DC. The **x** command assumes the top of the stack is an string of DC commands and executes it. The testing commands compare the top two elements on the stack and if the relation holds, execute the register that follows the relation. For example, to print the numbers 0-9,

```
[lip1+  si  li10>a]sa
0si  lax
```

Push-Down Registers and Arrays

These commands were designed for used by a compiler, not by people. They involve push-down registers and arrays. In addition to the stack that commands work on, DC can be thought of as having individual stacks for each register. These registers are operated on by the commands **S** and **L**. **S***x* pushes the top value of the main stack onto the stack for the register *x*. **L***x* pops the stack for register *x* and puts the result on the main stack. The commands **s** and **l** also work on registers but not as push-down stacks. **l** doesn't effect the top of the register stack, and **s** destroys what was there before.

The commands to work on arrays are : and ;. :*x* pops the stack and uses this value as an index into the array *x*. The next element on the stack is stored at this index in *x*. An index must be greater than or equal to 0 and less than 2048. ;*x* is the command to load the main stack from the array *x*. The value on the top of the stack is the index into the array *x* of the value to be loaded.

Miscellaneous Commands

The command ! interprets the rest of the line as a UNIX
command and passes it to UNIX to execute. One other compiler command is **Q**. This command uses the top of the stack as the number of levels of recursion to skip.

DESIGN CHOICES

The real reason for the use of a dynamic storage allocator was that a general purpose program could be (and in fact has been) used for a variety of other tasks. The allocator has some value for input and for compiling (i.e. the bracket [...] commands) where it cannot be known in advance how long a string will be. The result was that at a modest cost in execution time, all considerations of string allocation and sizes of strings were removed from the remainder of the program and debugging was made easier. The allocation method used wastes approximately 25% of available space.

The choice of 100 as a base for internal arithmetic seemingly has no compelling advantage. Yet the base cannot exceed 127 because of hardware limitations and at the cost of 5% in space, debugging was made a great deal easier and decimal output was made much faster.

The reason for a stack-type arithmetic design was to permit all DC commands from addition to subroutine execution to be implemented in essentially the same way. The result was a considerable degree of logical separation of the final program into modules with very little communication between modules.

The rationale for the lack of interaction between the scale and the bases was to provide an understandable means of proceeding after a change of base or scale when numbers had already been entered. An earlier implementation which had global notions of scale and base did not work out well. If the value of **scale** were to be interpreted in the current input or output base, then a change of base or scale in the midst of a computation would cause great confusion in the interpretation of the results. The current scheme has the advantage that the value of the input and output bases are only used for input and output, respectively, and they are ignored in all other operations. The value of scale is not used for any essential purpose by any part of the program and it is used only to prevent the number of decimal places resulting from the arithmetic operations from growing beyond all bounds.

The design rationale for the choices for the scales of the results of arithmetic were that in no case should any significant digits be thrown away if, on appearances, the user actually wanted them. Thus, if the user wants to add the numbers 1.5 and 3.517, it seemed reasonable to give him the result 5.017 without requiring him to unnecessarily specify his rather obvious requirements for precision.

On the other hand, multiplication and exponentiation produce results with many more digits than their operands and it seemed reasonable to give as a minimum the number of decimal places in the operands but not to give more than that number of digits unless the user asked for them by specifying a value for **scale**. Square root can be handled in just the same way as multiplication. The operation of division gives arbitrarily many decimal places and there is simply no way to guess how many places the user wants. In this case only, the user must specify a **scale** to get any decimal places at all.

The scale of remainder was chosen to make it possible to recreate the dividend from the quotient and remainder. This is easy to implement; no digits are thrown away.

References

[1]   L. L. Cherry, R. Morris, *BC − An Arbitrary Precision Desk-Calculator Language.*

[2]   K. C. Knowlton, *A Fast Storage Allocator,* Comm. ACM **8**, pp. 623-625 (Oct. 1965).

BC — An Arbitrary Precision Desk-Calculator Language

Lorinda Cherry

Robert Morris

Bell Laboratories
Murray Hill, New Jersey 07974

ABSTRACT

BC is a language and a compiler for doing arbitrary precision arithmetic on the PDP-11 under the UNIX† time-sharing system. The output of the compiler is interpreted and executed by a collection of routines which can input, output, and do arithmetic on indefinitely large integers and on scaled fixed-point numbers.

These routines are themselves based on a dynamic storage allocator. Overflow does not occur until all available core storage is exhausted.

The language has a complete control structure as well as immediate-mode operation. Functions can be defined and saved for later execution.

Two five hundred-digit numbers can be multiplied to give a thousand digit result in about ten seconds.

A small collection of library functions is also available, including sin, cos, arctan, log, exponential, and Bessel functions of integer order.

Some of the uses of this compiler are

— to do computation with large integers,

— to do computation accurate to many decimal places,

— conversion of numbers from one base to another base.

November 12, 1978

---

†UNIX is a Trademark of Bell Laboratories.

Introduction

BC is a language and a compiler for doing arbitrary precision arithmetic on the UNIX† time-sharing system [1]. The compiler was written to make conveniently available a collection of routines (called DC [5]) which are capable of doing arithmetic on integers of arbitrary size. The compiler is by no means intended to provide a complete programming language. It is a minimal language facility.

There is a scaling provision that permits the use of decimal point notation. Provision is made for input and output in bases other than decimal. Numbers can be converted from decimal to octal by simply setting the output base to equal 8.

The actual limit on the number of digits that can be handled depends on the amount of storage available on the machine. Manipulation of numbers with many hundreds of digits is possible even on the smallest versions of UNIX.

The syntax of BC has been deliberately selected to agree substantially with the C language [2]. Those who are familiar with C will find few surprises in this language.

Simple Computations with Integers

The simplest kind of statement is an arithmetic expression on a line by itself. For instance, if you type in the line:

    142857 + 285714

the program responds immediately with the line

    428571

The operators −, *, /, %, and ˆ can also be used; they indicate subtraction, multiplication, division, remaindering, and exponentiation, respectively. Division of integers produces an integer result truncated toward zero. Division by zero produces an error comment.

Any term in an expression may be prefixed by a minus sign to indicate that it is to be negated (the 'unary' minus sign). The expression

    7+−3

is interpreted to mean that −3 is to be added to 7.

More complex expressions with several operators and with parentheses are interpreted just as in Fortran, with ˆ having the greatest binding power, then * and % and /, and finally + and −. Contents of parentheses are evaluated before material outside the parentheses. Exponentiations are performed from right to left and the other operators from left to right. The two expressions

---

†UNIX is a Trademark of Bell Laboratories.

470

a^b^c and a^(b^c)

are equivalent, as are the two expressions

a*b*c and (a*b)*c

BC shares with Fortran and C the undesirable convention that

a/b*c is equivalent to (a/b)*c

Internal storage registers to hold numbers have single lower-case letter names. The value of an expression can be assigned to a register in the usual way. The statement

x = x + 3

has the effect of increasing by three the value of the contents of the register named x. When, as in this case, the outermost operator is an =, the assignment is performed but the result is not printed. Only 26 of these named storage registers are available.

There is a built-in square root function whose result is truncated to an integer (but see scaling below). The lines

x = sqrt(191)
x

produce the printed result

13

Bases

There are special internal quantities, called 'ibase' and 'obase'. The contents of 'ibase', initially set to 10, determines the base used for interpreting numbers read in. For example, the lines

ibase = 8
11

will produce the output line

9

and you are all set up to do octal to decimal conversions. Beware, however of trying to change the input base back to decimal by typing

ibase = 10

Because the number 10 is interpreted as octal, this statement will have no effect. For those who deal in hexadecimal notation, the characters A—F are permitted in numbers (no matter what base is in effect) and are interpreted as digits having values 10−15 respectively. The statement

ibase = A

will change you back to decimal input base no matter what the current input base is. Negative and large positive input bases are permitted but useless. No mechanism has been provided for the input of arbitrary numbers in bases less than 1 and greater than 16.

The contents of 'obase', initially set to 10, are used as the base for output numbers. The lines

obase = 16
1000

will produce the output line

3E8

which is to be interpreted as a 3-digit hexadecimal number. Very large output bases are permitted, and they are sometimes useful. For example, large numbers can be output in groups of five digits by setting 'obase' to 100000. Strange (i.e. 1, 0, or negative) output bases are handled appropriately.

Very large numbers are split across lines with 70 characters per line. Lines which are continued end with \. Decimal output conversion is practically instantaneous, but output of very large numbers (i.e., more than 100 digits) with other bases is rather slow. Non-decimal output conversion of a one hundred digit number takes about three seconds.

It is best to remember that 'ibase' and 'obase' have no effect whatever on the course of internal computation or on the evaluation of expressions, but only affect input and output conversion, respectively.

Scaling

A third special internal quantity called 'scale' is used to determine the scale of calculated quantities. Numbers may have up to 99 decimal digits after the decimal point. This fractional part is retained in further computations. We refer to the number of digits after the decimal point of a number as its scale.

When two scaled numbers are combined by means of one of the arithmetic operations, the result has a scale determined by the following rules. For addition and subtraction, the scale of the result is the larger of the scales of the two operands. In this case, there is never any truncation of the result. For multiplications, the scale of the result is never less than the maximum of the two scales of the operands, never more than the sum of the scales of the operands and, subject to those two restrictions, the scale of the result is set equal to the contents of the internal quantity 'scale'. The scale of a quotient is the contents of the internal quantity 'scale'. The scale of a remainder is the sum of the scales of the quotient and the divisor. The result of an exponentiation is scaled as if the implied multiplications were performed. An exponent must be an integer. The scale of a square root is set to the maximum of the scale of the argument and the contents of 'scale'.

All of the internal operations are actually carried out in terms of integers, with digits being discarded when necessary. In every case where digits are discarded, truncation and not rounding is performed.

The contents of 'scale' must be no greater than 99 and no less than 0. It is initially set to 0. In case you need more than 99 fraction digits, you may arrange your own scaling.

The internal quantities 'scale', 'ibase', and 'obase' can be used in expressions just like other variables. The line

    scale = scale + 1

increases the value of 'scale' by one, and the line

    scale

causes the current value of 'scale' to be printed.

The value of 'scale' retains its meaning as a number of decimal digits to be retained in internal computation even when 'ibase' or 'obase' are not equal to 10. The internal computations (which are still conducted in decimal, regardless of the bases) are performed to the specified number of decimal digits, never hexadecimal or octal or any other kind of digits.

Functions

The name of a function is a single lower-case letter. Function names are permitted to collide with simple variable names. Twenty-six different defined functions are permitted in addition to the twenty-six variable names. The line define a(x){

begins the definition of a function with one argument. This line must be followed by one or more statements, which make up the body of the function, ending with a right brace }. Return of control from a function occurs when a return statement is executed or when the end of the function is reached. The return statement can take either of the two forms

    return
    return(x)

In the first case, the value of the function is 0, and in the second, the value of the expression in parentheses.

   Variables used in the function can be declared as automatic by a statement of the form

    auto x,y,z

There can be only one 'auto' statement in a function and it must be the first statement in the definition. These automatic variables are allocated space and initialized to zero on entry to the function and thrown away on return. The values of any variables with the same names outside the function are not disturbed. Functions may be called recursively and the automatic variables at each level of call are protected. The parameters named in a function definition are treated in the same way as the automatic variables of that function with the single exception that they are given a value on entry to the function. An example of a function definition is

        define a(x,y){
            auto z
            z = x*y
            return(z)
        }

The value of this function, when called, will be the product of its two arguments.

   A function is called by the appearance of its name followed by a string of arguments enclosed in parentheses and separated by commas. The result is unpredictable if the wrong number of arguments is used.

   Functions with no arguments are defined and called using parentheses with nothing between them: b().

   If the function a above has been defined, then the line

    a(7,3.14)

would cause the result 21.98 to be printed and the line

    x = a(a(3,4),5)

would cause the value of x to become 60.

Subscripted Variables

   A single lower-case letter variable name followed by an expression in brackets is called a subscripted variable (an array element). The variable name is called the array name and the expression in brackets is called the subscript. Only one-dimensional arrays are permitted. The names of arrays are permitted to collide with the names of simple variables and function names. Any fractional part of a subscript is discarded before use. Subscripts must be greater than or equal to zero and less than or equal to 2047.

   Subscripted variables may be freely used in expressions, in function calls, and in return statements.

   An array name may be used as an argument to a function, or may be declared as automatic in a function definition by the use of empty brackets:

```
f(a[])
define f(a[])
auto a[]
```

When an array name is so used, the whole contents of the array are copied for the use of the function, and thrown away on exit from the function. Array names which refer to whole arrays cannot be used in any other contexts.

Control Statements

The 'if', the 'while', and the 'for' statements may be used to alter the flow within programs or to cause iteration. The range of each of them is a statement or a compound statement consisting of a collection of statements enclosed in braces. They are written in the following way

```
if(relation) statement
while(relation) statement
for(expression1; relation; expression2) statement
```

or

```
if(relation) {statements}
while(relation) {statements}
for(expression1; relation; expression2) {statements}
```

A relation in one of the control statements is an expression of the form

```
x>y
```

where two expressions are related by one of the six relational operators $<$, $>$, $<=$, $>=$, $==$, or $!=$. The relation $==$ stands for 'equal to' and $!=$ stands for 'not equal to'. The meaning of the remaining relational operators is clear.

BEWARE of using $=$ instead of $==$ in a relational. Unfortunately, both of them are legal, so you will not get a diagnostic message, but $=$ really will not do a comparison.

The 'if' statement causes execution of its range if and only if the relation is true. Then control passes to the next statement in sequence.

The 'while' statement causes execution of its range repeatedly as long as the relation is true. The relation is tested before each execution of its range and if the relation is false, control passes to the next statement beyond the range of the while.

The 'for' statement begins by executing 'expression1'. Then the relation is tested and, if true, the statements in the range of the 'for' are executed. Then 'expression2' is executed. The relation is tested, and so on. The typical use of the 'for' statement is for a controlled iteration, as in the statement

```
for(i=1; i<=10; i=i+1) i
```

which will print the integers from 1 to 10. Here are some examples of the use of the control statements.

```
define f(n){
auto i, x
x=1
for(i=1; i<=n; i=i+1) x=x*i
return(x)
}
```

The line

```
f(a)
```

will print *a* factorial if *a* is a positive integer. Here is the definition of a function which will compute values of the binomial coefficient (m and n are assumed to be positive integers).

```
define b(n,m){
auto x, j
x=1
for(j=1; j<=m; j=j+1) x=x*(n−j+1)/j
return(x)
}
```

The following function computes values of the exponential function by summing the appropriate series without regard for possible truncation errors:

```
scale = 20
define e(x){
        auto a, b, c, d, n
        a = 1
        b = 1
        c = 1
        d = 0
        n = 1
        while(1==1){
                a = a*x
                b = b*n
                c = c + a/b
                n = n + 1
                if(c==d) return(c)
                d = c
        }
}
```

Some Details

There are some language features that every user should know about even if he will not use them.

Normally statements are typed one to a line. It is also permissible to type several statements on a line separated by semicolons.

If an assignment statement is parenthesized, it then has a value and it can be used anywhere that an expression can. For example, the line

```
(x=y+17)
```

not only makes the indicated assignment, but also prints the resulting value.

Here is an example of a use of the value of an assignment statement even when it is not parenthesized.

```
x = a[i=i+1]
```

causes a value to be assigned to x and also increments i before it is used as a subscript.

The following constructs work in BC in exactly the same manner as they do in the C language. Consult the appendix or the C manuals [2] for their exact workings.

x = y = z is the same as	x = (y = z)
x = + y	x = x + y
x = − y	x = x − y
x = * y	x = x*y
x = / y	x = x/y
x = % y	x = x%y
x = ^ y	x = x^y
x + +	(x = x + 1) − 1
x − −	(x = x − 1) + 1
+ + x	x = x + 1
− − x	x = x − 1

Even if you don't intend to use the constructs, if you type one inadvertently, something correct but unexpected may happen.

WARNING! In some of these constructions, spaces are significant. There is a real difference between x = −y and x = −y. The first replaces x by x − y and the second by −y.

Three Important Things

1. To exit a BC program, type 'quit'.

2. There is a comment convention identical to that of C and of PL/I. Comments begin with '/*' and end with '*/'.

3. There is a library of math functions which may be obtained by typing at command level

    bc −l

This command will load a set of library functions which, at the time of writing, consists of sine (named 's'), cosine ('c'), arctangent ('a'), natural logarithm ('l'), exponential ('e') and Bessel functions of integer order ('j(n,x)'). Doubtless more functions will be added in time. The library sets the scale to 20. You can reset it to something else if you like. The design of these mathematical library routines is discussed elsewhere [3].

If you type

    bc file ...

BC will read and execute the named file or files before accepting commands from the keyboard. In this way, you may load your favorite programs and function definitions.

Acknowledgement

The compiler is written in YACC [4]; its original version was written by S. C. Johnson.

References

[1]   K. Thompson and D. M. Ritchie, *UNIX Programmer's Manual,* Bell Laboratories, 1978.

[2]   B. W. Kernighan and D. M. Ritchie, *The C Programming Language,* Prentice-Hall, 1978.

[3]   R. Morris, *A Library of Reference Standard Mathematical Subroutines,* Bell Laboratories internal memorandum, 1975.

[4]   S. C. Johnson, *YACC − Yet Another Compiler-Compiler.* Bell Laboratories Computing Science Technical Report #32, 1978.

[5]   R. Morris and L. L. Cherry, *DC − An Interactive Desk Calculator.*

Appendix

1. Notation

In the following pages syntactic categories are in *italics*; literals are in **bold**; material in brackets [] is optional.

2. Tokens

Tokens consist of keywords, identifiers, constants, operators, and separators. Token separators may be blanks, tabs or comments. Newline characters or semicolons separate statements.

2.1. Comments

Comments are introduced by the characters /* and terminated by */.

2.2. Identifiers

There are three kinds of identifiers — ordinary identifiers, array identifiers and function identifiers. All three types consist of single lower-case letters. Array identifiers are followed by square brackets, possibly enclosing an expression describing a subscript. Arrays are singly dimensioned and may contain up to 2048 elements. Indexing begins at zero so an array may be indexed from 0 to 2047. Subscripts are truncated to integers. Function identifiers are followed by parentheses, possibly enclosing arguments. The three types of identifiers do not conflict; a program can have a variable named **x**, an array named **x** and a function named **x**, all of which are separate and distinct.

2.3. Keywords

The following are reserved keywords:

ibase	**if**
obase	**break**
scale	**define**
sqrt	**auto**
length	**return**
while	**quit**
for	

2.4. Constants

Constants consist of arbitrarily long numbers with an optional decimal point. The hexadecimal digits $A - F$ are also recognized as digits with values $10 - 15$, respectively.

3. Expressions

The value of an expression is printed unless the main operator is an assignment. Precedence is the same as the order of presentation here, with highest appearing first. Left or right associativity, where applicable, is discussed with each operator.

3.1. Primitive expressions

3.1.1. Named expressions

Named expressions are places where values are stored. Simply stated, named expressions are legal on the left side of an assignment. The value of a named expression is the value stored in the place named.

3.1.1.1. *identifiers*

Simple identifiers are named expressions. They have an initial value of zero.

3.1.1.2. *array-name* [*expression*]

Array elements are named expressions. They have an initial value of zero.

3.1.1.3. scale, ibase and obase

The internal registers **scale**, **ibase** and **obase** are all named expressions. **scale** is the number of digits after the decimal point to be retained in arithmetic operations. **scale** has an initial value of zero. **ibase** and **obase** are the input and output number radix respectively. Both **ibase** and **obase** have initial values of 10.

3.1.2. Function calls

3.1.2.1. *function-name* ([*expression* [, *expression*...]])

A function call consists of a function name followed by parentheses containing a comma-separated list of expressions, which are the function arguments. A whole array passed as an argument is specified by the array name followed by empty square brackets. All function arguments are passed by value. As a result, changes made to the formal parameters have no effect on the actual arguments. If the function terminates by executing a return statement, the value of the function is the value of the expression in the parentheses of the return statement or is zero if no expression is provided or if there is no return statement.

3.1.2.2. sqrt (*expression*)

The result is the square root of the expression. The result is truncated in the least significant decimal place. The scale of the result is the scale of the expression or the value of **scale**, whichever is larger.

3.1.2.3. length (*expression*)

The result is the total number of significant decimal digits in the expression. The scale of the result is zero.

3.1.2.4. scale (*expression*)

The result is the scale of the expression. The scale of the result is zero.

3.1.3. Constants

Constants are primitive expressions.

3.1.4. Parentheses

An expression surrounded by parentheses is a primitive expression. The parentheses are used to alter the normal precedence.

3.2. Unary operators

The unary operators bind right to left.

3.2.1. − *expression*

The result is the negative of the expression.

3.2.2. + + *named-expression*

The named expression is incremented by one. The result is the value of the named expression after incrementing.

3.2.3. − − *named-expression*

The named expression is decremented by one. The result is the value of the named expression after decrementing.

3.2.4. *named-expression* + +

The named expression is incremented by one. The result is the value of the named expression before incrementing.

3.2.5. *named-expression* − −

The named expression is decremented by one. The result is the value of the named expression before decrementing.

3.3. Exponentiation operator

The exponentiation operator binds right to left.

3.3.1. *expression* ˆ *expression*

The result is the first expression raised to the power of the second expression. The second expression must be an integer. If a is the scale of the left expression and b is the absolute value of the right expression, then the scale of the result is:

$$\min (a \times b, \max (\mathbf{scale}, a))$$

3.4. Multiplicative operators

The operators *, /, % bind left to right.

3.4.1. *expression* * *expression*

The result is the product of the two expressions. If a and b are the scales of the two expressions, then the scale of the result is:

$$\min (a + b, \max (\mathbf{scale}, a, b))$$

3.4.2. *expression* / *expression*

The result is the quotient of the two expressions. The scale of the result is the value of **scale**.

3.4.3. *expression* % *expression*

The % operator produces the remainder of the division of the two expressions. More precisely, $a\%b$ is $a - a/b*b$.

The scale of the result is the sum of the scale of the divisor and the value of **scale**

3.5. Additive operators

The additive operators bind left to right.

3.5.1. *expression + expression*

The result is the sum of the two expressions. The scale of the result is the maximun of the scales of the expressions.

3.5.2. *expression − expression*

The result is the difference of the two expressions. The scale of the result is the maximum of the scales of the expressions.

3.6. assignment operators

The assignment operators bind right to left.

3.6.1. *named-expression = expression*

This expression results in assigning the value of the expression on the right to the named expression on the left.

3.6.2. *named-expression = + expression*

3.6.3. *named-expression = − expression*

3.6.4. *named-expression = * expression*

3.6.5. *named-expression = / expression*

3.6.6. *named-expression = % expression*

3.6.7. *named-expression = ˆ expression*

The result of the above expressions is equivalent to "named expression = named expression OP expression", where OP is the operator after the = sign.

4. Relations

Unlike all other operators, the relational operators are only valid as the object of an **if**, **while**, or inside a **for** statement.

4.1. *expression < expression*

4.2. *expression > expression*

4.3. *expression < = expression*

4.4. *expression > = expression*

4.5. *expression = = expression*

4.6. *expression != expression*

5. Storage classes

There are only two storage classes in BC, global and automatic (local). Only identifiers that are to be local to a function need be declared with the **auto** command. The arguments to a function are local to the function. All other identifiers are assumed to be global and available to all functions. All identifiers, global and local, have initial values of zero. Identifiers declared as **auto** are allocated on entry to the function and released on returning from the function. They therefore do not retain values between function calls. **auto** arrays are specified by the array name followed by empty square brackets.

Automatic variables in BC do not work in exactly the same way as in either C or PL/I. On entry to a function, the old values of the names that appear as parameters and as automatic variables are pushed onto a stack. Until return is made from the function, reference to these names refers only to the new values.

6. Statements

Statements must be separated by semicolon or newline. Except where altered by control statements, execution is sequential.

6.1. Expression statements

When a statement is an expression, unless the main operator is an assignment, the value of the expression is printed, followed by a newline character.

6.2. Compound statements

Statements may be grouped together and used when one statement is expected by surrounding them with { }.

6.3. Quoted string statements

"any string"

This statement prints the string inside the quotes.

6.4. If statements

if (*relation*) *statement*

The substatement is executed if the relation is true.

6.5. While statements

while (*relation*) *statement*

The statement is executed while the relation is true. The test occurs before each execution of the statement.

6.6. For statements

for (*expression*; *relation*; *expression*) *statement*

The for statement is the same as
first-expression
while (*relation*) {
    statement
    last-expression
}

All three expressions must be present.

6.7. Break statements

break

> **break** causes termination of a **for** or **while** statement.

6.8. Auto statements

auto *identifier* [*,identifier*]

> The auto statement causes the values of the identifiers to be pushed down. The identifiers can be ordinary identifiers or array identifiers. Array identifiers are specified by following the array name by empty square brackets. The auto statement must be the first statement in a function definition.

6.9. Define statements

define ([*parameter* [*,parameter* ...]]) {
> *statements* }

> The define statement defines a function. The parameters may be ordinary identifiers or array names. Array names must be followed by empty square brackets.

6.10. Return statements

return

return (*expression*)

> The return statement causes termination of a function, popping of its auto variables, and specifies the result of the function. The first form is equivalent to **return** (0). The result of the function is the result of the expression in parentheses.

6.11. Quit

> The quit statement stops execution of a BC program and returns control to UNIX when it is first encountered. Because it is not treated as an executable statement, it cannot be used in a function definition or in an **if, for,** or **while** statement.

UNIX† Assembler Reference Manual

Dennis M. Ritchie

Bell Laboratories
Murray Hill, New Jersey 07974

0. Introduction

This document describes the usage and input syntax of the UNIX PDP-11 assembler *as*. The details of the PDP-11 are not described.

The input syntax of the UNIX assembler is generally similar to that of the DEC assembler PAL-11R, although its internal workings and output format are unrelated. It may be useful to read the publication DEC-11-ASDB-D, which describes PAL-11R, although naturally one must use care in assuming that its rules apply to *as*.

As is a rather ordinary assembler without macro capabilities. It produces an output file that contains relocation information and a complete symbol table; thus the output is acceptable to the UNIX link-editor *ld*, which may be used to combine the outputs of several assembler runs and to obtain object programs from libraries. The output format has been designed so that if a program contains no unresolved references to external symbols, it is executable without further processing.

1. Usage

as is used as follows:

as [−u] [−o *output*] *file₁* ...

If the optional "−u" argument is given, all undefined symbols in the current assembly will be made undefined-external. See the **.globl** directive below.

The other arguments name files which are concatenated and assembled. Thus programs may be written in several pieces and assembled together.

The output of the assembler is by default placed on the file *a.out* in the current directory; the "−o" flag causes the output to be placed on the named file. If there were no unresolved external references, and no errors detected, the output file is marked executable; otherwise, if it is produced at all, it is made non-executable.

2. Lexical conventions

Assembler tokens include identifiers (alternatively, "symbols" or "names"), temporary symbols, constants, and operators.

2.1 Identifiers

An identifier consists of a sequence of alphanumeric characters (including period " . ", underscore " _ ", and tilde "˜" as alphanumeric) of which the first may not be numeric. Only the first eight characters are significant. When a name begins with a tilde, the tilde is discarded and that occurrence of the identifier generates a unique entry in the symbol table which can match no other occurrence of the identifier. This feature is used by the C compiler to place

---

† UNIX is a Trademark of Bell Laboratories.

483

names of local variables in the output symbol table without having to worry about making them unique.

2.2 Temporary symbols

A temporary symbol consists of a digit followed by "f" or "b". Temporary symbols are discussed fully in §5.1.

2.3 Constants

An octal constant consists of a sequence of digits; "8" and "9" are taken to have octal value 10 and 11. The constant is truncated to 16 bits and interpreted in two's complement notation.

A decimal constant consists of a sequence of digits terminated by a decimal point ".". The magnitude of the constant should be representable in 15 bits; i.e., be less than 32,768.

A single-character constant consists of a single quote "'" followed by an ASCII character not a new-line. Certain dual-character escape sequences are acceptable in place of the ASCII character to represent new-line and other non-graphics (see *String statements*, §5.5). The constant's value has the code for the given character in the least significant byte of the word and is null-padded on the left.

A double-character constant consists of a double quote """ followed by a pair of ASCII characters not including new-line. Certain dual-character escape sequences are acceptable in place of either of the ASCII characters to represent new-line and other non-graphics (see *String statements*, §5.5). The constant's value has the code for the first given character in the least significant byte and that for the second character in the most significant byte.

2.4 Operators

There are several single- and double-character operators; see §6.

2.5 Blanks

Blank and tab characters may be interspersed freely between tokens, but may not be used within tokens (except character constants). A blank or tab is required to separate adjacent identifiers or constants not otherwise separated.

2.6 Comments

The character "/" introduces a comment, which extends through the end of the line on which it appears. Comments are ignored by the assembler.

3. Segments

Assembled code and data fall into three segments: the text segment, the data segment, and the bss segment. The text segment is the one in which the assembler begins, and it is the one into which instructions are typically placed. The UNIX system will, if desired, enforce the purity of the text segment of programs by trapping write operations into it. Object programs produced by the assembler must be processed by the link-editor *ld* (using its "−n" flag) if the text segment is to be write-protected. A single copy of the text segment is shared among all processes executing such a program.

The data segment is available for placing data or instructions which will be modified during execution. Anything which may go in the text segment may be put into the data segment. In programs with write-protected, sharable text segments, data segment contains the initialized but variable parts of a program. If the text segment is not pure, the data segment begins immediately after the text segment; if the text segment is pure, the data segment begins at the lowest 8K byte boundary after the text segment.

The bss segment may not contain any explicitly initialized code or data. The length of the bss segment (like that of text or data) is determined by the high-water mark of the location counter within it. The bss segment is actually an extension of the data segment and begins immediately after it. At the start of execution of a program, the bss segment is set to 0. Typically the bss segment is set up by statements exemplified by

    lab: . = .+10

The advantage in using the bss segment for storage that starts off empty is that the initialization information need not be stored in the output file. See also *Location counter* and *Assignment statements* below.

4. The location counter

One special symbol, " . ", is the location counter. Its value at any time is the offset within the appropriate segment of the start of the statement in which it appears. The location counter may be assigned to, with the restriction that the current segment may not change; furthermore, the value of " . " may not decrease. If the effect of the assignment is to increase the value of " . ", the required number of null bytes are generated (but see *Segments* above).

5. Statements

A source program is composed of a sequence of *statements*. Statements are separated either by new-lines or by semicolons. There are five kinds of statements: null statements, expression statements, assignment statements, string statements, and keyword statements.

Any kind of statement may be preceded by one or more labels.

5.1 Labels

There are two kinds of label: name labels and numeric labels. A name label consists of a name followed by a colon (:). The effect of a name label is to assign the current value and type of the location counter " . " to the name. An error is indicated in pass 1 if the name is already defined; an error is indicated in pass 2 if the " . " value assigned changes the definition of the label.

A numeric label consists of a digit 0 to 9 followed by a colon (:). Such a label serves to define temporary symbols of the form "nb" and "nf", where n is the digit of the label. As in the case of name labels, a numeric label assigns the current value and type of " . " to the temporary symbol. However, several numeric labels with the same digit may be used within the same assembly. References of the form "nf" refer to the first numeric label "n:" *f*orward from the reference; "nb" symbols refer to the first "n :" label *b*ackward from the reference. This sort of temporary label was introduced by Knuth [*The Art of Computer Programming, Vol I: Fundamental Algorithms*]. Such labels tend to conserve both the symbol table space of the assembler and the inventive powers of the programmer.

5.2 Null statements

A null statement is an empty statement (which may, however, have labels). A null statement is ignored by the assembler. Common examples of null statements are empty lines or lines containing only a label.

5.3 Expression statements

An expression statement consists of an arithmetic expression not beginning with a keyword. The assembler computes its (16-bit) value and places it in the output stream, together with the appropriate relocation bits.

5.4 Assignment statements

An assignment statement consists of an identifier, an equals sign (=), and an expression. The value and type of the expression are assigned to the identifier. It is not required that the type or value be the same in pass 2 as in pass 1, nor is it an error to redefine any symbol by assignment.

Any external attribute of the expression is lost across an assignment. This means that it is not possible to declare a global symbol by assigning to it, and that it is impossible to define a symbol to be offset from a non-locally defined global symbol.

As mentioned, it is permissible to assign to the location counter " . ". It is required, however, that the type of the expression assigned be of the same type as " . ", and it is forbidden to decrease the value of " . ". In practice, the most common assignment to " . " has the form ". = . + n" for some number n; this has the effect of generating n null bytes.

5.5 String statements

A string statement generates a sequence of bytes containing ASCII characters. A string statement consists of a left string quote " < " followed by a sequence of ASCII characters not including newline, followed by a right string quote " > ". Any of the ASCII characters may be replaced by a two-character escape sequence to represent certain non-graphic characters, as follows:

\n	NL	(012)
\s	SP	(040)
\t	HT	(011)
\e	EOT	(004)
\0	NUL	(000)
\r	CR	(015)
\a	ACK	(006)
\p	PFX	(033)
\\	\	
\>	>	

The last two are included so that the escape character and the right string quote may be represented. The same escape sequences may also be used within single- and double-character constants (see §2.3 above).

5.6 Keyword statements

Keyword statements are numerically the most common type, since most machine instructions are of this sort. A keyword statement begins with one of the many predefined keywords of the assembler; the syntax of the remainder depends on the keyword. All the keywords are listed below with the syntax they require.

6. Expressions

An expression is a sequence of symbols representing a value. Its constituents are identifiers, constants, temporary symbols, operators, and brackets. Each expression has a type.

All operators in expressions are fundamentally binary in nature; if an operand is missing on the left, a 0 of absolute type is assumed. Arithmetic is two's complement and has 16 bits of precision. All operators have equal precedence, and expressions are evaluated strictly left to right except for the effect of brackets.

6.1 Expression operators

The operators are:

(blank)   when there is no operand between operands, the effect is exactly the same as if a "+" had appeared.

+   addition

−   subtraction

*   multiplication

\/   division (note that plain "/" starts a comment)

8   bitwise **and**

| bitwise **or**

\>   logical right shift

\<   logical left shift

%   modulo

! $a!b$ is a **or** (**not** b); i.e., the **or** of the first operand and the one's complement of the second; most common use is as a unary.

^   result has the value of first operand and the type of the second; most often used to define new machine instructions with syntax identical to existing instructions.

Expressions may be grouped by use of square brackets "[ ]". (Round parentheses are reserved for address modes.)

6.2 Types

The assembler deals with a number of types of expressions. Most types are attached to keywords and used to select the routine which treats that keyword. The types likely to be met explicitly are:

undefined
Upon first encounter, each symbol is undefined. It may become undefined if it is assigned an undefined expression. It is an error to attempt to assemble an undefined expression in pass 2; in pass 1, it is not (except that certain keywords require operands which are not undefined).

undefined external
A symbol which is declared **.globl** but not defined in the current assembly is an undefined external. If such a symbol is declared, the link editor *ld* must be used to load the assembler's output with another routine that defines the undefined reference.

absolute   An absolute symbol is defined ultimately from a constant. Its value is unaffected by any possible future applications of the link-editor to the output file.

text   The value of a text symbol is measured with respect to the beginning of the text segment of the program. If the assembler output is link-edited, its text symbols may change in value since the program need not be the first in the link editor's output. Most text symbols are defined by appearing as labels. At the start of an assembly, the value of " ." is text 0.

data   The value of a data symbol is measured with respect to the origin of the data segment of a program. Like text symbols, the value of a data symbol may change during a subsequent link-editor run since previously loaded programs may have data segments. After the first **.data** statement, the value of " ." is data 0.

bss   The value of a bss symbol is measured from the beginning of the bss segment of a program. Like text and data symbols, the value of a bss symbol may change during a subsequent link-editor run, since previously loaded programs may have bss segments. After the first **.bss** statement, the value of " ." is bss 0.

external absolute, text, data, or bss

> symbols declared **.globl** but defined within an assembly as absolute, text, data, or bss symbols may be used exactly as if they were not declared **.globl**; however, their value and type are available to the link editor so that the program may be loaded with others that reference these symbols.

register

> The symbols

> **r0 ... r5**
> **fr0 ... fr5**
> **sp**
> **pc**

> are predefined as register symbols. Either they or symbols defined from them must be used to refer to the six general-purpose, six floating-point, and the 2 special-purpose machine registers. The behavior of the floating register names is identical to that of the corresponding general register names; the former are provided as a mnemonic aid.

other types

> Each keyword known to the assembler has a type which is used to select the routine which processes the associated keyword statement. The behavior of such symbols when not used as keywords is the same as if they were absolute.

6.3 Type propagation in expressions

When operands are combined by expression operators, the result has a type which depends on the types of the operands and on the operator. The rules involved are complex to state but were intended to be sensible and predictable. For purposes of expression evaluation the important types are

> undefined
> absolute
> text
> data
> bss
> undefined external
> other

The combination rules are then: If one of the operands is undefined, the result is undefined. If both operands are absolute, the result is absolute. If an absolute is combined with one of the "other types" mentioned above, or with a register expression, the result has the register or other type. As a consequence, one can refer to r3 as "r0+3". If two operands of "other type" are combined, the result has the numerically larger type An "other type" combined with an explicitly discussed type other than absolute acts like an absolute.

Further rules applying to particular operators are:

+   If one operand is text-, data-, or bss-segment relocatable, or is an undefined external, the result has the postulated type and the other operand must be absolute.

−   If the first operand is a relocatable text-, data-, or bss-segment symbol, the second operand may be absolute (in which case the result has the type of the first operand); or the second operand may have the same type as the first (in which case the result is absolute). If the first operand is external undefined, the second must be absolute. All other combinations are illegal.

^   This operator follows no other rule than that the result has the value of the first operand and the type of the second.

others
It is illegal to apply these operators to any but absolute symbols.

7. Pseudo-operations

The keywords listed below introduce statements that generate data in unusual forms or influence the later operations of the assembler. The metanotation

[stuff] ...

means that 0 or more instances of the given stuff may appear. Also, boldface tokens are literals, italic words are substitutable.

7.1 .byte *expression* [, *expression*] ...

The *expression*s in the comma-separated list are truncated to 8 bits and assembled in successive bytes. The expressions must be absolute. This statement and the string statement above are the only ones that assemble data one byte at at time.

7.2 .even

If the location counter "." is odd, it is advanced by one so the next statement will be assembled at a word boundary.

7.3 .if *expression*

The *expression* must be absolute and defined in pass 1. If its value is nonzero, the .if is ignored; if zero, the statements between the .if and the matching .endif (below) are ignored. .if may be nested. The effect of .if cannot extend beyond the end of the input file in which it appears. (The statements are not totally ignored, in the following sense: .ifs and .endifs are scanned for, and moreover all names are entered in the symbol table. Thus names occurring only inside an .if will show up as undefined if the symbol table is listed.)

7.4 .endif

This statement marks the end of a conditionally-assembled section of code. See .if above.

7.5 .globl *name* [, *name*] ...

This statement makes the *names* external. If they are otherwise defined (by assignment or appearance as a label) they act within the assembly exactly as if the .globl statement were not given; however, the link editor *ld* may be used to combine this routine with other routines that refer these symbols.

Conversely, if the given symbols are not defined within the current assembly, the link editor can combine the output of this assembly with that of others which define the symbols. As discussed in §1, it is possible to force the assembler to make all otherwise undefined symbols external.

7.6 .text

7.7 .data

7.8 .bss

These three pseudo-operations cause the assembler to begin assembling into the text, data, or bss segment respectively. Assembly starts in the text segment. It is forbidden to assemble any code or data into the bss segment, but symbols may be defined and "." moved about by assignment.

7.9 .comm *name* , *expression*

Provided the *name* is not defined elsewhere, this statement is equivalent to

> .globl name
> name = expression ^ name

That is, the type of *name* is "undefined external", and its value is *expression*. In fact the *name* behaves in the current assembly just like an undefined external. However, the link-editor *ld* has been special-cased so that all external symbols which are not otherwise defined, and which have a non-zero value, are defined to lie in the bss segment, and enough space is left after the symbol to hold *expression* bytes. All symbols which become defined in this way are located before all the explicitly defined bss-segment locations.

8.   Machine instructions

Because of the rather complicated instruction and addressing structure of the PDP-11, the syntax of machine instruction statements is varied. Although the following sections give the syntax in detail, the machine handbooks should be consulted on the semantics.

8.1 Sources and Destinations

The syntax of general source and destination addresses is the same. Each must have one of the following forms, where *reg* is a register symbol, and *expr* is any sort of expression:

syntax	words	mode
reg	0	$00 + reg$
(*reg*) +	0	$20 + reg$
− (*reg*)	0	$40 + reg$
expr (*reg*)	1	$60 + reg$
(*reg*)	0	$10 + reg$
* *reg*	0	$10 + reg$
* (*reg*) +	0	$30 + reg$
* − (*reg*)	0	$50 + reg$
* (*reg*)	1	$70 + reg$
* *expr* (*reg*)	1	$70 + reg$
expr	1	67
$*expr*	1	27
* *expr*	1	77
* $*expr*	1	37

The *words* column gives the number of address words generated; the *mode* column gives the octal address-mode number. The syntax of the address forms is identical to that in DEC assemblers, except that "*" has been substituted for "@" and "$" for "#"; the UNIX typing conventions make "@" and "#" rather inconvenient.

Notice that mode "*reg" is identical to "(reg)"; that "*(reg)" generates an index word (namely, 0); and that addresses consisting of an unadorned expression are assembled as pc-relative references independent of the type of the expression. To force a non-relative reference, the form "*$expr" can be used, but notice that further indirection is impossible.

8.3 Simple machine instructions

The following instructions are defined as absolute symbols:

clc
clv
clz
cln
sec
sev
sez
sen

They therefore require no special syntax. The PDP-11 hardware allows more than one of the "clear" class, or alternatively more than one of the "set" class to be or-ed together; this may be expressed as follows:

clc | clv

8.4 Branch

The following instructions take an expression as operand. The expression must lie in the same segment as the reference, cannot be undefined-external, and its value cannot differ from the current location of " ." by more than 254 bytes:

br	blos	
bne	bvc	
beq	bvs	
bge	bhis	
blt	bec	(= bcc)
bgt	bcc	
ble	blo	
bpl	bcs	
bmi	bes	(= bcs)
bhi		

bes ("branch on error set") and bec ("branch on error clear") are intended to test the error bit returned by system calls (which is the c-bit).

8.5 Extended branch instructions

The following symbols are followed by an expression representing an address in the same segment as " .". If the target address is close enough, a branch-type instruction is generated; if the address is too far away, a jmp will be used.

jbr	jlos
jne	jvc
jeq	jvs
jge	jhis
jlt	jec
jgt	jcc
jle	jlo
jpl	jcs
jmi	jes
jhi	

jbr turns into a plain jmp if its target is too remote; the others (whose names are contructed by replacing the "b" in the branch instruction's name by "j") turn into the converse branch over a jmp to the target address.

8.6 Single operand instructions

The following symbols are names of single-operand machine instructions. The form of address expected is discussed in §8.1 above.

clr	sbcb
clrb	ror
com	rorb
comb	rol
inc	rolb
incb	asr
dec	asrb
decb	asl
neg	aslb
negb	jmp
adc	swab
adcb	tst
sbc	tstb

8.7 Double operand instructions

The following instructions take a general source and destination (§8.1), separated by a comma, as operands.

mov
movb
cmp
cmpb
bit
bitb
bic
bicb
bis
bisb
add
sub

8.8 Miscellaneous instructions

The following instructions have more specialized syntax. Here *reg* is a register name, *src* and *dst* a general source or destination (§8.1), and *expr* is an expression:

jsr	*reg,dst*	
rts	*reg*	
sys	*expr*	
ash	*src*, *reg*	(or, **als**)
ashc	*src*, *reg*	(or, **alsc**)
mul	*src*, *reg*	(or, **mpy**)
div	*src*, *reg*	(or, **dvd**)
xor	*reg*, *dst*	
sxt	*dst*	
mark	*expr*	
sob	*reg*, *expr*	

sys is another name for the **trap** instruction. It is used to code system calls. Its operand is required to be expressible in 6 bits. The expression in **mark** must be expressible in six bits, and the expression in **sob** must be in the same segment as " . ", must not be external-undefined, must be less than " . ", and must be within 510 bytes of " . ".

8.9   Floating-point unit instructions

The following floating-point operations are defined, with syntax as indicated:

cfcc		
setf		
setd		
seti		
setl		
clrf	*fdst*	
negf	*fdst*	
absf	*fdst*	
tstf	*fsrc*	
movf	*fsrc, freg*	(= ldf)
movf	*freg, fdst*	(= stf)
movif	*src, freg*	(= ldcif)
movfi	*freg, dst*	(= stcfi)
movof	*fsrc, freg*	(= ldcdf)
movfo	*freg, fdst*	(= stcfd)
movie	*src, freg*	(= ldexp)
movei	*freg, dst*	(= stexp)
addf	*fsrc, freg*	
subf	*fsrc, freg*	
mulf	*fsrc, freg*	
divf	*fsrc, freg*	
cmpf	*fsrc, freg*	
modf	*fsrc, freg*	
ldfps	*src*	
stfps	*dst*	
stst	*dst*	

fsrc, *fdst*, and *freg* mean floating-point source, destination, and register respectively. Their syntax is identical to that for their non-floating counterparts, but note that only floating registers 0-3 can be a *freg*.

The names of several of the operations have been changed to bring out an analogy with certain fixed-point instructions. The only strange case is **movf**, which turns into either **stf** or **ldf** depending respectively on whether its first operand is or is not a register. Warning: **ldf** sets the floating condition codes, **stf** does not.

9.   Other symbols

9.1   ..

The symbol " .." is the *relocation counter*. Just before each assembled word is placed in the output stream, the current value of this symbol is added to the word if the word refers to a text, data or bss segment location. If the output word is a pc-relative address word that refers to an absolute location, the value of " .." is subtracted.

Thus the value of " .." can be taken to mean the starting memory location of the program. The initial value of " .." is 0.

The value of " .." may be changed by assignment. Such a course of action is sometimes necessary, but the consequences should be carefully thought out. It is particularly ticklish to change " .." midway in an assembly or to do so in a program which will be treated by the loader, which has its own notions of " ..".

9.2 System calls

System call names are not predefined. They may be found in the file */usr/include/sys.s*

10. Diagnostics

When an input file cannot be read, its name followed by a question mark is typed and assembly ceases. When syntactic or semantic errors occur, a single-character diagnostic is typed out together with the line number and the file name in which it occurred. Errors in pass 1 cause cancellation of pass 2. The possible errors are:

)	parentheses error
]	parentheses error
>	string not terminated properly
*	indirection (*) used illegally
.	illegal assignment to " . "
A	error in address
B	branch address is odd or too remote
E	error in expression
F	error in local ("f" or "b") type symbol
G	garbage (unknown) character
I	end of file inside an .if
M	multiply defined symbol as label
O	word quantity assembled at odd address
P	phase error— " . " different in pass 1 and 2
R	relocation error
U	undefined symbol
X	syntax error

IMPLEMENTATION, MAINTENANCE, AND MISCELLANEOUS

Setting Up Unix — Seventh Edition

Charles B. Haley
Dennis M. Ritchie

Bell Laboratories
Murray Hill, New Jersey 07974

The distribution tape can be used only on a DEC PDP11/45 or PDP11/70 with RP03, RP04, RP05, RP06 disks and with a TU10, TU16, or TE16 tape drive. It consists of some preliminary bootstrapping programs followed by two file system images; if needed, after the initial construction of the file systems individual files can be extracted. (See restor(1))

If you are set up to do it, it might be a good idea immediately to make a copy of the tape to guard against disaster. The tape is 9-track 800 BPI and contains some 512-byte records followed by many 10240-byte records. There are interspersed tapemarks.

The system as distributed contains binary images of the system and all the user level programs, along with source and manual sections for them—about 2100 files altogether. The binary images, along with other things needed to flesh out the file system enough so UNIX will run, are to be put on one file system called the 'root file system'. The file system size required is about 5000 blocks. The file second system has all of the source and documentation. Altogether it amounts to more than 18,000 512-byte blocks.

Making a Disk From Tape

Perform the following bootstrap procedure to obtain a disk with a root file system on it.

1. Mount the magtape on drive 0 at load point.

2. Mount a formatted disk pack on drive 0.

3. Key in and execute at 100000

TU10	TU16/TE16
012700	Use the DEC ROM or other
172526	means to load block 1
010040	(i.e. second block) at 800 BPI
012740	into location 0 and transfer
060003	to 0.
000777	

   The tape should move and the CPU loop. (The TU10 code is *not* the DEC bulk ROM for tape; it reads block 0, not block 1.)

4. If you used the above TU10 code, halt and restart the CPU at 0, otherwise continue to the next step.

5. The console should type

   Boot
   :

Copy the magtape to disk by the following procedure. The machine's printouts are shown in italic, explanatory comments are within ( ). Terminate each line you type by carriage return or line-feed. There are two classes of tape drives: the name 'tm' is used for the TU10, and 'ht' is used for the TU16 or TE16. There are also two classes of disks: 'rp' is used for the RP03, and 'hp' is used for the RP04/5/6.

If you should make a mistake while typing, the character '#' erases the last character typed up to the beginning of the line, and the character '@' erases the entire line typed. Some consoles cannot print lower case letters, adjust the instructions accordingly.

> (bring in the program mkfs)
> :tm(0,3)   (use 'ht(0,3)' for the TU16/TE16)
> *file system size:* 5000
> *file system:* rp(0,0)   (use 'hp(0,0)' for RP04/5/6)
> *isize = XX*
> *m/n = XX*
> (after a while)
> *exit called*
> *Boot*
> *:*

This step makes an empty file system.

6.   The next thing to do is to restore the data onto the new empty file system. To do this you respond to the ':' printed in the last step with

> (bring in the program restor)
> :tm(0,4)   ('ht(0,4)' for TU16/TE16)
> *tape?* tm(0,5)   (use 'ht(0,5)' for TU16/TE16)
> *disk?* rp(0,0)   (use 'hp(0,0)' for RP04/5/6)
> *Last chance before scribbling on disk.* (you type return)
> (the tape moves, perhaps 5-10 minutes pass)
> *end of tape*
> *Boot*
> *:*

You now have a UNIX root file system.

Booting UNIX

You probably have the bootstrap running, left over from the last step above; if not, repeat the boot process (step 3) again. Then use one of the following:

> :rp(0,0)rptmunix   (for RP03 and TU10)
> :rp(0,0)rphtunix   (for RP03 and TU16/TE16)
> :hp(0,0)hptmunix   (for RP04/5/6 and TU10)
> :hp(0,0)hphtunix   (for RP04/5/6 and TU16/TE16)

The machine should type the following:

> *mem = xxx*
> #

The *mem* message gives the memory available to user programs in bytes.

UNIX is now running, and the 'UNIX Programmer's manual' applies; references below of the form X(Y) mean the subsection named X in section Y of the manual. The '#' is the prompt from the Shell, and indicates you are the super-user. The user name of the super-user is 'root' if you should find yourself in multi-user mode and need to log in; the password is also 'root'.

To simplify your life later, rename the appropriate version of the system as specified above plain 'unix.' For example, use mv (1) as follows if you have an RP04/5/6 and a TU16 tape:

> mv hphtunix unix

In the future, when you reboot, you can type just

> hp(0,0)unix

to the ':' prompt.   (Choose appropriately among 'hp', 'rp', 'ht', 'tm' according to your configuration).

You now need to make some special file entries in the dev directory. These specify what sort of disk you are running on, what sort of tape drive you have, and where the file systems are. For simplicity, this recipe creates fixed device names. These names will be used below, and some of them are built into various programs, so they are most convenient. However, the names do not always represent the actual major and minor device in the manner suggested in section 4 of the Programmer's Manual. For example, 'rp3' will be used for the name of the file system on which the user file system is put, even though it might be on an RP06 and is not logical device 3. Also, this sequence will put the user file system on the same disk drive as the root, which is not the best place if you have more than one drive. Thus the prescription below should be taken only as one example of where to put things. See also the section on 'Disk layout' below.

In any event, change to the dev directory (cd(1)) and, if you like, examine and perhaps change the makefile there (make (1)).

> cd /dev
> cat makefile

Then, use one of

> make rp03
> make rp04
> make rp05
> make rp06

depending on which disk you have. Then, use one of

> make tm
> make ht

depending on which tape you have. The file 'rp0' refers to the root file system; 'swap' to the swap-space file system; 'rp3' to the user file system. The devices 'rrp0' and 'rrp3' are the 'raw' versions of the disks. Also, 'mt0' is tape drive 0, at 800 BPI; 'rmt0' is the raw tape, on which large records can be read and written; 'nrmt0' is raw tape with the quirk that it does not rewind on close, which is a subterfuge that permits multifile tapes to be handled.

The next thing to do is to extract the rest of the data from the tape. Comments are enclosed in ( ); don't type these. The number in the first command is the size of the file system; it differs between RP03, RP04/5, and RP06.

> /etc/mkfs /dev/rp3 74000   (153406 if on RP04/5, 322278 on RP06)
> (The above command takes about 2-3 minutes on an RP03)
> dd if=/dev/nrmt0 of=/dev/null bs=20b files=6   (skip 6 files on the tape)
> restor rf /dev/rmt0 /dev/rp3   (restore the file system)
> (Reply with a 'return' (CR) to the 'Last chance' message)
> (The restor takes about 20-30 minutes)

All of the data on the tape has been extracted.

You may at this point mount the source file system (mount(1)). To do this type the following:

> /etc/mount /dev/rp3 /usr

The source and manual pages are now available in subdirectories of /usr.

The above mount command is only needed if you intend to play around with source on a single user system, which you are going to do next. The file system is mounted automatically when multi-user mode is entered, by a command in the file /etc/rc. (See 'Disk Layout' below).

Before anything further is done the bootstrap block on the disk (block 0) should be filled in. This is done using the command

        dd if=/usr/mdec/rpuboot of=/dev/rp0 count=1

if you have the RP03, or

        dd if=/usr/mdec/hpuboot of=/dev/rp0 count=1

if you have an RP04/5/6. Now the DEC disk bootstraps are usable. See Boot Procedures(8) for further information.

Before UNIX is turned up completely, a few configuration dependent exercises must be performed. At this point, it would be wise to read all of the manuals (especially 'Regenerating System Software') and to augment this reading with hand to hand combat.

Reconfiguration

The UNIX system running is configured to run with the given disk and tape, a console, and no other device. This is certainly not the correct configuration. You will have to correct the configuration table to reflect the true state of your machine.

It is wise at this point to know how to recompile the system. Print (cat(1)) the file /usr/sys/conf/makefile. This file is input to the program 'make(1)' which if invoked with 'make all' will recompile all of the system source and install it in the correct libraries.

The program mkconf(1) prepares files that describe a given configuration (See mkconf(1)). In the /usr/sys/conf directory, the four files xyconf were input to mkconf to produce the four versions of the system xyunix. Pick the appropriate one, and edit it to add lines describing your own configuration. (Remember the console typewriter is automatically included; don't count it in the kl specification.) Then run mkconf; it will generate the files l.s (trap vectors) c.c (configuration table), and mch0.s. Take a careful look at l.s to make sure that all the devices that you have are assembled in the correct interrupt vectors. If your configuration is non-standard, you will have to modify l.s to fit your configuration.

There are certain magic numbers and configuration parameters imbedded in various device drivers that you may want to change. The device addresses of each device are defined in each driver. In case you have any non-standard device addresses, just change the address and recompile. (The device drivers are in the directory /usr/sys/dev.)

The DC11 driver is set to run 4 lines. This can be changed in dc.c.

The DH11 driver is set to handle 3 DH11's with a full complement of 48 lines. If you have less, or more, you may want to edit dh.c.

The DN11 driver will handle 4 DN's. Edit dn.c.

The DU11 driver can only handle a single DU. This cannot be easily changed.

The KL/DL driver is set up to run a single DL11-A, -B, or -C (the console) and no DL11-E's. To change this, edit kl.c to have NKL11 reflect the total number of DL11-ABC's and NDL11 to reflect the number of DL11-E's. So far as the driver is concerned, the difference between the devices is their address.

All of the disk and tape drivers (rf.c, rk.c, rp.c, tm.c, tc.c, hp.c, ht.c) are set up to run 8 drives and should not need to be changed. The big disk drivers (rp.c and hp.c) have partition tables in them which you may want to experiment with.

After all the corrections have been made, use 'make(1)' to recompile the system (or recompile individually if you wish: use the makefile as a guide). If you compiled individually, say 'make unix' in the directory /usr/sys/conf. The final object file (unix) should be moved to the root, and then booted to try it out. It is best to name it /nunix so as not to destroy the working system until you're sure it does work. See Boot Procedures(8) for a discussion of booting. Note: before taking the system down, always (!!) perform a sync(1) to force delayed output to the disk.

Special Files

Next you must put in special files for the new devices in the directory /dev using mknod(1). Print the configuration file c.c created above. This is the major device switch of each device class (block and character). There is one line for each device configured in your system and a null line for place holding for those devices not configured. The essential block special files were installed above; for any new devices, the major device number is selected by counting the line number (from zero) of the device's entry in the block configuration table. Thus the first entry in the table bdevsw would be major device zero. This number is also printed in the table along the right margin.

The minor device is the drive number, unit number or partition as described under each device in section 4 of the manual. For tapes where the unit is dial selectable, a special file may be made for each possible selection. You can also add entries for other disk drives.

In reality, device names are arbitrary. It is usually convenient to have a system for deriving names, but it doesn't have to be the one presented above.

Some further notes on minor device numbers. The hp driver uses the 0100 bit of the minor device number to indicate whether or not to interleave a file system across more than one physical device. See hp(4) for more detail. The tm and ht drivers use the 0200 bit to indicate whether or not to rewind the tape when it is closed. The 0100 bit indicates the density of the tape on TU16 drives. By convention, tape special files with the 0200 bit on have an 'n' prepended to their name, as in /dev/nmt0 or /dev/nrmt1. Again, see tm(4) or ht(4).

The naming of character devices is similar to block devices. Here the names are even more arbitrary except that devices meant to be used for teletype access should (to avoid confusion, no other reason) be named /dev/ttyX, where X is some string (as in '00' or 'library'). The files console, mem, kmem, and null are already correctly configured.

The disk and magtape drivers provide a 'raw' interface to the device which provides direct transmission between the user's core and the device and allows reading or writing large records. The raw device counts as a character device, and should have the name of the corresponding standard block special file with 'r' prepended. (The 'n' for no rewind tapes violates this rule.) Thus the raw magtape files would be called /dev/rmtX. These special files should be made.

When all the special files have been created, care should be taken to change the access modes (chmod(1)) on these files to appropriate values (probably 600 or 644).

Floating Point

UNIX only supports (and really expects to have) the FP11-B/C floating point unit. For machines without this hardware, there is a user subroutine available that will catch illegal instruction traps and interpret floating point operations. (See fptrap(3).) To install this subroutine in the library, change to /usr/src/libfpsim and execute the shell files

        compall
        mklib

The system as delivered does not have this code included in any command, although the operating system adapts automatically to the presence or absence of the FP11.

Next, a floating-point version of the C compiler in /usr/src/cmd/c should be compiled using the commands:

```
cd /usr/src/cmd/c
make fc1
mv fc1 /lib/fc1
```

This allows programs with floating point constants to be compiled. To compile floating point programs use the '−f' flag to cc(1). This flag ensures that the floating point interpreter is loaded with the program and that the floating point version of 'cc' is used.

Time Conversion

If your machine is not in the Eastern time zone, you must edit (ed(1)) the file /usr/sys/h/param.h to reflect your local time. The manifest 'TIMEZONE' should be changed to reflect the time difference between local time and GMT in minutes. For EST, this is 5*60; for PST it would be 8*60. Finally, there is a 'DSTFLAG' manifest; when it is 1 it causes the time to shift to Daylight Savings automatically between the last Sundays in April and October (or other algorithms in 1974 and 1975). Normally this will not have to be reset. When the needed changes are done, recompile and load the system using make(1) and install it. (As a general rule, when a system header file is changed, the entire system should be recompiled. As it happens, the only uses of these flags are in /usr/sys/sys/sys4.c, so if this is all that was changed it alone needs to be recompiled.)

You may also want to look at timezone(3) (/usr/src/libc/gen/timezone.c) to see if the name of your timezone is in its internal table. If needed, edit the changes in. After timezone.c has been edited it should be compiled and installed in its library. (See /usr/src/libc/(mklib and compall)) Then you should (at your leisure) recompile and reinstall all programs that use it (such as date(1)).

Disk Layout

If there are to be more file systems mounted than just the root and /usr, use mkfs(1) to create any new file system and put its mounting in the file /etc/rc (see init(8) and mount(1)). (You might look at /etc/rc anyway to see what has been provided for you.)

There are two considerations in deciding how to adjust the arrangement of things on your disks: the most important is making sure there is adequate space for what is required; secondarily, throughput should be maximized. Swap space is a critical parameter. The system as distributed has 8778 (hpunix) or 2000 (rpunix) blocks for swap space. This should be large enough so running out of swap space never occurs. You may want to change these if local wisdom indicates otherwise.

The system as distributed has all of the binaries in /bin. Most of them should be moved to /usr/bin, leaving only the ones required for system maintenance (such as icheck, dcheck, cc, ed, restor, etc.) and the most heavily used in /bin. This will speed things up a bit if you have only one disk, and also free up space on the root file system for temporary files. (See below).

Many common system programs (C, the editor, the assembler etc.) create intermediate files in the /tmp directory, so the file system where this is stored also should be made large enough to accommodate most high-water marks. If you leave the root file system as distributed (except as discussed above) there should be no problem. All the programs that create files in /tmp take care to delete them, but most are not immune to events like being hung up upon, and can leave dregs. The directory should be examined every so often and the old files deleted.

Exhaustion of user-file space is certain to occur now and then; the only mechanisms for controlling this phenomenon are occasional use of du(1), df(1), quot(1), threatening messages of the day, and personal letters.

The efficiency with which UNIX is able to use the CPU is largely dictated by the configuration of disk controllers. For general time-sharing applications, the best strategy is to try to split user files, the root directory (including the /tmp directory) and the swap area among three controllers.

Once you have decided how to make best use of your hardware, the question is how to initialize it. If you have the equipment, the best way to move a file system is to dump it (dump(1)) to magtape, use mkfs(1) to create the new file system, and restore (restor(1)) the tape. If for some reason you don't want to use magtape, dump accepts an argument telling where to put the dump; you might use another disk. Sometimes a file system has to be increased in logical size without copying. The super-block of the device has a word giving the highest address which can be allocated. For relatively small increases, this word can be patched using the debugger (adb(1)) and the free list reconstructed using icheck(1). The size should not be increased very greatly by this technique, however, since although the allocatable space will increase the maximum number of files will not (that is, the i-list size can't be changed). Read and understand the description given in file system(5) before playing around in this way. You may want to see section rp(4) for some suggestions on how to lay out the information on RP disks.

If you have to merge a file system into another, existing one, the best bet is to use tar(1). If you must shrink a file system, the best bet is to dump the original and restor it onto the new filesystem. However, this might not work if the i-list on the smaller filesystem is smaller than the maximum allocated inode on the larger. If this is the case, reconstruct the filesystem from scratch on another filesystem (perhaps using tar(1)) and then dump it. If you are playing with the root file system and only have one drive the procedure is more complicated. What you do is the following:

1.   GET A SECOND PACK!!!!

2.   Dump the current root filesystem (or the reconstructed one) using dump(1).

3.   Bring the system down and mount the new pack.

4.   Retrieve the WECo distribution tape and perform steps 1 through 5 at the beginning of this document, substituting the desired file system size instead of 5000 when asked for 'file system size'.

5.   Perform step 6 above up to the point where the 'tape' question is asked. At this point mount the tape you made just a few minutes ago. Continue with step 6 above substituting a 0 (zero) for the 5.

New Users

Install new users by editing the password file /etc/passwd (passwd(5)). This procedure should be done once multi-user mode is entered (see init(8)). You'll have to make a current directory for each new user and change its owner to the newly installed name. Login as each user to make sure the password file is correctly edited. For example:

```
ed /etc/passwd
$a
joe::10:1::/usr/joe:
.
w
q
mkdir /usr/joe
chown joe /usr/joe
login joe
ls —la
login root
```

This will make a new login entry for joe, who should be encouraged to use passwd(1) to give himself a password. His default current directory is /usr/joe which has been created. The delivered password file has the user *bin* in it to be used as a prototype.

Multiple Users

If UNIX is to support simultaneous access from more than just the console terminal, the file /etc/ttys (ttys(5)) has to be edited. To add a new terminal be sure the device is configured and the special file exists, then set the first character of the appropriate line of /etc/ttys to 1 (or add a new line). Note that init.c will have to be recompiled if there are to be more than 100 terminals. Also note that if the special file is inaccessible when init tries to create a process for it, the system will thrash trying and retrying to open it.

File System Health

Periodically (say every day or so) and always after a crash, you should check all the file systems for consistency (icheck, dcheck(1)). It is quite important to execute sync (8) before rebooting or taking the machine down. This is done automatically every 30 seconds by the update program (8) when a multiple-user system is running, but you should do it anyway to make sure.

Dumping of the file system should be done regularly, since once the system is going it is very easy to become complacent. Complete and incremental dumps are easily done with dump(1). Dumping of files by name is best done by tar(1) but the number of files is somewhat limited. Finally if there are enough drives entire disks can be copied using cp(1), or preferably with dd(1) using the raw special files and an appropriate block size.

Converting Sixth Edition Filesystems

The best way to convert file systems from 6th edition (V6) to 7th edition (V7) format is to use tar(1). However, a special version of tar must be prepared to run on V6. The following steps will do this:

1. change directories to /usr/src/cmd/tar

2. At the shell prompt respond

        make v6tar

    This will leave an executable binary named 'v6tar'.

3. Mount a scratch tape.

4. Use tp(1) to put 'v6tar' on the scratch tape.

5. Bring down V7 and bring up V6.

6. Use tp (on V6) to read in 'v6tar'. Put it in /bin or /usr/bin (or perhaps some other preferred location).

7. Use v6tar to make tapes of all that you wish to convert. You may want to read the manual section on tar(1) to see whether you want to use blocking or not. Try to avoid using full pathnames when making the tapes. This will simplify moving the hierarchy to some other place on V7 if desired. For example

        chdir /usr/ken
        v6tar c .

    is preferable to

        v6tar c /usr/ken

8. After all of the desired tapes are made, bring down V6 and reboot V7. Use tar(1) to read in the tapes just made.

Odds and Ends

The programs dump, icheck, quot, dcheck, ncheck, and df (source in /usr/source/cmd) should be changed to reflect your default mounted file system devices. Print the first few lines of these programs and the changes will be obvious. Tar should be changed to reflect your desired default tape drive.

Good Luck

Charles B. Haley
Dennis M. Ritchie

REGENERATING SYSTEM SOFTWARE

Charles B. Haley

Dennis. M. Ritchie
Bell Laboratories
Murray Hill, New Jersey 07974

Introduction

This document discusses how to assemble or compile various parts of the UNIX† system software. This may be necessary because a command or library is accidentally deleted or otherwise destroyed; also, it may be desirable to install a modified version of some command or library routine. A few commands depend to some degree on the current configuration of the system; thus in any new system modifications to some commands are advisable. Most of the likely modifications relate to the standard disk devices contained in the system. For example, the df(1) ('disk free') command has built into it the names of the standardly present disk storage drives (e.g. '/dev/rf0', '/dev/rp0'). Df(1) takes an argument to indicate which disk to examine, but it is convenient if its default argument is adjusted to reflect the ordinarily present devices. The companion document 'Setting up UNIX' discusses which commands are likely to require changes.

Where Commands and Subroutines Live

The source files for commands and subroutines reside in several subdirectories of the directory /usr/src. These subdirectories, and a general description of their contents, are

cmd	Source files for commands.
libc/stdio	Source files making up the 'standard i/o package'.
libc/sys	Source files for the C system call interfaces.
libc/gen	Source files for most of the remaining routines described in section 3 of the manual.
libc/crt	Source files making up the C runtime support package, as in call save-return and long arithmetic.
libc/csu	Source for the C startup routines.
games	Source for (some of) the games. No great care has been taken to try to make it obvious how to compile these; treat it as a game.
libF77	Source for the Fortran 77 runtime library, exclusive of IO.
libI77	Source for the Fortran 77 IO runtime routines.
libdbm	Source for the 'data-base manager' package *dbm* (3).
libfpsim	Source for the floating-point simulator routine.
libm	Source for the mathematical library.

---

†UNIX is a Trademark of Bell Laboratories.

libplot   Source for plotting routines.

Commands

The regeneration of most commands is straightforward. The 'cmd' directory will contain either a source file for the command or a subdirectory containing the set of files that make up the command. If it is a single file the command

    cd /usr/src/cmd
    cmake cmd_name

suffices. (Cmd_name is the name of the command you are playing with.) The result of the cmake command will be an executable version. If you type

    cmake −cp cmd_name

the result will be copied to /bin (or perhaps /etc or other places if appropriate).

If the source files are in a subdirectory there will be a 'makefile' (see make(1)) to control the regeneration. After changing to the proper directory (cd(1)) you type one of the following:

make all   The program is compiled and loaded; the executable is left in the current directory.

make cp   The program is compiled and loaded, and the executable is installed. Everything is cleaned up afterwards; for example .o files are deleted.

make cmp   The program is compiled and loaded, and the executable is compared against the one in /bin.

Some of the makefiles have other options. Print (cat(1)) the ones you are interested in to find out.

The Assembler

The assembler consists of two executable files: /bin/as and /lib/as2. The first is the 0-th pass: it reads the source program, converts it to an intermediate form in a temporary file '/tmp/atm0?', and estimates the final locations of symbols. It also makes two or three other temporary files which contain the ordinary symbol table, a table of temporary symbols (like 1:) and possibly an overflow intermediate file. The program /lib/as2 acts as an ordinary multiple pass assembler with input taken from the files produced by /bin/as.

The source files for /bin/as are named '/usr/src/cmd/as/as1?.s' (there are 9 of them); /lib/as2 is produced from the source files '/usr/src/cmd/as/as2?.s'; they likewise are 9 in number. Considerable care should be exercised in replacing either component of the assembler. Remember that if the assembler is lost, the only recourse is to replace it from some backup storage; a broken assembler cannot assemble itself.

The C Compiler

The C compiler consists of seven routines: '/bin/cc', which calls the phases of the compiler proper, the compiler control line expander '/lib/cpp', the assembler ('as'), and the loader ('ld'). The phases of the C compiler are '/lib/c0', which is the first phase of the compiler; '/lib/c1', which is the second phase of the compiler; and '/lib/c2', which is the optional third phase optimizer. The loss of the C compiler is as serious as that of the assembler.

The source for /bin/cc resides in '/usr/src/cmd/cc.c'. Its loss alone (or that of c2) is not fatal. If needed, prog.c can be compiled by

```
/lib/cpp prog.c >temp0
/lib/c0 temp0 temp1 temp2
/lib/c1 temp1 temp2 temp3
as − temp3
ld −n /lib/crt0.o a.out −lc
```

The source for the compiler proper is in the directory /usr/src/cmd/c. The first phase (/lib/c0) is generated from the files c00.c, ..., c05.c, which must be compiled by the C compiler. There is also c0.h, a header file *included* by the C programs of the first phase. To make a new /lib/c0 use

    make c0

Before installing the new c0, it is prudent to save the old one someplace.

The second phase of C (/lib/c1) is generated from the source files c10.c, ..., c13.c, the include-file c1.h, and a set of object-code tables combined into table.o. To generate a new second phase use

    make c1

It is likewise prudent to save c1 before installing a new version. In fact in general it is wise to save the object files for the C compiler so that if disaster strikes C can be reconstituted without a working version of the compiler.

In a similar manner, the third phase of the C compiler (/lib/c2) is made up from the files c20.c and c21.c together with c2.h. Its loss is not critical since it is completely optional.

The set of tables mentioned above is generated from the file table.s. This '.s' file is not in fact assembler source; it must be converted by use of the *cvopt* program, whose source and object are located in the C directory. Normally this is taken care of by make(1). You might want to look at the makefile to see what it does.

UNIX

The source and object programs for UNIX are kept in four subdirectories of */usr/sys*. In the subdirectory *h* there are several files ending in '.h'; these are header files which are picked up (via '#include ...') as required by each system module. The subdirectory *dev* consists mostly of the device drivers together with a few other things. The subdirectory *sys* is the rest of the system. There are files of the form LIBx in the directories sys and dev. These are archives (ar(1)) which contain the object versions of the routines in the directory.

Subdirectory *conf* contains the files which control device configuration of the system. *L.s* specifies the contents of the interrupt vectors; *c.c* contains the tables which relate device numbers to handler routines. A third file, *mch.s*, contains all the machine-language code in the system. A fourth file, *mch0.s*, is generated by mkconf(1) and contains flags indicating what sort of tape drive is available for taking crash dumps.

There are two ways to recreate the system. Use

    cd /usr/sys/conf
    make unix

if the libraries /usr/sys/dev/LIB2 and /usr/sys/sys/LIB1, and also c.o and l.o, are correct. Use

    cd /usr/sys/conf
    make all

to recompile everything and recreate the libraries from scratch. This is needed, for example, when a header included in several source files is changed. See 'Setting Up UNIX' for other information about configuration and such.

When the make is done, the new system is present in the current directory as 'unix'. It should be tested before destroying the currently running '/unix', this is best done by doing something like

    mv /unix /ounix
    mv unix /unix

If the new system doesn't work, you can still boot 'ounix' and come up (see boot(8)). When you have satisfied yourself that the new system works, remove /ounix.

To install a new device driver, compile it and put it into its library. The best way to put it into the library is to use the command

    ar uv LIB2 x.o

where x is the routine you just compiled. (All the device drivers distributed with the system are already in the library.)

Next, the device's interrupt vector must be entered in l.s. This is probably already done by the routine mkconf(1), but if the device is esoteric or nonstandard you will have to massage l.s by hand. This involves placing a pointer to a callout routine and the device's priority level in the vector. Use some other device (like the console) as a guide. Notice that the entries in l.s must be in order as the assembler does not permit moving the location counter '.' backwards. The assembler also does not permit assignation of an absolute number to '.', which is the reason for the '. = ZERO+100' subterfuge. If a constant smaller than 16(10) is added to the priority level, this number will be available as the first argument of the interrupt routine. This stratagem is used when several similar devices share the same interrupt routine (as in dl11's).

If you have to massage l.s, be sure to add the code to actually transfer to the interrupt routine. Again use the console as a guide. The apparent strangeness of this code is due to running the kernel in separate I&D space. The *call* routine saves registers as required and prepares a C-style call on the actual interrupt routine named after the 'jmp' instruction. When the routine returns, *call* restores the registers and performs an rti instruction. As an aside, note that external names in C programs have an underscore ('_') prepended to them.

The second step which must be performed to add a device unknown to mkconf is to add it to the configuration table /usr/sys/conf/c.c. This file contains two subtables, one for block-type devices, and one for character-type devices. Block devices include disks, DECtape, and magtape. All other devices are character devices. A line in each of these tables gives all the information the system needs to know about the device handler; the ordinal position of the line in the table implies its major device number, starting at 0.

There are four subentries per line in the block device table, which give its open routine, close routine, strategy routine, and device table. The open and close routines may be nonexistent, in which case the name 'nulldev' is given; this routine merely returns. The strategy routine is called to do any I/O, and the device table contains status information for the device.

For character devices, each line in the table specifies a routine for open, close, read, and write, and one which sets and returns device-specific status (used, for example, for stty and gtty on typewriters). If there is no open or close routine, 'nulldev' may be given; if there is no read, write, or status routine, 'nodev' may be given. Nodev sets an error flag and returns.

The final step which must be taken to install a device is to make a special file for it. This is done by mknod(1), to which you must specify the device class (block or character), major device number (relative line in the configuration table) and minor device number (which is made available to the driver at appropriate times).

The documents 'Setting up Unix' and 'The Unix IO system' may aid in comprehending these steps.

The Library libc.a

The library /lib/libc.a is where most of the subroutines described in sections 2 and 3 of the manual are kept. This library can be remade using the following commands:

```
cd /usr/src/libc
sh compall
sh mklib
mv libc.a /lib/libc.a
```

If single routines need to be recompiled and replaced, use

```
cc −c −O x.c
ar vr /lib/libc.a x.o
rm x.o
```

The above can also be used to put new items into the library. See ar(1), lorder(1), and tsort(1).

The routines in /usr/src/cmd/libc/csu (C start up) are not in libc.a. These are separately assembled and put into /lib. The commands to do this are

```
cd /usr/src/libc/csu
as − x.s
mv a.out /lib/x
```

where x is the routine you want.

Other Libraries

Likewise, the directories containing the source for the other libraries have files compall (that recompiles everything) and mklib (that recreates the library).

System Tuning

There are several tunable parameters in the system. These set the size of various tables and limits. They are found in the file /usr/sys/h/param.h as manifests ('#define's). Their values are rather generous in the system as distributed. Our typical maximum number of users is about 20, but there are many daemon processes.

When any parameter is changed, it is prudent to recompile the entire system, as discussed above. A brief discussion of each follows:

NBUF   This sets the size of the disk buffer cache. Each buffer is 512 bytes. This number should be around 25 plus NMOUNT, or as big as can be if the above number of buffers cause the system to not fit in memory.

NFILE   This sets the maximum number of open files. An entry is made in this table every time a file is 'opened' (see open(2), creat(2)). Processes share these table entries across forks (fork(2)). This number should be about the same size as NINODE below. (It can be a bit smaller.)

NMOUNT   This indicates the maximum number of mounted file systems. Make it big enough that you don't run out at inconvenient times.

MAXMEM   This sets an administrative limit on the amount of memory a process may have. It is set automatically if the amount of physical memory is small, and thus should not need to be changed.

MAXUPRC   This sets the maximum number of processes that any one user can be running at any one time. This should be set just large enough that people can get work done but not so large that a user can hog all the processes available (usually by accident!).

NPROC   This sets the maximum number of processes that can be active. It depends on the demand pattern of the typical user; we seem to need about 8 times the number of terminals.

NINODE   This sets the size of the inode table. There is one entry in the inode table for every open device, current working directory, sticky text segment, open file, and mounted device. Note that if two users have a file open there is still only one entry in the inode table. A reasonable rule of thumb for the size of this table is

$$\text{NPROC} + \text{NMOUNT} + (\text{number of terminals})$$

SSIZE   The initial size of a process stack. This may be made bigger if commonly run processes have large data areas on the stack.

SINCR   The size of the stack growth increment.

NOFILE   This sets the maximum number of files that any one process can have open. 20 is plenty.

CANBSIZ   This is the size of the typewriter canonicalization buffer. It is in this buffer that erase and kill processing is done. Thus this is the maximum size of an input typewriter line. 256 is usually plenty.

CMAPSIZ   The number of fragments that memory can be broken into. This should be big enough that it never runs out. The theoretical maximum is twice the number of processes, but this is a vast overestimate in practice. 50 seems enough.

SMAPSIZ   Same as CMAPSIZ except for secondary (swap) memory.

NCALL   This is the size of the callout table. Callouts are entered in this table when some sort of internal system timing must be done, as in carriage return delays for terminals. The number must be big enough to handle all such requests.

NTEXT   The maximum number of simultaneously executing pure programs. This should be big enough so as to not run out of space under heavy load. A reasonable rule of thumb is about

$$(\text{number of terminals}) + (\text{number of sticky programs})$$

NCLIST   The number of clist segments. A clist segment is 6 characters. NCLIST should be big enough so that the list doesn't become exhausted when the machine is busy. The characters that have arrived from a terminal and are waiting to be given to a process live here. Thus enough space should be left so that every terminal can have at least one average line pending (about 30 or 40 characters).

TIMEZONE   The number of minutes westward from Greenwich. See 'Setting Up UNIX'.

DSTFLAG   See 'Setting Up UNIX' section on time conversion.

MSGBUFS   The maximum number of characters of system error messages saved. This is used as a circular buffer.

NCARGS   The maximum number of characters in an exec(2) arglist. This number controls how many arguments can be passed into a process. 5120 is practically infinite.

HZ   Set to the frequency of the system clock (e.g., 50 for a 50 Hz. clock).

UNIX Implementation

K. Thompson

Bell Laboratories
Murray Hill, New Jersey 07974

ABSTRACT

This paper describes in high-level terms the implementation of the resident UNIX† kernel. This discussion is broken into three parts. The first part describes how the UNIX system views processes, users, and programs. The second part describes the I/O system. The last part describes the UNIX file system.

1. INTRODUCTION

The UNIX kernel consists of about 10,000 lines of C code and about 1,000 lines of assembly code. The assembly code can be further broken down into 200 lines included for the sake of efficiency (they could have been written in C) and 800 lines to perform hardware functions not possible in C.

This code represents 5 to 10 percent of what has been lumped into the broad expression "the UNIX operating system." The kernel is the only UNIX code that cannot be substituted by a user to his own liking. For this reason, the kernel should make as few real decisions as possible. This does not mean to allow the user a million options to do the same thing. Rather, it means to allow only one way to do one thing, but have that way be the least-common divisor of all the options that might have been provided.

What is or is not implemented in the kernel represents both a great responsibility and a great power. It is a soap-box platform on "the way things should be done." Even so, if "the way" is too radical, no one will follow it. Every important decision was weighed carefully. Throughout, simplicity has been substituted for efficiency. Complex algorithms are used only if their complexity can be localized.

2. PROCESS CONTROL

In the UNIX system, a user executes programs in an environment called a user process. When a system function is required, the user process calls the system as a subroutine. At some point in this call, there is a distinct switch of environments. After this, the process is said to be a system process. In the normal definition of processes, the user and system processes are different phases of the same process (they never execute simultaneously). For protection, each system process has its own stack.

The user process may execute from a read-only text segment, which is shared by all processes executing the same code. There is no *functional* benefit from shared-text segments. An *efficiency* benefit comes from the fact that there is no need to swap read-only segments out because the original copy on secondary memory is still current. This is a great benefit to interactive programs that tend to be swapped while waiting for terminal input. Furthermore, if two processes are executing simultaneously from the same copy of a read-only segment, only one copy needs to reside in primary memory. This is a secondary effect, because simultaneous

---

†UNIX is a Trademark of Bell Laboratories.

512

execution of a program is not common. It is ironic that this effect, which reduces the use of primary memory, only comes into play when there is an overabundance of primary memory, that is, when there is enough memory to keep waiting processes loaded.

All current read-only text segments in the system are maintained from the *text table*. A text table entry holds the location of the text segment on secondary memory. If the segment is loaded, that table also holds the primary memory location and the count of the number of processes sharing this entry. When this count is reduced to zero, the entry is freed along with any primary and secondary memory holding the segment. When a process first executes a shared-text segment, a text table entry is allocated and the segment is loaded onto secondary memory. If a second process executes a text segment that is already allocated, the entry reference count is simply incremented.

A user process has some strictly private read-write data contained in its data segment. As far as possible, the system does not use the user's data segment to hold system data. In particular, there are no I/O buffers in the user address space.

The user data segment has two growing boundaries. One, increased automatically by the system as a result of memory faults, is used for a stack. The second boundary is only grown (or shrunk) by explicit requests. The contents of newly allocated primary memory is initialized to zero.

Also associated and swapped with a process is a small fixed-size system data segment. This segment contains all the data about the process that the system needs only when the process is active. Examples of the kind of data contained in the system data segment are: saved central processor registers, open file descriptors, accounting information, scratch data area, and the stack for the system phase of the process. The system data segment is not addressable from the user process and is therefore protected.

Last, there is a process table with one entry per process. This entry contains all the data needed by the system when the process is *not* active. Examples are the process's name, the location of the other segments, and scheduling information. The process table entry is allocated when the process is created, and freed when the process terminates. This process entry is always directly addressable by the kernel.

Figure 1 shows the relationships between the various process control data. In a sense, the process table is the definition of all processes, because all the data associated with a process may be accessed starting from the process table entry.

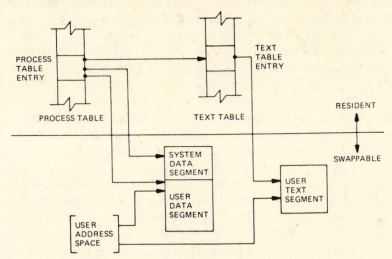

Fig. 1—Process control data structure.

2.1. Process creation and program execution

Processes are created by the system primitive **fork**. The newly created process (child) is a copy of the original process (parent). There is no detectable sharing of primary memory between the two processes. (Of course, if the parent process was executing from a read-only text segment, the child will share the text segment.) Copies of all writable data segments are made for the child process. Files that were open before the **fork** are truly shared after the **fork**. The processes are informed as to their part in the relationship to allow them to select their own (usually non-identical) destiny. The parent may **wait** for the termination of any of its children.

A process may **exec** a file. This consists of exchanging the current text and data segments of the process for new text and data segments specified in the file. The old segments are lost. Doing an **exec** does *not* change processes; the process that did the **exec** persists, but after the **exec** it is executing a different program. Files that were open before the **exec** remain open after the **exec**.

If a program, say the first pass of a compiler, wishes to overlay itself with another program, say the second pass, then it simply **exec**s the second program. This is analogous to a "goto." If a program wishes to regain control after **exec**ing a second program, it should **fork** a child process, have the child **exec** the second program, and have the parent **wait** for the child. This is analogous to a "call." Breaking up the call into a binding followed by a transfer is similar to the subroutine linkage in SL-5.[1]

2.2. Swapping

The major data associated with a process (the user data segment, the system data segment, and the text segment) are swapped to and from secondary memory, as needed. The user data segment and the system data segment are kept in contiguous primary memory to reduce swapping latency. (When low-latency devices, such as bubbles, CCDs, or scatter/gather devices, are used, this decision will have to be reconsidered.) Allocation of both primary and secondary memory is performed by the same simple first-fit algorithm. When a process grows, a new piece of primary memory is allocated. The contents of the old memory is copied to the new memory. The old memory is freed and the tables are updated. If there is not enough primary memory, secondary memory is allocated instead. The process is swapped out onto the secondary memory, ready to be swapped in with its new size.

One separate process in the kernel, the swapping process, simply swaps the other processes in and out of primary memory. It examines the process table looking for a process that is swapped out and is ready to run. It allocates primary memory for that process and reads its segments into primary memory, where that process competes for the central processor with other loaded processes. If no primary memory is available, the swapping process makes memory available by examining the process table for processes that can be swapped out. It selects a process to swap out, writes it to secondary memory, frees the primary memory, and then goes back to look for a process to swap in.

Thus there are two specific algorithms to the swapping process. Which of the possibly many processes that are swapped out is to be swapped in? This is decided by secondary storage residence time. The one with the longest time out is swapped in first. There is a slight penalty for larger processes. Which of the possibly many processes that are loaded is to be swapped out? Processes that are waiting for slow events (i.e., not currently running or waiting for disk I/O) are picked first, by age in primary memory, again with size penalties. The other processes are examined by the same age algorithm, but are not taken out unless they are at least of some age. This adds hysteresis to the swapping and prevents total thrashing.

These swapping algorithms are the most suspect in the system. With limited primary memory, these algorithms cause total swapping. This is not bad in itself, because the swapping does not impact the execution of the resident processes. However, if the swapping device must also be used for file storage, the swapping traffic severely impacts the file system traffic. It is exactly these small systems that tend to double usage of limited disk resources.

2.3. Synchronization and scheduling

Process synchronization is accomplished by having processes wait for events. Events are represented by arbitrary integers. By convention, events are chosen to be addresses of tables associated with those events. For example, a process that is waiting for any of its children to terminate will wait for an event that is the address of its own process table entry. When a process terminates, it signals the event represented by its parent's process table entry. Signaling an event on which no process is waiting has no effect. Similarly, signaling an event on which many processes are waiting will wake all of them up. This differs considerably from Dijkstra's P and V synchronization operations,[2] in that no memory is associated with events. Thus there need be no allocation of events prior to their use. Events exist simply by being used.

On the negative side, because there is no memory associated with events, no notion of "how much" can be signaled via the event mechanism. For example, processes that want memory might wait on an event associated with memory allocation. When any amount of memory becomes available, the event would be signaled. All the competing processes would then wake up to fight over the new memory. (In reality, the swapping process is the only process that waits for primary memory to become available.)

If an event occurs between the time a process decides to wait for that event and the time that process enters the wait state, then the process will wait on an event that has already happened (and may never happen again). This race condition happens because there is no memory associated with the event to indicate that the event has occurred; the only action of an event is to change a set of processes from wait state to run state. This problem is relieved largely by the fact that process switching can only occur in the kernel by explicit calls to the event-wait mechanism. If the event in question is signaled by another process, then there is no problem. But if the event is signaled by a hardware interrupt, then special care must be taken. These synchronization races pose the biggest problem when UNIX is adapted to multiple-processor configurations.[3]

The event-wait code in the kernel is like a co-routine linkage. At any time, all but one of the processes has called event-wait. The remaining process is the one currently executing. When it calls event-wait, a process whose event has been signaled is selected and that process returns from its call to event-wait.

Which of the runable processes is to run next? Associated with each process is a priority. The priority of a system process is assigned by the code issuing the wait on an event. This is roughly equivalent to the response that one would expect on such an event. Disk events have high priority, teletype events are low, and time-of-day events are very low. (From observation, the difference in system process priorities has little or no performance impact.) All user-process priorities are lower than the lowest system priority. User-process priorities are assigned by an algorithm based on the recent ratio of the amount of compute time to real time consumed by the process. A process that has used a lot of compute time in the last real-time unit is assigned a low user priority. Because interactive processes are characterized by low ratios of compute to real time, interactive response is maintained without any special arrangements.

The scheduling algorithm simply picks the process with the highest priority, thus picking all system processes first and user processes second. The compute-to-real-time ratio is updated every second. Thus, all other things being equal, looping user processes will be scheduled round-robin with a 1-second quantum. A high-priority process waking up will preempt a running, low-priority process. The scheduling algorithm has a very desirable negative feedback character. If a process uses its high priority to hog the computer, its priority will drop. At the same time, if a low-priority process is ignored for a long time, its priority will rise.

3. I/O SYSTEM

The I/O system is broken into two completely separate systems: the block I/O system and the character I/O system. In retrospect, the names should have been "structured I/O" and "unstructured I/O," respectively; while the term "block I/O" has some meaning, "character

I/O" is a complete misnomer.

Devices are characterized by a major device number, a minor device number, and a class (block or character). For each class, there is an array of entry points into the device drivers. The major device number is used to index the array when calling the code for a particular device driver. The minor device number is passed to the device driver as an argument. The minor number has no significance other than that attributed to it by the driver. Usually, the driver uses the minor number to access one of several identical physical devices.

The use of the array of entry points (configuration table) as the only connection between the system code and the device drivers is very important. Early versions of the system had a much less formal connection with the drivers, so that it was extremely hard to handcraft differently configured systems. Now it is possible to create new device drivers in an average of a few hours. The configuration table in most cases is created automatically by a program that reads the system's parts list.

3.1. Block I/O system

The model block I/O device consists of randomly addressed, secondary memory blocks of 512 bytes each. The blocks are uniformly addressed 0, 1, ... up to the size of the device. The block device driver has the job of emulating this model on a physical device.

The block I/O devices are accessed through a layer of buffering software. The system maintains a list of buffers (typically between 10 and 70) each assigned a device name and a device address. This buffer pool constitutes a data cache for the block devices. On a read request, the cache is searched for the desired block. If the block is found, the data are made available to the requester without any physical I/O. If the block is not in the cache, the least recently used block in the cache is renamed, the correct device driver is called to fill up the renamed buffer, and then the data are made available. Write requests are handled in an analogous manner. The correct buffer is found and relabeled if necessary. The write is performed simply by marking the buffer as "dirty." The physical I/O is then deferred until the buffer is renamed.

The benefits in reduction of physical I/O of this scheme are substantial, especially considering the file system implementation. There are, however, some drawbacks. The asynchronous nature of the algorithm makes error reporting and meaningful user error handling almost impossible. The cavalier approach to I/O error handling in the UNIX system is partly due to the asynchronous nature of the block I/O system. A second problem is in the delayed writes. If the system stops unexpectedly, it is almost certain that there is a lot of logically complete, but physically incomplete, I/O in the buffers. There is a system primitive to flush all outstanding I/O activity from the buffers. Periodic use of this primitive helps, but does not solve, the problem. Finally, the associativity in the buffers can alter the physical I/O sequence from that of the logical I/O sequence. This means that there are times when data structures on disk are inconsistent, even though the software is careful to perform I/O in the correct order. On non-random devices, notably magnetic tape, the inversions of writes can be disastrous. The problem with magnetic tapes is "cured" by allowing only one outstanding write request per drive.

3.2. Character I/O system

The character I/O system consists of all devices that do not fall into the block I/O model. This includes the "classical" character devices such as communications lines, paper tape, and line printers. It also includes magnetic tape and disks when they are not used in a stereotyped way, for example, 80-byte physical records on tape and track-at-a-time disk copies. In short, the character I/O interface means "everything other than block." I/O requests from the user are sent to the device driver essentially unaltered. The implementation of these requests is, of course, up to the device driver. There are guidelines and conventions to help the implementation of certain types of device drivers.

3.2.1. Disk drivers

Disk drivers are implemented with a queue of transaction records. Each record holds a read/write flag, a primary memory address, a secondary memory address, and a transfer byte count. Swapping is accomplished by passing such a record to the swapping device driver. The block I/O interface is implemented by passing such records with requests to fill and empty system buffers. The character I/O interface to the disk drivers create a transaction record that points directly into the user area. The routine that creates this record also insures that the user is not swapped during this I/O transaction. Thus by implementing the general disk driver, it is possible to use the disk as a block device, a character device, and a swap device. The only really disk-specific code in normal disk drivers is the pre-sort of transactions to minimize latency for a particular device, and the actual issuing of the I/O request.

3.2.2. Character lists

Real character-oriented devices may be implemented using the common code to handle character lists. A character list is a queue of characters. One routine puts a character on a queue. Another gets a character from a queue. It is also possible to ask how many characters are currently on a queue. Storage for all queues in the system comes from a single common pool. Putting a character on a queue will allocate space from the common pool and link the character onto the data structure defining the queue. Getting a character from a queue returns the corresponding space to the pool.

A typical character-output device (paper tape punch, for example) is implemented by passing characters from the user onto a character queue until some maximum number of characters is on the queue. The I/O is prodded to start as soon as there is anything on the queue and, once started, it is sustained by hardware completion interrupts. Each time there is a completion interrupt, the driver gets the next character from the queue and sends it to the hardware. The number of characters on the queue is checked and, as the count falls through some intermediate level, an event (the queue address) is signaled. The process that is passing characters from the user to the queue can be waiting on the event, and refill the queue to its maximum when the event occurs.

A typical character input device (for example, a paper tape reader) is handled in a very similar manner.

Another class of character devices is the terminals. A terminal is represented by three character queues. There are two input queues (raw and canonical) and an output queue. Characters going to the output of a terminal are handled by common code exactly as described above. The main difference is that there is also code to interpret the output stream as ASCII characters and to perform some translations, e.g., escapes for deficient terminals. Another common aspect of terminals is code to insert real-time delay after certain control characters.

Input on terminals is a little different. Characters are collected from the terminal and placed on a raw input queue. Some device-dependent code conversion and escape interpretation is handled here. When a line is complete in the raw queue, an event is signaled. The code catching this signal then copies a line from the raw queue to a canonical queue performing the character erase and line kill editing. User read requests on terminals can be directed at either the raw or canonical queues.

3.2.3. Other character devices

Finally, there are devices that fit no general category. These devices are set up as character I/O drivers. An example is a driver that reads and writes unmapped primary memory as an I/O device. Some devices are too fast to be treated a character at time, but do not fit the disk I/O mold. Examples are fast communications lines and fast line printers. These devices either have their own buffers or "borrow" block I/O buffers for a while and then give them back.

4. THE FILE SYSTEM

In the UNIX system, a file is a (one-dimensional) array of bytes. No other structure of files is implied by the system. Files are attached anywhere (and possibly multiply) onto a hierarchy of directories. Directories are simply files that users cannot write. For a further discussion of the external view of files and directories, see Ref. 4.

The UNIX file system is a disk data structure accessed completely through the block I/O system. As stated before, the canonical view of a "disk" is a randomly addressable array of 512-byte blocks. A file system breaks the disk into four self-identifying regions. The first block (address 0) is unused by the file system. It is left aside for booting procedures. The second block (address 1) contains the so-called "super-block." This block, among other things, contains the size of the disk and the boundaries of the other regions. Next comes the i-list, a list of file definitions. Each file definition is a 64-byte structure, called an i-node. The offset of a particular i-node within the i-list is called its i-number. The combination of device name (major and minor numbers) and i-number serves to uniquely name a particular file. After the i-list, and to the end of the disk, come free storage blocks that are available for the contents of files.

The free space on a disk is maintained by a linked list of available disk blocks. Every block in this chain contains a disk address of the next block in the chain. The remaining space contains the address of up to 50 disk blocks that are also free. Thus with one I/O operation, the system obtains 50 free blocks and a pointer where to find more. The disk allocation algorithms are very straightforward. Since all allocation is in fixed-size blocks and there is strict accounting of space, there is no need to compact or garbage collect. However, as disk space becomes dispersed, latency gradually increases. Some installations choose to occasionally compact disk space to reduce latency.

An i-node contains 13 disk addresses. The first 10 of these addresses point directly at the first 10 blocks of a file. If a file is larger than 10 blocks (5,120 bytes), then the eleventh address points at a block that contains the addresses of the next 128 blocks of the file. If the file is still larger than this (70,656 bytes), then the twelfth block points at up to 128 blocks, each pointing to 128 blocks of the file. Files yet larger (8,459,264 bytes) use the thirteenth address for a "triple indirect" address. The algorithm ends here with the maximum file size of 1,082,201,087 bytes.

A logical directory hierarchy is added to this flat physical structure simply by adding a new type of file, the directory. A directory is accessed exactly as an ordinary file. It contains 16-byte entries consisting of a 14-byte name and an i-number. The root of the hierarchy is at a known i-number (viz., 2). The file system structure allows an arbitrary, directed graph of directories with regular files linked in at arbitrary places in this graph. In fact, very early UNIX systems used such a structure. Administration of such a structure became so chaotic that later systems were restricted to a directory tree. Even now, with regular files linked multiply into arbitrary places in the tree, accounting for space has become a problem. It may become necessary to restrict the entire structure to a tree, and allow a new form of linking that is subservient to the tree structure.

The file system allows easy creation, easy removal, easy random accessing, and very easy space allocation. With most physical addresses confined to a small contiguous section of disk, it is also easy to dump, restore, and check the consistency of the file system. Large files suffer from indirect addressing, but the cache prevents most of the implied physical I/O without adding much execution. The space overhead properties of this scheme are quite good. For example, on one particular file system, there are 25,000 files containing 130M bytes of data-file content. The overhead (i-node, indirect blocks, and last block breakage) is about 11.5M bytes. The directory structure to support these files has about 1,500 directories containing 0.6M bytes of directory content and about 0.5M bytes of overhead in accessing the directories. Added up any way, this comes out to less than a 10 percent overhead for actual stored data. Most systems have this much overhead in padded trailing blanks alone.

4.1. File system implementation

Because the i-node defines a file, the implementation of the file system centers around access to the i-node. The system maintains a table of all active i-nodes. As a new file is accessed, the system locates the corresponding i-node, allocates an i-node table entry, and reads the i-node into primary memory. As in the buffer cache, the table entry is considered to be the current version of the i-node. Modifications to the i-node are made to the table entry. When the last access to the i-node goes away, the table entry is copied back to the secondary store i-list and the table entry is freed.

All I/O operations on files are carried out with the aid of the corresponding i-node table entry. The accessing of a file is a straightforward implementation of the algorithms mentioned previously. The user is not aware of i-nodes and i-numbers. References to the file system are made in terms of path names of the directory tree. Converting a path name into an i-node table entry is also straightforward. Starting at some known i-node (the root or the current directory of some process), the next component of the path name is searched by reading the directory. This gives an i-number and an implied device (that of the directory). Thus the next i-node table entry can be accessed. If that was the last component of the path name, then this i-node is the result. If not, this i-node is the directory needed to look up the next component of the path name, and the algorithm is repeated.

The user process accesses the file system with certain primitives. The most common of these are **open**, **create**, **read**, **write**, **seek**, and **close**. The data structures maintained are shown in Fig. 2.

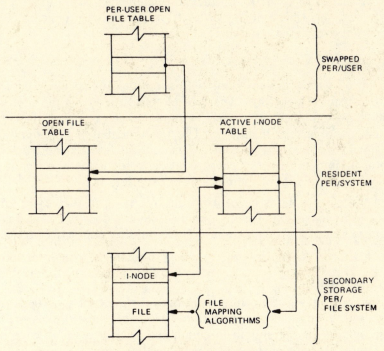

Fig. 2—File system data structure.

In the system data segment associated with a user, there is room for some (usually between 10 and 50) open files. This open file table consists of pointers that can be used to access corresponding i-node table entries. Associated with each of these open files is a current I/O pointer. This is a byte offset of the next read/write operation on the file. The system treats each read/write request as random with an implied seek to the I/O pointer. The user usually thinks of the file as sequential with the I/O pointer automatically counting the number of bytes that have been read/written from the file. The user may, of course, perform random I/O by setting the I/O pointer before reads/writes.

With file sharing, it is necessary to allow related processes to share a common I/O pointer and yet have separate I/O pointers for independent processes that access the same file. With these two conditions, the I/O pointer cannot reside in the i-node table nor can it reside in the list of open files for the process. A new table (the open file table) was invented for the sole purpose of holding the I/O pointer. Processes that share the same open file (the result of **forks**) share a common open file table entry. A separate open of the same file will only share the i-node table entry, but will have distinct open file table entries.

The main file system primitives are implemented as follows. **open** converts a file system path name into an i-node table entry. A pointer to the i-node table entry is placed in a newly created open file table entry. A pointer to the file table entry is placed in the system data segment for the process. **create** first creates a new i-node entry, writes the i-number into a directory, and then builds the same structure as for an **open**. **read** and **write** just access the i-node entry as described above. **seek** simply manipulates the I/O pointer. No physical seeking is done. **close** just frees the structures built by **open** and **create**. Reference counts are kept on the open file table entries and the i-node table entries to free these structures after the last reference goes away. **unlink** simply decrements the count of the number of directories pointing at the given i-node. When the last reference to an i-node table entry goes away, if the i-node has no directories pointing to it, then the file is removed and the i-node is freed. This delayed removal of files prevents problems arising from removing active files. A file may be removed while still open. The resulting unnamed file vanishes when the file is closed. This is a method of obtaining temporary files.

There is a type of unnamed FIFO file called a **pipe.** Implementation of **pipe**s consists of implied **seek**s before each **read** or **write** in order to implement first-in-first-out. There are also checks and synchronization to prevent the writer from grossly outproducing the reader and to prevent the reader from overtaking the writer.

4.2. Mounted file systems.

The file system of a UNIX system starts with some designated block device formatted as described above to contain a hierarchy. The root of this structure is the root of the UNIX file system. A second formatted block device may be mounted at any leaf of the current hierarchy. This logically extends the current hierarchy. The implementation of mounting is trivial. A mount table is maintained containing pairs of designated leaf i-nodes and block devices. When converting a path name into an i-node, a check is made to see if the new i-node is a designated leaf. If it is, the i-node of the root of the block device replaces it.

Allocation of space for a file is taken from the free pool on the device on which the file lives. Thus a file system consisting of many mounted devices does not have a common pool of free secondary storage space. This separation of space on different devices is necessary to allow easy unmounting of a device.

4.3. Other system functions

There are some other things that the system does for the user — a little accounting, a little tracing/debugging, and a little access protection. Most of these things are not very well developed because our use of the system in computing science research does not need them. There are some features that are missed in some applications, for example, better inter-process communication.

The UNIX kernel is an I/O multiplexer more than a complete operating system. This is as it should be. Because of this outlook, many features are found in most other operating systems that are missing from the UNIX kernel. For example, the UNIX kernel does not support file access methods, file disposition, file formats, file maximum size, spooling, command language, logical records, physical records, assignment of logical file names, logical file names, more than one character set, an operator's console, an operator, log-in, or log-out. Many of these things are symptoms rather than features. Many of these things are implemented in user software using the kernel as a tool. A good example of this is the command language.[5] Each user may have his own command language. Maintenance of such code is as easy as maintaining user code. The idea of implementing "system" code with general user primitives comes directly from MULTICS.[6]

References

1. R. E. Griswold and D. R. Hanson, "An Overview of SL5," *SIGPLAN Notices* **12**(4) pp. 40-50 (April 1977).

2. E. W. Dijkstra, "Cooperating Sequential Processes," pp. 43-112 in *Programming Languages*, ed. F. Genuys, Academic Press, New York (1968).

3. J. A. Hawley and W. B. Meyer, "MUNIX, A Multiprocessing Version of UNIX," M.S. Thesis, Naval Postgraduate School, Monterey, Cal. (1975).

4. D. M. Ritchie and K. Thompson, "The UNIX Time-Sharing System," *Bell Sys. Tech. J.* **57**(6) pp. 1905-1929 (1978).

5. S. R. Bourne, "UNIX Time-Sharing System: The UNIX Shell," *Bell Sys. Tech. J.* **57**(6) pp. 1971-1990 (1978).

6. E. I. Organick, *The MULTICS System,* M.I.T. Press, Cambridge, Mass. (1972).

The UNIX I/O System

Dennis M. Ritchie

Bell Laboratories
Murray Hill, New Jersey 07974

This paper gives an overview of the workings of the UNIX† I/O system. It was written with an eye toward providing guidance to writers of device driver routines, and is oriented more toward describing the environment and nature of device drivers than the implementation of that part of the file system which deals with ordinary files.

It is assumed that the reader has a good knowledge of the overall structure of the file system as discussed in the paper "The UNIX Time-sharing System." A more detailed discussion appears in "UNIX Implementation;" the current document restates parts of that one, but is still more detailed. It is most useful in conjunction with a copy of the system code, since it is basically an exegesis of that code.

Device Classes

There are two classes of device: *block* and *character*. The block interface is suitable for devices like disks, tapes, and DECtape which work, or can work, with addressable 512-byte blocks. Ordinary magnetic tape just barely fits in this category, since by use of forward and backward spacing any block can be read, even though blocks can be written only at the end of the tape. Block devices can at least potentially contain a mounted file system. The interface to block devices is very highly structured; the drivers for these devices share a great many routines as well as a pool of buffers.

Character-type devices have a much more straightforward interface, although more work must be done by the driver itself.

Devices of both types are named by a *major* and a *minor* device number. These numbers are generally stored as an integer with the minor device number in the low-order 8 bits and the major device number in the next-higher 8 bits; macros *major* and *minor* are available to access these numbers. The major device number selects which driver will deal with the device; the minor device number is not used by the rest of the system but is passed to the driver at appropriate times. Typically the minor number selects a subdevice attached to a given controller, or one of several similar hardware interfaces.

The major device numbers for block and character devices are used as indices in separate tables; they both start at 0 and therefore overlap.

Overview of I/O

The purpose of the *open* and *creat* system calls is to set up entries in three separate system tables. The first of these is the *u_ofile* table, which is stored in the system's per-process data area *u*. This table is indexed by the file descriptor returned by the *open* or *creat*, and is accessed during a *read, write,* or other operation on the open file. An entry contains only a pointer to the corresponding entry of the *file* table, which is a per-system data base. There is one entry in the *file* table for each instance of *open* or *creat*. This table is per-system because the same instance of an open file must be shared among the several processes which can result from *forks* after

---

†UNIX is a Trademark of Bell Laboratories.

the file is opened. A *file* table entry contains flags which indicate whether the file was open for reading or writing or is a pipe, and a count which is used to decide when all processes using the entry have terminated or closed the file (so the entry can be abandoned). There is also a 32-bit file offset which is used to indicate where in the file the next read or write will take place. Finally, there is a pointer to the entry for the file in the *inode* table, which contains a copy of the file's i-node.

Certain open files can be designated "multiplexed" files, and several other flags apply to such channels. In such a case, instead of an offset, there is a pointer to an associated multiplex channel table. Multiplex channels will not be discussed here.

An entry in the *file* table corresponds precisely to an instance of *open* or *creat;* if the same file is opened several times, it will have several entries in this table. However, there is at most one entry in the *inode* table for a given file. Also, a file may enter the *inode* table not only because it is open, but also because it is the current directory of some process or because it is a special file containing a currently-mounted file system.

An entry in the *inode* table differs somewhat from the corresponding i-node as stored on the disk; the modified and accessed times are not stored, and the entry is augmented by a flag word containing information about the entry, a count used to determine when it may be allowed to disappear, and the device and i-number whence the entry came. Also, the several block numbers that give addressing information for the file are expanded from the 3-byte, compressed format used on the disk to full *long* quantities.

During the processing of an *open* or *creat* call for a special file, the system always calls the device's *open* routine to allow for any special processing required (rewinding a tape, turning on the data-terminal-ready lead of a modem, etc.). However, the *close* routine is called only when the last process closes a file, that is, when the i-node table entry is being deallocated. Thus it is not feasible for a device to maintain, or depend on, a count of its users, although it is quite possible to implement an exclusive-use device which cannot be reopened until it has been closed.

When a *read* or *write* takes place, the user's arguments and the *file* table entry are used to set up the variables *u.u_base, u.u_count,* and *u.u_offset* which respectively contain the (user) address of the I/O target area, the byte-count for the transfer, and the current location in the file. If the file referred to is a character-type special file, the appropriate read or write routine is called; it is responsible for transferring data and updating the count and current location appropriately as discussed below. Otherwise, the current location is used to calculate a logical block number in the file. If the file is an ordinary file the logical block number must be mapped (possibly using indirect blocks) to a physical block number; a block-type special file need not be mapped. This mapping is performed by the *bmap* routine. In any event, the resulting physical block number is used, as discussed below, to read or write the appropriate device.

Character Device Drivers

The *cdevsw* table specifies the interface routines present for character devices. Each device provides five routines: open, close, read, write, and special-function (to implement the *ioctl* system call). Any of these may be missing. If a call on the routine should be ignored, (e.g. *open* on non-exclusive devices that require no setup) the *cdevsw* entry can be given as *nulldev;* if it should be considered an error, (e.g. *write* on read-only devices) *nodev* is used. For terminals, the *cdevsw* structure also contains a pointer to the *tty* structure associated with the terminal.

The *open* routine is called each time the file is opened with the full device number as argument. The second argument is a flag which is non-zero only if the device is to be written upon.

The *close* routine is called only when the file is closed for the last time, that is when the very last process in which the file is open closes it. This means it is not possible for the driver to maintain its own count of its users. The first argument is the device number; the second is a flag which is non-zero if the file was open for writing in the process which performs the final *close.*

When *write* is called, it is supplied the device as argument. The per-user variable *u.u_count* has been set to the number of characters indicated by the user; for character devices, this number may be 0 initially. *u.u_base* is the address supplied by the user from which to start taking characters. The system may call the routine internally, so the flag *u.u_segflg* is supplied that indicates, if *on,* that *u.u_base* refers to the system address space instead of the user's.

The *write* routine should copy up to *u.u_count* characters from the user's buffer to the device, decrementing *u.u_count* for each character passed. For most drivers, which work one character at a time, the routine *cpass( )* is used to pick up characters from the user's buffer. Successive calls on it return the characters to be written until *u.u_count* goes to 0 or an error occurs, when it returns −1. *Cpass* takes care of interrogating *u.u_segflg* and updating *u.u_count.*

Write routines which want to transfer a probably·large number of characters into an internal buffer may also use the routine *iomove(buffer, offset, count, flag)* which is faster when many characters must be moved. *Iomove* transfers up to *count* characters into the *buffer* starting *offset* bytes from the start of the buffer; *flag* should be *B_WRITE* (which is 0) in the write case. Caution: the caller is responsible for making sure the count is not too large and is non-zero. As an efficiency note, *iomove* is much slower if any of *buffer+offset, count* or *u.u_base* is odd.

The device's *read* routine is called under conditions similar to *write,* except that *u.u_count* is guaranteed to be non-zero. To return characters to the user, the routine *passc(c)* is available; it takes care of housekeeping like *cpass* and returns −1 as the last character specified by *u.u_count* is returned to the user; before that time, 0 is returned. *Iomove* is also usable as with *write;* the flag should be *B_READ* but the same cautions apply.

The "special-functions" routine is invoked by the *stty* and *gtty* system calls as follows: *(*p) (dev, v)* where *p* is a pointer to the device's routine, *dev* is the device number, and *v* is a vector. In the *gtty* case, the device is supposed to place up to 3 words of status information into the vector; this will be returned to the caller. In the *stty* case, *v* is 0; the device should take up to 3 words of control information from the array *u.u_arg[0...2].*

Finally, each device should have appropriate interrupt-time routines. When an interrupt occurs, it is turned into a C-compatible call on the devices's interrupt routine. The interrupt-catching mechanism makes the low-order four bits of the "new PS" word in the trap vector for the interrupt available to the interrupt handler. This is conventionally used by drivers which deal with multiple similar devices to encode the minor device number. After the interrupt has been processed, a return from the interrupt handler will return from the interrupt itself.

A number of subroutines are available which are useful to character device drivers. Most of these handlers, for example, need a place to buffer characters in the internal interface between their "top half" (read/write) and "bottom half" (interrupt) routines. For relatively low data-rate devices, the best mechanism is the character queue maintained by the routines *getc* and *putc.* A queue header has the structure

```
    struct {
          int     c_cc;    /* character count */
          char    *c_cf;   /* first character */
          char    *c_cl;   /* last character */
    } queue;
```

A character is placed on the end of a queue by *putc(c, &queue)* where *c* is the character and *queue* is the queue header. The routine returns −1 if there is no space to put the character, 0 otherwise. The first character on the queue may be retrieved by *getc(&queue)* which returns either the (non-negative) character or −1 if the queue is empty.

Notice that the space for characters in queues is shared among all devices in the system and in the standard system there are only some 600 character slots available. Thus device handlers, especially write routines, must take care to avoid gobbling up excessive numbers of characters.

The other major help available to device handlers is the sleep-wakeup mechanism. The call *sleep(event, priority)* causes the process to wait (allowing other processes to run) until the *event* occurs; at that time, the process is marked ready-to-run and the call will return when there is no process with higher *priority.*

The call *wakeup(event)* indicates that the *event* has happened, that is, causes processes sleeping on the event to be awakened. The *event* is an arbitrary quantity agreed upon by the sleeper and the waker-up. By convention, it is the address of some data area used by the driver, which guarantees that events are unique.

Processes sleeping on an event should not assume that the event has really happened; they should check that the conditions which caused them to sleep no longer hold.

Priorities can range from 0 to 127; a higher numerical value indicates a less-favored scheduling situation. A distinction is made between processes sleeping at priority less than the parameter *PZERO* and those at numerically larger priorities. The former cannot be interrupted by signals, although it is conceivable that it may be swapped out. Thus it is a bad idea to sleep with priority less than PZERO on an event which might never occur. On the other hand, calls to *sleep* with larger priority may never return if the process is terminated by some signal in the meantime. Incidentally, it is a gross error to call *sleep* in a routine called at interrupt time, since the process which is running is almost certainly not the process which should go to sleep. Likewise, none of the variables in the user area "*u.*" should be touched, let alone changed, by an interrupt routine.

If a device driver wishes to wait for some event for which it is inconvenient or impossible to supply a *wakeup,* (for example, a device going on-line, which does not generally cause an interrupt), the call *sleep(&lbolt, priority)* may be given. *Lbolt* is an external cell whose address is awakened once every 4 seconds by the clock interrupt routine.

The routines *spl4( ), spl5( ), spl6( ), spl7( )* are available to set the processor priority level as indicated to avoid inconvenient interrupts from the device.

If a device needs to know about real-time intervals, then *timeout(func, arg, interval)* will be useful. This routine arranges that after *interval* sixtieths of a second, the *func* will be called with *arg* as argument, in the style *(*func)(arg).* Timeouts are used, for example, to provide real-time delays after function characters like new-line and tab in typewriter output, and to terminate an attempt to read the 201 Dataphone *dp* if there is no response within a specified number of seconds. Notice that the number of sixtieths of a second is limited to 32767, since it must appear to be positive, and that only a bounded number of timeouts can be going on at once. Also, the specified *func* is called at clock-interrupt time, so it should conform to the requirements of interrupt routines in general.

The Block-device Interface

Handling of block devices is mediated by a collection of routines that manage a set of buffers containing the images of blocks of data on the various devices. The most important purpose of these routines is to assure that several processes that access the same block of the same device in multiprogrammed fashion maintain a consistent view of the data in the block. A secondary but still important purpose is to increase the efficiency of the system by keeping in-core copies of blocks that are being accessed frequently. The main data base for this mechanism is the table of buffers *buf.* Each buffer header contains a pair of pointers *(b_forw, b_back)* which maintain a doubly-linked list of the buffers associated with a particular block device, and a pair of pointers *(av_forw, av_back)* which generally maintain a doubly-linked list of blocks which are "free," that is, eligible to be reallocated for another transaction. Buffers that have I/O in progress or are busy for other purposes do not appear in this list. The buffer header also contains the device and block number to which the buffer refers, and a pointer to the actual storage associated with the buffer. There is a word count which is the negative of the number of words to be transferred to or from the buffer; there is also an error byte and a residual word count used to communicate information from an I/O routine to its caller. Finally, there is a flag word with bits indicating the status of the buffer. These flags will be discussed below.

Seven routines constitute the most important part of the interface with the rest of the system. Given a device and block number, both *bread* and *getblk* return a pointer to a buffer header for the block; the difference is that *bread* is guaranteed to return a buffer actually containing the current data for the block, while *getblk* returns a buffer which contains the data in the block only if it is already in core (whether it is or not is indicated by the *B_DONE* bit; see below). In either case the buffer, and the corresponding device block, is made "busy," so that other processes referring to it are obliged to wait until it becomes free. *Getblk* is used, for example, when a block is about to be totally rewritten, so that its previous contents are not useful; still, no other process can be allowed to refer to the block until the new data is placed into it.

The *breada* routine is used to implement read-ahead. it is logically similar to *bread,* but takes as an additional argument the number of a block (on the same device) to be read asynchronously after the specifically requested block is available.

Given a pointer to a buffer, the *brelse* routine makes the buffer again available to other processes. It is called, for example, after data has been extracted following a *bread.* There are three subtly-different write routines, all of which take a buffer pointer as argument, and all of which logically release the buffer for use by others and place it on the free list. *Bwrite* puts the buffer on the appropriate device queue, waits for the write to be done, and sets the user's error flag if required. *Bawrite* places the buffer on the device's queue, but does not wait for completion, so that errors cannot be reflected directly to the user. *Bdwrite* does not start any I/O operation at all, but merely marks the buffer so that if it happens to be grabbed from the free list to contain data from some other block, the data in it will first be written out.

Bwrite is used when one wants to be sure that I/O takes place correctly, and that errors are reflected to the proper user; it is used, for example, when updating i-nodes. *Bawrite* is useful when more overlap is desired (because no wait is required for I/O to finish) but when it is reasonably certain that the write is really required. *Bdwrite* is used when there is doubt that the write is needed at the moment. For example, *bdwrite* is called when the last byte of a *write* system call falls short of the end of a block, on the assumption that another *write* will be given soon which will re-use the same block. On the other hand, as the end of a block is passed, *bawrite* is called, since probably the block will not be accessed again soon and one might as well start the writing process as soon as possible.

In any event, notice that the routines *getblk* and *bread* dedicate the given block exclusively to the use of the caller, and make others wait, while one of *brelse, bwrite, bawrite,* or *bdwrite* must eventually be called to free the block for use by others.

As mentioned, each buffer header contains a flag word which indicates the status of the buffer. Since they provide one important channel for information between the drivers and the block I/O system, it is important to understand these flags. The following names are manifest constants which select the associated flag bits.

B_READ This bit is set when the buffer is handed to the device strategy routine (see below) to indicate a read operation. The symbol *B_WRITE* is defined as 0 and does not define a flag; it is provided as a mnemonic convenience to callers of routines like *swap* which have a separate argument which indicates read or write.

B_DONE This bit is set to 0 when a block is handed to the the device strategy routine and is turned on when the operation completes, whether normally as the result of an error. It is also used as part of the return argument of *getblk* to indicate if 1 that the returned buffer actually contains the data in the requested block.

B_ERROR This bit may be set to 1 when *B_DONE* is set to indicate that an I/O or other error occurred. If it is set the *b_error* byte of the buffer header may contain an error code if it is non-zero. If *b_error* is 0 the nature of the error is not specified. Actually no driver at present sets *b_error;* the latter is provided for a future improvement whereby a more detailed error-reporting scheme may be implemented.

B_BUSY This bit indicates that the buffer header is not on the free list, i.e. is dedicated to someone's exclusive use. The buffer still remains attached to the list of blocks associated with its device, however. When *getblk* (or *bread,* which calls it) searches the buffer list for a given device and finds the requested block with this bit on, it sleeps until the bit clears.

B_PHYS This bit is set for raw I/O transactions that need to allocate the Unibus map on an 11/70.

B_MAP This bit is set on buffers that have the Unibus map allocated, so that the *iodone* routine knows to deallocate the map.

B_WANTED This flag is used in conjunction with the *B_BUSY* bit. Before sleeping as described just above, *getblk* sets this flag. Conversely, when the block is freed and the busy bit goes down (in *brelse*) a *wakeup* is given for the block header whenever *B_WANTED* is on. This strategem avoids the overhead of having to call *wakeup* every time a buffer is freed on the chance that someone might want it.

B_AGE This bit may be set on buffers just before releasing them; if it is on, the buffer is placed at the head of the free list, rather than at the tail. It is a performance heuristic used when the caller judges that the same block will not soon be used again.

B_ASYNC This bit is set by *bawrite* to indicate to the appropriate device driver that the buffer should be released when the write has been finished, usually at interrupt time. The difference between *bwrite* and *bawrite* is that the former starts I/O, waits until it is done, and frees the buffer. The latter merely sets this bit and starts I/O. The bit indicates that *relse* should be called for the buffer on completion.

B_DELWRI This bit is set by *bdwrite* before releasing the buffer. When *getblk,* while searching for a free block, discovers the bit is 1 in a buffer it would otherwise grab, it causes the block to be written out before reusing it.

Block Device Drivers

The *bdevsw* table contains the names of the interface routines and that of a table for each block device.

Just as for character devices, block device drivers may supply an *open* and a *close* routine called respectively on each open and on the final close of the device. Instead of separate read and write routines, each block device driver has a *strategy* routine which is called with a pointer to a buffer header as argument. As discussed, the buffer header contains a read/write flag, the core address, the block number, a (negative) word count, and the major and minor device number. The role of the strategy routine is to carry out the operation as requested by the information in the buffer header. When the transaction is complete the *B_DONE* (and possibly the *B_ERROR)* bits should be set. Then if the *B_ASYNC* bit is set, *brelse* should be called; otherwise, *wakeup.* In cases where the device is capable, under error-free operation, of transferring fewer words than requested, the device's word-count register should be placed in the residual count slot of the buffer header; otherwise, the residual count should be set to 0. This particular mechanism is really for the benefit of the magtape driver; when reading this device records shorter than requested are quite normal, and the user should be told the actual length of the record.

Although the most usual argument to the strategy routines is a genuine buffer header allocated as discussed above, all that is actually required is that the argument be a pointer to a place containing the appropriate information. For example the *swap* routine, which manages movement of core images to and from the swapping device, uses the strategy routine for this device. Care has to be taken that no extraneous bits get turned on in the flag word.

The device's table specified by *bdevsw* has a byte to contain an active flag and an error count, a pair of links which constitute the head of the chain of buffers for the device *(b_forw, b_back)*, and a first and last pointer for a device queue. Of these things, all are used solely by the device driver itself except for the buffer-chain pointers. Typically the flag encodes the state of the device, and is used at a minimum to indicate that the device is currently engaged in transferring information and no new command should be issued. The error count is useful for counting retries when errors occur. The device queue is used to remember stacked requests; in the simplest case it may be maintained as a first-in first-out list. Since buffers which have been handed over to the strategy routines are never on the list of free buffers, the pointers in the buffer which maintain the free list *(av_forw, av_back)* are also used to contain the pointers which maintain the device queues.

A couple of routines are provided which are useful to block device drivers. *iodone(bp)* arranges that the buffer to which *bp* points be released or awakened, as appropriate, when the strategy module has finished with the buffer, either normally or after an error. (In the latter case the *B_ERROR* bit has presumably been set.)

The routine *geterror(bp)* can be used to examine the error bit in a buffer header and arrange that any error indication found therein is reflected to the user. It may be called only in the non-interrupt part of a driver when I/O has completed *(B_DONE* has been set).

Raw Block-device I/O

A scheme has been set up whereby block device drivers may provide the ability to transfer information directly between the user's core image and the device without the use of buffers and in blocks as large as the caller requests. The method involves setting up a character-type special file corresponding to the raw device and providing *read* and *write* routines which set up what is usually a private, non-shared buffer header with the appropriate information and call the device's strategy routine. If desired, separate *open* and *close* routines may be provided but this is usually unnecessary. A special-function routine might come in handy, especially for magtape.

A great deal of work has to be done to generate the "appropriate information" to put in the argument buffer for the strategy module; the worst part is to map relocated user addresses to physical addresses. Most of this work is done by *physio(strat, bp, dev, rw)* whose arguments are the name of the strategy routine *strat*, the buffer pointer *bp*, the device number *dev*, and a read-write flag *rw* whose value is either *B_READ* or *B_WRITE*. *Physio* makes sure that the user's base address and count are even (because most devices work in words) and that the core area affected is contiguous in physical space; it delays until the buffer is not busy, and makes it busy while the operation is in progress; and it sets up user error return information.

A Tour through the UNIX† C Compiler

D. M. Ritchie

Bell Laboratories
Murray Hill, New Jersey 07974

The Intermediate Language

Communication between the two phases of the compiler proper is carried out by means of a pair of intermediate files. These files are treated as having identical structure, although the second file contains only the code generated for strings. It is convenient to write strings out separately to reduce the need for multiple location counters in a later assembly phase.

The intermediate language is not machine-independent; its structure in a number of ways reflects the fact that C was originally a one-pass compiler chopped in two to reduce the maximum memory requirement. In fact, only the latest version of the compiler has a complete intermediate language at all. Until recently, the first phase of the compiler generated assembly code for those constructions it could deal with, and passed expression parse trees, in absolute binary form, to the second phase for code generation. Now, at least, all inter-phase information is passed in a describable form, and there are no absolute pointers involved, so the coupling between the phases is not so strong.

The areas in which the machine (and system) dependencies are most noticeable are

1. Storage allocation for automatic variables and arguments has already been performed, and nodes for such variables refer to them by offset from a display pointer. Type conversion (for example, from integer to pointer) has already occurred using the assumption of byte addressing and 2-byte words.

2. Data representations suitable to the PDP-11 are assumed; in particular, floating point constants are passed as four words in the machine representation.

As it happens, each intermediate file is represented as a sequence of binary numbers without any explicit demarcations. It consists of a sequence of conceptual lines, each headed by an operator, and possibly containing various operands. The operators are small numbers; to assist in recognizing failure in synchronization, the high-order byte of each operator word is always the octal number 376. Operands are either 16-bit binary numbers or strings of characters representing names. Each name is terminated by a null character. There is no alignment requirement for numerical operands and so there is no padding after a name string.

The binary representation was chosen to avoid the necessity of converting to and from character form and to minimize the size of the files. It would be very easy to make each operator-operand 'line' in the file be a genuine, printable line, with the numbers in octal or decimal; this in fact was the representation originally used.

The operators fall naturally into two classes: those which represent part of an expression, and all others. Expressions are transmitted in a reverse-Polish notation; as they are being read, a tree is built which is isomorphic to the tree constructed in the first phase. Expressions are passed as a whole, with no non-expression operators intervening. The reader maintains a stack; each leaf of the expression tree (name, constant) is pushed on the stack; each unary operator replaces the top of the stack by a node whose operand is the old top-of-stack; each binary

---

†UNIX is a Trademark of Bell Laboratories.

operator replaces the top pair on the stack with a single entry. When the expression is complete there is exactly one item on the stack. Following each expression is a special operator which passes the unique previous expression to the 'optimizer' described below and then to the code generator.

Here is the list of operators not themselves part of expressions.

EOF

marks the end of an input file.

BDATA *flag data ...*

specifies a sequence of bytes to be assembled as static data. It is followed by pairs of words; the first member of the pair is non-zero to indicate that the data continue; a zero flag is not followed by data and terminates the operator. The data bytes occupy the low-order part of a word.

WDATA *flag data ...*

specifies a sequence of words to be assembled as static data; it is identical to the BDATA operator except that entire words, not just bytes, are passed.

PROG

means that subsequent information is to be compiled as program text.

DATA

means that subsequent information is to be compiled as static data.

BSS

means that subsequent information is to be compiled as unitialized static data.

SYMDEF *name*

means that the symbol *name* is an external name defined in the current program. It is produced for each external data or function definition.

CSPACE *name size*

indicates that the name refers to a data area whose size is the specified number of bytes. It is produced for external data definitions without explicit initialization.

SSPACE *size*

indicates that *size* bytes should be set aside for data storage. It is used to pad out short initializations of external data and to reserve space for static (internal) data. It will be preceded by an appropriate label.

EVEN

is produced after each external data definition whose size is not an integral number of words. It is not produced after strings except when they initialize a character array.

NLABEL *name*

is produced just before a BDATA or WDATA initializing external data, and serves as a label for the data.

RLABEL *name*

is produced just before each function definition, and labels its entry point.

SNAME *name number*

is produced at the start of each function for each static variable or label declared therein. Subsequent uses of the variable will be in terms of the given number. The code generator uses this only to produce a debugging symbol table.

ANAME *name number*

Likewise, each automatic variable's name and stack offset is specified by this operator. Arguments count as automatics.

RNAME *name number*

Each register variable is similarly named, with its register number.

SAVE *number*

produces a register-save sequence at the start of each function, just after its label (RLABEL).

SETREG *number*

is used to indicate the number of registers used for register variables. It actually gives the register number of the lowest free register; it is redundant because the RNAME operators could be counted instead.

PROFIL

is produced before the save sequence for functions when the profile option is turned on. It produces code to count the number of times the function is called.

SWIT *deflab line label value ...*

is produced for switches. When control flows into it, the value being switched on is in the register forced by RFORCE (below). The switch statement occurred on the indicated line of the source, and the label number of the default location is *deflab*. Then the operator is followed by a sequence of label-number and value pairs; the list is terminated by a 0 label.

LABEL *number*

generates an internal label. It is referred to elsewhere using the given number.

BRANCH *number*

indicates an unconditional transfer to the internal label number given.

RETRN

produces the return sequence for a function. It occurs only once, at the end of each function.

EXPR *line*

causes the expression just preceding to be compiled. The argument is the line number in the source where the expression occurred.

NAME *class type name*

NAME *class type number*

indicates a name occurring in an expression. The first form is used when the name is external; the second when the name is automatic, static, or a register. Then the number indicates the stack offset, the label number, or the register number as appropriate. Class and type encoding is described elsewhere.

CON *type value*

transmits an integer constant. This and the next two operators occur as part of expressions.

FCON *type 4-word-value*

transmits a floating constant as four words in PDP-11 notation.

SFCON *type value*

transmits a floating-point constant whose value is correctly represented by its high-order word in PDP-11 notation.

NULL

indicates a null argument list of a function call in an expression; call is a binary operator whose second operand is the argument list.

CBRANCH *label cond*

produces a conditional branch.. It is an expression operator, and will be followed by an EXPR. The branch to the label number takes place if the expression's truth value is the same as that of *cond*. That is, if *cond*=*1* and the expression evaluates to true, the branch is taken.

binary-operator *type*

There are binary operators corresponding to each such source-language operator; the type of the result of each is passed as well. Some perhaps-unexpected ones are: COMMA, which is a right-associative operator designed to simplify right-to-left evaluation of function arguments; prefix and postfix $++$ and $--$, whose second operand is the increment amount, as a CON; QUEST and COLON, to express the conditional expression as 'a?(b:c)'; and a sequence of special operators for expressing relations between pointers, in case pointer comparison is different from integer comparison (e.g. unsigned).

unary-operator *type*

There are also numerous unary operators. These include ITOF, FTOI, FTOL, LTOF, ITOL, LTOI which convert among floating, long, and integer; JUMP which branches indirectly through a label expression; INIT, which compiles the value of a constant expression used as an initializer; RFORCE, which is used before a return sequence or a switch to place a value in an agreed-upon register.

Expression Optimization

Each expression tree, as it is read in, is subjected to a fairly comprehensive analysis. This is performed by the *optim* routine and a number of subroutines; the major things done are

1. Modifications and simplifications of the tree so its value may be computed more efficiently and conveniently by the code generator.

2. Marking each interior node with an estimate of the number of registers required to evaluate it. This register count is needed to guide the code generation algorithm.

One thing that is definitely not done is discovery or exploitation of common subexpressions, nor is this done anywhere in the compiler.

The basic organization is simple: a depth-first scan of the tree. *Optim* does nothing for leaf nodes (except for automatics; see below), and calls *unoptim* to handle unary operators. For binary operators, it calls itself to process the operands, then treats each operator separately. One important case is commutative and associative operators, which are handled by *acommute*.

Here is a brief catalog of the transformations carried out by by *optim* itself. It is not intended to be complete. Some of the transformations are machine-dependent, although they may well be useful on machines other than the PDP-11.

1. As indicated in the discussion of *unoptim* below, the optimizer can create a node type corresponding to the location addressed by a register plus a constant offset. Since this is precisely the implementation of automatic variables and arguments, where the register is fixed by convention, such variables are changed to the new form to simplify later processing.

2. Associative and commutative operators are processed by the special routine *acommute*.

3. After processing by *acommute,* the bitwise & operator is turned into a new *andn* operator; 'a & b' becomes 'a *andn* ~b'. This is done because the PDP-11 provides no *and* operator, but only *andn*. A similar transformation takes place for '=&'.

4. Relationals are turned around so the more complicated expression is on the left. (So that '2 > f(x)' becomes 'f(x) < 2'). This improves code generation since the algorithm prefers to have the right operand require fewer registers than the left.

5. An expression minus a constant is turned into the expression plus the negative constant, and the *acommute* routine is called to take advantage of the properties of addition.

6. Operators with constant operands are evaluated.

7. Right shifts (unless by 1) are turned into left shifts with a negated right operand, since the PDP-11 lacks a general right-shift operator.

8. A number of special cases are simplified, such as division or multiplication by 1, and shifts by 0.

The *unoptim* routine performs the same sort of processing for unary operators.

1. '*&x' and '&*x' are simplified to 'x'.

2. If *r* is a register and *c* is a constant or the address of a static or external variable, the expressions '*(r+c)' and '*r' are turned into a special kind of name node which expresses the name itself and the offset. This simplifies subsequent processing because such constructions can appear as the the address of a PDP-11 instruction.

3. When the unary '&' operator is applied to a name node of the special kind just discussed, it is reworked to make the addition explicit again; this is done because the PDP-11 has no 'load address' instruction.

4. Constructions like '*r++' and '*−−r' where *r* is a register are discovered and marked as being implementable using the PDP-11 auto-increment and -decrement modes.

5. If '!' is applied to a relational, the '!' is discarded and the sense of the relational is reversed.

6. Special cases involving reflexive use of negation and complementation are discovered.

7.   Operations applying to constants are evaluated.

The *acommute* routine, called for associative and commutative operators, discovers clusters of the same operator at the top levels of the current tree, and arranges them in a list: for 'a + ((b+c) + (d+f))' the list would be 'a,b,c,d,e,f'. After each subtree is optimized, the list is sorted in decreasing difficulty of computation; as mentioned above, the code generation algorithm works best when left operands are the difficult ones. The 'degree of difficulty' computed is actually finer than the mere number of registers required; a constant is considered simpler than the address of a static or external, which is simpler than reference to a variable. This makes it easy to fold all the constants together, and also to merge together the sum of a constant and the address of a static or external (since in such nodes there is space for an 'offset' value). There are also special cases, like multiplication by 1 and addition of 0.

A special routine is invoked to handle sums of products. *Distrib* is based on the fact that it is better to compute 'c1*c2*x + c1*y' as 'c1*(c2*x + y)' and makes the divisibility tests required to assure the correctness of the transformation. This transformation is rarely possible with code directly written by the user, but it invariably occurs as a result of the implementation of multidimensional arrays.

Finally, *acommute* reconstructs a tree from the list of expressions which result.

Code Generation

The grand plan for code-generation is independent of any particular machine; it depends largely on a set of tables. But this fact does not necessarily make it very easy to modify the compiler to produce code for other machines, both because there is a good deal of machine-dependent structure in the tables, and because in any event such tables are non-trivial to prepare.

The arguments to the basic code generation routine *rcexpr* are a pointer to a tree representing an expression, the name of a code-generation table, and the number of a register in which the value of the expression should be placed. *Rcexpr* returns the number of the register in which the value actually ended up; its caller may need to produce a *mov* instruction if the value really needs to be in the given register. There are four code generation tables.

Regtab is the basic one, which actually does the job described above: namely, compile code which places the value represented by the expression tree in a register.

Cctab is used when the value of the expression is not actually needed, but instead the value of the condition codes resulting from evaluation of the expression. This table is used, for example, to evaluate the expression after *if*. It is clearly silly to calculate the value (0 or 1) of the expression 'a = =b' in the context 'if (a= =b) ... '

The *sptab* table is used when the value of an expression is to be pushed on the stack, for example when it is an actual argument. For example in the function call 'f(a)' it is a bad idea to load *a* into a register which is then pushed on the stack, when there is a single instruction which does the job.

The *efftab* table is used when an expression is to be evaluated for its side effects, not its value. This occurs mostly for expressions which are statements, which have no value. Thus the code for the statement 'a = b' need produce only the approoriate *mov* instruction, and need not leave the value of *b* in a register, while in the expression 'a + (b = c)' the value of 'b = c' will appear in a register.

All of the tables besides *regtab* are rather small, and handle only a relatively few special cases. If one of these subsidiary tables does not contain an entry applicable to the given expression tree, *rcexpr* uses *regtab* to put the value of the expression into a register and then fixes things up; nothing need be done when the table was *efftab,* but a *tst* instruction is produced when the table called for was *cctab,* and a *mov* instruction, pushing the register on the stack, when the table was *sptab.*

The *rcexpr* routine itself picks off some special cases, then calls *cexpr* to do the real work. *Cexpr* tries to find an entry applicable to the given tree in the given table, and returns −1 if no such entry is found, letting *rcexpr* try again with a different table. A successful match yields a string containing both literal characters which are written out and pseudo-operations, or macros, which are expanded. Before studying the contents of these strings we will consider how table entries are matched against trees.

Recall that most non-leaf nodes in an expression tree contain the name of the operator, the type of the value represented, and pointers to the subtrees (operands). They also contain an estimate of the number of registers required to evaluate the expression, placed there by the expression-optimizer routines. The register counts are used to guide the code generation process, which is based on the Sethi-Ullman algorithm.

The main code generation tables consist of entries each containing an operator number and a pointer to a subtable for the corresponding operator. A subtable consists of a sequence of entries, each with a key describing certain properties of the operands of the operator involved; associated with the key is a code string. Once the subtable corresponding to the operator is found, the subtable is searched linearly until a key is found such that the properties demanded by the key are compatible with the operands of the tree node. A successful match returns the code string; an unsuccessful search, either for the operator in the main table or a compatble key in the subtable, returns a failure indication.

The tables are all contained in a file which must be processed to obtain an assembly language program. Thus they are written in a special-purpose language. To provided definiteness to the following discussion, here is an example of a subtable entry.

```
%n,aw
        F
        add     A2,R
```

The '%' indicates the key; the information following (up to a blank line) specifies the code string. Very briefly, this entry is in the subtable for '+' of *regtab;* the key specifies that the left operand is any integer, character, or pointer expression, and the right operand is any word quantity which is directly addressible (e.g. a variable or constant). The code string calls for the generation of the code to compile the left (first) operand into the current register ('F') and then to produce an 'add' instruction which adds the second operand ('A2') to the register ('R'). All of the notation will be explained below.

Only three features of the operands are used in deciding whether a match has occurred. They are:

1. Is the type of the operand compatible with that demanded?

2. Is the 'degree of difficulty' (in a sense described below) compatible?

3. The table may demand that the operand have a '*' (indirection operator) as its highest operator.

As suggested above, the key for a subtable entry is indicated by a '%,' and a comma-separated pair of specifications for the operands. (The second specification is ignored for unary operators). A specification indicates a type requirement by including one of the following letters. If no type letter is present, any integer, character, or pointer operand will satisfy the requirement (not float, double, or long).

b   A byte (character) operand is required.

w   A word (integer or pointer) operand is required.

f   A float or double operand is required.

d   A double operand is required.

l   A long (32-bit integer) operand is required.

Before discussing the 'degree of difficulty' specification, the algorithm has to be explained more completely. *Rcexpr* (and *cexpr*) are called with a register number in which to place their result. Registers 0, 1, ... are used during evaluation of expressions; the maximum register which can be used in this way depends on the number of register variables, but in any event only registers 0 through 4 are available since r5 is used as a stack frame header and r6 (sp) and r7 (pc) have special hardware properties. The code generation routines assume that when called with register n as argument, they may use $n+1$, ... (up to the first register variable) as temporaries. Consider the expression 'X+Y', where both X and Y are expressions. As a first approximation, there are three ways of compiling code to put this expression in register n.

1.   If Y is an addressible cell, (recursively) put X into register n and add Y to it.

2.   If Y is an expression that can be calculated in k registers, where k smaller than the number of registers available, compile X into register n, Y into register $n+1$, and add register $n+1$ to n.

3.   Otherwise, compile Y into register n, save the result in a temporary (actually, on the stack) compile X into register n, then add in the temporary.

The distinction between cases 2 and 3 therefore depends on whether the right operand can be compiled in fewer than k registers, where k is the number of free registers left after registers 0 through n are taken: 0 through $n-1$ are presumed to contain already computed temporary results; n will, in case 2, contain the value of the left operand while the right is being evaluated.

These considerations should make clear the specification codes for the degree of difficulty, bearing in mind that a number of special cases are also present:

z   is satisfied when the operand is zero, so that special code can be produced for expressions like 'x = 0'.

1   is satisfied when the operand is the constant 1, to optimize cases like left and right shift by 1, which can be done efficiently on the PDP-11.

c   is satisfied when the operand is a positive (16-bit) constant; this takes care of some special cases in long arithmetic.

a   is satisfied when the operand is addressible; this occurs not only for variables and constants, but also for some more complicated constructions, such as indirection through a simple variable, '*p++' where p is a register variable (because of the PDP-11's auto-increment address mode), and '*(p+c)' where p is a register and c is a constant. Precisely, the requirement is that the operand refers to a cell whose address can be written as a source or destination of a PDP-11 instruction.

e   is satisfied by an operand whose value can be generated in a register using no more than k registers, where k is the number of registers left (not counting the current register). The 'e' stands for 'easy.'

n   is satisfied by any operand. The 'n' stands for 'anything.'

These degrees of difficulty are considered to lie in a linear ordering and any operand which satisfies an earlier-mentioned requirement will satisfy a later one. Since the subtables are searched linearly, if a '1' specification is included, almost certainly a 'z' must be written first to prevent expressions containing the constant 0 to be compiled as if the 0 were 1.

Finally, a key specification may contain a '*' which requires the operand to have an indirection as its leading operator. Examples below should clarify the utility of this specification.

Now let us consider the contents of the code string associated with each subtable entry. Conventionally, lower-case letters in this string represent literal information which is copied directly to the output. Upper-case letters generally introduce specific macro-operations, some of which may be followed by modifying information. The code strings in the tables are written with tabs and new-lines used freely to suggest instructions which will be generated; the table-compiling program compresses tabs (using the 0200 bit of the next character) and throws away some of the new-lines. For example the macro 'F' is ordinarily written on a line by itself; but since its expansion will end with a new-line, the new-line after 'F' itself is dispensable. This is all to reduce the size of the stored tables.

The first set of macro-operations is concerned with compiling subtrees. Recall that this is done by the *cexpr* routine. In the following discussion the 'current register' is generally the argument register to *cexpr;* that is, the place where the result is desired. The 'next register' is numbered one higher than the current register. (This explanation isn't fully true because of complications, described below, involving operations which require even-odd register pairs.)

F   causes a recursive call to the *rcexpr* routine to compile code which places the value of the first (left) operand of the operator in the current register.

F1   generates code which places the value of the first operand in the next register. It is incorrectly used if there might be no next register; that is, if the degree of difficulty of the first operand is not 'easy;' if not, another register might not be available.

FS   generates code which pushes the value of the first operand on the stack, by calling *rcexpr* specifying *sptab* as the table.

Analogously,

S, S1, SS compile the second (right) operand into the current register, the next register, or onto the stack.

To deal with registers, there are

R   which expands into the name of the current register.

R1   which expands into the name of the next register.

R+   which expands into the the name of the current register plus 1. It was suggested above that this is the same as the next register, except for complications; here is one of them. Long integer variables have 32 bits and require 2 registers; in such cases the next register is the current register plus 2. The code would like to talk about both halves of the long quantity, so R refers to the register with the high-order part and R+ to the low-order part.

R−   This is another complication, involving division and mod. These operations involve a pair of registers of which the odd-numbered contains the left operand. *Cexpr* arranges that the current register is odd; the R− notation allows the code to refer to the next lower, even-numbered register.

To refer to addressible quantities, there are the notations:

A1   causes generation of the address specified by the first operand. For this to be legal, the operand must be addressible; its key must contain an 'a' or a more restrictive specification.

A2   correspondingly generates the address of the second operand providing it has one.

We now have enough mechanism to show a complete, if suboptimal, table for the + operator on word or byte operands.

```
%n,z
        F

%n,1
        F
        inc     R

%n,aw
        F
        add     A2,R

%n,e
        F
        S1
        add     R1,R

%n,n
        SS
        F
        add     (sp)+,R
```

The first two sequences handle some special cases. Actually it turns out that handling a right operand of 0 is unnecessary since the expression-optimizer throws out adds of 0. Adding 1 by using the 'increment' instruction is done next, and then the case where the right operand is addressible. It must be a word quantity, since the PDP-11 lacks an 'add byte' instruction. Finally the cases where the right operand either can, or cannot, be done in the available registers are treated.

The next macro-instructions are conveniently introduced by noticing that the above table is suitable for subtraction as well as addition, since no use is made of the commutativity of addition. All that is needed is substitution of 'sub' for 'add' and 'dec' for 'inc.' Considerable saving of space is achieved by factoring out several similar operations.

I   is replaced by a string from another table indexed by the operator in the node being expanded. This secondary table actually contains two strings per operator.

I'   is replaced by the second string in the side table entry for the current operator.

Thus, given that the entries for '+' and '−' in the side table (which is called *instab)* are 'add' and 'inc,' 'sub' and 'dec' respectively, the middle of of the above addition table can be written

```
%n,1
        F
        I'      R

%n,aw
        F
        I       A2,R
```

and it will be suitable for subtraction, and several other operators, as well.

Next, there is the question of character and floating-point operations.

B1   generates the letter 'b' if the first operand is a character, 'f' if it is float or double, and nothing otherwise. It is used in a context like 'movB1' which generates a 'mov', 'movb', or 'movf' instruction according to the type of the operand.

B2   is just like B1 but applies to the second operand.

BE   generates 'b' if either operand is a character and null otherwise.

BF   generates 'f' if the type of the operator node itself is float or double, otherwise null.

For example, there is an entry in *efftab* for the '=' operator

```
%a,aw
%ab,a
      IBE      A2,A1
```

Note first that two key specifications can be applied to the same code string. Next, observe that when a word is assigned to a byte or to a word, or a word is assigned to a byte, a single instruction, a *mov* or *movb* as appropriate, does the job. However, when a byte is assigned to a word, it must pass through a register to implement the sign-extension rules:

```
%a,n
      S
      IB1      R,A1
```

Next, there is the question of handling indirection properly. Consider the expression 'X + *Y', where X and Y are expressions. Assuming that Y is more complicated than just a variable, but on the other hand qualifies as 'easy' in the context, the expression would be compiled by placing the value of X in a register, that of *Y in the next register, and adding the registers. It is easy to see that a better job can be done by compiling X, then Y (into the next register), and producing the instruction symbolized by 'add (R1),R'. This scheme avoids generating the instruction 'mov (R1),R1' required actually to place the value of *Y in a register. A related situation occurs with the expression 'X + *(p+6)', which exemplifies a construction frequent in structure and array references. The addition table shown above would produce

```
[put X in register R]
mov     p,R1
add     $6,R1
mov     (R1),R1
add     R1,R
```

when the best code is

```
[put X in R]
mov     p,R1
add     6(R1),R
```

As we said above, a key specification for a code table entry may require an operand to have an indirection as its highest operator. To make use of the requirement, the following macros are provided.

F*   the first operand must have the form *X. If in particular it has the form *(Y + c), for some constant *c,* then code is produced which places the value of Y in the current register. Otherwise, code is produced which loads X into the current register.

F1* resembles F* except that the next register is loaded.

S*   resembles F* except that the second operand is loaded.

S1* resembles S* except that the next register is loaded.

FS* The first operand must have the form '*X'. Push the value of X on the stack.

SS* resembles FS* except that it applies to the second operand.

To capture the constant that may have been skipped over in the above macros, there are

#1   The first operand must have the form *X; if in particular it has the form *(Y + c) for c a constant, then the constant is written out, otherwise a null string.

#2   is the same as #1 except that the second operand is used.

Now we can improve the addition table above. Just before the '%n,e' entry, put

```
%n,ew*
        F
        S1*
        add     #2(R1),R
```

and just before the '%n,n' put

```
%n,nw*
        SS*
        F
        add     *(sp)+,R
```

When using the stacking macros there is no place to use the constant as an index word, so that particular special case doesn't occur.

The constant mentioned above can actually be more general than a number. Any quantity acceptable to the assembler as an expression will do, in particular the address of a static cell, perhaps with a numeric offset. If x is an external character array, the expression '$x[i+5] = 0$' will generate the code

```
mov     i,r0
clrb    x+5(r0)
```

via the table entry (in the '=' part of *efftab)*

```
%e*,z
        F
        I'B1    #1(R)
```

Some machine operations place restrictions on the registers used. The divide instruction, used to implement the divide and mod operations, requires the dividend to be placed in the odd member of an even-odd pair; other peculiarities of multiplication make it simplest to put the multiplicand in an odd-numbered register. There is no theory which optimally accounts for this kind of requirement. *Cexpr* handles it by checking for a multiply, divide, or mod operation; in these cases, its argument register number is incremented by one or two so that it is odd, and if the operation was divide or mod, so that it is a member of a free even-odd pair. The routine which determines the number of registers required estimates, conservatively, that at least two registers are required for a multiplication and three for the other peculiar operators. After the expression is compiled, the register where the result actually ended up is returned. (Divide and mod are actually the same operation except for the location of the result).

These operations are the ones which cause results to end up in unexpected places, and this possibility adds a further level of complexity. The simplest way of handling the problem is always to move the result to the place where the caller expected it, but this will produce unnecessary register moves in many simple cases; '$a = b*c$' would generate

```
mov     b,r1
mul     c,r1
mov     r1,r0
mov     r0,a
```

The next thought is used the passed-back information as to where the result landed to change the notion of the current register. While compiling the '=' operation above, which comes from a table entry like

```
%a,e
         S
         mov    R,A1
```

it is sufficient to redefine the meaning of 'R' after processing the 'S' which does the multiply. This technique is in fact used; the tables are written in such a way that correct code is produced. The trouble is that the technique cannot be used in general, because it invalidates the count of the number of registers required for an expression. Consider just 'a*b + X' where X is some expression. The algorithm assumes that the value of a*b, once computed, requires just one register. If there are three registers available, and X requires two registers to compute, then this expression will match a key specifying '%n,e'. If a*b is computed and left in register 1, then there are, contrary to expectations, no longer two registers available to compute X, but only one, and bad code will be produced. To guard against this possibility, *cexpr* checks the result returned by recursive calls which implement F, S and their relatives. If the result is not in the expected register, then the number of registers required by the other operand is checked; if it can be done using those registers which remain even after making unavailable the unexpectedly-occupied register, then the notions of the 'next register' and possibly the 'current register' are redefined. Otherwise a register-copy instruction is produced. A register-copy is also always produced when the current operator is one of those which have odd-even requirements.

Finally, there are a few loose-end macro operations and facts about the tables. The operators:

V   is used for long operations. It is written with an address like a machine instruction; it expands into 'adc' (add carry) if the operation is an additive operator, 'sbc' (subtract carry) if the operation is a subtractive operator, and disappears, along with the rest of the line, otherwise. Its purpose is to allow common treatment of logical operations, which have no carries, and additive and subtractive operations, which generate carries.

T   generates a 'tst' instruction if the first operand of the tree does not set the condition codes correctly. It is used with divide and mod operations, which require a sign-extended 32-bit operand. The code table for the operations contains an 'sxt' (sign-extend) instruction to generate the high-order part of the dividend.

H   is analogous to the 'F' and 'S' macros, except that it calls for the generation of code for the current tree (not one of its operands) using *regtab*. It is used in *cctab* for all the operators which, when executed normally, set the condition codes properly according to the result. It prevents a 'tst' instruction from being generated for constructions like 'if (a+b) ...' since after calculation of the value of 'a+b' a conditional branch can be written immediately.

All of the discussion above is in terms of operators with operands. Leaves of the expression tree (variables and constants), however, are peculiar in that they have no operands. In order to regularize the matching process, *cexpr* examines its operand to determine if it is a leaf; if so, it creates a special 'load' operator whose operand is the leaf, and substitutes it for the argument tree; this allows the table entry for the created operator to use the 'A1' notation to load the leaf into a register.

Purely to save space in the tables, pieces of subtables can be labelled and referred to later. It turns out, for example, that rather large portions of the the *efftab* table for the '=' and '=+' operators are identical. Thus '=' has an entry

```
%[move3:]
%a,aw
%ab,a
         IBE    A2,A1
```

while part of the '=+' table is

```
%aw,aw
%        [move3]
```

Labels are written as '%[... :]', before the key specifications; references are written with '% [...]' after the key. Peculiarities in the implementation make it necessary that labels appear before references to them.

The example illustrates the utility of allowing separate keys to point to the same code string. The assignment code works properly if either the right operand is a word, or the left operand is a byte; but since there is no 'add byte' instruction the addition code has to be restricted to word operands.

Delaying and reordering

Intertwined with the code generation routines are two other, interrelated processes. The first, implemented by a routine called *delay,* is based on the observation that naive code generation for the expression 'a = b++' would produce

```
mov    b,r0
inc    b
mov    r0,a
```

The point is that the table for postfix ++ has to preserve the value of *b* before incrementing it; the general way to do this is to preserve its value in a register. A cleverer scheme would generate

```
mov    b,a
inc    b
```

Delay is called for each expression input to *rcexpr,* and it searches for postfix ++ and −− operators. If one is found applied to a variable, the tree is patched to bypass the operator and compiled as it stands; then the increment or decrement itself is done. The effect is as if 'a = b; b++' had been written. In this example, of course, the user himself could have done the same job, but more complicated examples are easily constructed, for example 'switch (x++)'. An essential restriction is that the condition codes not be required. It would be incorrect to compile 'if (a++) ...' as

```
tst    a
inc    a
beq    ...
```

because the 'inc' destroys the required setting of the condition codes.

Reordering is a similar sort of optimization. Many cases which it detects are useful mainly with register variables. If *r* is a register variable, the expression 'r = x+y' is best compiled as

```
mov    x,r
add    y,r
```

but the codes tables would produce

```
mov    x,r0
add    y,r0
mov    r0,r
```

which is in fact preferred if *r* is not a register. (If *r* is not a register, the two sequences are the same size, but the second is slightly faster.) The scheme is to compile the expression as if it had been written 'r = x; r =+ y'. The *reorder* routine is called with a pointer to each tree that *rcexpr* is about to compile; if it has the right characteristics, the 'r = x' tree is constructed and passed recursively to *rcexpr;* then the original tree is modified to read 'r =+ y' and the calling instance of *rcexpr* compiles that instead. Of course the whole business is itself recursive so that more extended forms of the same phenomenon are handled, like 'r = x + y | z'.

Care does have to be taken to avoid 'optimizing' an expression like 'r = x + r' into 'r = x; r = + r'. It is required that the right operand of the expression on the right of the '=' be a ', distinct from the register variable.

The second case that *reorder* handles is expressions of the form 'r = X' used as a subexpression. Again, the code out of the tables for "x = r = y' would be

```
mov    y,r0
mov    r0,r
mov    r0,x
```

whereas if *r* were a register it would be better to produce

```
mov    y,r
mov    r,x
```

When *reorder* discovers that a register variable is being assigned to in a subexpression, it calls *rcexpr* recursively to compile the subexpression, then fiddles the tree passed to it so that the register variable itself appears as the operand instead of the whole subexpression. Here care has to be taken to avoid an infinite regress, with *rcexpr* and *reorder* calling each other forever to handle assignments to registers.

A third set of cases treated by *reorder* comes up when any name, not necessarily a register, occurs as a left operand of an assignment operator other than '=' or as an operand of prefix '++' or '−−'. Unless condition-code tests are involved, when a subexpression like '(a = + b)' is seen, the assignment is performed and the argument tree modified so that *a* is its operand; effectively 'x + (y = + z)' is compiled as 'y = + z; x + y'. Similarly, prefix increment and decrement are pulled out and performed first, then the remainder of the expression.

Throughout code generation, the expression optimizer is called whenever *delay* or *reorder* change the expression tree. This allows some special cases to be found that otherwise would not be seen.

A Tour Through the Portable C Compiler

S. C. Johnson

Bell Laboratories
Murray Hill, New Jersey 07974

Introduction

A C compiler has been implemented that has proved to be quite portable, serving as the basis for C compilers on roughly a dozen machines, including the Honeywell 6000, IBM 370, and Interdata 8/32. The compiler is highly compatible with the C language standard.[1]

Among the goals of this compiler are portability, high reliability, and the use of state-of-the-art techniques and tools wherever practical. Although the efficiency of the compiling process is not a primary goal, the compiler is efficient enough, and produces good enough code, to serve as a production compiler.

The language implemented is highly compatible with the current PDP-11 version of C. Moreover, roughly 75% of the compiler, including nearly all the syntactic and semantic routines, is machine independent. The compiler also serves as the major portion of the program *lint*, described elsewhere.[2]

A number of earlier attempts to make portable compilers are worth noting. While on CO-OP assignment to Bell Labs in 1973, Alan Snyder wrote a portable C compiler which was the basis of his Master's Thesis at M.I.T.[3] This compiler was very slow and complicated, and contained a number of rather serious implementation difficulties; nevertheless, a number of Snyder's ideas appear in this work.

Most earlier portable compilers, including Snyder's, have proceeded by defining an intermediate language, perhaps based on three-address code or code for a stack machine, and writing a machine independent program to translate from the source code to this intermediate code. The intermediate code is then read by a second pass, and interpreted or compiled. This approach is elegant, and has a number of advantages, especially if the target machine is far removed from the host. It suffers from some disadvantages as well. Some constructions, like initialization and subroutine prologs, are difficult or expensive to express in a machine independent way that still allows them to be easily adapted to the target assemblers. Most of these approaches require a symbol table to be constructed in the second (machine dependent) pass, and/or require powerful target assemblers. Also, many conversion operators may be generated that have no effect on a given machine, but may be needed on others (for example, pointer to pointer conversions usually do nothing in C, but must be generated because there are some machines where they are significant).

For these reasons, the first pass of the portable compiler is not entirely machine independent. It contains some machine dependent features, such as initialization, subroutine prolog and epilog, certain storage allocation functions, code for the *switch* statement, and code to throw out unneeded conversion operators.

As a crude measure of the degree of portability actually achieved, the Interdata 8/32 C compiler has roughly 600 machine dependent lines of source out of 4600 in Pass 1, and 1000 out of 3400 in Pass 2. In total, 1600 out of 8000, or 20%, of the total source is machine dependent (12% in Pass 1, 30% in Pass 2). These percentages can be expected to rise slightly as the compiler is tuned. The percentage of machine-dependent code for the IBM is 22%, for the Honeywell 25%. If the assembler format and structure were the same for all these machines, perhaps another 5-10% of the code would become machine independent.

These figures are sufficiently misleading as to be almost meaningless. A large fraction of the machine dependent code can be converted in a straightforward, almost mechanical way. On the other hand, a certain amount of the code requres hard intellectual effort to convert, since the algorithms embodied in this part of the code are typically complicated and machine dependent.

To summarize, however, if you need a C compiler written for a machine with a reasonable architecture, the compiler is already three quarters finished!

Overview

This paper discusses the structure and organization of the portable compiler. The intent is to give the big picture, rather than discussing the details of a particular machine implementation. After a brief overview and a discussion of the source file structure, the paper describes the major data structures, and then delves more closely into the two passes. Some of the theoretical work on which the compiler is based, and its application to the compiler, is discussed elsewhere.[4] One of the major design issues in any C compiler, the design of the calling sequence and stack frame, is the subject of a separate memorandum.[5]

The compiler consists of two passes, *pass1* and *pass2*, that together turn C source code into assembler code for the target machine. The two passes are preceded by a preprocessor, that handles the **#define** and **#include** statements, and related features (e.g., **#ifdef**, etc.). It is a nearly machine independent program, and will not be further discussed here.

The output of the preprocessor is a text file that is read as the standard input of the first pass. This produces as standard output another text file that becomes the standard input of the second pass. The second pass produces, as standard output, the desired assembler language source code. The preprocessor and the two passes all write error messages on the standard error file. Thus the compiler itself makes few demands on the I/O library support, aiding in the bootstrapping process.

Although the compiler is divided into two passes, this represents historical accident more than deep necessity. In fact, the compiler can optionally be loaded so that both passes operate in the same program. This "one pass" operation eliminates the overhead of reading and writing the intermediate file, so the compiler operates about 30% faster in this mode. It also occupies about 30% more space than the larger of the two component passes.

Because the compiler is fundamentally structured as two passes, even when loaded as one, this document primarily describes the two pass version.

The first pass does the lexical analysis, parsing, and symbol table maintenance. It also constructs parse trees for expressions, and keeps track of the types of the nodes in these trees. Additional code is devoted to initialization. Machine dependent portions of the first pass serve to generate subroutine prologs and epilogs, code for switches, and code for branches, label definitions, alignment operations, changes of location counter, etc.

The intermediate file is a text file organized into lines. Lines beginning with a right parenthesis are copied by the second pass directly to its output file, with the parenthesis stripped off. Thus, when the first pass produces assembly code, such as subroutine prologs, etc., each line is prefaced with a right parenthesis; the second pass passes these lines to through to the assembler.

The major job done by the second pass is generation of code for expressions. The expression parse trees produced in the first pass are written onto the intermediate file in Polish Prefix form: first, there is a line beginning with a period, followed by the source file line number and name on which the expression appeared (for debugging purposes). The successive lines represent the nodes of the parse tree, one node per line. Each line contains the node number, type, and any values (e.g., values of constants) that may appear in the node. Lines representing nodes with descendants are immediately followed by the left subtree of descendants, then the right. Since the number of descendants of any node is completely determined by the node number, there is no need to mark the end of the tree.

There are only two other line types in the intermediate file. Lines beginning with a left square bracket ('[') represent the beginning of blocks (delimited by { ... } in the C source); lines beginning with right square brackets (']') represent the end of blocks. The remainder of these lines tell how much stack space, and how many register variables, are currently in use.

Thus, the second pass reads the intermediate files, copies the ')' lines, makes note of the information in the '[' and ']' lines, and devotes most of its effort to the '.' lines and their associated expression trees, turning them turns into assembly code to evaluate the expressions.

In the one pass version of the compiler, the expression trees that are built by the first pass have been declared to have room for the second pass information as well. Instead of writing the trees onto an intermediate file, each tree is transformed in place into an acceptable form for the code generator. The code generator then writes the result of compiling this tree onto the standard output. Instead of '[' and ']' lines in the intermediate file, the information is passed directly to the second pass routines. Assembly code produced by the first pass is simply written out, without the need for ')' at the head of each line.

The Source Files

The compiler source consists of 22 source files. Two files, *manifest* and *macdefs*, are header files included with all other files. *Manifest* has declarations for the node numbers, types, storage classes, and other global data definitions. *Macdefs* has machine-dependent definitions, such as the size and alignment of the various data representations. Two machine-independent header files, *mfile1* and *mfile2*, contain the data structure and manifest definitions for the first and second passes, respectively. In the second pass, a machine dependent header file, *mac2defs*, contains declarations of register names, etc.

There is a file, *common*, containing (machine independent) routines used in both passes. These include routines for allocating and freeing trees, walking over trees, printing debugging information, and printing error messages. There are two dummy files, *comm1.c* and *comm2.c*, that simply include *common* within the scope of the appropriate pass1 or pass2 header files. When the compiler is loaded as a single pass, *common* only needs to be included once: *comm2.c* is not needed.

Entire sections of this document are devoted to the detailed structure of the passes. For the moment, we just give a brief description of the files. The first pass is obtained by compiling and loading *scan.c, cgram.c, xdefs.c, pftn.c, trees.c, optim.c, local.c, code.c*, and *comm1.c*. *Scan.c* is the lexical analyzer, which is used by *cgram.c*, the result of applying *Yacc*[6] to the input grammar *cgram.y*. *Xdefs.c* is a short file of external definitions. *Pftn.c* maintains the symbol table, and does initialization. *Trees.c* builds the expression trees, and computes the node types. *Optim.c* does some machine independent optimizations on the expression trees. *Comm1.c* includes *common*, that contains service routines common to the two passes of the compiler. All the above files are machine independent. The files *local.c* and *code.c* contain machine dependent code for generating subroutine prologs, switch code, and the like.

The second pass is produced by compiling and loading *reader.c, allo.c, match.c, comm1.c, order.c, local.c*, and *table.c*. *Reader.c* reads the intermediate file, and controls the major logic of the code generation. *Allo.c* keeps track of busy and free registers. *Match.c* controls the matching of code templates to subtrees of the expression tree to be compiled. *Comm2.c* includes the file *common*, as in the first pass. The above files are machine independent. *Order.c* controls the machine dependent details of the code generation strategy. *Local2.c* has many small machine dependent routines, and tables of opcodes, register types, etc. *Table.c* has the code template tables, which are also clearly machine dependent.

Data Structure Considerations.

This section discusses the node numbers, type words, and expression trees, used throughout both passes of the compiler.

The file *manifest* defines those symbols used throughout both passes. The intent is to use the same symbol name (e.g., MINUS) for the given operator throughout the lexical analysis, parsing, tree building, and code generation phases; this requires some synchronization with the *Yacc* input file, *cgram.y*, as well.

A token like MINUS may be seen in the lexical analyzer before it is known whether it is a unary or binary operator; clearly, it is necessary to know this by the time the parse tree is constructed. Thus, an operator (really a macro) called UNARY is provided, so that MINUS and UNARY MINUS are both distinct node numbers. Similarly, many binary operators exist in an assignment form (for example, $-=$), and the operator ASG may be applied to such node names to generate new ones, e.g. ASG MINUS.

It is frequently desirable to know if a node represents a leaf (no descendants), a unary operator (one descendant) or a binary operator (two descendants). The macro *optype(o)* returns one of the manifest constants LTYPE, UTYPE, or BITYPE, respectively, depending on the node number *o*. Similarly, *asgop(o)* returns true if *o* is an assignment operator number ($=$, $+=$, etc.), and *logop(o)* returns true if *o* is a relational or logical (&&, ||, or !) operator.

C has a rich typing structure, with a potentially infinite number of types. To begin with, there are the basic types: CHAR, SHORT, INT, LONG, the unsigned versions known as UCHAR, USHORT, UNSIGNED, ULONG, and FLOAT, DOUBLE, and finally STRTY (a structure), UNIONTY, and ENUMTY. Then, there are three operators that can be applied to types to make others: if *t* is a type, we may potentially have types *pointer to t, function returning t*, and *array of t's* generated from *t*. Thus, an arbitrary type in C consists of a basic type, and zero or more of these operators.

In the compiler, a type is represented by an unsigned integer; the rightmost four bits hold the basic type, and the remaining bits are divided into two-bit fields, containing 0 (no operator), or one of the three operators described above. The modifiers are read right to left in the word, starting with the two-bit field adjacent to the basic type, until a field with 0 in it is reached. The macros PTR, FTN, and ARY represent the *pointer to, function returning*, and *array of* operators. The macro values are shifted so that they align with the first two-bit field; thus PTR+INT represents the type for an integer pointer, and

$$ARY + (PTR<<2) + (FTN<<4) + DOUBLE$$

represents the type of an array of pointers to functions returning doubles.

The type words are ordinarily manipulated by macros. If *t* is a type word, *BTYPE(t)* gives the basic type. *ISPTR(t)*, *ISARY(t)*, and *ISFTN(t)* ask if an object of this type is a pointer, array, or a function, respectively. *MODTYPE(t,b)* sets the basic type of *t* to *b*. *DECREF(t)* gives the type resulting from removing the first operator from *t*. Thus, if *t* is a pointer to *t'*, a function returning *t'*, or an array of *t'*, then *DECREF(t)* would equal *t'*. *INCREF(t)* gives the type representing a pointer to *t*. Finally, there are operators for dealing with the unsigned types. *ISUNSIGNED(t)* returns true if *t* is one of the four basic unsigned types; in this case, *DEUNSIGN(t)* gives the associated 'signed' type. Similarly, *UNSIGNABLE(t)* returns true if *t* is one of the four basic types that could become unsigned, and *ENUNSIGN(t)* returns the unsigned analogue of *t* in this case.

The other important global data structure is that of expression trees. The actual shapes of the nodes are given in *mfile1* and *mfile2*. They are not the same in the two passes; the first pass nodes contain dimension and size information, while the second pass nodes contain register allocation information. Nevertheless, all nodes contain fields called *op*, containing the node number, and *type*, containing the type word. A function called *talloc()* returns a pointer to a new tree node. To free a node, its *op* field need merely be set to FREE. The other fields in the node will remain intact at least until the next allocation.

Nodes representing binary operators contain fields, *left* and *right*, that contain pointers to the left and right descendants. Unary operator nodes have the *left* field, and a value field called *rval*. Leaf nodes, with no descendants, have two value fields: *lval* and *rval*.

At appropriate times, the function *tcheck()* can be called, to check that there are no busy nodes remaining. This is used as a compiler consistency check. The function *tcopy(p)* takes a pointer *p* that points to an expression tree, and returns a pointer to a disjoint copy of the tree. The function *walkf(p,f)* performs a postorder walk of the tree pointed to by *p*, and applies the function *f* to each node. The function *fwalk(p,f,d)* does a preorder walk of the tree pointed to by *p*. At each node, it calls a function *f*, passing to it the node pointer, a value passed down from its ancestor, and two pointers to values to be passed down to the left and right descendants (if any). The value *d* is the value passed down to the root. *Fwalk* is used for a number of tree labeling and debugging activities.

The other major data structure, the symbol table, exists only in pass one, and will be discussed later.

Pass One

The first pass does lexical analysis, parsing, symbol table maintenance, tree building, optimization, and a number of machine dependent things. This pass is largely machine independent, and the machine independent sections can be pretty successfully ignored. Thus, they will be only sketched here.

Lexical Analysis

The lexical analyzer is a conceptually simple routine that reads the input and returns the tokens of the C language as it encounters them: names, constants, operators, and keywords. The conceptual simplicity of this job is confounded a bit by several other simple jobs that unfortunately must go on simultaneously. These include

- Keeping track of the current filename and line number, and occasionally setting this information as the result of preprocessor control lines.

- Skipping comments.

- Properly dealing with octal, decimal, hex, floating point, and character constants, as well as character strings.

To achieve speed, the program maintains several tables that are indexed into by character value, to tell the lexical analyzer what to do next. To achieve portability, these tables must be initialized each time the compiler is run, in order that the table entries reflect the local character set values.

Parsing

As mentioned above, the parser is generated by Yacc from the grammar on file *cgram.y*. The grammar is relatively readable, but contains some unusual features that are worth comment.

Perhaps the strangest feature of the grammar is the treatment of declarations. The problem is to keep track of the basic type and the storage class while interpreting the various stars, brackets, and parentheses that may surround a given name. The entire declaration mechanism must be recursive, since declarations may appear within declarations of structures and unions, or even within a **sizeof** construction inside a dimension in another declaration!

There are some difficulties in using a bottom-up parser, such as produced by Yacc, to handle constructions where a lot of left context information must be kept around. The problem is that the original PDP-11 compiler is top-down in implementation, and some of the semantics of C reflect this. In a top-down parser, the input rules are restricted somewhat, but one can naturally associate temporary storage with a rule at a very early stage in the recognition of that rule. In a bottom-up parser, there is more freedom in the specification of rules, but it is more difficult to know what rule is being matched until the entire rule is seen. The parser described by *cgram.c* makes effective use of the bottom-up parsing mechanism in some places (notably the treatment of expressions), but struggles against the restrictions in others. The usual result is that it is necessary to run a stack of values "on the side", independent of the Yacc value stack, in order to be able to store and access information deep within inner constructions, where the relationship of the rules being recognized to the total picture is not yet clear.

In the case of declarations, the attribute information (type, etc.) for a declaration is carefully kept immediately to the left of the declarator (that part of the declaration involving the name). In this way, when it is time to declare the name, the name and the type information can be quickly brought together. The "$0" mechanism of Yacc is used to accomplish this. The result is not pretty, but it works. The storage class information changes more slowly, so it is kept in an external variable, and stacked if necessary. Some of the grammar could be considerably cleaned up by using some more recent features of Yacc, notably actions within rules and the ability to return multiple values for actions.

A stack is also used to keep track of the current location to be branched to when a **break** or **continue** statement is processed.

This use of external stacks dates from the time when Yacc did not permit values to be structures. Some, or most, of this use of external stacks could be eliminated by redoing the grammar to use the mechanisms now provided. There are some areas, however, particularly the processing of structure, union, and enum declarations, function prologs, and switch statement processing, when having all the affected data together in an array speeds later processing; in this case, use of external storage seems essential.

The *cgram.y* file also contains some small functions used as utility functions in the parser. These include routines for saving case values and labels in processing switches, and stacking and popping values on the external stack described above.

Storage Classes

C has a finite, but fairly extensive, number of storage classes available. One of the compiler design decisions was to process the storage class information totally in the first pass; by the second pass, this information must have been totally dealt with. This means that all of the storage allocation must take place in the first pass, so that references to automatics and parameters can be turned into references to cells lying a certain number of bytes offset from certain machine registers. Much of this transformation is machine dependent, and strongly depends on the storage class.

The classes include EXTERN (for externally declared, but not defined variables), EXTDEF (for external definitions), and similar distinctions for USTATIC and STATIC, UFORTRAN and FORTRAN (for fortran functions) and ULABEL and LABEL. The storage classes REGISTER and AUTO are obvious, as are STNAME, UNAME, and ENAME (for structure, union, and enumeration tags), and the associated MOS, MOU, and MOE (for the members). TYPEDEF is treated as a storage class as well. There are two special storage classes: PARAM and SNULL. SNULL is used to distinguish the case where no explicit storage class has been given; before an entry is made in the symbol table the true storage class is discovered. Similarly, PARAM is used for the temporary entry in the symbol table made before the declaration of function parameters is completed.

The most complexity in the storage class process comes from bit fields. A separate storage class is kept for each width bit field; a k bit bit field has storage class k plus FIELD. This enables the size to be quickly recovered from the storage class.

Symbol Table Maintenance.

The symbol table routines do far more than simply enter names into the symbol table; considerable semantic processing and checking is done as well. For example, if a new declaration comes in, it must be checked to see if there is a previous declaration of the same symbol. If there is, there are many cases. The declarations may agree and be compatible (for example, an extern declaration can appear twice) in which case the new declaration is ignored. The new declaration may add information (such as an explicit array dimension) to an already present declaration. The new declaration may be different, but still correct (for example, an extern declaration of something may be entered, and then later the definition may be seen). The new declaration may be incompatible, but appear in an inner block; in this case, the old declaration is carefully hidden away, and the new one comes into force until the block is left. Finally, the declarations may be incompatible, and an error message must be produced.

A number of other factors make for additional complexity. The type declared by the user is not always the type entered into the symbol table (for example, if an formal parameter to a function is declared to be an array, C requires that this be changed into a pointer before entry in the symbol table). Moreover, there are various kinds of illegal types that may be declared which are difficult to check for syntactically (for example, a function returning an array). Finally, there is a strange feature in C that requires structure tag names and member names for structures and unions to be taken from a different logical symbol table than ordinary identifiers. Keeping track of which kind of name is involved is a bit of struggle (consider typedef names used within structure declarations, for example).

The symbol table handling routines have been rewritten a number of times to extend features, improve performance, and fix bugs. They address the above problems with reasonable effectiveness but a singular lack of grace.

When a name is read in the input, it is hashed, and the routine *lookup* is called, together with a flag which tells which symbol table should be searched (actually, both symbol tables are stored in one, and a flag is used to distinguish individual entries). If the name is found, *lookup* returns the index to the entry found; otherwise, it makes a new entry, marks it UNDEF (undefined), and returns the index of the new entry. This index is stored in the *rval* field of a NAME node.

When a declaration is being parsed, this NAME node is made part of a tree with UNARY MUL nodes for each *, LB nodes for each array descriptor (the right descendant has the dimension), and UNARY CALL nodes for each function descriptor. This tree is passed to the routine *tymerge*, along with the attribute type of the whole declaration; this routine collapses the tree to a single node, by calling *tyreduce*, and then modifies the type to reflect the overall type of the declaration.

Dimension and size information is stored in a table called *dimtab*. To properly describe a type in C, one needs not just the type information but also size information (for structures and enums) and dimension information (for arrays). Sizes and offsets are dealt with in the compiler by giving the associated indices into *dimtab*. *Tymerge* and *tyreduce* call *dstash* to put the discovered dimensions away into the *dimtab* array. *Tymerge* returns a pointer to a single node that contains the symbol table index in its *rval* field, and the size and dimension indices in fields *csiz* and *cdim*, respectively. This information is properly considered part of the type in the first pass, and is carried around at all times.

To enter an element into the symbol table, the routine *defid* is called; it is handed a storage class, and a pointer to the node produced by *tymerge*. *Defid* calls *fixtype*, which adjusts and checks the given type depending on the storage class, and converts null types appropriately. It then calls *fixclass*, which does a similar job for the storage class; it is here, for example, that register declarations are either allowed or changed to auto.

The new declaration is now compared against an older one, if present, and several pages of validity checks performed. If the definitions are compatible, with possibly some added information, the processing is straightforward. If the definitions differ, the block levels of the current and the old declaration are compared. The current block level is kept in *blevel*, an external variable; the old declaration level is kept in the symbol table. Block level 0 is for external declarations, 1 is for arguments to functions, and 2 and above are blocks within a function. If the current block level is the same as the old declaration, an error results. If the current block level is higher, the new declaration overrides the old. This is done by marking the old symbol table entry "hidden", and making a new entry, marked "hiding". *Lookup* will skip over hidden entries. When a block is left, the symbol table is searched, and any entries defined in that block are destroyed; if they hid other entries, the old entries are "unhidden".

This nice block structure is warped a bit because labels do not follow the block structure rules (one can do a **goto** into a block, for example); default definitions of functions in inner blocks also persist clear out to the outermost scope. This implies that cleaning up the symbol table after block exit is more subtle than it might first seem.

For successful new definitions, *defid* also initializes a "general purpose" field, *offset*, in the symbol table. It contains the stack offset for automatics and parameters, the register number for register variables, the bit offset into the structure for structure members, and the internal label number for static variables and labels. The offset field is set by *falloc* for bit fields, and *dclstruct* for structures and unions.

The symbol table entry itself thus contains the name, type word, size and dimension offsets, offset value, and declaration block level. It also has a field of flags, describing what symbol table the name is in, and whether the entry is hidden, or hides another. Finally, a field gives the line number of the last use, or of the definition, of the name. This is used mainly for diagnostics, but is useful to *lint* as well.

In some special cases, there is more than the above amount of information kept for the use of the compiler. This is especially true with structures; for use in initialization, structure declarations must have access to a list of the members of the structure. This list is also kept in *dimtab*. Because a structure can be mentioned long before the members are known, it is necessary to have another level of indirection in the table. The two words following the *csiz* entry in *dimtab* are used to hold the alignment of the structure, and the index in dimtab of the list of members. This list contains the symbol table indices for the structure members, terminated by a −1.

Tree Building

The portable compiler transforms expressions into expression trees. As the parser recognizes each rule making up an expression, it calls *buildtree* which is given an operator number, and pointers to the left and right descendants. *Buildtree* first examines the left and right descendants, and, if they are both constants, and the operator is appropriate, simply does the constant computation at compile time, and returns the result as a constant. Otherwise, *buildtree* allocates a node for the head of the tree, attaches the descendants to it, and ensures that conversion operators are generated if needed, and that the type of the new node is consistent with the types of the operands. There is also a considerable amount of semantic complexity here; many combinations of types are illegal, and the portable compiler makes a strong effort to check the legality of expression types completely. This is done both for *lint* purposes, and to prevent such semantic errors from being passed through to the code generator.

The heart of *buildtree* is a large table, accessed by the routine *opact*. This routine maps the types of the left and right operands into a rather smaller set of descriptors, and then accesses a table (actually encoded in a switch statement) which for each operator and pair of types causes an action to be returned. The actions are logical or's of a number of separate actions, which may be carried out by *buildtree*. These component actions may include checking the left side to ensure that it is an lvalue (can be stored into), applying a type conversion to the left or right operand, setting the type of the new node to the type of the left or right operand, calling various routines to balance the types of the left and right operands, and suppressing the ordinary conversion of arrays and function operands to pointers. An important operation is OTHER, which causes some special code to be invoked in *buildtree*, to handle issues which are unique to a particular operator. Examples of this are structure and union reference (actually handled by the routine *stref*), the building of NAME, ICON, STRING and FCON (floating point constant) nodes, unary * and &, structure assignment, and calls. In the case of unary * and &, *buildtree* will cancel a * applied to a tree, the top node of which is &, and conversely.

Another special operation is PUN; this causes the compiler to check for type mismatches, such as intermixing pointers and integers.

The treatment of conversion operators is still a rather strange area of the compiler (and of C!). The recent introduction of type casts has only confounded this situation. Most of the conversion operators are generated by calls to *tymatch* and *ptmatch*, both of which are given a tree, and asked to make the operands agree in type. *Ptmatch* treats the case where one of the operands is a pointer; *tymatch* treats all other cases. Where these routines have decided on the proper type for an operand, they call *makety*, which is handed a tree, and a type word, dimension offset, and size offset. If necessary, it inserts a conversion operation to make the types correct. Conversion operations are never inserted on the left side of assignment operators, however. There are two conversion operators used; PCONV, if the conversion is to a non-basic type (usually a pointer), and SCONV, if the conversion is to a basic type (scalar).

To allow for maximum flexibility, every node produced by *buildtree* is given to a machine dependent routine, *clocal*, immediately after it is produced. This is to allow more or less immediate rewriting of those nodes which must be adapted for the local machine. The conversion operations are given to *clocal* as well; on most machines, many of these conversions do nothing, and should be thrown away (being careful to retain the type). If this operation is done too early, however, later calls to *buildtree* may get confused about correct type of the subtrees; thus *clocal* is given the conversion ops only after the entire tree is built. This topic will be dealt with in more detail later.

Initialization

Initialization is one of the messier areas in the portable compiler. The only consolation is that most of the mess takes place in the machine independent part, where it is may be safely ignored by the implementor of the compiler for a particular machine.

The basic problem is that the semantics of initialization really calls for a co-routine structure; one collection of programs reading constants from the input stream, while another, independent set of programs places these constants into the appropriate spots in memory. The dramatic differences in the local assemblers also come to the fore here. The parsing problems are dealt with by keeping a rather extensive stack containing the current state of the initialization; the assembler problems are dealt with by having a fair number of machine dependent routines.

The stack contains the symbol table number, type, dimension index, and size index for the current identifier being initialized. Another entry has the offset, in bits, of the beginning of the current identifier. Another entry keeps track of how many elements have been seen, if the current identifier is an array. Still another entry keeps track of the current member of a structure being initialized. Finally, there is an entry containing flags which keep track of the current state of the initialization process (e.g., tell if a } has been seen for the current identifier.)

When an initialization begins, the routine *beginit* is called; it handles the alignment restrictions, if any, and calls *instk* to create the stack entry. This is done by first making an entry on the top of the stack for the item being initialized. If the top entry is an array, another entry is made on the stack for the first element. If the top entry is a structure, another entry is made on the stack for the first member of the structure. This continues until the top element of the stack is a scalar. *Instk* then returns, and the parser begins collecting initializers.

When a constant is obtained, the routine *doinit* is called; it examines the stack, and does whatever is necessary to assign the current constant to the scalar on the top of the stack. *gotscal* is then called, which rearranges the stack so that the next scalar to be initialized gets placed on top of the stack. This process continues until the end of the initializers; *endinit* cleans up. If a { or } is encountered in the string of initializers, it is handled by calling *ilbrace* or *irbrace*, respectively.

A central issue is the treatment of the "holes" that arise as a result of alignment restrictions or explicit requests for holes in bit fields. There is a global variable, *inoff*, which contains the current offset in the initialization (all offsets in the first pass of the compiler are in bits). *Doinit* figures out from the top entry on the stack the expected bit offset of the next identifier; it calls the machine dependent routine *inforce* which, in a machine dependent way, forces the assembler to set aside space if need be so that the next scalar seen will go into the appropriate bit offset position. The scalar itself is passed to one of the machine dependent routines *fincode* (for floating point initialization), *incode* (for fields, and other initializations less than an int in size), and *cinit* (for all other initializations). The size is passed to all these routines, and it is up to the machine dependent routines to ensure that the initializer occupies exactly the right size.

Character strings represent a bit of an exception. If a character string is seen as the initializer for a pointer, the characters making up the string must be put out under a different location counter. When the lexical analyzer sees the quote at the head of a character string, it returns the token STRING, but does not do anything with the contents. The parser calls *getstr*, which sets up the appropriate location counters and flags, and calls *lxstr* to read and process the contents of the string.

If the string is being used to initialize a character array, *lxstr* calls *putbyte*, which in effect simulates *doinit* for each character read. If the string is used to initialize a character pointer, *lxstr* calls a machine dependent routine, *bycode*, which stashes away each character. The pointer to this string is then returned, and processed normally by *doinit*.

The null at the end of the string is treated as if it were read explicitly by *lxstr*.

Statements

The first pass addresses four main areas; declarations, expressions, initialization, and statements. The statement processing is relatively simple; most of it is carried out in the parser directly. Most of the logic is concerned with allocating label numbers, defining the labels, and branching appropriately. An external symbol, *reached*, is 1 if a statement can be reached, 0 otherwise; this is used to do a bit of simple flow analysis as the program is being parsed, and also to avoid generating the subroutine return sequence if the subroutine cannot "fall through" the last statement.

Conditional branches are handled by generating an expression node, CBRANCH, whose left descendant is the conditional expression and the right descendant is an ICON node containing the internal label number to be branched to. For efficiency, the semantics are that the label is gone to if the condition is *false*.

The switch statement is compiled by collecting the case entries, and an indication as to whether there is a default case; an internal label number is generated for each of these, and remembered in a big array. The expression comprising the value to be switched on is compiled when the switch keyword is encountered, but the expression tree is headed by a special node, FORCE, which tells the code generator to put the expression value into a special distinguished register (this same mechanism is used for processing the return statement). When the end of the switch block is reached, the array containing the case values is sorted, and checked for duplicate entries (an error); if all is correct, the machine dependent routine *genswitch* is called, with this array of labels and values in increasing order. *Genswitch* can assume that the value to be tested is already in the register which is the usual integer return value register.

Optimization

There is a machine independent file, *optim.c*, which contains a relatively short optimization routine, *optim*. Actually the word optimization is something of a misnomer; the results are not optimum, only improved, and the routine is in fact not optional; it must be called for proper operation of the compiler.

Optim is called after an expression tree is built, but before the code generator is called. The essential part of its job is to call *clocal* on the conversion operators. On most machines, the treatment of & is also essential: by this time in the processing, the only node which is a legal descendant of & is NAME. (Possible descendants of * have been eliminated by *buildtree.*) The address of a static name is, almost by definition, a constant, and can be represented by an ICON node on most machines (provided that the loader has enough power). Unfortunately, this is not universally true; on some machine, such as the IBM 370, the issue of addressability rears its ugly head; thus, before turning a NAME node into an ICON node, the machine dependent function *andable* is called.

The optimization attempts of *optim* are currently quite limited. It is primarily concerned with improving the behavior of the compiler with operations one of whose arguments is a constant. In the simplest case, the constant is placed on the right if the operation is commutative. The compiler also makes a limited search for expressions such as

$$(x + a) + b$$

where *a* and *b* are constants, and attempts to combine *a* and *b* at compile time. A number of special cases are also examined; additions of 0 and multiplications by 1 are removed, although the correct processing of these cases to get the type of the resulting tree correct is decidedly nontrivial. In some cases, the addition or multiplication must be replaced by a conversion op to keep the types from becoming fouled up. Finally, in cases where a relational operation is being done, and one operand is a constant, the operands are permuted, and the operator altered, if necessary, to put the constant on the right. Finally, multiplications by a power of 2 are changed to shifts.

There are dozens of similar optimizations that can be, and should be, done. It seems likely that this routine will be expanded in the relatively near future.

Machine Dependent Stuff

A number of the first pass machine dependent routines have been discussed above. In general, the routines are short, and easy to adapt from machine to machine. The two exceptions to this general rule are *clocal* and the function prolog and epilog generation routines, *bfcode* and *efcode*.

Clocal has the job of rewriting, if appropriate and desirable, the nodes constructed by *buildtree*. There are two major areas where this is important; NAME nodes and conversion operations. In the case of NAME nodes, *clocal* must rewrite the NAME node to reflect the actual physical location of the name in the machine. In effect, the NAME node must be examined, the symbol table entry found (through the *rval* field of the node), and, based on the storage class of the node, the tree must be rewritten. Automatic variables and parameters are typically rewritten by treating the reference to the variable as a structure reference, off the register which holds the stack or argument pointer; the *stref* routine is set up to be called in this way, and to build the appropriate tree. In the most general case, the tree consists of a unary * node, whose descendant is a + node, with the stack or argument register as left operand, and a constant offset as right operand. In the case of LABEL and internal static nodes, the *rval* field is rewritten to be the negative of the internal label number; a negative *rval* field is taken to be an internal label number. Finally, a name of class REGISTER must be converted into a REG node, and the *rval* field replaced by the register number. In fact, this part of the *clocal* routine is nearly machine independent; only for machines with addressability problems (IBM 370 again!) does it have to be noticeably different,

The conversion operator treatment is rather tricky. It is necessary to handle the application of conversion operators to constants in *clocal*, in order that all constant expressions can have their values known at compile time. In extreme cases, this may mean that some simulation of the arithmetic of the target machine might have to be done in a cross-compiler. In the most common case, conversions from pointer to pointer do nothing. For some machines, however, conversion from byte pointer to short or long pointer might require a shift or rotate operation, which would have to be generated here.

The extension of the portable compiler to machines where the size of a pointer depends on its type would be straightforward, but has not yet been done.

The other major machine dependent issue involves the subroutine prolog and epilog generation. The hard part here is the design of the stack frame and calling sequence; this design issue is discussed elsewhere.[5] The routine *bfcode* is called with the number of arguments the function is defined with, and an array containing the symbol table indices of the declared parameters. *Bfcode* must generate the code to establish the new stack frame, save the return address and previous stack pointer value on the stack, and save whatever registers are to be used for register variables. The stack size and the number of register variables is not known when *bfcode* is called, so these numbers must be referred to by assembler constants, which are defined when they are known (usually in the second pass, after all register variables, automatics, and temporaries have been seen). The final job is to find those parameters which may have been declared register, and generate the code to initialize the register with the value passed on the stack. Once again, for most machines, the general logic of *bfcode* remains the same, but the contents of the *printf* calls in it will change from machine to machine. *efcode* is rather simpler, having just to generate the default return at the end of a function. This may be nontrivial in the case of a function returning a structure or union, however.

There seems to be no really good place to discuss structures and unions, but this is as good a place as any. The C language now supports structure assignment, and the passing of structures as arguments to functions, and the receiving of structures back from functions. This was added rather late to C, and thus to the portable compiler. Consequently, it fits in less well than the older features. Moreover, most of the burden of making these features work is placed on the machine dependent code.

There are both conceptual and practical problems. Conceptually, the compiler is structured around the idea that to compute something, you put it into a register and work on it. This notion causes a bit of trouble on some machines (e.g., machines with 3-address opcodes), but matches many machines quite well. Unfortunately, this notion breaks down with structures. The closest that one can come is to keep the addresses of the structures in registers. The actual code sequences used to move structures vary from the trivial (a multiple byte move) to the horrible (a function call), and are very machine dependent.

The practical problem is more painful. When a function returning a structure is called, this function has to have some place to put the structure value. If it places it on the stack, it has difficulty popping its stack frame. If it places the value in a static temporary, the routine fails to be reentrant. The most logically consistent way of implementing this is for the caller to pass in a pointer to a spot where the called function should put the value before returning. This is relatively straightforward, although a bit tedious, to implement, but means that the caller must have properly declared the function type, even if the value is never used. On some machines, such as the Interdata 8/32, the return value simply overlays the argument region (which on the 8/32 is part of the caller's stack frame). The caller takes care of leaving enough room if the returned value is larger than the arguments. This also assumes that the caller know and declares the function properly.

The PDP-11 and the VAX have stack hardware which is used in function calls and returns; this makes it very inconvenient to use either of the above mechanisms. In these machines, a static area within the called function is allocated, and the function return value is copied into it on return; the function returns the address of that region. This is simple to implement, but is non-reentrant. However, the function can now be called as a subroutine without being properly declared, without the disaster which would otherwise ensue. No matter what choice is taken, the convention is that the function actually returns the address of the return structure value.

In building expression trees, the portable compiler takes a bit for granted about structures. It assumes that functions returning structures actually return a pointer to the structure, and it assumes that a reference to a structure is actually a reference to its address. The structure assignment operator is rebuilt so that the left operand is the structure being assigned to, but the right operand is the address of the structure being assigned; this makes it easier to deal with

$$a = b = c$$

and similar constructions.

There are four special tree nodes associated with these operations: STASG (structure assignment), STARG (structure argument to a function call), and STCALL and UNARY STCALL (calls of a function with nonzero and zero arguments, respectively). These four nodes are unique in that the size and alignment information, which can be determined by the type for all other objects in C, must be known to carry out these operations; special fields are set aside in these nodes to contain this information, and special intermediate code is used to transmit this information.

First Pass Summary

There are may other issues which have been ignored here, partly to justify the title "tour", and partially because they have seemed to cause little trouble. There are some debugging flags which may be turned on, by giving the compiler's first pass the argument

$$-X[flags]$$

Some of the more interesting flags are −Xd for the defining and freeing of symbols, −Xi for initialization comments, and −Xb for various comments about the building of trees. In many cases, repeating the flag more than once gives more information; thus, −Xddd gives more information than −Xd. In the two pass version of the compiler, the flags should not be set when the output is sent to the second pass, since the debugging output and the intermediate code both go onto the standard output.

We turn now to consideration of the second pass.

Pass Two

Code generation is far less well understood than parsing or lexical analysis, and for this reason the second pass is far harder to discuss in a file by file manner. A great deal of the difficulty is in understanding the issues and the strategies employed to meet them. Any particular function is likely to be reasonably straightforward.

Thus, this part of the paper will concentrate a good deal on the broader aspects of strategy in the code generator, and will not get too intimate with the details.

Overview.

It is difficult to organize a code generator to be flexible enough to generate code for a large number of machines, and still be efficient for any one of them. Flexibility is also important when it comes time to tune the code generator to improve the output code quality. On the other hand, too much flexibility can lead to semantically incorrect code, and potentially a combinatorial explosion in the number of cases to be considered in the compiler.

One goal of the code generator is to have a high degree of correctness. It is very desirable to have the compiler detect its own inability to generate correct code, rather than to produce incorrect code. This goal is achieved by having a simple model of the job to be done (e.g., an expression tree) and a simple model of the machine state (e.g., which registers are free). The act of generating an instruction performs a transformation on the tree and the machine state; hopefully, the tree eventually gets reduced to a single node. If each of these instruction/transformation pairs is correct, and if the machine state model really represents the actual machine, and if the transformations reduce the input tree to the desired single node, then the output code will be correct.

For most real machines, there is no definitive theory of code generation that encompasses all the C operators. Thus the selection of which instruction/transformations to generate, and in what order, will have a heuristic flavor. If, for some expression tree, no transformation applies, or, more seriously, if the heuristics select a sequence of instruction/transformations that do not in fact reduce the tree, the compiler will report its inability to generate code, and abort.

A major part of the code generator is concerned with the model and the transformations, — most of this is machine independent, or depends only on simple tables. The flexibility comes from the heuristics that guide the transformations of the trees, the selection of subgoals, and the ordering of the computation.

The Machine Model

The machine is assumed to have a number of registers, of at most two different types: *A* and *B*. Within each register class, there may be scratch (temporary) registers and dedicated registers (e.g., register variables, the stack pointer, etc.). Requests to allocate and free registers involve only the temporary registers.

Each of the registers in the machine is given a name and a number in the *mac2defs* file; the numbers are used as indices into various tables that describe the registers, so they should be kept small. One such table is the *rstatus* table on file *local2.c*. This table is indexed by register number, and contains expressions made up from manifest constants describing the register types: SAREG for dedicated AREG's, SAREG|STAREG for scratch AREGS's, and SBREG and SBREG|STBREG similarly for BREG's. There are macros that access this information: *isbreg(r)* returns true if register number *r* is a BREG, and *istreg(r)* returns true if register number *r* is a temporary AREG or BREG. Another table, *rnames*, contains the register names; this is used when putting out assembler code and diagnostics.

The usage of registers is kept track of by an array called *busy*. *Busy[r]* is the number of uses of register *r* in the current tree being processed. The allocation and freeing of registers will be discussed later as part of the code generation algorithm.

General Organization

As mentioned above, the second pass reads lines from the intermediate file, copying through to the output unchanged any lines that begin with a ')', and making note of the information about stack usage and register allocation contained on lines beginning with ']' and '['. The expression trees, whose beginning is indicated by a line beginning with '.', are read and rebuilt into trees. If the compiler is loaded as one pass, the expression trees are immediately available to the code generator.

The actual code generation is done by a hierarchy of routines. The routine *delay* is first given the tree; it attempts to delay some postfix $++$ and $--$ computations that might reasonably be done after the smoke clears. It also attempts to handle comma (,) operators by computing the left side expression first, and then rewriting the tree to eliminate the operator. *Delay* calls *codgen* to control the actual code generation process. *Codgen* takes as arguments a pointer to the expression tree, and a second argument that, for socio-historical reasons, is called a *cookie*. The cookie describes a set of goals that would be acceptable for the code generation: these are assigned to individual bits, so they may be logically or'ed together to form a large number of possible goals. Among the possible goals are FOREFF (compute for side effects only; don't worry about the value), INTEMP (compute and store value into a temporary location in memory), INAREG (compute into an A register), INTAREG (compute into a scratch A register), INBREG and INTBREG similarly, FORCC (compute for condition codes), and FORARG (compute it as a function argument; e.g., stack it if appropriate).

Codgen first canonicalizes the tree by calling *canon*. This routine looks for certain transformations that might now be applicable to the tree. One, which is very common and very powerful, is to fold together an indirection operator (UNARY MUL) and a register (REG); in most machines, this combination is addressable directly, and so is similar to a NAME in its behavior. The UNARY MUL and REG are folded together to make another node type called OREG. In fact, in many machines it is possible to directly address not just the cell pointed to by a register, but also cells differing by a constant offset from the cell pointed to by the register. *Canon* also looks for such cases, calling the machine dependent routine *notoff* to decide if the offset is acceptable (for example, in the IBM 370 the offset must be between 0 and 4095 bytes). Another optimization is to replace bit field operations by shifts and masks if the operation involves extracting the field. Finally, a machine dependent routine, *sucomp*, is called that computes the Sethi-Ullman numbers for the tree (see below).

After the tree is canonicalized, *codgen* calls the routine *store* whose job is to select a subtree of the tree to be computed and (usually) stored before beginning the computation of the full tree. *Store* must return a tree that can be computed without need for any temporary storage locations. In effect, the only store operations generated while processing the subtree must be as a response to explicit assignment operators in the tree. This division of the job marks one of the more significant, and successful, departures from most other compilers. It means that the code generator can operate under the assumption that there are enough registers to do its job, without worrying about temporary storage. If a store into a temporary appears in the output, it is always as a direct result of logic in the *store* routine; this makes debugging easier.

One consequence of this organization is that code is not generated by a treewalk. There are theoretical results that support this decision.[7] It may be desirable to compute several subtrees and store them before tackling the whole tree; if a subtree is to be stored, this is known before the code generation for the subtree is begun, and the subtree is computed when all scratch registers are available.

The *store* routine decides what subtrees, if any, should be stored by making use of numbers, called *Sethi-Ullman numbers*, that give, for each subtree of an expression tree, the minimum number of scratch registers required to compile the subtree, without any stores into temporaries.[8] These numbers are computed by the machine-dependent routine *sucomp*, called by *canon*. The basic notion is that, knowing the Sethi-Ullman numbers for the descendants of a node, and knowing the operator of the node and some information about the machine, the Sethi-Ullman number of the node itself can be computed. If the Sethi-Ullman number for a tree exceeds the number of scratch registers available, some subtree must be stored. Unfortunately, the theory behind the Sethi-Ullman numbers applies only to uselessly simple machines and operators. For the rich set of C operators, and for machines with asymmetric registers, register pairs, different kinds of registers, and exceptional forms of addressing, the theory cannot be applied directly. The basic idea of estimation is a good one, however, and well worth applying; the application, especially when the compiler comes to be tuned for high code quality, goes beyond the park of theory into the swamp of heuristics. This topic will be taken up again later, when more of the compiler structure has been described.

After examining the Sethi-Ullman numbers, *store* selects a subtree, if any, to be stored, and returns the subtree and the associated cookie in the external variables *stotree* and *stocook*. If a subtree has been selected, or if the whole tree is ready to be processed, the routine *order* is called, with a tree and cookie. *Order* generates code for trees that do not require temporary locations. *Order* may make recursive calls on itself, and, in some cases, on *codgen*; for example, when processing the operators &&, ||, and comma (','), that have a left to right evaluation, it is incorrect for *store* examine the right operand for subtrees to be stored. In these cases, *order* will call *codgen* recursively when it is permissible to work on the right operand. A similar issue arises with the ? : operator.

The *order* routine works by matching the current tree with a set of code templates. If a template is discovered that will match the current tree and cookie, the associated assembly language statement or statements are generated. The tree is then rewritten, as specified by the template, to represent the effect of the output instruction(s). If no template match is found, first an attempt is made to find a match with a different cookie; for example, in order to compute an expression with cookie INTEMP (store into a temporary storage location), it is usually necessary to compute the expression into a scratch register first. If all attempts to match the tree fail, the heuristic part of the algorithm becomes dominant. Control is typically given to one of a number of machine-dependent routines that may in turn recursively call *order* to achieve a subgoal of the computation (for example, one of the arguments may be computed into a temporary register). After this subgoal has been achieved, the process begins again with the modified tree. If the machine-dependent heuristics are unable to reduce the tree further, a number of default rewriting rules may be considered appropriate. For example, if the left operand of a $+$ is a scratch register, the $+$ can be replaced by a $+=$ operator; the tree may then match a template.

To close this introduction, we will discuss the steps in compiling code for the expression

$$a += b$$

where *a* and *b* are static variables.

To begin with, the whole expression tree is examined with cookie FOREFF, and no match is found. Search with other cookies is equally fruitless, so an attempt at rewriting is made. Suppose we are dealing with the Interdata 8/32 for the moment. It is recognized that the left hand and right hand sides of the $+=$ operator are addressable, and in particular the left hand side has no side effects, so it is permissible to rewrite this as

$$a = a + b$$

and this is done. No match is found on this tree either, so a machine dependent rewrite is done; it is recognized that the left hand side of the assignment is addressable, but the right hand side is not in a register, so *order* is called recursively, being asked to put the right hand side of the assignment into a register. This invocation of *order* searches the tree for a match, and fails. The machine dependent rule for $+$ notices that the right hand operand is addressable; it decides to put the left operand into a scratch register. Another recursive call to *order* is made, with the tree consisting solely of the leaf *a*, and the cookie asking that the value be placed into a scratch register. This now matches a template, and a load instruction is emitted. The node consisting of *a* is rewritten in place to represent the register into which *a* is loaded, and this third call to *order* returns. The second call to *order* now finds that it has the tree

reg $+ b$

to consider. Once again, there is no match, but the default rewriting rule rewrites the $+$ as a $+=$ operator, since the left operand is a scratch register. When this is done, there is a match: in fact,

reg $+= b$

simply describes the effect of the add instruction on a typical machine. After the add is emitted, the tree is rewritten to consist merely of the register node, since the result of the add is now in the register. This agrees with the cookie passed to the second invocation of *order*, so this invocation terminates, returning to the first level. The original tree has now become

$a =$ **reg**

which matches a template for the store instruction. The store is output, and the tree rewritten to become just a single register node. At this point, since the top level call to *order* was interested only in side effects, the call to *order* returns, and the code generation is completed; we have generated a load, add, and store, as might have been expected.

The effect of machine architecture on this is considerable. For example, on the Honeywell 6000, the machine dependent heuristics recognize that there is an ''add to storage'' instruction, so the strategy is quite different; *b* is loaded in to a register, and then an add to storage instruction generated to add this register in to *a*. The transformations, involving as they do the semantics of C, are largely machine independent. The decisions as to when to use them, however, are almost totally machine dependent.

Having given a broad outline of the code generation process, we shall next consider the heart of it: the templates. This leads naturally into discussions of template matching and register allocation, and finally a discussion of the machine dependent interfaces and strategies.

The Templates

The templates describe the effect of the target machine instructions on the model of computation around which the compiler is organized. In effect, each template has five logical sections, and represents an assertion of the form:

If we have a subtree of a given shape (1), and we have a goal (cookie) or goals to achieve (2), and we have sufficient free resources (3), **then** we may emit an instruction or instructions (4), and rewrite the subtree in a particular manner (5), and the rewritten tree will achieve the desired goals.

These five sections will be discussed in more detail later. First, we give an example of a template:

```
ASG PLUS,    INAREG,
             SAREG,      TINT,
             SNAME,      TINT,
             0,          RLEFT,
             "           add         AL,AR\n",
```

The top line specifies the operator ($+=$) and the cookie (compute the value of the subtree into an AREG). The second and third lines specify the left and right descendants, respectively, of the $+=$ operator. The left descendant must be a REG node, representing an A register, and have integer type, while the right side must be a NAME node, and also have integer type. The fourth line contains the resource requirements (no scratch registers or temporaries needed), and the rewriting rule (replace the subtree by the left descendant). Finally, the quoted string on the last line represents the output to the assembler: lower case letters, tabs, spaces, etc. are copied *verbatim.* to the output; upper case letters trigger various macro-like expansions. Thus, **AL** would expand into the **A**ddress form of the **L**eft operand — presumably the register number. Similarly, **AR** would expand into the name of the right operand. The *add* instruction of the last section might well be emitted by this template.

In principle, it would be possible to make separate templates for all legal combinations of operators, cookies, types, and shapes. In practice, the number of combinations is very large. Thus, a considerable amount of mechanism is present to permit a large number of subtrees to be matched by a single template. Most of the shape and type specifiers are individual bits, and can be logically or'ed together. There are a number of special descriptors for matching classes of operators. The cookies can also be combined. As an example of the kind of template that really arises in practice, the actual template for the Interdata 8/32 that subsumes the above example is:

```
ASG OPSIMP, INAREG|FORCC,
            SAREG,                TINT|TUNSIGNED|TPOINT,
            SAREG|SNAME|SOREG|SCON,              TINT|TUNSIGNED|TPOINT,
            0,          RLEFT|RESCC,
            "           OI          AL,AR\n",
```

Here, OPSIMP represents the operators $+$, $-$, $|$, $\&$, and $\hat{}$. The **OI** macro in the output string expands into the appropriate **I**nteger **O**pcode for the operator. The left and right sides can be integers, unsigned, or pointer types. The right side can be, in addition to a name, a register, a memory location whose address is given by a register and displacement (OREG), or a constant. Finally, these instructions set the condition codes, and so can be used in condition contexts: the cookie and rewriting rules reflect this.

The Template Matching Algorithm.

The heart of the second pass is the template matching algorithm, in the routine *match*. *Match* is called with a tree and a cookie; it attempts to match the given tree against some template that will transform it according to one of the goals given in the cookie. If a match is successful, the transformation is applied; *expand* is called to generate the assembly code, and then *reclaim* rewrites the tree, and reclaims the resources, such as registers, that might have become free as a result of the generated code.

This part of the compiler is among the most time critical. There is a spectrum of implementation techniques available for doing this matching. The most naive algorithm simply looks at the templates one by one. This can be considerably improved upon by restricting the search for an acceptable template. It would be possible to do better than this if the templates were given to a separate program that ate them and generated a template matching subroutine. This would make maintenance of the compiler much more complicated, however, so this has not been done.

The matching algorithm is actually carried out by restricting the range in the table that must be searched for each opcode. This introduces a number of complications, however, and needs a bit of sympathetic help by the person constructing the compiler in order to obtain best results. The exact tuning of this algorithm continues; it is best to consult the code and comments in *match* for the latest version.

In order to match a template to a tree, it is necessary to match not only the cookie and the op of the root, but also the types and shapes of the left and right descendants (if any) of the tree. A convention is established here that is carried out throughout the second pass of the compiler. If a node represents a unary operator, the single descendant is always the "left" descendant. If a node represents a unary operator or a leaf node (no descendants) the "right" descendant is taken by convention to be the node itself. This enables templates to easily match leaves and conversion operators, for example, without any additional mechanism in the matching program.

The type matching is straightforward; it is possible to specify any combination of basic types, general pointers, and pointers to one or more of the basic types. The shape matching is somewhat more complicated, but still pretty simple. Templates have a collection of possible operand shapes on which the opcode might match. In the simplest case, an *add* operation might be able to add to either a register variable or a scratch register, and might be able (with appropriate help from the assembler) to add an integer constant (ICON), a static memory cell (NAME), or a stack location (OREG).

It is usually attractive to specify a number of such shapes, and distinguish between them when the assembler output is produced. It is possible to describe the union of many elementary shapes such as ICON, NAME, OREG, AREG or BREG (both scratch and register forms), etc. To handle at least the simple forms of indirection, one can also match some more complicated forms of trees; STARNM and STARREG can match more complicated trees headed by an indirection operator, and SFLD can match certain trees headed by a FLD operator: these patterns call machine dependent routines that match the patterns of interest on a given machine. The shape SWADD may be used to recognize NAME or OREG nodes that lie on word boundaries: this may be of some importance on word—addressed machines. Finally, there are some special shapes: these may not be used in conjunction with the other shapes, but may be defined and extended in machine dependent ways. The special shapes SZERO, SONE, and SMONE are predefined and match constants 0, 1, and −1, respectively; others are easy to add and match by using the machine dependent routine *special*.

When a template has been found that matches the root of the tree, the cookie, and the shapes and types of the descendants, there is still one bar to a total match: the template may call for some resources (for example, a scratch register). The routine *allo* is called, and it attempts to allocate the resources. If it cannot, the match fails; no resources are allocated. If successful, the allocated resources are given numbers 1, 2, etc. for later reference when the assembly code is generated. The routines *expand* and *reclaim* are then called. The *match* routine then returns a special value, MDONE. If no match was found, the value MNOPE is returned; this is a signal to the caller to try more cookie values, or attempt a rewriting rule. *Match* is also used to select rewriting rules, although the way of doing this is pretty straightforward. A special cookie, FORREW, is used to ask *match* to search for a rewriting rule. The rewriting rules are keyed to various opcodes; most are carried out in *order*. Since the question of when to rewrite is one of the key issues in code generation, it will be taken up again later.

Register Allocation.

The register allocation routines, and the allocation strategy, play a central role in the correctness of the code generation algorithm. If there are bugs in the Sethi-Ullman computation that cause the number of needed registers to be underestimated, the compiler may run out of scratch registers; it is essential that the allocator keep track of those registers that are free and busy, in order to detect such conditions.

Allocation of registers takes place as the result of a template match; the routine *allo* is called with a word describing the number of A registers, B registers, and temporary locations needed. The allocation of temporary locations on the stack is relatively straightforward, and will not be further covered; the bookkeeping is a bit tricky, but conceptually trivial, and requests for temporary space on the stack will never fail.

Register allocation is less straightforward. The two major complications are *pairing* and *sharing*. In many machines, some operations (such as multiplication and division), and/or some types (such as longs or double precision) require even/odd pairs of registers. Operations of the first type are exceptionally difficult to deal with in the compiler; in fact, their theoretical properties are rather bad as well.[9] The second issue is dealt with rather more successfully; a machine dependent function called *szty(t)* is called that returns 1 or 2, depending on the number of A registers required to hold an object of type *t*. If *szty* returns 2, an even/odd pair of A registers is allocated for each request.

The other issue, sharing, is more subtle, but important for good code quality. When registers are allocated, it is possible to reuse registers that hold address information, and use them to contain the values computed or accessed. For example, on the IBM 360, if register 2 has a pointer to an integer in it, we may load the integer into register 2 itself by saying:

        L   2,0(2)

If register 2 had a byte pointer, however, the sequence for loading a character involves clearing the target register first, and then inserting the desired character:

        SR   3,3
        IC   3,0(2)

In the first case, if register 3 were used as the target, it would lead to a larger number of registers used for the expression than were required; the compiler would generate inefficient code. On the other hand, if register 2 were used as the target in the second case, the code would simply be wrong. In the first case, register 2 can be *shared* while in the second, it cannot.

In the specification of the register needs in the templates, it is possible to indicate whether required scratch registers may be shared with possible registers on the left or the right of the input tree. In order that a register be shared, it must be scratch, and it must be used only once, on the appropriate side of the tree being compiled.

The *allo* routine thus has a bit more to do than meets the eye; it calls *freereg* to obtain a free register for each A and B register request. *Freereg* makes multiple calls on the routine *usable* to decide if a given register can be used to satisfy a given need. *Usable* calls *shareit* if the register is busy, but might be shared. Finally, *shareit* calls *ushare* to decide if the desired register is actually in the appropriate subtree, and can be shared.

Just to add additional complexity, on some machines (such as the IBM 370) it is possible to have "double indexing" forms of addressing; these are represented by OREGS's with the base and index registers encoded into the register field. While the register allocation and deallocation *per se* is not made more difficult by this phenomenon, the code itself is somewhat more complex.

Having allocated the registers and expanded the assembly language, it is time to reclaim the resources; the routine *reclaim* does this. Many operations produce more than one result. For example, many arithmetic operations may produce a value in a register, and also set the condition codes. Assignment operations may leave results both in a register and in memory. *Reclaim* is passed three parameters; the tree and cookie that were matched, and the rewriting field of the template. The rewriting field allows the specification of possible results; the tree is rewritten to reflect the results of the operation. If the tree was computed for side effects only (FOREFF), the tree is freed, and all resources in it reclaimed. If the tree was computed for condition codes, the resources are also freed, and the tree replaced by a special node type, FORCC. Otherwise, the value may be found in the left argument of the root, the right argument of the root, or one of the temporary resources allocated. In these cases, first the resources of the tree, and the newly allocated resources, are freed; then the resources needed by the result are made busy again. The final result must always match the shape of the input cookie; otherwise, the compiler error "cannot reclaim" is generated. There are some machine dependent ways of preferring results in registers or memory when there are multiple results matching multiple goals in the cookie.

The Machine Dependent Interface

The files *order.c*, *local2.c*, and *table.c*, as well as the header file *mac2defs*, represent the machine dependent portion of the second pass. The machine dependent portion can be roughly divided into two: the easy portion and the hard portion. The easy portion tells the compiler the names of the registers, and arranges that the compiler generate the proper assembler formats, opcode names, location counters, etc. The hard portion involves the Sethi−Ullman computation, the rewriting rules, and, to some extent, the templates. It is hard because there are no real algorithms that apply; most of this portion is based on heuristics. This section discusses the easy portion; the next several sections will discuss the hard portion.

If the compiler is adapted from a compiler for a machine of similar architecture, the easy part is indeed easy. In *mac2defs*, the register numbers are defined, as well as various parameters for the stack frame, and various macros that describe the machine architecture. If double indexing is to be permitted, for example, the symbol R2REGS is defined. Also, a number of macros that are involved in function call processing, especially for unusual function call mechanisms, are defined here.

In *local2.c*, a large number of simple functions are defined. These do things such as write out opcodes, register names, and address forms for the assembler. Part of the function call code is defined here; that is nontrivial to design, but typically rather straightforward to implement. Among the easy routines in *order.c* are routines for generating a created label, defining a label, and generating the arguments of a function call.

These routines tend to have a local effect, and depend on a fairly straightforward way on the target assembler and the design decisions already made about the compiler. Thus they will not be further treated here.

The Rewriting Rules

When a tree fails to match any template, it becomes a candidate for rewriting. Before the tree is rewritten, the machine dependent routine *nextcook* is called with the tree and the cookie; it suggests another cookie that might be a better candidate for the matching of the tree. If all else fails, the templates are searched with the cookie FORREW, to look for a rewriting rule. The rewriting rules are of two kinds; for most of the common operators, there are machine dependent rewriting rules that may be applied; these are handled by machine dependent functions that are called and given the tree to be computed. These routines may recursively call *order* or *codgen* to cause certain subgoals to be achieved; if they actually call for some alteration of the tree, they return 1, and the code generation algorithm recanonicalizes and tries again. If these routines choose not to deal with the tree, the default rewriting rules are applied.

The assignment ops, when rewritten, call the routine *setasg*. This is assumed to rewrite the tree at least to the point where there are no side effects in the left hand side. If there is still no template match, a default rewriting is done that causes an expression such as

$$a += b$$

to be rewritten as

$$a = a + b$$

This is a useful default for certain mixtures of strange types (for example, when *a* is a bit field and *b* an character) that otherwise might need separate table entries.

Simple assignment, structure assignment, and all forms of calls are handled completely by the machine dependent routines. For historical reasons, the routines generating the calls return 1 on failure, 0 on success, unlike the other routines.

The machine dependent routine *setbin* handles binary operators; it too must do most of the job. In particular, when it returns 0, it must do so with the left hand side in a temporary register. The default rewriting rule in this case is to convert the binary operator into the associated assignment operator; since the left hand side is assumed to be a temporary register, this preserves the semantics and often allows a considerable saving in the template table.

The increment and decrement operators may be dealt with with the machine dependent routine *setincr*. If this routine chooses not to deal with the tree, the rewriting rule replaces

$$x ++$$

by

$$((x += 1) - 1)$$

which preserves the semantics. Once again, this is not too attractive for the most common cases, but can generate close to optimal code when the type of x is unusual.

Finally, the indirection (UNARY MUL) operator is also handled in a special way. The machine dependent routine *offstar* is extremely important for the efficient generation of code. *Offstar* is called with a tree that is the direct descendant of a UNARY MUL node; its job is to transform this tree so that the combination of UNARY MUL with the transformed tree becomes addressable. On most machines, *offstar* can simply compute the tree into an A or B register, depending on the architecture, and then *canon* will make the resulting tree into an OREG. On many machines, *offstar* can profitably choose to do less work than computing its entire argument into a register. For example, if the target machine supports OREGS with a constant offset from a register, and *offstar* is called with a tree of the form

$$expr + const$$

where *const* is a constant, then *offstar* need only compute *expr* into the appropriate form of register. On machines that support double indexing, *offstar* may have even more choice as to how to proceed. The proper tuning of *offstar*, which is not typically too difficult, should be one of the first tries at optimization attempted by the compiler writer.

The Sethi-Ullman Computation

The heart of the heuristics is the computation of the Sethi-Ullman numbers. This computation is closely linked with the rewriting rules and the templates. As mentioned before, the Sethi-Ullman numbers are expected to estimate the number of scratch registers needed to compute the subtrees without using any stores. However, the original theory does not apply to real machines. For one thing, the theory assumes that all registers are interchangeable. Real machines have general purpose, floating point, and index registers, register pairs, etc. The theory also does not account for side effects; this rules out various forms of pathology that arise from assignment and assignment ops. Condition codes are also undreamed of. Finally, the influence of types, conversions, and the various addressability restrictions and extensions of real machines are also ignored.

Nevertheless, for a "useless" theory, the basic insight of Sethi and Ullman is amazingly useful in a real compiler. The notion that one should attempt to estimate the resource needs of trees before starting the code generation provides a natural means of splitting the code generation problem, and provides a bit of redundancy and self checking in the compiler. Moreover, if writing the Sethi-Ullman routines is hard, describing, writing, and debugging the alternative (routines that attempt to free up registers by stores into temporaries "on the fly") is even worse. Nevertheless, it should be clearly understood that these routines exist in a realm where there is no "right" way to write them; it is an art, the realm of heuristics, and, consequently, a major source of bugs in the compiler. Often, the early, crude versions of these routines give little trouble; only after the compiler is actually working and the code quality is being improved do serious problem have to be faced. Having a simple, regular machine architecture is worth quite a lot at this time.

The major problems arise from asymmetries in the registers: register pairs, having different kinds of registers, and the related problem of needing more than one register (frequently a pair) to store certain data types (such as longs or doubles). There appears to be no general way of treating this problem; solutions have to be fudged for each machine where the problem arises. On the Honeywell 66, for example, there are only two general purpose registers, so a need for a pair is the same as the need for two registers. On the IBM 370, the register pair (0,1) is used to do multiplications and divisions; registers 0 and 1 are not generally considered part of the scratch registers, and so do not require allocation explicitly. On the Interdata 8/32, after much consideration, the decision was made not to try to deal with the register pair issue; operations such as multiplication and division that required pairs were simply assumed to take all of the scratch registers. Several weeks of effort had failed to produce an algorithm that seemed to have much chance of running successfully without inordinate debugging effort. The difficulty of this issue should not be minimized; it represents one of the main intellectual efforts in porting the compiler. Nevertheless, this problem has been fudged with a degree of success on nearly a dozen machines, so the compiler writer should not abandon hope.

The Sethi-Ullman computations interact with the rest of the compiler in a number of rather subtle ways. As already discussed, the *store* routine uses the Sethi-Ullman numbers to decide which subtrees are too difficult to compute in registers, and must be stored. There are also subtle interactions between the rewriting routines and the Sethi-Ullman numbers. Suppose we have a tree such as

$$A - B$$

where *A* and *B* are expressions; suppose further that *B* takes two registers, and *A* one. It is possible to compute the full expression in two registers by first computing *B*, and then, using the scratch register used by *B*, but not containing the answer, compute *A*. The subtraction can then be done, computing the expression. (Note that this assumes a number of things, not the least of which are register-to-register subtraction operators and symmetric registers.) If the machine dependent routine *setbin*, however, is not prepared to recognize this case and compute the more difficult side of the expression first, the Sethi-Ullman number must be set to three. Thus, the Sethi-Ullman number for a tree should represent the code that the machine dependent routines are actually willing to generate.

The interaction can go the other way. If we take an expression such as

$$* (p + i)$$

where *p* is a pointer and *i* an integer, this can probably be done in one register on most machines. Thus, its Sethi-Ullman number would probably be set to one. If double indexing is possible in the machine, a possible way of computing the expression is to load both *p* and *i* into registers, and then use double indexing. This would use two scratch registers; in such a case, it is possible that the scratch registers might be unobtainable, or might make some other part of the computation run out of registers. The usual solution is to cause *offstar* to ignore opportunities for double indexing that would tie up more scratch registers than the Sethi-Ullman number had reserved.

In summary, the Sethi-Ullman computation represents much of the craftsmanship and artistry in any application of the portable compiler. It is also a frequent source of bugs. Algorithms are available that will produce nearly optimal code for specialized machines, but unfortunately most existing machines are far removed from these ideals. The best way of proceeding in practice is to start with a compiler for a similar machine to the target, and proceed very carefully.

Register Allocation

After the Sethi-Ullman numbers are computed, *order* calls a routine, *rallo*, that does register allocation, if appropriate. This routine does relatively little, in general; this is especially true if the target machine is fairly regular. There are a few cases where it is assumed that the result of a computation takes place in a particular register; switch and function return are the two major places. The expression tree has a field, *rall*, that may be filled with a register number; this is taken to be a preferred register, and the first temporary register allocated by a template match will be this preferred one, if it is free. If not, no particular action is taken; this is just a heuristic. If no register preference is present, the field contains NOPREF. In some cases, the result must be placed in a given register, no matter what. The register number is placed in *rall*, and the mask MUSTDO is logically or'ed in with it. In this case, if the subtree is requested in a register, and comes back in a register other than the demanded one, it is moved by calling the routine *rmove*. If the target register for this move is busy, it is a compiler error.

Note that this mechanism is the only one that will ever cause a register-to-register move between scratch registers (unless such a move is buried in the depths of some template). This simplifies debugging. In some cases, there is a rather strange interaction between the register allocation and the Sethi-Ullman number; if there is an operator or situation requiring a particular register, the allocator and the Sethi-Ullman computation must conspire to ensure that the target register is not being used by some intermediate result of some far-removed computation. This is most easily done by making the special operation take all of the free registers, preventing any other partially-computed results from cluttering up the works.

Compiler Bugs

The portable compiler has an excellent record of generating correct code. The requirement for reasonable cooperation between the register allocation, Sethi-Ullman computation, rewriting rules, and templates builds quite a bit of redundancy into the compiling process. The effect of this is that, in a surprisingly short time, the compiler will start generating correct code for those programs that it can compile. The hard part of the job then becomes finding and eliminating those situations where the compiler refuses to compile a program because it knows it cannot do it right. For example, a template may simply be missing; this may either give a compiler error of the form ''no match for op ...'' , or cause the compiler to go into an infinite loop applying various rewriting rules. The compiler has a variable, *nrecur*, that is set to 0 at the beginning of an expressions, and incremented at key spots in the compilation process; if this parameter gets too large, the compiler decides that it is in a loop, and aborts. Loops are also characteristic of botches in the machine-dependent rewriting rules. Bad Sethi-Ullman computations usually cause the scratch registers to run out; this often means that the Sethi-Ullman number was underestimated, so *store* did not store something it should have; alternatively, it can mean that the rewriting rules were not smart enough to find the sequence that *sucomp* assumed would be used.

The best approach when a compiler error is detected involves several stages. First, try to get a small example program that steps on the bug. Second, turn on various debugging flags in the code generator, and follow the tree through the process of being matched and rewritten. Some flags of interest are −e, which prints the expression tree, −r, which gives information about the allocation of registers, −a, which gives information about the performance of *rallo*, and −o, which gives information about the behavior of *order*. This technique should allow most bugs to be found relatively quickly.

Unfortunately, finding the bug is usually not enough; it must also be fixed! The difficulty arises because a fix to the particular bug of interest tends to break other code that already works. Regression tests, tests that compare the performance of a new compiler against the performance of an older one, are very valuable in preventing major catastrophes.

Summary and Conclusion

The portable compiler has been a useful tool for providing C capability on a large number of diverse machines, and for testing a number of theoretical constructs in a practical setting. It has many blemishes, both in style and functionality. It has been applied to many more machines than first anticipated, of a much wider range than originally dreamed of. Its use has also spread much faster than expected, leaving parts of the compiler still somewhat raw in shape.

On the theoretical side, there is some hope that the skeleton of the *sucomp* routine could be generated for many machines directly from the templates; this would give a considerable boost to the portability and correctness of the compiler, but might affect tunability and code quality. There is also room for more optimization, both within *optim* and in the form of a portable "peephole" optimizer.

On the practical, development side, the compiler could probably be sped up and made smaller without doing too much violence to its basic structure. Parts of the compiler deserve to be rewritten; the initialization code, register allocation, and parser are prime candidates. It might be that doing some or all of the parsing with a recursive descent parser might save enough space and time to be worthwhile; it would certainly ease the problem of moving the compiler to an environment where *Yacc* is not already present.

Finally, I would like to thank the many people who have sympathetically, and even enthusiastically, helped me grapple with what has been a frustrating program to write, test, and install. D. M. Ritchie and E. N. Pinson provided needed early encouragement and philosophical guidance; M. E. Lesk, R. Muha, T. G. Peterson, G. Riddle, L. Rosler, R. W. Mitze, B. R. Rowland, S. I. Feldman, and T. B. London have all contributed ideas, gripes, and all, at one time or another, climbed "into the pits" with me to help debug. Without their help this effort would have not been possible; with it, it was often kind of fun.

References

1. B. W. Kernighan and D. M. Ritchie, *The C Programming Language,* Prentice-Hall, Englewood Cliffs, New Jersey (1978).

2. S. C. Johnson, "Lint, a C Program Checker," Comp. Sci. Tech. Rep. No. 65 (1978).

3. A. Snyder, *A Portable Compiler for the Language C,* Master's Thesis, M.I.T., Cambridge, Mass. (1974).

4. S. C. Johnson, "A Portable Compiler: Theory and Practice," *Proc. 5th ACM Symp. on Principles of Programming Languages,* pp. 97-104 (January 1978).

5. M. E. Lesk, S. C. Johnson, and D. M. Ritchie, *The C Language Calling Sequence,* Bell Laboratories internal memorandum (1977).

6. S. C. Johnson, "Yacc — Yet Another Compiler-Compiler," Comp. Sci. Tech. Rep. No. 32, Bell Laboratories, Murray Hill, New Jersey (July 1975).

7. A. V. Aho and S. C. Johnson, "Optimal Code Generation for Expression Trees," *J. Assoc. Comp. Mach.* **23**(3) pp. 488-501 (1975). Also in *Proc. ACM Symp. on Theory of Computing,* pp. 207-217, 1975.

8. R. Sethi and J. D. Ullman, "The Generation of Optimal Code for Arithmetic Expressions," *J. Assoc. Comp. Mach.* **17**(4) pp. 715-728 (October 1970). Reprinted as pp. 229-247 in *Compiler Techniques,* ed. B. W. Pollack, Auerbach, Princeton NJ (1972).

9. A. V. Aho, S. C. Johnson, and J. D. Ullman, "Code Generation for Machines with Multiregister Operations," *Proc. 4th ACM Symp. on Principles of Programming Languages,* pp. 21-28 (January 1977).

A Dial-Up Network of UNIX™ Systems

D. A. Nowitz

M. E. Lesk

Bell Laboratories
Murray Hill, New Jersey 07974

ABSTRACT

A network of over eighty UNIX† computer systems has been established using the telephone system as its primary communication medium. The network was designed to meet the growing demands for software distribution and exchange. Some advantages of our design are:

- The startup cost is low. A system needs only a dial-up port, but systems with automatic calling units have much more flexibility.

- No operating system changes are required to install or use the system.

- The communication is basically over dial-up lines, however, hardwired communication lines can be used to increase speed.

- The command for sending/receiving files is simple to use.

Keywords: networks, communications, software distribution, software maintenance

August 18, 1978

---

†UNIX is a Trademark of Bell Laboratories.

1. Purpose

The widespread use of the UNIX† system[1] within Bell Laboratories has produced problems of software distribution and maintenance. A conventional mechanism was set up to distribute the operating system and associated programs from a central site to the various users. However this mechanism alone does not meet all software distribution needs. Remote sites generate much software and must transmit it to other sites. Some UNIX systems are themselves central sites for redistribution of a particular specialized utility, such as the Switching Control Center System. Other sites have particular, often long-distance needs for software exchange; switching research, for example, is carried on in New Jersey, Illinois, Ohio, and Colorado. In addition, general purpose utility programs are written at all UNIX system sites. The UNIX system is modified and enhanced by many people in many places and it would be very constricting to deliver new software in a one-way stream without any alternative for the user sites to respond with changes of their own.

Straightforward software distribution is only part of the problem. A large project may exceed the capacity of a single computer and several machines may be used by the one group of people. It then becomes necessary for them to pass messages, data and other information back an forth between computers.

Several groups with similar problems, both inside and outside of Bell Laboratories, have constructed networks built of hardwired connections only.[2, 3] Our network, however, uses both dial-up and hardwired connections so that service can be provided to as many sites as possible.

2. Design Goals

Although some of our machines are connected directly, others can only communicate over low-speed dial-up lines. Since the dial-up lines are often unavailable and file transfers may take considerable time, we spool all work and transmit in the background. We also had to adapt to a community of systems which are independently operated and resistant to suggestions that they should all buy particular hardware or install particular operating system modifications. Therefore, we make minimal demands on the local sites in the network. Our implementation requires no operating system changes; in fact, the transfer programs look like any other user entering the system through the normal dial-up login ports, and obeying all local protection rules.

We distinguish "active" and "passive" systems on the network. Active systems have an automatic calling unit or a hardwired line to another system, and can initiate a connection. Passive systems do not have the hardware to initiate a connection. However, an active system can be assigned the job of calling passive systems and executing work found there; this makes a passive system the functional equivalent of an active system, except for an additional delay while it waits to be polled. Also, people frequently log into active systems and request copying from one passive system to another. This requires two telephone calls, but even so, it is faster

---

†UNIX is a Trademark of Bell Laboratories.

than mailing tapes.

Where convenient, we use hardwired communication lines. These permit much faster transmission and multiplexing of the communications link. Dial-up connections are made at either 300 or 1200 baud; hardwired connections are asynchronous up to 9600 baud and might run even faster on special-purpose communications hardware.[4, 5] Thus, systems typically join our network first as passive systems and when they find the service more important, they acquire automatic calling units and become active systems; eventually, they may install high-speed links to particular machines with which they handle a great deal of traffic. At no point, however, must users change their programs or procedures.

The basic operation of the network is very simple. Each participating system has a spool directory, in which work to be done (files to be moved, or commands to be executed remotely) is stored. A standard program, *uucico*, performs all transfers. This program starts by identifying a particular communication channel to a remote system with which it will hold a conversation. *Uucico* then selects a device and establishes the connection, logs onto the remote machine and starts the *uucico* program on the remote machine. Once two of these programs are connected, they first agree on a line protocol, and then start exchanging work. Each program in turn, beginning with the calling (active system) program, transmits everything it needs, and then asks the other what it wants done. Eventually neither has any more work, and both exit.

In this way, all services are available from all sites; passive sites, however, must wait until called. A variety of protocols may be used; this conforms to the real, non-standard world. As long as the caller and called programs have a protocol in common, they can communicate. Furthermore, each caller knows the hours when each destination system should be called. If a destination is unavailable, the data intended for it remain in the spool directory until the destination machine can be reached.

The implementation of this Bell Laboratories network between independent sites, all of which store proprietary programs and data, illustratives the pervasive need for security and administrative controls over file access. Each site, in configuring its programs and system files, limits and monitors transmission. In order to access a file a user needs access permission for the machine that contains the file and access permission for the file itself. This is achieved by first requiring the user to use his password to log into his local machine and then his local machine logs into the remote machine whose files are to be accessed. In addition, records are kept identifying all files that are moved into and out of the local system, and how the requestor of such accesses identified himself. Some sites may arrange to permit users only to call up and request work to be done; the calling users are then called back before the work is actually done. It is then possible to verify that the request is legitimate from the standpoint of the target system, as well as the originating system. Furthermore, because of the call-back, no site can masquerade as another even if it knows all the necessary passwords.

Each machine can optionally maintain a sequence count for conversations with other machines and require a verification of the count at the start of each conversation. Thus, even if call back is not in use, a successful masquerade requires the calling party to present the correct sequence number. A would-be impersonator must not just steal the correct phone number, user name, and password, but also the sequence count, and must call in sufficiently promptly to precede the next legitimate request from either side. Even a successful masquerade will be detected on the next correct conversation.

3. Processing

The user has two commands which set up communications, *uucp* to set up file copying, and *uux* to set up command execution where some of the required resources (system and/or files) are not on the local machine. Each of these commands will put work and data files into the spool directory for execution by *uucp* daemons. Figure 1 shows the major blocks of the file transfer process.

File Copy

The *uucico* program is used to perform all communications between the two systems. It performs the following functions:

- Scan the spool directory for work.

- Place a call to a remote system.

- Negotiate a line protocol to be used.

- Start program *uucico* on the remote system.

- Execute all requests from both systems.

- Log work requests and work completions.

Uucico may be started in several ways;

a)   by a system daemon,

b)   by one of the *uucp* or *uux* programs,

c)   by a remote system.

Scan For Work

The file names in the spool directory are constructed to allow the daemon programs (*uucico, uuxqt*) to determine the files they should look at, the remote machines they should call and the order in which the files for a particular remote machine should be processed.

Call Remote System

The call is made using information from several files which reside in the uucp program directory. At the start of the call process, a lock is set on the system being called so that another call will not be attempted at the same time.

The system name is found in a "systems" file. The information contained for each system is:

[1]   system name,

[2]   times to call the system (days-of-week and times-of-day),

[3]   device or device type to be used for call,

[4]   line speed,

[5]   phone number,

[6]   login information (multiple fields).

The time field is checked against the present time to see if the call should be made. The *phone number* may contain abbreviations (e.g. "nyc", "boston") which get translated into dial sequences using a "dial-codes" file. This permits the same "phone number" to be stored at every site, despite local variations in telephone services and dialing conventions.

A "devices" file is scanned using fields [3] and [4] from the "systems" file to find an available device for the connection. The program will try all devices which satisfy [3] and [4] until a connection is made, or no more devices can be tried. If a non-multiplexable device is successfully opened, a lock file is created so that another copy of *uucico* will not try to use it. If the connection is complete, the *login information* is used to log into the remote system. Then a command is sent to the remote system to start the *uucico* program. The conversation between the two *uucico* programs begins with a handshake started by the called, *SLAVE*, system. The *SLAVE* sends a message to let the *MASTER* know it is ready to receive the system identification and conversation sequence number. The response from the *MASTER* is verified by the *SLAVE* and if acceptable, protocol selection begins.

Line Protocol Selection

The remote system sends a message

P *proto-list*

where *proto-list* is a string of characters, each representing a line protocol. The calling program checks the proto-list for a letter corresponding to an available line protocol and returns a *use-protocol* message. The *use-protocol* message is

U *code*

where code is either a one character protocol letter or a *N* which means there is no common protocol.

Greg Chesson designed and implemented the standard line protocol used by the uucp transmission program. Other protocols may be added by individual installations.

Work Processing

During processing, one program is the *MASTER* and the other is *SLAVE*. Initially, the calling program is the *MASTER*. These roles may switch one or more times during the conversation.

There are four messages used during the work processing, each specified by the first character of the message. They are

S   send a file,
R   receive a file,
C   copy complete,
H   hangup.

The *MASTER* will send *R* or *S* messages until all work from the spool directory is complete, at which point an *H* message will be sent. The *SLAVE* will reply with *SY*, *SN*, *RY*, *RN*, *HY*, *HN*, corresponding to *yes* or *no* for each request.

The send and receive replies are based on permission to access the requested file/directory. After each file is copied into the spool directory of the receiving system, a copy-complete message is sent by the receiver of the file. The message *CY* will be sent if the UNIX *cp* command, used to copy from the spool directory, is successful. Otherwise, a *CN* message is sent. The requests and results are logged on both systems, and, if requested, mail is sent to the user reporting completion (or the user can request status information from the log program at any time).

The hangup response is determined by the *SLAVE* program by a work scan of the spool directory. If work for the remote system exists in the *SLAVE's* spool directory, a *HN* message is sent and the programs switch roles. If no work exists, an *HY* response is sent.

A sample conversation is shown in Figure 2.

Conversation Termination

When a *HY* message is received by the *MASTER* it is echoed back to the *SLAVE* and the protocols are turned off. Each program sends a final "OO" message to the other.

4. Present Uses

One application of this software is remote mail. Normally, a UNIX system user writes "mail dan" to send mail to user "dan". By writing "mail usg!dan" the mail is sent to user "dan" on system "usg".

The primary uses of our network to date have been in software maintenance. Relatively few of the bytes passed between systems are intended for people to read. Instead, new programs (or new versions of programs) are sent to users, and potential bugs are returned to authors. Aaron Cohen has implemented a "stockroom" which allows remote users to call in and request software. He keeps a "stock list" of available programs, and new bug fixes and utilities are added regularly. In this way, users can always obtain the latest version of anything without bothering the authors of the programs. Although the stock list is maintained on a particular system, the items in the stockroom may be warehoused in many places; typically each program is distributed from the home site of its author. Where necessary, uucp does remote-to-remote copies.

We also routinely retrieve test cases from other systems to determine whether errors on remote systems are caused by local misconfigurations or old versions of software, or whether they are bugs that must be fixed at the home site. This helps identify errors rapidly. For one set of test programs maintained by us, over 70% of the bugs reported from remote sites were due to old software, and were fixed merely by distributing the current version.

Another application of the network for software maintenance is to compare files on two different machines. A very useful utility on one machine has been Doug McIlroy's "diff" program which compares two text files and indicates the differences, line by line, between them.[6] Only lines which are not identical are printed. Similarly, the program "uudiff" compares files (or directories) on two machines. One of these directories may be on a passive system. The "uudiff" program is set up to work similarly to the inter-system mail, but it is slightly more complicated.

To avoid moving large numbers of usually identical files, *uudiff* computes file checksums on each side, and only moves files that are different for detailed comparison. For large files, this process can be iterated; checksums can be computed for each line, and only those lines that are different actually moved.

The "uux" command has been useful for providing remote output. There are some machines which do not have hard-copy devices, but which are connected over 9600 baud communication lines to machines with printers. The *uux* command allows the formatting of the printout on the local machine and printing on the remote machine using standard UNIX command programs.

5. Performance

Throughput, of course, is primarily dependent on transmission speed. The table below shows the real throughput of characters on communication links of different speeds. These numbers represent actual data transferred; they do not include bytes used by the line protocol for data validation such as checksums and messages. At the higher speeds, contention for the processors on both ends prevents the network from driving the line full speed. The range of speeds represents the difference between light and heavy loads on the two systems. If desired, operating system modifications can be installed that permit full use of even very fast links.

Nominal speed	Characters/sec.
300 baud	27
1200 baud	100-110
9600 baud	200-850

In addition to the transfer time, there is some overhead for making the connection and logging in ranging from 15 seconds to 1 minute. Even at 300 baud, however, a typical 5,000 byte source program can be transferred in four minutes instead of the 2 days that might be required to mail a tape.

Traffic between systems is variable. Between two closely related systems, we observed 20 files moved and 5 remote commands executed in a typical day. A more normal traffic out of a single system would be around a dozen files per day.

The total number of sites at present in the main network is 82, which includes most of the Bell Laboratories full-size machines which run the UNIX operating system. Geographically, the machines range from Andover, Massachusetts to Denver, Colorado.

Uucp has also been used to set up another network which connects a group of systems in operational sites with the home site. The two networks touch at one Bell Labs computer.

6. Further Goals

Eventually, we would like to develop a full system of remote software maintenance. Conventional maintenance (a support group which mails tapes) has many well-known disadvantages.[7] There are distribution errors and delays, resulting in old software running at remote sites and old bugs continually reappearing. These difficulties are aggravated when there are 100 different small systems, instead of a few large ones.

The availability of file transfer on a network of compatible operating systems makes it possible just to send programs directly to the end user who wants them. This avoids the bottleneck of negotiation and packaging in the central support group. The "stockroom" serves this function for new utilities and fixes to old utilities. However, it is still likely that distributions will not be sent and installed as often as needed. Users are justifiably suspicious of the "latest version" that has just arrived; all too often it features the "latest bug." What is needed is to address both problems simultaneously:

1.   Send distributions whenever programs change.

2.   Have sufficient quality control so that users will install them.

To do this, we recommend systematic regression testing both on the distributing and receiving systems. Acceptance testing on the receiving systems can be automated and permits the local system to ensure that its essential work can continue despite the constant installation of changes sent from elsewhere. The work of writing the test sequences should be recovered in lower counseling and distribution costs.

Some slow-speed network services are also being implemented. We now have inter-system "mail" and "diff," plus the many implied commands represented by "uux." However, we still need inter-system "write" (real-time inter-user communication) and "who" (list of people logged in on different systems). A slow-speed network of this sort may be very useful for speeding up counseling and education, even if not fast enough for the distributed data base applications that attract many users to networks. Effective use of remote execution over slow-speed lines, however, must await the general installation of multiplexable channels so that long file transfers do not lock out short inquiries.

7. Lessons

The following is a summary of the lessons we learned in building these programs.

1.   By starting your network in a way that requires no hardware or major operating system changes, you can get going quickly.

2.   Support will follow use. Since the network existed and was being used, system maintainers were easily persuaded to help keep it operating, including purchasing additional hardware to speed traffic.

3.   Make the network commands look like local commands. Our users have a resistance to learning anything new: all the inter-system commands look very similar to standard UNIX system commands so that little training cost is involved.

4.   An initial error was not coordinating enough with existing communications projects: thus, the first version of this network was restricted to dial-up, since it did not support the various hardware links between systems. This has been fixed in the current system.

Acknowledgements

We thank G. L. Chesson for his design and implementation of the packet driver and protocol, and A. S. Cohen, J. Lions, and P. F. Long for their suggestions and assistance.

References

1. D. M. Ritchie and K. Thompson, "The UNIX Time-Sharing System," *Bell Sys. Tech. J.* **57**(6) pp. 1905-1929 (1978).

2. T. A. Dolotta, R. C. Haight, and J. R. Mashey, "UNIX Time-Sharing System: The Programmer's Workbench," *Bell Sys. Tech. J.* **57**(6) pp. 2177-2200 (1978).

3. G. L. Chesson, "The Network UNIX System," *Operating Systems Review* **9**(5) pp. 60-66 (1975). Also in *Proc. 5th Symp. on Operating Systems Principles*.

4. A. G. Fraser, "Spider — An Experimental Data Communications System," *Proc. IEEE Conf. on Communications*, p. 21F (June 1974). IEEE Cat. No. 74CH0859-9-CSCB.

5. A. G. Fraser, "A Virtual Channel Network," *Datamation*, pp. 51-56 (February 1975).

6. J. W. Hunt and M. D. McIlroy, "An Algorithm for Differential File Comparison," Comp. Sci. Tech. Rep. No. 41, Bell Laboratories, Murray Hill, New Jersey (June 1976).

7. F. P. Brooks, Jr., *The Mythical Man-Month,* Addison-Wesley, Reading, Mass. (1975).

Uucp Implementation Description

D. A. Nowitz

ABSTRACT

Uucp is a series of programs designed to permit communication between UNIX systems using either dial-up or hardwired communication lines. This document gives a detailed implementation description of the current (second) implementation of uucp.

This document is for use by an administrator/installer of the system. It is not meant as a user's guide.

October 31, 1978

Introduction

Uucp is a series of programs designed to permit communication between UNIX† systems using either dial-up or hardwired communication lines. It is used for file transfers and remote command execution. The first version of the system was designed and implemented by M. E. Lesk.[1] This paper describes the current (second) implementation of the system.

Uucp is a batch type operation. Files are created in a spool directory for processing by the uucp demons. There are three types of files used for the execution of work. *Data files* contain data for transfer to remote systems. *Work files* contain directions for file transfers between systems. *Execution files* are directions for UNIX command executions which involve the resources of one or more systems.

The uucp system consists of four primary and two secondary programs. The primary programs are:

uucp	This program creates work and gathers data files in the spool directory for the transmission of files.
uux	This program creates work files, execute files and gathers data files for the remote execution of UNIX commands.
uucico	This program executes the work files for data transmission.
uuxqt	This program executes the execution files for UNIX command execution.

The secondary programs are:

uulog	This program updates the log file with new entries and reports on the status of uucp requests.
uuclean	This program removes old files from the spool directory.

The remainder of this paper will describe the operation of each program, the installation of the system, the security aspects of the system, the files required for execution, and the administration of the system.

1. Uucp - UNIX to UNIX File Copy

The *uucp* command is the user's primary interface with the system. The *uucp* command was designed to look like *cp* to the user. The syntax is

    uucp [option] ... source ... destination

where the source and destination may contain the prefix *system-name!* which indicates the system on which the file or files reside or where they will be copied.

The options interpreted by *uucp* are:

    −d   Make directories when necessary for copying the file.

---

†UNIX is a Trademark of Bell Laboratories.
1 M. E. Lesk and A. S. Cohen, UNIX Software Distribution by Communication Link, private communication.

−c   Don't copy source files to the spool directory, but use the specified source when the actual transfer takes place.

−g*letter*   Put *letter* in as the grade in the name of the work file. (This can be used to change the order of work for a particular machine.)

−m   Send mail on completion of the work.

The following options are used primarily for debugging:

−r   Queue the job but do not start *uucico* program.

−s*dir*   Use directory *dir* for the spool directory.

−x*num*   *Num* is the level of debugging output desired.

The destination may be a directory name, in which case the file name is taken from the last part of the source's name. The source name may contain special shell characters such as "*?*[]*". If a source argument has a *system-name!* prefix for a remote system, the file name expansion will be done on the remote system.

The command

        uucp *.c usg!/usr/dan

will set up the transfer of all files whose names end with ".c" to the "/usr/dan" directory on the"usg" machine.

The source and/or destination names may also contain a ~*user* prefix. This translates to the login directory on the specified system. For names with partial path-names, the current directory is prepended to the file name. File names with ../ are not permitted.

The command

        uucp usg!~dan/*.h ~dan

will set up the transfer of files whose names end with ".h" in dan's login directory on system "usg" to dan's local login directory.

For each source file, the program will check the source and destination file-names and the system-part of each to classify the work into one of five types:

[1] Copy source to destination on local system.

[2] Receive files from other systems.

[3] Send files to a remote systems.

[4] Send files from remote systems to another remote system.

[5] Receive files from remote systems when the source contains special shell characters as mentioned above.

After the work has been set up in the spool directory, the *uucico* program is started to try to contact the other machine to execute the work (unless the −r option was specified).

Type 1

A *cp* command is used to do the work. The −d and the −m options are not honored in this case.

Type 2

A one line *work file* is created for each file requested and put in the spool directory with the following fields, each separated by a blank. (All *work files* and *execute files* use a blank as the field separator.)

[1] R

[2]   The full path-name of the source or a ˜user/path-name. The ˜*user* part will be expanded on the remote system.

[3]   The full path-name of the destination file. If the ˜*user* notation is used, it will be immediately expanded to be the login directory for the user.

[4]   The user's login name.

[5]   A "−" followed by an option list. (Only the −m and −d options will appear in this list.)

Type 3

For each source file, a *work file* is created and the source file is copied into a *data file* in the spool directory. (A "−c" option on the *uucp* command will prevent the *data file* from being made.) In this case, the file will be transmitted from the indicated source.) The fields of each entry are given below.

[1]   S

[2]   The full-path name of the source file.

[3]   The full-path name of the destination or ˜user/file-name.

[4]   The user's login name.

[5]   A "−" followed by an option list.

[6]   The name of the *data file* in the spool directory.

[7]   The file mode bits of the source file in octal print format (e.g. 0666).

Type 4 and Type 5

Uucp generates a *uucp* command and sends it to the remote machine; the remote *uucico* executes the *uucp* command.

2. Uux - UNIX To UNIX Execution

The *uux* command is used to set up the execution of a UNIX command where the execution machine and/or some of the files are remote. The syntax of the uux command is

        uux [−] [option] ... command-string

where the command-string is made up of one or more arguments. All special shell characters such as "<>|˜" must be quoted either by quoting the entire command-string or quoting the character as a separate argument. Within the command-string, the command and file names may contain a *system-name!* prefix. All arguments which do not contain a "!" will not be treated as files. (They will not be copied to the execution machine.) The "−" is used to indicate that the standard input for *command-string* should be inherited from the standard input of the *uux* command. The options, essentially for debugging, are:

    −r   Don't start *uucico* or *uuxqt* after queuing the job;

    −x*num*   Num is the level of debugging output desired.

The command

            pr abc | uux − usg!lpr

will set up the output of "pr abc" as standard input to an lpr command to be executed on system "usg".

Uux generates an *execute file* which contains the names of the files required for execution (including standard input), the user's login name, the destination of the standard output, and the command to be executed. This file is either put in the spool directory for local execution or sent to the remote system using a generated send command (type 3 above).

For required files which are not on the execution machine, *uux* will generate receive command files (type 2 above). These command-files will be put on the execution machine and executed by the *uucico* program. (This will work only if the local system has permission to put files in the remote spool directory as controlled by the remote *USERFILE.*)

The *execute file* will be processed by the *uuxqt* program on the execution machine. It is made up of several lines, each of which contains an identification character and one or more arguments. The order of the lines in the file is not relevant and some of the lines may not be present. Each line is described below.

User Line

U user system

where the *user* and *system* are the requester's login name and system.

Required File Line

F file-name real-name

where the *file-name* is the generated name of a file for the execute machine and *real-name* is the last part of the actual file name (contains no path information). Zero or more of these lines may be present in the *execute file*. The *uuxqt* program will check for the existence of all required files before the command is executed.

Standard Input Line

I file-name

The standard input is either specified by a "<" in the command-string or inherited from the standard input of the *uux* command if the "−" option is used. If a standard input is not specified, "/dev/null" is used.

Standard Output Line

O file-name system-name

The standard output is specified by a ">" within the command-string. If a standard output is not specified, "/dev/null" is used. (Note − the use of ">>" is not implemented.)

Command Line

C command [arguments] ...

The arguments are those specified in the command-string. The standard input and standard output will not appear on this line. All *required files* will be moved to the execution directory (a subdirectory of the spool directory) and the UNIX command is executed using the Shell specified in the *uucp.h* header file. In addition, a shell "PATH" statement is prepended to the command line as specified in the *uuxqt* program.

After execution, the standard output is copied or set up to be sent to the proper place.

3. Uucico - Copy In, Copy Out

The *uucico* program will perform the following major functions:

- Scan the spool directory for work.
- Place a call to a remote system.
- Negotiate a line protocol to be used.
- Execute all requests from both systems.
- Log work requests and work completions.

Uucico may be started in several ways;

a)   by a system daemon,

b)   by one of the *uucp, uux, uuxqt* or *uucico* programs,

c)   directly by the user (this is usually for testing),

d)   by a remote system. (The uucico program should be specified as the "shell" field in the "/etc/passwd" file for the "uucp" logins.)

When started by method a, b or c, the program is considered to be in *MASTER* mode. In this mode, a connection will be made to a remote system. If started by a remote system (method d), the program is considered to be in *SLAVE* mode.

The *MASTER* mode will operate in one of two ways. If no system name is specified (−s option not specified) the program will scan the spool directory for systems to call. If a system name is specified, that system will be called, and work will only be done for that system.

The *uucico* program is generally started by another program. There are several options used for execution:

−r1   Start the program in *MASTER* mode. This is used when *uucico* is started by a program or "cron" shell.

−s*sys*   Do work only for system *sys*. If −s is specified, a call to the specified system will be made even if there is no work for system *sys* in the spool directory. This is useful for polling systems which do not have the hardware to initiate a connection.

The following options are used primarily for debugging:

−d*dir*   Use directory *dir* for the spool directory.

−x*num*   *Num* is the level of debugging output desired.

The next part of this section will describe the major steps within the *uucico* program.

Scan For Work

The names of the work related files in the spool directory have format

        type . system-name grade number

where:

Type is an upper case letter, (*C* - copy command file, *D* - data file, *X* - execute file);

System-name is the remote system;

Grade is a character;

Number is a four digit, padded sequence number.

The file

        C.res45n0031

would be a *work file* for a file transfer between the local machine and the "res45" machine.

The scan for work is done by looking through the spool directory for *work files* (files with prefix "C."). A list is made of all systems to be called. *Uucico* will then call each system and process all *work files*.

Call Remote System

The call is made using information from several files which reside in the uucp program directory. At the start of the call process, a lock is set to forbid multiple conversations between the same two systems.

The system name is found in the *L.sys* file. The information contained for each system is;

[1]   system name,

[2]   times to call the system (days-of-week and times-of-day),

[3]   device or device type to be used for call,

[4]   line speed,

[5]   phone number if field [3] is *ACU* or the device name (same as field [3]) if not *ACU*,

[6]   login information (multiple fields),

The time field is checked against the present time to see if the call should be made.

The *phone number* may contain abbreviations (e.g. mh, py, boston) which get translated into dial sequences using the *L-dialcodes* file.

The *L-devices* file is scanned using fields [3] and [4] from the *L.sys* file to find an available device for the call. The program will try all devices which satisfy [3] and [4] until the call is made, or no more devices can be tried. If a device is successfully opened, a lock file is created so that another copy of *uucico* will not try to use it. If the call is complete, the *login information* (field [6] of *L.sys*) is used to login.

The conversation between the two *uucico* programs begins with a handshake started by the called, *SLAVE*, system. The *SLAVE* sends a message to let the *MASTER* know it is ready to receive the system identification and conversation sequence number. The response from the *MASTER* is verified by the *SLAVE* and if acceptable, protocol selection begins. The *SLAVE* can also reply with a "call-back required" message in which case, the current conversation is terminated.

Line Protocol Selection

The remote system sends a message

> P *proto-list*

where proto-list is a string of characters, each representing a line protocol.

The calling program checks the proto-list for a letter corresponding to an available line protocol and returns a *use-protocol* message. The *use-protocol* message is

> U *code*

where code is either a one character protocol letter or *N* which means there is no common protocol.

Work Processing

The initial roles (*MASTER* or *SLAVE*) for the work processing are the mode in which each program starts. (The *MASTER* has been specified by the "−r1" uucico option.) The *MASTER* program does a work search similar to the one used in the "Scan For Work" section.

There are five messages used during the work processing, each specified by the first character of the message. They are;

S   send a file,

R   receive a file,

C   copy complete,

X   execute a *uucp* command,

H   hangup.

The *MASTER* will send *R*, *S* or *X* messages until all work from the spool directory is complete, at which point an *H* message will be sent. The *SLAVE* will reply with *SY*, *SN*, *RY*, *RN*, *HY*, *HN*, *XY*, *XN*, corresponding to yes or no for each request.

The send and receive replies are based on permission to access the requested file/directory using the *USERFILE* and read/write permissions of the file/directory. After each file is copied into the spool directory of the receiving system, a copy-complete message is sent by the receiver of the file. The message *CY* will be sent if the file has successfully been moved from the temporary spool file to the actual destination. Otherwise, a *CN* message is sent. (In the case of *CN*, the transferred file will be in the spool directory with a name beginning with ''TM'.) The requests and results are logged on both systems.

The hangup response is determined by the *SLAVE* program by a work scan of the spool directory. If work for the remote system exists in the *SLAVE's* spool directory, an *HN* message is sent and the programs switch roles. If no work exists, an *HY* response is sent.

Conversation Termination

When a *HY* message is received by the *MASTER* it is echoed back to the *SLAVE* and the protocols are turned off. Each program sends a final ''OO'' message to the other. The original *SLAVE* program will clean up and terminate. The *MASTER* will proceed to call other systems and process work as long as possible or terminate if a −s option was specified.

4. Uuxqt - Uucp Command Execution

The *uuxqt* program is used to execute *execute files* generated by *uux*. The *uuxqt* program may be started by either the *uucico* or *uux* programs. The program scans the spool directory for *execute files* (prefix ''X.''). Each one is checked to see if all the required files are available and if so, the command line or send line is executed.

The *execute file* is described in the ''Uux'' section above.

Command Execution

The execution is accomplished by executing a *sh* −c of the command line after appropriate standard input and standard output have been opened. If a standard output is specified, the program will create a send command or copy the output file as appropriate.

5. Uulog - Uucp Log Inquiry

The *uucp* programs create individual log files for each program invocation. Periodically, *uulog* may be executed to prepend these files to the system logfile. This method of logging was chosen to minimize file locking of the logfile during program execution.

The *uulog* program merges the individual log files and outputs specified log entries. The output request is specified by the use of the following options:

−s*sys*   Print entries where *sys* is the remote system name;

−u*user* Print entries for user *user*.

The intersection of lines satisfying the two options is output. A null *sys* or *user* means all system names or users respectively.

6. Uuclean - Uucp Spool Directory Cleanup

This program is typically started by the daemon, once a day. Its function is to remove files from the spool directory which are more than 3 days old. These are usually files for work which can not be completed.

The options available are:

−d*dir*   The directory to be scanned is *dir*.

−m   Send mail to the owner of each file being removed. (Note that most files put into the spool directory will be owned by the owner of the uucp programs since the setuid bit will be set on these programs. The mail will therefore most often go to the owner of the uucp programs.)

−n *hours*	Change the aging time from 72 hours to *hours* hours.
−p *pre*	Examine files with prefix *pre* for deletion. (Up to 10 file prefixes may be specified.)
−x *num*	This is the level of debugging output desired.

7. Security

The uucp system, left unrestricted, will let any outside user execute any commands and copy in/out any file which is readable/writable by the uucp login user. It is up to the individual sites to be aware of this and apply the protections that they feel are necessary.

There are several security features available aside from the normal file mode protections. These must be set up by the installer of the *uucp* system.

- The login for uucp does not get a standard shell. Instead, the *uucico* program is started. Therefore, the only work that can be done is through *uucico*.

- A path check is done on file names that are to be sent or received. The *USERFILE* supplies the information for these checks. The *USERFILE* can also be set up to require call-back for certain login-ids. (See the "Files required for execution" section for the file description.)

- A conversation sequence count can be set up so that the called system can be more confident that the caller is who he says he is.

- The *uuxqt* program comes with a list of commands that it will execute. A "PATH" shell statement is prepended to the command line as specifed in the *uuxqt* program. The installer may modify the list or remove the restrictions as desired.

- The *L.sys* file should be owned by uucp and have mode 0400 to protect the phone numbers and login information for remote sites. (Programs uucp, uucico, uux, uuxqt should be also owned by uucp and have the setuid bit set.)

8. Uucp Installation

There are several source modifications that may be required before the system programs are compiled. These relate to the directories used during compilation, the directories used during execution, and the local *uucp system-name*.

The four directories are:

lib	(/usr/src/cmd/uucp) This directory contains the source files for generating the *uucp* system.
program	(/usr/lib/uucp) This is the directory used for the executable system programs and the system files.
spool	(/usr/spool/uucp) This is the spool directory used during *uucp* execution.
xqtdir	(/usr/spool/uucp/.XQTDIR) This directory is used during execution of *execute files.*

The names given in parentheses above are the default values for the directories. The italicized named *lib, program, xqtdir,* and *spool* will be used in the following text to represent the appropriate directory names.

There are two files which may require modification, the *makefile* file and the *uucp.h* file. The following paragraphs describe the modifications. The modes of *spool* and *xqtdir* should be made "0777".

Uucp.h modification

Change the *program* and the *spool* names from the default values to the directory names to be used on the local system using global edit commands.

Change the *define* value for $MYNAME$ to be the local *uucp* system-name.

makefile modification

There are several *make* variable definitions which may need modification.

INSDIR   This is the *program* directory (e.g. INSDIR = /usr/lib/uucp). This parameter is used if "make cp" is used after the programs are compiled.

IOCTL   This is required to be set if an appropriate *ioctl* interface subroutine does not exist in the standard "C" library; the statement "IOCTL = ioctl.o" is required in this case.

PKON   The statement "PKON = pkon.o" is required if the packet driver is not in the kernel.

Compile the system The command

```
make
```

will compile the entire system. The command

```
make cp
```

will copy the commands to the to the appropriate directories.

The programs *uucp*, *uux*, and *uulog* should be put in "/usr/bin". The programs *uuxqt*, *uucico*, and *uuclean* should be put in the *program* directory.

Files required for execution

There are four files which are required for execution, all of which should reside in the *program* directory. The field separator for all files is a space unless otherwise specified.

L-devices

This file contains entries for the call-unit devices and hardwired connections which are to be used by *uucp*. The special device files are assumed to be in the */dev* directory. The format for each entry is

```
line  call-unit  speed
```

where;

line   is the device for the line (e.g. cul0),

call-unit   is the automatic call unit associated with *line* (e.g. cua0), (Hardwired lines have a number "0" in this field.),

speed   is the line speed.

The line

```
cul0  cua0  300
```

would be set up for a system which had device cul0 wired to a call-unit cua0 for use at 300 baud.

L-dialcodes

This file contains entries with location abbreviations used in the *L.sys* file (e.g. py, mh, boston). The entry format is abb dial-seq

where;

    abb   is the abbreviation,

    dial-seq   is the dial sequence to call that location.

The line

            py 165—

would be set up so that entry py7777 would send 165—7777 to the dial-unit.

LOGIN/SYSTEM NAMES

It is assumed that the *login name* used by a remote computer to call into a local computer is not the same as the login name of a normal user of that local machine. However, several remote computers may employ the same login name.

Each computer is given a unique *system name* which is transmitted at the start of each call. This name identifies the calling machine to the called machine.

USERFILE

This file contains user accessibility information. It specifies four types of constraint;

    [1]   which files can be accessed by a normal user of the local machine,

    [2]   which files can be accessed from a remote computer,

    [3]   which login name is used by a particular remote computer,

    [4]   whether a remote computer should be called back in order to confirm its identity.

Each line in the file has the following format

     login,sys [c] path-name [path-name] ...

where;

    login   is the login name for a user or the remote computer,

    sys   is the system name for a remote computer,

    c   is the optional *call-back required* flag,

    path-name   is a path-name prefix that is acceptable for *user*.

The constraints are implemented as follows.

    [1]   When the program is obeying a command stored on the local machine, *MASTER* mode, the path-names allowed are those given for the first line in the *USERFILE* that has a login name that matches the login name of the user who entered the command. If no such line is found, the first line with a *null* login name is used.

    [2]   When the program is responding to a command from a remote machine, *SLAVE* mode, the path-names allowed are those given for the first line in the file that has the system name that matches the system name of the remote machine. If no such line is found, the first one with a *null* system name is used.

    [3]   When a remote computer logs in, the login name that it uses must appear in the *USERFILE*. There may be several lines with the same login name but one of them must either have the name of the remote system or must contain a *null* system name.

    [4]   If the line matched in ([3]) contains a "c", the remote machine is called back before any transactions take place.

The line

        u,m /usr/xyz

allows machine *m* to login with name *u* and request the transfer of files whose names start with "/usr/xyz".

The line

        dan, /usr/dan

allows the ordinary user *dan* to issue commands for files whose name starts with "/usr/dan".

The lines

        u,m /usr/xyz /usr/spool
        u, /usr/spool

allows any remote machine to login with name *u*, but if its system name is not *m*, it can only ask to transfer files whose names start with "/usr/spool".

The lines

        root, /
        , /usr

allows any user to transfer files beginning with "/usr" but the user with login *root* can transfer any file.

L.sys

Each entry in this file represents one system which can be called by the local uucp programs. The fields are described below.

system name

The name of the remote system.

time

This is a string which indicates the days-of-week and times-of-day when the system should be called (e.g. MoTuTh0800−1730).

The day portion may be a list containing some of

    Su Mo Tu We Th Fr Sa

or it may be *Wk* for any week-day or *Any* for any day.

The time should be a range of times (e.g. 0800−1230). If no time portion is specified, any time of day is assumed to be ok for the call.

device

This is either *ACU* or the hardwired device to be used for the call. For the hardwired case, the last part of the special file name is used (e.g. tty0).

speed

This is the line speed for the call (e.g. 300).

phone

The phone number is made up of an optional alphabetic abbreviation and a numeric part. The abbreviation is one which appears in the *L-dialcodes* file (e.g. mh5900, boston995−9980).

For the hardwired devices, this field contains the same string as used for the *device* field.

login

The login information is given as a series of fields and subfields in the format

expect send [expect send] ...

where; *expect* is the string expected to be read and *send* is the string to be sent when the *expect* string is received.

The expect field may be made up of subfields of the form

expect[−send−expect]...

where the *send* is sent if the prior *expect* is not successfully read and the *expect* following the *send* is the next expected string.

There are two special names available to be sent during the login sequence. The string *EOT* will send an EOT character and the string *BREAK* will try to send a BREAK character. (The *BREAK* character is simulated using line speed changes and null characters and may not work on all devices and/or systems.)

A typical entry in the L.sys file would be

sys Any ACU 300 mh7654 login uucp ssword: word

The expect algorithm looks at the last part of the string as illustrated in the password field.

9. Administration

This section indicates some events and files which must be administered for the *uucp* system. Some administration can be accomplished by *shell files* which can be initiated by *crontab* entries. Others will require manual intervention. Some sample *shell files* are given toward the end of this section.

SQFILE − sequence check file

This file is set up in the *program* directory and contains an entry for each remote system with which you agree to perform conversation sequence checks. The initial entry is just the system name of the remote system. The first conversation will add two items to the line, the conversation count, and the date/time of the most resent conversation. These items will be updated with each conversation. If a sequence check fails, the entry will have to be adjusted.

TM − temporary data files

These files are created in the *spool* directory while files are being copied from a remote machine. Their names have the form

TM.pid.ddd

where *pid* is a process-id and *ddd* is a sequential three digit number starting at zero for each invocation of *uucico* and incremented for each file received.

After the entire remote file is received, the *TM* file is moved/copied to the requested destination. If processing is abnormally terminated or the move/copy fails, the file will remain in the spool directory.

The leftover files should be periodically removed; the *uuclean* program is useful in this regard. The command

uuclean −pTM

will remove all *TM* files older than three days.

LOG — log entry files

During execution of programs, individual *LOG* files are created in the *spool* directory with information about queued requests, calls to remote systems, execution of *uux* commands and file copy results. These files should be combined into the *LOGFILE* by using the *uulog* program. This program will put the new *LOG* files at the beginning of the existing *LOGFILE*. The command

          uulog

will accomplish the merge. Options are available to print some or all the log entries after the files are merged. The *LOGFILE* should be removed periodically since it is copied each time new LOG entries are put into the file.

The *LOG* files are created initially with mode 0222. If the program which creates the file terminates normally, it changes the mode to 0666. Aborted runs may leave the files with mode 0222 and the *uulog* program will not read or remove them. To remove them, either use *rm*, *uuclean*, or change the mode to 0666 and let *uulog* merge them with the *LOGFILE*.

STST — system status files

These files are created in the spool directory by the *uucico* program. They contain information of failures such as login, dialup or sequence check and will contain a *TALKING* status when to machines are conversing. The form of the file name is

     STST.sys

where *sys* is the remote system name.

For ordinary failures (dialup, login), the file will prevent repeated tries for about one hour. For sequence check failures, the file must be removed before any future attempts to converse with that remote system.

If the file is left due to an aborted run, it may contain a *TALKING* status. In this case, the file must be removed before a conversation is attempted.

LCK — lock files

Lock files are created for each device in use (e.g. automatic calling unit) and each system conversing. This prevents duplicate conversations and multiple attempts to use the same devices. The form of the lock file name is

          LCK..str

where *str* is either a device or system name. The files may be left in the spool directory if runs abort. They will be ignored (reused) after a time of about 24 hours. When runs abort and calls are desired before the time limit, the lock files should be removed.

Shell Files

The *uucp* program will spool work and attempt to start the *uucico* program, but the starting of *uucico* will sometimes fail. (No devices available, login failures etc.). Therefore, the *uucico* program should be periodically started. The command to start *uucico* can be put in a "shell" file with a command to merge *LOG* files and started by a crontab entry on an hourly basis. The file could contain the commands

     program/uulog
     program/uucico   −r1

Note that the "−r1" option is required to start the *uucico* program in *MASTER* mode.

Another shell file may be set up on a daily basis to remove *TM*, *ST* and *LCK* files and *C.* or *D.* files for work which can not be accomplished for reasons like bad phone number, login changes etc. A shell file containing commands like

```
program/uuclean   −pTM −pC. −pD.
program/uuclean   −pST −pLCK −n12
```

can be used. Note the "−n12" option causes the *ST* and *LCK* files older than 12 hours to be deleted. The absence of the "−n" option will use a three day time limit.

A daily or weekly shell should also be created to remove or save old *LOGFILE*s. A shell like

```
cp spool/LOGFILE    spool/o.LOGFILE
rm spool/LOGFILE
```

can be used.

Login Entry

One or more logins should be set up for *uucp*. Each of the "/etc/passwd" entries should have the "*program*/uucico" as the shell to be executed. The login directory is not used, but if the system has a special directory for use by the users for sending or receiving file, it should as the login entry. The various logins are used in conjunction with the *USERFILE* to restrict file access. Specifying the *shell* argument limits the login to the use of uucp (*uucico*) only.

File Modes

It is suggested that the owner and file modes of various programs and files be set as follows.

The programs *uucp*, *uux*, *uucico* and *uuxqt* should be owned by the *uucp* login with the "setuid" bit set and only execute permissions (e.g. mode 04111). This will prevent outsiders from modifying the programs to get at a standard *shell* for the *uucp* logins.

The *L.sys*, *SQFILE* and the *USERFILE* which are put in the *program* directory should be owned by the *uucp* login and set with mode 0400.

On the Security of UNIX

Dennis M. Ritchie

Bell Laboratories
Murray Hill, New Jersey 07974

Recently there has been much interest in the security aspects of operating systems and software. At issue is the ability to prevent undesired disclosure of information, destruction of information, and harm to the functioning of the system. This paper discusses the degree of security which can be provided under the UNIX† system and offers a number of hints on how to improve security.

The first fact to face is that UNIX was not developed with security, in any realistic sense, in mind; this fact alone guarantees a vast number of holes. (Actually the same statement can be made with respect to most systems.) The area of security in which UNIX is theoretically weakest is in protecting against crashing or at least crippling the operation of the system. The problem here is not mainly in uncritical acceptance of bad parameters to system calls— there may be bugs in this area, but none are known— but rather in lack of checks for excessive consumption of resources. Most notably, there is no limit on the amount of disk storage used, either in total space allocated or in the number of files or directories. Here is a particularly ghastly shell sequence guaranteed to stop the system:

```
while : ; do
        mkdir x
        cd x
done
```

Either a panic will occur because all the i-nodes on the device are used up, or all the disk blocks will be consumed, thus preventing anyone from writing files on the device.

In this version of the system, users are prevented from creating more than a set number of processes simultaneously, so unless users are in collusion it is unlikely that any one can stop the system altogether. However, creation of 20 or so CPU or disk-bound jobs leaves few resources available for others. Also, if many large jobs are run simultaneously, swap space may run out, causing a panic.

It should be evident that excessive consumption of disk space, files, swap space, and processes can easily occur accidentally in malfunctioning programs as well as at command level. In fact UNIX is essentially defenseless against this kind of abuse, nor is there any easy fix. The best that can be said is that it is generally fairly easy to detect what has happened when disaster strikes, to identify the user responsible, and take appropriate action. In practice, we have found that difficulties in this area are rather rare, but we have not been faced with malicious users, and enjoy a fairly generous supply of resources which have served to cushion us against accidental overconsumption.

The picture is considerably brighter in the area of protection of information from unauthorized perusal and destruction. Here the degree of security seems (almost) adequate theoretically, and the problems lie more in the necessity for care in the actual use of the system.

Each UNIX file has associated with it eleven bits of protection information together with a user identification number and a user-group identification number (UID and GID). Nine of

---

†UNIX is a Trademark of Bell Laboratories.

the protection bits are used to specify independently permission to read, to write, and to execute the file to the user himself, to members of the user's group, and to all other users. Each process generated by or for a user has associated with it an effective UID and a real UID, and an effective and real GID. When an attempt is made to access the file for reading, writing, or execution, the user process's effective UID is compared against the file's UID; if a match is obtained, access is granted provided the read, write, or execute bit respectively for the user himself is present. If the UID for the file and for the process fail to match, but the GID's do match, the group bits are used; if the GID's do not match, the bits for other users are tested. The last two bits of each file's protection information, called the set-UID and set-GID bits, are used only when the file is executed as a program. If, in this case, the set-UID bit is on for the file, the effective UID for the process is changed to the UID associated with the file; the change persists until the process terminates or until the UID changed again by another execution of a set-UID file. Similarly the effective group ID of a process is changed to the GID associated with a file when that file is executed and has the set-GID bit set. The real UID and GID of a process do not change when any file is executed, but only as the result of a privileged system call.

The basic notion of the set-UID and set-GID bits is that one may write a program which is executable by others and which maintains files accessible to others only by that program. The classical example is the game-playing program which maintains records of the scores of its players. The program itself has to read and write the score file, but no one but the game's sponsor can be allowed unrestricted access to the file lest they manipulate the game to their own advantage. The solution is to turn on the set-UID bit of the game program. When, and only when, it is invoked by players of the game, it may update the score file but ordinary programs executed by others cannot access the score.

There are a number of special cases involved in determining access permissions. Since executing a directory as a program is a meaningless operation, the execute-permission bit, for directories, is taken instead to mean permission to search the directory for a given file during the scanning of a path name; thus if a directory has execute permission but no read permission for a given user, he may access files with known names in the directory, but may not read (list) the entire contents of the directory. Write permission on a directory is interpreted to mean that the user may create and delete files in that directory; it is impossible for any user to write directly into any directory.

Another, and from the point of view of security, much more serious special case is that there is a "super user" who is able to read any file and write any non-directory. The superuser is also able to change the protection mode and the owner UID and GID of any file and to invoke privileged system calls. It must be recognized that the mere notion of a super-user is a theoretical, and usually practical, blemish on any protection scheme.

The first necessity for a secure system is of course arranging that all files and directories have the proper protection modes. Traditionally, UNIX software has been exceedingly permissive in this regard; essentially all commands create files readable and writable by everyone. In the current version, this policy may be easily adjusted to suit the needs of the installation or the individual user. Associated with each process and its descendants is a mask, which is in effect and-ed with the mode of every file and directory created by that process. In this way, users can arrange that, by default, all their files are no more accessible than they wish. The standard mask, set by *login,* allows all permissions to the user himself and to his group, but disallows writing by others.

To maintain both data privacy and data integrity, it is necessary, and largely sufficient, to make one's files inaccessible to others. The lack of sufficiency could follow from the existence of set-UID programs created by the user and the possibility of total breach of system security in one of the ways discussed below (or one of the ways not discussed below). For greater protection, an encryption scheme is available. Since the editor is able to create encrypted documents, and the *crypt* command can be used to pipe such documents into the other text-processing programs, the length of time during which cleartext versions need be available is strictly limited.

The encryption scheme used is not one of the strongest known, but it is judged adequate, in the sense that cryptanalysis is likely to require considerably more effort than more direct methods of reading the encrypted files. For example, a user who stores data that he regards as truly secret should be aware that he is implicitly trusting the system administrator not to install a version of the crypt command that stores every typed password in a file.

Needless to say, the system administrators must be at least as careful as their most demanding user to place the correct protection mode on the files under their control. In particular, it is necessary that special files be protected from writing, and probably reading, by ordinary users when they store sensitive files belonging to other users. It is easy to write programs that examine and change files by accessing the device on which the files live.

On the issue of password security, UNIX is probably better than most systems. Passwords are stored in an encrypted form which, in the absence of serious attention from specialists in the field, appears reasonably secure, provided its limitations are understood. In the current version, it is based on a slightly defective version of the Federal DES; it is purposely defective so that easily-available hardware is useless for attempts at exhaustive key-search. Since both the encryption algorithm and the encrypted passwords are available, exhaustive enumeration of potential passwords is still feasible up to a point. We have observed that users choose passwords that are easy to guess: they are short, or from a limited alphabet, or in a dictionary. Passwords should be at least six characters long and randomly chosen from an alphabet which includes digits and special characters.

Of course there also exist feasible non-cryptanalytic ways of finding out passwords. For example: write a program which types out "login:" on the typewriter and copies whatever is typed to a file of your own. Then invoke the command and go away until the victim arrives.

The set-UID (set-GID) notion must be used carefully if any security is to be maintained. The first thing to keep in mind is that a writable set-UID file can have another program copied onto it. For example, if the super-user *(su)* command is writable, anyone can copy the shell onto it and get a password-free version of *su*. A more subtle problem can come from set-UID programs which are not sufficiently careful of what is fed into them. To take an obsolete example, the previous version of the *mail* command was set-UID and owned by the super-user. This version sent mail to the recipient's own directory. The notion was that one should be able to send mail to anyone even if they want to protect their directories from writing. The trouble was that *mail* was rather dumb: anyone could mail someone else's private file to himself. Much more serious is the following scenario: make a file with a line like one in the password file which allows one to log in as the super-user. Then make a link named ".mail" to the password file in some writable directory on the same device as the password file (say /tmp). Finally mail the bogus login line to /tmp/.mail; You can then login as the super-user, clean up the incriminating evidence, and have your will.

The fact that users can mount their own disks and t pes as file systems can be another way of gaining super-user status. Once a disk pack is mounted, the system believes what is on it. Thus one can take a blank disk pack, put on it anything desired, and mount it. There are obvious and unfortunate consequences. For example: a mounted disk with garbage on it will crash the system; one of the files on the mounted disk can easily be a password-free version of *su;* other files can be unprotected entries for special files. The only easy fix for this problem is to forbid the use of *mount* to unprivileged users. A partial solution, not so restrictive, would be to have the *mount* command examine the special file for bad data, set-UID programs owned by others, and accessible special files, and balk at unprivileged invokers.

Password Security: A Case History

Robert Morris

Ken Thompson

Bell Laboratories
Murray Hill, New Jersey 07974

ABSTRACT

This paper describes the history of the design of the password security scheme on a remotely accessed time-sharing system. The present design was the result of countering observed attempts to penetrate the system. The result is a compromise between extreme security and ease of use.

April 3, 1978

INTRODUCTION

Password security on the UNIX† time-sharing system [1] is provided by a collection of programs whose elaborate and strange design is the outgrowth of many years of experience with earlier versions. To help develop a secure system, we have had a continuing competition to devise new ways to attack the security of the system (the bad guy) and, at the same time, to devise new techniques to resist the new attacks (the good guy). This competition has been in the same vein as the competition of long standing between manufacturers of armor plate and those of armor-piercing shells. For this reason, the description that follows will trace the history of the password system rather than simply presenting the program in its current state. In this way, the reasons for the design will be made clearer, as the design cannot be understood without also understanding the potential attacks.

An underlying goal has been to provide password security at minimal inconvenience to the users of the system. For example, those who want to run a completely open system without passwords, or to have passwords only at the option of the individual users, are able to do so, while those who require all of their users to have passwords gain a high degree of security against penetration of the system by unauthorized users.

The password system must be able not only to prevent any access to the system by unauthorized users (i.e. prevent them from logging in at all), but it must also prevent users who are already logged in from doing things that they are not authorized to do. The so called "super-user" password, for example, is especially critical because the super-user has all sorts of permissions and has essentially unlimited access to all system resources.

Password security is of course only one component of overall system security, but it is an essential component. Experience has shown that attempts to penetrate remote-access systems have been astonishingly sophisticated.

Remote-access systems are peculiarly vulnerable to penetration by outsiders as there are threats at the remote terminal, along the communications link, as well as at the computer itself. Although the security of a password encryption algorithm is an interesting intellectual and mathematical problem, it is only one tiny facet of a very large problem. In practice, physical security of the computer, communications security of the communications link, and physical control of the computer itself loom as far more important issues. Perhaps most important of all is control over the actions of ex-employees, since they are not under any direct control and they may have intimate knowledge about the system, its resources, and methods of access. Good system security involves realistic evaluation of the risks not only of deliberate attacks but also of casual unauthorized access and accidental disclosure.

---

†UNIX is a Trademark of Bell Laboratories.

PROLOGUE

The UNIX system was first implemented with a password file that contained the actual passwords of all the users, and for that reason the password file had to be heavily protected against being either read or written. Although historically, this had been the technique used for remote-access systems, it was completely unsatisfactory for several reasons.

The technique is excessively vulnerable to lapses in security. Temporary loss of protection can occur when the password file is being edited or otherwise modified. There is no way to prevent the making of copies by privileged users. Experience with several earlier remote-access systems showed that such lapses occur with frightening frequency. Perhaps the most memorable such occasion occurred in the early 60's when a system administrator on the CTSS system at MIT was editing the password file and another system administrator was editing the daily message that is printed on everyone's terminal on login. Due to a software design error, the temporary editor files of the two users were interchanged and thus, for a time, the password file was printed on every terminal when it was logged in.

Once such a lapse in security has been discovered, everyone's password must be changed, usually simultaneously, at a considerable administrative cost. This is not a great matter, but far more serious is the high probability of such lapses going unnoticed by the system administrators.

Security against unauthorized disclosure of the passwords was, in the last analysis, impossible with this system because, for example, if the contents of the file system are put on to magnetic tape for backup, as they must be, then anyone who has physical access to the tape can read anything on it with no restriction.

Many programs must get information of various kinds about the users of the system, and these programs in general should have no special permission to read the password file. The information which should have been in the password file actually was distributed (or replicated) into a number of files, all of which had to be updated whenever a user was added to or dropped from the system.

THE FIRST SCHEME

The obvious solution is to arrange that the passwords not appear in the system at all, and it is not difficult to decide that this can be done by encrypting each user's password, putting only the encrypted form in the password file, and throwing away his original password (the one that he typed in). When the user later tries to log in to the system, the password that he types is encrypted and compared with the encrypted version in the password file. If the two match, his login attempt is accepted. Such a scheme was first described in [3, p.91ff.]. It also seemed advisable to devise a system in which neither the password file nor the password program itself needed to be protected against being read by anyone.

All that was needed to implement these ideas was to find a means of encryption that was very difficult to invert, even when the encryption program is available. Most of the standard encryption methods used (in the past) for encryption of messages are rather easy to invert. A convenient and rather good encryption program happened to exist on the system at the time; it simulated the M-209 cipher machine [4] used by the U.S. Army during World War II. It turned out that the M-209 program was usable, but with a given key, the ciphers produced by this program are trivial to invert. It is a much more difficult matter to find out the key given the cleartext input and the enciphered output of the program. Therefore, the password was used not as the text to be encrypted but as the key, and a constant was encrypted using this key. The encrypted result was entered into the password file.

ATTACKS ON THE FIRST APPROACH

Suppose that the bad guy has available the text of the password encryption program and the complete password file. Suppose also that he has substantial computing capacity at his disposal.

One obvious approach to penetrating the password mechanism is to attempt to find a general method of inverting the encryption algorithm. Very possibly this can be done, but few successful results have come to light, despite substantial efforts extending over a period of more than five years. The results have not proved to be very useful in penetrating systems.

Another approach to penetration is simply to keep trying potential passwords until one succeeds; this is a general cryptanalytic approach called *key search*. Human beings being what they are, there is a strong tendency for people to choose relatively short and simple passwords that they can remember. Given free choice, most people will choose their passwords from a restricted character set (e.g. all lower-case letters), and will often choose words or names. This human habit makes the key search job a great deal easier.

The critical factor involved in key search is the amount of time needed to encrypt a potential password and to check the result against an entry in the password file. The running time to encrypt one trial password and check the result turned out to be approximately 1.25 milliseconds on a PDP-11/70 when the encryption algorithm was recoded for maximum speed. It is takes essentially no more time to test the encrypted trial password against all the passwords in an entire password file, or for that matter, against any collection of encrypted passwords, perhaps collected from many installations.

If we want to check all passwords of length n that consist entirely of lower-case letters, the number of such passwords is 26^n. If we suppose that the password consists of printable characters only, then the number of possible passwords is somewhat less than 95^n. (The standard system "character erase" and "line kill" characters are, for example, not prime candidates.) We can immediately estimate the running time of a program that will test every password of a given length with all of its characters chosen from some set of characters. The following table gives estimates of the running time required on a PDP-11/70 to test all possible character strings of length n chosen from various sets of characters: namely, all lower-case letters, all lower-case letters plus digits, all alphanumeric characters, all 95 printable ASCII characters, and finally all 128 ASCII characters.

n	26 lower-case letters	36 lower-case letters and digits	62 alphanumeric characters	95 printable characters	all 128 ASCII characters
1	30 msec.	40 msec.	80 msec.	120 msec.	160 msec.
2	800 msec.	2 sec.	5 sec.	11 sec.	20 sec.
3	22 sec.	58 sec.	5 min.	17 min.	43 min.
4	10 min.	35 min.	5 hrs.	28 hrs.	93 hrs.
5	4 hrs.	21 hrs.	318 hrs.		
6	107 hrs.				

One has to conclude that it is no great matter for someone with access to a PDP-11 to test all lower-case alphabetic strings up to length five and, given access to the machine for, say, several weekends, to test all such strings up to six characters in length. By using such a program against a collection of actual encrypted passwords, a substantial fraction of all the passwords will be found.

Another profitable approach for the bad guy is to use the word list from a dictionary or to use a list of names. For example, a large commercial dictionary contains typicallly about 250,000 words; these words can be checked in about five minutes. Again, a noticeable fraction of any collection of passwords will be found. Improvements and extensions will be (and have been) found by a determined bad guy. Some "good" things to try are:

- The dictionary with the words spelled backwards.

- A list of first names (best obtained from some mailing list). Last names, street names, and city names also work well.

- The above with initial upper-case letters.

- All valid license plate numbers in your state. (This takes about five hours in New Jersey.)

- Room numbers, social security numbers, telephone numbers, and the like.

The authors have conducted experiments to try to determine typical users' habits in the choice of passwords when no constraint is put on their choice. The results were disappointing, except to the bad guy. In a collection of 3,289 passwords gathered from many users over a long period of time;

15 were a single ASCII character;

72 were strings of two ASCII characters;

464 were strings of three ASCII characters;

477 were string of four alphamerics;

706 were five letters, all upper-case or all lower-case;

605 were six letters, all lower-case.

An additional 492 passwords appeared in various available dictionaries, name lists, and the like. A total of 2,831, or 86% of this sample of passwords fell into one of these classes.

There was, of course, considerable overlap between the dictionary results and the character string searches. The dictionary search alone, which required only five minutes to run, produced about one third of the passwords.

Users could be urged (or forced) to use either longer passwords or passwords chosen from a larger character set, or the system could itself choose passwords for the users.

AN ANECDOTE

An entertaining and instructive example is the attempt made at one installation to force users to use less predictable passwords. The users did not choose their own passwords; the system supplied them. The supplied passwords were eight characters long and were taken from the character set consisting of lower-case letters and digits. They were generated by a pseudo-random number generator with only 2^{15} starting values. The time required to search (again on a PDP-11/70) through all character strings of length 8 from a 36-character alphabet is 112 years.

Unfortunately, only 2^{15} of them need be looked at, because that is the number of possible outputs of the random number generator. The bad guy did, in fact, generate and test each of these strings and found every one of the system-generated passwords using a total of only about one minute of machine time.

IMPROVEMENTS TO THE FIRST APPROACH

1. Slower Encryption

Obviously, the first algorithm used was far too fast. The announcement of the DES encryption algorithm [2] by the National Bureau of Standards was timely and fortunate. The DES is, by design, hard to invert, but equally valuable is the fact that it is extremely slow when implemented in software. The DES was implemented and used in the following way: The first eight characters of the user's password are used as a key for the DES; then the algorithm is used to encrypt a constant. Although this constant is zero at the moment, it is easily accessible and can be made installation-dependent. Then the DES algorithm is iterated 25 times and the resulting 64 bits are repacked to become a string of 11 printable characters.

2. Less Predictable Passwords

The password entry program was modified so as to urge the user to use more obscure passwords. If the user enters an alphabetic password (all upper-case or all lower-case) shorter than six characters, or a password from a larger character set shorter than five characters, then the program asks him to enter a longer password. This further reduces the efficacy of key search.

These improvements make it exceedingly difficult to find any individual password. The user is warned of the risks and if he cooperates, he is very safe indeed. On the other hand, he is not prevented from using his spouse's name if he wants to.

3. Salted Passwords

The key search technique is still likely to turn up a few passwords when it is used on a large collection of passwords, and it seemed wise to make this task as difficult as possible. To this end, when a password is first entered, the password program obtains a 12-bit random number (by reading the real-time clock) and appends this to the password typed in by the user. The concatenated string is encrypted and both the 12-bit random quantity (called the *salt*) and the 64-bit result of the encryption are entered into the password file.

When the user later logs in to the system, the 12-bit quantity is extracted from the password file and appended to the typed password. The encrypted result is required, as before, to be the same as the remaining 64 bits in the password file. This modification does not increase the task of finding any individual password, starting from scratch, but now the work of testing a given character string against a large collection of encrypted passwords has been multiplied by 4096 (2^{12}). The reason for this is that there are 4096 encrypted versions of each password and one of them has been picked more or less at random by the system.

With this modification, it is likely that the bad guy can spend days of computer time trying to find a password on a system with hundreds of passwords, and find none at all. More important is the fact that it becomes impractical to prepare an encrypted dictionary in advance. Such an encrypted dictionary could be used to crack new passwords in milliseconds when they appear.

There is a (not inadvertent) side effect of this modification. It becomes nearly impossible to find out whether a person with passwords on two or more systems has used the same password on all of them, unless you already know that.

4. The Threat of the DES Chip

Chips to perform the DES encryption are already commercially available and they are very fast. The use of such a chip speeds up the process of password hunting by three orders of magnitude. To avert this possibility, one of the internal tables of the DES algorithm (in particular, the so-called E-table) is changed in a way that depends on the 12-bit random number. The E-table is inseparably wired into the DES chip, so that the commercial chip cannot be used. Obviously, the bad guy could have his own chip designed and built, but the cost would be unthinkable.

5. A Subtle Point

To login successfully on the UNIX system, it is necessary after dialing in to type a valid user name, and then the correct password for that user name. It is poor design to write the login command in such a way that it tells an interloper when he has typed in a invalid user name. The response to an invalid name should be identical to that for a valid name.

When the slow encryption algorithm was first implemented, the encryption was done only if the user name was valid, because otherwise there was no encrypted password to compare with the supplied password. The result was that the response was delayed by about one-half second if the name was valid, but was immediate if invalid. The bad guy could find out whether a particular user name was valid. The routine was modified to do the encryption in either case.

CONCLUSIONS

On the issue of password security, UNIX is probably better than most systems. The use of encrypted passwords appears reasonably secure in the absence of serious attention of experts in the field.

It is also worth some effort to conceal even the encrypted passwords. Some UNIX systems have instituted what is called an "external security code" that must be typed when dialing into the system, but before logging in. If this code is changed periodically, then someone with an old password will likely be prevented from using it.

Whenever any security procedure is instituted that attempts to deny access to unauthorized persons, it is wise to keep a record of both successful and unsuccessful attempts to get at the secured resource. Just as an out-of-hours visitor to a computer center normally must not only identify himself, but a record is usually also kept of his entry. Just so, it is a wise precaution to make and keep a record of all attempts to log into a remote-access time-sharing system, and certainly all unsuccessful attempts.

Bad guys fall on a spectrum whose one end is someone with ordinary access to a system and whose goal is to find out a particular password (usually that of the super-user) and, at the other end, someone who wishes to collect as much password information as possible from as many systems as possible. Most of the work reported here serves to frustrate the latter type; our experience indicates that the former type of bad guy never was very successful.

We recognize that a time-sharing system must operate in a hostile environment. We did not attempt to hide the security aspects of the operating system, thereby playing the customary make-believe game in which weaknesses of the system are not discussed no matter how apparent. Rather we advertised the password algorithm and invited attack in the belief that this approach would minimize future trouble. The approach has been successful.

References

[1] Ritchie, D.M. and Thompson, K. The UNIX Time-Sharing System. *Comm. ACM* **17** (July 1974), pp. 365-375.

[2] *Proposed Federal Information Processing Data Encryption Standard.* Federal Register (40FR12134), March 17, 1975

[3] Wilkes, M. V. *Time-Sharing Computer Systems.* American Elsevier, New York, (1968).

[4] U. S. Patent Number 2,089,603.

A Short Glossary of the UNIX System

M. D. McIlroy

This glossary covers major terms that have special meaning for the UNIX system. It excludes ordinary terms of art such as "ASCII", "compiler", "address space", or "byte". It also excludes most terms peculiar to a single part of UNIX, e.g. "diversion" (troff), "enumeration" (C), or "pattern space" (sed).

a.out the default name of a freshly compiled *executable file*, pronounced "a-dot-out"; historically a.out signified assembler output; cf. *object file*.

absolute pathname same as *full pathname*.

alarm a *signal* scheduled by the clock.

archive 1. a collection of data gathered from several *files* into one file. 2. especially, such a collection gathered by *ar*(1) for use as a *library*.

argument 1. a string made available to a *process* upon *executing* a *file*. 2. a string in a *command*, which the *shell* will pass to the command program as an argument (sense 1).

ASCII file same as *text file*.

automatic persistent only during the invocation of a procedure, said of data belonging to a *process;* automatic data occupies the *stack segment;* cf. *static*.

background running independently of a terminal, said of a *process;* converse of *foreground*.

block the basic unit of *buffering* in the *kernel*, 512 bytes in the 7th edition.

block device a *device* upon which a *file system* (sense 1) can be *mounted*, typically a permanent storage device such as a tape or disk drive, so called because data transfers to the device occur by *blocks;* cf. *character device*.

boot to start the operating system, so called because the *kernel* must bootstrap itself from secondary store into an empty machine.

boot block the first block of a *file system* (sense 1), which is reserved for a *booting* program for the *device*.

break 1. an out-of-band signal on an asynchronous data line arising from the "break" or "interrupt" key on a terminal; before *logging in* a break causes a change in baud rate; thereafter it is interpreted as an *interrupt*. 2. a control statement in the C language. 3. the *program break*. 4. in *troff*(1), a point in running text where a new line must begin.

bss segment see *segment*.

buffer 1. a staging area for input-output where arbitrary-length transactions are collected into convenient units for system operations; the *file system* (sense 3) uses buffers, as does *stdio*. 2. to use buffers.

buffer pool a region of store available to the *file system* (sense 3) for holding *blocks;* all but *raw* (sense 2) input-output for *block devices* goes through the buffer pool so read and write operations may be independent of device blocks.

cbreak a mode of terminal input in which every character not a *special character* becomes available to a *read*(2) operation as soon as it is typed, instead of being *buffered* up to a *newline* or *EOT* character.

character 1. a unit of store, usually 8 bits; a byte. 2. a token of the ASCII code, with octal value between 0 and 0177.

character device a *device* upon which a *file system* (sense 1) cannot be *mounted*, such as a terminal or the *null device*.

child process see *fork*.

close to make an *open file* unavailable for input or output; converse of *open*.

command 1. an instruction to the *shell*, usually to run a *program* (sense 1). 2. by extension, any *executable file*, especially a *utility program*.

command file same as *shell script*.

control character an ASCII character with octal code 0-037 or 0177, which does not print but may otherwise affect the behavior of a terminal; cf. *special character*.

control terminal the terminal associated with a *process* from which the process may receive *interrupt*, *quit*, and *hangup* signals; cf. *process group*.

cooked not *raw* (sense 1); terminal input is usually cooked.

core file a *core image* of a terminated *process* saved for debugging; a core file is created under the name "core" in the *current directory* of the process.

core image a copy of all the *segments* of an executing program; the copy may exist in main store, in the *swap area*, or in a *core file*.

create to *open* a file for writing, bringing it into existence as a *plain file* if necessary, and discarding any data it may have contained previously; cf. *unlink*.

current directory, working directory the directory from which *relative pathnames* begin; a current directory is associated with each *process*.

daemon a *background* process, often perpetual, that performs a system-wide public function, e.g. *calendar*(1) and *cron*(8); the affected spelling is an ancient legacy.

data segment see *segment*.

data space, D-space see *separate*.

device 1. a *file* (sense 2) that is not a *plain file* or a *directory*, such as a tape drive, a terminal, a span of *blocks* on a disk drive, or the *null device*; a *special file*. 2. a physical input-output unit.

directory a catalog of *filenames*; the organizing principle of the *file system* (sense 2), a directory consists of *entries* which specify further *files* (sense 2, including directories), and constitutes a node of the *directory tree*.

directory entry, entry 1. an association of a name with an *inode number* appearing as an element of a *directory*. 2. the name part of such an association.

directory hierarchy, directory tree the tree of all *directories*, in which each is reachable from the *root* via a chain of *subdirectories*.

echo to transmit characters received from a terminal back to it; the technique of echoing to a *full duplex* terminal provides acknowledgement of typed input.

effective userid see *set userid*.

end of file the condition of the *read pointer* being past the last character of an *open file*; end of file is signified by a read operation returning zero bytes, or by an EOF return from functions of the *stdio* package; end of file may be simulated from a terminal by typing EOT (control-D) after a *newline*.

entry see *directory entry*.

environment 1. a set of strings, distinct from the *arguments*, made available to a *process* when it *executes* a *file*; the environment is usually inherited across *exec*(2) operations. 2. a specific environment (sense 2) maintained by the *shell*. 3. a nebulously identified way of doing things, as in "interactive environment": deprecated usage, not always expunged from these manuals.

EOT, EOT character 1. the ASCII "end of transmission" character, control-D, octal code 04. 2. a character that ends (and is excluded from) data obtained by *read*(2) from a terminal; EOT at the beginning of a line causes the *end of file* condition.

epoch the zero of UNIX clocks, 00:00:00 Greenwich Mean Time, January 1, 1970.

erase character a *special character* (sense 2), which, when received from a terminal, is deleted together with the character immediately preceding it on the line; usually defaulted to "#" or backspace, the erase character may be changed by *stty*(1); cf. *kill character*.

escape character 1. The ASCII character ESC, octal 033. 2. a *special character* that may cause the following character to have other than its usual meaning; the default escape character in terminal input is "\".

executable file, object program 1. an object file that is ready to be copied into the address space of a *process* to run as the code of that process. 2. a file that has execute *permission*, either an *executable file* or a *shell script*.

execute 1. (informally) run a *program*. 2. replace the *text segment* and *data segments* of a *process* with a given *program* (sense 1).

exit to terminate a *process*; exit is voluntary, in contrast to *kill*.

exit status, return code an integer value denoting the outcome of a *process*, including an indication of the cause of termination.

external known beyond the scope of a single compilation, said of names of data and functions in a program.

file 1. in general, a potential source of input or destination for output. 2. most specifically, an *inode* and/or associated contents, i.e. a *plain file*, a *special file*, or a *directory*. 3. a *directory entry*; several directory entries may name the same file (sense 2). 4. most loosely, a *plain file*.

file descriptor a conventional integer quantity that designates an *open file*; cf. *stream*.

file system 1. a collection of *files* that can be *mounted* on a block *special file*; each file of a file system appears exactly once in the *i-list* of the file system and is accessible via some *path* from the *root* directory of the file system. 2. the collection of all *files* on a computer. 3. the part of the kernel that deals with file systems (sense 1).

filename 1. a *pathname*. 2. the last component name in a pathname.

filter a *program* (sense 1) that reads from the *standard input* and writes on the *standard output*, so called because it can be used as a data-transformer in a *pipeline*.

flag an *option* for a *command*.

flush to empty a *buffer*, for example to throw away unwanted input-output upon *interrupt* or to release output from the clutches of *stdio*.

foreground running under direct control of a terminal, said of a *process*; converse of *background*.

fork to split one *process* into two, the **parent process** and **child process,** with separate, but initially identical, *text, data,* and *stack segments*.

free list in a *file system* (sense 1), the list of *blocks* that are not occupied by data.

full duplex 1. capable of carrying information simultaneously in both directions, said of a communication channel. 2. transmitting what is typed while printing what is received, said of a terminal, or of terminal communication; cf. *half duplex* and *echo*.

global same as *external*.

group 1. a set of *permissions* alternative to *owner* permissions for access to a *file*. 2. a set of *userids* that may assume the privileges of a group (sense 1). 3. the *groupid* of a *file*.

groupid an integer value, usually associated with one or more *login names*; as the *userid* of a process becomes the *owner* of files *created* by the process, so the groupid of a process becomes the *group* (sense 3) of such files.

half duplex 1. capable of carrying information in both directions, but not simultaneously, said of a communication channel. 2. transmitting (usually typing what is transmitted) and receiving, but not simultaneously, said of a terminal; cf. *full duplex*.

hangup a *signal* indicating that a user's terminal has been disconnected.

here file in a *shell script*, literally given input data for a *command*; here files are introduced by "<<".

hole a gap in a *plain file* caused by *seeking* while writing; *read*(2) takes data in holes to be zero; a *block* in a hole occupies no space in its *file system*.

home directory 1. the *current directory* established for each user upon *logging in*. 2. a part of the *environment* maintained by the *shell*, used in particular for a default destination for the *cd* command.

i-list the index to a *file system* (sense 1) listing all the *inodes (files)* of the file system; cf. *inode number*.

include file a *file*, usually containing shared data declarations, that is to be copied into source programs as they are compiled.

inode an element of a *file system* (sense 1); an inode specifies all properties of a particular *file* and locates the file's contents, if any.

inode number, i-number the position of an *inode* in the *i-list* of a *file system* (sense 1).

instruction space, I-space see *separate*.

interrupt 1. a *signal* that normally terminates a *process*, caused by a *break* (sense 1) or an *interrupt character;* cf. *quit*. 2. loosely, any *signal*.

interrupt character a character (normally ASCII DEL) that, when typed on a *control terminal*, causes an *interrupt*.

kernel the UNIX system proper; resident code that implements the *system calls*.

kill 1. a particular *signal* guaranteed to terminate a *process*. 2. by extension, to send any *signal* to a *process*. 3. the *kill character*.

kill character a *special character*, which, when received from a terminal, is deleted together with all preceding characters on the line; defaulted to "@", the kill character may be changed by *stty*(1); cf. *erase character*.

library an *archive* of *object files* from which the *link editor* may select functions and data as needed.

line in a *text file*, a sequence of bytes terminated by a *newline*.

link 1. to add an entry for an existing *file* to a directory; converse of *unlink*. 2. by extension, a *directory entry*.

link count the number of *directory entries* that pertain to an *inode;* a *file* ceases to exist when its link count becomes zero and it is not *open*.

link editor, loader the utility *ld*(1), which combines separately compiled *object files* into single *executable files*.

loader same as *link editor*.

log in to identify one's self as a user and start a computing session.

login 1. the *program* that controls logging in. 2. the act of *logging in*.

login name the name by which a person identifies himself upon *logging in;* cf. *userid*.

makefile a list of dependencies among files and recipes for updating them, usually by recompilation, used by *make*(1) to maintain self-consistent software.

mode, file mode the *permissions* of a *file;* colloquially referred to by a 3-digit octal number, e.g. "a 755 file"; see *chmod*(1).

mount to extend the *directory hierarchy* by associating the *root* of a *file system* (sense 1) with a *directory entry* in an already mounted file system; converse is **unmount,** spelled "umount".

namelist same as *symbol table*.

newline the combined function of carriage return and line feed, represented by the ASCII character LF, octal value 012; separates *lines* in a *text file;* newline is evoked by the "return" key on most terminals.

nice mode 1. the priority level of a *process*. 2. a low priority level, so called because the *process* gives way to others.

null device a
device (sense 1) that always yields *end of file* on reading and discards all data written on it.

object file a *file* of machine language code and data; object files are produced from source programs by compilers and from other object files and *libraries* by the *link editor;* an object file that is ready to run is an *executable file*.

other 1. a set of *permissions* regulating access to a *file* by processes with *userid* different from the *owner* and *groupid* different from the *group* of the file. 2. the customary name of the default *group* (sense 2) assigned upon *login*.

open to make a *file* available for writing or reading, with the *write pointer* or *read pointer* positioned at byte 0; converse of *close*; cf. *create*.

open file 1. the destination for input or output obtained by *opening* a *file* or creating a *pipe*; a *file descriptor*; open files are shared across *forks* and persist across *executes*. 2. loosely, a file that has been opened, however an open file (sense 1) need not exist in a *file system* (sense 1), and a file (sense 2) may be the destination of several *open files* simultaneously.

option an *argument* that affects the way a *command* works; option names customarily begin with "−".

owner the *userid* of the *process* that created a *file*; the owner has distinctive *permissions* for a file.

parent directory the *directory* next nearer the *root* than a given directory; the inverse of a *subdirectory*; the parent of a given directory appears in it as the *entry* "..".

parent process see *fork*.

password a secret word used to confirm a user's right to *log in* under a particular *userid*; passwords are encrypted by a one-way algorithm and kept in the *password file*.

password file a record of all *login names* with the *password, userid, groupid, home directory*, and *shell* (sense 2) for each, used to control access to the system.

path, pathname a chain of names designating a *file*; a **relative pathname** leads from the *current directory*, for example, a path to *directory* A, thence to directory B, thence to *file* C is denoted A/B/C; a **full pathname** begins at the *root*, indicated by an initial "/", as in /A/B/C.

permission a right to access a *file* in a particular way: read, write, execute (or look up in, if a directory); permissions are granted separately to *owner, group*, and *others*. **permission bit** a permission, so called because each permission is encoded into one bit in an *inode*.

pipe a direct input-output connection between *processes*, whereby data written on an *open file* in one process becomes available for reading in another.

pipeline a sequence of *programs* (sense 1) connected by *pipes*.

plain file a *file* that is neither a *special file* nor a *directory*; plain files are the customary repository of data.

priority see *nice mode*.

process a connected sequence of computation; a process is characterized by a *core image* with instruction location counter, *current directory*, a set of *open files*, *control terminal, userid*, and *groupid*.

process group a set of processes that share a *control terminal* and among which *signals* may be broadcast by *kill*(2); a process group is created upon *logging in* and augmented by *forking*.

process number, process id an integer that identifies a *process*.

profile 1. an optional *shell script*, ".profile", conventionally used by the *shell* upon *logging in* to establish the *environment* (sense 3) and other working conditions customary to a particular user. 2. to collect a histogram of values of the instruction location counter of a *process*.

program 1. an *executable file*. 2. a running process. 3. all the usual meanings.

program break the first address beyond the *static* data accessible to a *process*; the program break may be adjusted by *sbrk*(2).

quit a *signal* that normally terminates a *process*, caused by a **quit character** (normally control-\); quit differs from *interrupt* in that quit creates a *core file* for the terminated process.

random library a *library* that contains an index to *external* names; a library is made into a random library by *ranlib*(1); nonrandom libraries must be carefully ordered for the *link editor* to cope with cross references among the subroutines.

raw 1. a mode of terminal input in which every character typed is passed to a reading *process* and *special characters* lose their special character; converse of *cooked*. 2. said of input-output to a *raw device*.

raw device a *block device*, read and write operations to which are not buffered, and are synchronized to natural records of the physical device.

read ahead to fill input *buffers* in the *kernel* in advance of read(2) operations.

read pointer the number of the next byte that *read*(2) would normally obtain from an *open file;* same as *write pointer*.

real userid see *set userid*.

regular expression 1. an expression denoting a set of strings in a notation due to Kleene. 2. especially, a restricted and modified form regular expression used for pattern-matching in *ed*(1), *grep*(1), etc.

relative pathname see *pathname*.

relocation bits, relocation information information in an *object file* that tells the *link editor* how to adjust addresses when combining it with other *object files;* "bits" is a fossilized misnomer.

return code same as *exit status*.

root a distinguished directory that constitutes the origin of the *directory hierarchy;* the root of an entire UNIX system has the conventional *pathname* "/".

runcom a *shell script*, obsolete.

schedule to assign resources — main store and CPU time — to *processes*. **scheduler** a permanent *process*, with *process number* 1, and associated *kernel* facilities that do scheduling.

search path in the *shell*, a list of *pathnames* of *directories* that determines the meaning of a *command* name; a command name is prefixed with members of the search path in turn until a pathname of an *executable file* results.

seek to set the *read pointer* or *write pointer* to a specified place in an *open file*.

segment a contiguous range of the address space of a *process* with consistent store access capabilities; the four segments are (i) the **text segment,** occupied by executable code, (ii) the **data segment,** occupied by *static* data that is specifically initialized, (iii) the **bss segment,** occupied by static data that is initialized by default to zero values, and (iv) the **stack segment,** occupied by *automatic* data, see *stack;* sometimes (ii), (iii), and (iv) are collectively called data segments.

separate 1. a mode of operating a PDP-11 in which the *text segment* and the *data segments* of a process have distinct address spaces; a given address value refers to a store location in the **instruction space** when accessing an instruction and in the **data space** when accessing data. 2. intended to use separate address spaces, said of an *executable file*.

set userid a special *permission* for an *executable file* that causes a *process* executing it to have the access rights of the *owner* of the file; the owner's *userid* becomes the **effective userid** of the process, distinguished from the **real userid** under which the process began. **set userid bit** the associated *permission bit*.

shared text a *text segment*, one copy of which may be used simultaneously by more than one *process*.

shell 1. the program *sh*(1), which causes other programs to be executed on *command;* the shell is usually started on a user's behalf when the user *logs in*. 2. by analogy, any program started upon logging in.

shell script, command file a *file* of *commands* taken as input to the *shell*.

signal an exceptional occurrence that causes a *process* to terminate or divert from the normal flow of control; cf. *interrupt, kill*.

sleep to cease activity for a specified time, or until a *signal* occurs, said of a *process*.

special character a character, which, when typed at a terminal, modifies the input or affects the behavior of *processes* for which that terminal is the *control terminal;* examples are the *interrupt character, erase character,* and *EOT character*.

special file an *inode* that designates a *device*, further categorized as either (i) a **block special file** describing a *block device*, or (ii) a **character special file** describing a *character device*.

spool to collect and serialize output from multiple *processes* competing for a single output service.

spooler a *daemon* that spools. **spool area** a *directory* in which a spooler collects work.

stack a *segment* of the address space into which *automatic* data and subroutine linkage information is allocated in last-in-first-out fashion; the stack occupies the largest data addresses and grows downward towards *static* data.

strip remove the *symbol table* and *relocation bits* from an *executable file*.

standard input, standard output, standard error *open files*, customarily available when a *process* begins, with *file descriptors* 0, 1, 2 and *stdio* names "stdin", "stdout", "stderr"; where possible, utilities by default read from the standard input, write on the standard output, and place error comments on the standard error file.

static persistent throughout a process, said of data; static data occupies the *data segment* and the *bss segment;* cf. *automatic.*

status see *exit status.*

stdio, standard input-output a collection of functions for formatted and character-by-character input-output at a higher level than the basic *read, write,* and *open*(1) operations; stdio is described in Volume 1, Section 3S.

sticky file a special *permission* for a *shared text* file that causes a copy of the *text segment* to be retained in the *swap area* to improve system response. **sticky bit** the associated *permission bit.*

stream an *open file* with *buffering* superimposed by the *stdio* package.

subdirectory a *directory* that appears as an *entry* in another.

super block the second *block* in a *file system* (sense 1), which describes the allocation of space in the file system; cf. *boot block.*

super-user *userid* 0, which can access any *file* regardless of *permissions* and can perform certain privileged *system calls,* e.g. setting the clock.

swap to move the *core image* of an executing program between main and secondary store to make room for other *processes.*

swap area the part of secondary store to which *core images* are *swapped;* the swap area is disjoint from the *file system.*

symbol table information in an *object file* about the names of data and functions in that file; the symbol table and *relocation bits* are used by the *link editor* and by the debugger *adb*(1).

system call a basic operation performed by the UNIX kernel; system calls are described in Volume 1, Section 2.

text see *text file, segment.*

text file, ASCII file a *file,* the bytes of which are understood to be in ASCII code.

text segment see *segment.*

umask a list of *permissions* that will be denied for files *created* by a *process,* so called because the list is expressed as a *mode* bit mask.

UNIX the name of an operating system, not an acronym for anything; a trademark of Bell Laboratories, UNIX should be used as an adjective: "UNIX system", "UNIX software", "UNIX editor", etc.

unlink to remove an *entry* from a *directory;* converse to *link* and *create.*

usenet an informal, nationwide computer network based on *uucp*(1).

userid an integer value, usually associated with a *login name;* the userid of a *process* becomes the *owner* of files *created* by the process and descendent *(forked)* processes.

utility, utility program a standard, generally useful, permanently available *program.*

wait to suspend running until the termination of another *process;* only a *parent process* can wait for one of its *child processes.*

working directory same as *current directory.*

write behind to *buffer* data for writing to a *device* at a convenient time without holding up the computation of a writing *process.*

write pointer the number of the next byte that *write*(2) would normally fill in an *open file;* same as *read pointer.*

"a" format code, in Fortran 77, 417
accents, 130
accept action, of Yacc parser, 360, 374
access control scheme, 23
 See also security
accounting, 9
active processes, determination of, 8
adb, 3, 11, 52
 address maps, 345–346
 advanced breakpoint usage, 329–331
 and combinations of formatting requests, 332–334
 command summary, 350
 and conversion of values from one representation to another, 334
 current address dot, 324–325
 and debugging A core image, 326–327
 and debugging C programs, 326–331
 and directory and i-node dumps, 334, 349
 and example of C program with pointer bug, 337–338
 expressions, 350
 formats, 325, 350
 and formatting and patching, 347–348
 general form of requests, 325
 and ilist dump, 334
 invocation of, 324
 and maps, 331–332
 and multiple function C program for stack trace illustration, 339–340
 multiple functions, 327
 output for C program with breakpoints, 344
 and patching files, 335
 problems with, 335–336
 and setting breakpoints, 328–329
 tabs decoding, 341–343
 usage, 323, 324
addition, DC, 464
additive operators
 BC, 480
 in C language, 253–254
addresses
 number of, commands in sed and, 443–444
 and selection of lines for editing with sed, 442–444
Advanced Editing on UNIX, 55
algorithmic languages, 13
allocator, DC, 463–464
alphabetic sorting, 8, 45
alternate returns, in Fortran 77, 412
alternative notation, tbl command for, 161
ampersand (&), 71
 at end of command line, 48
 and shell, 83
 as special character in ed, 64
append command "a," 55–56, 88–89
arbitrary characters, Lex, 391
archives
 creation, 10
 maintenance, 10
 retrieval, 10
 updating by date, 10
arguments
 in Fortran 77, 408–409
 and M4 macro processor, 436
 and macros in nroff/troff, 210
 in UNIX program, 302
 values between calls, in Fortran 77, 411–412
 See also dummy procedure arguments; macros with arguments
arithmetic, 18
 in C language, 249
 and DC, 464
 and M4 micro processor, 436–437
 and troff, 239–240
 and Yacc, 367–369, 378–379
arithmetic test, 18
arrays
 awk, 456
 in Fortran 77, 413
 operations in C language with, 269
(as) Assembler, 10
 blank and tab characters, 484
 comments, 484
 constants, 484
 diagnostics, 494

expressions, 486–489
 identifiers, 483–484
 lexical conventions, 483
 location counter, 485
 machine instructions, 490–493
 operators, 484
 pseudo-operations, 489–490
 regeneration, 507
 relocation counter, 493
 segments, 484–485
 statements, 485–486
 system calls, 494
 usage, 423
ASCII
 conversion to card-image form, 18
 conversion to paper tape form, 18
ASCII files, sorting or merging, 17
assignment operators
 BC, 480
 in C language, 255–256
 older forms of, lint detection of, 283–284
assignment statements, as, 486
assignments, awk, 455
at-sign (@)
 as symbol in copy, 41
 and typing errors, 41
awk, 17, 50
 actions, 454–456
 design, 456–457
 execution times for programs vs. sed and lex, 459
 field variables, 455
 implementation, 457
 patterns, 453–454
 printing, 453
 records and fields, 452–453
 regular expressions, 454
 usage, 452, 457

Backgammon, 18
background commands, 83
backslash character (\), 68
 and ed, 63
 erasing, 41
backspaces
 list command and visibility of, 66
 in nroff/troff, 214
backup, 8–9
bar, in mathematical typesetting, 151
bases, in BC language, 471–472
BC language, 13, 469–482
 assignment statements, 475
 and bases, 471–472
 comment convention, 476
 constants, 477
 control statements, 474–475, 481–482
 exiting, 476
 expressions, 477–480
 functions, 472–473
 identifiers, 477
 keywords, 477
 and library of math functions, 476
 notation, 477
 scaling, 472
 storage classes, 481
 subscripted variables, 473–474
 tokens, 477
 usage, 469, 470
BEGIN pattern, awk, 453
bibliographic citations, 16
binary initialization constants, in Fortran 77, 405
bitwise AND operator, in C language, 254
bitwise exclusive OR operator, in C language, 254
bitwise inclusive OR operator, in C language, 255
BJ, 18
Blackjack, 18
blank interpretation, 92
blank characters, as, 484
blank lines, in Fortran 77 and 66, 411
blanks, in numeric input fields, and formatted I/O of Fortran 77, 417
block. See compound statement
block data statements, in Fortran 77, 411
block device drivers, 527–528
block device interface, 525–527
block if, in Fortran 77, 415

block I/O system, 516
BNF syntax specifications, 14
Boolean operations, and Fortran 77, 406
boxes, 129
braces
 in C language, 261
 in mathematical typesetting, 140–141, 149
brackets, 70–71
 calculation of sizes, 16
 large, in nroff/troff, 216
break, in Ratfor, 428
"break" key, 40–41
 and stopping programs, 42
break statement
 in C language, 264
 and lint, 280–281
 in Ratfor, 426
breakpoints
 ADB output for, 344
 ADB setting of, 328–329
 advanced usage with ADB, 329–331
buffer, 24
 printing contents of, 57–58

c command, 61–62
C compiler, 529–543
 code generation, 534–542
 delaying and reordering, 542–543
 expression optimization, 532–534
 and intermediate language, 529–532
 list of operators, 530–532
 regeneration, 507–508
 See also portable C compiler
C language, 3
 anachronisms, 271
 arithmetic conversions in, 250–251
 arithmetic types in, 249
 and BC language, 470
 characters in, 250
 comments in, 247
 compiler control lines in, 267–268
 constant expressions in, 270
 constants in, 248
 conversions, 250
 conversions of floating values to integral types in, 250
 debugging, see ADB
 declarations in, 256–262
 expressions in, 251–256
 external definitions in, 265–266
 float and double in, 250
 and Fortran 77 compiler, 403
 hardware characteristics, 248–249
 identifiers in, 247, 249
 implicit declarations in, 268
 initialization in, 260–261
 integers in, 249, 250
 keywords, 247–248
 and Lex, see Lex
 lexical conventions, 247
 lint program checker, see lint
 lvalues, 250
 objects, 250
 operations with arrays, pointers, and subscripts in, 269
 operations with explicit pointer conversions with, 269–270
 operations with functions in, 268–269
 operations with structures and unions in, 268
 pointers and integers in, 250
 portability considerations with, 270
 and prog, 292–293
 programming in, 51–52
 recent changes in, 277
 scope rules in, 266
 stack trace for, 11
 statements in, 262–265
 storage classes, 249
 strings in, 248
 supporting programs with, 52
 syntax notation, 249, 272–276
 type names in, 261–262
 typedef in, 262
 unsigned integers in, 250
 usage, 247
 See also UNIX programming; Yacc
CAI scripts
 advantages of, 109

CAI scripts (*continued*)
  available, 109
  description of, 112–113
  sample dialog from basic files script, 111
  See also LEARN
calendar printing, 18
calling in, 121
calls. *See* commands
card-guessing game, 19
caret. *See* circumflex
case notation, 88–89
cat, 6, 44
cc command, 402
  and MAKE, 11
change command "c," 61–62
character classes, Lex, 391
character constants
  in C language, 248
  in Fortran 77, 413–414, 416
character counts, 17
  and ed, 56–57
  and Lex, 392–393
character data type, in Fortran 77, 412
character device drivers, 523–525
character input streams, lexical processing
  of. *See* Lex
character I/O system, 516, 517
character patterns, searching for, 11
character sequences, in mathematical typesetting, 155
character sets, Lex, 399
character size, in nroff/troff, 198, 204–206
character strings
  assignment in Fortran 77, 405, 414
  concatenation in Fortran 77, 414
  and initialization of portable C compiler,
    553
character throughput, of UNIX dial-up network, 574–575
character translations, 17
  nroff/troff commands for, 199, 214
characters
  C language, 249, 250
  nonportable, line and, 282
  in Lex, 391
  repeated tbl commands for, 162
Checkers, 18
Chess, 18
child process, 27
  and implementation of shell, 30–31
chmod command, 87
circumflex "^", 69, 148
close, 520
  in Fortran, 77, 419
  in I/O library, 308–310
code generation, for C compiler, 534–542,
  556–560
colon, in Fortran 77 I/O operation, 416
column entries, and tbl input commands,
  159, 161
comfile, commands in, 31
command files, 30
  locating, 28
command line, 28
command separators, 30
commands, 74
  ADB, 350
  awk, 452
  background, 83
  in BC language, 476
  compiled output for DC, 464–467
  for compiling and loading Fortran and For-
    tran-related files, 402
  DC, 461–463
  for document typing, 126, 132
  ed, 55, 64
  errors in, 56
  execution by shell, 103–104
  execution by uucp, 584
  failing to execute, 100–101
  and file names, 84–85
  filter, 84
  format with sed, 441
  GCOS on Lex, 396
  grouping, 94
  immune to hanging up terminal, 7
  input-output redirection, 83–84
  interactive, 4
  and make, 295–296
  mistaken, 41
  nroff and troff, 198–202
  pipe and connection of standard input and
    output of, 84
  and prompting, 86
  running in low or high priority, 7
  running and reporting timing information
    on, 11
  sed, 441–442

shell, 86, 104
shell as, 30
simple, 83
speed of typing, 41
of Standard I/O Library, 319–322
substitution, 98–100
tbl input, 159–163, 174
typing, 41, 122
UNIX, regeneration of, 507
and UNIX dial-up network, 571
and whole-line oriented functions in sed,
  444–445
See also Program running
commas
  in C language, 256
  in formatted input of Fortran 77, 406
comments
  as, 484
  in BC language, 476, 477
  in C language, 247
  in nroff/troff, 215
Communications, 9–10
  mail command, 42
  writing to other users, 42
compiler control lines in C language, 267
compiler-compiler. *See* Yacc
compilers, 14
  See also C compiler
compound statement, in C language, 262–
  263
computer–aided instruction, 43
concatenation
  of character strings in Fortran 77, 414
  string, awk, 456
conditional acceptance of input in nroff/troff,
  219
conditional assembly, 10
conditional compilation, in C language, 267–
  268
"conditional jump" instructions, 10
conditional operator, in C language, 255
conditional statement
  in C language, 263
  in troff, 241–242
Connect time report, publishing cumulative,
  9
constants
  as, 484
  in BC, 477
  in C language, 248, 270
  in Fortran 77, 414
context addresses, and sed, 443
context searching, 60–62, 72
  and substitute function of sed, 445–447
context sensitivity of Lex, 391–392
continue statement, in C language, 264
control characters, in nroff/troff, 215
control-d sequence, 42
control flow statements, and Ratfor language,
  421
converson operators, and portable C compiler, 554–555
conversions, in C language, 250–251
copy in, copy out, and uucp uncico program,
  581–584
core image, ADB debugging of, 326–327
cp command, 6, 44
create, in I/O Library, 308–310
create command, 24, 26, 520, 523
cref, 50
cross-references (cref), 50
current address, in ADB, 324–325

daemon programs, and UNIX dial-up network, 571, 572
date, on document, 130
DC, 13, 460–468
  addition, 464
  and BC language, *see* BC language
  commands, 461–463, 464–467
  and computations with integers, 470–471
  description, 461
  design choices, 467–468
  division, 465
  dynamic string storage allocator, 463–464
  exponentiation, 465
  input conversion and base, 466
  interactive interface to, 13
  internal arithmetic, 464
  internal registers and programming, 466
  multiplication, 465
  numbers, 461
  output commands, 466
  output format and base, 466
  push-down registers and arrays, 467
  remainder, 465
  square root, 465
  stack commands, 466

subroutine definitions and calls, 466
subtraction, 464
  Yacc specification for, 378–379
debugging, 3, 32, 52
  of C programs, *see* lint
  interactive, 11
  of M4 macro processor, 438
  of portable C compiler, 566–567
  shell procedures, 95
  See also ADB
declarations
  in C language, 256–262, 273–274
  corresponding Fortran and C, 407
  in Fortran 77, 412, 413
  Yacc, 355–356
DECtape files
  replacing or deleting, 9
  updating by date, 7
default
  in Fortran 77, 417
  Lex, 392
  tbl command for, 161
default suffix list, and make, 296
default transformation paths, and make, 296–
  297
define statement, in Ratfor, 429
definitions, for frequently used string of
  characters, 153–154
  See also external definitions; source defini-
    tions
"delete" character, 32
deletion of lines, 59
DES chips, 600
description files, make and, 294–299
Desk calculator (DC). *See* DC
device resolution, nroff and troff, 203
diablo-mechanism terminals, fancy printing
  on, 16
diacritical marks, 16, 151
  in mathematical typesetting, 141
diagnostics, *as*, 494
dictionary, search for words with specified
  prefix in, 14
diff, 17, 50
DIGIT, in Yacc, 359–360
directories, 22
  and ADB, 334
  checking consistency of, 9
  manipulation of, 6–7
directory/dev, 22
disk, making from tape, 497–498
disk drivers, 517
displays, and advanced ADB usage, 332–
  334
  See also tables
diversions, in nroff/troff, 198–199, 210–211,
  242–243
division, DC, 465
do loops, in Fortran 77, 406, 412
do statement
  in C language, 263
  in Ratfor, 425–426
document changing
  and accents, 130
  and registers, 130
document formatting, 14–16
document preparation, 14, 49–51
  and file size, 50
  supporting programs for, 50
document typing, 126–130
  beginning, 126
  and boxing words or lines, 129
  and changeable registers, 137
  commands for, 132, 134
  cover sheets and first pages, 126
  and dating, 130
  displays, 129, 136
  and double columns, 136
  and equations, 131, 137
  examples of, 134–137
  and footnotes, 129, 136
  and headings, 127, 135
  and indented paragraphs, 128
  internal memorandum example, 135
  and italics or underlining, 128–129
  and keeping tables or blocks of lines on
    same page, 129–130
  and keeps, 136
  list, 136
  mathematics, 135
  and multi-column formats, 127
  and multiple indents, 136
  and nroff/troff commands, 130
  and page headings, 127
  and paragraph indents, 126
  references for further study, 131
  register names, 132
  and signature line, 130

tables, 129, 137
and text, 126
documentation conventions, for Fortran 77
  compiler, 403
dollar sign "$," 68–69
  and Yacc, 357–359
dots, 73–74, 324–325
double, in C language, 250
double columns, 136
double complex data type, and Fortran 77,
  404
double precision alignment, and Fortran 77
  compiler, 406–407
Drawing lines and characters, in troff, 235–
  236
Dummy procedure arguments, and Fortran 77
  compiler, 407
dumping, 9
  ADB and, 349
  postmortem, 11

e command, 78
  and reading text from file, 56–57
echo command, 7, 85, 103, 392
ed, 14, 43–44
  and additions to end of file, 77–78
  and append command "a", 55–56
  change command "c", 61–62
  and changing name of file, 76
  compared with sed, 441
  and context searching, 60–62
  and copying files, 76–77
  and copying lines, 80
  cut and paste operations, 78–80
  and deleting lines, 59
  and editing scripts, 80–81
  entering and creating text exercise, 56
  and error messages, 56
  and escape command, 80
  and global commands, 62, 75–78
  grep program and, 80
  and insert command "i", 61–62
  inserting one file into another, 78
  interrupting, 75
  and joining lines, 71–72
  leaving, 56
  line addressing in, 72–75
  marking lines, 79
  method of learning, 55
  and moving lines around, 79
  and moving text around, 62
  and print command "p," 57–58
  and printing contents of buffer, 57–58
  and printing files, 44
  and publication lists, 192–193
  and putting files together, 77
  and quit command, 56
  and read command "r," 57
  and reading text from file exercise, 56–57
  removing files, 77
  and RETURN, 55
  and sed, 17, 81
  and special characters, 63–64, 66–72
  starting with, 55
  and substituting newlines, 71
  summary of commands and line numbers,
    64
  and text creation, 55–56
  and text modification, 59–60
  and write command, 56
  and writing out part of file, 78–79
  and writing text out as a file, 56
edg, 89–90
edit command (e), and reading text from file,
  56–57
editing codes, positional, in Fortran 77, 416
egrep, 456
else statement, in Ratfor language, 423–424
end=, err=, and instat= clauses, in Fortran
  77, 416
end macro, in nroff/troff, 225
END pattern, awk, 453
ENTRY statement, in Fortran 77, 411–412
enumeration type, in C language, 277
environment switching, nroff/troff commands
  for, 200, 219–220
EOF. See control-d sequence
eqn, 16, 50, 131
  checking for errors in, 16
  and mathematical typesetting, 140–144
  use with tbl, 163–164
  See also mathematical typesetting
equations, 137
  displayed, 147
  example of, 154
  in-line, shorthand for, 153
  lining up, 151–152
equality operators, in C language, 254

equivalence statements, in Fortran 77, 405–
  406
escape command, 80
escape sequences, nroff/troff, 201
error correction
  I/O library and, 306, 310–311
  in mathematical typesetting, 155–156
  nroff/troff and, 221
  shell and, 100–103
  Yacc and, 360, 369–371, 374
  See also text modification
evaluations, in shell, 99–100
events, automatic reminder service for, 10
exec, 514
execl, 311–312
execute primitive, 27–28
execv, 311–312
exit command, 101
  of BC program, 476
  in UNIX programming, 306
explicit long constants, in C language, 248
explicit pointer conversions, operations in C
  language with, 269–270
exponentiation
  in BC, 479
  DC, 465
  in Fortran 77, 414
expression operators, as, 487
expression optimization, for C compiler,
  532–534
expression statements
  as, 485
  in C language, 262
expression trees, building with portable C
  compiler, 547, 551–552, 555–556
expressions
  ADB, 350
  as, 486–489
  awk, 454, 455
  in BC, 477–480
  of C compiler, 529–530
  in C language, 272–273
  complicated, lint evaluation of, 284
  in Fortran 77, 413–414
  repeated, in Lex, 391
external data definitions, in C language,
  265–266, 275

fields
  awk, 452–453, 455
  nroff/troff commands for, 199, 213–214
file archives
  managing on magnetic or DECtape, 9
  retrieval from, 9
  See also I/O library, 304–306
file descriptor 1, 28–29
file descriptor 2, 29
file descriptors, 24
  I/O Library, 306–307
file formats, in Fortran 77, 409–410
file inclusion, in C language, 267
file manipulation, 6
  and M4 micro processor, 437
file modes, for uucp, 591
file names
  changing, 76
  choosing, 44–47
  for Fortran 77 compiler, 402
  generation of, 84–85
  manipulation of, 6–7
file pointer, 304, 305
file switching, input/output, in nroff/troff,
  220
file systems, 21–25, 518–521
  access control scheme, 23
  amount of free space on, 8
  attachment of device containing to tree of
    directories, 8
  checking consistency of, 9
  conversion from UNIX 6th to 7th edition,
    504
  creation, 502–503
  directories, 22
  dumping, 9
  implementation of, 25–26
  and I/O calls, 24
  making new, 8
  ordinary files, 21
  removable, 23
  repairing damage to, 9
  restoring dumped, 9
  special files, 22–23
  See also Files
Filep, 24
files
  additions at end of, 77–78
  binary search for lines with specified pre-
    fix, 17

bringing into agreement, 17
collapsing successive duplicate lines into
  one line, 17
combining, 17
combining into archives and libraries, 10
comparing, 6
comparison, and UNIX dial-up network,
  574
concatenation into standard output, 6
copying, 6, 44, 76–77
creation of, 43
  in current directory, 83
determination of kind of information in, 8
dumping, 11
examination of, 11
encrypting and decrypting, 14
expunging from file system, 9
identification of common lines in, 17
input/output switching, nroff/troff commands for, 200
insertion into another file, 78
line, word and character counts in, 17
listing names of, 8, 9, 43–44
locating, 46–47
modification for uucp installation, 585–589
moving, 44, 76
naming, 22
partial printing, 6
patching with ADB, 335
preconnected in Fortran 77, 410
printing, 6, 44
putting together, 77
reading text from, 56–57
reading and writing, 78
recommended size of, 50
remote input or output into or out of local,
  10
removal, 44
removing, 77
replacement of terminal with, 47
replacing or deleting from archives, 10
reporting inaccessible, 9
with reverse line feeds, canonicalizing for
  one-pass printing, 16
searching, see also inverted indexes
splitting, 6
sum of words of, 6
transmission to another time-sharing system, 10
translation of data, 6
and UNIX dial-up network, 572
UNIX to UNIX communication, uucp and,
  578–580
updating, see make
writing out part of, 78–79
writing text out as, 56
filters, 4, 18, 29, 84
Fish, 19
flags
  Fortran 77 compiler, 402–403
  and make, 296
  names for selection of, 526–527
float, in C language, 250
floating constants, in C language, 248
floating patterns, searching for, 11
floating point, single and double-precision, in
  C language, 249
floating point unit, and UNIX, 501–502
floating values, conversions to integral type
  in C language, 250
flow-of-control
  and awk, 456
  and lint, 280–281
  and sed, 449–450
font changes
  in mathematical typesetting, 150–151
  tbl command for, 161
font size, nroff/troff commands for, 198
fonts, in nroff/troff, 226, 233
footnotes, 129, 136
  in nroff/troff, 224–225
for loop notation, 87–88
for statement
  in C language, 263
  in Ratfor, 427–428
foreign words, accents in, 130
fork, 34, 312–313
  and implementation of shell, 30–31
  and UNIX process creation, 514
fork primitive, 31
fork system call, 27
formats
  in ADB, 325, 347–348, 350
  in Fortran 77, 415
  multi-column, 127
  nroff and troff, 203
formatting packages, 49
Formulae, vertical "piling" of, 16

FORREW, and rewriting rules, 563–564
Fortran 77 language, 3, 403–407
  alternate returns in, 412, 415
  and automatic storage, 404
  binary initialization constants, 405
  blank lines in, 411
  and Boolean operations and UNIX com-
      mand arguments, 406
  character strings, 405
  and commas in formatted input, 406
  compared with Fortran 68, 411–420
  conversion of, 13
  declarations in, 412–413
  deletion of extended range, 411
  do loops in, 412
  and double complex data type, 404
  ENTRY statement in, 411–412
  equivalence statements, 405–406
  executable statements in, 415
  expressions in, 413–414
  features deleted from Fortran 66, 411
  formatted I/O in, 416–417
  and implicit undefined statements, 404
  include statement, 405
  input/output, 415–420
  inquire statements, 419–420
  and internal files, 404
  and old Hollerith notation, 405
  and one-trip do loops, 406
  open statement in, 418–419
  program and block data statements, 411
  rational proprocessor for, *see* Ratfor lan-
      guage
  and recursion of procedures, 404
  return statement in, 428
  and short integers, 406
  source input format, 404–405
Fortran 77 compiler, 401–420
  argument lists, 408–409
  command for compiling and loading files,
      402
  and corresponding Fortran and C declara-
      tions, 407
  documentation conventions, 403
  and double precision alignment, 406–407
  and dummy procedure arguments, 407
  file formats, 409–410
  file name suffixes, 402
  flags, 402–403
  and Fortran 77, *see* Fortran 77
  implementation strategy, 403
  interface with C procedures, 407–409
  portability considerations, 409
  and pre-connected files and file positions,
      410
  and procedure names, 407
  and return values, 408
  usage, 402–403
  violations of standard by, 406–407
Fortune, 18
Fortune cookies, 18
fractions, 149
fred command, 97
free-form input, in Ratfor, 428–429
fseek routine, 409
functions
  in BC language, 472–473
  built-in, awk, 455
  flow-of-control functions, 449–450
  operations in C language with, 268–269
  sed, 444–450
  unused, lint and, 279–280, 281
  whole-line oriented, sed and, 444–445
  See also input/output function

g command, 75–76
games, 18–19
  logging in to, 32
GCOS typesetter
  Lex commands on, 496
  and M4 macro processor, *see* M4 macro
      processor
  printing mathematical document on, 156
get functions. *See* hold and get functions
global commands, 62, 75–76
  multi-line, 76
  and rearranging lines, 72
global data structure of portable C computer,
      547–548
"global" size or font, 150–151
goto statement, in C language, 264
grammar rules
  ambiguity and conflicts in, Yaac and,
      364–367
  Ratfor, 430
  Yacc, 355–357
graphics, 3, 18
graph, 18

Greek letters, 155
  and EQN, 16
  in mathematical typesetting, 148
  in troff, 244
grep, 17, 50, 80, 84, 456
  and shell, 89–90
gross statistics, printing, 9

hanging numbers. *See* indented paragraphs
Hangman, 18
hardware, 4, 21
  of C language, 248–249
hat. *See* circumflex
header and footer macros, and nroff/troff,
      222–223
headings, 127
  and nroff/troff, 223
here document, 89–90
hold and get functions, sed, 449
"holes," in bit fields of portable C compiler,
      553
Hollerith notation, and Fortran 77, 405, 411
horizontal lines, tbl command for, 160, 162
horizontal place, marking in nroff/troff, 216
hunt program
  option arguments recognized by, 179–180
  and retrieving items from index, 179–180
hyphenation, nroff/troff commands for, 199,
      217–218

I Ching, 18
IBEX
  accounting, 9
  backup and maintenance, 8–9
  communication, 9–10
identifiers
  as, 483–484
  in BC language, 477
  in C language, 247, 249
if command, 93–94
  nested in Ratfor, 424
if-else ambiguity, in Ratfor, 424–425
if-than-else statement. *See* block if
ilist of file system, 25, 26
  ADB dump of, 334
Images, processes and, 27–28
Implementation, of Ratfor, 430–431
  See also UNIX implementation
implicit declarations
  in C language, 268
  in Fortran 77, 412
include statements
  in Fortran 77, 405
  in Ratfor, 429–430
indents, 126
  multiple, 136
  in nroff/troff, 198, 209, 234
indexes
  construction of, 175, 176
  key word in context, 14
  of references, 178
  See also inverted indexes; publication lists
information handling, 17–18
Initialization, 31
  in C language, 260–261
  older forms of, lint detection of, 283–284
  and portable C compiler, 552–553
  See also binary initialization constants
i-node, 25
  making for special file, 8
input, conditional acceptance of, nroff/troff
      commands for, 199–200
input conversion
  DC, 466
  formatted, 10
input form, in nroff/troff, 203
input-line functions, multiple, sed and, 448
input/output conventions
  nroff/troff, 199
  and sed, 447–448
  Yacc, 372
input output redirection, 83–84
input spaces, in mathematical typesetting,
      147–148
inquire statement, 409
  in Fortran 77, 419–420
insertions, 61–62
  from standard output, nroff/troff com-
      mands for, 200, 220
integer arithmetic, evaluation of, 14
integer constants, in C language, 248
integer patterns, searching for, 11
integer sizes, in C language, 249
integers
  in C language, 250
  computations in DC language, 470–471
  factoring, 18
  short, in Fortran 77, 406

integrals
  in mathematical typesetting, 150
Interactive programs, 4
internal files, in formatted I/O of Fortran 77,
      418
internal registers, of DC, 466
Interpreter, interactive, 13
"interrupt" key, 40–41
  and stopping program 42
interrupt signal, 32, 104
intrinsic statement, in Fortran 77, 413
i-number, 25
inverted index
  check for bad drops, 177
  and coordination level searching, 177
  generating to list of record tags and keys,
      176
  hash and invert process, 178–179
  and mkey program, 178
  preparation of, 175, 176
  and searching, 175–180
  and updating publication lists, 188–195
I/O system, 3, 5, 304–306, 522–528
  block and character, 515–517, 522
  and block device interface, 525–527
  and block device drivers, 527–528
  bottom level on UNIX system, 306–311
  buffered character-by-character, 10
  calls, 319–322
  and character device drivers, 523–525
  character devices, 517
  character lists, 517
  direct access in Fortran 77, 418
  and disk drivers, 517
  and error handling, 306, 310–311
  and execl and execv, 311–312
  and execution of program from within
      another, 311–315
  and file access, 304–306
  forcing to completion, 9
  and fork and wait, 312–313
  formatted in Fortran 77, 416–417
  Fortran, 409–410
  and Fortran 77 compiler, 403
  general usage, 319
  and Lex, 393–394, 396, 399
  and miscellaneous I/O functions, 306
  open, creat, close, and unlink in, 308–310
  overview, 522–523
  and pipes, 313–315
  random access in, 310
  read and write in, 307–308
  and signals and program faults, 315–318
  and "system" function, 311
Is-It, 44
italics, 128–129
iw.m integer output code, in Fortran 77, 417

j command, 71–72

k command, 79
keeps, 136
key-making program mkey, 178
keyword parameters in shell
  and parameter substitution, 97–98
  and parameter transmission, 97
  substitution, 99–100
keyword statements, *as*, 486
keywords
  and automatic storage of Fortran 77, 404
  in BC language, 477
  in C language, 247–248
  in mathematical typesetting, 154–155
  reserved, specifications for Yacc and,
      373–374
knowledge tests, 18

l command, 66
labeled statement, in C language, 264
labels, *as*, 485
leaders, in nroff/troff, 199, 213
learn, 43
  advantages of CAI scripts, 109
  available CAI scripts for, 109
  directory structure for, 115
  disadvantages of, 119
  educational assumptions and design, 110–
      112
  experience with, 114, 118–119
  and interpretation of scripts, 114–118
  sample lesson, 116–117
  See also CAI scripts
left context sensitivity, lex, 398–399
Lex, 3, 14, 52, 457
  actions, 392–394
  and ambiguous source rules, 394
  bugs, 400
  character set, 399

compilation of source program with, 395–396

context sensitivity, 391–392

definitions of regular expressions, 390–392

execution time for program vs. awk and sed, 459

format of source, 390

GCOS commands, 396

and left context sensitivity, 398–399

and make, 11

source definitions, 395

source format summary, 399–400

source program example, 396–398

TSO commands and, 396

usage, 388–389

and Yacc, 396

lexical analysis, 14

and portable C compiler, 548

and Yacc, 359–360

See also Lex; Yacc

lexical conventions, *as*, 483

lexical scope, in C language, 266

library declaration files, and lint, 287

library libc.a, regeneration, 510

ligatures, in nroff/troff, 214

line length, in nroff/troff, 198, 209, 234

line numbers

default, 73

in nroff/troff, 218

and sed, 443

line protocol selection, and UNIX dial-up network, 573

lines

beginning of, circumflex and, 69

in C language, 268

changes and insertions, in, 61–62

copying, 80

deletion of, 59

drawing in troff, 216–217, 235–236

duplicate, 17

identification of common lines in two files, 17

joined together, 71–72

marking, 79

moving around, 72, 79

satisfying pattern used in ed, 17

with specified prefix, binary search in sorted file for, 17

splitting into two or more shorter lines, 71

See also blank lines; horizontal lines; vertical lines; output line numbering

link edit, 11

linking, 22

lint, 52

and assignments of longs to ints, 282

communicating with, 286–287

and detection of variables used before setting, 280

and evaluation of complex expression, 284

and flow of control, 280–281

implementation of, 284–285

and library declaration files, 287

and nonportable character use, 282

and older forms of assignment operators and initialization, 283–284

options, 290

and pointer alignment, 284

portability of, 285–286

problems with, 287–288

and strange constructions, 283

and type casts, 282

and type checking, 281–282

and unused and unreturned function values, 281

and unused variables and functions, 279–280

usage, 278, 279

local motions, in troff, 235–236

local variables, set and unused, 280

location counter, *as*, 485

lock files of uucp, 590

log entry files of uucp, 590

logging in, 40–41, 121

logging out, 42, 122

logical AND operator, in C language, 255

logical OR operator, in C language, 255

LOGIN, 5

login, 9, 40–41, 121

and password security, 600

and shell, 86

and uucp, 585, 591

longs, assignments to ints, lint and, 282

lookall command, 175, 177

looping, 32

lower case devices, and UNIX, 40

ls command, 8, 43–44

lseek, in I/O Library, 310

ltypes, in C language, 250

m command, 62, 79

M4 macro processor, 14, 433–439

and arguments, 436

and arithmetic built-ins, 436–437

basic operations, 434

built-ins summary, 439

conditionals, 437–438

and defining macros, 434–435

features, 433

and file manipulation, 437

printing, 438

and quoting, 435–436

and system command, 437

usage, 434

machine instruction statements, *as*, 490–493

macro definitions, make and, 294–295, 296

macro processors, 13–14

See also M4 macro processor

macros

defining, M4 macro processor and, 434–435

in nroff/troff, 198–199, 209–210, 220–221, 237–238, 240–241

and type words of portable C compiler, 547

mail, 5, 91

announcing presence of, 9

reading and sending, 42

mailing, 9

maintenance, 8–9

make, 3, 11, 52

basic features, 292–294

command usage, 295–296

and description files and substitutions, 294–295

example of use of, 297–299

implicit rules, 296–297

problems with, 299

and updating target file, 292–294

usage, 291, 292

man command, 95–96

manuscript layout package (MS), 15–16

maps, and ADB, 331–332, 345–346

mark command k, 79

MASTER. *See* Unix dial-up network

mathematical function library, 10

mathematics typesettting, 135, 138–156

and assembly language design, 139–143

big brackets, 152

braces for grouping in, 149

character sequences in, 155

diacritical marks, 151

difficulties of, 138–139

and displayed equations, 147, 154

and eqn, 147

error correction, 155–156

experience with, 143–144

and extra spaces, 154

fractions, 149

Greek letters in, 155

and input spaces, 147–148

keywords and precedences, 154–155

and language theory, 142–143

and languages, 146

lining up equations in, 151–152

matrices, 153

and output spaces, 148

and phototypesetter, 139

piles in, 152–153

printing on UNIX typesetter, 156

quotes in, 151

and shorthand for frequently used string of characters, 153–154

and shorthand for in-line equations 153

and sizes and fonts, 141, 150–151

square roots, 149–150

subscripts and superscripts, 148–149

summation, integral, 150

symbols, special names, and Greek alphabet in, 148

words know to eqn, 155

matrices, 153

vertical piling of formulae for, 16

mazes, 18

measurements, conversion between scales of, 18

messages, mailing to users, 9

metacharacters, 67–68

ampersand "&", 71

backslash (\ ), 68

brackets, 70–71

circumflex "^", 69

dollar sign "$," 68–69

removal of special meaning, 85–86

shell, 107

star "*", 69–70

mixed mode expressions, in Fortran 77, 414

mkey program, 178

flag arguments reorganized by, 178

motions, local horizontal and vertical, nroff/troff and, 215–216

mount system request, 23, 26

move command "m," 62

multiple columns, 127

in nroff/troff, 223–224

multiple users of UNIX, setting up for, 504

multiplication, DC, 465

multiplicative operators

in BC, 479

in C language, 253

multitasking, and command separators, 30

ms macro package, 3, 15–16

See also Document typing

namelist of object program printing, 11

neqn, 16, 50

new users of UNIX, installation of, 503

newlines

concealed, in nroff/troff, 215

in mathematical typesetting, 147–148

next statment, in Ratfor, 426, 428

Nonprogrammers, and eqn, 16

nonsense arrangements, protection against, 8

novelties. *See* games

nroff, 3, 15–16, 49–51

applications, 196

commands, 130, 198–202

invoking, 196–197

and neqn, 16

options and effects, 196–197

and ul, 71

See also document typing; nroff/troff

nroff/troff

backspacing, 214

changes since 1976 manual in, 229

comments and concealed newlines in, 215

conditional acceptance of input, 219

control characters in, 215

diversions in, 210–211

environment switching in, 219–220

escape sequences for characters, indicators and functions, 201

fields in, 213–214

font and character size control, 204–206

font style examples, 226

footnotes in, 224–225

form of input, 203

formatter and device resolution, 203

hyphenation in, 217–218

indenting, 209

input character translations, 214

input naming conventions for special characters, 227–228

input/output file switching, 220

insertions from standard input, 220

large brackets in, 216

last page, 225

ligatures, 214

line drawing, in, 216–217

line length, 209

local horizontal and vertical motions in, 215–216

macros and strings, 209–210, 220–221

marking horizontal place in, 216

multiple column output, 223–224

number registers, 202, 212–213, 229

numerical notation, 204

numerical parameter input, 203–204

output and error messages, 221

output line numbering, 218

overstriking, 214, 216

page control, 206–207

page margins, 222–223

paragraphs and headings, 223

tabs and leaders, 213

text filling, adjusting, and centering, 207–208

three-part titles in, 218

transparent throughput in, 215

traps, 211–212

underlining, 214–215

vertical spacing, 208–209

width function, 216

zero-width characters in, 216

nroff/troff commands

alphabetical request and section number cross references, 200

for conditional acceptance of input, 199–200

environment switching, 200

hyphenation, 199

indenting, 198

input/output conventions and character translations, 199

input/output file switching, 200

nroff/troff commands *(continued)*
insertions from standard input, 200
line length, 198
macros, strings, diversion, and position
traps, 198–199
number registers, 199
for output line numbering, 199
for page control, 198
tabs, leaders, and fields, 199
for text filling, adjusting and centering,
198
for three-part titles, 199
for vertical spacing, 198
null statements
as, 485
in C language, 266
number conversions, 10
number-guessing game, 18
number registers
and arithmetic in troff, 239–240
in nroff/troff, 199, 202, 212–213, 229
numbers
and DC, 263, 461
graphs, 18
nroff/troff, 204

object codes, creation of, 10
object files,
combining, 11
placement for loading, 11
printing namelist of, 11
removal of relocation and symbol table information from, 11
reporting core requirements of, 11
open command, 26, 520, 523
in Fortran 77, 418–419
in I/O Library, 308–310
open system call, 25
operators
of C compiler, list of, 530–532
Lex, 390–391
optional plus signs, in formatted I/O of Fortran 77, 416–417
output
and filter, 84
from nroff/troff, 221
output commands, DC, 466
output conversion, formatted, 10
output formats, 11
DC, 466
output line numbering, nroff/troff commands
for, 199
overstriking, in nroff/troff, 214, 216

p command, 66
and printing contents of buffer, 57–58
–p option of refer, 187
page control, in nroff/troff, 198, 206–
207
page headings of documents, 127
page margins, and nroff/troff, 222–223
page numbering, in troff, 238–239
pages, last, in nroff/troff, 225
paragraph indents, 126, 128
nroff/troff and, 223
parameter statement, in Fortran 77, 413
parent process, 27
and implementation of shell, 30–31
parentheses, 30
in BC, 478
parse tree, Yacc, 358–359
parsing
by portable C compiler, 549
Yacc. *See* Yacc parser
password, 5
changing, 5
password security, 595–601
and DES chips, 600
first scheme for, 597–599
improvements to, 599–601
and login, 600
and salted passwords, 600
and selection of passwords, 600
and UNIX system vulnerability, 597
patching, 11
and ADB, 335, 347–348
pathname of file, 22, 46–47
pattern matching, 88–89
pattern scanning, and AWK, 17, 453–454
period
actual instead of "match anything," 68
and append command, 56
piles, and mathematical typesetting, 141,
152–153
pipes, 27, 48, 80, 84, 313–315
implementation of, 520
plus signs, optional, in formatted I/O of Fortran 77, 416–417

point size changes
tbl command for, 161
in troff, 232–233
pointer alignment, lint and, 284
pointer bug, ADB and, 337–338
pointers
integers added to or subtracted from, in C
language, 250
operations in C language with, 269
portable C compiler, 544–567
bugs, 566–567
and code generation, 556–560
data structure of, 547–548
description of, 544–545
and expression tree building, 551–552
first pass summary, 556
improvements needed for, 567
and initialization, 552–553
and lexical analyzer, 548
and machine dependent interface, 563
machine dependent routines, 554–556
optimization, 553–554
overview, 545–546
and parsing, 548–549
pass one of, 548
passes of, 545–546
and register allocation, 566
register allocation routines and allocation
strategy, 562–563
registers, 557
and rewriting rules, 563–564
and Sethi-Ullman computation, 564–566
source files of, 546
statements, 553
storage classes, 549
and symbol table maintenance, 550–551
template matching algorithm of, 561–562
templates, 560
position traps, nroff/troff commands for,
198–199
positional editing codes, in Fortran 77, 416
pr, 6, 44
Precedence relations, 14
in mathematical typesetting, 154–155
preparagraph spacing, in nroff/troff, 223
preprocessor, in C language, 275–276
primary expressions, in C language, 251–252
print command,
awk, 453
and printing contents of buffer, 57–58
printing, 6
and M4 macro process, 438
procedure names, in Fortran 77, 404, 407
processes
communication via pipes, 27
defined, 27
fork system call and, 27
images and, 27–28
synchronization, 28
termination, 28
processid, 27, 28
prof, 11, 52
program faults, and I/O Library, 315–318
programs
execution of, 7–8, 27–28
stopping, 42
Yacc, 356
Programming, 51–52
in C, 51–52
and shell, 51
with UNIX, *see* UNIX programming
See also awk; C language
project, changes in, 5
prompts, 41, 86
shell, 92
pseudo-operations, *as,* 489–490
publication lists
fields of citation, 190
format of data base entries, 188–190
printing, 194–195
updating, 188–195
updating and reindexing, 190–194
push-down registers and arrays, DC, 467
pwd command, 8, 46

q command, 43
quicksort, 10
quit command (q), 56, 315
quit signal, 32, 103
Quiz, 18
quotes
in mathematical typesetting, 151
and M4 macroprocessor, 435–436
in shell, 99–100
and special meaning of metacharacters,
85–86

random access, in I/O Library, 310
random number generator, 10

Ratfor, 3, 52
break statement in, 428
break and next in, 426
control flow statements, 421
cosmetic facilities, 428
and deficiencies with Fortran, 422
define statement, 429
design, 422–423
do statement, 425–426
else statement, 423–424
experience with, 431–432
for statement in, 427–428
free-form input in, 428–429
if-else ambiguity in, 424–425
implementation, 430–431
include statement, 429–430
nested if's in, 424
next statement in, 428
problems with, 420
repeat until statement, 428
statement grouping in, 423
switch statement, 425
translations in, 429
while statement in, 426–427
See also Lex
raw block-device I/O system, 528
read, 7
in I/O Library, 307–308
read-ahead, 41
read call, 24, 26
read command (r), and reading text from
file, 57
read statements, end=, err=, and instat=
clauses in Fortran 77, 416
reconfiguration of UNIX, 500–501
records, awk, 452–453
reduce action, of Yacc parser, 360–361
refer, 3, 16, 50
collecting references, 185–187
key letters recognized by, 182–183
options, 186–187
and reference files, 182–185
and selecting and formatting references for
troff, 181–182
refer preprocessor, 175
references
and indented paragraphs, 128
indexing, 178
refer and, 182–187
selecting and formatting for troff, 181–182
register allocation routines, of portable C
compiler, 562–563, 566
registers, 132
alternation for document typing, 130
changes in, 137
regular expressions, Lex, 390–392
REJECT action, in Lex, 394
relational expressions
awk, 454
BC, 480
in C language, 254
relocation counter symbol, *as,* 493
remainders, and DC, 465
remote systems, calling up, 10
repeat until statement, in Ratfor, 428
repetitions, ampersand and elimination of,
71
report generation, and awk, 457
requests, in ADB, 325
reserved words, shell, 107
retrieval from archives, 10
RETURN
ed and, 55
and logging in, 41
return statement
in C language, 264
in Fortran, 428
in Fortran 77, 415
return values, in Fortran 77, 408
rewriting rules, and portable C compiler,
563–564
roff, 14–15
and ul, 71
root directory, 22
root file system, and making disk from tape,
497–498

s command, 66–67, 74
save statement, in Fortran 77, 413
scaling, and BC language, 472, 478
scan command, 102–103
scheduling
one-shot action, 8
regular actions, 8
scheduling algorithm of UNIX, 515
scope of externals, in C language, 266
scope rules, in C language, 266
scripts, 80–81

searching
  with inverted index, 176–177
  and lookall command, 177
  repeated, 73
  and retrieving, 179–180
  See also inverted indexes
Security
  encrypt and decrypt files for, 14
  optional encryption for, 14
  and passwords, 5
  and UNIX dial-up network, 571, 592–594
  and uucp, 585
  See also password security
sed, 81, 456
  addresses and selection of lines for editing, 442–444
  command format, 441
  execution time for programs vs. awk and lex, 459
  flow-of-control functions, 449–450
  functions, 444–450
  hold and get functions, 449
  input/output functions, 447–448
  and multiple input-line functions, 448
  order of application of editing commands, 442
  overall operation of, 441–442
  and substitute function, 445–447
  usage, 440, 441
seek, 520
segments, *as*, 484–485
semicolon
  and line addressing, 74–75
  and separation of commands, 30, 48
sequence check file of uucp, 589
Sethi-Ullman computation, 563
  and portable C compiler, 564–566
sharp sign (#)
  as symbol in copy, 41
  and typing errors, 41
shell, 4, 7, 9, 28–32
  and background commands, 83
  capabilities, 48–49
  and case notation, 88–89
  as command, 30
  command execution, 103–104
  command grouping, 94
  and command separators, 30
  command substitution, 98–99
  debugging procedures, 95
  error correction, 100–101
  escape to during editing, 14
  evaluations and quoting, 99–100
  and familiarity with UNIX, 83
  fault handling, 101–103
  features of, 3, 82
  and file name generation, 84–85
  filters, 29, 84
  and for loop notation, 87–88
  functions of, 7
  grammar, 106
  and grep, 89–90
  and here document, 89–90
  if command, 93–94
  implementation of, 30–31
  and initialization, 31
  and input output redirection, 83–84
  invoking, 104
  keyword parameters, 97
  and login, 86
  and man command, 95–96
  metacharacters and reserve words, 107
  other programs as, 32
  parameter substitution, 97–98
  parameter transmission, 97
  pipelines, 84
  procedures, 87
  and programming, 51
  and prompting, 86, 92
  and quoting, 85–86
  scan command, 102–103
  simple commands, 83
  and standard I/O, 28–29
  string-valued variables, 90–92
  and test command, 92
  and trap and touch commands, 102
  and UNIX signals, 101–102
  and while loop, 92–93
shell accounting report, publishing, 9
shell conditionals, tests for use in, 7
shell files of uucp, 590–591
shift action, of Yacc parser, 360
shift operators, in C language, 254
signals, and I/O library, 315–318
signature line, 130
simple commands, 83
size changes, 11
  in mathematical typesetting, 150

slashes, in file system, 22
SLAVE. *See* UNIX dial-up network
Software, 21
  See also UNIX software regeneration
sort, 17, 50
sorting files, 17
source definitions, Lex, 390, 395
source files, of portable C compiler, 546
source input format
  for Fortran 77, 404–405
  Lex, summary of, 399–400
source modifications, and uucp installation, 585–589
source program, Lex, example of, 396–398
spaces
  between columns, 160–161
  determination of usage, 8
  in mathematical typesetting, 140, 147–148
  reporting duplicate use of, 9
  retrieval of, 9
  See also vertical spacing
special characters, 16, 63–64, 66–72
  and EQN, 16
  input naming conventions in nroff/troff, 227–228
  and list command "l", 66
  metacharacters, 67–68
  substitute command s, 66–67
  in troff, 233–234, 244
  undo command u, 67
  See also metacharacters
special files
  creation for UNIX, 501
  making i-node for, 8
special names, in mathematical typesetting, 148
specifications for Lex, 394
specifications for Yaac, 355–356, 372–374
  and input style, 372
  and left recursion, 372–373
  and lexical decisions, 373
  and reserved words, 373–374
spell, 14, 18, 50
spelling errors, 50
  locating, 14
  and substitute command "s", 59–60, 67
spool directory cleanup, uucp, 584–585
square roots, 141, 149–150, 465
stack commands, DC, 466
stack trace illustration, ADB and, 339–340
standard input, in UNIX programming, 302–304
Standard I/O, 28–29
standard output, in UNIX programming, 302–304
star "*", 69–70
statements
  as, 485–486
  BC, 481–482
  in C language, 262–265, 274–275
  control, in BC language, 474–475
  executable in Fortran 77, 415
  flow-of-control, awk, 456
  grouping in Ratfor language, 423
  and portable C compiler, 553
  program and block data, in Fortran 77, 411
static, and automatic storage of Fortran 77, 404
status inquiries, 8
stderr, in UNIX programming, 306
storage allocator, 10
storage classes
  BC, 481
  in C language, 256–257
  of portable C compiler, 549
String computations, 7
string concatenation, awk, 456
string statements, *as*, 486
strings
  awk, 455
  in C language, 248
  in nroff/troff, 198–199, 209–210, 220–221, 236–237
  See also character strings
  structure specifiers, in C language, 258–260, 268, 277
  subdirectories of UNIX, contents of, 506–507
subroutines
  definitions and calls in DC, 466
  in Fortran 77, 411
subscripts, 148–149
  in C language, 269
  calculation of size changes for, 16
  in Fortran 77, 414
substitute command "s", 59–60, 66–67
substitution, undoing, 67

subtraction, on DC, 464
substrings, in Fortran 55, 414
summations, 150
superscripts, 148–149
super-user
  and access control scheme, 23
  temporarily becoming, 9
swapping process, and user control of UNIX, 514
switch statement
  in C language, 263–264
  and portable C compiler, 553
  in Ratfor, 424, 425
Switches, setting for logging in, 40–41
symbol table maintenance, and portable C compiler, 550–551
symbols
  in mathematical typesetting, 148
  temporary, *as*, 484
syntax, in C language, 249, 272–276
system calls, *as*, 494
system command, of M4 macro processor, 437
"system" function, of I/O Library, 311

t command, 80
tab characters, *as*, 484
table of contents, printing, 9, 10
tables, 129, 137
  kept on same page, 129–130
  See also tbl
tabs, 5, 41
  ADB decoding, 341–343
  list command and visibility of, 66
  in nroff/troff, 199, 213, 235
  setting, 5
tape, making disk from, 497–498
tbl, 3, 16, 50, 158–174, 235
  applications, 151
  data commands, 162–163
  input command options, 159–163
  input format, 158
  input-output examples, 164–173
  list of command characters and words, 174
  usage, 163–164
  use with eqn, 163–164
template matching algorithms, of portable C compiler, 561–562
templates, of portable C compiler, 560
temporal sorting of names of files, 8
temporary data files of uucp, 589
Terminal, 5–6
  calling in on, 121
  connecting, 121
  printing name of, 8
terminal communication, establishing, 10
terminals
  strange behavior, 41
  types of, 121
termination of process, 8, 28
  of shell procedures, 101–102
terminology, 122
test command, 7, 92
Text
  changes and insertions, 61–62
  filling, adjusting, and centering, nroff/troff commands for, 198, 207–208
  interrupted, in nroff/troff, 207–208
  "kept in a buffer," 55
  modification, 59–60
  moving, 62
text blocks in tables, tbl command for, 162–163
text creation, and ed, 55–56
text editors, interactive compared with noninteractive, 441
  See also ed; sed
Tic-tac-toe, 18
timing information
  construction of profile of time spent per routine, 11
  reporting, 11
  See also accounting
Time, 8, 11, 52
Time conversions, 10, 502
titles, three-part, in nroff/troff, 199, 218, 238–239
token names, in Yacc, 355
token numbers, and lexical analyzer of Yacc, 359–360
tokens
  in BC language, 477
  in C language, 247, 267
touch command, 93–94
tr, 17, 50
translations, 6
  Ratfor and, 429
transparent throughput, in nroff/troff, 215

trap command, 102
traps, 32
    in nroff/troff, 211–212
Tree of directories
    attaching device containing file system to,
        8
    removal of file system contained on device
        from, 8
troff, 3, 15–16, 49–51
    applications, 196
    commands, 130, 198–202
    conditionals in, 241–242
    description, 230
    diversions in, 242–243
    drawing lines and characters in, 235–236
    eqn and, 16
    fonts, 233
    general usage of, 231–232
    Greek letters in, 244
    indents and line lengths, 234
    invoking, 196–197
    local motions in, 235–236
    macros in, 237–238
    macros with arguments in, 240–241
    and mathematical language design, 139–
        143
    and mathematical typesetting, 146
    number registers and arithmetic in, 239–
        240
    options and effects, 196–197
    phototypesetter character set, 244
    and phototypesetting mathematics, 139
    point sizes in, 232–233
    removal of commands from input, 16
    strings in, 236–237
    and tables. See tbl
    tabs in, 234–235
    titles, pages and numbering in, 238–239
    selecting and formatting references for,
        181–182
    special characters in, 233–234
    vertical spacing in, 232–233
    See also document typing; nroff/troff
TSO commands, and Lex, 396, 400
TX command line option to tbl, 163
type, lint checking of, 281–282
type casts, and lint, 282
type names, in C language, 261–262
type specifiers, in C language, 257
typedef, in C language, 262
typeface, of portable C computer, 547
typesetting
    checking TROFF page layout prior to, 16
    fancy printing, 16
    in huge letters, 18
Typesetting preprocessors, 16
Typesetting programs, 14–16
typing. See document typing
typo, 14, 50

ul command, 71
unary operators, expressions with in C lan-
    guage, 252–253
underlining, 128–129
    in nroff/troff, 214–215
undo command u, 67
union specifiers, in C language, 258–260
unions, operations in C language with, 268
UNIX
    advantages, 32–34
    and algorithmic languages, 13
    applications, 20–21, 34
    basic starting information, 121–122
    commands typing, 122
    compilers, 14
    computer-aided instruction on, see LEARN
    creation of files, 43
    document formatting, 14–16
    document typing, see Document typing
    file manipulation, 6
    games and novelties, 18–19
    graphics, 18
    hardware, 4
    hardware and software, 21
    implementation of, see UNIX implementa-
        tion
    information handling, 17–18
    languages used with, 52
    logging in, 40–41
    and M4 macro processor, see M4 macro
        processor
    macroprocessing, 13–14
    manipulation of directories and file names,
        6–7

operating system, 4–12
    processes and images, 27–28
    program development tools, 10
    programs available under, 21
    running programs, 7–8
    security, see password security
    and sed, see sed
    shell, 28–32
    software for, 4–5
    status inquiries, 8
    summary of features, 3–17
    terminal handling, 5–6
    terminals dealing with, 40
    terminology, 122
    text processing, 14–16
    traps, 32
    user access control, 5
    variants, 40
UNIX dial-up network, 569–575
    "active" and "passive" systems on, 570–
        571
    advantages of, 569
    basic operation of, 571
    call remote system, 572
    design goals, 570–571
    and file copy, 572
    goals of, 575
    lessons of, 575
    line protocol selection, 573
    performance, 574–575
    present uses, 573–574
    processing, 571
    purpose of, 570
    and security, 571
    and work processing, 573
    and uucp, see uucp implementation
UNIX implementation, 512–521
    and C code and assembly code, 512
    and file system, 518–521
    and I/O system, 515–517
    and process creation and program execu-
        tion, 514
    and process synchronization and schedul-
        ing, 515
    and user process control, 512–515
UNIX login name, 40
UNIX PDP-11 assembler as. See as
Unix Programmer's Manual, The, 11–12,
        40
    on-line, 43
    and file descriptors, 306–307
    and low-level I/O, 306–311
    program arguments, 302
    "standard input and output", 302–304
    and Standard I/O Library, 304–306
UNIX, setting up, 497–505
    booting, 498–500
    and checking and dumping of file system,
        504
    and conversion of file systems from 6th to
        7th edition, 504
    and disk layout, 502–503
    and floating point unit, 501–502
    and installation of new users, 503
    making disk from tape, 497–498
    and multiple users, 504
    and program changes, 505
    and reconfiguration, 500–501
    and special files, 501
    and time conversion, 502
UNIX shell. See Shell
UNIX software regeneration, 506–511
    and assembler, 507
    and C compiler, 507–508
    and commands, 507
    and library libc.a, 510
    and source and object programs, 508–509
    and subdirectories of source files for com-
        mands and subroutines, 506–507
    and system tuning, 510–511
UNIX text editor. See ed
UNIX typesetter, printing mathematical
    documents on, 156
UNIX to UNIX copy, 10
unlink, 520
    in I/O library, 310
unoptim routine, for C compiler, 533
unsigned integers, in C language, 249, 250
User
    identification of, 8
    logged in, names of, 83
    signing on, 5
user-group identification number (GID), and
    UNIX security, 592–594

user identification number (UID), 23
    and UNIX security, 592–594
uucico program, and copy in, copy out, 581–
        584
uucp implementation, 3, 10, 577–592
    and administration, 589–591
    and command execution, 584
    and copy in, copy out, 581–584
    and file modes, 591
    installation, 585–589
    log inquiry with uulog, 584
    and login entry, 591
    primary and secondary programs of, 578
    and security, 585
    and spool directory cleanup, 584–585
    and UNIX to UNIX execution, 580–581
    and UNIX to UNIX file copy, 578–580
uulog, and uucp log inquiry, 584
uux command, and UNIX to UNIX execu-
    tion with uucp, 580–581
uuxqt program, and uucp command execu-
    tion, 584

v command, 62, 75–76
values
    ADB conversion of, 334
    unrepresentable, in formatted I/O of For-
        tran 77, 417
variables
    awk, 455
    local and global, symbolic reference to, 11
    string-valued, 90–92
    unused, lint and, 279–280
    used before setting, lint detection of, 280
vertical lines, tbl command for, 160
vertical spacing
    in nroff/troff, 198, 208–209
    tbl command fora changes in, 161
    in troff, 232–233
vertical spanning, tbl command for, 161, 162

w command, 74
wait, 7, 312–313, 514
    and implementation of shell, 31
    and init, 31
wc, 17, 50
while loop, 92–93
while statement
    in C language, 263
    in Ratfor, 426–427
who command, 8, 83
width function, in nroff/troff, 216
Word count, 17
Word-guessing game, 18
Word list, spelling error location and, 14
Working directory, printing name of, 8
write, 10
    in I/O Library, 308
Write call, 26
write command (w), 56
write statements, end=, err=, and instat=
    clauses in Fortran, 77, 416
writing, to other users, 42

Yacc, 14
    accessing values in enclosing rules, 374
    actions performed with grammar rules,
        357–359
    advanced topics, 374–376
    ambiguous and conflicting grammar rules,
        364–367, 382–386
    basic specifications, 355–357
    error handling, 369–371
    grammar rules, 354
    input syntax, 380–381
    languages used with, 353
    Lex and, 392, 396
    lexical analysis, 354–355, 359–360
    literals and synonyms, 387
    and make, 11
    and parsing of arithmetic expressions,
        367–369
    parser, 360–374
    simulating error and accept in actions, 374
    specification for desk calculator, 378–379
    specification preparations, 372–374
    support for arbitrary value types, 374–375
    usage, 354–355
yacc compiler-compiler, 52
yyleng, in Lex, 392
yytext, in Lex, 392, 393

zero-width characters, in nroff/troff, 216